NATIONAL
TELEVISION
VIOLENCE
STUDY
Volume 1

NATIONAL
TELEVISION
VIOLENCE
STUDY

Volume 1

SAGE Publications
International Educational and Professional Publisher
Thousand Oaks London New Delhi

For information address:

SAGE Publications, Inc.
2455 Teller Road
Newbury Park, California 91320
E-mail: order@sagepub.com

SAGE Publications Ltd.
6 Bonhill Street
London EC2A 4PU
United Kingdom

SAGE Publications India Pvt. Ltd.
M-32 Market
Greater Kailash I
New Delhi 110 048 India

Printed in the United States of America

ISBN 0-7619-0801-3 (hardcover)
ISBN 0-7619-0802-1 (paperback)

98 99 00 01 02 03 10 9 8 7 6 5 4 3 2

Acquiring Editor:	Margaret Seawell
Editorial Assistant:	Renee Piernot
Keylining:	Tina Hill
Cover Designer:	Ravi Balasuriya
Print Buyer:	Anna Chin

CONTENTS

*Dr. Barbara J. Wilson, Dr. Dale Kunkel, Dr. Dan Linz, Dr. James Potter,
Dr. Ed Donnerstein, Stacy L. Smith, Eva Blumenthal, Timothy Gray*

PART II. TELEVISION VIOLENCE IN "REALITY" PROGRAMMING: UNIVERSITY OF TEXAS, AUSTIN STUDY 269

Dr. Charles Whitney, Dr. Ellen Wartella, Dr. Dominic LaSorsa,
Dr. Wayne Danielson, Adriana Olivarez, Rafael Lopez, Marlies Klijn

*Dr. Frank Biocca, Dr. Jane Brown, Fuyan Shen, Jay M. Bernhardt,
Leandro Batista, Karen Kemp, Greg Makris, Dr. Mark West, Dr. James Lee,
Howard Straker, Dr. Henry Hsiao, Elena Carbone*

ACKNOWLEDGMENTS

University of California, Santa Barbara

This project could not have been completed without the advice and support of many individuals to whom we are deeply grateful.

First are our colleagues, both faculty and graduate students, in the Department of Communication at the University of California, Santa Barbara. This department has built an extraordinary intellectual community, with the common bond being a tremendous respect for contributions to knowledge in our field. Those of us involved in this study know we have at times been indulgent and disruptive as we pursued our singular goal of making this the best project possible. From patience and small favors to major conceptual contributions, all of our colleagues have in one way or another helped us in our work. We thank each and every one of you. We are particularly grateful to Dr. Howard Giles, department chair, for both his administrative and intellectual support. In addition, the insightful comments of Dr. James Bradac have often helped to inspire our thinking.

The strength and support of the university professional staff who work with us have been an invaluable asset for the project. We are in great debt to the staff of the Department of Communication and the Law & Society Program at UCSB, particularly Betty Fisk, for their help in the project's administration. In addition, very special recognition must go to Faye Nennig, our own administrative assistant, who has been creative, caring, tireless, and incredibly efficient. As we have set a hectic pace inventing tasks that require people, space, equipment, and other resources, Faye has sprinted along with us, managing the project's endeavors and keeping the machinery of this project running. Thanks also to Carrie Colvin, who has done a superb job managing our data entry, and to Mike Berry, who worked on many early aspects of the project during his leave from the University of Bath.

Throughout this project we have been helped constantly by our colleagues at the three other NTVS sites. To (1) Dr. Ellen Wartella, Dr. Charles Whitney, Dr. Dominic Lasorsa, and Dr. Wayne Danielson of the University of Texas; (2) Dr. Joanne Cantor of the University of Wisconsin; and (3) Dr. Frank Biocca and Dr. Jane Brown of the University of North Carolina, we offer our sincere appreciation. While facing many demands and challenges from their own study's agenda, each of these scholars found the time to contribute important ideas and critiques of our work that have challenged us, have stimulated us, and have certainly helped to strengthen our research and its presentation in this report. In addition, we have been impressed with the dedication of the graduate research assistants who have collaborated with our faculty colleagues at the other sites: Adrianna Olivarez, Shannon Campbell, Rafael Lopez, Saam Haddad, and Marlies Klijn from the University of Texas; Kris Harrison from the University of Wisconsin and Fuyuan Shen, Jay Bernhardt, Leandro Batista, Karen Kemp, Greg Makris, Howard Straker, and Elena Carbone from the University of North Carolina.

This project also required the time and dedication of the staff of Mediascope. To Marcy Kelly, Bill Boyd, Vickie Valice, Stephanie Carbone, and Elena Sweet, we owe thanks for coordinating and administering a project that has proved to be bigger than any of its architects ever imagined. We especially thank Joel Federman, former Research Director at Mediascope, for his continued support and scholarly insights. He is a valued colleague who has contributed immensely to this project from day one, starting with the design of the research all the way through to the writing of this report. At another level, his interpersonal skills have amazed us as he has resolved many of the contentious issues that inevitably emerge when many strong-willed people are forced to work together on a project about which they all care passionately. Now that the management of the overall NTVS project has moved from Mediascope to UCSB, we are pleased that Joel has agreed to join us here and to continue his role as research coordinator among the four NTVS sites.

Throughout the 18 months that this project has evolved, we have reported our progress and gained valuable feedback from an impressive group that comprises the NTVS Board of Advisors. This study has benefitted from their comments as well as their commitment to insure that our research findings make an important contribution to the TV violence debate. To each of these members we extend our sincere appreciation:

Dr. Trina Anglin	Society for Adolescent Medicine
Char Beals	Cable and Telecommunications: A Marketing Society
Darlene Chavez	National Education Association
Belva Davis	American Federation of Television and Radio Artists
Dr. Del Elliot	American Society of Criminology andAmerica Sociological Association
Moctesuma Esparza	Caucus for Producers, Writers, and Directors
Carl Gottlieb	Writers Guild of America
Dr. Robert McAfee	American Medical Association
E. Michael McCann	American Bar Association
Dorothea Petrie	Producers Guild of America
Dr. Robert Phillips	American Psychiatric Association
Gene Reynolds	Directors Guild of America
Dr. Donald Roberts	International Communication Association
Dr. Don Shifrin	American Academy of Pediatrics
Dr. Barbara Staggers	National Children's Hospital Association
Jeanette Weis	National Parent-Teachers Association
Dr. Brian Wilcox	American Psychological Association

More far afield, we are in debt to many colleagues who have shared with us ideas and perspectives that have helped us with our work. In particular, we want to thank Dr. Barrie Gunter of the University of Sheffield, Dr. Horace Newcomb of the University of Texas, and Dr. George Gerbner of the University of Pennsylvania.

We also wish to acknowledge the National Cable Television Association for its financial support and cooperation regarding the conduct of this research. To oversimplify, we've been given everything we've asked for and otherwise been left alone to do our work the best we know how, which is exactly as it should be. We are especially thankful to Winston (Tony) Cox, the dynamic leader of the cable industry committee that initiated this project, for reminding us from time to time that our report must speak to real-world issues as much as to theoretical constructs. And our primary contact at NCTA, Vice President for Research Cynthia Brumfield, has earned our respect by demonstrating consistently throughout the project that she and her organization understand and fully honor our guarantee of independence for this research.

Finally, we offer our warmest, heartfelt thanks to all of the undergraduate students who have worked on this project. Collectively, they have provided a range a important contributions. Some gave us essential feedback on our first attempts at categorizing violent depictions, which helped to shape and refine our content analysis framework. Others helped to manage our sample of thousands of hours of television content. Many performed more specialized tasks, and most all mastered our obviously complex codebook. That task alone required months of dedication before one could even begin the actual work of coding programs for violence. We recognize that without their contributions there would be no report. We thank you all.

Research Assistants (Coding and Lab Supervision)

Bennett, Carolyn	Braun, Alan	Cox, Steve
Foderaro, Bill	Foley, Jeff	Fraser, Mandy
Fuson, Andrea	Goette, Ulla	Ishibashi, Chris
Pinto, Jessica	Roudebush, Lori	Schwartz, Julie
Spaniardi, Amy	Williams, Michelle	

Coding

Banville, Michelle	Beaulieu, Cynthia	Benedict, Aloha
Butler, Christy	Cannon, Steve	Carter, Terri
Cassuto, Denise	Chambliss, Marlene	Chan, Bryan
Channing, Kristi	Collins, Kimberly	Fier, Timothy
Gargaro, Catherine	George, Jenni-Marie	Goodhue, Liz
Green, Tara	Grossman, Jamie	Haase, Derek
Holman, Joy	Johannsen, River	Kearnaghan, Jason
Lindstrom, Brett	Liu, Sue	Malouf, Diana
McCabe, Susan	Merin, Lori	Miklusak, Courtney
Moore, Jay	Murano, Jill	Nelson, Akane
Panek, Kristina	Rhee, Karen	Romero, Victoria
Rusher, Julie	Sanger, Kristin	Scarlett, Jennifer
Senter, Tracy	Sherman, Jesse	Siemens, Jennifer
Sullivan, Brendan	Teichmann, Michael	Thompson, Analisa
Valpredo, Michael	Vincent, Colin	von Hoetzendorff, Meg
Wood, J. Paige		

Data Entry

Appel, Mike	Bates, Cheryl	Cardona, Anel
Silvas, Carlos	Woo, Nancy	

University of Texas, Austin

We add our thanks to those already acknowledged in the University of California at Santa Barbara report, most especially to Winston (Tony) Cox and Cynthia Brumfield at the National Cable Television Association, to the NTVS Board of Advisors, to Professor George Gerbner of the University of Pennsylvania, and to Joel Federman, the research director at Mediascope. We must also express our deepest gratitude to our colleagues at the University of California, Santa Barbara, Profs. Edward Donnerstein, Dale Kunkel, Daniel Linz, James Potter, and Barbara Wilson, and to the UCSB graduate research assistants, Eva Blumenthal, Timothy Gray, and particularly Stacy Smith.

At the University of Texas, Profs. Horace Newcomb, Janet Staiger and Marilyn Schultz have helped us immeasurably, as have Robert Risher, Jackie Srnensky and Anne Reed in the Office of the Dean of the College of Communication. Three graduate research assistants, Shannon Campbell, Saam Haddad and Sam Moore, made important contributions in the early stages of the project. Without their help, and that of our student coders--Patrick Aziz, Meredith Butler, Alison Cabral, Ben Chorush, Sylvana Fierro, Shane Miller, Neil Pollner, Diane Quest, Arlene Rivero, Pamela Rivero, Felipe Stevenson, Liza Trevino, Alice Tsai, and Lisa Wyatt--this project would never have become a reality.

We thank you all.

University of Wisconsin, Madison

The authors would first like to thank the National Cable Television Association for providing the support for this project, and for letting us do the research in a truly independent fashion. Without this support, the research in its current form would not have been possible. Thanks also to Mediascope, and especially to Marcy Kelly and Joel Federman, for their support and guidance, to the members of the NTVS Advisory Board, and to all the researchers at the other three sites.

We would like to thank Kurt Kiefer, Director of External Research for the Madison Metropolitan School District, for approving our proposal for testing students in the Madison Schools. We would especially like to thank Robert Pelligrino, Principal of Velma Hamilton Middle School, Booker Gardner, Principal of Van Hise Elementary School, Jan Dowden, Principal of Sennett Middle School, and Anthony Middlebrooks, director of AfterSchool Daycare, for their wonderful cooperation and enthusiastic support of this project.

We would also like to express our gratitude to Marina Krcmar for the creative and energetic way she helped conceptualize and conduct Study II, and to Nick Van Straten for the enormous energy he put into preparing, planning, and running Study III. Many thanks are also due to Amy Nathanson, who helped in innumerable ways with the research and report preparation; to Eugenia Peck for help with coding; to Debbie Hanson for the enormous amount of work she has had to do to keep track of the purchasing and the personnel on this project; to Linda Henzl for her creative and thorough secretarial support; and to Dave Fritsch and the other engineers for patiently advising us on our equipment needs, setting up our equipment, and keeping it running in top form. We would also like to thank the other graduate and undergraduate students who helped with the project by interviewing children: Patricia Cicero, Debbie Cohen, Paul Dearlove, Elizabeth Glinski, Linda Godbold, Heather Haskins, Andrea Jellinek, Mike Kaye, Courtney Kurtin, Matt Liegel, Ryan Lingsweiler, Wai-Mei Loon, Rebecca McAfee, Matt McCoy, Mike McCoy, Jennifer Metz, Lisa Mleczko, Lindsay Morrow, Elizabeth Navis, Michelle Oppermann, Michael Pallett, Erik Peterson, Jennifer Samp, Kelly Sarauer, Samantha Schaul, Jeff Shapack, Jennifer Slone, Brian Smith, Andy Sowle, Anne Sprague, Courtney Stillman, Sandie Traxler, Jonna Walsh, and Tiffany Zimmermann.

We would like to thank the wonderful children for their cooperation during this project; to thank their parents for allowing their children to be participants; and to extend our appreciation to the college students who took part as well.

University of North Carolina, Chapel Hill

The research team at the University of North Carolina at Chapel Hill would like to offer sincere thanks to the following individuals: Cynthia Brumfield, Tony Cox and the National Cable Television Association for their willingness to support our research efforts; Marcy Kelly, Joel Federman and the staff at Mediascope for their contributions in administering the project; Dr. Donald Roberts and the members of the NTVS Advisory Council for overseeing the research; and all of our fellow NTVS researchers from the University of California at Santa Barbara, the University of Texas at Austin, and the University of Wisconsin at Madison for their support and participation in our work.

We would also like to thank the following individuals for lending their support and resources to our studies: Bob Stepno, graduate assistant; Dr. Richard Rideout, director of the Division of Youth Services for the North Carolina Department of Human Resources; Mr. Sterlin Holt, director, and Dr. Janet Clarke-McLean, senior psychologist, at the C.A. Dillon School, Butner, NC; Mr. David Holdzkom, executive director of Research, Development and Accountability, Durham (NC) Public Schools; Mr. Brandon Smith, principal, and Ms. Judith Bell, teacher; and all of the students who participated in the studies; Richard Cole, dean, and Ms. Judy Meade, business manager, UNC-CH School of Journalism and Mass Communication; Dr. Donald Wood, contract specialist, UNC-CH; and Prof. Frances Campbell, chair, Academic Affairs Institutional Review Board.

INTRODUCTION

Joel Federman
Center for Communication and Social Policy
University of California, Santa Barbara

The National Television Violence Study (NTVS) is a three year effort to assess violence on television. The project, which began in June 1994, involves the participation of media scholars at four university sites, an oversight Council of representatives from national policy organizations, and project administration and coordination. It is funded by the National Cable Television Association. This volume represents the first year research findings of the project.

Project Overview

Each of the universities makes a unique contribution to the study. Scholars at the University of California, Santa Barbara conduct a content analysis of violence in series, daytime, movies, specials, children's shows, and music videos. The University of Texas at Austin provides a similar analysis of violence in reality programs, including tabloid news, talk shows, police shows, and documentaries. The University of Wisconsin, Madison analyzes the role of violence ratings and advisories used on television, including their effect on the viewing decisions of parents and children. The University of North Carolina, Chapel Hill, conducts studies of the effectiveness of anti-violence public service announcements and educational initiatives produced by the television industry.

The project also involves the efforts of an oversight Council, whose role is to assure the integrity and independence of the study, provide advice and counsel to the researchers, endorse the validity of the study and identify implications from the findings. The Council is comprised of representatives from eighteen national organizations that have an interest or concern with the impact of television on society. These organizations represent the professions of education, medicine, law, psychology and communication; one third of the Council members are from the entertainment industry.

The project's administration and coordination was undertaken initially by Mediascope, Inc., a nonprofit organization that promotes constructive depictions of health and social issues in mass media. This included convening the NTVS Council; arranging for a series of meetings with representatives of television industry; coordinating the research effort; releasing the study's first annual report; and managing the videotaping of more than 6,000 programs for the first two years of the content analysis. Beginning in July 1996, the coordination of the study was transferred to the Center for Communication and Social Policy at the University of California, Santa Barbara.

Intellectual Framework

There are many ways that violence on television can be assessed. The National Television Violence Study takes a public health approach to the issue, treating violence as a partially preventable social ill.

The study does not exaggerate the importance of televised violence among the myriad contributors to violence in society. It recognizes that the causes of violence are manifold, and include biological and psychological factors, as well as broader social and cultural ones. Among these, however, television violence has been recognized as a significant factor contributing to violent and aggressive antisocial behavior by an overwhelming majority of the scientific community, including such organizations as the American Psychological Association, American Medical Association, the Surgeon General's Advisory Committee on Television and Behavior and the National Institute of Mental Health.

It is also recognized that televised violence does not have a uniform effect on viewers. The relationship between viewing violence and subsequent behavior depends both on the nature of the depiction and the makeup of the audience. In some cases, the same portrayal of violence may have different effects on different audiences. For example, graphically portrayed violence may elicit fear in some viewers and aggression in others. Peer influences, family role models, social and economic status, educational level and the availability of weapons can each significantly alter the likelihood of a particular reaction to viewing violence on television.

Through primary and secondary research, the study examines the landscape of television, as well as the interaction between the medium and its audience, and attempts to illuminate those factors which positively or negatively alter the risk of viewing violence. The study highlights a mass of scientific evidence regarding the differential effects on audiences of various kinds of violent portrayals. It identifies aspects of those portrayals for which there is clear evidence of a risk of harmful effects on audiences, and then analyzes a representative sample of television to determine the relative presence of those factors. Such factors include the reason for the violence, the nature of the perpetrator and target, the consequences of the violence, its extent or graphicness, presence of rewards, punishments, weapons or humor, and the degree of realism of the portrayal. The study also asks whether violence ratings and advisories can alter viewer choices about violent programming, and how anti-violence messages in programs and public service announcements can be crafted to maximum effect.

The Report

Public concern about violence in the media, particularly television, has become highly politicized. The television industry has become a focal point for attention in the national attempt to redress the enormous social and personal costs of violence. While it would be an error in judgment to place the burden of blame for violence on a single social institution, the study emphasizes the fact that the effect of thousands of messages conveyed through the most powerful medium of mass communication cannot be underestimated.

The following report was conducted with the goal of encouraging more responsible television programming and viewing. It is hoped that it will also contribute to a larger societal strategy of violence prevention, helping to mitigate the terrible price in pain, suffering, and lives lost to violence in America each year.

PART I

TELEVISION VIOLENCE AND ITS CONTEXT: UNIVERSITY OF CALIFORNIA, SANTA BARBARA STUDY

Dr. Barbara J. Wilson
Dr. Dale Kunkel
Dr. Dan Linz
Dr. James Potter
Dr. Ed Donnerstein
Stacy L. Smith
Eva Blumenthal
Timothy Gray

SUMMARY

Violence on television may be presented in many different forms or settings. It may be performed by heroic characters or villains. It may be rewarded or it may be punished. Violence may occur without much pain and suffering, or it may cause tremendous physical anguish. It may be shown close-up or at a distance.

These and other similar variations represent the context of television violence. Such contextual features hold important implications for the influence of violent depictions on the audience. Some types of depictions pose a substantial risk of harmful effects for viewers, whereas other portrayals may be pro-social and actually beneficial for the audience.

This study has two primary goals: (1) to identify the contextual features associated with violent depictions that most significantly increase the risk of a harmful effect on the audience, and; (2) to analyze the television environment in depth to report on the nature and extent of violent depictions, focusing in particular on the relative presence of the most problematic portrayals.

The foundation for this content analysis was a review of the entire body of existing scientific knowledge regarding the impact of televised violence. This analysis identified three primary types of harmful effects associated with viewing television violence: learning aggressive attitudes and behaviors, becoming desensitized to real-world violence, and developing unrealistic fear of being victimized by violence. The risk of such effects occurring is influenced strongly by the contextual patterns in the ways by which violence is depicted.

In order to accurately assess the important contextual elements in television content, it is necessary to consider multiple levels of analysis. This study analyzed violent content at three distinct levels: (1) how characters interact with one another when violence occurs (labeled a violent interaction); (2) how violent interactions are grouped together (labeled a violent scene), and (3) how violence is presented in the context of the overall program.

Programs on 23 of the most frequently viewed broadcast and cable television channels were randomly selected for analysis over a 20 week period. The study monitored programs between the hours of 6:00 a.m. and 11:00 p.m., a total of 17 hours a day across seven days of the week. In total, the project examined approximately 2500 hours of television that includes 2693 programs, representing one of the largest and most representative samples of television ever studied using scientific content analysis procedures.

The key findings of the study were that: (1) the context in which most violence is presented on television poses risks for viewers; (2) the negative consequences of violence are not often portrayed in violent programming; (3) perpetrators go unpunished in most scenes of violence; (4) violent programs rarely employ an anti-violent theme; and (5) on the positive side, television violence is usually not explicit or graphic. The study offers recommendations for parents, television producers, and public policy-makers.

Chapter 1

INTRODUCTION TO THE PROJECT

It is well established by scientific research that exposure to televised violence contributes to a range of anti-social or harmful effects on many viewers. It is also the case that not all research on the impact of violent depictions produces evidence of a negative effect on the audience. We believe that much of the variability in the findings can be traced to differences in the nature of the violent depictions studied.

Obviously, there is a vast array of approaches to presenting violent material. In terms of its visual presentation, the violence may occur on-screen and be shown graphically, or it may occur off-screen but be clearly implied. Violent acts may be shown close-up or at a distance. There are also differences in scripting of characters who commit violence and their reasons for doing so. And there are differences in the depiction of the results of violence, including both the pain and suffering of victims as well as the outcomes for the perpetrator. Simply put, not all portrayals of violence are the same; they vary in many important ways.

The goal of this research project is two-fold: first, we seek to identify the contextual features associated with violent depictions that most significantly increase the risk of a harmful effect on the audience; and second, we then analyze the television environment in depth to report on the nature and extent of violent depictions, focusing in particular on the relative presence of the most problematic portrayals.

To accomplish the first goal, we have reviewed the entire body of existing scientific knowledge regarding the impact of televised violence. Drawing conclusions as warranted from this evidence, we have devised an elaborate framework for evaluating the important contextual features associated with violent depictions. We have then established systematic procedures for measuring the presence of these features across the full diversity of types of television content.

To accomplish our second goal, we have collected what we believe to be the largest and most representative sample of television content ever evaluated by a single research project. Over the period from October, 1994 to June, 1995, we have randomly selected programs on 23 television channels to create a composite week of content for each source. We monitored programs between the hours of 6:00 am and 11:00 pm, a total of 17 hours a day across seven days of the week, yielding a sum of approximately 119 hours per channel. The 23 channels we studied represent the television sources most frequently viewed by the American public, with the exception that we did not evaluate sports or news and thus omitted channels such as CNN and ESPN. In total, we have collected approximately 2500 hours of television programming that includes 3185 programs.

Our findings focus on the levels of violence that are found on all sources of television content, including the broadcast networks; independent broadcast; public broadcast; basic cable; and premium cable. We also address variability in the presence of violence in different program types or genres, including children's programming; and at different times of day and night. Throughout all of our analyses, we emphasize the importance of the context in which violence is depicted, separating portrayals that pose the greatest risk to viewers from those that are pro-social and would likely discourage violence.

This research was commissioned and funded by the National Cable Television Association. Although industry sponsored, this project has been conducted solely and independently by researchers at the University of California, Santa Barbara, along with the help of our colleagues at the University of Texas, University of Wisconsin, and University of North Carolina. At the outset of the project, we were guaranteed complete freedom and autonomy to pursue our research in whatever fashion we deemed appropriate. Throughout all phases of this study, that independence was never compromised even an inch. No industry figure, or anyone else for that matter, ever attempted to influence our methods, our findings, or our conclusions.

The report we present here reflects the collective wisdom of five senior faculty and three graduate student researchers. The five senior faculty have devoted their entire careers to the study of media effects. Several are experts on violence, others are experts on child development, and across the entire group we have published more than 300 research articles in leading scientific journals in the field, along with numerous books, and many hundreds of papers and related reports. The findings we have produced for this report represent the identical work that would have emerged had this project been funded by the government, by a philanthropist, or by our university. We stake our collective reputations on its accuracy and legitimacy. We have strived to be fair in assessing all aspects of the industry, including cable and broadcasting, evenly.

This report represents the first of three annual evaluations that will be conducted using the unique analytical framework we have devised. As such, we will be able to track precisely changes over time in the relative presence of violent depictions deemed most problematic for influencing the audience. We hope that this information will offer a meaningful commentary on the state of violence on American television for parents, policy makers, and the media industry.

Chapter 2

THE EFFECTS OF EXPOSURE TO MEDIA VIOLENCE

We live in a violent society. As a nation we rank first among all developed countries in the world in homicides per capita. The pervasiveness of violence is staggering, particularly involving children and adolescents. For example, consider the following statistics cited by the American Psychological Association (1993):

- Every five minutes a child is arrested for a violent crime.
- Gun related violence takes the life of an American child every three hours.
- Every day over 100,000 children carry guns to schools.
- In a recent survey of fifth graders in New Orleans, more than 50% report being a victim of violence, and 70% have seen weapons being used.
- Adolescents account for 24% of all violent crimes leading to arrest. The rate has increased over time for the age groups 12-19, and is down for age groups 35 and older.
- Among individuals age 15 to 24 years old, homicide is the second leading cause of death, and for African American youth it is the leading cause.
- A child growing up in Chicago is 15 times more likely to be murdered than a child growing up in Northern Ireland.

What accounts for these alarming figures? There is universal agreement that many factors contribute to violent behavior, such as gangs, drugs, guns, poverty, and racism. Violence is truly multifaceted, such that these factors may independently and interactively combine to generate antisocial behavior. Groups like the American Psychological Association, American Medical Association, National Academy of Science, and Centers for Disease Control and Prevention have all recently examined the perplexing problem of the causes of violence. While recognizing the complexity in determining the causes of violent behavior, all of these groups have concluded that the mass media bear some responsibility for contributing to real world violence. Viewing media violence is not the only, nor even the most important, contributor to violent behavior. Furthermore, it is not every act of violence in the media that raises concern, nor every child or adult who is affected. But there is clear evidence that exposure to media violence contributes in significant ways to violence in society. This conclusion is based on careful and critical readings of the social science research collected over the last 40 years.

While media violence may not be the single most important contributor to aggression, there is wide consensus that it may be the one factor that is the easiest to mitigate. To devise solutions to the problem of media violence, two fundamental issues need to be addressed: what types of violent material are the most problematic; and what types of violence exist on television. This report addresses information at both of these levels, providing a detailed analysis of violence on television that is framed according to all existing scientific knowledge that informs us about the effects of media violence on the audience.

In this section of the report, we provide an overview of the existing knowledge about the relationship between exposure to media violence and real world aggressive behavior. We also summarize the theoretical models that account for these findings. Collectively, this research evidence forms the foundation for the concerns about media violence.

What Does the Research Community Conclude?

Over the past few decades many governmental and professional organizations have conducted exhaustive reviews of the scientific literature on the relationship between media violence and aggressive behavior. These investigations have consistently documented how media violence, across various genres, is related to the aggressive behavior of many children, adolescents, and adults, as well as an influence on perceptions and attitudes about violence.

Two early, major reports from the government's leading public health agencies, the 1972 Surgeon General's Report and the 1982 National Institute of Mental Health review, concluded that television occupied a significant role in the lives of both children and adults. Both of these reports were emphatic in their claim that many types of televised violence can influence aggressive behavior. The Surgeon General's Report concluded that there was a consistent and significant correlation between viewing televised violence and subsequent aggression. This finding emerged across many different measures of aggressive behavior and across different methodological approaches (e.g., experimental evidence, longitudinal field studies) to studying the problem. The Surgeon General's research made clear that there was a direct, causal link between exposure to televised violence and subsequent aggressive behavior by the viewer.

The NIMH report, which followed ten years later, added significantly to the conclusions of the Surgeon General. First, the age range of the effects was extended to include preschoolers and older adolescents, and the findings were generalized to girls as well as to boys. Secondly, and perhaps more important, it was established that viewers learn more than aggressive behavior. They learn to fear being a victim. Heavy viewing may lead to aggression, but for some individuals it will lead to fear and apprehension about being victimized by aggression. It is more than aggressive behavior, the report concluded, that should be of concern.

In recent years additional reports, particularly from the Centers for Disease Control (1991), National Academy of Science (1993), and the American Psychological Association (1993) have lent further support to the conclusion that the mass media contribute to aggressive attitudes and behavior. The most comprehensive of these reports comes from the American Psychological Association, which established a Commission on Youth and Violence to exhaustively examine the scientific literature on the causes and prevention of violence. Like previous investigations into violence, the role of the mass media was considered, and the conclusions reached were similar. Specifically, the APA report concluded that:

1. Nearly four decades of research on television and other media have documented the almost universal exposure of American children to high levels of media violence.

2. There is absolutely no doubt that those who are heavy viewers of this violence demonstrate increased acceptance of aggressive attitudes and increased aggressive behavior.

This correlation between violence viewing and aggressive behavior is fairly stable over time, place, and demographics (Donnerstein, Slaby & Eron, 1994; Huesmann & Eron, 1986), and also across varieties of television genres (Paik & Comstock, 1994). An examination of hundreds of experimental and longitudinal studies supports the position that viewing violence in the mass media is related to aggressive behavior (Huston et al., 1992). More important, naturalistic field studies and cross national studies support the position that the viewing of televised aggression leads to increases in subsequent aggression and that such behavior can become part of a lasting behavioral pattern (Huesmann & Eron, 1986). Aggressive habits learned early in life form the foundation for later behavior. Aggressive children who have trouble in school and with relating to peers tend to watch more television; the violence they see there, in turn, reinforces their tendency toward aggression. These effects are both short-term and long-lasting. In fact, Huesmann and his colleagues (i.e., Huesmann, 1986; Huesmann, Eron, Lefkowitz, & Walder, 1984) found a clear and significant relationship between early exposure to televised violence at age eight and adult aggressive behavior (measured by seriousness of criminal acts) 22 years later. As Huesmann (1986) noted:

> Aggressive habits seem to be learned early in life, and once established, are resistant to change and predictive of serious adult antisocial behavior. If a child's observation of media violence promotes the learning of aggressive habits, it can have harmful lifelong consequences. Consistent with this theory, early television habits are in fact correlated with adult criminality (pp. 129-130).

Consequently, children's exposure to violence in the mass media, particularly at young ages, can have lifelong consequences.

In addition to increasing violent behavior toward others, viewing violence on television changes attitudes and behaviors in response to violence in significant ways. Even those who do not themselves behave violently are affected by their viewing of violence in two significant ways.

First, prolonged viewing of media violence can lead to emotional desensitization toward real world violence and the victims of violence, which can result in callous attitudes toward violence directed at others and a decreased likelihood to take action on behalf of the victim when violence occurs (Donnerstein, Slaby, & Eron, 1994). Research on desensitization to media violence has shown that although observers react initially with relatively intense physiological responses to scenes of violence, habituation can occur with prolonged or repeated exposure and this habituation can carry over to other settings (Thomas, Horton, Lippincott, & Drabman, 1977). Once viewers are emotionally "comfortable" with violent content, they may also evaluate media violence more favorably in other domains (Linz, Donnerstein, & Penrod, 1988).

Second, viewing violence can increase the fear of becoming a victim of violence, with a resultant increase in self-protective behaviors and increased mistrust of others. Research by Gerbner and his colleagues (e.g., Gerbner, Gross, Signiorelli & Morgan, 1986) has shown that heavy viewers of media violence tend to have a perception of social reality which matches that presented in the media. That is, heavy viewers tend to see the world as more crime-ridden and dangerous, and are more fearful of walking alone in their own neighborhoods. Furthermore, viewing violence increases viewers' appetites for becoming involved in violence or exposing themselves to violence (APA, 1993).

In summary, the research literature over the last three decades has been highly consistent in its findings in three major areas of effects associated with exposure to media violence. First, there is increased violence toward others due primarily to the effect of <u>learning and imitation</u>. Second, there is increased callousness toward violence among others, which has commonly been labeled the <u>desensitization</u> effect. And third, there is increased <u>fearfulness</u> (both in the short and long term) about becoming a victim of violence, often referred to as the "mean world syndrome" by Gerbner and his colleagues. In the following section we will address the major theoretical explanations for these effects.

What Theoretical Models Account for these Effects?

<u>Learning and Imitation</u>

As we noted earlier, there is general consensus that viewers learn both aggressive attitudes and behaviors from exposure to media violence. From a scientific perspective, that means such relationships can be predicted with strong confidence. It is a separate but equally important scientific question to explain the process by which these effects occur. Theoretical models are devised to provide that information.

<u>**Social learning theory**</u>. One of the most important models that explains how learning and imitation of violence occur via the media is Social Learning Theory (Bandura, 1971). This theory asserts that modes of response are acquired either through direct experience or indirectly through the observation of models, such as those presented in the mass media. Through the observation of mass media models the observer comes to learn which behaviors are "appropriate"-- that is, which behaviors will later be rewarded, and which will be punished. Implicit in this approach is the assumption that most human behavior is directed toward attaining some anticipated reward.

Many laboratory studies have demonstrated that children and adults acquire novel behaviors by observing models (Bandura, 1965; Bandura, Ross & Ross, 1961, 1963a, 1963b; Berkowitz & Geen, 1967; Liebert & Baron, 1972). Typically these studies have involved showing children or adults an aggressive model who is either rewarded or punished for aggressive behavior. After watching a model who is positively reinforced for aggression, the observers are more likely to behave in a similar manner. These studies indicate that viewing a model's aggressive behavior disinhibits, or encourages, aggressive behavior.

Research outside the laboratory, primarily field studies, has also supported the social learning model (Comstock & Paik, 1991). For example, Huesmann and Eron (1986) suggest that aggression, as a characteristic way of solving problems, is learned at a young age and becomes more impervious to change as the child grows older. In a longitudinal study to examine the long term effects of television violence on aggressive and criminal behavior, Huesmann, Eron, Lefkowitz & Walder (1984) studied a group of youth over a 22 year period. This study collected data on aggression and television viewing when the subjects were 8, 18, and 30 years old. The researchers found evidence of a longitudinal effect that spanned the 22 years from age 8 to age 30. For boys, early television violence viewing correlated with self-reported aggression at age 30 and added significantly to the prediction of serious criminal arrests accumulated by age 30. These effects occurred independently of social class, intellectual capability, and parenting variables (Huesmann, 1986). Huesmann and Eron (1986) concluded that early exposure to television violence stimulates aggression, and that early aggression is a statistical precursor of later criminal behavior. These researchers find a longitudinal relationship between habitual childhood exposure to television violence and adult crime. Their analyses suggest that approximately 10 percent of the variability in later criminal behavior can be attributed to television violence.

The learning theory approach to explaining mass media effects has gained wide acceptance among media scholars. Most research in recent years has centered on the particular variables which facilitate the acquisition of aggressive responses through observational learning. A detailed discussion of these "contextual" variables which mediate the influence of aggressive models will be presented in Chapter 3.

Priming effects theory. In the last decade, a new theoretical proposal has emerged which serves to complement the more traditional learning theories' account of the effects of exposure to violent media. Berkowitz (1984) and his colleagues (Berkowitz & Rogers, 1986) have proposed that many media effects are immediate, transitory and relatively short-lived. They have offered an explanation for these effects grounded in cognitive psychology theory (Neisser, 1967). Basically, the explanation is that when people witness an event through the media, ideas are "activated" and for a short period of time tend to prime or evoke other semantically related thoughts. After an idea is activated there is a greater likelihood that it and associated thought elements will come to mind again. This process of thought activation has been termed a "priming effect." Berkowitz suggests, for instance, that aggressive ideas brought on by viewing violence in the mass media can prime other semantically related thoughts. Once these additional thoughts have come to mind they influence aggressive responding in a variety of ways.

Berkowitz's explanation is appealing because it provides a way of unifying several tangents of mass media research by invoking one relatively simple explanation.

For example, one of the contextual variables we will examine later is the observer's identification with media characters who commit violence. This theoretical model suggests that viewers who identify with certain actors may be vividly imagining themselves as these characters and thinking of themselves as carrying out the depicted actions. Identification with characters in the mass media should activate high imagery thoughts and the subsequent priming of these thoughts might influence subsequent behavior. It is as if viewers draw a lesson from what they see: "What happens on the screen might also happen to me if I engage in the same behavior."

Many studies provide evidence that the activation of aggressive ideas through exposure to media violence primes other aggression-related thoughts, which in turn may have important social consequences. For example, a study by Carver, Ganellan, Froming and Chambers (1983) presented participants with a brief film depicting a hostile interaction between a business man and his secretary; afterwards, subjects evaluated an ambiguous person as more hostile than did those who had not seen the film. In another experiment (Berkowitz, Parker & West; cited in Berkowitz, 1973) children who read aggressive comic books were more likely to choose words with aggressive connotations to complete sentences later presented by the experimenters than subjects who had read neutral comics. Other studies have shown that people who have witnessed certain types of violent media (e.g., depictions of sexual violence) are more likely to report they would use violence in interpersonal situations (Malamuth & Check, 1981). There is also evidence to suggest that being primed with aggressive thoughts often leads to aggressive acts. Carver et al. (1983) showed that men who were induced to have aggressive thoughts delivered the most intense electric shocks to other men. Other studies (e.g., Worchel, 1972) have shown similar results.

The social developmental model. From either the modeling or the cognitive theoretical perspective, media depictions of violence have a high likelihood of being emulated. One issue that can be taken with these theories, however, is that they are primarily one-directional. Media effects are presumed to arise from the environment and to influence individuals in the audience. There is little attempt to account for audience expectations, more active construal of messages, or the continued interaction of the viewer with the mass media. This one-sided approach leaves many important questions unaddressed. What are the consequences of viewing media violence for future interest in violent media? Once the individual has been exposed to media violence, does he or she seek further violence viewing? And how can we explain the fact that some individuals are affected by televised violence differently than others? We can address these questions with a recent theoretical model that emphasizes the reciprocal nature of the viewer and his or her interest in media violence, and which also adds consideration of individual viewer characteristics in explaining media effects. This model is the developmental theory of media violence effects proposed by Huesmann (1986).

Huesmann draws upon ideas in social cognition to explain the effects of televised violence, especially the notion that learning the appropriate course of action in a situation involves the retention of behavioral rules or "scripts." In this model, as in social learning theory, behavioral strategies learned through watching violent television are tried in the immediate environment and, if reinforced, are retained and used again. The most important contribution of the social developmental model proposed by Huesmann, however, is the explication of personal and interpersonal factors as intervening variables that link violence viewing and aggressive behavior.

Past empirical research has established five variables as particularly important in maintaining the television viewing-aggression relationship (Huesmann, 1986). These key factors are the child's (1) intellectual achievement, (2) social popularity, (3) identification with the television characters, (4) belief in the realism of the violence shown on television, and (5) amount of fantasizing about aggression. According to Huesmann, a heavy diet of television violence sets into motion a sequence of processes, based on these personal and interpersonal factors, that results in many viewers becoming not only more aggressive but also developing increased interest in seeing more television violence.

Research suggests that children who have poorer academic skills behave more aggressively. They also watch television with greater frequency, watch more violent programs, and believe violent programs are more accurate portrayals of life (Huesmann & Eron, 1986). Huesmann speculates that aggressiveness interferes with the social interactions between the viewer and his or her teachers and peers that are needed in order to develop academic potential. Slow intellectual achievement may therefore be related to heightened television violence viewing in two ways. First, heightened television viewing in general may interfere with intellectual achievement (Lefkowitz, Eron, Walder, & Huesmann, 1977). Children who cannot obtain gratification from success in school may turn to television shows to obtain vicariously the successes they cannot otherwise achieve. Aggressive children may also be substantially less popular with their peers (Huesmann & Eron 1986). Longitudinal analyses suggest, however, that the relationship between unpopularity and aggression is bidirectional. Not only do more aggressive children become less popular, but less popular children seem to become more aggressive. In addition, less popular children view more television and therefore see more violence on television.

Identification with television characters may also be important. Children who perceive themselves as like television characters are more likely to be influenced by the aggressive scripts they observe (Huesmann, Lagerspetz, & Eron 1984). This may be particularly true for boys. At the same time, more aggressive children tend to identify with aggressive characters, and those who identify more with television characters behave more aggressively.

For an aggressive behavioral script to be encoded in memory and maintained, it must be salient to a child. Huesmann speculates that realistic depictions are the most salient depictions. If a violent action is perceived as totally unrealistic, it is likely to receive less attention than material which is more directly pertinent to the viewer. Early investigations of televised violence have emphasized perceived reality as a determinant of imitative effects (e.g., Feshbach, 1972). Later investigations by Huesmann and his colleagues have confirmed that the relation between violence viewing and aggression is heightened for children who believe the violence is representative of real life (Huesmann et al., 1984).

Finally, the maintenance of aggressive scripts might be accomplished through the rehearsal of these scripts in the child's mind, which is facilitated by continued exposure to media violence. Research has shown that children's self-reports of violent fantasies are positively correlated with both aggression and greater television viewing (Huesmann & Eron, 1986).

Desensitization

Over the years, research on affective reactions to violent messages has been concerned with the possibility that continued exposure to violence in the mass media will undermine feelings of concern, empathy, or sympathy viewers might have toward victims of actual violence. The early research on desensitization to media violence involved exposure to rather mild forms of television violence for relatively short periods of time (Cline, Croft, & Courrier, 1973; Thomas, 1982; Thomas, Horton, Lippencott, & Drabman, 1977). These studies indicated that heavy viewers of media violence showed less physiological reactivity to violent film clips compared to light viewers; that general physiological arousal decreases as viewers watched more violent media; and that children as well as adults are susceptible to this effect.

Research on longer term exposure and more graphic forms of violence has shown further desensitization effects. For example, Linz, Donnerstein, and Penrod (1984, 1987) measured the reactions of college-age men to films portraying violence against women (mostly in a sexual context) viewed across a five-day period. Comparisons of first and last day reactions to the films showed that, with repeated exposure, initial levels of self-reported anxiety decreased substantially. Furthermore, subjects' perceptions of the films also changed from the first day to the last day. Material that was previously judged to be violent and degrading to women was seen as significantly less so by the end of the exposure period. Subjects also indicated that they were less depressed and that they enjoyed the material more with repeated exposure. Most importantly, these effects generalized to a victim of sexual assault presented in a videotaped reenactment of a rape trial. Subjects who were exposed to the violent films rated the victim as less severely injured compared to a no-exposure control group. In a similar study (Linz, Donnerstein & Penrod, 1988), subjects were also less sympathetic to the rape victim portrayed in the trial and less able to empathize with rape victims in general, compared to no-exposure control subjects and to subjects who viewed non-violent films.

Linz et al. (1984, 1988) suggested that the viewers in these studies become increasingly comfortable, or desensitized, to what are initially anxiety provoking situations. Further, it was suggested that self-awareness of reductions in anxiety and emotional arousal may be instrumental in the formation of new perceptions and attitudes about the violence portrayed in the films. These views may then be carried over to other contexts. This position is similar to that offered in the behavioral treatment of pathological fears from exposure therapy.

In therapy, simply exposing a patient to the situations or objects he or she is frightened of diminishes the anxiety or negative affect that was once evoked by the problem stimulus. Foa and Kozak (1986) have speculated that a patient's perception of his or her own habituation in the presence of a feared stimulus plays an important role in helping the patient become comfortable with that stimulus. Self-awareness of reduced anxiety may provide the patient with information that helps to facilitate a reduction in fear. That awareness might also facilitate changes in the negative valence associated with the feared stimulus. Patients may then begin to evaluate the "badness" of the feared stimuli in a less exaggerated manner.

Similar processes may operate when subjects are exposed repeatedly to graphic media violence. Once viewers are emotionally "comfortable" with the violent content of the films, they may also evaluate the film more favorably in other domains. Material originally believed to be offensive or degrading to the victims of violence may be evaluated as less so with continued exposure. A reduction in the level of anxiety may also blunt viewers' awareness of the frequency and intensity of violence in the films. Reductions in anxiety may serve to decrease sensitivity to emotional cues associated with each violent episode and thereby reduce viewers' perceptions of the amount of violence in the films. Consequently, by the end of an extensive exposure period, viewers may perceive aggressive films as less violent than they had initially. These altered perceptual and affective reactions may then be carried over into judgments made about victims of violence in other more realistic settings.

Fear

The viewing of media violence can lead to fear reactions such as a general fear of crime or victimization that are quite stable over time. There can also be more transitory reactions such as immediate emotional fright when viewing graphic terror. These effects can occur in both children and adults.

One concept that accounts for the more stable, long-term reactions can be grouped under the rubric of "media cultivation effects." Initially developed by George Gerbner (e.g., Gerbner, 1969; Gerbner & Gross, 1976; Gerbner, Gross, Morgan & Signorielli, 1994), cultivation theory presumes that extensive, cumulative television exposure shapes viewers' perceptions of social reality. The assumption is that individuals develop beliefs about the "real world" from observing the world of television. Researchers have suggested that people store media information automatically (Shapiro, 1991) and subsequently utilize it to formulate their perceptions and beliefs about the world (Harris, 1994). As Tan (1986) notes, this influence on people's conceptions of social reality may be one of the most important mass media effects.

The media, and in particular television, communicate facts, norms, and values about our social world. For many people television is the main source of information about critical aspects of their social environment. Learning about violence in the news and in fictional programming may lead to the belief that the world is generally a scary and dangerous place. Gerbner and colleagues have presented elaborate evidence that heavy viewers of television believe the world they live in is more violent and unsafe than do light viewers. For example, heavy viewers evidence greater fear of walking alone at night; greater estimations of the prevalence of violence; and greater overall fear of crime (Gerbner & Gross, 1976). These results indicate that the media can cultivate fear, and this effect has been found with both children and adult viewers.

While most of the research on cultivation has been correlational in nature, there is also experimental evidence to support the effect. For example, Bryant, Carveth, and Brown (1981) demonstrated that the cultivation effect could be obtained in an experimental situation, even within a short period of time. Subjects in this study were assigned to a six week TV diet of either light or heavy viewing, but with an added twist. Those who were assigned to the heavy viewing condition were divided into two groups: one that saw only justified violence in which the "good guys" won, and the other which saw only unjustified violence in which the "bad guys" got away with their violence. Results indicated that subjects in the heavy viewing/unjustified condition showed the highest increases in anxiety and perceived likelihood of being a victim of crime, in comparison to the other groups. This study suggests that the viewing of media violence can have short as well as long-term influence on fear reactions.

We should note that cultivation theory has been criticized on both methodological and conceptual grounds (Hirsch, 1980, 1981a, 1981b; Newcomb, 1978; Potter, 1993; Rubin, Perse & Taylor, 1988). Some argue that the theory is simplistic and that a number of mediating factors influence cultivation (Wilson, 1995). For example, factors such as experience with crime, motivations for viewing television, and overall cognitive ability seem to be important factors influencing the cultivation effect. Comstock and Paik (1991) note that the effects might not be cumulative at all as suggested by cultivation theory. Instead, they suggest:

> Exposure to violent television stimuli may simply activate or heighten the likelihood of recall of thoughts of a more pessimistic nature. Frequency of exposure in this instance may not be a measure of the history of viewing but the likelihood of recent exposure to violence or distressing events in entertainment, news, or other programming. (pp. 185-186)

From another perspective, Gunter (1994) notes that the cultivation effect may be program-specific rather than the result of total television viewing. Specific programs, such as crime-related shows, would be most influential in affecting perceptions of crime. In addition, the effects may be due to how viewers perceive and interpret the content, particularly if they view the program as being more realistic (Potter, 1986). Individuals may also selectively attend to programs which reinforce their perception of the world (Gunter, 1994).

In a recent overview of cultivation theory, Gerbner and his colleagues address some of these concerns:

> The elements of cultivation do not originate with television or appear out of a void. Layers of social, personal, and cultural contexts also determine the shape, scope, and degree of the contribution television is likely to make. Yet, the meaning of those contexts and factors are in themselves

aspects of the cultivation process. That is, although a viewer's gender, or age, or class makes a difference in perspective, television viewing can make a similar and interacting difference....The interaction is a continuous process (as is cultivation) beginning with infancy and going on from cradle to grave (Gerbner, Gross, Morgan & Signorielli, 1994, p. 23).

For cultivation theory, television viewing is a life-long process. Whether television shapes or merely maintains beliefs about the world is not as important as its role in a dynamic process that leads to enduring and stable assumptions about the world, particularly violence.

For children, however, some fear effects may be more specific and urgent. Fright reactions to violent forms of media can be immediate and dramatic, and quite specific to particular content. Child-viewers may scream or hide their face in their hands. Later, nightmares and recurring thoughts may keep both child and parent awake at night (Wilson & Cantor, 1985). There is a growing body of evidence that both younger and older children can experience strong emotional reactions, including fear responses, from viewing media depictions of crime, violence, physical injury, or danger (Cantor, 1994; Cantor & Wilson, 1988; Wilson, 1995).

Most research on children's emotional reactions emphasizes immediate impacts, although some evidence suggests that the effects of viewing scary or frightening media can last several days or weeks (Cantor, 1994). While most of these longer-lasting effects may be relatively mild, they may sometimes be acute and disabling, like severe anxiety states, lasting up to several weeks (Mathai, 1983). As Cantor (1994) notes, transitory fright reactions occur in a large proportion of children, with more enduring reactions affecting an "appreciable" minority of viewers.

To account for these fear reactions, it appears that a stimulus generalization process is operating. Although the viewer is in no "real" danger from viewing a violent media depiction, the reaction is fundamentally the same (although less intense) as if the experience had been encountered in the real world.

Overall, fear reactions to violent portrayals are experienced by both children and adults, and occur as a function of both immediate exposure as well as the accumulation of viewing over time.

Summary: Effects of Exposure

In this chapter, we have reviewed extensive research which establishes that exposure to televised violence contributes to aggressive behavior, to desensitization to violence, and to fear responses in some viewers. This evidence represents the scientific basis for concern about the effects of televised violence on the audience. In the next chapter, we turn to a more specific task -- that of identifying the specific contextual features which heighten the probability that a given depiction of violence will generate one of these three types of effects.

Chapter 3

THE IMPORTANCE OF CONTEXT

The research reviewed in Chapter 2 indicates that television violence can have at least three types of harmful effects on viewers and that different types of content are capable of producing such effects. However, not all violent portrayals are equal with regard to the risk they might pose. Consider, for example, a documentary about gangs that contains scenes of violence in order to inform audiences about this societal problem. The overall message about violence in such a program is likely to be quite different from that of an action-adventure movie featuring a violent hero. The documentary actually may discourage aggression whereas the action-adventure movie may seem to glamorize it. A comparison of a film like *Schindler's List* about the Holocaust with a film like *The Terminator* illustrates this difference.

Such a contrast underscores the importance of considering the context within which violence is portrayed. Indeed, the television industry itself has long recognized that violence can have different meanings depending upon how it is presented within a program. In a recent policy statement, the National Cable Television Association (1993, p. 1) stipulated that:

> ... the gratuitous use of violence depicted as an easy and convenient solution to human problems is harmful to our industry and to society. We therefore discourage and will strive to reduce the frequency of such exploitative uses of violence while preserving our right to show programs that convey the real meaning and consequences of violent behavior.

Similarly, the Network Television Association (1992) issued standards for the depiction of violence that warn against showing, among other things, "callousness or indifference to suffering," "scenes where children are victims," and "portrayals of the use of weapons or implements readily accessible" to children. Most of these programming guidelines focus on contextual cues and the different ways that violence can be portrayed.

The significance of context is highlighted not only by television industry guidelines, but also by academic research. Most of the major theoretical perspectives discussed in the previous chapter explicitly recognize that contextual cues influence audience reactions to a media portrayal. Bandura's social learning theory, in particular its most recent revisions (Bandura, 1986), postulates that a viewer's interpretation of a message mediates imitation and learning. Such interpretations are in part a function of contextual cues like the type of model who engages in violence and the consequences delivered to that model. Berkowitz's priming theory focuses on how specific features of a violent portrayal, such as the type of perpetrator involved, can instigate aggressive thoughts and memories in a viewer.

In addition to theoretical support, several major reviews of social science research demonstrate that some depictions are more likely than others to pose risks for viewers (Comstock & Paik, 1991; Gunter, 1994; Wilson, Linz, & Randall, 1990). For example, Comstock and Paik (1991) examined much of the experimental literature and concluded that three dimensions of a portrayal are important in predicting whether a program is likely to facilitate aggression among viewers: 1) how efficacious or successful the violence is, 2) how normative or justified the violence appears, and 3) how pertinent the violence is to the viewer.

Although such dimensions are useful summary devices, they are too broad to form the basis of a classification scheme that can be used consistently and accurately in a content analysis. Moreover, the dimensions are tied to only one outcome--the learning of aggressive attitudes and behaviors. Unfortunately, most previous reviews of the literature (e.g., Comstock & Paik, 1991; Gunter, 1994) have paid virtually no attention to how context might influence outcomes such as audience fear and desensitization.

Thus, prior to developing our content coding scheme for this project, we conducted our own careful and exhaustive search of the social science research. Our goal was threefold: 1) to update previous reviews of the social science research literature, 2) to identify specific features rather than broad dimensions of a violent portrayal that have been consistently documented to influence viewers, and 3) to focus not only on how context influences the learning of aggression but also on how it affects fear and desensitization.

Our search concentrated primarily on experimental studies that manipulated some contextual feature in a violent portrayal and then assessed one of the three outcomes of interest here: subjects' learning of aggression, fear, or desensitization. Although we included correlational and longitudinal evidence in building our framework, we focused most closely on experiments because of their high internal validity and control. With the experimental methodology, we could be most confident in drawing conclusions about the causal effect of a specific context factor. In addition, we scrutinized how each context factor was operationalized or measured in the experiments because these specifications formed the basis for how we defined context in our coding scheme.

Our literature search included books, technical reports, conference papers, journal articles, dissertations, and review pieces. We included studies of adults as well as children. In all, our data base contains over 80 experiments, several review chapters on media violence, and a few meta-analyses of the experimental work. As mentioned above, we also relied on several correlational studies to support the experimental evidence. In the next section, we present the context factors that emerged from our review.

Set of Contextual Factors

Our comprehensive review revealed nine contextual factors that influence audience reactions to violent portrayals: 1) the nature of the perpetrator, 2) the nature of the target, 3) the reason for the violence, 4) the presence of weapons, 5) the extent and graphicness of the violence, 6) the degree of realism of the violence, 7) whether the violence is rewarded or punished, 8) the consequences of violence, and 9) whether humor is involved in violence. The research findings regarding each factor are discussed below, with an indication whether a given contextual feature affects learning of aggression, desensitization, and/or fear, and if so, how. Although some of the factors increase the probability that a violent portrayal will pose risks to viewers, other factors decrease that probability. A summary of these relationships is presented in Table 1.

Before examining each context factor individually, three overall observations from our literature review should be noted. First, most of the experimental studies have focused on imitation or learning of aggression as the outcome variable. Only a few have used fear or desensitization as the outcome. Thus, we know much more about what types of contextual features pose risks for the learning of aggression than we do about what types facilitate fear or desensitization. Table 1 illustrates these gaps in our knowledge. The question-mark symbols, which indicate that there are no experimental studies to address the impact of that context factor on a particular outcome, are most prevalent in the columns referring to fear and desensitization.

The second overall observation is that there is a great deal of overlap in the findings regarding adult viewers and child viewers. In other words, the same types of contextual cues that influence older viewers also influence younger viewers. This congruence will be illustrated in the review below.

Third, although the types of factors that affect older and younger viewers are the same, the *ways* in which these contextual cues operate sometimes differ across age. In particular, several of the contextual cues are interpreted differently by younger children than by older children and adults, resulting in slightly different predicted effects. These developmental differences will be considered later in this chapter.

In the discussion below, we will focus on what we know about each factor rather than what we do not know. Consequently, if fear and/or desensitization are not mentioned in the discussion of a particular factor, then it can be assumed that there is no controlled research relevant to this potential outcome, as indicated in Table 1.

Nature of Perpetrator

When a violent event occurs in a program, typically there is a character or group of characters who can be identified as the perpetrator. The meaning of the violence is closely connected to the characteristics of the perpetrator. For example, viewers are likely to interpret a gunshot from the star of a popular police series differently than a gunshot from a criminal. Indeed, characters are integral to the plot of any program and viewers form strong evaluations of the things that characters do or say in a scene (Hoffner & Cantor, 1991). Character evaluations have important implications for how a viewer ultimately will respond to a particular portrayal. Research indicates that both children and adults are more likely to attend to and learn from models who are perceived as attractive (Bandura, 1986, 1994). Thus, a perpetrator of violence who is attractive or

Table 1

**Predicted Impact of Contextual Factors
on Three Outcomes of Exposure to Media Violence**

	Outcomes of Media Violence		
Contextual Factors	**Learning Aggression**	**Fear**	**Desensitization**
Attractive Perpetrator	Δ		
Attractive Target		Δ	
Justified Violence	Δ		
Unjustified Violence	t	Δ	
Presence of Weapons	Δ		
Extensive/Graphic Violence	Δ	Δ	Δ
Realistic Violence	Δ	Δ	
Rewards	Δ	Δ	
Punishments	t	t	
Pain/Harm Cues	t		
Humor	Δ		Δ

Note. Predicted effects are based on review of social science research on contextual features of violence. Blank spaces indicate that there is inadequate research to make a prediction.

> Δ = likely to *increase* the outcome
> t = likely to *decrease* the outcome

engaging is likely to be a more potent role model for viewers than is a neutral or unattractive character.

What types of characters are perceived as attractive in entertainment programming? Studies suggest that viewers assign more positive ratings to characters who act prosocially or helpful than to characters who are cruel (Hoffner & Cantor, 1985; Zillmann & Cantor, 1977). Moreover, children as young as 4 years of age can distinguish between prototypically good and bad characters in a television program (Berndt & Berndt, 1975; Liss, Reinhardt, & Fredricksen, 1983).

One exaggerated form of a good character is the superhero who engages in violent means in order to battle evil. *Wonder Woman*, the *Power Rangers*, *Superman*, and the *Ninja Turtles* are just a few examples of this popular type of protagonist. Liss et al. (1983) found that children who were exposed to a cartoon featuring a violent superhero subsequently were more likely to act aggressively than were those who watched a violent cartoon without a superhero. Interestingly, even adults are susceptible to hero influence. In one experiment (Perry & Perry, 1976), male undergraduates who were encouraged to identify with the victor of a filmed prize fight were subsequently more aggressive than those encouraged to imagine themselves as the loser in the film. Other studies also have documented that identification with the hero in a violent portrayal increases aggressive behavior among adult viewers (Leyens & Picus, 1973; Turner & Berkowitz, 1972).

In addition to heros, viewers also are attracted to characters who are perceived as similar to themselves. Perceived similarity to a character can be a function of shared demographic characteristics such as sex and age (Jose & Brewer, 1984). For example, boys are more likely to attend to and imitate male perpetrators, whereas girls respond more strongly to female characters (Bandura, 1986; Bandura, Ross, & Ross, 1963a). Furthermore, children are more likely to engage in aggression after watching a violent child character than a violent adult character (Hicks, 1965). However, any type of cue in a portrayal that is pertinent to the viewer's own circumstances can prompt aggressive behavior among both children and adults (Berkowitz & Geen, 1966, 1967; Geen & Berkowitz, 1966; Josephson, 1987).

To summarize, the nature of the perpetrator is an important consideration in terms of imitation and learning. Consistent with this assertion, a recent meta-analysis of 217 experimental studies found that violent programs have a stronger effect on viewer aggression when they feature perpetrators with whom audiences can identify (Paik & Comstock, 1994). Viewers certainly rely on a multitude of cues in determining who is attractive or likeable in a program. To date, research has documented that perpetrators who are benevolent, heroic, or demographically similar to the viewer are potent role models in entertainment programming.

Nature of Target

Just as the nature of the perpetrator is an important contextual feature of violence, so is the nature of the target. Once again, viewers are more likely to react strongly to a target who is perceived as likeable or attractive. Consider a scene in which a likeable star of a detective series is about to be shot. Exchanging the popular detective with a malicious criminal illustrates the importance of the target in terms of audience reactions.

Interestingly, the nature of the target is most likely to influence audience fear rather than learning. Research indicates that viewers feel concern for characters who are perceived as attractive and often share such characters' emotional experiences (Zillmann, 1980, 1991). This type of empathic responding has been found with characters who are benevolent or heroic (Comisky & Bryant, 1982; Zillmann & Cantor, 1977), as well as characters who are perceived to be similar to the viewer (Feshbach & Roe, 1968; Tannenbaum & Gaer, 1965). Thus, a well-liked character can encourage audience involvement. When such a character is threatened or attacked in a violent scene, viewers are likely to experience increased anxiety and fear.

Reason for Violence

How we interpret an act of violence is dependent to a great extent on a character's motives or reasons for engaging in such behavior (Gunter, 1985; Hoffner & Cantor, 1991). For example, a father may shoot someone who is trying to kidnap his child. Certain motives such as self-defense and defense of a loved one seem justified, and viewers may even cheer when a character kills the kidnapper. In contrast, a character who shoots a bank teller for not getting the money out of a drawer fast enough is likely to be judged as malicious and not receive much sympathy from a viewer.

Research suggests that motives also can influence a viewer's tendency to learn or imitate aggression. In a series of studies by Berkowitz and others (e.g., Berkowitz & Geen, 1967; Berkowitz & Powers, 1979), adult subjects were given different descriptions about a perpetrator and target prior to viewing the same violent scene. Those in the justified violence conditions typically were told that a sympathetic perpetrator had been previously harmed or wronged and now is retaliating. In the unjustified violence condition, the perpetrator was cast as someone who attacks innocent people out of hate or greed. The results consistently showed that angered subjects who viewed a film scene portraying violence as justified subsequently behaved more aggressively than did those who viewed less justified violence (Berkowitz & Geen, 1967; Berkowitz & Powers, 1979; Berkowitz & Rawlings, 1963; Geen & Stonner, 1973, 1974; Hoyt, 1970). Moreover, exposure to unjustified violence actually *reduced* aggressive tendencies compared to a control group receiving no information about the motive (Berkowitz & Powers, 1979; Geen, 1981).

The impact of justification has been documented with fictional as well as more realistic programming (Meyer, 1972), and with adult as well as child viewers (Liss et al., 1983). In fact, a recent meta-analysis of 217 media studies documents that a justified portrayal of violence can enhance aggressive behavior among viewers (Paik & Comstock, 1994).

Based on this research, we can infer that television violence that is motivated by protection or retaliation, to the extent that it appears to be justified, should facilitate viewer aggression. Researchers have speculated that when violence is portrayed as morally proper or somehow beneficial, it lowers a viewer's inhibitions against aggression (Jo & Berkowitz, 1994). The prototypical "justified" scenario is the hero who employs violence to protect society against villainous characters. In contrast, violence that is undeserved or purely malicious should decrease the risk of audience imitation or learning of aggression.

Does the reason or motive for violence have other effects on the audience? It seems reasonable to assume that viewers are more likely to be frightened by television violence that is undeserved or targeted against innocent victims. Such portrayals may make the audience feel more personally vulnerable. One study provides some indirect evidence for this idea (Bryant et al., 1981). In this experiment, adult subjects who viewed action-adventure shows featuring unjust violence were more anxious than were those who viewed violent programs emphasizing justice. The primary difference between these depictions centered on whether violence was punished in the end, but criminals who go unpunished may appear even more unjust in their motives, particularly if they have gotten away with violence against innocent victims. Clearly, further research is needed here but we can tentatively conclude that unjustified violence is likely to be more scary than violence that is socially sanctioned or somehow altruistic.

Presence of Weapons

A variety of methods and tools can be used to enact violence against a target on television. A perpetrator can use natural means such as punching with a fist or slapping with a hand. Alternatively, a perpetrator can use a weapon like a gun or a knife or a more unconventional tool like a frying pan or a chain saw. Berkowitz (1984, 1990) has argued that certain visual cues in a film can activate or "prime" aggressive thoughts and behaviors in a viewer, and that weapons can function as such cues.

In support of this idea, a recent meta-analysis of 56 published experiments found that the presence of weapons, either pictorially or in the natural environment, significantly enhanced aggression among angered as well as non-angered subjects (Carlson, Marcus-Newhall, & Miller, 1990). In particular, studies have found that exposure to slides or pictures of weapons significantly increased aggressive behavior in male and female adults (Leyens & Parke, 1974; Page & O'Neal, 1977). Similarly, the mere presence of actual firearms in a naturalistic environment can enhance aggression among adults in controlled studies (Berkowitz & LePage, 1967; Turner, Layton, & Simons, 1975).

Presumably for ethical reasons, no studies have been done on the impact of weapon cues on young children. However, one experiment found that adolescents became more aggressive against a target when in the presence of weapons than in the presence of neutral stimuli (Frodi, 1975). It seems reasonable to assume that conventional weapons can prompt the same types of aggressive tendencies in younger viewers.

According to Berkowitz (1990) and others (e.g., Leyens & Parke, 1974), weapons like guns and knives are more likely than unconventional means to instigate or prime aggression in viewers because they are commonly associated with previous violent events stored in memory. Thus, a television portrayal that features traditional weapons poses the greatest risk for the so-called "weapons effect" on audiences.

Extent and Graphicness of Violence

Television programs and especially movies vary widely in the extent and graphicness of the violence they contain. A violent interaction between a perpetrator and a target can last only a few seconds and be shot from a distance or it can persist for several minutes and involve many close-ups on the action. The media industry recognizes this difference when it provides ratings and advisories for certain programs. As an illustration, the Motion Picture Association of America's film rating system assigns an R rating to a movie when violence is "rough" or "persistent," whereas PG is used when the violence is not "strong" or "cumulative" (Valenti, 1987). When other countries such as Great Britain import American movies, they often cut or edit out violence that is considered too extensive or graphic (Gray & Berry, 1994).

Research suggests that audiences can be influenced by the extent and explicitness of violent portrayals. Most attention has been devoted to the impact of extensive or repeated violence on viewer desensitization. For example, several early studies on adults showed that physiological arousal to prolonged scenes of brutality steadily declines over time during exposure to a 17-minute film (Lazarus & Alfert, 1964; Lazarus, Speisman, Mordkoff, & Davison, 1962; Speisman, Lazarus, Mordkoff, & Davison, 1964). Moreover, even children have been shown to exhibit such physiological desensitization over time during exposure to a violent film, with the decrement being strongest for those who were heavy viewers of TV violence (Cline, Coft, & Courrier, 1973).

More recently, studies have examined what happens when subjects are exposed to extensive media violence over several viewing sessions. In a study by Linz, Donnerstein, & Penrod (1988). male undergraduates were exposed to five full-length "slasher" movies (e.g., *Friday the 13th, Part 2*; *Texas Chainsaw Massacre*) over a period of two weeks. After each film, emotional reactions, perceptions of violence in the films, and attitudes toward female victims in the films were measured. The results revealed that subjects perceived less violence in the films and evaluated the films as less degrading to women after repeated exposure. A subsequent study replicated these finding. Subjects who were shown three slasher films across a five-day period exhibited a progressive decrease in arousal and in sensitivity to the violence in the films across the exposure period (Mullin & Linz, 1995). Thus, exposure to extensive violence, either within a single program or across several programs, produces decreased arousal and sensitivity to violence in both children and adults. This is the desensitization effect.

Does extensive or repeated violence influence the other two effects of concern, the learning of aggression and fear? Only one experiment could be found that actually varied the *amount* of exposure to TV violence and then measured aggression (Parke,

Berkowitz, Leyens, West, & Sebastian, 1977). Adolescent juvenile delinquents residing in minimum security institutions were exposed either to five full-length violent films, five neutral films, a single violent film, or a single neutral film. Contrary to expectations, multiple exposures to filmed violence resulted in *less* aggressive behavior than did the single exposure. However, the researchers noted that this unexpected effect was likely due to a substantial difference between the two groups in initial aggressiveness, and thus little information can be gleaned from this study.

Although not experimental, other evidence suggests that exposure to extensive violence in the media should actually promote the learning of aggression. Huesmann and his colleagues have conducted several longitudinal surveys demonstrating that the more TV violence children watch in a given year, the more likely they are to behave aggressively in subsequent years (Huesmann, 1986; Huesmann et al., 1984). Furthermore, Huesmann's developmental model, social learning theory, and Berkowitz's cognitive script theory all predict that heavy exposure to a variety of violent models and behaviors on television will foster the development of well-established scripts and routines for responding aggressively.

The impact of extent and graphicness of violence on fear, however, is less obvious. One could argue that prolonged exposure to explicit scenes of violence will enhance fright reactions among viewers. Alternatively, if the images are constant and repeated within a program, a viewer could become desensitized and feel *less* upset over time. An experiment by Ogles and Hoffner (1987) suggests that extensive exposure to violence promotes rather than diminishes fear. Male undergraduates were randomly assigned to view five slasher films (e.g., *Toolbox Murders*, *Maniac*) over a two-week period or two slasher films within a one-week period. Subjects in the extended exposure condition perceived significantly more crime in the real world and felt personally more vulnerable to it, and these perceptions correlated with feelings of fear. These findings taken together with the research reviewed earlier on cultivation effects indicate that viewing extensive violence is likely to be frightening.

Clearly, more research on extent and graphicness is needed, with special attention to the conditions under which fear versus emotional blunting is most likely to occur. For example, are viewers more likely to desensitize if the violent images are redundant rather than constantly changing? Is desensitization more likely if violence is continual and uninterrupted rather than sporadic or interspersed throughout a program? Finally, how long does desensitization persist compared to fear? One recent study suggests that habituation is a relatively short-term effect and that viewers' sensitivity and arousal to violence may rebound fairly quickly (Mullin & Linz, 1995). These questions warrant further examination.

Realism of Violence

Another important attribute or contextual factor concerns the degree of realism associated with a violent portrayal. Public reaction to televised images of the Rodney King beatings and the more recent bombing of a federal building in Oklahoma illustrates that realistic scenes of violence can have a significant impact on viewers. But violence in a fictional context also can be differentiated in terms of degrees of realism. Indeed, movies like *The Silence of the Lambs* and *Goodfellas* seem to cause more concern about violence in our culture than do movies like *Star Wars* (Plagens, Miller, Foote, & Yoffe, 1991), largely because of this factor.

Such public concern is supported by research findings. Several studies indicate that realistic portrayals of violence can pose more risks for viewers than unrealistic ones. For example, Berkowitz and Alioto (1973) found that exposure to a war film led to more aggression among adult males when it was described as a documentary than when it was labeled a Hollywood production. Subsequent studies showed that a film of a campus fistfight that was introduced as something that actually happened led to greater aggression among college-aged males than did the same fight when it was described as staged (Geen, 1975; Thomas & Tell, 1974).

Not only adults but also children seem to respond to the realism of violence. In a study of 6- to 10-year-olds, a television program portraying human violence led to more aggressive behavior than did one showing animated violence (Hapkiewicz & Stone, 1974). However, it is difficult to draw firm conclusions from this study because the more "realistic" program in this case was the *Three Stooges* and its violent content presumably varied in many important ways from the *Mighty Mouse* cartoon. In a more controlled study by Feshbach (1972), 9- to 11-year-old children were exposed to the same campus riot footage that was described either as part of a news story or as a Hollywood film. Children who perceived the content to be more realistic subsequently behaved more aggressively. Atkin (1983) obtained similar results when 10- to 13-year-olds viewed the same violent scene presented within an actual newscast versus, as compared to viewing the scene within a movie promo.

All of these studies suggest that realistic violence is a more potent elicitor of aggressive behavior than fictional portrayals. Researchers have hypothesized that viewers can more easily identify with perpetrators who are realistic and that such portrayals may more readily reduce inhibitions against aggression because they are so applicable to real-life situations (Atkin, 1983; Jo & Berkowitz, 1994).

The realism of a portrayal also can influence viewers' fear reactions to violence. In one early study, Lazarus, Opton, Nomikos, and Rankin (1965) found that adults were less physiologically aroused to a movie showing gory accidents when the events had been introduced as fake compared to no such introduction. Subsequent studies have demonstrated that adults are far more emotionally aroused by violent scenes that are perceived to have actually happened than if the same scenes are believed to be fictional (Geen, 1975; Geen & Rakosky, 1973).

Children also can be frightened by realistic depictions. In one experiment, children who thought that a threatening creature depicted in a movie actually existed in their city were more frightened by the scene than were those who did not believe the creature was a realistic threat (Cantor & Hoffner, 1990). Additionally, several surveys have shown that programs that depict events that could possibly happen in real life are more frightening to older children than are programs featuring clearly fantastic events (Cantor & Sparks, 1984; Sparks, 1986).

To summarize, the research reviewed here suggests that more realistic portrayals of violence can foster the learning of aggressive attitudes and behaviors among children as well as adults. Realistic depictions of brutality also can elevate viewers' fear responses. Based on this contextual factor, one might expect that cartoon or fantasy violence on television is relatively harmless. After all, such depictions obviously are not very authentic. However, research on very young children cautions against such a conclusion. In fact, what seems unrealistic to adults and older children may appear to be quite real to a younger child. We will shortly turn our focus to the topic of developmental differences in how children understand television. Some of our contextual factors take on special consideration when the audience is composed primarily of younger children.

Rewards and Punishments

A critical feature of any violent portrayal concerns whether the aggressive behavior is reinforced or rewarded. Violent characters on television can be rewarded in several ways--they may obtain money or property, they may acquire power, or they may win the admiration of others. They may even exhibit self-reinforcement by feeling proud or exhilarated after an aggressive act. Several previous content analyses of television suggest that much of the violence in entertainment programming involves characters who are rewarded or successful (Potter & Ware, 1987; Williams, Zabrack, & Joy, 1982).

According to social learning theory, observers are more likely to learn a behavior that is rewarded than one that is punished (Bandura, 1986). In a series of famous Bobo doll studies (e.g., Bandura, 1965; Bandura, Ross, & Ross, 1961, 1963b), Bandura consistently found that children exposed to an aggressive film model who was rewarded were significantly more likely to behave aggressively than were children exposed to an aggressive model who was punished. In most of this research, toys, cookies, and/or adult approval were used as rewards in the films, whereas the removal of toys, spanking, and/or adult disapproval were used as punishments. Other studies have documented similar effects for rewards and punishments on children's imitative behavior (Rosekrans & Hartup, 1967; Walters & Parke, 1964; Walters, Parke, & Cane, 1965).

Media violence need not be explicitly rewarded or punished, however, in order to have an impact on learning. Research indicates children may imitate a model's antisocial behavior so long as there is no explicit punishment delivered to the model, presumably because the lack of punishment actually serves as a sanction for such behavior (Bandura, 1965; Walters & Parke, 1964). Thus, the absence of punishment for violence seems to be a sufficient condition for fostering imitation, generating essentially the same effect as when violence is rewarded.

Reinforcements not only influence children but also adults. In one experiment, Lando and Donnerstein (1978) found that exposure to violence that was portrayed as "successful" significantly increased aggressive behavior among undergraduates, whereas exposure to unsuccessful violence actually decreased aggression. More recently, Paik and Comstock's (1994) meta-analysis provides evidence for the idea that rewarded violence facilitates aggression among both child and adult viewers.

In general, rewarded violence or violence that is not overtly punished fosters the learning of aggressive attitudes and behavior among viewers. In contrast, portrayals of punished violence can serve to inhibit or reduce the learning of aggression. Can such reinforcements affect other audience responses besides aggression? One experimental study mentioned previously examined the impact of rewards and punishments on fear. Bryant, Carveth, and Brown (1981) exposed adults to six weeks of action-adventure programs that depicted either just endings in which violence was punished or unjust endings where violence went unpunished. Subjects who viewed violence that went unpunished were significantly more anxious and more pessimistic about the consequences of real-life violence than were those who saw the just endings. Thus, programs that punish criminals who are violent and ultimately restore justice can decrease viewer aggression as well as viewer fear.

Consequences of Violence

Another important contextual feature of media violence concerns whether the consequences of aggressive actions are depicted. Gerbner (1992) has criticized television for displaying a predominance of what he calls "happy violence," or portrayals that do not show any pain or tragic consequences to the victims and their loved ones. Indeed, several studies suggest that viewers interpret violent scenes with observable harm and pain as more serious and more violent than scenes showing no such consequences (Gunter, 1983, 1985).

Cries of pain and other signs of suffering can affect not only interpretations but also imitation of aggression. Numerous experiments have found that adults who are exposed to overt, intense pain cues from a victim subsequently behave less aggressively than do those who see no such pain cues (Baron, 1971a, 1971b; Gorenson, 1969; Sanders & Baron, 1975; Schmutte & Taylor, 1980). The assumption is that pain cues inhibit aggression by eliciting sympathy and reminding the viewer of social norms against violence. Children also have been shown to be influenced by the consequences of violence. In one experiment, boys who viewed a violent film clip that showed explicit injuries and blood subsequently were less aggressive than were those who saw a violent clip with no such consequences (Wotring & Greenberg, 1973).

It should be noted that a few studies actually have found that pain cues can sometimes enhance or facilitate aggression (Baron, 1979; Dubanoski & Kong, 1977; Swart & Berkowitz, 1976). However, such effects have been restricted to subjects who are highly angered or prone to aggression and are placed in situations where other environmental cues are present to prompt aggressive behavior. Thus, for most viewers the explicit depiction of psychological and physical harm in violent portrayals is likely to inhibit the learning of aggressive attitudes and behaviors.

Humor

Portrayals of violence on television often are cast in a humorous light. Slapstick shows like *The Three Stooges* and cartoons such as *The Road Runner* are obvious examples in which almost every act of violence has a comical tone to it. But even dramatic action-adventure programs can contextualize violence with humor. For example, Dirty Harry challenged criminals to shoot first by saying "Go ahead ... make my day," and the Terminator offered the infamous "Hasta la vista, baby" before killing an enemy. Indeed, one previous content analysis by Williams et al. (1982) found a high incidence of humor in television programs that were violent.

What impact does the addition of humor to a violence scene have on the viewer? Of all the contextual variables that have been examined, we know the least about humor. For one thing, there are many types of humor that can be used in a portrayal. A perpetrator could crack a joke while harming someone, the violent act itself can be shown as farcical, or the target could over-react with pain to a slight injury. Moreover, humor can come in a variety of forms such as sarcasm, a witty remark, a nonverbal gesture, or a funny story. To further complicate the situation, an entire program can be funny or humor can be restricted to violent scenes. Unfortunately, there is no systematic research to date that examines all these various manifestations of humor.

The few studies that have been conducted on humor and aggression offer a mixed set of findings. For instance, Baron and Ball (1974) exposed angered and nonangered subjects either to humorous magazine cartoons or to nonhumorus pictures before allowing them to aggress against a confederate. Results revealed that the humorous material significantly reduced subsequent aggressive behavior among the angered subjects but had no impact on nonangered subjects. In contrast, other studies suggest that humor can sometimes facilitate aggression. Mueller and Donnerstein (1977) found that exposure to highly arousing jokes on an audiotape produced significantly more aggressive behavior among angered subjects than did exposure to milder jokes. A subsequent study revealed similar effects for a humorous movie clip (Mueller & Donnerstein, 1983). Taken together, these findings suggest some forms of mild humor are capable of reducing aggression by distracting or creating a positive mood (Berger, 1988; Zillmann & Bryant, 1991), whereas other more intense forms of humor can instigate aggression because they are arousing.

The key limitation of this research is that it focuses on the impact of humor alone on aggressive behavior, and not the impact of humor in the context of a violent portrayal. What is needed is a controlled study that exposes subjects to the same violent episode with and without humorous overtones. Our literature search revealed no such experiments. However, we found two studies that are closer to the issue at hand because they deal with hostile or aggressive humor rather than more neutral forms of comedy. In one of these studies, undergraduates were first angered or not angered and then listened to a tape recording of either a nonhostile comedian or a hostile comedian (Berkowitz, 1970). Results revealed that the hostile humor which included numerous insults to university coeds significantly increased aggressive responses among both angered and nonangered subjects.

In the second study (Baron, 1978), subjects were exposed to either 10 still picture cartoons featuring hostile humor, 10 cartoons featuring nonhostile humor, or 10 nonhumorous pictures. Several of the hostile cartoons actually depicted physical violence. For both angered and nonangered subjects, the hostile humor significantly increased electric shocks delivered to a confederate, whereas nonhostile humor decreased such aggression. These two experiments alone provide the strongest evidence that humor combined with violence actually can foster aggression.

Several mechanisms can be used to explain such a facilitative effect of humor on aggression. Humor might elevate a viewer's arousal level over that attained by violence alone, and increased arousal has been shown to facilitate aggression (Zillmann, 1979). Humor could serve as a reinforcement or reward for violence, especially if the perpetrator is funny or admired for his or her wit. And humor may diminish the seriousness of the violence and therefore undermine the inhibiting effects of harm and pain cues in a scene (Deckers & Carr, 1986). However, we should underscore that our conclusion about the facilitative effect of humor on aggression is tentative until more systematic research on the impact of a violent scene with and without different forms of humor is undertaken.

Some research on audience perceptions of violence suggests that humor also may foster desensitization. Gunter (1985) and Sander (1995) have found that adults actually perceive violent scenes that contain humor to be less aggressive and less brutal than are similar scenes without comedic tones. Thus, we tentatively conclude that humor can trivialize violence and its consequences, though clearly further research is needed.

Developmental Differences in the Processing of Television Content

The preceding discussion establishes that both child and adult viewers are influenced by the nine context factors indicated above. Moreover, each factor affects children and adults in the same way or direction. For example, rewarded violence *increases* the likelihood of learning of aggression regardless of the age of the viewer, whereas punished violence *decreases* that risk. Nevertheless, some unique concerns regarding the viewer's interpretation of context come into play when considering very young age groups.

Admittedly, many television programs are not designed for young children. In fact, some movies and television series carry parental advisories indicating that the content may be inappropriate for younger age groups. Yet there is no doubt that younger age groups often are in the audience when adult-oriented programs are shown (Condry, 1989). Because children view television at all times of the day and because policy-makers and parents seem most concerned about the youngest viewers in the audience (Broder, 1995; Hundt, 1995; Lacayo, 1995), we have designed certain aspects of our content analysis to take into account this special age group. In particular, two contextual factors, reality of the violence and the reinforcements associated with violence, pose unique concerns for young viewers.

As children develop, they bring different cognitive skills and different amounts of social experience to the new situations they encounter. Several influential perspectives such as Piaget's (1952, 1960) theory of cognitive development and more recent models of information processing (e.g., Flavell, 1985; Siegler, 1991) support this idea. Based on their level of development and maturity, younger children can be expected to interpret or make sense of television in a somewhat different way than will their older counterparts. There are no precise age differences associated with these changes because children exhibit substantial variation in how and when they develop various skills. However, most research reveals marked differences between 2- to 6-year-olds and 7- to 12-year-olds both in the strategies that are used to make sense of new information and in the memory limits that constrain the amount of information that can be considered (Kail, 1990; Siegler, 1991).

For our purposes, we will focus on just two cognitive strategies or skills that are important for television comprehension. The first concerns children's understanding of fantasy and reality. A number of studies have documented developmental differences in the ability to distinguish real from fantasy or pretend (e.g., Morison & Gardner, 1978; Taylor & Howell, 1973). For instance, preschoolers have a greater tendency than older children to believe in magical and supernatural creatures (Rosengren, Kalish, Hickling, & Gelman, 1994), and are often swayed by how things appear rather than how things really are (Flavell, 1986).

Several researchers have tried to extend these developmental findings to perceptions about television. Studies generally show that children's perceptions about the realism of television portrayals are complex and multidimensional in nature, depending on factors such as the genre or type of program, the production cues, and the social realism or similarity of the content to real life (Potter, 1988; Wright, Huston, Reitz, & Piemyat, 1994). Regardless of what aspect of reality is measured, however, developmental differences typically are found. In general, younger children judge characters or actions as "real" simply because they have observed their physical presence through television's "magic window" (Hawkins, 1977). As children develop, they increasingly consider a wider range of cues, including whether the events and characters *possibly* could occur in real life (Dorr, 1983; Wright et al., 1994).

What implications does this have for television violence? Clearly, a fantastic portrayal of violence might be discounted as unrealistic by older children and adults, but perceived as very real by younger children. As an illustration, one study found that preschoolers who were exposed to a violent cartoon model were just as aggressive afterwards as those who watched a human model displaying the same violent acts (Bandura, Ross, & Ross, 1963a). Moreover, numerous studies show that young children readily imitate violent cartoon characters such as *Batman* (Friedrich & Stein, 1973; Steuer, Applefield, & Smith, 1971) and superheros with magical powers like the *Power Rangers* (Boyatzis, Matillo, & Nesbitt, 1995).

These findings underscore the importance of *perceived* reality for the viewer. In spite of the fact that realistic depictions of violence pose more risks for all viewers, younger children make these judgments differently than do older children and adults. Thus, we cannot discount cartoon or fantasy violence when considering younger audiences.

The second cognitive skill that is relevant to television viewing is the capacity to draw inferences and connect scenes. Television plots are stories that require the viewer to make causal links between scenes and to fill in gaps in information. Research suggests that older children are better able than younger children to integrate pieces of information together from stories and narrations, and then to draw inferences from such information (Schmidt, Schmidt, & Tomalis, 1984; Thompson & Myers, 1985). Likewise, older children are better able to coherently link scenes together from a television program (Collins, 1979, 1983).

This developmental pattern has important implications for the context factor dealing with rewards and punishments. Many action-adventure programs feature criminals or bad guys who get away with violence early on in a program. These characters often are not caught or punished until the end of the program when the plot is resolved. In other words, violence is rewarded in the short run and if it is punished at all, this negative reinforcement is not depicted until much later.

Research suggests that the *timing* of punishments is a critical factor for younger children. In one study (Collins, 1973), third, sixth, and tenth graders watched a program in which a crime was either punished immediately after it occurred or punished later, after a four-minute commercial break. The findings revealed that the youngest group was more likely to respond aggressively when the punishment was separated from the violence than when it was temporally contiguous to it. In contrast, the separation manipulation had no impact on the two older groups. Therefore, in order to be an effective deterrent for younger children, punishments must occur in close proximity to the violent action in a program.

To summarize, younger children may respond to two context factors in somewhat different ways than will older children and adults. Younger viewers are more likely to perceive fantasy and animated violence as realistic, thus increasing the risk of imitation and fear when this age group is exposed to such content. They also are less able to link scenes together that are temporally separated. Thus, punishments may not serve as effective inhibitors of imitation and aggression unless such restraints are depicted in the same scene or immediately adjacent to the violence. These special contingencies will be of interest when we consider the 2- to 6-year-old audience and when we examine children's programming in particular.

Summary: Contextual Patterns

The research reviewed above establishes clearly that certain depictions of television violence pose more of a risk for viewers than do others. Specifically, nine different contextual cues or message factors have been documented as important influences on audience reactions. Because the experimental studies to date have only tested these context factors in isolation from one another, we have no solid information about which factors may be most critical or how such factors might interact with one another. For example, it might be that pain and harm cues are more influential when shown within a realistic portrayal of violence than in the context of a fantasy program.

Until more detailed analyses are conducted, we must assume that each factor is somehow important to the overall risk associated with a given portrayal. In that case, a violent program that contains several contextually-based risk factors presumably is more problematic than a portrayal featuring only one. The context factors can be examined collectively to reveal certain patterns of portrayals in a program that would affect the potential risk for the audience. A careful review of Table 1 reveals such patterns. For example, a portrayal that poses the greatest risk for the learning of aggression would feature an attractive perpetrator who is motivated by morally proper reasons; who engages in repeated violence that seems realistic, is rewarded, and employs conventional weapons; and whose violent actions produce no visible harm or pain and are accompanied by humor. In contrast, a portrayal that may actually inhibit or reduce the risk of learning aggression would feature an unattractive perpetrator who is motivated by greed or hatred, who commits violence that produces strong negative consequences for the victims, and who is ultimately punished for this aggression.

Somewhat different risk patterns exist for the other outcomes of concern, desensitization and fear. A portrayal that poses the greatest risk for desensitization would contain violence that is repeated or extensive and that is depicted as humorous. A portrayal that poses the greatest risk for audience fear would feature violence that is aimed at an attractive or likeable target, that seems unjustified, that is extensive and realistic, and that goes unpunished.

Although each context variable is important in its own right, television programming is likely to reveal certain combinations of factors such as those described above. One of the primary goals of this study is to detect whether these patterns exist and if so, to identify where they are most likely to be found. For example, if the themes described above are more commonly found in certain types of programs, then we can draw conclusions about the potential risks and/or benefits associated with different genres of television. Such themes or templates also may be more pervasive on certain types of channels or in certain time slots during the day. If so, parents and educators can use such findings to make more informed decisions about what children should and should not view. Such findings also can help us to teach children to be more critical viewers of television content.

Chapter 4

THE CONTENT ANALYSIS FRAMEWORK

Researchers have analyzed violence on television for as long as the medium has existed (cf., Clark & Blankenberg, 1972; Gerbner, Gross, Signorielli, Morgan, & Jackson-Beeck, 1979; Greenberg, Edison, Korzenny, Fernandez-Collado, & Atkin, 1980; Head, 1954; Lichter & Amundson, 1992, 1994; Potter & Ware, 1987; Schramm, Lyle, & Parker, 1961; Smythe, 1954; Williams, Zabrack, & Joy, 1982). Most of these studies have examined all types of television content, although some have focused more narrowly on children's programming (Poulos, Harvey, & Liebert, 1976) or music videos, a genre with strong appeal to youth (Baxter, Riemer, Landini, Leslie, & Singletary, 1985; Brown & Campbell, 1986; Sherman & Dominick, 1986; Sommers-Flanagan, Sommers-Flanagan & Davis, 1993). The monitoring of violence also has been undertaken by citizen activists ("NCTV says," 1983) and by the television industry itself (Columbia Broadcasting System, 1980).

In this chapter, we review the approaches that have been employed previously to examine the topic of televised violence. Our goal here is to describe the range of findings in this research area and to illustrate how the differences in findings can be traced to methodological decisions made by the various researchers. These methodological decisions reflect differences in defining violence, selecting the units for analyzing violence, and selecting the sample of television programming to be studied. To the extent that these decisions vary across studies, there inevitably will be corresponding differences in the findings produced by the research.

For example, if one study defines violence to include comic or slapstick actions, its count of violence will yield a higher figure than would a comparable study that excluded such actions in its definition. A study that focuses on individual violent acts as the unit of analysis will likely result in a higher count of violence than a study that uses much larger units of analysis such as the scene. And a study that includes certain genres known for very high rates of violence, such as action/adventure movies and cartoons, will produce a higher rate of violence than a study that uses a more narrow sample that excludes such genres. Therefore, the results of a given content analysis are strongly influenced by the definition of violence, the units of analysis, and the sample.

We begin this chapter by describing the range of previous findings regarding the amount of violence on television. We then present an analysis of various studies to illustrate how methodological decisions have influenced the nature of the results. Next, we overview how context has been addressed in past assessments of television violence. Finally, we provide an overview of the major methodological decisions made in planning this study to show how we have built on the strengths of the previous research while at the same time avoiding many of the limitations of those studies.

Range of Previous Findings

Since the late 1960s, George Gerbner and his colleagues have conducted the most consistent and widely cited assessments of the amount of violence on American television (e.g., Gerbner, Gross, Morgan, & Signorielli, 1980). On average they have found that violence occurs at a rate of 5.4 acts per hour (Signorielli, 1990). Studies in both the U.S. and Britain (Cumberbatch, Lee, Hardy, & Jones, 1987) that used Gerbner's definition of violence have consistently found 4 to 6 violent acts per hour of prime time programming, with substantially more on American children's cartoons.

Higher rates of violence are reported in many other content analyses. For example, a study by the National Coalition on Television Violence ("NCTV says," 1983), found 9.7 violent acts per hour of U.S. programming. Williams, Zabrack, and Joy (1982) found 18.5 aggressive acts per hour of U.S. and Canadian programming. Potter and his colleagues (1995) found an average of 36.6 acts of aggression per hour. Greenberg and his colleagues (1980) reported a rate of 38 acts of anti-social behavior per hour.

What can account for such a wide range of findings? In the following sections, we will show that the differences in the reported rates are influenced strongly by the differences in definitions of violence, the selection of a unit of analysis, and the sample of television programs.

Definition of Violence

There is no single commonly accepted definition of violence in the research literature. Violence is treated as a construct. That is, different researchers have different ways to assemble elements into their definitions. For example, Gerbner's definition of television violence focused on the act or threat of physical violence. He defined violence as "the overt expression of physical force (with or without a weapon) against self or other, compelling action against one's will on pain of being hurt or killed, or actually hurting or killing" (see Gerbner, Gross, Morgan & Signorielli, 1980). This definition is limited to overt physical acts and has produced findings of about 5-6 acts per hour over many years.

Williams, Zabrack, and Joy (1982) used a wider concept of aggression defined as "behavior that inflicts harm, either physically or psychologically, including explicit or implicit threats and nonverbal behavior" (p. 366). Using this broader definition, which includes verbal aggression, they found 18.5 aggressive acts per hour in a mix of U.S. and Canadian programming.

Potter and his colleagues (1995) used a still broader definition: "any action that serves to diminish something in a physical, psychological, social, or emotional manner." The victim of aggression could be a person or a non-human entity (e.g., animal, object, or society), and likewise, the perpetrator could fall within any one of these types. They found an average of 36.6 acts per hour, of which 13.2 were physical in nature.

Greenberg and his colleagues (1980) also used a broad conception in studying violence, including verbal acts of aggression and anti-social behaviors such as deceit. Their study reported 38 acts per hour, 12 of which were physical forms. Like the Williams et al. (1982) and the Potter et al. (1995) studies, the Greenberg definition allows for the inclusion of verbal aggression as well as physical violence.

As these examples demonstrate, the broader the definition, the greater the number of violent behaviors that will be indicated by research. The key elements that broaden a definition are the inclusion of verbal as well as physical violence, the inclusion of accidents as well as intentional acts, and the inclusion of threats as well as acts that involve actual harm.

Selecting Units of Analysis

Most of the findings noted above focus on the number of acts of violence. In these studies, a violent act typically begins with the presence of some action that meets the definition of violence and ends when that discrete action is completed. For example, if a cowboy pulls his gun and kills the sheriff, the act begins with the pulling of the gun and it ends when the sheriff falls down dead. Whether this lasts one second or one minute, it is still one act.

In contrast to coding discrete acts as they occur, some researchers divide a program into narrative scenes. If a scene contains violence it is coded as "yes," and if it does not, it is coded as "no." This is what Lichter and Amundson (1994) did in their one-day study of violence commissioned by TV Guide. When they report that violence occurred at the rate of 10.7 scenes per hour during evening prime-time in 1992, they are not reporting average numbers of acts. If a scene contained 1, 5, 10, or any number of violent acts, the scene would simply be coded as violent, and their count would increase by only one scene, thereby sacrificing a great deal of precision.

The selection of a unit of analysis substantially influences the findings of any content analysis study. For example, consider a 5-minute scene depicting a bar-room brawl where 100 punches are thrown before the mass of combatants tumbles outside on the street where one person draws a gun and shoots another. If we select a very narrow unit of analysis, then each punch might be counted along with the shooting, with each given equal weight. If instead we choose a very broad unit of analysis such as a scene, then all these acts would be collapsed together and simply be counted as one unit -- a single violent scene. We could select a mid-level unit of analysis, but then we would face the challenge of constructing rules for chunking some behaviors together while separating others into distinct units. The decisions about unitizing have a direct influence on the numbers that are tallied in reporting the amount of violence observed on television.

Sampling

Although most previous content analyses examined a sample of one week of television programming, there is still wide variation in the nature of the samples gathered.

For example, Gerbner's basic approach was to rely upon a single intact week of network programming. All programs on each network were sampled during a consecutive seven-day period, with the time slots limited to prime-time and Saturday morning hours. One possible concern with this approach is that the week selected may not be representative of the overall television season. Signorielli, Gross, and Morgan (1982) acknowledge this concern, and seek to overcome it by reporting that no significant differences were found for most measures when comparing one week of their data to seven weeks of data gathered in 1976.

Greenberg et al. (1980) examined a composite week of prime-time programming, spreading the taping process out over a four-week period. This approach reduces the risk of gathering an unrepresentative sample due to a limited time frame in which the material is gathered. Like Gerbner, however, Greenberg collected essentially the same overall amount of content -- approximately 60-80 hours of programming for each year's entire analysis. Approximately 22 hours were devoted to each of the three existing broadcast networks that were studied. The time periods sampled were the same as those used by Gerbner: prime-time and Saturday morning hours.

Potter et al. (1995) also used a composite week of television programming, but they sampled four networks (ABC, NBC, CBS, and Fox) from 6 p.m. to midnight, for a total of 168 hours of programming. Their sample, which was collected over a three-month period, was larger than that of Gerbner or Greenberg because of the addition of a fourth network (Fox) and the addition of early fringe (6 p.m. to 8 p.m.) and late fringe (11 p.m. to midnight) hours. But Potter et al. did not include any Saturday morning programs, thus omitting a heavy concentration of cartoons that typically contain a substantial amount of violence.

Lichter and Amundson (1994) used a sample that was broader in its inclusion of 10 channels: the broadcast networks ABC, CBS, NBC, Fox, and PBS; an independent broadcast station; and cable-delivered channels WTBS, USA, MTV, and HBO. It also included more day-parts in its span from 6 a.m. to midnight. However, it was severely limited in its reliance on a single day of programming taped simultaneously on all 10 channels to represent an entire year.

Larger samples are generally superior to smaller ones, because the inclusion of more programs across more day-parts and days is more likely to be representative of the total population of television programming. This is especially clear when we understand that the patterns of violence are relatively stable year to year, but not necessarily day-part to day-part or day to day. To illustrate the importance of this point, we will reexamine the findings from three studies that were conducted across multiple years.

Gerbner's findings are relatively stable from 1967 to 1985, with between 65% and 80% of prime-time programs containing some violence, and between 89% and 98% of all Saturday morning children's shows also containing violence over a 20 year period (Signorielli, 1990). Greenberg et al.'s (1980) findings also show stable rates of violence across time, averaging 14.5 acts per hour in 1975-76; 15.2 acts per hour in 1976-77; and 14.1 per hour in 1977-78. Consistent with Gerbner, Greenberg et al. reported that

Saturday morning children's programming was substantially more violent than prime-time content. Across the three-year study, acts of physical aggression took place at a rate of 22.9 per hour (1975-76); 25.2 per hour (1976-77); and 21.2 per hour (1977-78) during Saturday morning children's programs.

In contrast, Lichter and Amundson (1994) reported a very large fluctuation of violence, but they examined only a single day to represent each of their two years. Their overall number of violent scenes was 31% higher in 1994 than 1992, with some time periods experiencing increases of more than 200%. If accurate and representative, such evidence would point to huge, unexplained shifts in the level of televised violence across these two years. In fact, this instability is most likely a function of the small size of the sample that was used to represent each of the two years studied. Had they chosen a different day to represent each of those two years, the resulting pattern might well have indicated a dramatic drop in violence. This sampling base is not adequate to establish stability in the levels of violence that naturally vary somewhat from day to day. In conclusion, broader based samples with more days, more day-parts, and more channels are more representative of a year's television programming.

Contextual Variables

Although most content analyses of violence focus on the frequency of acts, some have also gathered information on the manner in which violence is presented. The variables that capture this type of information have been regarded as "contextual" variables. Since his earliest content analyses, Gerbner has gathered information about the demographic characteristics (e.g., gender, ethnic background, age group) of both the perpetrators and victims of violence. Over time, content analysts have become more and more interested in these contextual characteristics and have added new variables to the list. For example, when Dominick (1973) counted criminal acts on prime-time, he also gathered information on the motives for the acts and how those acts were resolved. Williams, Zabrack, and Joy (1982) assessed the harmfulness of violence to the victim. Potter and Ware (1987) examined four contextual variables: motivation, reward, justification, and portrayal of the characters (hero, villain, or neutral). More recently, Potter et al. (1995) analyzed 21 contextual variables including reward, intentionality, motivation, remorse, consequences, humor, presentational style, and demographic profiles of the perpetrators and victims. Mustonen and Pulkkinen (1993) developed 37 contextual variables. Many of these were the same concepts as used in the Potter et al. study (although operationalized differently), but there were also some additional variables such as graphicness, intensity, duration, and attractiveness.

Contextual variables have been useful in extending content analysis findings beyond a simple counting of violent acts. However, to date, researchers have selected particular contextual variables for inclusion in their study primarily on the basis of face validity. That is, a variable is deemed important if it appears to be relevant as a factor influencing how viewers make sense of a violent act. There is a need to move beyond the criterion of simple face validity in selecting the attributes examined when studying television violence. Researchers need to construct a unified set of variables that meet a higher criterion of predictive validity. In short, it is important to design a content analysis of violence that will include all the contextual characteristics that have been demonstrated, through experimental research, to influence viewers' reactions to violent portrayals.

This study strives to meet that challenge. In the remainder of this chapter, we outline the basic framework for the present research, providing a useful overview of our methods for the non-technical reader. In the subsequent chapter, we provide a complete explication of our research methods that will be of greatest interest to those more skilled in the practice of research.

Overview of the Present Research

Violence can be depicted in a variety of ways, and we have presented substantial evidence that differences in the context of a portrayal hold important implications for its impact on viewers. These differences in portrayals and their related implications for influencing the audience represent the heart of our interest in undertaking a long-term commitment to the study of televised violence. The goal of our project is to distinguish portrayals of violence most likely to contribute to effects generally considered as anti-social or harmful from portrayals that may be less problematic, if not in some cases even beneficial. As previously noted, the areas of effects upon which we will concentrate are: the learning of aggressive attitudes and behaviors, desensitization, and fear. To accomplish our goal, we have crafted a content analysis framework that we believe is uniquely sensitive to the context in which depictions of televised violence occur.

Definition of Violence

The most critical aspect for any study of television violence is the definition that is employed to identify acts classified as "violent." Our fundamental definition of violence places emphasis on three key elements: intention to harm, the physical nature of harm, and the involvement of animate beings. Violence is defined as any overt depiction of a credible threat of physical force or the actual use of such force intended to physically harm an animate being or group of beings. Violence also includes certain depictions of physically harmful consequences against an animate being or group that occur as a result of unseen violent means. Thus, there are three primary types of violent depictions: credible threats, behavioral acts and harmful consequences.

This definition insures that depictions classified as violent represent actual physical aggression directed against living beings. Such physical action lies at the heart of any conception of violence, and limiting our definition to this type of portrayal (as opposed to including, for example, verbal aggression that might intimidate) renders it a conservative measure of violence on television.

Units of Analysis

In order to capture thorough information about the context of each violent act, it is essential that acts not be viewed in isolation; rather, each act should be considered as part of an ongoing exchange between characters, and each exchange must also be situated within the larger setting of the program as a whole. The richest meaning of any portrayal is found in larger units or chunks, rather than in individual acts. We plan to tap into these larger units of meaning through several different and novel techniques.

First, although we count as violence any act which fits the definition indicated above, we classify acts collectively as part of a larger, superordinate unit of analysis known as a violent incident. A violent incident involves an interaction between a perpetrator (P), an act (A), and a target (T), yielding the convenient acronym PAT as the label for this summary unit. We track and report collectively all violence within the same PAT framework, and refer to this as the PAT level of analysis. For each PAT incident, we ascertain an array of contextual information particular to that exchange that helps us to estimate the likely impact of the depiction.

Second, we gather and report additional descriptive information about the context of violent depictions at the scene level. A violent scene encompasses an interrelated series of violent incidents that occur without a meaningful break in the flow of actual or imminent violence. Analysis at this level affords the opportunity to examine relationships between discrete violent acts. Does one violent act trigger another? Does violence escalate in seriousness from one act to another? These and other related questions can be assessed by examining scene-level information.

Finally, we also examine violent content at the program level. It is important to consider the larger meaning or message that is conveyed by a program, and to do so accurately requires assessment at this level. Some critics have argued that previous studies have failed to differentiate the violence in an artistic or historical program from the violence contained in an entertaining action-adventure program. Both types of programs may contain numerous acts of violence when the focus is at the micro-level of analysis. However, the overall narrative of an historical or educational program may be to condemn the evilness of violence, whereas the action-adventure show may seem to glorify violence. For example, the broadcast network program *Kids Killing Kids* first presented situations resulting in youth violence, but then replayed each scene a second time, illustrating non-violent alternatives to conflict resolution. An analysis of content of *Kids Killing Kids* at the micro-level would reveal that it ranks very high in terms of frequency of violent acts. Yet the overall message of the movie, when viewed at the program level, is an anti-violence one.

By analyzing violence at all three of these levels -- the incident or PAT level, the scene level, and the program level -- we hope to provide the most rich and meaningful data regarding the nature and extent of violent portrayals yet presented by the scientific community. These units of analysis represent a novel framework devised specifically for this project. Both this overall framework for analysis as well as the individual context measures that are assessed at each of the appropriate levels were refined over roughly a six-month period during which the principal investigators evaluated their validity and reliability. The measures that have survived this process are theoretically grounded, consistent with all existing scientific research assessing the effects of televised violence, and as we will demonstrate, can be applied consistently by different coders who are assigned to evaluate television program content.

Measures

The preceding chapter on "The Importance of Context" has foregrounded most areas in which we have crafted measures that will be used to describe the most important aspects of violent depictions. These measures include assessment of the type of violent depiction (credible threats, behavioral acts and harmful consequences); the means by which violence is accomplished (e.g., type of weapon); the extent and graphicness of the violent portrayal; characteristics of the perpetrator and target; the reason for the violence; the consequences of the violence (e.g., pain, harm); the rewards or punishments associated with violence; the degree of realism of the violence; and the use of humor in depictions of violence. In addition, a judgment regarding the overall narrative purpose of each program is applied to help further contextualize any violent depictions. Details regarding the range of values for each measure and the procedures for judging specific content are included in the subsequent chapter of this report.

Coding of Content

Each program included in the sample was evaluated by one of 55 undergraduate research assistants who were trained as coders. Prior to the beginning of the coding process in which judgments are recorded for each of the content measures included in the overall study, coders received approximately 40 hours of classroom training and 20 hours of laboratory practice in recording their observations properly. Only coders who demonstrated strong proficiency with our measures at the completion of training were allowed to continue with the project.

Once the actual process of evaluating videotapes began, coders were assigned randomly to code taped programs. They performed their work in small, individual rooms in a laboratory at UCSB. The consistency of judgments across coders was monitored on a bi-weekly basis throughout all periods of data collection, and the results of these reliability tests are reported in Chapter 5. This monitoring insured that the quality of the judgments that were recorded for each tape was consistently high.

Sample

There are two major features that set our sample apart from other content analyses. First, it is significantly larger than most previous studies of television violence. The typical sample size in the studies cited previously in this chapter is in the range of 80-120 hours per year examined. In contrast, this project sampled nearly 2500 hours of material. The sample includes programming from 6 a.m. until 11 p.m. across a total of 23 different channels (affiliates of the four leading commercial broadcast networks; a public broadcasting affiliate; three independent commercial broadcast stations, 12 basic cable channels, and three premium cable channels).

Second, rather than sampling intact days or weeks of programming, we selected each individual program randomly from a population of all programs appearing from October 1994 to June 1995. Therefore, our sample technically involves literally thousands of sampling units (programs) rather than the more traditional seven units (days). When a sample relies on large units like entire days, there is a greater risk of an anomalous event occurring (e.g., a breaking news story) that could make that block of seven units of programming unrepresentative. In contrast, an anomalous event occurring in one of several thousand units would have much less impact on the overall representativeness of the sample.

Our sample includes most forms of programming on television. However, we did not analyze all shows for violence. Excluded were the genres of religious programming, game shows, instructional shows, home shopping, sports, and newscasts. Consequently, the cable program services CNN and ESPN were excluded entirely from the study. All of these exclusions were stipulated in the research contract with the study's funder, the National Cable Television Association.

Conclusion

This chapter has presented a brief review of the previous content analyses of televised violence in order to illuminate the key decisions in the design of those studies. We then provided a summary of the key aspects in the design of our study. Now we want to highlight the key innovations of our research. These innovations are in the areas of definition of violence, units of analyses, sampling, reliability, and the consideration of context.

Our definition of violence moves beyond a narrow focus on the behavioral act, including credible threats and depictions of harmful consequences of unseen violence. As for units of analyses, we provide for a simultaneous, multiple level (PAT, sequence, and program) examination. Our sample of programs is far more broad than any other scientific content analysis. Our reliability design is particularly complex because of our use of so many coders and the elaborate nature of our measures. And finally, our focus on contextual variables is grounded strongly in the effects literature, so we can be confident of the importance of the content attributes we have selected for study.

In the following chapter, we detail the intricacies of our methods and measures in a thorough fashion that will be of greatest interest to those in the research community who wish to scrutinize our procedures. After the complete presentation of our methods in Chapter 5, we turn to the report of our content analysis findings in Chapter 6.

Chapter 5

DESCRIPTION OF METHODS

In the previous chapter, we provided a basic overview of the framework for this study. In this chapter, we offer a detailed explication of the methods employed in the present research. We begin with information about the sample, then turn to the content measures, and finally the coding and reliability of our data.

We believe that the sample for this study represents a significant improvement over the methodologies employed by past research. Our approach includes a broad range of programming, including most major sources of cable and broadcast television. The sheer size of the sample is approximately 25-30 times larger than most previous studies, with a total of approximately 2,500 hours of content. But most importantly, we employ a scientific model for selecting the material included in the sample, thus maximizing the generalizability of our findings to the overall television environment.

Sample of Programs

The population of interest here is theoretically all programs on television. As a practical matter, however, it is rarely possible for any researcher to truly examine an entire population. Instead, a sample is drawn that is meant to represent the overall population. Some samples accomplish this goal better than others.

Basic Parameters of the Sample

The sampling frame for the present investigation is defined by four parameters: channels, program types, sampling times (i.e., times of day), and sampling periods (i.e., times of year).

Channel. Twenty-three channels were included in the sample. The channels consist of the following different types: commercial broadcast networks, commercial broadcast independents, the public broadcasting network, basic cable, and premium cable. More specifically, the channels listed in Table 2 were included in each group.

All monitoring for each channel was conducted in the Los Angeles market. For the commercial broadcast networks, their Los Angeles affiliates were sampled. These include KABC, KCBS, KTTV for Fox, and KNBC. We did not differentiate between material aired on these stations that originated from the network as opposed to non-network material presented at the discretion of the local affiliate. Thus, what we really have sampled is network affiliate programming, which includes mostly network content but also some syndicated material that would air during fringe hours. If we had focused solely on network content, we would have excluded many hours of programming that is watched by large numbers of people. We suspect that there is not much variation from one network affiliate to another in terms of how these fringe hours are filled (i.e., mostly syndicated content). Furthermore, for the average viewer it is not always easy or meaningful to differentiate between network and local affiliate programming when both are delivered on the same channel. Therefore, we have chosen to include all network affiliate content in the study and to classify it as network programming. This provides the most comprehensive assessment because it allows us to analyze all television programming that is delivered to the public.

Table 2

List of Channels in Sample

Commercial Broadcast	Independent Broadcast	Public Broadcast	Basic Cable	Premium Cable
ABC	KCAL	KCET	A&E	Cinemax
CBS	KCOP		AMC	HBO
Fox	KTLA		BET	Showtime
NBC			Cartoon Network	
			Disney	
			Family Channel	
			Lifetime	
			Nickelodeon	
			TNT	
			USA	
			VH-1	
			MTV	

Similarly, we recognize that our sample of PBS programming from the local affiliate in Los Angeles, KCET, will include some small amount of content that is not network-originated. It would be difficult to monitor any PBS affiliate without encountering this concern. In essence, the issue here is the same as with the commercial network affiliates, and we have resolved it in the same fashion. We have monitored all programming on the affiliate and will report it as public broadcasting content.

For the independent stations, the three major outlets in the market were sampled. Because the independents' share of the Los Angeles market is dominated by these three stations, and because most all nationally syndicated programming airs in the market, we are reasonably confident that our sample includes virtually all of the first-run syndicated content available nation-wide. During the 1994-95 television season, two new network services were unveiled: Warner and Paramount. Each of these services began to deliver a "part-time" slate of programs, and this content was aired in the Los Angeles market on two of the independent stations we sampled. Because of the modest scope of the programming efforts, and the lack of any established "identity" for these networks that would trigger any particular audience expectations, we have chosen to treat these programs the same as any other syndicated content aired on independent stations. Thus, this material is included in the overall findings for the independent stations category.

The cable channels included in the sample were chosen because of their significant audience reach. Program services that are typically marketed as part of a cable subscriber package without any additional per channel cost are classified as "basic cable" services. Services that require an additional per-channel fee are classified as premium cable channels. During the period when this study was being conducted, The Disney Channel began to alter its marketing from a premium to a basic cable service. Though not yet implemented in all markets, this shift is well underway. Consequently, we have chosen to include Disney during this transition year in the basic service category where it will ultimately reside.

Program type. Religious programs, game shows, "infomercials" or home shopping material, instructional programs, sports, and news (see University of Texas report for boundaries of "news" category) were excluded from analysis in the study. To maintain the integrity of the sample design and its representativeness of the overall television environment, these programs were included in the sample grid whenever they were selected by the random draw that created our composite week of programming (that process is detailed below). However, none of these program types were examined for violence. Their exclusion was established by the original contract for this research.

Time of day. All programs listed in TV Guide from 6:00 am until 10:59 pm were eligible for inclusion in the sample (a total of 17 hours per day).

Sampling period. A set of 20 weeks beginning October 8th, 1994 and ending June 9, 1995 was chosen as the sampling period. (See Table 3 for a list of the specific sample weeks). The time periods around certain holidays (Thanksgiving, Christmas, and Easter) were excluded from the sampling frame. Holiday specials and non-regular programming presumed to be variable from year to year were therefore eliminated. The sampling period was of sufficient length to allow for the inclusion of five network "sweep" weeks. Summer weeks were not included in the sample period in order to avoid the over-inclusion of programs due to repeated scheduling.

Given the large number of channels, the broad span of weeks, and the 17 hours per channel per day that define the sample of programs, the present study is much more comprehensive than the sample examined in other studies. For comparative purposes it is useful to note that the most widely cited content analysis conducted previously, that of Gerbner and his colleagues, encompassed only a single week of prime time and Saturday morning programs per year.

Obtaining a Representative Sample of the Program Population

Rather than being selected on the basis of convenience as in most other content analysis studies, the programs chosen in the present study were selected with a modified version of the equal probability of selection method (EPSEM). With this method of

Table 3

Year 1 Sample Weeks

Week Number	Dates
1	October 8-October 14
2	October 15-October 21
3	October 22-October 28
4	October 29-November 4
5	November 5-November 11
6	December 3-December 9
7	January 14-January 20
8	January 21-January 27
9	January 28-February 3
10	February 4-February 10
11	February 11-February 17
12	March 4-March 10
13	March 11-March 17
14	March 18-March 24
15	April 22-April 28
16	April 29-May 5
17	May 6-May 12
18	May 20-May 26
19	May 27-June 2
20	June 3-June 9

selection every program has an equal chance, or opportunity, to appear in the sample. This method insures that a subset of the population of television programs that is *representative* of the entire population of programs is obtained for analysis.

A sample is representative of the population from which it is selected if the aggregate characteristics of the sample closely approximate those same aggregate characteristics in the population. Usually social scientists select groups of people for study. For a sample of individuals to be representative of a larger population of people it must contain essentially the same variations and in the same relative proportions as also exist in the overall population. If the population contains a certain proportion of women and a certain proportion of men, then a representative sample would consist of that same proportion of men and women. Similarly if the population of interest was comprised of two children for every eight adults, a representative sample would contain a similar ratio of children and adults.

This logic can be applied equally well to the population of television programs. For example, if the population of television programs contains a given proportion of situation comedies, then a representative sample of programs would also contain approximately that same proportion. Although no sample is ever perfectly representative of the population from which it is drawn, a basic principle of probability sampling is that a sample will be more representative of the population from which it was selected if all members of the population have an equal chance of being selected.

Equal probability samples are more representative because they avoid the *biases* of convenience samples. For example, the riskiest strategy a researcher wishing to study a population of U.S. residents could pursue would be to walk around his or her neighborhood and interview the first 100 people that could be found. This kind of method is sometimes used by untrained researchers, but it has serious problems. Obviously, the 100 people interviewed by happenstance may share very few characteristics of U.S. residents in general.

The same risks are encountered in selecting television programs for study. Simply selecting programs that are convenient for study (i.e., examining only the first couple of programs in a season, or choosing to examine a single day of programming) risks selecting programs that are not "typical" of the larger population from which they have been chosen. Examining programs only in the beginning of the season is risky because programming strategies may shift during times of the year, such as during ratings "sweeps" periods. Selecting a single day for monitoring raises a significant risk that one particularly violent movie or other program would be shown that day and have a major impact on the overall findings. In fact, the possibilities for inadvertent sampling bias are endless and not always obvious. The only technique that guards against bias is the equal probability selection method.

The strength of the method employed in this study is that the sample is representative because every program has an approximately equal chance of being included. This method of selection offers an additional benefit. Because they are chosen randomly, each program can be said to be "independent" of every other program in the sample. This independence among sampling units permits us to make the strongest possible statistical comparisons between groups of programs that might be distinguished by time-of-day or type of channel, for example.

Program selection. Two half-hour time slots (defined by hour of day and day of week) were randomly selected for each channel during each week that the sampling occurred. Once a time slot was selected, the TV Guide was consulted and the program corresponding to that time slot was entered into a scheduling grid several days before the target week programming began. Programs were retained in the sample in their entirety regardless of the number of time slots they occupied. For example, if the time slot 1:30 pm, Tuesday was randomly selected and an hour long program which began at 1:00 pm was identified in the TV Guide, that program was selected for inclusion in the sample and permitted to occupy two half-hour time slots (1:00 pm - 2:00 pm). Our procedure thus can be said to be a modified version of an EPSEM because the sample is actually self-weighted by length of program. An hour long program has twice the probability of being included in the final sample as a half-hour program.

This taping schedule was transmitted to an independent television taping contractor, Killingsworth Inc. of Long Beach, California, where the programs were taped. Once taped, the content was shipped to the University of California, Santa Barbara where it was checked for completeness, picture and sound quality. Programs found to be incomplete or for which sound or picture quality were inadequate were dropped from the sample and the time slot was re-sampled. Table 4 shows the total number of programs sampled by channel.

Preemptions. Only scheduled programming was included in the sample. Programs that were preempted by news bulletins or special reports that exceeded five minutes in length per half hour of programming were excluded from the sample. The largest number of preemptions were due to the O.J. Simpson trial which was heavily covered by Los Angeles area independent broadcasters.

Program overlap. Sampling by half-hour unit resulted in some program overlap due to the availability of half-hour time slots which were "sandwiched" between programs already in the sample. These programs were taped in their entirety and included in the sample. Table 4 lists the number and percentage of program overlap by channel. Premium channels with a high proportion of movie programming accounted for the highest overlap. Overall, 14% of the programs included in the sample overlap with other programs.

Programs exceeding the 6:00 am-11:00 pm time-of-day frame. Programs which began before 6:00 am or continued beyond 11:00 pm were taped in their entirety when they were selected by the sampling process. For example, a program that was selected for sampling for the 10:00 pm block that ran 90 minutes would be included even though its final half-hour aired after 11:00 pm.

Table 4
Breakdown of Programs and Exclusions in Sample

Channel	Number of programs	Not Coded	% Not Coded	Taping Errors	% Taping Errors	Program Overlap	% overlap
ABC	137	40	29%	3	2%	6	4%
CBS	143	54	38%	6	4%	17	12%
NBC	129	48	37%	3	2%	13	10%
FOX	163	26	16%	14	9%	12	7%
PBS	163	12	7%	4	2%	12	7%
KCAL	162	55	34%	3	2%	9	6%
KCOP	147	28	19%	3	2%	7	5%
KTLA	104	41	39%	8	8%	22	21%
A & E	95	0	0%	3	3%	4	4%
AMC	82	0	0%	2	2%	47	57%
BET	133	29	22%	5	4%	3	2%
CAR	171	0	0%	9	5%	10	6%
DIS	166	0	0%	8	5%	14	8%
FAM	174	58	33%	5	3%	15	9%
LIF	145	51	36%	7	5%	16	11%
MTV	153	13	8%	4	3%	22	14%
NIK	229	2	1%	9	4%	9	4%
TNT	94	2	2%	7	7%	21	22%
USA	143	33	23%	3	2%	27	19%
VH-1	181	0	0%	11	6%	30	17%
HBO	104	0	0%	1	1%	42	40%
MAX	81	0	0%	3	4%	48	59%
SHO	86	0	0%	9	10%	43	50%
Total	3185	492	15%	130	4%	449	14%

Summary Description of the Sample

A composite week of programming. The sampling procedure described above resulted in a seven-day composite week of programming. Virtually all shows in the regular program schedule for each channel appear in the final composite week. As noted above, the random selection method insures that this composite is theoretically more representative of a "typical" week of cable television programming than an arbitrary selected actual week of programming. Further, the number of independently sampled programs is large enough to make scientifically valid comparisons between violent content in various categories of programming and across times of day.

Total program count. The taped sample includes a total of 3,185 programs. A complete grid of all programs selected for inclusion in the sample appears in Appendix 1 of this report. A total of 130 programs (4%) were removed from the sample due to taping errors or other technical problems. Table 4 includes a breakdown of missing program blocks by cable channel. Missing half-hour program blocks occur most frequently for Showtime (10%) and Fox (9%).

Sample exclusions. Of the total 3,185 programs, 492 (15%) are religious programs, game shows, sports, "infomercials", instructional shows and breaking news, and thus were not included in the coding analyses.

Overall Summary

The sample for the present study has several strengths that distinguish it from previous content analyses. Because the method of selection is based on probability and because the parameters of the sample (17 hours per day, 20 weeks, 23 channels) are so broad, a composite week has been assembled that can be said to be more representative of a typical week of television programming than past research efforts. A sample of programming selected in this fashion permits a more accurate estimation of the amount and type of violent programming in a given year. This method is also particularly valuable for insuring accuracy in comparing levels over time. With this method, we are able to accurately track increases or decreases in violence precisely from year to year.

Content Measures

We now turn to the measures that are applied in our analysis of the content collected by our sampling strategy. In this section we deal with three main topics. The first topic, that of defining violence, isolates the depictions that will be the focus of further analysis. The second topic, units of analysis, establishes the framework within which we operate in structuring our assessment of violent depictions. The third topic, contextual measures, details the specific judgments that are recorded for each case of violence that we observe.

Definition of Violence

Our fundamental definition of violence places emphasis on a number of elements, including intention to harm, the physical nature of harm, and the involvement of animate beings. We use the following definition of violence in this study:

> Violence is defined as any overt depiction of a credible threat of physical force or the actual use of such force intended to physically harm an animate being or group of beings. Violence also includes certain depictions of physically harmful consequences against an animate being or group that occur as a result of unseen violent means.

Thus, there are three primary types of violent depictions: credible threats, behavioral acts and harmful consequences. The key concepts embodied in this definition warrant some explanation and rationale.

Intention to harm. Intentionality is obviously a private, internal psychological state that is not open to direct observation. Nonetheless, it is the focus of how most humans seek to make sense of their world; that is, they attribute intentionality to the actions of others. If viewers could not attribute intentions to the actions of television characters they observed, the content would hold little interest for them. Consequently, program creators seek to convey motives and intentions to the audience in order for a story to make sense. We believe character intent related to behaviors that threaten or harm others can be inferred from the context of the portrayal and classified reliably.

The concept of intention is an essential aspect of our definition. If intentions were not addressed, many harmful behaviors not reasonably considered as aggressive might otherwise be classified as violent. All accidental harm would be included, as might the actions of surgeons and dentists, neither of which has been associated with harmful psychological effects on the audience. Conversely, it is important that we not exclude acts that attempt to cause harm but which prove unsuccessful. Such acts are clearly aggressive. They could be learned, and could contribute to fear responses in the audience as well as increased socialization to aggression. Only through a consideration of intent can such actions be properly classified as falling within our definition of violence.

Physical harm. One might reasonably assert that verbal assaults that intimidate or physical acts that are meant to cause psychological or emotional harm (e.g., embarrassment, humiliation) should be considered as violence. Certainly such actions are aggressive and may in some cases be associated with anti-social impacts on the audience.

We have chosen, however, to draw the line for our definition of violence at a point which is supported most strongly and unequivocally by the existing base of research evidence, rather than to grapple for the edge of that boundary. Physical harm or the threat thereof is at the root of all conceptions of violence and of most operationalizations of the concept in past research (Baron & Richardson, 1994;

Reiss & Roth, 1993). By employing this approach, we can be confident that our definition of violence is a conservative one, and that our findings will not artificially inflate any estimates of the overall amount of violence on television.

Given that physical harm represents a key dimension in our basic definition of violence, it is important to recognize two key extensions of this concept. One is that credible threats of physical harm must be considered as violent because just as with a harmful act, they too may contribute to fear responses in the audience (Cantor, 1991) as well as increased priming of aggressive thoughts and behaviors (Berkowitz, 1984; Berkowitz & Rogers, 1986). A second application is that violent actions that are not portrayed overtly but can be inferred clearly from the depiction of the harmful consequences (e.g., police respond to the scene of a shooting and find a victim bleeding to death) also should be considered as violence because of their likelihood of contributing to anti-social effects such as fear (Wilson, 1995; Wilson & Cantor, 1985).

It is important to note that although our definition of violence will include a range of acts including credible threats, behavioral acts, and depictions of harmful consequences of unseen violence, we do not mean to assert that there is equivalence in terms of harmfulness across this range of depictions. For example, consider a portrayal in which violence occurs off-screen, with only the result of that violence (such as a bloody nose or lip from a blow to the face) depicted instead of the actual act itself. This depiction would be captured by our measures as an example of harmful consequences, yet would likely pose less concern, at least from a social learning or modeling standpoint, than would an overt depiction of the implied behavioral act.

Animate beings as perpetrator and target. Harm can be caused to individuals by many forces other than the actions of living beings. For example, a person could be injured by an act of nature such as a tornado or lightning bolt. Although these actions might contribute to fear on the part of some viewers, in particular young children, they would not raise concerns in terms of socialization to or modeling of aggression. Consistent with our previous point that intention to harm is a fundamental aspect in our definition of violence, we believe that at least one animate being capable of possessing intentions must be involved as a perpetrator in order to have an instance of violence.

Similarly, an animate being must be a target in order to meet our definition of violence. Individuals often hit or kick inanimate objects in aggressive fashion. Sometimes this reflects spontaneous anger and other times a premeditated intention to damage a target's possessions. In either case, intent to physically harm something living is missing, and thus we would not consider these examples of violence as we have defined it. Again we must note that some such examples of violence against property would certainly be associated with anti-social influences on the audience. Nonetheless, some examples of property damage, such as putting a sledge hammer to an old car at the county fair, could be entirely benign when considered in context. Most importantly, the research evidence documenting the anti-social effects of violence against living beings is compelling, while no comparable body of direct evidence exists regarding the impacts of violence against inanimate objects. Given our desire to measure violence in conservative fashion, we have stipulated that an animate being must be targeted for harm in order for violence to occur.

Of course, the television world is inhabited by a wide range of creatures not all of whom naturally occur on Earth. These include everything from *Smurfs* to *Teenage Mutant Ninja Turtles* to *Biker Mice from Mars*, to name a few children's program characters; beings from other planets such as *Superman* or *Alf*; fictional monsters such as *King Kong* or *Godzilla*; or even fantasy characters such as anthropomorphized flowers or trees that walk and talk. We will consider animate beings to include humans (either real or animated), animals, supernatural creatures, and anthropomorphized characters of all kinds. Although any of these will count as animate, we do not mean to imply they are all necessarily equivalent. In our assessment of the context in which violence occurs, information about the type of characters involved as well as specific attributes associated with particular characters will be important considerations.

Three forms of violence. A violent action is any depiction that qualifies as violence according to our basic definition. We have classified violent actions into three primary types: credible threats of violence, behavioral acts, and depictions of harmful consequences of violence.

First, a credible threat is an overt behavior which threatens the use of violence. The behavior may be either verbal or nonverbal. A credible threat occurs when a perpetrator evidences a serious intent to harm a target by either directly communicating the threat verbally or by displaying violent means in a threatening manner. For example, a directly communicated credible threat is when someone says menacingly, "I'll slash your throat." A common example of a threat using a display of violent means is when someone aims a gun at another.

Second, a behavioral act is an overt action using violent physical force against another. These types of acts may employ weapons, ordinary objects, or the perpetrator's own natural means. Common examples of behavioral acts using weapons include stabbings, shootings, and the use of explosives. Ordinary objects used to commit behavioral acts could include beer bottles, chairs, or lead pipes; the common characteristic is that the object is not normally associated with use as a weapon. Finally, punches, kicks, and bites are examples of behavioral acts using natural means.

Third, harmful consequences are depictions of the victims of violence when the violence is clearly implied but not portrayed overtly as it occurs. An example of this type of violence is when two detectives arrive on a scene to find a murder victim lying in a pool of blood. Depictions of harmful consequences are coded only when a program does not include any portion of the violent act, but rather depicts only its physical aftermath. If in the above example the program had shown the victim actually being shot and then later it shows the detectives arriving and encountering the body, we would count the original act as a violent behavioral act, but would not count the harmful consequences as a separate act of violence. In this way, we avoid "double-counting" of any violent actions. Harmful consequences count as violence only when the behavioral act is implied and never shown.

Units of Analysis

The judgments and observations we have recorded for each instance of violence are organized into three distinct levels, or units of analysis. These three levels include: (1) the violent interaction, or PAT level; (2) the scene level; and (3) the program level. The PAT level is the most microscopic of the three.

PAT level. All violent incidents can be said to represent an interaction between a perpetrator (P) who performs a type of act (A) directed at a target (T). For example, a hijacker with a bomb strapped to his back who threatens a planeload of passengers would be categorized at the PAT level in the following manner: P = hijacker, A = credible threat, T = passengers on the plane. A CIA agent who shoots a handgun at a group of terrorists would be unitized as: P = CIA agent, A = behavioral act, T = terrorists.

When a violent action occurs, it is coded first as a PAT case or observation. The information recorded for that case encompasses all of the violent actions directed by a particular perpetrator at a particular target within the same scene, so long as the type of act remains the same. Recall that type of act refers to credible threat, behavioral act, and depiction of harmful consequences. Brief threats that are followed immediately by a violent behavioral act are not considered as independent actions, but rather are recorded as a violent behavioral act and thus constitute a single PAT. However, a threat that was followed through with a violent behavior at a later point in time would represent two separate PATs -- one for the threat and one for the behavioral act. Even though the P and T remained constant, the change in A (type of act) requires a new PAT. Generally speaking, a different PAT case results whenever there is a significant change in any one of the three elements of the violent interaction: the perpetrator, the act, or the target.

Obviously, not all violent interactions display the same characteristics or contextual features. For our purposes, it is vital to evaluate all violent interactions at their most microscopic level because we need to take into account numerous aspects of the context of each portrayal in order to estimate its potential for influencing the audience. Consider the following example: a law enforcement officer is assaulted by a fleeing felon, who tries to stab the officer in order to escape from the scene of the crime. The officer responds by shooting the suspect in order to save her own life. In this exchange, there are two very different motives for violence. There may also be other important differences, such as the nature of the characters committing the violence, the way in which the violent actions are depicted on-screen, and the consequences of each person's actions. To capture these important differences, we must be able to evaluate the nature of each character's involvement in violence, including what actions they have performed, their reasons for violence, and so on. To accomplish this, we must view each PAT interaction as a separate case.

One PAT would be recorded with the criminal as the P and the officer as the T, with a separate PAT representing the officer as the P and the criminal as the T when the officer responded to the initial assault with more violence. In this example, there is a different reason for violence by the officer than by the criminal. If the entire interaction between the two was recorded as a single unit, that information would be lost or diminished. The obvious qualitative differences inherent within different interactions led to the construction of the PAT unit.

Because perpetrators and targets may come in single, multiple, or implied forms, precise operational rules were crafted in order to maintain the integrity of the PAT unit across a wide range of situations. For example, when a group of people such as a military squad operate collectively to accomplish a common goal, their actions are considered as representing a single P. Similarly, it is important to distinguish interactions such as a credible threat from an implied perpetrator (i.e., an anonymous ransom note) from a visual depiction of a graphic and imitatable behavioral act performed by a heroic character. The details of these and other rules for coding observations are included in the complete version of the codebook, which is contained in Appendix 2 of this report.

Scene level. The second and intermediate level of analysis is called a scene. A violent scene is defined as a related series of violent behaviors, actions or depictions of harmful consequences of violence that occur without a significant break in the flow of actual or imminent violence. In other words, the actions maintain a narrative flow in which a sequence of actions are connected or related to one another. Therefore, violent sequences typically occur in the same general setting among the same characters or types of characters. One or many PAT interactions may occur within a given scene.

A great deal of rich contextual information that may not necessarily be present at the microscopic PAT level, such as the presence of rewards or punishments for violence, can be captured at this intermediate level of analysis. Also measured at this level is the explicitness or graphicness of the violent depictions.

A violent scene begins whenever any action that fulfills the definition of violence is observed. A scene ends whenever a significant break occurs within the scene. A significant break occurs when the imminent threat of violence ceases to exist or when there is an interruption in the time, place, or setting that would reflect what is commonly referred to as a scene change. Again, specific operational rules have been crafted to facilitate consistency in judgments across coders. For example, films often include "cut-aways," or shifts back and forth between events occurring simultaneously at two separate locations. When this occurs, scene shifts or cut-aways that continue for a period of 30 seconds or more are considered significant breaks.

Program level. The macro-ordinate unit of analysis is an entire program. While it is important to evaluate violent interactions at both the PAT and scene level in order to capture vital contextual differences between different interactions, it is also important to evaluate content at the broader level of overall themes or messages represented in a show. We believe the judgments at this level very nearly approximate some of the overall messages that average adult viewers would obtain after watching an entire program. For example, an evil character may be punished for violence only at the end of a program, but not at the time the violence was committed. The PAT and scene measures would not capture this punishment because they are focused on the character's actions (PAT level) and the related developments that occur within the scene in which those actions are depicted (scene level). A measure of punishments for violence at the program level is needed to complement our analysis at the more microscopic PAT and scene level.

Most programs consist of one thematic story or unfolding narrative whose beginning, middle and end is presented across a scheduled block of time. These programs typically begin and end their time slots with production credits and/or conventions (e.g., teasers, previews). Examples of these types of programs are situation comedies dramas, soap operas, and movies.

Some other types of programs, however, feature two or more self-contained stories whose unfolding narratives are each presented independently of one another. Each of these segments represents only a portion of the overall time devoted to a scheduled program, yet each is an independent "story." The plotline, characters, and/or geographical locations in each segment tend to vary from one story to the next. A good example of this would be a magazine format show such as the long-running Sunday night program *Sixty Minutes*. We refer to such content as a <u>segmented program</u>.

Segmented programs also typically begin and end their time slots with standard production credits and/or conventions (e.g., teasers, previews). However, each independent story nested within the program is introduced and separated in some way from other stories by some form of production credits and/or conventions. For example, a narrator or program host might introduce each segment. Examples of these types of programs are music videos, news magazines, certain reality-based programs, and some cartoon shows. For material classified as a segmented program, the program level variables are assessed for each segment within that particular program in order to capture the differences which may exist between discrete segments in a program.

Contextual Measures

In order to measure the contextual factors presented in Chapter 3, two types of variables were created: violence-related and character-related variables. In the next three sections, each violence-related contextual measure will be defined and explicated at the PAT, scene, and program level of analysis. Then, each of the character-related contextual variables designed to capture the qualities of the perpetrators and targets involved in violence will be conceptually and operationally defined.

PAT level context variables. The first contextual factor assessed at the PAT level was the perpetrator's primary <u>reason</u> or motive for engaging in violence. This variable was assessed at the most micro-level of analysis because a perpetrator's reason for acting violently may vary as a function of the target s/he is confronting. There were six possible values for this measure: protection of life, retaliation, anger, personal gain, mental instability, and other.

As Chapter 3 indicates, violence that is "justified" may pose a greater risk to viewers than "unjustified" aggressive actions. In an effort to assess justified violence, four categories of reasons are collapsed at the level of analysis. Violence that is accomplished in an effort to "protect life" or to "retaliate" for a previous act of violence is usually socially sanctioned in a typical plot. As such, these two reasons will form the variable "justified" violence. Alternatively, aggressive actions that seem to be motivated by "personal gain" or "mental instability" are more likely to appear "unjustified." Consequently, these two reasons will be collapsed in an effort to examine "unjustified" violence.

The second contextual variable assessed the <u>means</u> used in each violent interaction. Means were defined as any object, weapon or device that perpetrators used to threaten and/or harm targets. There were six categories of means: natural means (using a character's normal physical capabilities such as striking with a fist), unconventional weapons (striking with a chair or bottle), conventional weapons non-firearms (police baton, knife), handheld firearms (gun, pistol), heavy weaponry (submarines, tanks), and bombs (timer, remote). For any given violent interaction, each different type of means used by a perpetrator against a particular target was captured.

In addition to assessing the type/s, the <u>extent</u> of each means used also was recorded. Extent was measured within each means category for a given interaction. There were five values for the extent variable: one (single example of act), some (between two and nine examples of the act), many (between 10 and 20 examples of the act), and extreme (over 20 examples of the act).

The next three contextual factors measured the immediate consequences of each violent interaction. Conceptually, consequences referred to the amount of physical harm and pain that a target incurred as a result of violence. Two types of harm were measured for each violent interaction: depicted harm and likely harm. Subsequent comparison of these two measures allows us to draw inferences about the relative degree of realism associated with specific portrayals.

The evaluation of <u>depicted harm</u> was based on two specific factors: the amount of physical injury done to a target's body, and the target's ability to function after experiencing violence. In some cases of unrealistic depictions, such as in cartoons, these two elements are often in conflict. That is, a character may be flattened like a pancake by a steamroller, but then pop right up and walk away unfazed. In such cases, the depicted harm would be judged as minimal because the target continued to function seemingly without harm even though suffering temporary disconfiguration of the body. There were four possible values for depicted harm: none, mild, moderate, or extreme.

A measure of <u>likely harm</u>, on the other hand, assessed the level of physical injury and incapacitation that would likely occur if the same violent means were targeted toward a human in real life. To judge this, an inference had to be drawn about the potential seriousness of the means used. The values for likely harm were the same as those for depicted harm.

In addition to depicted and likely harm, the amount of <u>depicted pain</u> a target experienced as a result of violence was also assessed. Conceptually, pain was defined as the audible (i.e., screams, moans, yells, gasps) or visible (i.e., facial expressions, physical reactions such as clutching of a wound/injury) expression of physical suffering that occurred as a result of violence. Pain had four possible values: none, mild, moderate, and extreme. If there was no opportunity to observe a target's pain either during or immediately after experiencing violence, the measure was not assesed.

Finally, violent behaviors were assessed for instances of sexual assault. Sexual assault was defined as violence that occurred in conjunction with intimate physical contact involving sexual and/or erotic overtones; or other erotic touching or physical contact intended to arouse or sexually gratify the perpetrator against a target's will. If any of these elements were present either immediately before, during or after a violent act, then the act was coded as including sexual assault.

Scene level context variables. At the scene level, several violence-related contextual variables were assessed. These variables were judged after the coder had viewed the entire scene *and* the one that immediately followed it. Scene measures are particularly salient for assessing impacts on young viewers, who are much better at comprehending cause/effect relationships (such as rewards/punishments) that are closely linked in a program than when they are separated more distantly. Coders always watched the scene that immediately followed the violent scene prior to making their contextual judgments at this level of analysis. If a violent scene was followed by a commercial break, by definition, no subsequent scene existed and the coder was instructed to simply assess the following variables at the end of the scene.

The first contextual factor at the scene level assessed the rewards that were associated with a perpetrator's violent action. A reward was defined as any verbal or nonverbal reinforcement that was given to or taken by a perpetrator for acting violently. The presence or absence of three types of rewards were assessed at this level: self praise, praise from others, or material rewards.

Similarly, punishments associated with violent actions were also measured at the scene level. Conceptually, a punishment was defined as any verbal or nonverbal sign of disapproval or disappointment that was expressed towards a perpetrator for acting violently. The presence or absence of four specific types of punishments was assessed at the scene level: self condemnation, condemnation from others, nonviolent condemnation, violent condemnation.

The next contextual factor assessed at the scene level was graphicness. Three types of graphicness were assessed. The first factor assessed the explicitness of the violent behavioral act and the second measured the explicitness of the means to target impact. Explicitness was defined as the focus, concentration or level of detail with which violence was presented. The camera focus for each of these variables was coded as either shown up-close, shown long-shot, or not shown at all.

In addition to assessing explicitness, the amount of blood and gore displayed within each scene was also measured. This variable evaluated the degree or quantity of blood, gore, and/or dismemberment that was depicted within a violent scene. There were four levels of graphicness: none, mild, moderate and extreme.

The last contextual factor assessed at this level was humor. As indicated in Chapter 3, very little research has been conducted on the effects of humor presented within the context of violence. Due to the paucity of research in this area, we adopted a very broad conceptualization of this variable. Humor was defined as those verbal or nonverbal words, actions and/or behaviors that a character engaged in that were intended to amuse either the self, another character or characters, and/or the viewer. Humor, regardless of the type, was simply coded as either present or absent within each violent scene.

Program level context variables. At the program level, several global or macro-level contextual variables were measured. These variables were ascertained by the coder only at the end of each program viewed. The first variable was designed to assess the program's purpose for including violence within its unfolding narrative. More specifically, this variable measured whether or not the program contained an "anti-violence theme."

A program was judged to possess an anti-violence theme if it illustrated that using violence is morally and/or socially wrong. Operationally, an anti-violence theme was coded as present if any of the following conditions were met within the context of the unfolding narrative: 1) alternatives to violent actions were presented and/or discussed throughout the program; 2) main characters repeatedly discussed the negative consequences of violence; 3) the physical pain and emotional suffering that results from violence were clearly emphasized; or 4) punishments for violence clearly and consistently outweighed rewards. If a program did not fit one of these criteria, then it was coded as having no anti-violence theme.

The next two contextual variables assessed the degree of realism surrounding the presentation of violence and its negative effects. The purpose of these program level contextual variables was to identify and discriminate those programs that present violence in a realistic context from those that present violence in a fantastic context.

Operationally, each program was evaluated for its level of realism. The coder assessed whether the content represented: 1) actual reality (i.e., programs that show footage of actual, real life events); 2) re-creation of reality (i.e., reenacted events that are presented similarly to how they actually occurred); 3) fiction (i.e., creative constructions not based upon actual events, yet depicting actions and events that could possibly occur; and 4) fantasy (i.e., programs containing characters that could not possibly exist or events that could not possibly happen in the real world as we know it).

The second measure of realism assessed the presentational style of each program. This variable indicates whether a program was presented via animation, live action, or a mix of both formats.

Although research evidence indicates that more realistic portrayals of violence put most viewers at a greater risk in terms of learning aggressive acts, research also suggests that realistically depicting the negative consequences that result from engaging in violence inhibits viewers from learning and/or modeling aggressive actions. In an effort to assess how each program presented the long-term pain and suffering that results from violence, the next contextual factor, harm/pain was assessed at the end of each program viewed. This program level variable was defined much more broadly to include not only physical harm, but also emotional, financial, and psychological suffering that is experienced as a result of violence.

Those programs that presented pain/harm as a result of violence in the same scene or in the immediately adjacent scene were coded as presenting the consequences of violence in a "short-term" fashion. Those programs that depicted pain/harm later in the program were coded as presenting the consequences of violence in a "long-term/extended" fashion. Those programs that did not present any harm/pain within the context of the plot, were coded as presenting "no harm" as a result of violence.

The next program level contextual factor assessed the overall pattern of punishments that were delivered to all good, bad, and good and bad (to be defined below) characters involved in violence. The focus of this variable was to ascertain the patterns with which different types of characters (i.e., all of the good characters or all of the bad characters) received punishment for acting violently in a program. All good, bad and both good and bad characters that engaged in violence were coded as being punished in one of the following patterns: punished throughout an entire program, punished at the end only, never or rarely punished, or not punished by any one of the above patterns.

Character context variables. In addition to assessing the nature and consequences surrounding violent acts, several character-related context variables were crafted in an effort to gain rich, descriptive data about the perpetrators and targets involved in violence. All characters, whether they instigated violence or received it, were coded for both demographic and attributive qualities. In terms of demographics, characters were assessed for type (i.e., human, animal, supernatural creature, anthropomorphized animal, anthropomorphized supernatural being), form (single, multiple, implied), size if a multiple unit (2; 3-9; 10-99; 100-999; 1000 or more), sex (male, female, can't tell), age (child, teen, adult, elderly, can't tell) and apparent ethnicity (i.e., white, hispanic, black, native american, asian/pacific islander, or middle eastern).

In addition to these demographic data, characters were assessed in terms of specific attributive qualities. The following contextual features were crafted in an effort to measure the "attractiveness" of the characters who engaged in violence. First, a character's "goodness" or "badness" was evaluated. Good characters were defined as those who acted benevolently, helped others, and/or were motivated to consider the needs of others before themselves. Bad characters, on the other hand, were those who acted primarily in their own self-interest, emphasized their own needs, and had very little regard for others. Those characters who were both good and bad were those that displayed a balance of both characteristics in a program. And finally, those characters who were either 1) not featured long enough to ascertain their orientation towards others or 2) their orientation could not be determined from the context of the plot, were coded as "neutral."

Each character was also assessed for hero status. As indicated in the literature review, heros are characters that children and adults are most likely to identify with and potentially imitate. In order to clearly differentiate heros from good characters, we crafted a very narrow definition of this variable. A character was only coded as a hero if he/she/it met all of the following criteria: 1) appeared as one of the primary characters in the program's plot-line, 2) the character's role in the program was to protect others from becoming victims of violence, and 3) the character engaged in helping of others above and beyond the call of duty. All characters who did not meet this definition were coded as a "non-hero."

Coding and Reliability

The coding of data for this project was performed by undergraduate students at the University of California, Santa Barbara. Individuals were recruited in the Department of Communication, and screened to obtain those with the strongest academic records. To perform coding work, individuals had to master all aspects of our codebook, which explicates all of our variables and measures in detail at both the conceptual and operational levels. This training was accomplished through a number of complementary processes. We began with approximately 40 hours of instruction for all coders in a class setting. We then added small group training sessions. Throughout the entire training process, coders regularly practiced applying our measures by individually coding programs in our lab. Feedback on these practice sessions was provided individually, in small groups, and to the entire class of coders as appropriate to the training task.

With any content analysis methodology, researchers must demonstrate that their coders have made decisions consistently. In other words, if several coders are asked to view the same program, they should apply the definitions and measures of violence in the same way, and their resulting judgments regarding the presence or absence of violence should show high agreement. Thus, the designing of a good test of inter-coder reliability is an important part of making a case for the quality of data. The result of such a test is a series of reliability coefficients ranging between a possible 1.0 for perfect inter-coder agreement to .00 indicating no consistency.

Our testing for the reliability of coders was conducted in two phases. In the first phase, we monitored the decision-making of the coders in order to determine when they were fully trained and able to begin coding of actual data to be used in the analyses. Here the focus was on the coders themselves and their aptitude in internalizing all the coding rules. The second phase consisted of two different prongs. The first was an examination of the patterns in the coded data themselves so as to determine the degree of reliability, and hence the quality, of the data. For this analysis, we shifted the focus from individual coders to individual decision points in the process of coding. The second prong involved an assessment focused again on the coders' performance so as to spot fatigue or other problems that might diminish the quality of the data. Both of these different aspects of the second phase were conducted concurrently throughout the duration of the coding process. The same raw data were employed for both of the prongs, but they were analyzed in different ways. The details of these procedures are explicated below.

Initial Diagnostic Testing

Once the coding scheme was sufficiently developed to warrant initial testing, we began a series of diagnostic coding exercises.

Purpose. The initial diagnostic testing provided a check on the training. It consisted of a series of coding exercises that were designed to (1) determine the extent to which coders were consistent in applying the coding rules as written, and (2) identify those coders who had missed key elements in the training. In the development of the coding scheme, we were guided by the principle of providing coding rules at a sufficient level of detail along with concrete examples so that all coders would be able to make consensus decisions about any violent content they might encounter. How well were we achieving this goal? In order to answer this question, we needed to conduct diagnostic testing.

Also, we were concerned that all 40 coders might not have internalized the training to an equally high degree. So we needed to identify those coders who were having problems applying the coding rules so that they could receive some additional training.

Of course the two purposes of the diagnostic testing are interrelated. For example, if we found that all coders were having trouble with a particular coding decision, then we would need to determine if the problem could be traced to the way the coding rule was written or if the problem was traceable instead to training. However, if instead we found that the majority of the coders were applying a particular rule consistently, then we could conclude that those few coders who were not part of the majority needed remedial training. If a large number of coders applied a coding rule consistently one way while another large number of coders applied it consistently another way, we concluded that the rule was ambiguous and required rewriting.

Procedures. Each diagnostic test followed six steps. First, a program was selected to serve as a good challenge for a particular aspect of the coding scheme being tested. Second, all coders were assigned to code the program individually. Third, the coding data were collected and arranged into 40-column matrices comparing the decisions by all coders. For PAT level codes, a matrix was constructed for each PAT level variable. Each of these matrices was 40 columns wide, and the number of lines corresponded to the largest number of acts any coder identified. We could then compare the extent to which each coder recognized the same number of violent acts. A coder who missed coding a violent act was able to be easily identified by the missing PAT line in the matrix. A set of matrices was also constructed for each variable at the scene level. These scene level matrices were 40 columns wide, and the number of lines corresponded to the number of scenes the coders identified within a program. The program level codes were all entered into a single program level matrix for a show. The program level matrix was 40 columns wide, and the number of lines corresponded to the number of variables coded at the program level. Thus, at the end of this third step in the procedure, we had a set of matrices for the PAT level codes, a set of matrices for the scene level codes, and a single program level matrix.

Fourth, the appropriate coding values were entered in the matrices. For example, on the scene level reward matrix, a "1" was entered into a cell for every coder who decided that the scene did not depict the violence as being rewarded and therefore coded "no" for the reward variable. Coders who decided that the violence in a scene was rewarded had a "2" entered in the appropriate matrix. Then for each line in a matrix, we determined the mode, which is the most prevalent code used by the 40 coders. The modal frequency was then divided by 40 to arrive at the percentage of agreement of codes on that one line. For example, if a given scene (one line of data in the scene matrix) displayed 36 codes of "1" and the remaining four codes as "2," then the mode is clearly "1" which occurs 36 times. This means that 90% of the coders agreed on this code for this scene. Finally, by summing all the modal frequencies for each line on the matrix and dividing by the total number of coding decisions exhibited in the matrix, we arrive at the total percentage of agreement for that variable. This procedure was repeated for each PAT and scene level matrix. For the program level matrix, the total percentages of agreement were computed for each line, because each line contained the total data for each program level variable.

Fifth, for each variable, the percentages of agreement were reported to the planning group. We used the convention in the content analysis literature of regarding .70 as a minimum acceptable percentage of agreement, and if we found a percentage that was lower than .70, it was a signal of a coding problem. With all problems, we solicited feedback from the coders to try to ascertain the root of the problem as being either: (a) unclear directions in the code book, (b) incomplete training of all coders, or (c) inconsistent training where some coders understood the decision while others did not. The group members studied the patterns in the matrices of the problem variables and brainstormed about possible solutions to the inconsistencies. Many of these discussions resulted in revisions to the preliminary coding rules. In certain instances we found that a few coders were consistently making wrong coding decisions, and these coders were targeted for further training. In some instances, the members of the planning group did not feel confident in identifying a problem, and had to rely upon results of the next step before deciding how to improve the consistency of coding decisions.

Sixth, the coders were debriefed. Discussions were stimulated among coders, either in the full group or in sub-sets, focusing on the coding decisions that were diagnosed as being a problem. Often the program that was coded was re-screened so that coders could talk through their decision-making processes. These discussions served two purposes. One purpose was to give members of the planning team feedback about the coding process so that they could pinpoint causes of inconsistent decision-making. The other purpose was to highlight points where decision-making was done consistently so as to reinforce those good decisions and to show the inconsistent coders how their decisions should have been made.

The series of diagnostic tests. For our first year study, we employed two groups of coders to generate our data, and thus pursued two series of tests. This first series included eight rounds as follows:

Round 1.1   A 12-minute segment of the cartoon *Tom & Jerry* was selected for coding for the first diagnostic test. The coders limited their analysis to PAT level variables.

Round 1.2:   Coders analyzed PAT variables in an episode of *Hawkeye*.

Round 1.3:   Coders analyzed PAT, scene, and program (character codes only) level codes in episodes of four programs: *Remington Steele, Tales from the Crypt, MacGyver*, and *Looney Tunes*.

Round 1.4:   Coders tested four program level variables (narrative purpose, realism, harm/pain, and rewards/punishments) for episodes of three programs: *Tales from the Crypt, The Rifleman*, and *Power Rangers*. The discussions from these results served to make changes in the codes for harm/pain as well as rewards/punishments.

Round 1.5:   Coders tested program level codes on episodes of *Starsky & Hutch* and *Magnum, P.I.* The reward/punishment code continued to be a problem and additional changes were made with it.

Rounds 1.6 & 1.7:   Coders looked at an episode of *Silk Stalkings* for PAT level analysis. A few problems in dealing with multiple perpetrators and targets were discovered, so additional rules were written to help coders distinguish when multiple characters were acting in concert or independently. Coders received additional training. The following week these new rules and retraining were tested on the same program.

Round 1.8:   Coders analyzed an episode of *Magnum, P.I.* and a segment of the *Looney Tunes* cartoon. All variables at the PAT, scene, and program levels were coded.

Near the end of this process, we began testing on a second group of coders who joined the project. This second group required only three rounds of testing, because by this point our training procedures were more efficient and the codebook was complete. We had corrected the problems encountered during the first round of training. The three rounds of testing with the second group of coders overlapped with rounds 1.7 and 1.8 of the original coders. This was done so that the data from the two groups of coders could be compared. The second group of coders performed almost at the same level as the first group, indicating that the code book and training procedures were working well.

Round 2.1:   Coders analyzed an episode of *Starsky and Hutch*.

Round 2.2:   Coders analyzed an episode of *Silk Stalkings*. This was the same episode that the first group had coded in Rounds 1.6 and 1.7. This group of second round coders exhibited far fewer problems with multiple perpetrators and multiple targets than the first-round coders had in round 1.6.

<u>Round 2.3</u>:   Coders examined an episode of *Magnum, P. I.* and coded at all three levels. They also coded a segment of the *Looney Tunes* cartoon.

At this point, we had achieved acceptable levels of reliability consistently exceeding .70 on most variables. We then deemed the training phase complete, and the actual coding of programs began.

The coding process was conducted by randomly assigning individual coders to programs. Coders viewed each show alone in a video lab and could watch the entire program or any segment of it as many times as necessary to ascertain the required coding judgments. Data for each program were obtained from the observations of a single coder. For this reason, it is essential to demonstrate that the coding process maintained a strong and consistent level of performance over time in order to insure the quality of the data. The next section describes how we monitored the reliability in coding of the data upon which the findings of this study are based.

Checking the Quality of Data

Procedure. The coding process required roughly 20 weeks (not counting holidays and break periods) to complete. During each week when coding was conducted, half of the active coders independently evaluated the same program. Their coding judgments were then compared for reliability assessment purposes. Thus, the decision-making of each coder was checked once during each two-week period.

The programs selected for reliability assessments were randomly chosen within each genre. All genres were examined at least twice. Two examples of each genre were tested in back-to-back weeks so that each coder's performance would be evaluated across the complete range of program content. Table 5 presents the list of randomly selected programs used for the reliability tests.

The sections that follow lay out the conceptual basis and operational aspects of our reliability assessments. After the appropriate details are explicated, the findings of our assessments are presented.

Conceptualization of reliability. Because the coding scheme developed in this project is very complex, coders had to make many different types of decisions when examining a show. It is best to categorize these decisions as existing at two distinct levels. The first level focuses on unitizing, that is, the identification of PATs and scenes. The second level is concerned with the degree of consistency among coders in choosing the same value for a given variable. In total we have 38 variables. Below, we explain the purpose and procedures for evaluating reliability at both of these levels.

Unitizing. This is a critical part of the coding process. In this study, unitizing refers to the process of identifying each PAT and each scene. If coders agree at the beginning and ending point of each PAT and each scene, then they are consistently identifying our units of analysis.

Table 5

Programs Randomly Selected for the Continuing Reliability Tests

Genre	Program Name
Children's Series	Top Cat
Children's Series	Captain Planet
Drama Series	Rockford Files
Drama Series	Lou Grant
Movie	God Is My Co-Pilot
Movie	Coma
Drama Series	Sherlock Holmes
Drama Series	Wild, Wild West
Drama Series	Days of Our Lives
Drama Series	Young and the Restless
Comedy Series	Designing Women
Comedy Series	Fresh Prince
Reality-Based	Cops
Reality-Based	Real Stories of Highway Patrol
Music Video	Yo MTV Rap
Music Video	VH1 Video

The fundamental building block of the coding scheme is the PAT -- a single interaction involving violence. Every time a coder observed an act of violence, s/he created a line of data that included the string of values on the variables that had to be coded at this level. In evaluating the unitizing process, we are not focusing on the string of numbers selected; instead we are focusing on the number of PAT lines a coder creates -- that is, the number of violent interactions the coder perceives to exist in the program.

If all coders have the same number of PAT lines on their coding form for a show and if those PAT lines refer to the same acts, then there is perfect agreement. To reiterate, both conditions must be met for perfect agreement. If coders differ on the number of PAT lines, then there is not perfect agreement. If coders all have the same number of PAT lines, but if there is disagreement about what those PATs are, then there is not perfect agreement.

For each show coded, the determination of PAT level reliability began with the construction of a matrix. This matrix was composed of one column for every coder and one line for every PAT identified by those coders. For purposes of illustration, let's say that there are 12 coders, so the PAT reliability matrix would have 12 columns. If the first coder perceived eight PAT lines, then the matrix would start with 8 lines, and the resulting matrix would have 96 cells (12 x 8 = 96). An "X" to indicate agreement would be placed in each of the eight cells in the first coder's column, because this coder recorded each of those 8 acts of violence. If the remaining 11 coders each recorded the same 8 acts of violence, they would each have 8 X's in their columns. This matrix would then have 96 X's -- one in every possible cell. Such a pattern indicates total agreement among all coders on all acts of violence. What if the PAT reliability matrix did not display a full set of X's? This would indicate some disagreement. The fewer X's, the greater the disagreement.

How can we report a useful indicator of the degree of agreement? It is not sufficient to sum all the X's and divide by the number of cells in the matrix, because the X's indicate position, not agreement. For example, let's say we have nine coders, each of whom sees only one PAT line in a program, and they all agree that it is the same PAT. However, let's say that a tenth coder sees 3 PATs, one of which is the same as the other nine coders have seen. In this case, there are 10 X's on the first line to indicate that all 10 coders saw the first PAT, but on each of the next two lines of the matrix, there is an X only in the column of coder 10. Thus the matrix has 30 cells and 12 X's for a simple agreement ratio of 40%. Clearly this figure underestimates the situation where we have complete agreement among nine out of 10 coders.

What we have done to avoid this problem is to report three descriptors: the Agreement Mode, the range of PATs, and a Close Interval around the Agreement Mode (CIAM). An example will illustrate what we mean by the "Agreement Mode." If we have 10 coders and one reported 7 PAT lines, seven reported 8 PAT lines, one reported 9 PAT lines, and one reported 11 PAT lines, the mode would be 8 PAT lines because that is the number reported by the greatest number of coders. Thus 70% of the coders are at this mode. If all seven coders had the same 8 PAT lines, then the agreement mode is 8.

In many cases, not all coders were at the Agreement Mode, so we also report the range of PAT lines exhibited by the set of coders. The smaller the range, the tighter the pattern of agreement. But sometimes the range can be misleading as an indicator of how much variation there is in a distribution. For example, let's say that we have 10 coders: three have 4 PAT lines, five have 5 PAT lines, one has 6 PAT lines, and one has 12 PAT lines. The range here is from 4 to 12 PAT lines, which appears to signal a wide range of disagreement. However, 90% of the coders are within one PAT line of the mode. So we also compute a Close Interval around the Agreement Mode (CIAM). We operationalized "close to the agreement mode" as those judgments that were within one PAT line on either side of the agreement mode. For example, if the agreement mode were 4, we would include in the CIAM each of the following: (a) other coders who also saw 4 PATs but disagreed on one of the PATs, (b) other coders who saw only 3 PATs but each of those 3 match PATs in the set of the 4 PATs that determine the Agreement Mode, and (c) other coders who had 5 PATs where 4 of those 5 PATs were identical to the four that determine the Agreement Mode. When the Agreement Mode is greater than five, we establish the width of the CIAM as 20% on either side of the mode. For example, if the Agreement Mode is 10, we include coders who exhibit no more than two disagreements with the coders at the Agreement Mode.

The procedure explained above for determining the Agreement Mode and the CIAM for PAT lines is the same with scenes. For each show coded, a scene level matrix was constructed, where there was a column for each coder and a line for each scene identified. We then computed and reported an Agreement Mode, a range, and a CIAM for scenes for each program.

Selecting values on the coding variables. Now we turn our attention to the consistency among coders in choosing a value on each coding variable. Our coding scheme contains a total of 38 variables: 12 at the program level, 13 for each scene within each program, and 13 for each PAT within each scene. At the program level, the coder judged the overall narrative purpose (from among 2 values), realism of the program (4), harm/pain (3), style of presentation (3), punishment of bad characters (5), punishment of good characters (5), and punishment of mixed (good and bad) characters (5). Also, each character who was involved (either as a perpetrator or victim) in violence was coded for type (7), sex (4), ethnicity (9), good/bad (6), and hero status (4).

At the scene level, the coder judged whether there was a reward of self praise (from among 2 values), praise from other (2), and material praise (2); whether there was punishment of self condemnation (2), condemnation from another (2), nonviolent action (2), and violent actions (2); whether there was explicitness of the action itself (4) and means-to-target impact (4); degree of graphicness (5), and humor (2). Also, the characters were coded for age (6) and physical strength (6).

At the PAT level, each act was coded for type (from among 4 values), means used (8), extent of means (5), harm depicted (7), harm likely (7), pain (7), visual depiction (2), and sexual assault (2). The perpetrator was coded for type (4), size if multiple (6), and reason for committing the violence (6). Finally, each target was coded for type (3) and size if multiple (6).

The reliability for coding variables was assessed in the following manner. At the program level, the modal value was identified for each variable. The number of coders at the modal value was divided by the total number of coders, thus computing a percentage of agreement.

At the scene and PAT levels, each line of the matrix was examined for its modal value. All coders at the modal value were counted and this number was written in the margin. These margin numbers were summed down all the rows of a matrix. This sum was divided by all the decisions reflected in the matrix, and the resulting fraction was the percentage of agreement among coders on that variable.

The computation of the reliability coefficient for scene and PAT level is more complicated than the computation for the program level codes because of the unitizing issues described above. At the PAT level analysis, the first step starts with the PAT level matrix of coders. This becomes a template of cells. This template is used to build 13 PAT matrices, one for each variable coded at the PAT level. For each line in each matrix, the modal value is identified; thus the reliability testing is based on a norm determined by the coders, not a prescribed criterion value. The number of coders selecting the modal value is entered in the margin of the matrix. These margin numbers (one for each PAT line) are summed and then divided by the number of cells in the matrix. This proportion is the percentage of agreement. These percentages of agreement were then converted into reliability coefficients by using a PRE (proportional reduction of error) procedure.

The term "percentage of agreement" is used several times in the above section. This is simply the number of times coders actually agreed divided by the number of times they could have possibly agreed. The larger the number, the better the agreement.

Although percentage of agreement is often a useful indicator of consistency, it is an incomplete measure, particularly for complex judgments. With complex measures, some context is needed to better interpret the meaning of the statistic. Below, we describe two ways of providing this context: employing a proportional reduction of error technique and providing an inferential context for interpreting our reliability calculations.

Proportional reduction of error. A percentage of agreement reflects a combination of two elements: real agreement (uniformity in decision-making due to training) and error agreement (selection of the same codes by chance alone). If two coders looked at the same show and had to decide whether there was violence in a scene, the probability that they would agree by chance alone is 50%. If we cannot correct for chance agreement, then the percentages of agreement are inflated by error.

How do we correct for chance agreement? We modified the Scott's pi formula to account for multiple coders performing the same task. We took the percentages of agreement and converted them into reliability coefficients by using a proportional reduction of error (PRE) procedure using the following formula:

$$\text{Reliability coefficient} = \frac{A-P}{1-P}$$

Where: A = percentage of agreement
P = proportion of agreement due to chance

This formula is essentially pi as developed by Scott (1955). However, Scott's pi is limited to pairs of coders and does not allow for a test of multiple coders on the same task. Therefore, the formula needed to be adapted, specifically the proportion of agreement due to chance or P. To compute such a probability, we developed the following formula from probability theory using binomial decisions.

$$P = \frac{N!}{M!\,(N-M)!}\,(p^M)(q^{N-M})$$

Where: N = the number of coders in a test
M = the number of coders who agree
p = probability of choosing the option on which there is agreement
q = probability of not choosing the option on which there is agreement

The sum of p and q is 1. For example, if coders are given a choice between two options, then p is .5 and q is also .5. If coders are given a choice among three options, then p is .33 and q is .67 (the probability of choosing either of the two options not chosen by the plurality of coders). The formula for P computes the probability of agreement among N coders. Once this probability of agreement by chance alone is determined, it is entered in the previous formula so that its effect is proportionally reduced from the percentage of agreement.

Inferential context. A second context for interpreting the consistency is to use inferential procedures to compute a confidence level for reliability coefficients. In the content analysis literature, authors will arbitrarily select a certain value (usually about .70) as being a minimum acceptable reliability coefficient, then demonstrate that their coefficients surpass this minimum. While this strategy at first may appear to demonstrate acceptable strength, it really has no intrinsic meaning; it acquires meaning only as a convention when most scholars agree to use it.

We wanted to develop a better strategy for several reasons. First, a 70% agreement is much easier to achieve when using two coders than when using a much larger group as we planned to do. And second, we wanted to avoid arbitrary cut-off points and instead put the interpretation of our coefficients on a firmer foundation. Therefore we chose to use an inferential procedure to determine the probability that each of our reliability coefficients could have occurred by chance alone.

For each coding decision, we computed a z score using the following formula:

$$Z = \frac{X - \mu}{\sigma} \qquad \begin{aligned} \mu &= pn \\ \sigma &= \sqrt{pqn} \end{aligned}$$

Where: p = the probability of a single coder selecting the modal value
q = the probability of a single coder not selecting the modal value
n = number of coders in test
X = upper real limit of number of coders at mode

Then we looked up z in a Unit Normal Table. This indicates the probability of obtaining the observed level of agreement by chance alone. For example, let's say we ran a test with 12 coders who had to choose among four options and that seven of those coders all chose the same option. Using the above procedure, we would find that the chance of getting 58.3% agreement (7 out of 12 agreeing on the same option out of four) would be less than one in a thousand or $p < .001$. With only two options available, we would need an agreement of 10 out of 12 (83.3%) in order to have this same high level of confidence ($p < .001$) that this pattern could not have occurred by chance alone.

In summary, three procedures were used for reliability testing. First, agreement on the unitizing for PATs was assessed for each show. Second, agreement on the unitizing for scenes was assessed for each show. And third, the selection of codes (at program, scene, and PAT levels) was assessed. We realize the importance of going beyond reporting simple percentages of agreement, because they can be misleading. In our procedures we do both of the following: (1) convert percentages of agreement into reliability coefficients by removing the error portion of the agreement, and (2) report the confidence level we have that each reliability coefficient could have occurred by chance alone.

Results of reliability testing. The results of the reliability testing indicate that coders were generally consistent in their decisions. Their consistency in unitizing was quite good given the complexity of the task and the number of coders involved (see Table 6). There was always a range in the number of sequences, but in over half of the tests, 100% of coders fell within the 20% interval around the mode. Likewise with PATs, there was always a range in the number of violent interactions, but coders usually clustered tightly around the mode. Across all of the programs examined for reliability, most coders were able to agree on the number of PATs (83% median agreement) and scenes (100% median agreement) within the 20% interval around the mode.

As for the consistency of coding the variables within units, we first computed a level of confidence for each of our 608 reliability coefficients (38 variables on each of 16 programs in the reliability test). Out of those 608 coefficients, only 33 (5.4%) were too small to attain statistical significance (p < .05). This proportion is almost exactly what we should expect by chance alone.

The reliability on each of the 38 variables was quite high as indicated by the median level of agreement that ranged from a low of .63 to a high of 1.0 (see Tables 7-9). Half of these medians are above .94, which is very good for a task of this magnitude and with so many coders. On only five of the 38 variables was the median reliability lower than .80. Four of these were program level codes of harm/pain (median of .70), punishment of bad characters (.64), punishment of good characters (.63), and the judgment about whether a character was good or bad (.75). The other relatively low reliability was on the variable for perpetrator reason (.75), which was coded at the PAT level.

Check for Fatigue in Coder Performance

Consistency over time in coding practices is essential for establishing the reliability of the data. Therefore, as noted above, we conducted a continual check to spot instances of coder fatigue as soon as possible and to make any necessary corrections. Using the same reliability data as that reported in the preceding section, but analyzing it from a different perspective, we were able to assess the performance of individual coders relative to the performance of the overall group.

Table 6

Reliability Coefficients for PAT and Sequence Range and Mode

Title	PAT range	PAT mode/%	PAT mode +/- 20%	Sequence range	Sequence mode/%	Sequence Mode +/- 20%
Top Cat (N=14)	7-12	9/-	57%	4-5	5/64%	100%
Captain Planet (N=12)	7-21	18/-	55%	4-11	7/50%	50%
Rockford Files (N=15)	5-10	6/40%	73%	4-6	4/87%	93%
Lou Grant (N=9)	1-4	3/33%	89%	1-3	3/44%	89%
God is My Co-Pilot (N=9)	13-19	17/11%	78%	4-5	4/44%	100%
Coma (N=11)	5-8	6/27%	91%	3-5	4/55%	100%
Sherlock Holmes (N=9)	6-9	7/11%	67%	3-4	4/78%	100%
Wild Wild West (N=9)	18-24	24/-	75%	7-10	9/44%	89%
Days Of Our Lives (N=7)	1-7	3/-	43%	1-3	3/43%	71%
The Young & the Restless (N=12)	2-3	2/50%	100%	1-2	2/92%	100%
Designing Women (N=9)	2-4	2/56%	89%	1-2	1/89%	100%
Fresh Prince of Bel Air (N=11)	2-4	3/55%	100%	1-3	2/55%	100%
Cops (N=16)	1-4	2/69%	88%	1-2	1/75%	100%
Real Stories of the Highway Patrol (N=10)	3-7	3/40%	70%	2-5	2/80%	100%
Yo MTV Raps (N=10)	2-11	4/20%	40%	2-9	4/30%	50%
VH-1 Videos (N=10)	4-13	11/10%	50%	4-8	5/10%	60%

Table 7: Reliability Coefficients for PAT Context Variables

Title	Type of act	Means used	Extent of means used	Harm depicted	Harm likely	Pain	Visual depiction
Top Cat (N=14)	.99	.94	.91	.81	.78	.84	.99
Captain Planet (N=12)	1.0	.88	.86	.87	.85	.88	.97
Rockford Files (N=15)	1.0	.90	.85	.73	.83	.72	.98
Lou Grant (N=9)	1.0	.81	1.0	.92	.88	.92	.96
God is My Co-Pilot (N=9)	1.0	.89	.73	.84	.88	.66	.99
Coma (N=11)	1.0	.89	.65	.84	.84	.72	1.0
Sherlock Holmes (N=9)	1.0	.92	.80	.76	.75	.71	.97
Wild Wild West (N=9)	1.0	.96	.89	.85	.74	.80	1.0
Days Of Our Lives (N=7)	1.0	.90	.85	.90	.70	.95	1.0
The Young & the Restless (N=12)	1.0	.79	.88	.79	.79	.79	1.0
Designing Women (N=9)	1.0	.71	.70	.51*	.62	.62	.80
Fresh Prince of Bel Air (N=11)	1.0	.93	.96	.93	.89	.89	.89
Cops (N=16)	1.0	.97	.91	.91	.88	.82	.94
Real Stories of the Highway Patrol (N=10)	1.0	1.0	.92	.95	.95	.95	1.0
Yo MTV Raps (N=10)	1.0	.96	.98	.82	.84	.82	.98
VH1 Videos (N=10)	1.0	.99	.96	.79	.77	.80	.98
Overall Range (N=173)	.99-1.0	.71-1.0	.65-1.0	.51-.95	.62-.95	.62-.95	.80-1.0
Overall Median (N=173)	1.0	.90	.88	.84	.83	.81	.98

Title	Sexual assault	Perpetrator type	Perpetrator size (if multiple)	Perpetrator reason	Target type	Target size (if multiple)
Top Cat (N=14)	1.0	.96	.87	.75	.99	.89
Captain Planet (N=12)	1.0	.99	.88	.84	.95	.85
Rockford Files (N=15)	1.0	.99	.98	.70	.96	.96
Lou Grant (N=9)	1.0	1.0	.92	.81	1.0	.96
God is My Co-Pilot (N=9)	1.0	.98	.82	.62	.98	.83
Coma (N=11)	1.0	.97	.97	.75	1.0	1.0
Sherlock Holmes (N=9)	1.0	.98	.95	.61	1.0	.97
Wild Wild West (N=9)	.99	.97	.95	.80	.98	.97
Days Of Our Lives (N=7)	.95	1.0	.85	.65	1.0	.85
The Young & the Restless (N=12)	1.0	1.0	.92	1.0	1.0	.92
Designing Women (N=9)	1.0	.90	1.0	.81	1.0	1.0
Fresh Prince of Bel Air (N=11)	.96	.86	.96	.96	.93	.93
Cops (N=16)	1.0	.94	.94	.73	.91	.97
Real Stories of the Highway Patrol (N=10)	1.0	1.0	1.0	.89	1.0	.92
Yo MTV Raps (N=10)	1.0	.95	.95	.63	.96	.93
VH1 Videos (N=10)	1.0	.96	.96	.68	.93	.93
Overall Range (N=173)	.95	.86-1.0	.86-1.0	.61-1.0	.91	.83-1.0
Overall Median (N=173)	1.0	.97	.97	.75	.98	.93

Key: * = p> .05   unstarred coefficients   = p<.05

Table 8: Reliability Coefficients for Scene Character and Context Variables

Title	Character age	Character physical strength	Rewards self praise	Rewards praise from	Rewards material praise	Punishments self condemnation	Punishments condemnation from other
Top Cat (N=14)	.86	.88	.88	.95	.95	.98	.92
Captain Planet (N=12)	.89	.91	.77	.63	.89	1.0	.96
Rockford Files (N=15)	.93	.98	.93	1.0	.85	1.0	.97
Lou Grant (N=9)	1.0	.79	.85	.95	1.0	.95	.69*
God is My Co-Pilot (N=9)	.92	.97	.87	.82	.93	1.0	.73*
Coma (N=11)	.91	.98	.89	1.0	1.0	.91	.88
Sherlock Holmes (N=9)	.97	.91	.94	.80	1.0	1.0	.84
Wild Wild West (N=9)	.98	.92	.85	.94	.97	1.0	.85
Days Of Our Lives (N=7)	1.0	1.0	.78*	.93	1.0	.93	.63*
The Young & the Restless (N=12)	1.0	1.0	.91	1.0	1.0	1.0	1.0
Designing Women (N=9)	.95	.86	1.0	1.0	1.0	.76*	1.0
Fresh Prince of Bel Air (N=11)	.86	.84	1.0	1.0	.82	1.0	.94
Cops (N=16)	1.0	.95	.95	.95	.95	.95	.90
Real Stories of the Highway Patrol (N=10)	1.0	1.0	1.0	1.0	.77	1.0	.95
Yo MTV Raps (N=10)	.98	.98	1.0	1.0	.94	.98	.92
VH-1 Videos (N=10)	1.0	.96	.97	.97	1.0	1.0	.98
Overall Range (N=173)	.86-1.0	.79-1.0	.77-1.0	.63-1.0	.77-1.0	.76-1.0	.63-1.0
Overall Median (N=173)	.97	.95	.93	.95	.96	1.0	.92

Title	Punishments nonviolent action	Punishments violent action	Explicitness violent action	Explitiness focus on impact	Graphicness	Humor
Top Cat (N=14)	.98	.94	.86	.82	.89	.91
Captain Planet (N=12)	.85	.93	.89	.91	1.0	.96
Rockford Files (N=15)	.98	.98	.97	.85	.97	.72
Lou Grant (N=9)	.80	.95	.90	.86	.81	.74*
God is My Co-Pilot (N=9)	.93	.76*	.54*	.78	.75	.93
Coma (N=11)	.87	1.0	.89	.84	.93	.98
Sherlock Holmes (N=9)	.84	.97	.97	.97	.80	.84
Wild Wild West (N=9)	1.0	.77*	.95	.94	.99	.88
Days Of Our Lives (N=7)	.63*	1.0	.87	.87	.87	.87
The Young & the Restless (N=12)	1.0	1.0	.83	.64	.65	1.0
Designing Women (N=9)	.76*	.88	.89	.89	.89	1.0
Fresh Prince of Bel Air (N=11)	1.0	1.0	.89	1.0	1.0	1.0
Cops (N=16)	.80	1.0	.85	.85	.85	1.0
Real Stories of the Highway Patrol (N=10)	.55*	.77	1.0	.86	.86	1.0
Yo MTV Raps (N=10)	.73*	.96	.92	.88	.94	1.0
VH-1 Videos (N=10)	.98	.95	.76	.85	.88	.80
Overall Range (N=173)	.55-1.0	.77-1.0	.54-1.0	.64-1.0	.65-1.0	.72-1.0
Overall Median (N=173)	.86	.96	.89	.86	.88	.95

Key: * = p>.05   unstarred coefficients = p<.05

Table 9: Reliability Coefficients for Program Character and Context Variables

	Narrative purpose	Realism	Harm/Pain	Style	Punishments bad	Punishments good
Top Cat (N=14)	1.0	.86	.64	1.0	.79	.71
Captain Planet (N=12)	1.0	1.0	.92	1.0	.56	1.0
Rockford Files (N=15)	1.0	1.0	.80	1.0	.87	.59
Lou Grant (N=9)	.41*	1.0	.54	1.0	.66	.78
God is My Co-Pilot (N=9)	1.0	.78	.67	1.0	.51*	.89
Coma (N=11)	1.0	1.0	.73	1.0	.51*	.82
Sherlock Holmes (N=9)	1.0	1.0	.54	1.0	.66	.66
Wild Wild West (N=9)	.89	.54	.54	.89	.13*	.54*
Days Of Our Lives (N=7)	1.0	.54	.54	1.0	1.0	.51*
The Young & the Restless (N=12)	1.0	1.0	1.0	1.0	.44*	.44*
Designing Women (N=9)	1.0	1.0	.36*	1.0	.66	.51*
Fresh Prince of Bel Air (N=11)	.71*	1.0	.91	1.0	.91	.35*
Cops (N=16)	.81	.94	.69	1.0	.69	.75
Real Stories of the Highway Patrol (N=10)	.55*	.66	1.0	1.0	.47*	1.0
Yo MTV Raps (N=10)	1.0	.94	.82	1.0	.62	.53*
VH-1 Videos (N=10)	.96	.85	.73	1.0	.40*	.76
Overall Range (N=173)	.41-1.0	.54-1.0	.36-1.0	.89-1.0	.13-1.0	.35-1.0
Overall Median (N=173)	1.0	.97	.70	1.0	.64	.63

Title	Punishments good/bad	Character type	Character sex	Character ethnicity	Character good/bad	Character hero status
Top Cat (N=14)	.19*	.99	1.0	.91	.73	1.0
Captain Planet (N=12)	.56	.76	.96	.84	.80	.90
Rockford Files (N=15)	.80	1.0	1.0	.99	.90	1.0
Lou Grant (N=9)	.30*	1.0	1.0	1.0	.49	1.0
God is My Co-Pilot (N=9)	1.0	1.0	.93	.98	.76	.90
Coma (N=11)	.91	1.0	1.0	1.0	.83	.92
Sherlock Holmes (N=9)	1.0	.96	.96	.96	.72	.94
Wild Wild West (N=9)	1.0	.93	.98	.99	.78	.92
Days Of Our Lives (N=7)	.70	.79	1.0	1.0	.86	1.0
The Young & the Restless (N=12)	.75	1.0	.91	1.0	.57	1.0
Designing Women (N=9)	.51*	1.0	1.0	1.0	.44	1.0
Fresh Prince of Bel Air (N=11)	.82	1.0	.97	.97	.75	.86
Cops (N=16)	.88	1.0	1.0	.93	.78	.98
Real Stories of the Highway Patrol (N=10)	.89	1.0	.97	1.0	.94	.81
Yo MTV Raps (N=10)	.75	1.0	.96	.94	.63	1.0
VH-1 Videos (N=10)	.88	1.0	.91	.91	.53	.93
Overall Range (N=173)	.19-1.0	.76-1.0	.91-1.0	.84-1.0	.44-.94	.81-1.0
Overall Median (N=173)	.81	1.0	.97	.96	.75	.93

Key: * = p>.05   unstarred coefficients = p<.05

For each reliability test, three indexes of quality were constructed: one for program coding, one for scene coding, and one for PAT coding. Each time a coder was in the modal group on a coding decision, he/she earned a point. If coders were close to the mode, they could earn partial points (see Table 10). Thus, coders who amassed the greatest number of points on an index were ranked the highest on consistency and were regarded as the best coders. Coders who had low index scores were regarded as the least consistent compared to other coders.

For the tests in which the range between the best coders and the least consistent coders was small and the overall reliability coefficients remained high, we were assured that coder fatigue had not occurred. When that gap widened, however, we had to make a subjective judgment about the performance of individual coders who fell at the bottom of our index. Our first method of dealing with inconsistent coders was to retrain them in the areas where they were diagnosed as having difficulty making proper judgments. In most cases this worked well, and the subsequent coding work was found to be consistent. When this was the case, we retained the individual as a coder on the project.

In the two instances when a coder could not be retrained successfully to produce consistent coding, s/he was removed from coding responsibilities. In this situation, data generated by a problem coder was discarded back to the time of the previous test of reliability for which that coder had demonstrated satisfactory performance.

Table 10: Computation of Coder Index

Program Level -- Context

M	Narrative purpose (2)
M	Realism (4)
M+	Harm/pain (3)
M	Style of presentation (3)
M	Punishments: Bad character (5)
M	Punishments: Good character (5)
M	Punishments: Good and bad character (5)

Program Level - Characters

	Character type (7)
M	Character sex (4)
M	Character ethnicity (9)
	Character good/bad (6)
	Character hero status (4)

Scene Level -- Characters

M	Perpetrator age (6)
M	Perpetrator physical strength (6)
M	Target age (6)

Scene Level -- Context

M	Reward: Self praise (2)
M	Reward: Praise from other (2)
M	Reward: Material praise (2)
M	Punishment: Self condemnation (2)
M	Punishment: Condemnation from another (2)
M	Punishment: Non-violent action (2)
M	Punishment: Violent actions (2)
M+	Explicitness: Action itself (4)
M+	Explicitness: Means-to-target impact (4)
M+	Degree of graphicness (5)
M	Humor (2)

PAT Level -- Context

M	Type of act (4)
M+	Means used (8)
M+	Extent of means (5)
M+	Harm depicted (7)

M+	Harm likely (7)
M+	Pain (7)
M	Visual depiction (2)
M	Sexual assault (2)

PAT Level -- Characters

M	Perpetrator type (4)
M+	Perpetrator size, if multiple (6)
M?	Perpetrator reason for committing the violence (6)
M	Target type (3)
M+	Target size, if multiple (6)

M = Modal response earns 1 point; non-modal responses earn no points.

M+ = Modal response earns 1 point. Also, divide the list of possible values on the variable into two categories: (a) none (codes that indicate the absence of the characteristic named by the variable) and (b) some (a list of codes that indicate the presence of a the characteristic to varying degrees). Then consider the following rules:

RULE 1: If the modal response is a "none" code, then all non-modal responses earn no points.

RULE 2: If the modal response is a value from a "some" distribution, then selection of a coding value directly adjacent (in a heirarchy of values, i.e.,one, few, some, many) to the modal response earns 1/2 point UNLESS the adjacent response has crossed the line into a "none" code, in which case it earns no points.

Chapter 6

RESULTS

This Results Chapter is organized into five sections. In the first section, we provide an introduction to our overall plan of analysis. In the second section, we describe the basic patterns concerning the presence of violence. The third section examines the context in which violence is portrayed. In the fourth section, we report on programming that features an anti-violence theme. Finally, the chapter concludes with a brief summary of our major findings.

Before proceeding, we underscore two caveats that frame our results. First, we did not code every program in our sample, which is a complete composite week of programming for 23 channels from 6 a.m. to 11 p.m. As mentioned previously, several types of programming were not stipulated in our contract with NCTA (e.g., news, religious programs, instructional shows). These programs collectively represent only 15% of the programs we randomly sampled for the composite week. Still, when interpreting our findings, readers should be aware that this small percentage is not part of our final sample of *coded* programs.

Second, we want to emphasize the importance of interpreting our findings accurately. **The results should always be framed in terms of the correct unit of analysis.** Some of the findings below pertain to *programs* as the unit of analysis, because a particular variable was coded at the program level. For example, style of presentation was coded at the program level so all results pertaining to this variable refer to the *percentage of programs* that feature animation or live action. In contrast, some of the findings pertain to *violent scenes* as the unit of analysis, because a particular variable was coded at the scene level. For example, graphicness was coded at the scene level so all results pertaining to this variable refer to *percentage of violent scenes* that feature graphic violence. Lastly, some of the findings pertain to *violent interactions* as the unit of analysis, because a particular variable was coded at the most micro level or unit of analysis in our study. For instance, the type of means employed in violence was coded at the interaction level, so that all results pertaining to this variable refer to the *percentage of violent interactions* that involve a particular means like guns. We encourage the reader to consider carefully each finding in terms of its correct unit of analysis (i.e., program, scene, interaction).

Plan of Analysis

Our plan of analysis is structured into three areas of focus: presence of violence, context of the violence, and presence of anti-violence themes. In examining the presence of violence on television, we highlight both its prevalence and its distribution. Prevalence addresses the question of how widespread violence is on television. In other words, what percentage of programs contain violence? In contrast, the concept of distribution refers to the range in the frequency of violence across programs. Although many programs may contain violence (prevalence), a program that features only one violent interaction is very different from a program that contains 10 interactions.

After we present the general patterns of prevalence and distribution from the entire sample of coded programs, we assess whether those patterns hold across different locations in the composite week of programming. We created four "locator variables" that partition the total sample into meaningful subgroups. The locator variables allow us to determine if the violence is more likely to occur during particular spots in the programming schedule. Our locator variables are: channel type, program genre, daypart, and type of day (i.e., weekday or weekend).

As for channel type, the 23 channels in the sample were arranged into five groups as follows: (1) *broadcast networks*, which include ABC, CBS, Fox, and NBC; (2) *public broadcast*, which includes PBS; (3) *independent broadcast*, which includes KTLA, KCOP, and KCAL; (4) *basic cable*, which includes Arts & Entertainment, American Movie Classics, Black Entertainment Television, Cartoon Network, The Family Channel, Lifetime, Music TV, Nickelodeon, Turner Network Television, USA Network, VH-1, and The Disney Channel; and (5) *premium cable*, which includes Cinemax, Home Box Office, and Showtime.

As for the genre locator variable, we classified all the different types of programs in our sample into six groups: drama series, comedy series, movies, music videos, reality-based programs, and children's series. For a list of examples of programs in each of these six genres, see Table 11.

The locator variable dealing with daypart was constructed by dividing the 17-hour sampling frame (6:00 a.m. to 11:00 p.m.) into five time periods: *early morning* (6:00 a.m. to 9:00 p.m.), *mid-day* (9:00 a.m. to 3:00 p.m.), *late afternoon* (3:00 p.m. to 6:00 p.m.), *early evening* (6:00 p.m. to 8:00 p.m.), and *prime time* (8:00 p.m. to 11:00 p.m.). The type of day locator variable was constructed by dividing the seven days of the week into two groups: weekday and weekend.

In all analyses involving locator variables, we essentially are searching for differences. For example, does the prevalence or distribution of violence differ significantly across the five types of channels or across the six genres of programming? To answer such a question, we looked for two types of significance: statistical and substantive. Statistical significance refers to how much confidence we have that the patterns we observe in the sample accurately reflect the patterns in the entire population of all television programming. To assess statistical significance, we computed a chi-square statistic for the pattern of data across each locator variable. Each chi square has an accompanying probability value (p), which indicates the level of confidence we have that the pattern is not due to chance or error. For example, if the p-value is $p < .001$ it means that there is less than one chance in 1,000 that this pattern is a result of error. Virtually all analyses of differences in this report are statistically significant at $p < .05$.

Table 11

Drama Series	Channel	Date	Day	Time
Magnum PI	KTLA	11/1/94	Tuesday	10:00am-11:00am
Rifleman	FAM	1/21/95	Saturday	3:00pm-3:30pm
How the West was Won	TNT	3/13/95	Monday	11:00am-12:00pm
Little House on the Prairie	KTLA	10/24/94	Monday	11:00am-12:00pm
In the Heat of the Night	TNT	3/10/95	Saturday	4:00pm-5:00pm
Remington Steele	A&E	10/19/94	Wednesday	1:00pm-2:00pm
Babylon 5	KCOP	1/26/95	Thursday	8:00pm-9:00pm
Vanishing Son	KTLA	3/11/95	Saturday	9:00pm-10:00pm
Kung Fu	TNT	2/9/95	Thursday	10:00am-11:00am
Charlie's Angels	TNT	10/14/94	Friday	9:00am-10:00am

Comedy Series	Channel	Date	Day	Time
Roc	BET	12/9/94	Friday	5:00pm-5:30pm
Andy Griffith	FOX	1/17/95	Tuesday	10;30am-11:00am
Designing Women	LIF	3/10/95	Friday	1:00pm-1:30pm
Murphy Brown	CBS	2/13/95	Monday	9:00pm-9:30pm
The State	MTV	3/23/95	Thursday	7:30pm-8:00pm
Friends	NBC	11/10/94	Thursday	8:30pm-9:00pm
Comicview	BET	3/13/95	Monday	5:30pm-6:00pm
I Love Lucy	FOX	2/4/95	Saturday	5:00pm-5:30pm
Brady Bunch	KTLA	1/18/95	Wednesday	12:00pm-12:30pm
Bewitched	NIK	3/20/95	Monday	8:30pm-9:00pm

Children's Series	Channel	Date	Day	Time
Auggie Doggie	CAR	1/25/95	Wednesday	12:00pm-12:30pm
Muppet Babies	NIK	3/24/95	Friday	4:00pm-4:30pm
Heathcliff	CAR	11/8/94	Tuesday	7:00am-7:30am
Daisy-Head Mayzie	TNT	2/5/95	Sunday	4:00pm-4:30pm
Under the Umbrella Tree	DIS	10/26/94	Wednesday	7:00am-7:30am

Captain Planet	KCAL	3/7/95	Tuesday	6:30am-7:00am
Gumby	NIK	1/25/95	Wednesday	2:00pm-2:30pm
Beetlejuice	NIK	2/12/95	Sunday	8:30am-9:00am
Cartoon Express	USA	10/26/94	Wednesday	9:00am-10:00am

Music

Video Countdown	MTV	10/28/94	Friday	8:00pm-10:00pm
Top 21 Countdown	VH-1	10/14/94	Friday	4:00pm-6:00pm
Rude Awakening	MTV	3/9/95	Thursday	6:00am-7:00am
Last Word	VH-1	3/4/95	Saturday	10:30am-11:00am
Rap City	BET	12/8/94	Thursday	1:30pm-3:30pm
Videos	MTV	1/27/95	Friday	6:00pm-6:30pm
Top Jams Countdown	MTV	11/6/94	Sunday	4:00pm-6:00pm
Top 10 Countdown	VH-1	1/22/95	Sunday	10:00pm-11:00pm
Video Vibrations	BET	10/12/94	Wednesday	12:00pm-2:00pm

Movies

Cocktail	USA	1/15/95	Tuesday	3:00pm-5:00pm
2001 A Space Odyssey	HBO	10/31/94	Monday	4:00pm-6:30pm
Stay Tuned	HBO	10/15/94	Saturday	9:30am-11:00am
An Affair to Remember	AMC	1/18/95	Wednesday	9:30pm-11:30pm
It's a Mad Mad World	TNT	11/5/94	Saturday	6:00pm-10:00pm
Beyond Betrayal	CBS	10/11/94	Tuesday	9:00pm-11:00pm
The Power of One	MAX	12/5/94	Monday	4:00pm-6:30pm
Weekend at Bernie's II	HBO	10/20/94	Thursday	7:30pm-9:00pm

Reality-Based

Highway Patrol	CBS	4/30/95	Sunday	5:00pm-5:30pm
Cops	FOX	10/13/94	Thursday	6:30pm-7:00pm
Oprah	ABC	3/14/95	Tuesday	3:00pm-4:00pm
Rescue 911	FAM	10/10/94	Monday	9:00pm-10:00pm

However, not all of the differences that are statistically significant are necessarily meaningful. For instance, if a table reveals that 55% of all programs contain violence whereas only 50% of comedy series contain violence, should we conclude that this difference of 5% is meaningful? Our answer is no, because we view 5% as being too small for us to regard as a notable difference. To assess substantive significance (our second type of significance), we examined the magnitude of difference in percentages. Unless we observe a difference of at least 10% between the overall pattern across all programming (i.e., industry average) and the pattern found for a specific subgroup of programming, we are not prepared to argue that there is a substantive difference. Differences of 10% to 19% are regarded as moderate differences, whereas differences of 20% or more are regarded as substantial. Although these cut-points are somewhat arbitrary, we use them because they are a helpful tool in summarizing important differences that might exist in the programming schedule.

Our second task in the analysis plan is to describe the context in which the violence is portrayed. Our contextual analysis is organized around the major context variables described above in Chapter 3: the nature of the perpetrator of violence, the nature of the target, the reason for the violence, means used (weapons), extent of violence, graphicness, realism, rewards/punishments, consequences, and humor. For each contextual variable, we present the overall pattern across all programming, and then we present any important differences that emerge as a function of the four locator variables.

The final task in our analysis plan is to assess anti-violence themes in television programming. In particular, we are concerned with how many programs feature such a theme and how such themes may be used. This analysis differs somewhat from the quantitative focus that characterizes the sections pertaining to the presence and context of violence. Our analysis of anti-violence themes focuses instead on detailed descriptions of sample programs that feature an anti-violence theme. Our goal is to illustrate how writers and producers in the television industry can creatively portray violence in order to emphasize its negative consequences for society.

Presence of Violence

In this section, we deal with general patterns of prevalence and distribution of violence across all programming. Then we turn to an analysis of differences in these patterns by locator variables. The section concludes with an examination of the topics of sexual violence and violence advisories.

Prevalence of Violence

The issue of prevalence addresses the question: What percentage of the coded television programs contain violence? If a program contained one or more acts of violence, we regarded it as a violent program for purposes of our prevalence analysis. By this criterion, 57% of all programs in our sample were classified as violent; the remaining 43% of programs contained no portrayals that qualified as violence given our definition.

Recall that our definition of violence has three main components: (1) behavioral acts, (2) credible threats, and (3) harmful consequences of unseen violence. Although most accidents were not coded because they lacked the most important element of our definition (intent to harm), accidental violence *was* included in situations where a character experienced unintentional harm as a result of ongoing violence.

A total of more than 18,000 violent interactions were observed in our sample of programming. What is the most prevalent form of violence in these interactions? Two thirds of the violent incidents (66%) on television feature behavioral acts of aggression (see Figure 1). In other words, a majority of violent interactions involve a perpetrator committing an actual physical act of violence. Far fewer of the violent interactions involve credible threats (29%), where the perpetrator demonstrates a clear intent to physically harm the target and has the means ready to do so, but for some reason does not follow through immediately. Much more rare (3%) are interactions involving harmful consequences of unseen violence, or instances where an injured victim is depicted but the violence itself is not shown on screen. Also quite rare are accidents (2%), where targets are unintentionally harmed in the course of ongoing violence.

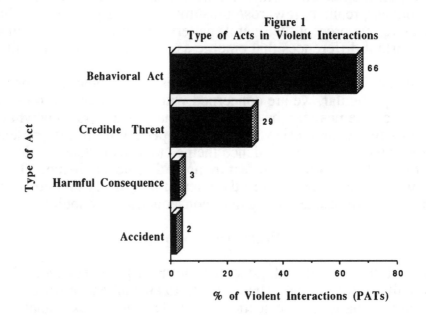

Figure 1
Type of Acts in Violent Interactions

Distribution of Violence

The issue of distribution addresses the question: What is the range of violent interactions across programs? Our goal in answering this question is to be able to contrast those programs that display only one or two violent interactions with those that feature many violent incidents. As we mentioned in Chapter 5, some programs are segmented, meaning that they contain independent stories or narrative units within a larger framework (e.g., *Looney Tunes*, *60 Minutes*). For distribution analyses, we use the program segment as our base of comparison. Although most programs are composed of a single segment (e.g., movies, drama series, situation comedies), the overall $\underline{N}$ in our analyses is slightly larger when treating segmented programs as individual units.

Violent programs differ quite a bit in terms of the number of violent interactions they contain. In particular, the frequency of violent interactions per program ranges from 1 to 88. However, most of the programs cluster at the lower end of the frequency distribution, with 15% of programs containing only one violent interaction, 12% containing two, and 10% containing three. This means that slightly more than one third of all violent programs contain between one and three violent interactions. Another one third contain between four and eight violent interactions, and the remaining one third feature nine or more violent interactions.

We must emphasize that a violent interaction does not necessarily mean that a single act of violence occurs. Instead, it means that a particular perpetrator committed some amount of violence against a particular target. If, for example, a criminal fires a gun six times in rapid succession at a hero, coders recorded this as a single violent interaction rather than six independent acts of violence. The information about multiple gun shots is captured by a variable called "extent" (discussed below in the context section of this chapter). Thus, when we report that one third of the programs feature nine or more violent interactions, we mean that these shows contain nine or more separate violent incidents involving different perpetrator and target combinations. This statistic tells us nothing about the number of individual behavioral acts *within* each incident, so it is not comparable to other studies that report on the rate of violent acts per hour or per program.

Analysis by Locator Variables

Now we turn our attention to *where* violence is located in the programming schedule. For both prevalence and distribution, there are significant differences across channel types and program genres. Differences also exist, but to a lesser extent, across dayparts and type of day.

Channel type. In terms of prevalence, programming on premium cable is more likely to contain violence than the industry average of 57% (see Figure 2). In contrast, programming on the broadcast networks is less likely to contain violence, and the percent of violent programs on public broadcast is even lower. From this point on, all the differences we highlight in the results section have met the statistical criterion of $p < .05$ according to a chi-square test of frequencies, as well as a more conservative criterion of substantive significance. Recall that to be substantively significant, we stipulated that there must be a minimum of 10% difference between an observed percentage on a locator variable and the overall pattern or average across all programming.

As for distribution, public broadcast exhibits the smallest range of violent interactions per program (from 1 to 29), followed by the broadcast networks (1 to 35), basic cable (1 to 64), independent broadcast (1 to 69), and premium cable (1 to 88). Recall that in our sample of violent programs, about one third of the programs have one to three violent interactions ("low"), one third have four to eight interactions ("medium"), and one third have nine or more ("high"). When we break down programs by channel type and compare across these three groupings, we find some interesting patterns (see Figure 3). Premium cable and independent broadcast each have a very large percentage of programs containing a *high* number of violent interactions. In contrast, programming on the broadcast networks is more likely to feature a *low* number of violent interactions.

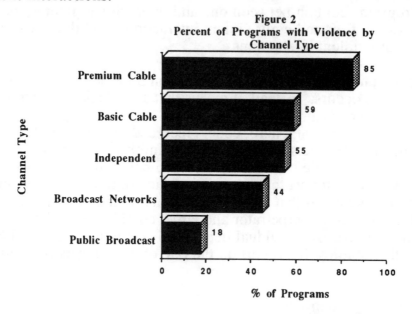

Figure 2
Percent of Programs with Violence by Channel Type

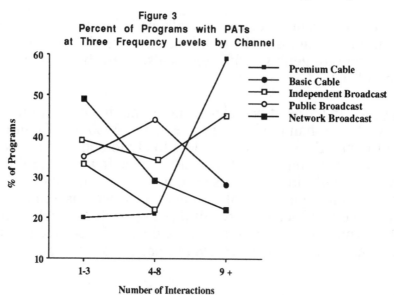

Figure 3
Percent of Programs with PATs at Three Frequency Levels by Channel

Program genre. The prevalence findings also vary significantly by program genre. A higher percentage of movies and drama series contain violence compared to the industry average, whereas fewer comedy series, reality-based shows, and music videos contain violence (see Figure 4). It is not surprising that the movie genre would display the greatest prevalence given that premium cable, which is dominated by films, also has the highest prevalence among the channel types. Somewhat unexpectedly, reality-based program are less likely to be violent, although we must underscore that this genre not only includes programs like *Cops* and *American Justice*, but also talk shows and documentaries which may be less likely to feature aggression. Music videos often are criticized for being violent, but our data show that only a third of them contain violence. Perhaps the most violent examples of this genre capture critics' attention and the numerous nonviolent, performance videos get underrepresented.

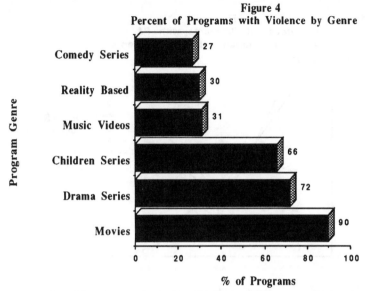

Figure 4
Percent of Programs with Violence by Genre

The pattern on distribution of violence generally parallels the pattern on prevalence. Concerning the ranges, movies exhibit the widest range of violent interactions (1 to 88 per program), followed by dramatic series (1 to 41) and children's series (1 to 40). Comedy series and reality-based programs feature a smaller range of violent interactions (1 to 26 for each). The lowest range is found for music videos (1 to 18), which is not surprising given the fact that videos almost never last for more than four or five minutes. When we compare the genres across levels of frequency, we see that most music videos and comedy series feature a "low" number of violent interactions (see Figure 5). In contrast, nearly two thirds of reality-based programs and movies contain a "high" number of violent interactions.

Daypart and type of day. In general, programs shown on the weekends have a slightly higher prevalence (62%) compared to programs shown on weekdays (55%). An examination of the prevalence of violent programs across daypart reveals that almost all percentages are very close to the overall average of 57%. There are only two minor deviations from this norm. In the early morning time slot (6:00-9:00 a.m.) during weekdays, only 45% of all programs contain violence, whereas in the late afternoon (3:00-6:00 p.m.) on weekends, 68% of programs are violent.

Summary of Prevalence and Distribution

The majority (57%) of programs in a composite week of television contain some violence. Furthermore, most of the violent incidents on television involve behavioral acts of aggression rather credible threats or implied violence. The highest percentages of violent programs are found on premium cable and within the genre of movies specifically; this is also where the highest frequencies of violent interactions are displayed. In contrast, the lowest percentage of violent programming is found on the broadcast networks and especially on public broadcast. Violence is less likely in comedy series, music videos, and reality-based programs. These channel types and genres also are characterized by relatively few violent interactions per program.

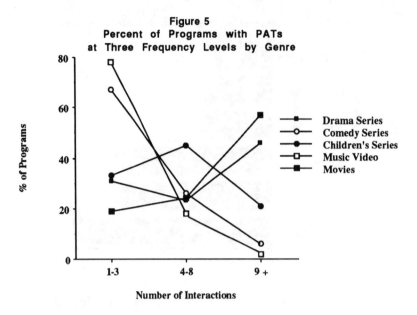

Figure 5
Percent of Programs with PATs
at Three Frequency Levels by Genre

Prevalence of Sexual Violence

The probability of encountering a sexual assault within a violent incident is very low. On average, less than 1% of violent interactions in our sample involve a sexual assault. There are too few examples of these depictions to identify any variation by channel type, genre, daypart, and type of day.

Prevalence of Advisories

As indicated in the site report from the University of Wisconsin, Madison, very few of all coded programs in our sample contain any type of advisory or content code. We followed up on this analysis by examining *only* those programs that were coded as violent. Specifically, our findings reveal that among those programs featuring any violence, 15% are preceded by an advisory or content code. In other words, viewers are rarely advised about programs that contain violence.

However, the presence of advisories or content codes differs substantially across channel type and genre. As seen in Figure 6, three fourths of the violent programs on premium cable are preceded by some type of viewer advisory. In striking contrast, very few of the violent programs on the four other channel types contain an advisory or content code.

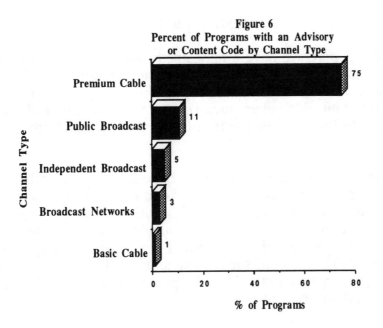

Figure 6
Percent of Programs with an Advisory
or Content Code by Channel Type

With respect to genre, violent movies are substantially more likely to contain an advisory or content code than the overall average, whereas violent children's series, violent drama series, and violent comedy series are less likely (see Figure 7). Reality-based programs are not different from the industry norm in terms of the presence of advisories or content codes, though very few of them contain such warnings.

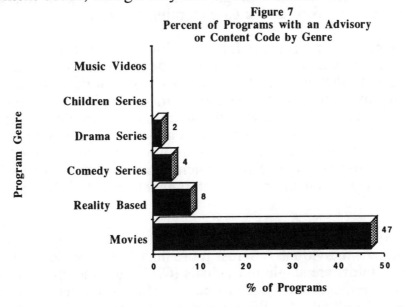

Figure 7
Percent of Programs with an Advisory
or Content Code by Genre

The presence of advisories or content codes does not differ much in terms of daypart and type of day, with one exception. Violent programs featured during prime time (8-11 p.m.) on the weekend (26%) are more likely than the industry average (16%) to be preceded by some type of advisory or content code.

Contextual Factors

Throughout this report, we have emphasized that the heart of this study is to assess the nature or context of violent portrayals. The preceding section describes what proportion of programs contain violence as well as how many violent interactions occur in different types of content. However, such figures tell us nothing about *how* that violence is portrayed. In this section, we turn to the analyses that provide us with that information.

When analyzing context, each program was coded as a separate unit or narrative story. However, as we noted previously, some programs are segmented, meaning that they contain independent stories or narrative units within a larger framework. Because these segments each contain their own narrative purpose, different characters, and a different story line, they were treated as individual programs, for purposes of applying the contextual variables. Thus, for all subsequent statistical analyses, the overall $\underline{N}$ (number of programs) is larger than the $\underline{N}$ in the preceding analyses because segments were treated as independent programs.

Nature of the Perpetrator

The nature of the perpetrator of violence is an important consideration in terms of imitation and learning. As demonstrated in Chapter 3, research indicates that perpetrators who are attractive or who are demographically similar to the viewer are potent role models in entertainment programming. Violent interactions that feature these types of models are more likely to increase learning of aggression.

Coders identified a perpetrator for *each* violent interaction in a program. Summing across all the violent interactions provides a profile of the characters that is weighted according to the number of interactions in which they are involved. For example, if a program features two characters, a male who is the aggressor in eight violent interactions and a female who is the aggressor in two violent incidents, we would report that 80% of the perpetrators are male and 20% are female. This weighting is appropriate because our focus is a behavioral one. Thus, we are interested in describing the attributes (such as character demographics) associated with violent interactions, rather than focusing on characters independent of the extent of their behaviors.

Perpetrators could be classified as single individuals, groups of individuals, or implied (unidentified) individuals. Across more than 18,000 violent interactions, two thirds of the perpetrators are single individuals (67%), and therefore are relatively easy to code in terms of demographics and attributes. Most of the remaining perpetrators (30%) are groups of individuals. We represent each group as "one" perpetrator in our data because, by our definition, groups act collectively against a target. Like individuals, each group is assigned a value on the demographics and the character attribute variables. When individuals in a group are not homogenous on a particular characteristic (e.g., some men and some women), coders identified the perpetrator as "mixed" on that variable.

As seen from the above breakdown, only 3% of the perpetrators of violence are implied or unknown. In subsequent analyses, percentages do not always add to 100 because implied as well as mixed perpetrators could not be assigned demographic and attribute characteristics. Also, some perpetrators were coded as "can't tell" when a trait or characteristic was impossible to ascertain (e.g., sex of an alien creature).

Type of character. Coders classified each perpetrator according to one of five character types: human, animal, anthropomorphized animal, supernatural creature, or anthropomorphized supernatural creature. As seen in Figure 8, almost three fourths of perpetrators of violence are human characters (71%). Two other categories account for nearly all the remaining perpetrators: anthropomorphized animals (12%) and anthropomorphized supernatural creatures (10%). Supernatural creatures and animals are rarely involved as perpetrators of violence. In other words, most of the perpetrators of aggression on television are humans or human-like characters. According to the research reviewed in Chapter 3, these characters should be easier for viewers to identify with than those who do not resemble humans.

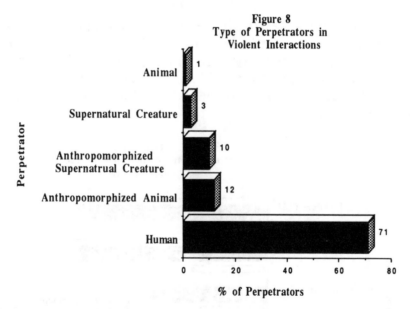

Figure 8
Type of Perpetrators in
Violent Interactions

In addition to the overall patterns across all programming, we assessed each character variable by program genre and by channel type. We did not, however, look at character variables in terms of daypart and type of day because preliminary analyses suggested no meaningful differences here, especially in light of the number of time slots and number of categories for each character variable.

Type of perpetrator varies across genre and channel type. For every program genre except children's series, nearly all perpetrators of violence are humans. In contrast, almost half of the perpetrators in children's series are anthropomorphized (48%) and only 40% are humans. This pattern is reflective of the high proportion of cartoons that constitute children's programming (see Figure 9).

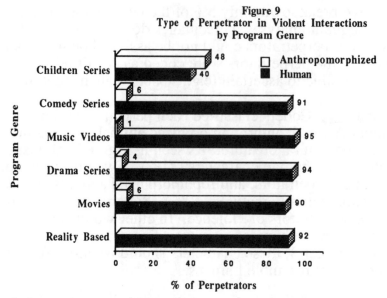

Figure 9
Type of Perpetrator in Violent Interactions
by Program Genre

In terms of channel type, nearly all the perpetrators featured on public broadcast are humans (see Figure 10). Premium cable also displays a higher proportion of human perpetrators than the overall industry average. In comparison, independent broadcast is *less* likely to feature human perpetrators, and *more* likely to show anthropomorphized creatures as aggressors. Such a finding is indicative of a higher concentration of cartoons on this channel type.

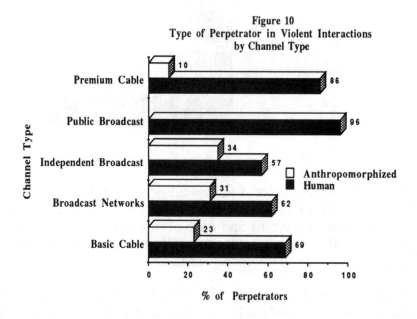

Figure 10
Type of Perpetrator in Violent Interactions
by Channel Type

Sex. More than three fourths of the perpetrators in violent interactions are male (78%), whereas only 9% are female. This robust pattern does not differ across genre or channel type.

Age. Coders judged the approximate age of each perpetrator as one of the following: child (0-12 years), teen (13-20 years), adult (21-64 years), or elderly (65 years or older). As seen in Figure 11, three fourths of the perpetrators in violent interactions are adults (76%). Teens make up the next largest category, though only 5% of perpetrators fall into this age group. Very few perpetrators of violence on television are children (2%) or elderly (1%).

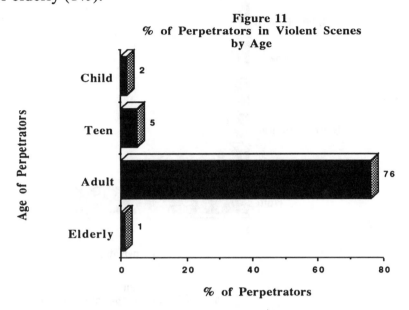

Figure 11
% of Perpetrators in Violent Scenes by Age

Age of perpetrator does not differ across the five channel types. Differences emerge as a function of genre, however. Drama series contain a higher proportion of adult perpetrators (90%) than the overall industry norm (76%). In contrast, children's series feature a lower proportion of adult perpetrators (60%). Nevertheless, the lower percentage of adults does *not* translate into more child or teen perpetrators in such programming, as might be expected. Instead, many of the perpetrators in children's series cannot be classified in terms of age, presumably because their supernatural or anthropomorphized qualities make chronological age difficult to ascertain.

Apparent ethnicity. The perpetrator's apparent ethnicity was coded for human characters only as: White, Hispanic, Black, Asian, Native American, or Middle Eastern. As seen in Figure 12, approximately three fourths of the perpetrators of violence on television are White (76%). Only 5% of the perpetrators are Black, 3% are Native American, 3% are Asian, 2% are Hispanic, and 1% are Middle Eastern.

Character ethnicity varies by program genre. Music videos and reality-based programs are substantially less likely to feature White perpetrators compared to the industry average (see Figure 13), and *more* likely to show Black perpetrators. This latter finding is most pronounced for music videos, where over one third of the perpetrators are Black (38%) compared to a 5% industry norm.

In terms of channel type, the only difference that emerges is that broadcast networks are *less* likely to feature White perpetrators (65%) than the overall average

(76%). This pattern is accounted for by the fact that slightly more Black perpetrators show up on the broadcast networks (13%), although according to our criterion this latter difference is not substantively significant (i.e., at least 10% different from the margin).

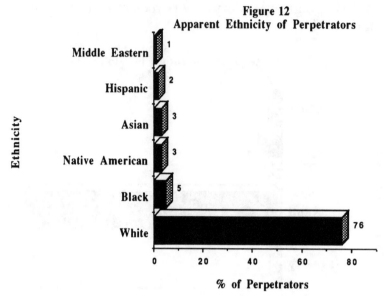

Figure 12
Apparent Ethnicity of Perpetrators

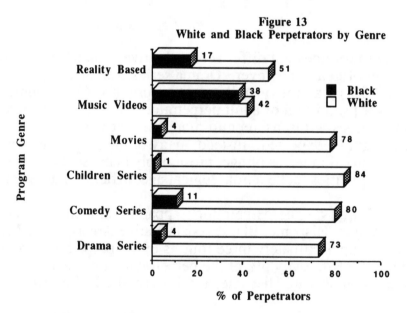

Figure 13
White and Black Perpetrators by Genre

Hero. Most perpetrators do *not* qualify as heroes (93%) according to our data. Given our rather strict definition, only 6% of all perpetrators on television are primary characters who go above and beyond the call of duty to protect others. No differences are found in this pattern by genre or channel type.

Good/bad. Coders judged each perpetrator as good, bad, *both* good and bad (blended), or neutral (neither good nor bad). A bad character was defined as an animate being who is motivated primarily by self-interest, whereas a good character was defined as one who is motivated by a concern for others. Our findings reveal that nearly half of the perpetrators of violence on television are bad characters (45%). As seen in Figure 14, only 24% of perpetrators are good characters. A much smaller proportion of perpetrators are *both* good and bad (13%). Taken together, then, approximately 37% of the perpetrators of violence have some good qualities with which a viewer might identify (% of good plus % of blended). To round out the findings, only 14% of perpetrators are purely neutral (14%).

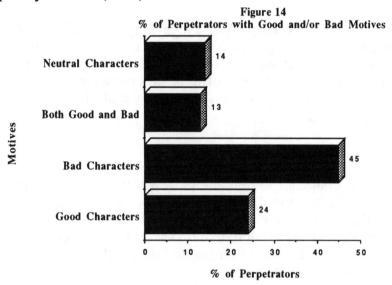

Figure 14
% of Perpetrators with Good and/or Bad Motives

This overall pattern characterizes perpetrators across all five channel types. The only difference pertains to one of the program genres--music videos. In music videos, a higher proportion of the perpetrators are neutral (33%), whereas a lower proportion are good (13%) or bad (31%) compared to the overall average. Clearly, the brief duration of most videos makes it more difficult to ascertain the motives of characters, making the neutral category a more viable option.

Summary of perpetrators. The typical perpetrator of violence on television is a human character who is adult, white, and male. Most often, the perpetrator is *not* a hero, and in fact is likely to be a "bad" rather than a "good" character. However, more than one third of all perpetrators have some good qualities that could make them attractive, and therefore potent role models for viewers.

The profile of the typical perpetrator varies some by genre. Children's series are more likely to feature anthropomorphized or human-like perpetrators and less likely to feature actual humans as aggressors compared to other genres. But this pattern is not surprising given the preponderance of cartoons within this genre. Music videos and reality-based programs also show some differences in the nature of the perpetrator. In particular, both genres feature a higher proportion of Black perpetrators and a lower proportion of White perpetrators compared to the overall pattern. In fact, music videos contain almost equal proportions of Black and White perpetrators. Music videos also are less likely than other genres to feature "bad" or "good" characters as perpetrators, and more likely to portray perpetrators as "neutral."

Fewer differences are present for channel type. Public broadcast and premium cable are more likely than the norm to feature human perpetrators, whereas independent broadcast is less likely to show humans as perpetrators, primarily because of the number of cartoons on this channel type. The only other finding of substance is that the broadcast networks are less likely to feature White perpetrators compared to the overall industry norm.

One final point should be emphasized regarding the findings. All of the percentages reported here refer only to perpetrators of violence and not to every character in a program. Because we coded only those characters involved in violence, we cannot use our data to describe the profile of all characters on television, nor can we directly compare our percentages to an overall base of all characters featured on television.

Nature of the Target

The target is the character or characters to whom violence is directed. The nature of the target of violence is an important consideration in terms of audience fear. Research indicates that viewers feel concern for and share emotional experiences with characters who they perceive as attractive and similar to themselves. As a result, when an attractive or well-liked character is threatened or attacked in a violent scene, viewers are likely to experience anxiety or fear.

Coders identified a target for each violent interaction in a program. As was done with perpetrators, summing across all the violent interactions provides a profile of the characters that is weighted according to the number of interactions in which they are victims. For example, if a program features two characters, an adult who is the object of violence in nine interactions and a child who is the object in one violent interaction, we would report that 90% of the targets are adults and 10% are children.

Across more than 18,000 violent interactions, almost 71% of targets are single individuals (69%), and only 29% are groups of individuals. As with the perpetrator data, each group of targets is assessed as a single unit on the demographic and character attribute variables. If individuals in a group are not homogenous on a particular characteristic (e.g., ethnicity), then coders identified the target as "mixed" on that variable. The remaining 2% of the targets of violence are implied or unidentifiable. As a reminder, percentages reported below do not always add to 100 because of implied and "mixed" targets as well as those who were coded as "can't tell" for certain variables.

Type of character. As seen in Figure 15, the vast majority of targets in violent interactions are human characters (70%). Two other categories account for most of the other targets: anthropomorphized animals (14%) and anthropomorphized supernatural creatures (9%). Supernatural creatures and animals rarely are involved as targets of violence. It should be noted that this pattern is almost identical to that of the perpetrators. Overall then, most of the victims of aggression on television are humans or human-like characters who presumably are easier for viewers to identify with than non-humans.

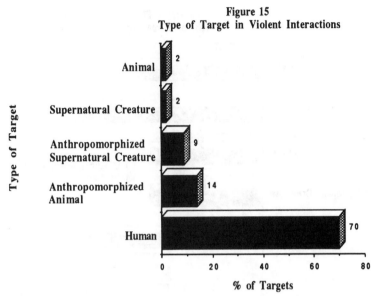

Figure 15
Type of Target in Violent Interactions

When examining genre, we see that 90% or more of all targets are human in drama series, movies, comedy series, reality-based programs, and music videos (see Figure 16). In striking contrast, children's series feature a substantially lower proportion of human targets and a higher proportion of anthropomorphized characters as targets. Again, this difference is consistent with the fact that much of children's programming is comprised of cartoons.

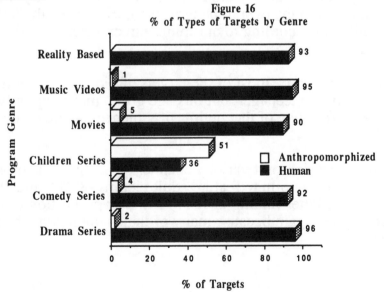

Figure 16
% of Types of Targets by Genre

In terms of channel type, nearly all the targets shown on public broadcast are humans (see Figure 17). Likewise, premium cable features a higher proportion of humans as targets compared to the overall margin. Yet the broadcast networks and independent broadcast contain a smaller proportion of human targets, and a greater proportion of anthropomorphized targets. Again, this pattern is indicative of more cartoons on these types of channels.

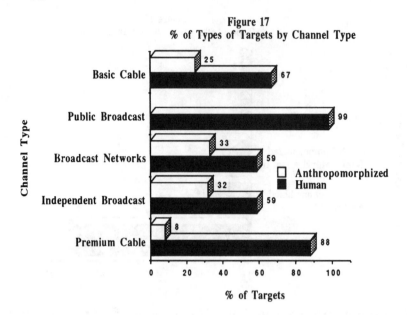

Figure 17
% of Types of Targets by Channel Type

Sex. Just as with perpetrators, the vast majority of targets of violence are male (75%). In spite of public concern that women may be singled out as victims on television, only 9% of the targets in our sample are female. This pattern generally does not differ across channel type or across genre, with one exception. In reality-based programs, a lower proportion of targets are male (59%), and a slightly higher percentage are female (14%) compared to the overall pattern (9%). However, the latter difference is not substantively significant according to our minimum criterion of 10% difference from the overall industry average.

Age. As with perpetrators, most of the targets of violence are adults (72%). The next most common victim is a teenager, but this age group makes up only 7% of all targets (see Figure 18). Very few of the victims of violence on television are children (3%) or elderly (1%).

The age of the target does not vary by channel type. In terms of genre, drama series are more likely than the norm to feature adult victims (89%), and children's series are less likely (54%). The latter finding is due to a higher proportion of targets who cannot be classified by age, again because many of the characters in children's series are anthropomorphized.

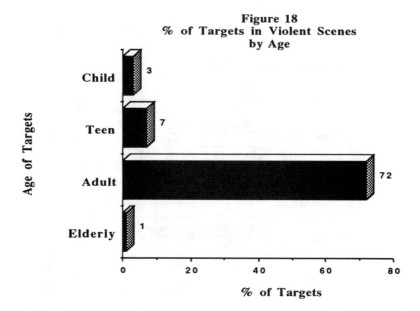

Figure 18
% of Targets in Violent Scenes
by Age

Apparent ethnicity. As seen in Figure 19, more than three fourths of the targets of violence on television are White (77%). Only 6% of the targets are Black, and the remaining groups each account for 3% or less of the victims.

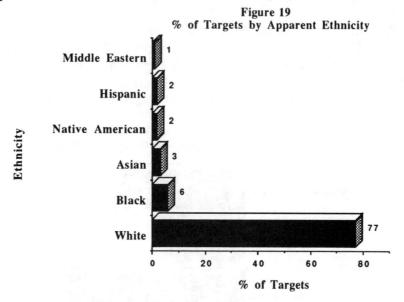

Figure 19
% of Targets by Apparent Ethnicity

In spite of the overall predominance of white victims, ethnicity does vary by program genre. Music videos and reality-based programs are substantially *less* likely to feature White victims compared to the industry average (see Figure 20), and music videos are substantially *more* likely to display Black victims. In fact, targets are almost equally split between Black and White characters when looking at music videos. Target ethnicity does not vary by channel type.

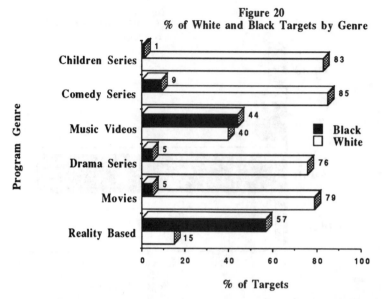

Figure 20
% of White and Black Targets by Genre

Hero. Targets of violence typically are <u>not</u> heroes. Only 6% of victims meet our strict definition of what constitutes this type of character (i.e., primary character who goes above and beyond the call of duty to protect others in a program). This finding does not differ across genre or channel type.

Good/bad. Our findings suggest that almost one third of targets can be described as good characters (31%). As seen in Figure 21, another third of the targets are bad characters (31%). Only 12% can be classified as both good and bad, and 21% are best described as neutral. Taken together, then, almost half of the victims of violence on television (42%) possess some good qualities that might encourage a viewer to identify with them.

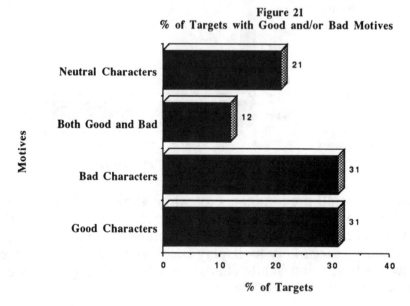

Figure 21
% of Targets with Good and/or Bad Motives

There are no differences in this variable as a function of channel type. In terms of genre, targets in comedy series are more likely to be neutral when compared to the overall margin. Furthermore, targets in music videos are substantially more likely to be neutral and less likely to be good. This latter finding presumably is a function of the difficulty in fully developing the motives or nature of characters in such brief programming.

Summary of targets. The profile of the typical target of television violence is nearly identical to that for the average perpetrator. Most targets are humans, and most are adult White males. Thus, the prototypical scenario for violence on television is an adult white male attacking another adult White male. The fact that so many of the profile variables look identical for both perpetrators and targets suggests that most of the characters involved in violence are simultaneously aggressing and being aggressed against. In other words, most targets turn around and fight back.

Like perpetrators, very few targets are heroes. However, almost half of the targets of violence on television possess some good qualities that might encourage viewer identification. Indeed, targets are slightly more likely to be good characters than are perpetrators. As discussed in Chapter 3, viewers are more likely to experience fear when violence is directed toward an attractive or well-liked victim. Our findings suggest that a majority of violent interactions involve good characters as targets and thus have the potential to cause anxiety in viewers.

There are some differences in the nature of the target across genre, and by in large these parallel the findings for perpetrators. Children's series are more likely to feature anthropomorphized or human-like victims and less likely to feature actual humans as the target of violence compared to other genres. Even so, research reviewed above suggests that younger children are quite responsive to animated and unrealistic characters so we cannot conclude that such depictions are somehow less problematic in terms of viewer fear. Music videos and reality-based programs also show some differences in the nature of the target. Both genres feature a lower proportion of White victims, and music videos in particular display a higher proportion of Black victims compared to the overall pattern. Lastly, music videos as well as comedy series are more likely than other genres to feature "neutral" victims who cannot be classified as either good or bad.

In terms of channel type, public broadcast and premium cable are more likely to feature human targets compared to the overall margin, whereas the broadcast networks and independent broadcast are more likely to contain anthropomorphized victims. Again, these patterns are roughly parallel to the perpetrator findings.

We must remind readers that the same caveat described in the perpetrator section holds for the target findings. All of the percentages here refer only to targets of violence and not to every character in a program. Because we coded only those characters involved in violence, we cannot use our data to describe the profile of *all* characters on television.

Reasons for Violence

For every violent interaction, coders assessed the reason or motive for the perpetrator's aggression against a particular target. Reasons were coded into one of six categories: protection of life, anger, retaliation, personal gain, mental instability, or other. The "other" category was used whenever the perpetrator's motive did not fit into one of the five specific options, or whenever the program did not provide enough information to determine the perpetrator's reason (e.g., the perpetrator was not shown).

The findings reveal that violence on television is generally motivated by one of three reasons--personal gain, anger, or protection of life (see Figure 22). Specifically, 30% of the violence is committed by perpetrators for personal gain, such as obtaining material goods (e.g., money), power, or affection. Another 24% of the violence is committed because the perpetrator feels anger over something the target did or said. And 26% of the violence is committed by a perpetrator in order to protect the self or another character. In contrast, very little of the violence on television is motivated by mental instability (5%) or retaliation for an act of previous violence in an earlier scene of the program (2%). The remaining 14% of violent interactions fell into the "other" category, because they could not be clearly classified into one of the five reasons outlined above.

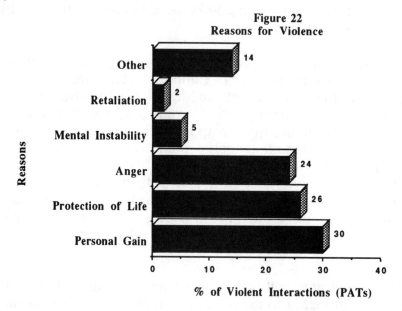

Figure 22
Reasons for Violence

Reasons for violence do not vary much across the locator variables. Compared to other channel types, the violence on public broadcast is less likely to be motivated by personal gain or protection, and more likely to be motivated by some "other" or unknown reason. However, there is so little violence on PBS that this differential pattern should be interpreted with caution.

There also are some differences in the reasons across the program genres. Compared to the overall industry norm, violence in comedy series is more likely to be committed because of anger. In comparison, violence in music videos is less likely to be motivated by protection of life, and more likely to occur for some "other" reason. The fact that much of the violence in music videos was classified as "other" is not entirely surprising. Because of the brief nature and production format of most videos (e.g., quick cuts to numerous images), a perpetrator's reason for acting violently may be difficult to ascertain. Reasons for violence do not fluctuate across dayparts or type of day.

As discussed in Chapter 3, research suggests that violence portrayed as justified or somehow morally sanctioned poses a greater risk for viewers than does violence that appears unjustified. We collapsed categories of reasons in order to make this comparison. Violence that is committed to protect life or to retaliate for a previous act of aggression is likely to appear as justified within the context of a typical plot. In contrast, violence that is enacted for personal gain or because of mental instability is likely to seem unjustified. Anger, the only remaining reason, is more difficult to classify because some violence motivated by anger may appear justified (e.g., perpetrator shoves a target who is burning down his house), whereas some may not (e.g., perpetrator shoots a target because of a sarcastic remark). Thus, we excluded all interactions motivated by anger in the analysis of justification.

When reasons are collapsed as indicated (excluding the category "other"), nearly half of the violent interactions portray violence as justified (44%) and half portray it as unjustified (56%). There are no differences across channel type in the depiction of justified violence. In terms of genre, music videos are *less* likely than other types of content to portray violence as justified, consistent with the finding above that protection of life is less likely to be a motive for violence in this genre. There are no differences in justified violence across daypart or type of day.

To summarize, almost one third of the violence on television is committed for instrumental purposes and almost one fourth is motivated by anger. In other words, perpetrators routinely use violence as a way to obtain resources or deal with their emotions. The only other reason that accounts for a substantial amount of violence (one fourth) is to protect life. When reasons are classified in terms of justification, almost half of the violent interactions appear justified and half seem unjustified. This pattern is fairly consistent across channels, genre, daypart, and type of day.

Means/Presence of Weapons

For each violent interaction, the means or method that a perpetrator used to engage in violence was coded. Means were classified into one of seven categories: natural means, unconventional weapon, handheld firearm, conventional handheld weapon other than firearm, heavy weaponry, bombs, or means unknown. Coders recorded all the different means that a perpetrator uses against the same target. However, in nearly all of the violent interactions in our sample (89%), the perpetrator uses only one form of means against a target. Thus, the findings report the primary means employed in each violent interaction.

The most prevalent method perpetrators use to enact violence on television is natural means (see Figure 23). Indeed, 40% of all violent interactions involve perpetrators using their own bodies to commit violence, such as hitting, punching, or kicking the target. When weapons are used, handheld firearms (i.e., guns) are the most common. In fact, guns are used in 25% of all violent interactions. The next most common form of weapon used is unconventional objects that are not traditionally associated with violence (e.g., rope, chair). Perpetrators use unconventional weapons in 20% of violent interactions. In contrast, bombs (2%), heavy weaponry like tanks and missiles (3%), and conventional handheld weapons other than guns (8%) are rarely used.

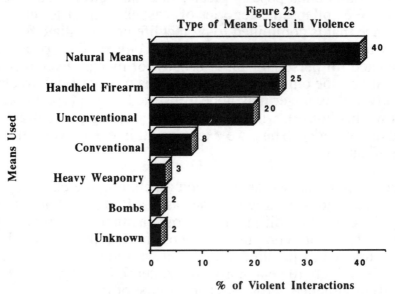

Figure 23
Type of Means Used in Violence

% of Violent Interactions

Because the two most prevalent means (natural means and guns) also are of most interest theoretically, we will now focus on them more specifically. Violence by natural means warrants special attention because conceivably it is more imitable by a viewer given that it does not require a special object or weapon. Guns have special significance because of the potential priming effect associated with such conventional weapons (see Chapter 3).

Do these two types of means differ across the locator variables? Our data indicate that there are no differences in the use of natural means or the use of guns across channel type. There are, however, some significant differences in use of these two means across program genres. Compared to all types of content, natural means are used *more* often in music videos, and *less* often in reality-based programs (see Figure 24).

Guns, on the other hand, are used *more* often in reality-based programs and drama series, and *less* often in children's series. Therefore, music videos pose the highest risk for imitating behaviors like hitting and kicking, whereas reality-based programs and drama series present the highest risk of weapon priming. There are no differences in the use of natural means or guns across daypart and type of day.

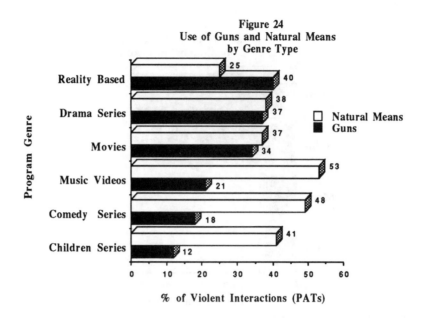

Figure 24
Use of Guns and Natural Means
by Genre Type

Extent of Violence

For each violent interaction in a program, the amount or extent of repeated violence was examined. This measure applies to behavioral acts only, and is not applicable to credible threats or harmful consequences. For extent, coders were trained to counted the number of times a behavioral act was repeated by a perpetrator against the same target within the same scene. The range of times was coded as follows: one, some (2 to 9 times), many (10 to 20 times), or extreme (21 or more times). For example, a perpetrator might punch a target 15 times and this would be coded as a single violent interaction involving "natural means" (punch with fist) with an extent of "many" (hitting 15 times). In cases where behavioral acts are interconnected and thus impossible to count individually, like a wrestling match or automatic gunfire, coders judged extent based on the amount of time the behavior lasted, using the same four categories (see Chapter 5).

Coders were trained to assess extent for each means or method of violence employed in a particular interaction. However, as mentioned above, nearly all of the violent interactions involve only one type of means (89%). Thus, the analyses of extent include the primary means only.

Our data indicate that 43% of the violent interactions involve only one act of aggression (see Figure 25). Put another way, nearly 60% of the violent interactions on television involve repeated or extended behavioral violence. In particular, 42% of the violent interactions feature "some" violence, 9% involve "many" acts of violence, and 7% involve "extreme" amounts of violence.

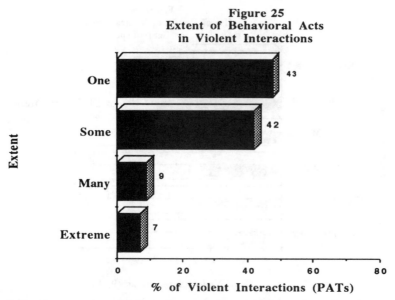

Figure 25
Extent of Behavioral Acts
in Violent Interactions

In terms of the locator variables, there are no differences in the extent or repetition of violence across the five channel types. In contrast, extent of violence differs as a function of program genre. In particular, reality-based programs are more likely to contain repeated violence than are the other types of content (see Figure 26). It is important to point out that children's series do not differ from other genres in terms of the extent of violence shown. There are no significant differences in the extent of violence by daypart or type of day.

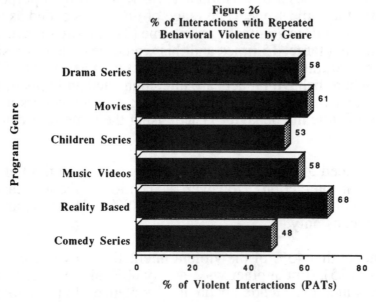

Figure 26
% of Interactions with Repeated
Behavioral Violence by Genre

Overall, a majority of violent interactions on television feature repeated or extensive aggression, though very few could be classified as extreme. Furthermore, reality-based programs are more likely than other genres to feature extended behavioral violence.

Graphicness of Violence

Graphicness of violence was measured in terms of the *explicitness* of the violence and in terms of the amount of *blood and gore* shown. Explicitness refers to the focus or concentration on the details of violence. Blood and gore refers to the amount of bloodshed and carnage shown. Both types of measures were assessed at the level of each violent scene. In other words, coders considered all violent interactions in a scene before judging overall explicitness and blood/gore.

Given its definition, explicitness is applicable only to behavioral violence, and not to credible threats or harmful consequences of unseen violence. Two types of explicitness were assessed: 1) explicitness of the violent behavioral act itself (i.e., the level of detailed focus on the perpetrator using the means or weapon), and 2) explicitness of means-to-target impact (i.e., the level of detailed focus on the means or weapon impacting and damaging the target's body). Both types of explicitness were coded into one of three categories: close-up focus, long-shot focus, or not shown at all.

Our findings reveal that very little of the violence on television is explicit. In particular, only 3% of all violent scenes contain a close-up focus on behavioral acts of violence, and only 2% of violent scenes feature a close-up focus on the impact of violence on a target's body (see Figure 27). In other words, it is very rare to see a close up shot of a fist hitting a person or a bullet entering a body. The channel, genre, daypart, and type of day locators revealed no differences in this overall finding.

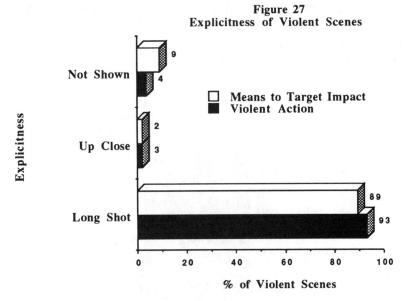

Figure 27
Explicitness of Violent Scenes

The other measure of graphicness deals with the amount of blood and gore shown. Amount of graphicness was classified into one of four categories: none, mild, moderate, or extreme. Our findings reveal that the vast majority of violent scenes on television depict no blood and gore (85%). As can be seen in Figure 28, very few of the scenes contain a "mild" amount of blood and gore (6%), or a "moderate" amount (6%). And almost none of the scenes depict an "extreme" amount of blood and gore (3%).

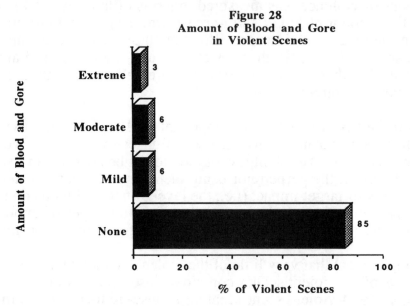

Figure 28
Amount of Blood and Gore
in Violent Scenes

Some variability exists, however, in where this bloodshed and carnage is found. For the analyses involving locator variables, the categories of "mild," "moderate," and "extreme" were combined because of their low frequencies. The analyses, then, look at the percent of scenes that contain *any* blood and gore versus *none*. Approximately 15% of all violent scenes contain some blood and gore. In terms of channel, viewers are more likely to encounter blood and gore in violent scenes featured on premium cable (see Figure 29). All other types of channels do not differ from the industry average on this measure.

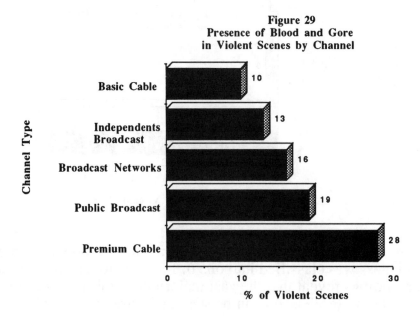

Figure 29
Presence of Blood and Gore
in Violent Scenes by Channel

As for genre, movies are more likely than the industry average to contain blood and gore within violent scenes. In contrast, bloodshed is virtually nonexistent in children's series (see Figure 30). Finally, blood and gore are more likely to be found in prime time hours than in any other time slot during the week (see Figure 31). There are no differences in the depiction of bloodshed across dayparts during the weekend.

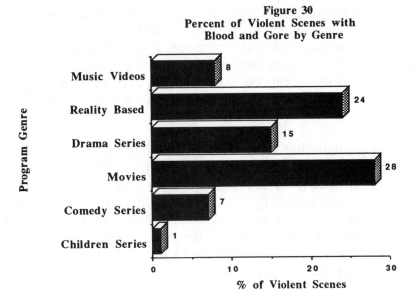

Figure 30
Percent of Violent Scenes with
Blood and Gore by Genre

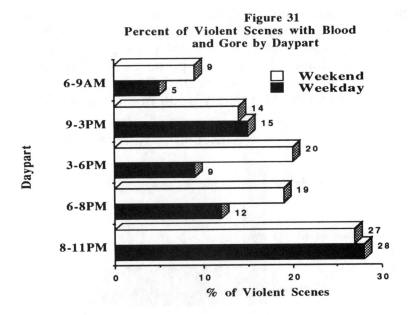

Figure 31
Percent of Violent Scenes with Blood
and Gore by Daypart

To summarize, the most robust finding here is that only a small percentage of violent scenes on television can be described as graphic. There are very few close-ups of violent behaviors or of victims as they are injured. In addition, not much bloodshed and carnage is depicted. But this is not to say that all programming shares equally in this relatively positive pattern. When blood and gore is portrayed, it is most likely to be found on premium cable, on movies, and in prime-time hours during the weekdays.

Realism

As discussed in Chapter 3, research indicates that viewers who perceive television violence as realistic are more likely to be influenced by it. But what is real? Answering such a question requires that we consider several features of realism as well as the developmental level or age of the viewer. Consequently, we cannot simply label a particular portrayal as real or unreal, but we can array certain features of a program on a continuum where we can safely argue that some depictions reflect reality more than do others.

One feature of realism that we coded was the degree of authenticity of the characters and events on television. For each program, coders judged whether the characters and events represented actual reality, re-created reality, fiction, or fantasy. In the television world, some shows present actual events from real life (e.g., a documentary), and these portrayals usually are regarded as more realistic than re-enactments of real events (e.g., *Rescue 911*). Re-enactments typically are more realistic than fictional programs, which feature fabricated events. In turn, fictional programs are more realistic than fantasy shows, because the former portray events that are at least *possible* in real life.

Our findings reveal that almost half of the violent programs in our sample can be classified as fantasy (49%). As seen in Figure 32, most of the remaining programs fall into the fictional category (43%). Only 4% of violent programs involve actual reality and only 4% depict re-creations of reality. For purposes of subsequent analyses, we collapsed the later three categories into an "realistic" grouping which represents all programs based on events that could possibly occur in the real world (51% total).

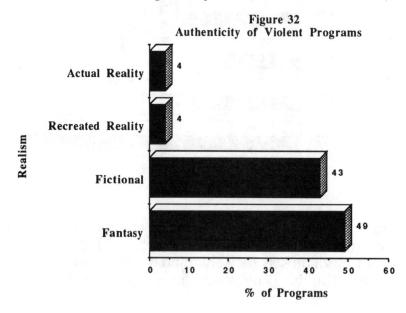

Figure 32
Authenticity of Violent Programs

When we analyze authenticity by channel type, we see that public broadcast and premium cable feature substantially more programs involving realistic violence than the industry average (see Figure 33). In contrast, independent broadcast is more likely to feature fantasy violence compared to the industry norm.

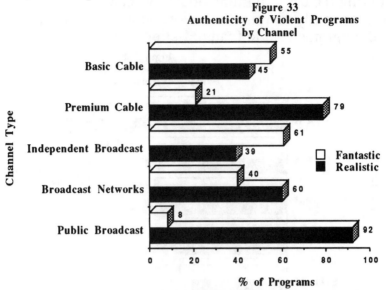

Figure 33
Authenticity of Violent Programs
by Channel

The analysis by genre reveals some differential patterns in terms of authenticity (see Figure 34). As might be expected, all reality-based programs are classified as involving realistic characters and events. When compared to the industry average, music videos, drama series, movies, and comedy series also are more likely to feature realistic events. In contrast, nearly all of the violent programs in children's series feature fantastic or impossible events and characters. Moreover, of all the programs featuring fantasy in our sample, 89% of them are in the single genre of children's series. In other words, fantasy violence is almost exclusively found in programs targeted to young viewers.

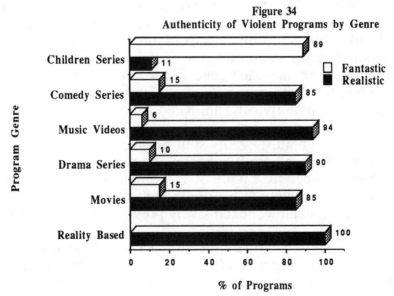

Figure 34
Authenticity of Violent Programs by Genre

Consistent with this pattern, fantasy programs are also limited to a particular time of day. For both weekday and weekend, violent programs that feature fantasy or impossible events are most likely to be found in the early morning time slot (see Figure 35). Again, this scheduling difference is presumably due to the concentration of children's series during the early morning hours. In general, the percentage of fantasy programs drops after the early morning time slot and is at its lowest during prime time, where most violent programs tend to feature fictional events.

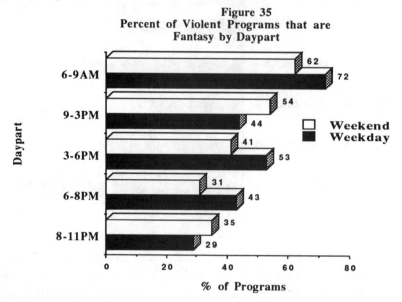

Figure 35
Percent of Violent Programs that are
Fantasy by Daypart

Now we turn our attention to another feature of realism, the style of presentation. This variable refers to the of production format that might influence how reality is assessed by viewers. Some producers use human actors in live-action scenes, whereas others use animated characters and settings. Still others use a combination of live action and animation. If characters and events are animated, it is more likely that viewers will regard them as being unrealistic. There are exceptions, however. As noted in Chapter 3, younger children respond to many animated characters as if they were real. Also, some animated characters like Bart Simpson may seem more realistic even to adult viewers compared to a non-animated character like the Terminator. Still, we contend that characters and events that are animated generally seem less real than human characters and live action. Coders rated the style of each violent program using three values: live action, animated action, or both live and animated action.

Violent programs are almost evenly split between live action (51%) and animated action (46%). Only 3% contain both live action and animation. This pattern differs a bit when we look at channel type (see Figure 36). Compared to the industry average, broadcast networks are more likely to feature violence in live action, and public broadcast and premium cable almost exclusively present violent programs in live action.

When we look at genre, nearly all the violence on children's series is animated (see Figure 37). Furthermore, nearly all (97%) of the animated programs containing violence are in the single category of children's series. The remaining genres all are substantially more likely to feature live action violence compared to the industry average, which is lower simply because of children's series.

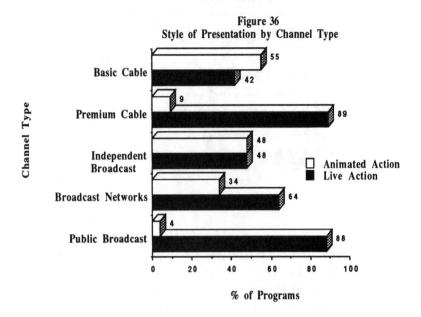

Figure 36
Style of Presentation by Channel Type

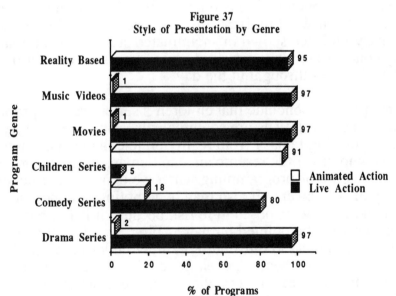

Figure 37
Style of Presentation by Genre

As for daypart, programs with animated violence are more prevalent in the early morning time slot on both weekdays and the weekend (see Figure 38). Animated violence drops off throughout the day, although it drops more gradually on the weekends than on weekdays. By prime time, the pattern shifts dramatically to a higher percentage of live action violence.

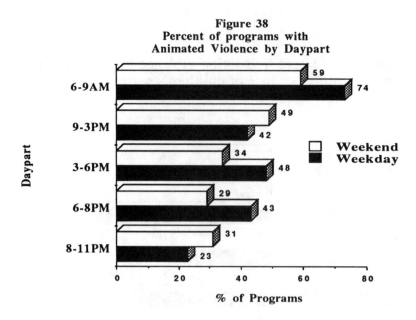

Figure 38
Percent of programs with
Animated Violence by Daypart

In summary, our two ways of assessing realism (degree of authenticity and style of presentation) result in very similar patterns. Overall, very few violent programs in our sample involve real or re-created events. Instead, most of the violent programs fall into one of two categories: fictional or fantasy. In terms of style of presentation, programs divide almost equally between live action and animated violence. However, the location of these depictions is very much tied to certain genres. Five of the six genres feature realistic violence that is conveyed in live action. Alternatively, children's programs contain mostly fantasy violence shown in an animated style. This animated fantasy violence is mostly concentrated in the early morning hours before children go to school (6-9 a.m.), and then declines throughout the day.

It may be tempting to conclude that children's series are less problematic than other genres because their portrayals are so unrealistic. However, very young children have difficulty distinguishing fantasy from reality on television and often readily imitate animated characters who bear little resemblance to humans (see Chapter 3). Thus, we cannot exonerate this genre of programming when we consider the developmental capabilities of many of its viewers. It also may be tempting to conclude that much of the violence targeted to adult viewers poses little risk because it is not based on real life events. Two caveats should be pointed out here. First, we did not assess any hard news programming (per our contract) so our findings surely underrepresent the amount of real-life violence on television. Second, even fictional violence, which is the norm in adult programming, can seem realistic to a viewer because the events and characters are feasible in real life.

Rewards and Punishments

Rewards and punishments for violence were coded at the end of each violent scene as well as at the end of each program. The scene coding allows us to examine reinforcements for violence that are delivered during or immediately after aggression occurs. The program coding allows us to assess the pattern of reinforcements across the entire program.

In the majority of violent scenes (58%), aggression is neither rewarded nor punished when it occurs (see Figure 39). A much smaller proportion of scenes shows violence as being explicitly punished (19%) or rewarded (15%), and even fewer depict violence as *both* rewarded and punished (8%). As demonstrated in Chapter 3, violence that goes unpunished poses the greatest risk for viewers in terms of learning aggressive attitudes and behaviors. Taken together, our findings indicate that almost three fourths of the violent scenes on television (73%) portray no punishments for violence within the immediate context of when it occurs. This robust pattern holds across all types of genres, including children's series. The pattern also holds across different types of channels, and across dayparts and type of day.

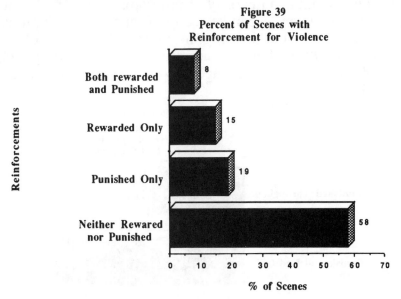

Figure 39
Percent of Scenes with
Reinforcement for Violence

What types of rewards and punishments typically are depicted? We classified rewards as involving self-praise that a perpetrator expresses after acting violently, praise from other characters, and material goods that are received as a consequence of violence (e.g., money, jewelry). A given violent scene could feature one or all of these types of rewards. Although rewards do not occur very often in the immediate context of violence, the most common forms involve self-praise and praise from other. In particular, the perpetrator expresses personal satisfaction for violence in 14% of all violent scenes, whereas other characters express approval in 10% of all scenes. Only 6% of all scenes depict material rewards for violence.

Punishments were classified as involving self-condemnation that a perpetrator expresses for acting violently, condemnation from others, nonviolent action to stop or penalize violence, and violent action by a third party to terminate further violence. A given scene could feature one or more of these types of punishments. Although punishments do not occur very often in the immediate context of violence, the most common forms involve condemnation expressed by characters other than the perpetrator (16% of all scenes) and violent action taken by a third party to stop violence (12% of all scenes). Only 9% of the violent scenes feature a nonviolent action to penalize violence, and virtually none of the scenes (3%) show a perpetrator feeling remorse over violence.

At the program level, reinforcements were examined as well. However, here we focused only on the presence or absence of punishment because of its importance for inhibiting viewers' learning of aggression. Coders assessed the overall pattern of punishments delivered to good perpetrators, to bad perpetrators, and to perpetrators who are both good and bad. It should be noted that reliabilities for these measures are somewhat lower than for other program-level variables so the data should be interpreted with some caution.

Our findings reveal that in a majority of programs (62%), bad characters are punished for violence. However, as can be seen in Figure 40, such punishments typically are delivered at the end of the program (40%). Only 23% of programs depict bad characters as punished throughout the narrative. The remaining 37% of the programs feature bad characters who engage in violence and are "never or rarely" punished for their behavior.

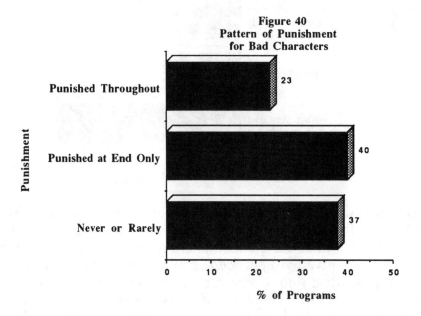

This pattern of punishments for bad characters generally holds across channel type, daypart, and type of day. Several differences emerge, however, when looking at the patterns of punishments by genre. Specifically, drama series are *more* likely to show the bad characters being disciplined or chastised, whereas comedy series, music videos, and reality-based programs are *less* likely to depict bad characters as punished (see Figure 41).

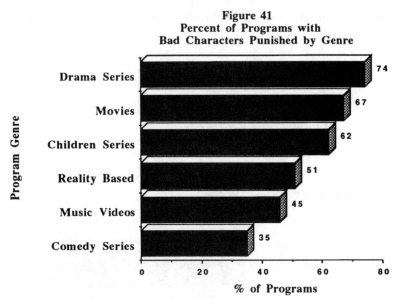

Figure 41
Percent of Programs with
Bad Characters Punished by Genre

The findings above indicate that in most television programming, bad characters are eventually punished. Yet the picture looks quite different for good characters. Good characters who engage in violence are punished in only 15% of all programs (see Figure 42). In other words, in the vast majority of programs good characters never feel remorse, nor are they reprimanded or hindered by others when they engage in violence. This robust pattern is stable across the five channel types and six genres of programming. It also is found consistently across all dayparts during the weekday and weekend.

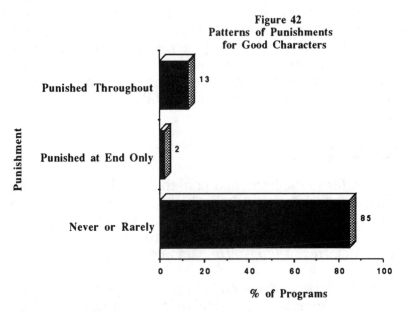

Figure 42
Patterns of Punishments
for Good Characters

Slightly fewer programs feature characters who are both good and bad. Such characters more commonly are found in movies than in the other program genres. The pattern of punishments for these characters is similar to the pattern for purely good characters. Blended characters (both good and bad) who engage in violence are punished in only 33% of the programs (see Figure 43). This pattern is fairly consistent across the locator variables, especially given the low frequency of such characters in violent programming.

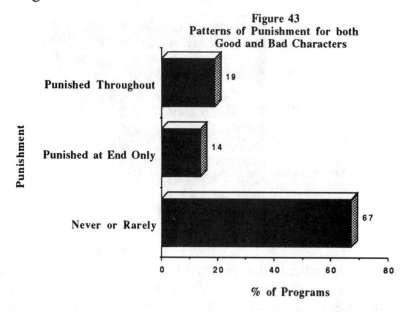

Figure 43
Patterns of Punishment for both
Good and Bad Characters

In sum, the vast majority of violence on television is *not* punished at the time it occurs or immediately after within a scene. Punishments more typically occur later in the program, particularly toward the end of the plot. But this pattern is true only for bad characters. Good characters who engage in violence are rarely punished at all on television, and characters who are both good and bad typically are not punished either. Thus, the characters that children are most likely to identify with are rarely discouraged or punished for acting aggressively. These patterns are fairly consistent across all locator variables, with a few exceptions pertaining to genre. Most importantly, drama series are more likely to feature bad characters being punished for violence, whereas comedy series, reality-based programs, and music videos are less likely to portray bad characters as punished.

Consequences of Violence

Consequences refer to the harm and pain that result from violent actions. We coded the consequences of violence at both the interaction and the program level. Coding at the interaction level allows us to examine the *immediate* consequences of violence at the time that it occurs. Coding at the program level enables us to assess the aftermath of violence in terms of *long-term* pain and suffering.

For each violent interaction, we coded harm and pain separately. Because our definition of violence is grounded in physical as opposed to psychological damage, we coded harm and pain for behavioral acts and harmful consequences only. By definition, credible threats could not result in physical injury so pain and harm were not coded for any of these types of interactions. For harm, we assessed: (1) the amount of physical injury that is actually *depicted* on screen, and (2) the amount of *likely* injury that would have occurred if the violence had been enacted against a human in real life. Both of these measures of harm had four possible values: none, mild, moderate, or extreme. Coders also noted when the target literally is not shown in the program such that depicted harm could not be ascertained.

Our findings indicate that across all violent interactions, 44% depict *no* physical injury to the target. In an additional 3% of the violent interactions, the target is not even shown on screen (camera moves away or the scene changes abruptly). Thus, almost half of violent incidents (47%) on television contain no observable indications of harm to the victim (see Figure 44). This finding is particularly important given that the research suggests that harm and pain cues inhibit viewers' learning of aggression (see Chapter 3). To round out these findings, approximately 22% of the violent interactions show mild harm to the target, 12% show moderate harm, and 18% depict harm as extreme.

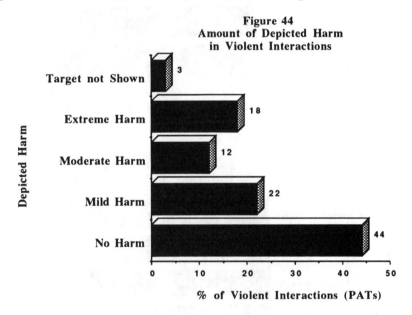

Figure 44
Amount of Depicted Harm
in Violent Interactions

Some differences in depicted harm emerge across the locator variables. In terms of channel type, broadcast networks are more likely to show *no* harm to victims compared to the industry average (see Figure 45). For genre, children's series are significantly more likely to portray *no* observable harm to victims of violence (see Figure 46). On the other hand, movies are less likely to circumvent harm cues. No differences in depicted harm occur across daypart and type of day.

In addition to depicted harm, we also measured likely harm in order to locate those interactions that portrayed less harm to the target than they should have, given the seriousness of the violence. To accomplish this, we developed a new variable called *unrealistic harm*, defined as any instance in which the degree of depicted harm (none, mild, moderate, extreme) is less than the degree of likely harm in real life (mild, moderate, extreme). An example would be a farcical depiction of a target who is hit over the head with an sledgehammer and walks away with only a small lump on the forehead. This type of injury would be coded as "mild" for depicted harm but "extreme" for likely harm in real life. Such a violent interaction would be characterized as showing unrealistic harm. This constructed variable allows us more accuracy in gauging the degree of authenticity of the harm depicted on television.

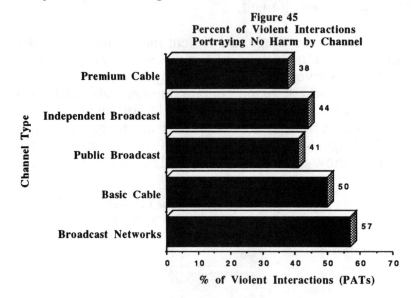

Figure 45
Percent of Violent Interactions
Portraying No Harm by Channel

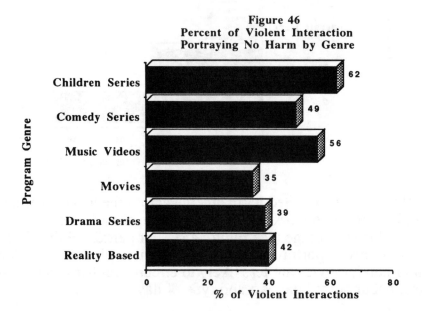

Figure 46
Percent of Violent Interaction
Portraying No Harm by Genre

Overall, only 35% of all violent interactions portray unrealistic harm on television. In other words, almost two thirds of the violent incidents feature a realistic portrayal of the degree of injury to the victim. The portrayal of unrealistic harm differs, however, across channel type. Compared to the overall pattern, public broadcast and premium cable are *less* likely to feature unrealistic harm (see Figure 47). The pattern for unrealistic harm also differs with respect to program genre. As seen in Figure 48, reality-based programs, movies, and drama series all contain the lowest proportion of interactions featuring unrealistic harm. Arguably, the most important finding is that children's series contain the highest percentage of unrealistic depictions of harm. In fact, more than half of the violent interactions in children's series portray an unrealistic amount of injury to the victim. There are no differences in the occurrence of unrealistic harm across daypart or type of day.

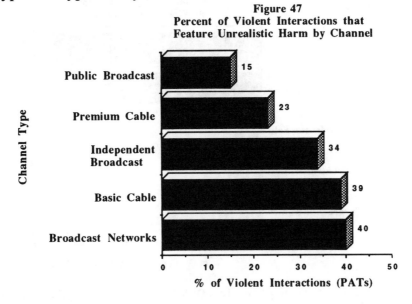

Figure 47
Percent of Violent Interactions that
Feature Unrealistic Harm by Channel

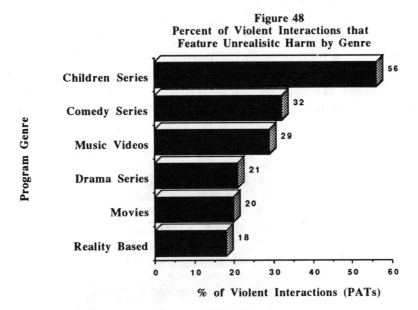

Figure 48
Percent of Violent Interactions that
Feature Unrealisitc Harm by Genre

Like harm, depicted pain was coded at the level of each violent interaction. The amount of depicted pain ranged from none (no verbal or nonverbal expressions of pain, anguish, or suffering) to extreme (expression of intense, enduring, and protracted pain and suffering). Our findings reveal that across all violent interactions, 50% depict the target experiencing no pain. In an additional 8% of the interactions, the target is not even shown on screen so pain cues could not be assessed (i.e., camera moved away or the scene changed). Therefore, a total of 58% of all violent interactions show no observable pain to the victim (see Figure 49). Rounding out the findings, mild pain is depicted in 30% of the violent interactions, moderate pain is depicted in 7%, and extreme pain is shown in 6% of the violent interactions.

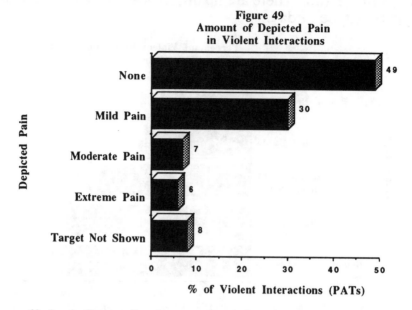

Figure 49
Amount of Depicted Pain
in Violent Interactions

These overall depictions of pain are consistent across dayparts and type of day. Yet some interesting differences emerge when we examine program genres (see Figure 50). Although a clear majority of violent interactions depict no pain, music videos, reality-based programs, and children's series are even *more* likely to show no observable pain cues to the victim. In fact, over three fourths of violent interactions in music videos and nearly 70% of the interactions in reality-based programs and children's series show no pain cues to the target. Depicted pain also differs as a function of channel type. Public broadcast is slightly more likely to show no pain than the industry norm.

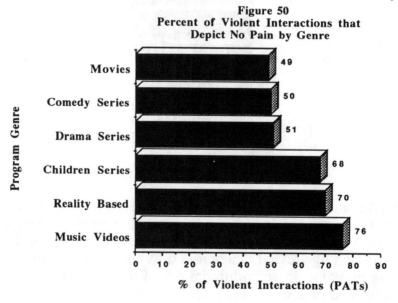

Figure 50
Percent of Violent Interactions that
Depict No Pain by Genre

In addition to coding harm and pain for each violent interaction, the consequences of violence were coded at the program level. This measure provided an overall judgment about harm and pain combined. It asked coders to consider not only the physical harm and pain experienced as a result of violence, but also the emotional, psychological, and financial costs to the participants, their families, and the community at large. Coders assessed the extent of harm and pain depicted across the entire program, indicating whether such consequences generally were: (1) *not shown* at all, (2) *short-term* or immediate in nature (limited to within the violent scene or immediately thereafter), or (3) *long-term* in nature (displayed throughout the program).

Our findings indicate that almost one third of all programs (32%) can be characterized as showing no negative consequences of violence. As can be seen in Figure 51, slightly more than half of the programs depict short-term negative consequences of violence (52%), and only 16% depict more long-term pain and suffering associated with violence.

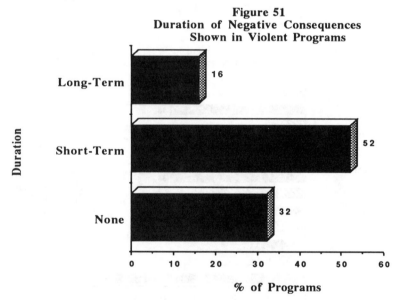

Figure 51
Duration of Negative Consequences
Shown in Violent Programs

The pattern of negative consequences does not differ by daypart or type of day, but there are some differences for the other two locator variables. As for channel type, premium cable features more programs that depict the long-term negative consequences of violence, and fewer programs that show no consequences at all compared to the industry average (see Figure 52).

In terms of genre, music videos are substantially more likely to show *no* negative outcomes of violence compared to the industry average. On the other hand, drama series and especially movies are more likely to portray the long-term repercussions of violence than the industry norm (see Figure 53). Perhaps the most notable finding is that children's series are *less* likely to portray the extended negative consequences of violence.

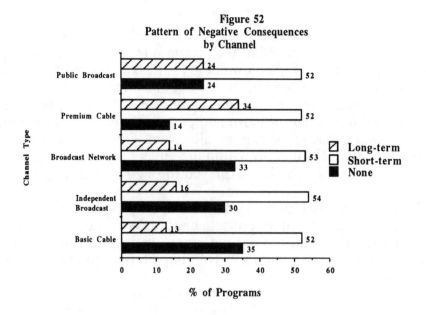

Figure 52
Pattern of Negative Consequences
by Channel

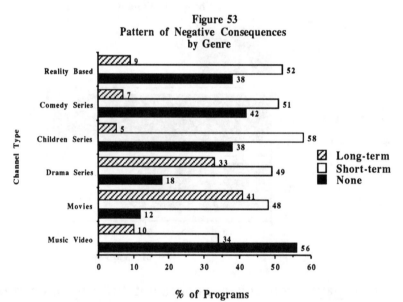

Figure 53
Pattern of Negative Consequences
by Genre

In summary, most violent interactions on television contain no observable harm or pain cues to the victim. This pattern is especially true of children's series, in which much of the harm that is depicted is unrealistic when compared to what would happen in real life if such aggressive actions were to occur. On the overall program level, about one third of the programs do not portray any physical, emotional, psychological, or financial consequences of violence. When such consequences are shown, they are for the most part depicted as short-term in nature. Of all the channel types, premium cable is the most likely to portray the negative outcomes of violence. Of all genres, movies and drama series are the most likely to feature the serious repercussions of violence, whereas children's series are the least likely to show such consequences.

Humor

The presence or absence of humor was assessed within each violent scene. Our findings reveal that humor frequently accompanies violence on television. Indeed, humor is present in 39% of all violent scenes. This relatively high rate is fairly consistent across channel types, with one exception. In public broadcast, only 8% of violent scenes are contextualized with humor (see Figure 54).

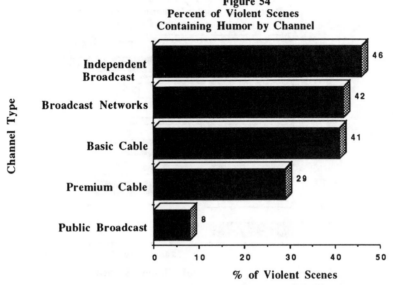

Figure 54
Percent of Violent Scenes
Containing Humor by Channel

When we compare the use of humor across different genres, we see some considerable differences (see Figure 55). As might be expected, humor accompanies violence substantially more often in children's series and comedy series, and substantially less often in music videos, reality-based programs, and drama series. Humor also is less likely to be present in violence scenes featured in movies, though this difference is not as great.

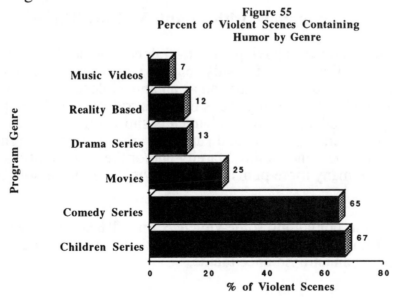

Figure 55
Percent of Violent Scenes Containing
Humor by Genre

The daypart and type of day analyses also reveal some differences, although not as dramatic as the genre analysis. Humor is featured in violent scenes more often during early morning hours, and less often during prime time hours (see Figure 56), and this pattern holds for weekday as well as weekend. These differences presumably are due in part to the distribution of program types within these day parts; children's series commonly are found in the early morning hours, whereas drama series and reality-based programs are often shown during prime time.

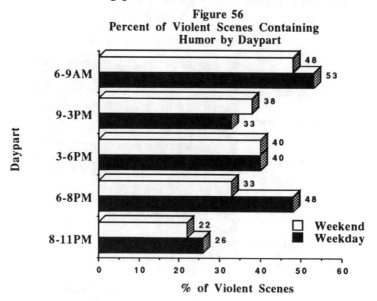

Figure 56
Percent of Violent Scenes Containing Humor by Daypart

In sum, many of the violent scenes on television are portrayed in some form of comedic context which, according to research cited in Chapter 3, may serve to undermine the seriousness of aggression. Humorous violence is most often found in children's series and in comedy series, and generally during early morning (6 a.m. to 9 a.m.) programming.

Programming with an Anti-Violence Theme

Programs were coded as having an anti-violence theme if the overall message was that violence is destructive or wrong. This concept was operationalized using four different criteria. In order to be categorized as an anti-violence theme at least one of the following patterns had to be a strong focus of the narrative: (1) alternatives to violence are discussed or presented, (2) the main characters show reluctance or remorse for committing acts of violence, (3) pain and suffering are depicted throughout, and some attention is devoted to how the victims' family and/or the community is affected, or (4) on balance, there are many more punishments for violence throughout the program than there are rewards.

Of all programs containing some violence, only 4% strongly feature an anti-violence theme. Table 12 contains examples of various types of programs that emerge in our sample as having an anti-violence theme.

Table 12

Examples of Programs in Sample Containing an Anti-violence Theme by Genre

Genre	Title of Program	Channel	Time
Children's Series	Beetlejuice	NIK	4:00 - 5:00 pm
	Bullwinkle	NIK	7:00 - 7:30 am
	G-Force	CAR	3:00 - 3:30 pm
	Ghostwriter	PBS	4:00 - 4:30 pm
	Josie and the Pussycats	CAR	9:00 - 9:30 pm
	Mighty Max	KCAL	7:30 - 8:00 am
	Muppet Babies	NIK	4:00 - 4:30 pm
	Rin Tin Tin K-9 Cop	FAM	6:00 - 6:30 pm
Comedy Series	Doogie Howser	KTLA	5:00 - 5:30 pm
	Roseanne	KCOP	6:00 - 6:30 pm
	Fresh Prince of Bel-Air	NBC	8:00 - 8:30 pm
Drama Series	Beverly Hills 90210	FOX	8:00 - 9:00 pm
	CHIPS	TNT	9:00 - 10:00 pm
	In the Name of Love	LIF	10:30 - 11:00 pm
	Kung Fu	TNT	4:00 - 5:00 pm
	Mystery	PBS	9:00 - 10:00 pm
	Star Trek Deep Space	KCOP	9:00 - 10:00 pm
	University Hospital	KCOP	9:00 - 10:00 pm
Movies	Airborne	HBO	6:00 - 8:00 am
	Avalon	SHO	5:00 - 7:30 pm
	Avenging Angel	TNT	5:00 - 7:00 pm
	Ordinary Magic	HBO	4:30 - 6:30 pm
	Pollyanna	DIS	7:00 - 9:30 pm
	Project X	MAX	12:00 - 2:00 pm
	Romeo & Juliet	AMC	6:00 - 8:30 pm
	South Central	HBO	8:00 - 10:00 pm
	Snowy River	FAM	6:00 - 7:00 am
	The Toy Tiger	AMC	5:30 - 8:00 pm
	Toys	HBO	4:00 - 6:00 pm
	Twins	KTLA	8:00 - 10:00 pm
	Woman With a Past	HBO	12:30 - 2:00 pm

Reality-Based	American Justice	A&E	6:00 - 7:00 pm
	Cops	FOX	6:30 - 7:30 pm
	Frontline	PBS	9:30 - 11:30 pm
	Rescue 911	FAM	9:00 - 10:00 pm
	Jenny Jones	KCOP	11:00 - 12:00 pm
	To the Contrary	PBS	1:00 - 1:30 pm
Music Videos	Don't Tell Me	MTV	7:30 - 9:00 am
	I Miss You	MTV	10:00 - 12:00 pm
	I Remember	MTV	7:30 - 9:00 am
	I Remember	MTV	1:30 - 1:30 pm
	If Anything Ever Happened	BET	12:00 - 1:30 pm
	If Anything Ever Happened	BET	6:00 - 8:00 pm
	Stevie Wonder and		
	Black History Month	VH1	2:00 - 2:30 pm
	Zombie	MTV	7:30 - 9:00 am
	Zombie	MTV	7:30 - 9:00 am
	Zombie	MTV	7:30 - 9:00 am
	Voices against		
	Violence Segment	VH1	5:00 - 5:30 pm

Our analyses by locator variables reveal that the presence of an anti-violence theme does not vary across the different program genres. Nor does the presence of an anti-violence theme differ across daypart or type of day. Nevertheless, there is a difference as a function of channel type. Compared to the industry norm, public broadcast is more likely to feature programs with an anti-violence theme (see Figure 57). Yet very few programs contain violence on this channel so such a difference should be interpreted with caution.

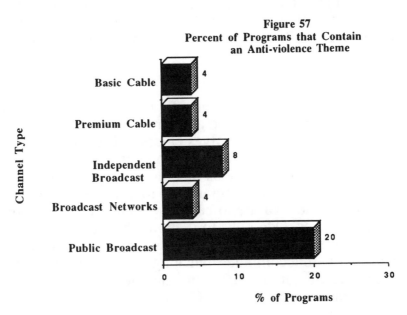

Figure 57
Percent of Programs that Contain an Anti-violence Theme

Below we present a brief description of several of the programs in our sample that carry an anti-violence theme. We present these to illustrate how violence can be used in a prosocial manner in entertainment programming. Such descriptions should be informative to parents and educators who want to be able to distinguish violent programs that pose risks for children from those that might be prosocial or educational. In addition, these descriptions should be informative for writers and producers who are seeking creative ways to portray conflict in a socially responsible manner.

Children's Series

Beetlejuice is a half-hour cartoon that features a ghost-like character named Beetlejuice who loves to play jokes and has supernatural powers. His best friend is a young girl named Lydia who delights in his games and his magic. This particular episode aired on Nickelodeon at 4:30 p.m. and focuses on Halloween. Beetlejuice and Lydia discover that a neighborhood witch has taken Lydia's cat, so the two are forced to crash a witches' Halloween party to retrieve the animal. Beetlejuice and Lydia disguise themselves as witches and join in the festivities while trying to find the cat. When the witches discover the disguise, they threaten to harm Beetlejuice and Lydia with their magical powers. Just as the witches are ready to attack, Lydia reminds them of how Beetlejuice managed to spark up their party and make it more fun. Beetlejuice then challenges the witches: "Don't use your magic on evil, use magic for fun!" The witches realize that Beetlejuice has been a good addition to their party and they decide not to hurt him or Lydia. Instead, the witches proceed to use their magic to play party games.

Of the four ways that could be used to emphasize anti-violence, this program is a good example of the first--the presentation and discussion of alternatives to violence. In this case, both of the main characters, Beetlejuice and Lydia, persuade the angry witches to use their powers to have fun instead of to hurt others. The witches turn from nasty, evil creatures to fun-loving party goers after they accept this nonviolent alternative. Interestingly, this cartoon contains 12 violent interactions, most of which occur before Beetlejuice and Lydia are able to convince the witches to change their behavior.

Drama Series

Star Trek: Deep Space Nine is a science fiction series based on the original *Star Trek* program. This particular episode aired at 9 p.m. on KCOP, one of the independent channels in our sample. The episode involves Quark's discovery of a humanoid baby on a nearby space wreckage. The baby is brought on board and rapidly develops into an adult. Dr. Bashir's scientific testing reveals that the creature is not a humanoid at all, but rather a Jem'Hadar that is genetically programmed to kill. During the remainder of the episode, Odo tries to teach the creature to be non-violent. Whenever the Jem'Hadar displays aggressive tendencies, Odo talks to it about channeling those impulses and about alternative ways to release frustration. For example, Odo tries to get the creature to smile and to work out with a computer punching machine when he feels aggressive. Odo manages to keep the creature from hurting anyone on the spaceship, but it eventually escapes to search for its own people.

Like the program described above, the anti-violence theme in this episode is conveyed primarily through talk and discussion about nonviolent alternatives. In fact, there are very few behavioral acts of violence in this episode, though the creature manages to threaten others. Odo, a primary character in the series, is shown in several different scenes trying to teach non-violence and peace to an aggressively predisposed Jem'Hadar. Taken together, the cartoon example presented above and the drama series described here demonstrate that genres typically containing violence can be entertaining while still featuring conflict in a prosocial manner.

Comedy Series

Fresh Prince of Bel Air is a situation comedy featuring an African American teenager (Will) who moved from the inner city to Bel Air, California to live with his wealthy aunt and uncle. The series is shown at 8 p.m. on NBC. In this episode, Will and his cousin Carlton are robbed at gunpoint at an automated teller machine. The robber shoots at the two cousins and hits Will. The remainder of the program focuses on the difficulties that the family experiences because of this violent crime. Will is dangerously close to being paralyzed and is in the hospital for the latter half of the show. The family waits in agony until they find out that he will recover. In the meantime, Carlton is traumatized by the violent experience and decides in anger to start carrying a gun. In the final scene, Will lays in his hospital bed and begs Carlton to give up the gun, saying "that's not your way ... that's them." Carlton finally gives him the gun and the program closes as Will empties the bullets from the gun and breaks down in tears.

Of the four possible ways to convey anti-violence, the first and third are used in this episode. The serious consequences of violence are repeatedly depicted. The victim (Will) is shown in physical pain, has a nightmare about the crime, and is in the hospital for the entire episode. His family is emotionally upset and Will's girlfriend sleeps on the chair near his bed, because she refuses to leave the hospital. Though Will still cracks an occasional joke, he points out that humor helps him deal with the trauma. In contrast, Carlton finds no humor in the situation and reprimands Will several times for his jokes. All in all, this is a very serious episode in spite of the fact that it is a situation comedy. In addition to showing pain and harm, alternatives to violence are emphasized in this episode when Will pleads emotionally with Carlton to not become violent like the criminal who robbed them. For example, he tells Carlton that carrying a gun is not a solution to the problem.

Two other points are worth mentioning. This program contains only two violent interactions in spite of the fact that the entire plot focuses on violence. Moreover, the robber is never visually shown to the viewers, but rather is kept off-screen. Thus, there is no explicit visual depiction of the violent act. The other point is that NBC aired an anti-violence Public Service Announcement during one of the commercial breaks in this episode. Though this project does not include an analysis of commercial material, it is worth mentioning this instance because of the reinforcement value of showing an anti-violence PSA within an anti-violence program. The PSA features Eriq La Salle, an actor from *ER*, saying "Everyone has a right to get angry but you don't have a right to fight. Walk away. Chill. You win."

Music Video

The music video *You Gotta Be* by Ahmad aired on BET at 12:30 p.m. in our sample. This rap video tells the story of a young man who tries to resist his own gang's criminal behavior. After he is threatened by his fellow gang members, he reluctantly goes to a mini-mart with them and tries to rob the store. In the process, he is shot by the store clerk. The video then shows the man lying on the floor of the store as medics frantically work to save his life. In the next scene, he sings as he lays in his open casket. Meanwhile, his gang is arrested by the police and sent to prison. The gang members are then shown being assaulted in the prison by older inmates.

This 4-minute video uses the second and fourth way of emphasizing non-violence: the perpetrator shows reluctance while engaging in violence, and the violence is punished throughout the scenario. In this video, the young man is threatened into going along with his gang. As he rides in the car, he expresses anguish and concern. In addition, all of the perpetrators are seriously punished for their actions. The main character is killed and dramatically speaks from his coffin. The other gang members are immediately arrested and sent to prison. The lyrics remind the audience that all of this happened "cuz you gotta be rough ... gotta be tough."

Made-For-TV Movie

A Cry for Help was shown on the Lifetime channel at 5 p.m. It is based on the true story of Tracy Thurman who was tragically beaten by her husband. The movie was preceded by an advisory stating that it contains graphic scenes that may be "too intense for some viewers." The movie opens dramatically with Tracy's husband attacking her with a knife. Then the movie jumps back in time and tells how this couple met, fell in love, and married. The relationship is characterized from the beginning by threats and physical abuse. Though Tracy leaves her husband early on, the police do not treat her complaints very seriously and often do little to protect her against her husband. After Tracy's husband stalks her for months, he attacks her viciously, slashing her face and jumping on her neck as a policeman helplessly stands by. After the attack, the husband is sent to prison and Tracy then sues the police department. She wins the suit, and the case results in the passage of the "Thurman Law" in Connecticut, stipulating that police must treat domestic partners no differently than any other accused perpetrators of violence.

Unlike most of the other examples, this movie contains extensive and repeated violence. In fact, 12 different violent interactions were coded, and they all involved extensive violence. However, the movie also features a strong anti-violence theme. This theme is conveyed primarily through dramatic portrayals of the pain, fear, and suffering of the victims. Most notably, Tracy is terrorized throughout the movie by her husband, and even their baby son seems traumatized by his presence. In addition, close-ups of her painful bruises and black eyes are shown after each beating. In the husband's final attack, Tracy is seriously hurt, and her recovery in the hospital is depicted in graphic detail. At first she is paralyzed from the neck down. When she finally regains movement in her body, she limps when she walks and has no use of one arm. Moreover, an ugly scar runs down her face and neck. She spends so much time in the hospital that her son hardly recognizes her when she comes home. The violence also affects Tracy's friends and family, who agonize over the abuse and are frightened themselves of the violent husband.

In addition to painful consequences, an anti-violence theme is conveyed through the punishment of violence. Throughout the program, the husband is portrayed as a sick and possessive individual. Though the police do little at first, Tracy's friends publicly condemn the husband as does Tracy's attorney. In the end, the husband is sentenced to 20 years in prison for the attack. Furthermore, a second trial results in public condemnation of the police department for overlooking domestic abuse. The final scene provides a transition back to "real life" by reminding viewers that a new law was passed in Connecticut to ensure that domestic partners are arrested immediately for such abuse.

Theatrically-Released Movie

South Central was released in the theaters in 1992 and subsequently was aired by one of the premium channels in our sample. The movie aired on HBO, at 8 p.m. HBO clearly labeled the film as having received an R rating from the MPAA. In addition, HBO gave the film its own ratings indicating that it contained "violence, adult content, and graphic language." The movie tells the story of Bobby, an African American from South Central Los Angeles, who is a gang member. The movie opens as Bobby is released from the county jail and goes home to meet his newborn son. He resumes his gang activity soon thereafter, but because of his new responsibility as a father, he experiences reluctance and regret in his role as a gang member. After being threatened by a rival gang, Bobby gets involved in a violent shootout and is sent back to prison for killing a man. Over his years in prison, he agonizes about his young son who is becoming involved with gangs. Bobby finally gets out of prison after educating himself and vowing to give up violence. He then finds his son, promises to be a better father, and successfully urges his son to give up the gang affiliation.

Like *A Cry for Help*, this movie contains numerous violent events (19 violent interactions) but still conveys an overall anti-violence theme. In fact, the plot features all four of the ways that anti-violence can be shown. First, alternatives to violence are emphasized. In prison, Bobby meets a fellow inmate who teaches him to control his anger and to read the works of nonviolent heros. The inmate convinces Bobby that the only way to get out of prison and help his son is to eliminate violence from his life. Second, Bobby shows remorse when he engages in gang violence and seems to be struggling to avoid it in the early part of the movie. He even tries to stay away from his fellow gang members. Third, the painful consequences of violence are emphasized throughout. Bobby's girlfriend is unable financially or emotionally to raise her child alone while Bobby is in prison. She becomes addicted to drugs, and her 10-year-old son's involvement with the gang intensifies. While trying to steal a car radio, the son is shot in the back and almost dies. The movie portrays the son's slow and painful recovery in the hospital including several scenes of difficult physical therapy and repeated views of the large scar on his back. Fourth, the story line continually stresses immediate and harsh punishment for violence. Bobby is shown being released from county jail in the beginning of the movie and spends the latter half of it in prison. Prison life is portrayed as rough and full of violence. The movie is a good example of a multi-pronged effort at depicting the realistic and negative consequences of gang violence in society.

Summary of Results

This section provides an overview of the main findings of this project. Three questions guided our study: 1) How much violence is on television and where is it located? 2) What is the nature or context of violence on television? 3) How often is violence used in an educational or prosocial manner to promote an anti-violence message? In this summary section, we will focus on the most robust findings rather than detailing all the patterns across all the locator variables.

Presence of Violence

* 57% of coded programs contain some violence.
    * Premium cable is more likely to contain violence, whereas the broadcast networks and particularly public broadcasting are less likely.
    * Movies and drama series are more likely to contain violence, whereas comedy series, reality-based programs, music videos are less likely.

* About two thirds of the violence involves behavioral acts of aggression.
    * Only one third involves credible threats.
    * Very little involves harmful consequences of unseen violence.

Distribution of Violence

* About one third of violent programs contain nine or more violent interactions. The highest frequencies of violent interactions are found on:
        * premium cable and independent broadcast;
        * movies and reality-based programs.

Context or Nature of Violent Portrayals

* Perpetrators of violence are:
        * overwhelmingly human, adult in age, white, and male;
        * more often characterized as bad rather than good;
        * typically *not* heros.

* Targets of violence are similar to perpetrators.

* Most violence is committed for one of three reasons:
        * personal gain;
        * anger;
        * protection.

* Nearly half of the violence on television is portrayed as justified.

* Guns on television:
        * are used in about one quarter of all violent interactions;
        * are used most often in reality-based programs and drama series.

* How extensive is violence?
    * The majority of violent interactions involve *repeated* behavioral acts of aggression;
    * 16% of violent interactions include 10 or more acts of aggression against a victim.

* How graphic is violence?
  • Most violence is *not* shown in close-up shots.
  • Blood and gore are rarely shown on television.
  • Blood and gore are most often seen on premium cable, and in movies.

* How realistic is violence?
  • Very little of TV violence is based on actual events in the real world, but most events seem fairly realistic in that they *could* happen in real life.
  • Fantasy or unrealistic violence is rare except in children's series.

* Rewards and punishments:
  • The vast majority of violence is *not* punished at the time that it occurs within a scene.
  • Punishments more typically occur toward the end of the program, but only for bad characters.
  • Good characters who engage in violence are rarely punished at all.
  • Characters who engage in violence almost never show remorse.

* Consequences of violence:
  • Roughly half of the violent interactions on TV contain no observable harm or pain to the victim
  • Children's series contain the highest percentage of unrealistic depictions of harm.
  • Almost one third of violent programs portray *no* negative consequences of violence.
  • Very few programs depict the long-term negative repercussions of violence.

* Humor:
  • 39% of all violent scenes contain humor.
  • Humor is more often linked to violence in children's series and comedy series.

* Only 4% of all programs with violence feature a strong anti-violence theme.

Overall, our findings indicate that violence is more likely to be found on premium cable and within the genres of movies and drama series. However, the context of violence or the way in which it is portrayed does not differ substantially across channels or genres. Violence typically involves behavioral acts that are perpetrated by white males against other white males. Acts of aggression often are repeated and frequently involve guns. Violence is typically sanitized on television. It is rarely punished in the immediate context in which it occurs and it rarely results in observable harm to the victims. In fact, violence is often funny on television. In other words, the serious consequences of violence are frequently ignored.

Chapter 7

DISCUSSION

The previous chapter presented an inventory of results for individual context factors. In this chapter, we put these findings into perspective by synthesizing patterns across television programming overall as well as within particular genres and types of channels. To set the stage for this task, we revisit some of the basic background and goals of the study. We then present a synthesis of our findings, followed by a discussion of their implications for the three harmful effects of exposure to television violence: imitation/learning, fear, and desensitization. Next, we summarize where these risks are greatest according to our locator variables: program genre, type of channel, daypart, and type of day. We discuss the strengths and limitations of this study, and finally, we offer a set of recommendations to be considered by the television industry, policy-makers, and parents.

Background and Goals of Study

Concern about televised violence is an enduring issue with a long history. The roots of the concern precede the medium's existence, tracing back historically to early studies of motion pictures' influence on the audience. By the time television had penetrated most American households in the 1950s, Congress had already begun to hold hearings to address the issue, although little scientific evidence was available at the time to help inform the discussion. Since then, a great deal of research has been conducted on the influence of television violence on viewers.

Today, there is no longer a debate about the conclusion that television violence contributes to aggressive attitudes and behaviors, to desensitization, and to fear in many viewers. The level of agreement concerning this evidence is reflected in many recent major reports and policy documents that have reviewed all of the available research. These reports have, in turn, influenced public opinion on the issue and contributed to a heightened sense of urgency to seek steps to address the concerns about television violence.

We have designed a framework for analyzing violent depictions that is built on existing scientific knowledge about the impact of media violence. Our review of the research revealed nine contextual factors that heighten the risk of learning, desensitization and fear effects. These include: 1) the nature, or qualities of the perpetrator, 2) the nature of the target, or victim, 3) the reason for the violence, 4) the presence of weapons, 5) the extent and graphicness of the violence, 6) the degree of realism of the violence, 7) whether the violence is rewarded or punished, 8) the consequences of the violence, and 9) whether humor is involved in the violence. Rather than merely counting up all incidents of violence, thereby implicitly equating them with one another, we have strived to differentiate violent depictions according to these context features.

We recognize that in order to fully capture these contextual features in a content analysis, we must be sensitive to how these elements manifest themselves within a violent program. In particular, some context features occur at the level of interactions between characters. Others can be understood only by considering the entire program as a unit of analysis. For example, a victim might not express pain during a violent attack, but he or she may be portrayed later in the plot as suffering emotionally and financially. In other words, context factors often are revealed as a plot unfolds.

To accommodate these different aspects of a program, we have analyzed television content at three distinct levels: 1) how characters interact with one another when violence occurs (which we label a violent interaction); 2) how violent interactions are grouped together (which we label as a violent scene), and 3) how violence is presented in the context of the overall program (which we label program-level analysis). In sum, we have assessed violent depictions at multiple levels, taking into account the differing message characteristics that have been established by previous research as influential in shaping the effects of television violence.

Our goal in conducting this research is to provide the most thorough and elaborate description of the contextual elements associated with television violence yet produced by the scientific community. Our approach offers another important dimension too. By pursuing our content evaluation with an analytic framework that is grounded in existing knowledge about television violence effects, this study can do more than merely describe. Each of our contextual measures is associated with some degree of risk or benefit. Certain contextual elements in a violent portrayal may enhance the harmful effects of exposure, whereas others may ameliorate negative effects. Thus, we have the capability to differentiate depictions of violence most likely to cause concern from those portrayals that should be less problematic, if not in some cases even beneficial.

Summary of Major Findings

The full inventory of results was described in the previous chapter. Here, we synthesize all those individual results into a list of major findings. This list presents a general picture of the world of television violence. Figure 58 presents a summary of our findings for the television environment as a whole.

* Violence is found extensively across the television landscape.

The majority of programs (57%) in our composite sample of television contain some violence. When violence is found in a program, it is rarely an isolated, single occurrence. We observed more than 18,000 violent interactions across all programming. But only a small percentage (15%) of violent programs contain only one violent interaction. In contrast, one third of violent programs feature between five and eight violent interactions, and one third contain nine or more violent interactions.

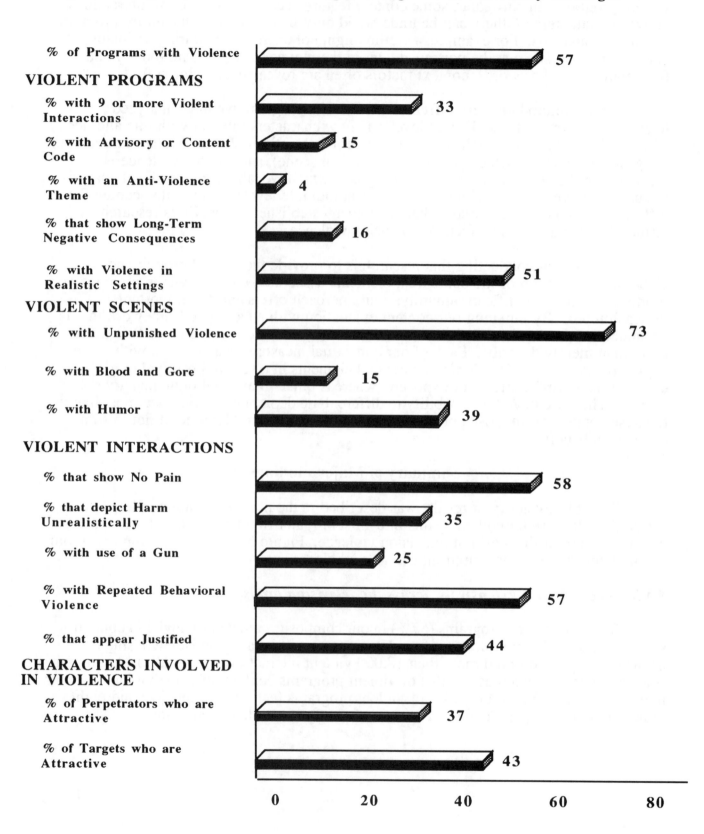

Figure 58
Major Findings Across Television Programming Overall: Industry Averages

% of Programs with Violence — 57

VIOLENT PROGRAMS

% with 9 or more Violent Interactions — 33

% with Advisory or Content Code — 15

% with an Anti-Violence Theme — 4

% that show Long-Term Negative Consequences — 16

% with Violence in Realistic Settings — 51

VIOLENT SCENES

% with Unpunished Violence — 73

% with Blood and Gore — 15

% with Humor — 39

VIOLENT INTERACTIONS

% that show No Pain — 58

% that depict Harm Unrealistically — 35

% with use of a Gun — 25

% with Repeated Behavioral Violence — 57

% that appear Justified — 44

CHARACTERS INVOLVED IN VIOLENCE

% of Perpetrators who are Attractive — 37

% of Targets who are Attractive — 43

0   20   40   60   80

* Warnings about violence are not often presented.

Among programs that contain violence, only 15% are preceded with any sort of advisory or content code. This figure seems very low given the substantial amount of violence on television, the sheer number of violent interactions within some programs, and the extent of behavioral aggression often shown.

* Despite the high frequency of violence on television, it is extremely rare for a program to emphasize an anti-violence theme.

Only 4% of all violent programs have a strong anti-violence theme. In order for a program to have been classified as having an anti-violence theme, it had to meet one of the following criteria: (1) alternatives to violent actions are presented throughout the program; (2) main characters repeatedly discuss the negative consequences of violence; (3) the physical pain and emotional suffering that results from violence are emphasized; or (4) punishments for violence clearly and consistently outweigh rewards. The study identified some noteworthy examples of each of these elements, but their overall presence in television programming was extremely low.

* In about three fourths of all violent scenes, perpetrators go unpunished.

Within a violent scene, perpetrators are rarely punished for their actions. In fact, perpetrators "get away" with violence in 73% of violent scenes. One of the clearest findings of this study is that a very high proportion of violent scenes lack any form of punishment for the perpetrators. This means the world of television is not only violent -- it also consistently sanctions its violence. We find a slightly different pattern, however, when the entire program is considered. Punishment is more frequently shown at the program level. A majority of bad characters (62%) are punished, though this occurs primarily toward the end of the plot. In contrast, good characters rarely are punished for engaging in violence. Thus, the characters with whom viewers, in particular children, are most likely to identify are rarely discouraged for acting aggressively at the time they engage in their violent behavior.

* Very little of the violence on television is graphic or explicit.

Only 3% of all scenes involve a close-up focus on violent acts, and only 2% include a close-up of the impact of violence on a victim's body. The large majority of violent scenes contain no blood and gore (85%), with very few (3%) depicting extreme amounts of bloodshed.

* Violence is often portrayed as humorous.

More than one third of all violent scenes portray aggression in a humorous context (39%). This could include anything from a perpetrator cracking a joke after engaging in violence to a slapstick depiction of aggression, though particular types of humor were not distinguished.

* In a high proportion of violence, the consequences are not portrayed realistically.

More than half of all violent interactions (58%) fail to show the victim experiencing any signs of pain. Furthermore, almost half of all violent interactions (47%) present no observable indication of harm to the victim.

In addition to measuring the harm actually depicted, we also estimated the likely harm that would occur if the same violence was enacted against a human in real life. A comparison of depicted harm with likely harm allows us to identify those portrayals that are unrealistic in their depiction of harm. For example, a farcical skit in which a character is hit over the head with a sledgehammer and walks away with only a small lump on the forehead would be classified as "mild" for depicted harm but "extreme" for likely harm in real life. Such a depiction would be coded as showing unrealistic harm. Overall, roughly one third of all violent interactions (35%) portray harm unrealistically.

The consequences of violence also were examined at the overall program level. Here, only 16% of all programs portray the serious, long-term consequences of violence, such as emotional, financial and physical suffering. In sum, characters often show no pain or harm at the time that violence occurs. And one third of the depictions actually depict harm unrealistically given the nature or seriousness of the violence. Very few programs deal with the long-term repercussions of violence to victims and their families.

* In one fourth of the violent interactions, a gun is used.

The most prevalent method to enact violence is by natural means (40%). However, when weapons are used handheld guns are the most common device. Handguns are the primary weapon in 25% of all violent interactions. Given the number of violent interactions observed across a single week of content on 23 channels, this means that literally thousands of examples of handgun use are portrayed on television each week.

* In a majority of violent interactions, the perpetrator engages in repeated acts of violence.

The perpetrator engages in multiple acts of behavioral violence in nearly 60% of all violent interactions. In other words, perpetrators hit, kick, punch, or shoot repeatedly when trying to harm a victim. Thus, our total of more than 18,000 violent interactions actually represents a much higher number of individual acts of violence.

* Nearly half of the violence on television appears justified.

For every violent interaction, the perpetrator's reason for violence was examined. The findings indicate that violence is mostly associated with three motives: personal gain (30%), such as obtaining money, power, or affection; protection of self and others (26%), which would include the actions of most police officers and heroes; and anger (24%). When collapsing these reasons in terms of justification, nearly half of the violent interactions portray violence that could be interpreted as justified (44%) and half portray it as unjustified (56%).

Attractive characters often are involved in violence.

Research suggests that viewers will identify with characters that are perceived as attractive or similar to themselves. We assessed characters in terms of how good or bad they are and in terms of their demographic characteristics. We defined a "good" character as one who considers the needs of others, whereas a "bad" character is motivated primarily by self-interest. Nearly half of all perpetrators are bad (45%), with about one fourth (24%) categorized as good. A much smaller proportion of perpetrators are *both* good and bad, or blended in nature (13%). Taken together, approximately 37% of the perpetrators of violence have some good qualities with which a viewer might identify (% of good plus % of blended).

Our findings suggest that almost one third of targets can be described as good characters (31%). Another third of the targets are bad characters (31%). Only 12% can be classified as both good and bad. Taken together, then, almost half of the victims of violence on television (43%) possess some good qualities that might encourage a viewer to identify with them.

Characters involved in violence also were coded for demographic characteristics. The typical perpetrator of violence on television is a human character (71%) whose apparent race is white (76%), age is adult (76%), and sex is male (78%). The target profile is almost identical to the perpetrator profile; targets are usually human characters (70%) who are white (77%), adult (72%), and male (75%).

Risks to Viewers

As we noted earlier in this report, there is general consensus that exposing viewers to media violence may result in at least three anti-social effects. Viewers may learn aggressive attitudes and behaviors from exposure to media violence. Research also indicates that continued exposure to violence in the mass media will undermine feelings of concern, empathy or sympathy viewers might have toward victims of actual violence (i.e., desensitization effects). Finally, the viewing of media violence can lead to fear reactions such as general fear of crime or victimization as well as immediate emotional fright. The results found for many of the contextual characteristics lead us to believe that violence on television is presented to viewers in a way that may produce learning of aggression, desensitization to violence and fear effects. We will now frame our discussion of the overall findings of this study in terms of these three effects.

Before proceeding with a discussion of the findings in light of these effects, one caveat should be mentioned. The implications of the present study for learning, desensitization, and fear effects are slightly less straightforward than we may prefer due to several gaps in the violence effects research literature. As we will note below, several of the contextual features that are important for one effect are equally important for another. In other words, contextual features that have potential learning effects or desensitization effects also have implications for fear effects in viewers. However, in at least one instance, a contextual feature that increases the likelihood of one effect additionally decreases the likelihood for another. That is, portrayals of unjustified violence may reduce the probability of learning aggression, yet increase the probability of a heightened fear response in viewers. Furthermore, the effects of several contextual factors are known only for one of the three harmful outcomes but not for all of them. Until more integrative research is conducted on the effects of media violence, we are left with no choice but to treat fear, learning and desensitization as independent effects.

Learning Aggressive Behavior

The findings of this study suggest that most violent portrayals on television have features that increase the potential for learning of aggression. First, a very high percentage (73%) of violent scenes do not show the perpetrator being punished for committing violence. Second, in a majority (58%) of the interactions, the target shows no pain. Third, in over half of the programs (51%), the violence is presented as plausible or possible in real life. Fourth, approximately 37% of the perpetrators of violence have some good qualities with which the viewers might identify. Finally, only 16% of programs with violence depict any long-term negative consequences.

Given this pattern of context variable findings, what are viewers likely to learn from these portrayals? The apparent message is that violence is not a particularly painful or harmful behavior even when engaged in multiple times. Further, viewers may learn that violence poses no long-term repercussions to the victim and his or her community at large. Finally, viewers are learning that those characters who commit violence are rarely punished for their actions.

The portrayal of rewards and punishments is probably the most important of all contextual factors for viewers as they interpret the meaning of what they see on television. Viewers who would otherwise think of a class of behaviors such as violence as bad, over time will learn that those behaviors are good (e.g., useful, successful, or desirable) if they are repeatedly and consistently portrayed as rewarded or unpunished.

From a developmental perspective, the timing of punishments can be particularly important for young child viewers. Younger children are likely to have difficulty linking the punishments at the end of a program with an earlier act that occurred at the outset of the show. Thus the violence will appear to go unpunished.

Finally, a substantial number of perpetrators of violence on television have characteristics with which the viewer may identify. The probability of aggressive behavior following exposure to media violence is increased when these characteristics are present.

Desensitization Effects

In the majority of interactions (57%), the perpetrator engages in an extensive amount or at least in repeated acts of violence. Further, a substantial portion of scenes involve humor (39%). Repeated exposure to extensive media violence may increase viewer desensitization and this effect is more likely when the violence is presented in a context in which it is trivialized or made humorous. This study suggests that there is a moderate possibility of desensitization effects for average viewers of televised violence. Yet, it should be noted that only a small percentage of scenes contain blood and gore (15%), which could also increase desensitization.

Fear Effects

A very high percentage (73%) of violent scenes do not show the perpetrator being punished for committing violence. This has implications for the learning of aggression, as we noted above, but it also has implications for fear effects. Research indicates that viewers shown violence that goes unpunished are significantly more likely to become anxious and possibly fearful. Viewers also are more likely to be frightened by television violence that is undeserved or targeted against innocent victims. Our study reveals that 44% of violent interactions are classified as justified. Conversely, 56% of violent interactions are unjustified. Although justified violence may increase learning effects, unjustified violence potentially increases fear effects. A majority of violent interactions also involve repeated acts of behavioral violence. As noted above, viewing extensive violence is likely to lead to desensitization. It is also likely to increase fear effects -- at least in the short term. Because most violent interactions (57%) involve repeated acts of behavioral violence, there is substantial likelihood of pervasive fear effects.

Only 8% of the programs in our study that include violence could be classified as "real life" events -- that is, events that truly happened in the real world. A substantial proportion of the programs (43%) fall into the fictional category, which includes programs that portray events that are at least possible in real life. The combination of these two categories (resulting in a total of 51%) offers a better indication of the amount of violence that appears realistic. When violent programming is perceived as realistic, it heightens the risk of a fear effect on the audience.

Summary of Effects Concerns

In summary, our findings reveal that the majority of programs contain at least some violence. Generally, violence portrayed on television goes unpunished and is not typically followed by depictions of pain or negative consequences for victims. When violence is shown, it is often repeated, and frequently is portrayed in a context that makes it seem humorous or trivial. Finally, most violent portrayals seem realistic as opposed to fantastic. Taken together, and viewed in light of the effects literature, these findings imply a substantial potential for learning of aggression, desensitization to violence, and fear among viewers who see televised violence. Unfortunately, within the television environment generally, there is little attempt to educate or warn the viewer about violence. A very small number of programs (4%) contain an anti-violence theme. Further, when one looks for warnings about violence across the television spectrum, few are found. Among programs that contain violence only 15% are preceded with an advisory or content code.

Profiles Across Locator Variables

Although the preceding sections address patterns throughout the television world in general, this section shifts the focus to our locator variables to identify where the risks are highest and lowest. Our three locator variables are: (1) the source of the content, represented by channel type; (2) the type of content, represented by commonly understood categories of television programs, or genres; and (3) the scheduling of the content, distinguishing patterns that vary by different times of day or days of the week (i.e., weekdays vs. weekends).

Profile of Violence Across Channel Types

The sample of programming examined in the study encompasses most major sources of television content available to the American public: broadcast networks, public broadcast, independent broadcast, basic cable, and premium cable. Table 13 presents a graphical summary of differences across types of channels. The left-hand column of numbers reflects the overall industry-wide average for each variable indicated. Deviations from those overall averages are indicated for each channel type by symbols that reflect any meaningful deviation from the norm.

Moderate deviations (represented in the table by one circle) are defined as a difference of between 10-19 percentage points above or below the industry-wide average on any measure. Substantial deviations (represented in the table by two circles) require a difference of at least 20 percentage points from the average. We use symbols rather than numbers in order to make the patterns as easy as possible to discern. The darkened symbols represent deviations from the industry norms that hold adverse implications -- that is, they increase the risk of a harmful effects to viewers. The clear symbols represent deviations from industry norms in a positive, or socially desirable direction.

Broadcast networks. The broadcast networks feature a lower proportion of programs with violence compared to the industry norm. They are also less likely to contain program with numerous violent interactions. However, across most of the contextual variables their programming is close to the industry average. The only deviation is in the use of program advisories and content codes. In particular, broadcast networks are less likely to feature these messages than the industry average.

Public broadcast. PBS has the lowest overall percentage of programs with violence. It also is moderately less likely to present show with numerous violent interactions. Public broadcast also presents more than the average amount of programs with anti-violence themes. It is particularly strong in two areas: avoiding humor associated with violence, and avoiding violence that depicts harm unrealistically. The major concern associated with public broadcast is that it presents substantially more than the average percentage of its violence in realistic settings.

TABLE 13 : PROFILE OF VIOLENCE ACROSS CHANNEL TYPE

	Overall %	Broadcast Networks	Public Broadcast	Independent Broadcast	Basic Cable	Premium Cable
Programs with Violence	57	○	○○	◉	◉	●●

Of Those Programs That Contain Violence. . .

% with 9 or more **Violent Interactions**	33	○	○	●	◉	●●
% with Advisory or **Content Code**	15	●	◉	◉	●	○○
% with an Anti- **Violence Theme**	4	◉	○	◉	◉	◉
% that Show Long-term **Negative Consequences**	16	◉	◉	◉	◉	○
% with Violence in **Realistic Settings**	51	◉	●●	○	◉	●●

Of Those Scenes That Contain Violence. . .

% with Unpunished **Violence**	73	◉	◉	◉	◉	◉
% with **Blood & Gore**	15	◉	◉	◉	◉	●
% with **Humor**	39	◉	○○	◉	◉	◉

When a Violent Interaction Occurs. . .

% that Show **No Pain**	58	◉	●	◉	◉	◉
% that Depict **Unrealistic Harm**	35	◉	○○	◉	◉	○
% with **Use of a Gun**	25	◉	◉	◉	◉	◉
% with Repeated **Behavioral Violence**	57	◉	◉	◉	◉	◉
% that **Appear Justified**	44	◉	◉	◉	◉	◉

Of those Characters Involved in Violence . . .

% of Perpetrators **who are Attractive**	37	◉	◉	◉	◉	◉
% of Targets **who are Attractive**	43	◉	◉	◉	◉	◉

○○ = Substantially Better than Industry Average
○   = Moderately Better than Industry Average
◉   = Industry Average
●   = Moderately Worse than Industry Average
●● = Substantially Worse than Industry Average

Independent broadcast. Independent broadcast differs from industry averages in two important ways. First, they are moderately above the norm in presenting programs with a high number of violent interactions. Second, they are moderately below the norm in presenting violence in realistic settings.

Basic cable. On all of the key measures assessing the nature and amount of violence, basic cable channels are close to the industry-wide average with one exception. Basic cable is less likely that the industry norm to present advisories or content codes for violent programming.

Premium cable. Premium cable channels presents the highest proportion of violent programs. It is also the most likely to feature programs with numerous violent interactions. However, premium cable channels are substantially better than average at providing advisories or content codes for violent programming. The substantial risk factor associated with their violent programming is that a high proportion of it is presented in realistic settings. They are also moderately high in presenting programs with blood and gore. On the positive side, premium cable is moderately better than the norm at showing long-term negative consequences of violence and in avoiding shows that depict harm unrealistically.

Profile of Violence Across Program Genres

The sample of content examined in the study encompasses the complete diversity of television programming, with the exceptions noted previously of news, sports, and a handful of show types that would be unlikely to include any violence (e.g., game shows, religious programming). We have organized our sample of programs into six basic types, or genres: drama series, comedies, children's series, movies, reality-based content, and music videos. Table 14 presents the findings by the genre locator variable.

Notice that in Table 14 that there are more deviations from the industry-wide norm across genres than there are across channel types. It is not surprising that different genres exhibit different treatments of violence because they tend to revolve around different formulas in terms of plot and characterization. Because most channel types exhibit several different genres on a regular basis, the differences may be "washed out" in a channel type comparison.

Drama series. Dramas are moderately more likely to contain violence than the industry average. They also are more likely to feature numerous violence interactions and to depict the use of guns. Dramatic series are substantially more likely to portray violence in realistic settings. This genre's strong points involve portraying the long-term consequences of violence, avoiding unrealistic depictions of harm, and in particular avoiding humor with violence.

TABLE 14: PROFILE OF VIOLENCE ACROSS PROGRAM GENRE

	Overall %	Drama Series	Comedy Series	Children's Series	Movies	Reality Based	Music Videos
Programs with Violence	57	●	○○	◉	●●	○○	○○
Of Those Programs That Contain Violence. . .							
% with 9 or more Violent Interactions	33	●	○○	○	●●	●●	○○
% with Advisory or Content Code	15	●	●	●	○○	◉	●
% with Anti-Violence Theme	4	◉	◉	◉	◉	◉	◉
% that Show Long-term Negative Consequences	16	○	◉	●	○○	◉	◉
% with Violence in Realistic Settings	51	●●	●●	○○	●●	●●	●●
Of Those Scenes That Contain Violence . . .							
% with Unpunished Violence	73	◉	◉	◉	◉	◉	◉
% with Blood & Gore	15	◉	◉	○	●	◉	◉
% with Humor	39	○○	●●	●●	○	○○	○○
When a Violent Interaction Occurs . . .							
% that Show No Pain	58	◉	◉	●	◉	●	●
% that Depict Unrealistic Harm	35	○	◉	●●	○	○	◉
% with Use of a Gun	25	●	◉	○	◉	●	◉
% with Repeated Behavioral Violence	57	◉	◉	◉	◉	●	◉
% that Appear Justified	44	◉	◉	◉	◉	◉	○
Of those Characters Involved in Violence . . .							
% of Perpetrators who are Attractive	37	◉	◉	◉	◉	○	○
% of Targets who are Attractive	43	◉	◉	◉	◉	○	○○

○○ = Substantially Better than Industry Average
○ = Moderately Better than Industry Average
◉ = Industry Average
● = Moderately Worse than Industry Average
● ● = Substantially Worse than Industry Average

Comedy series. Not surprisingly, comedy series are substantially less likely to include violence and less likely to feature numerous violent interactions. These shows are substantially worse in terms of presenting violence in a humorous context, and presenting violence in realistic settings.

Children's series. Children's programs are 9% above the overall average for the percentage of programs with violence, which just missed our 10% criterion for differences that would be considered meaningful. The risk factors for this genre are the use of humor with violence, unrealistic depictions of the harms of violence, failing to show pain from victims of violence, and failing to show the long-term consequences of violence. The positive aspects are that blood and gore are moderately below average, as is violence involving guns. The one substantially positive element is that most depictions of violence avoid realistic settings, although the importance of this factor is minimized by our knowledge that younger children lack have difficulty discriminating fantasy from reality in television programming.

Movies. Movies as a genre have the highest percentage of programs with violence and the highest proportion of programs with numerous violent interactions. Movies portray violence in realistic settings much more than the norm and depict graphic blood and gore moderately above average. The positive features of movies are that long-term consequences are portrayed substantially more often, and that humorous violence and unrealistic harm are avoided. Movies are the most likely to receive an advisory or content code (note this does not include an MPAA rating) of any genre.

Reality-based programs. This genre includes news magazines, documentaries, and talk shows as well as police-based reality programs. The diversity of the genre helps to explain why this category includes a substantially lower than average proportion of shows (30%) containing violence. However, those programs that do contain violence are substantially more likely to feature numerous violent interactions and with those interactions, repeated acts of behavioral violence. Other risk factors in this genre include depictions of violence in realistic settings, depictions of violence without victim pain, and depictions of violence involving guns. The positive aspects are that these programs are below average in the use of humorous violence, unrealistic depictions of harm, and depictions of violence featuring attractive perpetrators and targets.

Music videos. Slightly less than one third of music videos (31%) contain any violence, which is substantially below the overall average. Each music video is considered a discrete narrative unit or segment, and most of these are relatively short in length. This helps account for the finding that this genre is substantially less likely to present numerous violent interactions within each segment. Risks associated with context include a high proportion of violence in realistic settings and depictions of violence that show no pain. The positive aspects are that the videos avoid violence with humor, avoid violence that appears justified, and are below average in depicting attractive perpetrators and targets of violence.

Differences in Violence by Scheduling

Surprisingly little variation that could be considered meaningful was observed across the overall schedule in the nature and amount of violence on television. The few areas with any important differences are reported here.

Day-part. An examination across day-parts indicates that the prevalence of violence generally holds very close to the overall average of 57%. The one exception is that weekday early mornings (6:00-9:00 a.m.) are moderately lower, averaging only 45% of all programs containing violence.

In terms of content attributes, violent fantasy programs are found at certain times in the schedule more than others. These shows, which depict the lowest level of realism in their portrayals of violence, tend to air during the mornings on both weekdays and weekends. This scheduling pattern is presumably due to the concentration of children's series during the early morning hours. Animated fantasy violence is concentrated in the early morning hours before children go to school (6:00-9:00 a.m.) and then declines throughout the day.

In addition, humor is featured in violent scenes more often during the early morning hours, and less often during prime-time hours.

Day. Late afternoons (3:00-6:00 p.m.) on weekends (68%) are substantially above average in programs that contain violence.

Conclusions About Patterns of Violence by Source, Content, and Scheduling

There are some notable differences in the presentation of violence across channels. Public broadcasting is less likely to feature programs with violence, and when violent depictions are included they are frequently presented in a manner that reduces their risk of harmful effects. The broadcast networks have a smaller percentage of programs with violence than the industry average. Yet when violence is included, the context of those portrayals is not any different than that found across television overall. Violence is found most frequently and in greater amounts on premium cable channels. Although violence is higher on premium cable, it is noteworthy that these channels in large part present advisories and content codes that identify their violent material. This practice is in contrast to other sources, which tend to employ violence advisories infrequently if at all.

Moving past the cross-channel differences in the prevalence of violence and the use of advisories, perhaps the most striking finding is the overall lack of variation across channels in the contextual aspects of televised violence. Notwithstanding a small number of notable exceptions (e.g., public broadcasting is much better than the rest of the industry at avoiding violence with humor and at avoiding unrealistic depictions of harm), there is very little diversity in the contextual aspects of violence across channel types. With only occasional exceptions, the context of televised violence follows the consistent pattern that was documented in the analysis above that assessed television programming as a whole.

There is more substantial variation in the nature and amount of violence associated with the six genre categories this study examined. For example, children's programming is the worst overall in depicting the long-term negative consequences of violence and in portraying unrealistically low levels of harm. Other distinctive differences include: movies depict blood and gore most often; violence involving handguns appears most frequently in drama and reality-based programs; and violence in music videos is relatively low and avoids a number of contextual risk factors such as humor, violence without pain, and violence that appears justified.

It should be noted that the pattern of findings for channel type and genre are sometimes related. Consider these two key findings. First, at the level of channel type differences, premium cable presents programming with violence more often than other channels, and also presents programming with a greater number of violent interactions than other channels. Second, at the level of content differences, movies as a genre contain violence more often than other program categories and also contain a greater number of violent interactions than other program types. Given that premium cable programming consists largely of movies, the channel type findings naturally mirror the patterns that exist for that particular type of content. And given the length of movies compared to most other television genres that employ 30 or 60 minute formats, it is not surprising that movies rank the highest in terms of number of violent interactions per program.

Finally, very few differences in the patterns of violence were found across day-part and type of day. Most important here is that there are no substantial differences in levels of violence during prime-time as compared to other times of day when children are more likely to be viewing without adult supervision.

Strengths and Limitations of the Study

Overview of Strengths of the Project

This content analysis of violence has several unique strengths. Below we list several methodological and conceptual features of this project that merit attention.

The large amount of television content examined. The first strength of this project is that its analysis is based on an extremely large sample of programs. Our sampling process captured a total of 3185 programs; with exclusions for content not included in the study (e.g., news, sports), we analyzed a total of 2693 programs. That amount is roughly 20 times larger than any previously published scientific content analysis of television violence of which we are aware. In general, larger samples of programming are superior to smaller ones, because the inclusion of a wider range of programs makes the sample more likely to be representative of the total population of television programming.

The sampling procedure. We have constructed a method of selecting our programs in a purely random manner. Unlike other studies that typically tape a day or week of intact programming, we selected each individual program randomly from the population of all programs appearing from October 1994 to June 1995. Therefore our sample involves thousands of *independent* sampling units (programs) rather than the traditional one (i.e., day) or seven independent units (i.e., days) used in other studies. This insures that our composite of programs is representative of television programming generally and greatly reduces the possibility of misleading findings due to anomalous days or weeks in which violence might be abnormally high or low.

Violence in context. We have moved the focus of research away from simple counts of violent acts and place it instead on the implications of the violence for harmful effects as indicated by certain contextual factors. In this study we analyzed violence on a myriad of levels. Our selection of contextual factors grew out of an exhaustive survey of the entire body of scientific evidence on the effects of television violence on viewer behavior. Among the factors included in our analysis are the nature of the perpetrator and target, the reason for violence, the presence of weapons, the extent and graphicness of violence, the realism of violence, the rewards and punishments associated with the violence, consequences of the violence, and the presence of humor. We have concentrated on these contextual features because they are associated with violent depictions that increase the risk of a harm to the audience -- specifically, learning and imitation effects, desensitization effects, and fear effects. The importance of these factors and these effects has been confirmed by public health organizations such as American Psychological Association, the National Academy of Science, and the Centers for Disease Control.

Definition of violence. Our definition of violence places emphasis on three key elements: intention to harm, the physical nature of the harm, and the involvement of animate beings. This conceptualization of violence has the advantage of moving beyond a narrow focus on behavioral acts to include credible threats of violence and instances of harmful consequences of unseen violence. This definition insures that depictions classified as violent represent actual physical aggression directed against living beings. This is a strength because it renders our definition an appropriately conservative measure of violence on television compared to other content analyses.

Multiple units of analysis. In order to capture thorough information about the context of each violent act, it is essential that acts of violence not be viewed in isolation. One of the fundamental strengths of this study is that each act is considered as part of an ongoing exchange between characters, and each exchange between characters is situated within the larger setting of a scene and, ultimately, a program. With this approach, we can capture microscopic details as well as macroscopic concepts embedded in the content under examination.

Procedures for establishing coder reliability. In employing a content analysis methodology, researchers must demonstrate that coders have made decisions consistently. If coders are asked to view the same program, they should apply the definitions and measures of violence in the same way and their resulting judgments regarding the presence or absence of violence should show high agreement. The strength of this study is that we tested for the reliability of coders in several phases. First, we tested our training procedures to determine if television viewers could apply our coding rules. Second, we systematically checked the quality to make certain our data base was of high quality. To do this, we checked for consistency among coders in determining the presence of violence in a program, unitizing, and selecting values on the coding variables. Third, we continually monitored coder performance through the entire length of the coding phase of the project in order to identify any coder fatigue.

Capability for longitudinal analyses. We feel confident that we have measured violence with a set of precise, robust and well conceptualized contextual variables applied to a representative sample of television programs. Only by accomplishing this in the first year of analyses is it possible to accurately compare changes in programming over time from year to year. Laying this foundation allows us to follow through systematically with our procedures and measure trends precisely from this base in the future.

Acknowledgment of Limitations

No study is without its limitations and ours is no exception. We describe five of the most important limitations below.

Exclusion of other elements of context. Our choice of contextual variables is circumscribed in the sense that we deliberately focused on only those factors that have been identified in the scientific literature as contributing to our three effects of concern -- imitation, desensitization and fear. Otherwise, we might have examined additional variables. For example, many scholars have argued that television violence should be understood in the context of gender relations, or in light of institutional racism, or with regard to the fact that television programming is a product of a particular political or economic system. We chose not to investigate the content of television from any of these perspectives. Our study is more narrowly focused on public health effects. Undoubtedly, much of the richness associated with locating television violence within larger societal institutions is lost by using this approach. We will leave it to others to supplement our analyses with assessments at other levels.

No focus on verbal aggression. We recognize that some forms of harmful violence may involve verbal rather than physical abuse. However, we were uncomfortable with the prospect of including this form of violence in our analyses. There are two reasons for our position. First, the scientific literature on the effects of exposure to verbal violence does not clearly establish harmful effects, in part because of the lack of attention devoted to the topic. Second, the need to clearly define at an operational level the boundaries of what verbal behaviors would be considered "violent" likely poses an insurmountable obstacle to measuring such actions.

No evaluation of certain types of programs for violence. The genres of news, sports, religious programming, game shows, instructional shows, and home shopping were excluded from our analyses by our contract with the National Cable Television

Association. Consequently, the program services CNN and ESPN were omitted entirely from the study. Some may argue that sports programming is extremely violent and that this genre should have been included in our analyses. Certainly it is important to consider news programming in assessing the overall levels of violence on television, notwithstanding the fact that simple prescriptions about reducing the levels of violence could never be easily applied to news content because of its important informational function for society. We agree that news programs warrant analyses and recommend that this be pursued in the future.

Our coders are drawn from a narrow segment of the population. The coders employed for this study are students at the University of California, Santa Barbara. Thus, the full spectrum of possible economic, cultural, racial, and social backgrounds are not well represented in our group of coders. This is a potential disadvantage because the perceptions of any communication content are influenced by each individual's background and life experiences, and the work of coding is essentially recording the perceptions that one derives from television, albeit within a highly structured measurement framework. To the extent that our judgments are susceptible to socio-cultural influence, a more diverse group of coders may have provided a more representative viewpoint for interpreting television content.

Unreliability of certain variables. Although our reliability coefficients are generally excellent (87% of the median reliabilities were stronger than .80), several were somewhat weak. For example, the punishment of bad characters (.64) and punishment of good characters (.63) variables defined the low end of our range of median reliability coefficients. We should point out that other content analyses of violence regard coefficients as small as .60 as acceptable.

Recommendations

The findings of this particular study, coupled with the extensive body of research evidence upon which the content analysis is based, provide a foundation for some general prescriptions that could improve the current situation. The recommendations offered here address several different audiences for this report: the television industry, public policy-makers, and parents, all of whom have an important interest in the topic of television violence.

For the Television Industry

* Produce more programs that avoid violence; if a program does contain violence, keep the number of violent incidents low.

No one can ignore the issue of the overall amount of violence that exists on television, and the cumulative exposure to violence that average viewers inevitably encounter. We do not advocate that all violence be eliminated from television, nor do we profess to know exactly how much is "too much." We trust that interested observers will monitor changes over time in the levels of violence that are measured by this study and will encourage appropriate efforts to limit the presentation of televised violence. Our recommendation is simply to begin efforts to cut back.

This is indeed a long term goal. The amount of violence on television has been high since its beginnings almost 50 years ago. A substantial reduction in the amount of violence will not happen in one or two years. It will take time for the television industry to accept that the American viewing public will enjoy programming with lower amounts of violence. In the short term, we suggest that producers working in those genres where violence is particularly high (movies, drama series, and reality-based shows) begin working to bring their levels of violence closer to the industry averages. This, of course, would begin to reduce that industry average, and over time would contribute to lower norms for the overall level of televised violence.

* Be creative in showing ...   **- more violent acts being punished.**

- more negative consequences -- both short and long-term -- for violent acts.

- more alternatives to the use of violence in solving problems.

- less justification for violent actions.

This recommendation recognizes that violence is not likely to be declared "off limits." Our focus is on promoting its presentation, when violence is deemed essential, in a manner that should reduce its risk of negative influence on the audience. Much of the portrayal of violence on television is formulaic, a finding that is reflected in the consistency of some of our results on the contextual variables. We encourage producers to move beyond the "old formula" where a bad character stirs things up with repeated acts of violence; where the suffering of victims is seldom shown; and where the bad character continually gets away with the violent action until a good character retaliates with violence of his or her own.

* When violence is presented, consider greater emphasis on a strong anti-violence theme.

There are a number of ways to do this. Among the most obvious are: (1) present alternatives to violent actions throughout the program; (2) show main characters repeatedly discussing the negative consequences of violence; (3) emphasize the physical pain and emotional suffering that results from violence; and (4) show that punishments for violence clearly and consistently outweigh rewards.

* Increase the use of program advisories or content codes before violent programming.

We realize that an audience exists for violent programming, and that such shows will persist to some degree. Many violent programs pose a risk to the audience and that risk should be communicated as clearly as possible. Premium channels consistently provide program advisories, but there are many violent programs on other types of channels that are not identified for the audience. When we recommend warnings, we do not mean a simple statement that the program contains violence. Rather, we suggest something more substantial and specific that warns potential viewers about the context of the violence in addition to its presence.

For Public Policy-makers

This study was stimulated in large part because of the current policy debate about violence on television. Numerous policy alternatives have been proposed, including the V-chip technology, a "safe harbor" approach that would channel violent programming to certain hours of the day, and a violence report card that would identify the sponsors of violent programming. This study does not argue for or against any specific proposal to address the issue. Rather, it provides information to help policy-makers better understand the problems associated with violence on television. It also establishes a benchmark for comparisons over time in the levels of televised violence.

Because our data are oriented more to specifying the nature and extent of the problem of televised violence than to identifying the most appropriate solution, we cannot endorse any specific policy proposal. Our recommendations to policy-makers are therefore at a more fundamental level.

* Continue to monitor the nature and extent of violence on television.

Evidence of the harmful effects associated with televised violence is well established overall and well documented in the initial sections of this study. The stakes are high in terms of the social implications in this realm not so much because of the strength of the effects of viewing violence but more because of the fact that most everyone watches, most people watch a lot, and most of television contains violence. The effects are pervasive and cumulative. The importance of the issue warrants continued attention to help sensitize the television industry as well as to help alert and inform the public.

* Recognize that context is an essential aspect of television violence.

Treating all acts of violence as if they are the same disregards a rich body of scientific knowledge about media effects. An appreciation of key contextual factors is crucial for understanding the impact of televised violence on the audience. Furthermore, an appreciation of these elements may contribute to more effective policies should any regulatory action be pursued. At the base of any policy proposal in this realm is the need to define violence and, assuming that not all violence is to be treated equally, to differentiate types of violent depictions that pose the greatest cause for concern. This requires the careful consideration of the contextual elements we have identified in this study.

For Parents

The ultimate consumers of the information in this report are the nation's television viewers. Of particular concern are parents of young children, who often express helplessness in the face of 50 channels of programming across seven days a week. Our study was originally crafted and designed to help families make more informed decisions about television violence, and toward this end we have several recommendations for parents.

* Be aware of the three potential risks associated with viewing television violence.

Evidence of the potential harmful effects associated with viewing violence on television is well established and fully documented in this report. Most attention has been devoted to the impact of television violence on the learning of aggressive attitudes and behaviors. Though not all children will imitate media violence, certain children who are exposed to repeated depictions of a particular nature are at risk for such learning. Arguably more pervasive and often underemphasized are the other two risks associated with television violence: fear and desensitization. A clear understanding of these three effects will help parents to appreciate the role of television in children's socialization.

* Consider the context of violent depictions in making viewing decisions for children.

As demonstrated in this study, not all violent portrayals are the same. Some depictions pose greater risks for children than do others, and some may even be educational. When considering a particular program, think about whether violence is rewarded or punished, whether heroes or good characters engage in violence, whether violence appears to be justified or morally sanctioned, whether the serious negative consequences of violence are portrayed, and whether humor is used.

* Consider your child's developmental level when making viewing decisions.

Throughout this study, we underscore the important of the child's developmental level or cognitive ability in making sense of television. Very young children are less able to distinguish reality from fantasy on television. Thus, for preschoolers and younger elementary schoolers, animated violence, cartoon violence, and fantasy violence cannot be dismissed or exonerated because it is unrealistic. Indeed, many younger children strongly identify with superheroes and fantastic cartoon characters who regularly engage in violence. Furthermore, younger children have difficulty connecting nonadjacent scenes together and drawing causal inferences about the plot. Therefore, punishments, pain cues, or serious consequences of violence that are shown later in a program, well after the violent act, may not be comprehended fully by a young child.

For younger viewers, then, it is particularly important that contextual features like punishment and pain be shown *within* the violent scene.

* Recognize that different program genres and channel types pose different risks for children.

Our findings suggest that children's series may be particularly problematic, especially for younger viewers. Such programming is characterized by unrealistic depictions of harm, frequent use of humor in the context of violence, and little attention to the long-term negative consequences of violence. Although it is tempting for adults to dismiss cartoons as fantasy, these contextual features enhance the risk of imitation of aggression for younger viewers. In addition to genre differences, the type of channel has important ramifications for violence. Premium cable contains more violence than the industry norm, but it also depicts the serious consequences of violence more often. In contrast, public broadcast contains less violence overall. These differences should be taken into account when planning a family's media environment and viewing habits.

* Watch television with your child and encourage critical evaluation of the content.

Of all the recommendations we could make, perhaps the most important is to watch television with your child. The only way to ensure that a child appreciates the contextual aspects of violence is to teach a child while viewing. Parents can help a child to understand that violence in the real world may result in more serious injury and may have more long-term repercussions than what is shown on television. Parents also can help children to recognize that there non-violent strategies exist for solving problems in society.

Appendix 1

National Television Violence Study

Sample of Programs for Content Analysis

1994 - 1995

NATIONAL TELEVISION VIOLENCE STUDY

SAMPLE OF PROGRAMS FOR CONTENT ANALYSIS

The following scheduling grid displays the 3,185 programs that were randomly sampled across 23 channels from the time period of October 1994 to June 1995. Of the total 3,185 programs, 15% were classified as religious programs, game shows, infomercials, instructional shows or breaking news. As specified by contract with the National Cable Television Association, these five program types were not coded, but were included in the sample so that a representative week of television programming could be compiled. A total of 130 programs (4%) were removed from the sample due to taping errors or other technical problems. The time slots they occupy on the grid are left blank. The total number of programs coded for violence is 2,693.

Overlap among programs within time slots occurs in the composite week due to the sampling procedure employed. Approximately 14% of programs in the sample overlap with other programs. Program overlap is shaded gray on the grid. All statistical comparisons are based on proportions, therefore the effects of program overlap are controlled for in the study's analyses. For further explication of the sampling procedures see the Methods section of the UCSB Scientific Paper.

Legend for Scheduling Grid

Δ = ADVISORY

Advisories refer to those short messages that precede programs. Advisories can take a variety of forms, but typically involve advocating caution or discretion regarding the upcoming program (e.g., "viewer discretion advised"). Most of these messages are communicated both orally and by the display of written text.

¥ = MOTION PICTURE ASSOCIATION OF AMERICA (MPAA) RATING

MPAA Ratings refer to those ratings given to movies by the Motion Picture Association of America. The only MPAA ratings that were observed in this sample were "G: General audiences," "PG: Parental discretion advised," "PG-13: Parents strongly cautioned," and "R: Restricted."

«» = VIOLENCE CODE

Violence codes refer to those specific content codes developed to indicate the nature of the content to appear in the program. Although the codes used in the sample apply to language, adult content, nudity, and rape, as well as violence, only the violence codes are displayed on the grid. They are "MV: Mild violence," "V: Violence," and "GV: Graphic violence."

A&E	SATURDAY	SUNDAY	MONDAY	TUESDAY	WEDNESDAY	THURSDAY	FRIDAY
6:00 am	Behind the Veil... Nuns 5/6	Breakfast with the Arts 1/22	McCloud 10/31	Columbo 10/25	McCloud 2/8	McMillan & Wife 11/3	Columbo 5/26
6:30 am							
7:00 am	Civil War Journal 10/22		McCloud 3/20				
7:30 am				Columbo 5/23			
8:00 am	David L. Wolper Presents 11/5	All My Sons 1/15	Remington Steele 1/30		Banacek 5/24	Remington Steele 2/9	Remington Steele 5/12
8:30 am							
9:00 am	20th Century 10/15		Police Story 3/13	Police Story 2/14	Police Story 5/17	Police Story 6/1	Police Story 11/11
9:30 am							
10:00 am	Investigative Reports 3/4	Funeral In Berlin 10/30	Rockford Files 4/24	Rockford Files 3/7	Rockford Files 1/25	Rockford Files 5/4	Rockford Files 10/14
10:30 am							
11:00 am	American Justice 3/11		△ Columbo 1/16	McCloud 3/14	McMillan & Wife 10/26	Columbo 10/13	McCloud 12/9
11:30 am							
12:00 pm	Last Day 4/22	Road Games 2/5					
12:30 pm			Columbo 1/23	Banacek 4/25	Remington Steele 10/19	Remington Steele 3/23	Remington Steele 6/2
1:00 pm							
1:30 pm							
2:00 pm	The Lindbergh Kidnapping Case 1/14	Time Machine 10/9	Lou Grant 2/6	Lou Grant 1/24	Lou Grant 5/31	Lou Grant 3/16	Lou Grant 10/28
2:30 pm							
3:00 pm		In Search Of 12/4	Police Story 5/1	Police Story 11/8	Police Story 3/15	Police Story 1/26	Police Story 4/28
3:30 pm							
4:00 pm	Home Again 1/21		Rockford Files 10/17	Rockford Files 10/11	Rockford Files 11/2	Rockford Files 2/16	Rockford Files 10/21
4:30 pm							
5:00 pm	The Mountain Men 3/18	Money for Nothing 10/23	Biography 3/6	Biography 11/1	Biography 6/7	Biography 3/9	Biography 2/17
5:30 pm							
6:00 pm			Sherlock Holmes 5/8	Inspector Morris 10/18	American Justice 11/9	Atlantic Record Story 10/20	Investigative Reports 3/17
6:30 pm							
7:00 pm		Civil War Journal 3/5	Lovejoy 5/15				Ancient Mysteries 2/3
7:30 pm							
8:00 pm	Evening at the Improv 1/28	Caroline's Comedy Hour 1/29	Law & Order 2/13	Law & Order 3/21	Law & Order 10/12	Law & Order 1/19	Law & Order 1/27
8:30 pm							
9:00 pm	Seven Days in May 2/11	Cuban Missile Crisis 10/16	Biography 10/10	Biography 1/31	Biography 1/18	Biography 10/27	Biography 3/24
9:30 pm							
10:00 pm			Sherlock Holmes Mysteries 11/7	Winds of War 5/2	American Justice 2/15	The Last Years of Marvin Gaye 2/2	Investigative Reports 6/9
10:30 pm							

Key: △ Advisory   ¥ MPAA Rating   «» Violence Code

162

ABC	SATURDAY	SUNDAY	MONDAY	TUESDAY	WEDNESDAY	THURSDAY	FRIDAY
6:00 am	Pigasso's Place 10/22	Topper 2/5	News 5/1	News 11/8	News 11/9	News 6/1	News 1/27
6:30 am	Kid's View 2/4	Main Floor 2/5					
7:00 am	Sonic the Hedgehog 2/11	Infomercial 6/4	Good Morning America 3/20	Good Morning America 2/7	Good Morning America 5/10	Good Morning America 10/27	Good Morning America 10/28
7:30 am	Free Willy 3/18	Infomercial 6/4					
8:00 am	Cryptkeeper 3/4	Good Morning America Sunday 1/22					
8:30 am	Reboot 3/4						
9:00 am	Bump in the Night 3/11	Vista L.A. 1/29	Regis & Kathie Lee 5/8	Regis & Kathie Lee 10/11	Regis & Kathie Lee 5/3		Regis & Kathie Lee 2/17
9:30 am	Fudge 3/11	Front Runners 3/19					
10:00 am	Bugs Bunny & Tweety 10/22	L.A. Extra 5/14	Mike & Maty 3/6		Mike & Maty 2/1	Mike & Maty 5/4	Mike & Maty 12/9
10:30 am		Vista L.A. 5/21					
11:00 am	Cro 1/28	Wall Street Journal 10/9	Loving 5/29	Loving 5/16	Loving 10/26	Loving 10/27	Loving 5/5
11:30 am	Weekend Special 2/4	This Week 10/23	News 5/29	News 11/1	News 3/15	News 11/10	News 5/12
12:00 pm	College Football 10/15		All My Children 1/16	All My Children 1/17	All My Children 10/19	All My Children 3/9	All My Children 11/4
12:30 pm		Lighter Side 4/30					
1:00 pm		Dog Sled Racing 4/30	One Life to Live 3/13	One Life to Live 1/31	One Life to Live 5/31	One Life to Live 2/2	One Life to Live 3/10
1:30 pm							
2:00 pm		Discover California 10/9	General Hospital 10/24	General Hospital 10/25	General Hospital 3/22	General Hospital 2/16	General Hospital 4/28
2:30 pm		Auto Racing 5/14					
3:00 pm		Figure Skating 5/7	Oprah 5/15	Oprah 3/14	Oprah 10/26	Oprah 3/23	Oprah 1/20
3:30 pm							
4:00 pm	Senior Golf 1/28		News 4/24	News 1/24	News 11/2	News 10/20	News 10/21
4:30 pm				News 3/21			
5:00 pm	Peggy Fleming's Ice Stories 1/21	City View 4/23	News 1/30	News 5/30	News 1/25	News 3/16	News 2/3
5:30 pm		City View 10/16					
6:00 pm	News 10/29	News 10/16	NFL Football 10/17	News 3/7	News 5/24	News 3/16	News 5/19
6:30 pm		Siskel & Ebert 10/30		ABC News 3/7	ABC News 4/26	ABC News 5/25	ABC News 3/24
7:00 pm	Jeopardy 1/14	Home Videos 4/23		Jeopardy 2/14	Jeopardy 5/17		Jeopardy 10/14
7:30 pm	Wheel of Fortune 2/11	Home Videos 3/19		Wheel of Fortune 10/25	Wheel of Fortune 2/15	Wheel of Fortune 11/3	Wheel of Fortune 5/12
8:00 pm	Summertime Switch 10/8	Lois & Clark 3/12		Full House 11/1	Behind Closed Doors 2/8	Columbo 5/18	Family Matters 3/17
8:30 pm				Me & the Boys 2/14	All American Girl 10/19		Sister Sister 4/28
9:00 pm		Texas Justice Part I 2/12	Texas Justice Part II 2/13	Home Improvement 4/25	Grace Under Fire 5/24	The Commish 2/9	Step By Step 5/5
9:30 pm				Ellen 4/25	Coach 5/17		On Our Own 3/24
10:00 pm	The Commish 11/5			△ NYPD Blue 10/18	Prime Time 2/15	Day One 5/11	20/20 2/10
10:30 pm							

Key: △ Advisory   ¥ MPAA Rating   «» Violence Code

AMC

Time	SATURDAY	SUNDAY	MONDAY	TUESDAY	WEDNESDAY	THURSDAY	FRIDAY
6:00 am							A Farewell To Arms 5/12
6:30 am	A Night in Casablanca 10/15	The All American 1/29		The Great Man 1/24	What a Way to Go 2/15		
7:00 am							The Sign of the Cross 10/21
7:30 am		The Perfect Furlough 6/4				The Redhead of Wyoming 2/2	
8:00 am	Silver City 1/28	Homeward Bound 10/16	Stand In 10/17	The Barbarian & the Geisha 1/31	Babes In Toyland 10/26		
8:30 am							The Kid from Left Field 2/17
9:00 am							
9:30 am	Saps At Sea 2/11	Gunfight at the OK Corral 1/22				Up In Arms 11/10	Wyoming Mail 1/27
10:00 am	The Buccaneer 10/29		King Kong 10/31	The Tin Star 5/16	I Was a Male War Bride 3/22		
10:30 am						The Best Years of Our Lives 10/27	
11:00 am		Anna Karenina 5/7					Target Unknown 11/11
11:30 am	Laurel & Hardy 10/8			The Glory Brigade 12/6			
12:00 pm	The Buccaneer (cont.)		Fall of the Roman Empire Part I & II 10/10	Out of the Past 5/2	Caribbean 10/26		
12:30 pm							The Plainsman 2/10
1:00 pm	Fort Apache 10/22	Soldier of Fortune 5/21		Wait 'til the Sun Shines, Nellie 5/9	Stars & Stripes 12/7		
1:30 pm						A New Kind of Love 1/26	
2:00 pm				I Married a Monster from Outer Space 10/18			Follow the Sun 10/14
2:30 pm		Singapore 3/12				Ride the Pink Horse 2/9	
3:00 pm	Call Northside 777 6/3		What a Way to Go 2/6		Eldorado 10/12		
3:30 pm		The Great Race 4/30		Call of the Wild 3/21		Newsreels 2/2	
4:00 pm						Ride a Crooked Trail 3/9	Detective Story 12/9
4:30 pm	The Day the Earth Stood Still 1/14	The Girl Can't Help It 11/7		The Black Orchid 10/25	Sorry Wrong Number 11/2		
5:00 pm		Yankee Pasha 6/4					
5:30 pm					Lady Sings the Blues 3/15	The Geisha Boys 3/23	
6:00 pm	Romeo & Juliet 1/21	My Favorite Wife 5/14	The Toy Tiger 2/13			The Last Time I Saw Paris 11/3	His Kind of Woman 11/4
6:30 pm							
7:00 pm	Bang the Drum Slowly 12/3			The Song of Bernadette 2/7	On the Riviera 2/1		
7:30 pm							
8:00 pm			A Connecticut Yankee in NY 1/16			It's Only Money 3/16	Singapore 1/20
8:30 pm		The Island 10/30			The Odd Couple 2/8		
9:00 pm		A New Kind of Love 6/4	The Duel at Silver Creek 3/6			Forever Amber 10/13	The Snows of Kilimanjaro 2/3
9:30 pm	Anna Karenina 11/5			War Arrow 1/17	An Affair to Remember 1/18		
10:00 pm	Once Upon a Time in the West 3/18	Love Nest 2/12				Tell Me that You Love Me 2/16	Street Scenes: NY on Film 10/28
10:30 pm			Istanbul 12/5	A Farewell to Arms 2/14	Stage Door 11/9		The Snows of Kilimanjaro (con't)

Key: Δ Advisory   ¥ MPAA Rating   «» Violence Code

BET	SATURDAY	SUNDAY	MONDAY	TUESDAY	WEDNESDAY	THURSDAY	FRIDAY
6:00 am	Story Porch 1/14	Bobby Jones Gospel 10/23	Roc 5/15	Roc 11/1	Roc 5/31	Roc 2/16	Roc 2/17
6:30 am	Video Soul 12/3		What's Happenin' 1/30	What's Happenin' 2/14	What's Happenin' 3/15	What's Happenin' 3/9	What's Happenin' 3/10
7:00 am			What's Happenin' 1/16	What's Happenin' 1/31	What's Happenin' 3/15	What's Happenin' 3/9	What's Happenin' 4/28
7:30 am		Video Gospel 1/29	Screen Scene 3/20	Screen Scene 11/1	Screen Scene 10/19	Screen Scene 6/8	Sanford & Son 3/17
8:00 am	Rap City 2/11	Lead Story 4/30	In Your Ear 10/17	In Your Ear 11/8	In Your Ear 11/9	In Your Ear 11/10	In Your Ear 1/27
8:30 am		Our Voices 2/12					
9:00 am	Teen Summit 5/13						
9:30 am		Infomercial 11/6					
10:00 am	Campus All Star Challenge 10/22	Infomercial 3/19	Video Soul 5/1	Video Soul 10/11	Video Soul 2/1	Video Soul 11/3	Video Soul 10/28
10:30 am	Infomercial 5/20	Infomercial 3/19					
11:00 am	One on One 10/22	Infomercial 4/23					
11:30 am	Infomercial 5/20	Infomercial 5/14					
12:00 pm	Caribbean Rhythms 4/29	Infomercial 11/6	Video Vibrations 11/7	Video Vibrations 1/17	Video Vibrations 10/12	Video Vibrations 6/1	Video Vibrations 6/2
12:30 pm		Infomercial 3/12					
1:00 pm	Out All Night 10/29						
1:30 pm	Roc 10/29	Infomercial 2/5					
2:00 pm	BET Shopping 3/4	Infomercial 1/15	Rap City 10/31	Rap City 1/24	Rap City 2/8		Rap City 5/26
2:30 pm		Infomercial 5/14					
3:00 pm		Infomercial 3/5					
3:30 pm		Infomercial 5/21	Screen Scene 10/24	Screen Scene 10/18	Screen Scene 10/19	Screen Scene 10/13	News 12/9
4:00 pm		Infomercial 5/21	What's Happenin' 1/16	What's Happenin' 2/7	What's Happenin' 11/9	What's Happenin' 1/19	What's Happenin' 3/17
4:30 pm		Infomercial 1/15	Out All Night 5/15	Sanford & Son 11/8	Out All Night 10/26	Sanford & Son 1/19	What's Happenin' 2/17
5:00 pm	Infomercial 2/4	Infomercial 10/9	Roc 3/13	Roc 1/31	Roc 10/26	Roc 2/2	Roc 12/9
5:30 pm	Black Enterprise Golf & Tennis 10/15	Bobby Jones Gospel 10/16	Comic View 3/13	Comic View 1/17	Comic View 2/15	Comic View 2/2	Comic View 10/24
6:00 pm			Video Soul 10/10	Video Soul 10/18	Big 15 Kick-Off Jam 1/25	Video Soul 6/1	Video Soul 10/21
6:30 pm	Video Soul 11/5	Video Gospel 3/5			Video Soul 3/22		
7:00 pm		Color Code 10/9					
7:30 pm		Lead Story 10/30					
8:00 pm	Infomercial 1/21	Our Voices 5/7	Roc 10/24	Roc 5/30	Roc 5/3	Roc 5/4	Roc 10/14
8:30 pm	Infomercial 1/21	Infomercial 4/30	Jazz Central 2/6	Jazz Central 10/25	Jazz Central 3/8	Jazz Central 10/20	Jazz Central 2/3
9:00 pm	Off the Court 5/27	Infomercial 10/30					
9:30 pm		Infomercial 10/30					
10:00 pm	Midnight Love 10/8	Infomercial 1/29					
10:30 pm		Infomercial 5/28	Comic View 11/7	Comic View 2/14	Comic View 5/3	Comic View 10/13	

Key: Δ Advisory   ¥ MPAA Rating   «» Violence Code

CAR	SATURDAY	SUNDAY	MONDAY	TUESDAY	WEDNESDAY	THURSDAY	FRIDAY
6:00 am	Quick Draw McGraw 10/29	Wacky Races 5/7	The Smurfs 1/16	Smurfs 1/24	Smurfs 2/15	Smurfs 2/2	Smurfs 2/3
6:30 am	Augie Doggie 10/29	Perils of. . . 4/23					
7:00 am	Boomerang 10/22	Don Coyote 1/29	Boomerang 10/10	Heathcliff 11/8	Funky Phantom 5/3	Heathcliff 10/20	Heathcliff 10/21
7:30 am		Young Robin Hood 3/5			A Pup Named Scooby Doo 3/15	A Pup Named Scooby Doo 5/18	Top Cat 11/4
8:00 am		Pirates of Dark Water 2/12		Paw Paws 2/14	Paw Paws 4/26	Paw Paws 2/9	Paw Paws 2/17
8:30 am		Centurions 10/9		Shirt Tales 3/7	Shirt Tales 3/22	Shirt Tales 5/4	Shirt Tales 5/5
9:00 am	Pirates of Dark Water 1/21	Scooby Doo 10/9	Snorks 1/30	Snorks 3/14	A Pup Named Scooby Doo 10/12	Snorks 5/11	Snorks 2/17
9:30 am			Back to Bedrock 4/24	Pound Puppies 10/11	Back to Bedrock 5/3	Back to Bedrock 6/1	Back to Bedrock 1/20
10:00 am		Hong Kong Phooey 12/4	Richie Rich 1/23	Fantastic Max 11/8	Richie Rich 4/26	Richie Rich 5/18	Richie Rich 3/24
10:30 am		Clue Club 4/23	Flintstone Kids 2/6	Flintstone Kids 3/7	Flintstone Kids 2/8	Flintstone Kids 2/9	Flintstone Kids 10/21
11:00 am	Thundarr 5/27	Cartoon Network Dog Bowl 1/29	Down wit' Droopy D 3/13	Down wit' Droopy D 2/7	Down wit' Droopy D 10/19	Down wit' Droopy D 11/3	Down wit' Droopy D 12/9
11:30 am	Fantastic Four 5/27						
12:00 pm	Captain Planet 4/22	Buford & Galloping Ghost 4/30	Augie Doggie 4/24	Yuckie Duck 5/2	Augie Doggie 1/25	Augie Doggie 1/19	Augie Doggie 11/4
12:30 pm	Centurions 2/4		Josie & the Pussycats 10/10	Plasticman 1/31	Plasticman 3/8	Plasticman 2/16	Plasticman 4/28
1:00 pm	Super Adventures 2/11	Hokey Wolf Marathon 4/30	James Bond Jr. 3/20	James Bond Jr. 3/21	Godzilla 10/12	James Bond Jr. 5/4	James Bond Jr. 3/24
1:30 pm			Pirates of Dark Water 5/8	Pirates of Dark Water 2/14	Thundarr 11/2	Pirates of Dark Water 1/26	Pirates of Dark Water 4/28
2:00 pm	Godzilla 1/14	Secret Squirrel Marathon 2/5	Super Adventures 10/24	Super Adventures 11/1	Super Adventures 3/22	Super Adventures 10/13	Super Adventures 1/20
2:30 pm	Captain Planet 4/22						
3:00 pm	Something Old, Something New 6/3	Porky Pig 11/6	G-Force 2/13	G-Force 3/14	G-Force 1/18	G-Force 3/9	Centurions 10/14
3:30 pm	Dynomutt 3/18		Johnny Quest 5/8	Johnny Quest 11/1	Johnny Quest 3/8	Johnny Quest 3/16	Johnny Quest 2/10
4:00 pm	Turbo Teen 10/15	Swat Kats 1/15	Scooby Doo 5/29	Scooby Doo 10/25	Scooby Doo 10/26	Scooby Doo 3/9	Scooby Doo 3/10
4:30 pm		2 Stupid Dogs 2/5					
5:00 pm	Moxy Pirate 5/6	Moxy Pirate 1/22	Flintstones 11/7	Flintstones 10/18	Flintstones 11/2	Flintstones 1/19	Flintstones 10/14
5:30 pm	Scooby & Scrappy 1/14	Top Cat 2/12	Impossibles 5/1	Jetson's Marathon 5/9		Jetsons 3/23	2 Stupid Dogs 1/27
6:00 pm	Flintstones 1/28	Mr. Spims Theater 3/19	Bugs & Daffy Tonight 10/17	Bugs & Daffy Tonight 1/17	Bugs & Daffy Tonight 11/9	Bugs & Daffy Tonight 4/27	
6:30 pm	Jetsons 3/18	Moxy Pirate 3/5					
7:00 pm		Wait Till Your Father Gets Home 10/16			Bugs & Daffy Tonight 1/18	Scooby Doo 6/1	
7:30 pm	Bugs & Daffy 10/8					Tom & Jerry 5/11	
8:00 pm	2 Stupid Dogs 2/4	Tom & Jerry 10/23			2 Stupid Dogs 10/19	2 Stupid Dogs 10/20	Space Ghost 10/28
8:30 pm	2 Stupid Dogs 5/6		Scooby Doo 2/13	Scooby Doo 10/11	Scooby Doo 5/24	Scooby Doo 5/25	Moxy Pirate 3/17
9:00 pm	Super Adventures 11/5	Popeye 10/30	Toonheads 3/6		Space Ghost 5/31	Amazing Chan Clan 10/27	Josie & the Pussycats 3/17
9:30 pm				Popeye 5/16	Late Night Black & White 5/24	Banana Splits 12/8	Cinco de Mayo 5/5
10:00 pm			Flintstones 3/20	Flintstones 5/30	Down wit' Droopy D 6/7	Cartoons 5/25	Butch Cassidy 5/12
10:30 pm		Cartoons 5/15					Banana Splits 5/12

Key: Δ Advisory   ¥ MPAA Rating   «» Violence Code

CBS	SATURDAY	SUNDAY	MONDAY	TUESDAY	WEDNESDAY	THURSDAY	FRIDAY
6:00 am	What's Up Network 5/6	Singsation 11/6	CBS News 1/16		News 2/8	News 6/8	CBS News 3/17
6:30 am	Madison's Adventures 3/4	Kenneth Copeland 10/23	CBS News 10/10	CBS News 5/9		CBS News 4/7	CBS News 4/28
7:00 am	Little Mermaid 3/18		CBS This Morning 10/17	CBS This Morning 10/25	CBS This Morning 5/10	CBS This Morning 6/8	
7:30 am	Beethoven 5/13	Sunday Morning 5/14					
8:00 am	Aladdin 4/29						
8:30 am	Ninja Turtles 3/18						
9:00 am	Wildcats 10/8	College Basketball 1/29	Guiding Light 5/29	Guiding Light 5/2	Guiding Light 3/22	Guiding Light 5/18	Guiding Light 5/26
9:30 am	Garfield & Friends 5/6	Bob Navarro's Journal 10/9					
10:00 am	Wild Cats 5/13	College Basketball (con't)	The Price is Right 10/31		The Price is Right 11/9	The Price is Right 11/3	The Price is Right 10/28
10:30 am	Garfield & Friends 11/5						
11:00 am	Eye on Sports 2/11	Sports Show 5/7	The Young & the Restless 3/13	The Young & the Restless 3/7	The Young & the Restless 5/24	The Young & the Restless 1/26	The Young & the Restless 5/19
11:30 am							
12:00 pm		Infomercial 1/15	News 4/24	News 2/14	News 3/22	News 6/8	News 1/20
12:30 pm		Golf 4/23	The Bold & the Beautiful 5/15	The Bold & the Beautiful 11/1	The Bold & the Beautiful 4/26	The Bold & the Beautiful 3/23	The Bold & the Beautiful 1/20
1:00 pm	Travel Travel 10/29	College Basketball 2/12	As the World Turns 5/22	As the World Turns 3/14	As the World Turns 5/31	As the World Turns 5/4	As the World Turns 12/9
1:30 pm	Golf 4/22						
2:00 pm	Eye on Sports 1/21	Golf (con't)	Guiding Light 11/7	Guiding Light 1/31	Family Feud 6/7	Guiding Light 2/2	Family Feud 6/2
2:30 pm					Love Connection 4/26		Love Connection 6/2
3:00 pm	Infomercial 10/22	L.A. Stories 4/30	Geraldo 5/8	Schoolbreak Special 3/21	Geraldo 3/15	Hard Copy 3/23	Geraldo 10/21
3:30 pm	Infomercial 10/22	Martha Stewart 1/22				Geraldo 6/8	
4:00 pm	Court TV 10/29	Highway Patrol 11/6	News 6/5	News 5/16		News 10/13	News 4/28
4:30 pm	Highway Patrol 10/8	High Tide 5/21	News 3/20	News 5/16	News 6/7		News 5/5
5:00 pm	News 3/11	Highway Patrol 4/30	News 10/24	News 10/18	News 2/15	News 10/20	News 5/12
5:30 pm	CBS News 3/11	CBS News 4/23					
6:00 pm	Entertainment Tonight 1/28	News 12/4	CBS News 11/7	Election Coverage 11/8	CBS News 3/15	CBS News 4/27	CBS News 2/10
6:30 pm			Highway Patrol 4/24	Highway Patrol 11/1	Highway Patrol 11/2	Highway Patrol 6/8	Highway Patrol 10/14
7:00 pm	Renegade 3/4	60 Minutes 10/30	Hard Copy 5/1	Election Coverage (con't)	Hard Copy 5/17	Hard Copy 6/8	Hard Copy 12/9
7:30 pm			Entertainment Tonight 1/16		Entertainment Tonight 5/17	Entertainment Tonight 2/9	Entertainment Tonight 2/10
8:00 pm	Dr. Quinn Medicine Woman 2/4	Murder, She Wrote 10/16	The Nanny 5/15	Rescue 911 2/7	George Wendt 3/8	Due South 12/8	NCAA Basketball 3/24
8:30 pm			Dave's World 2/13		A League of Their Own 5/3		
9:00 pm	Five Mrs. Buchanons 10/15	The Piano Lesson 2/5	Murphy Brown 2/13	Beyond Betrayal 10/11	Touched by an Angel 10/26	Eye to Eye 6/1	
9:30 pm	Dr. Quinn (con't)		Cybill 3/20				
10:00 pm	Walker, Texas Ranger 1/14		Northern Exposure 10/10		48 Hours 11/2	48 Hours 2/16	
10:30 pm							

Key: Δ Advisory   ¥ MPAA Rating   «» Violence Code

DIS	SATURDAY	SUNDAY	MONDAY	TUESDAY	WEDNESDAY	THURSDAY	FRIDAY
6:00 am	Music Box 1/28	Music Box 1/29	Mousercise 3/6	Mousercise 5/9	Mousercise 3/15	Mousercise 2/9	Mousercise 4/28
6:30 am	Dumbo's Circus 1/28	Dumbo's Circus 3/12	Mouse Tracks 5/22	Mouse Tracks 1/31	Mouse Tracks 5/10	Mouse Tracks 2/16	Mouse Tracks 5/19
7:00 am	Pooh Corner 3/18	Pooh Corner 10/9	Under the Umbrella Tree 10/10	Under the Umbrella Tree 5/23	Under the Umbrella Tree 10/26	Under the Umbrella Tree 3/23	Under the Umbrella Tree 3/24
7:30 am	Mother Goose Stories 11/5		Wonderland 3/13	Wonderland 1/24		Wonderland 2/9	Wonderland 5/5
8:00 am	My Little Pony Tales 5/20	My Little Pony Tales 11/6	Adventures of Winnie 2/13		Adventures of Winnie 5/17	Adventures of Winnie 4/27	Adventures of Winnie 10/28
8:30 am	Care Bears 2/11	Care Bears 10/16	Care Bears 1/16	Care Bears 4/25		Care Bears 5/25	Care Bears 5/5
9:00 am	Charlie 5/13	Charlie 2/12	Gummi Bears 10/31	Gummi Bears 5/30	Gummi Bears 5/10	Gummi Bears 1/19	Gummi Bears 1/20
9:30 am	Quack Attack 5/13	Quack Attack 4/30	Pooh Corner 10/31	Pooh Corner 3/14	Pooh Corner 2/3	Pooh Corner 5/4	Pooh Corner 2/3
10:00 am		Here Comes the Littles 10/16		Dumbo's Circus 1/24	Dumbo's Circus 2/8	Dumbo's Circus 1/19	Dumbo's Circus 4/28
10:30 am	The Wiz 10/15		Fraggle Rock 2/6	Fraggle Rock 4/25	Fraggle Rock 3/15	Fraggle Rock 5/25	Fraggle Rock 3/17
11:00 am		Brown Bears Wedding 1/15	My Little Pony Tales 5/15	My Little Pony Tales 2/14	My Little Pony Tales 4/26	My Little Pony Tales 2/2	My Little Pony Tales 5/19
11:30 am			Mouse Tracks 10/24	Mouse Tracks 11/1	Mouse Tracks 5/3	Mouse Tracks 6/1	Mouse Tracks 3/10
12:00 pm		Baby-sitters Club 2/12	Gryphon 12/5	Wuzzies 5/16	Fraggle Rock 1/18	Marsupilami 10/27	Lunch Box 5/26
12:30 pm	Frankenweenie 10/15	Kids Inc. 10/9		Mother Goose Stories 5/2	Secret Life of Toys 10/19	Really Rosie 10/13	Music Box 10/28
1:00 pm	Danger Bay 4/22	Mickey Mouse 3/19		The Further Adventures of the Wilderness Family 3/7			
1:30 pm	Zorro 2/11	Ocean Girl 4/30	Alice in Wonderland 10/17		Frogs 10/12	The Wiz 10/20	To Catch a Yeti 1/27
2:00 pm	Elfego Baca 5/6	Torkelsons 1/15					
2:30 pm		Sinbad 3/12		New Adventures of Winnie 11/1			Muppet Caper 5/26
3:00 pm	Hardy Boys 3/11	Faerie Tale Theatre 10/30	Gummi Bears 2/6	Gummi Bears 2/7	Gummi Bears 3/22	Gummi Bears 2/16	Gummi Bears 2/3
3:30 pm	Miracle of the White Stallion 11/5		Quack Attack 4/24	Quack Attack 5/23	Quack Attack 11/2	Quack Attack 4/27	
4:00 pm			Fraggle Rock 5/8	Fraggle Rock 2/14	Fraggle Rock 1/25	Fraggle Rock 11/3	Hunting Instinct 1/20
4:30 pm	Walt Disney World 10/29	Cool Runnings 5/7	Under the Umbrella Tree 5/15	Under the Umbrella Tree 2/7	Under the Umbrella Tree 3/8	Under the Umbrella Tree 3/23	
5:00 pm			Kids Inc. 5/8	Kids Inc. 5/9	Kids Inc. 4/26	Kids Inc. 10/13	Rock N Roll Mom 5/12
5:30 pm	Δ The Dark Crystal 10/29		Mickey Mouse Club 1/16			Mickey Mouse Club 3/16	
6:00 pm		Avonlea 3/5	Charlie Brown 1/23	Charlie Brown 5/16	Faerie Tale Theatre 11/2	Baby-sitters Club 5/18	
6:30 pm			Almost Home 3/6	For Better or Worse 10/25		Eerie, Indiana 11/10	Muppet Christmas Carol 12/9
7:00 pm			Sinbad 3/13				
7:30 pm	Polly--Comin' Home 3/18	Hocus Pocus 12/4	Ocean Girl 10/24	Here Come the Littles 10/11		Woof 3/9	Fantastic Voyage 10/14
8:00 pm			Avonlea 5/1		Pollyanna 2/15		
8:30 pm	Walt Disney World (con't)			Walt Disney 5/2		Old Curiosity Shop 5/4	
9:00 pm		Pollyanna 1/22		Δ D-Day to Berlin 6/6		Δ Roger Daltry: Music of the Who 1/26	Hey There Yogi Bear 2/17
9:30 pm	Billy Joel 1/21	Δ David Bowie 3/19			Disney World Inside 11/9		
10:00 pm		Fun & Feel of the Fifties 1/29	Mr. Hobbs Takes a Vacation 11/7	Mr. Deeds Goes to Town 5/30	Wonder Man 2/1		Much Ado About Nothing 10/21
10:30 pm	Nine to Five 3/4					Sound of Julie Andrews 5/11	

Key: Δ Advisory   ¥ MPAA Rating   «» Violence Code

168

FAM	SATURDAY	SUNDAY	MONDAY	TUESDAY	WEDNESDAY	THURSDAY	FRIDAY
6:00 am	Infomercial 5/20	Infomercial 4/30	Cable Health Club 10/24	Cable Health Club 2/7	Cable Health Club 5/31	Cable Health Club 10/27	Cable Health Club 10/28
6:30 am	Backyard America 5/6	Life Today 10/16					
7:00 am	American Baby 3/4	Coral Ridge 1/15	Popeye 3/13	Popeye 1/31	Popeye 5/31	Popeye 1/26	Popeye 3/24
7:30 am	Healthy Kid 5/6		Inspector Gadget 5/8	Inspector Gadget 11/1	Inspector Gadget 4/26	Inspector Gadget 2/9	Inspector Gadget 2/3
8:00 am	Madeline 2/11	Popeye & Son 1/15	XUXA 5/15	XUXA 2/7	XUXA 5/10	XUXA 4/27	XUXA 1/20
8:30 am	Wishkid 10/8	Heathcliff 1/29	Prince Valiant 3/20	Prince Valiant 5/23	Prince Valiant 6/7	Prince Valiant 5/11	Prince Valiant 1/27
9:00 am	Mario All Stars 3/18	Madeline 4/23	Let's Make a Deal 3/13	Let's Make a Deal 10/11	Let's Make a Deal 3/15	Let's Make a Deal 2/2	Let's Make a Deal 10/21
9:30 am	Maximum Drive 4/29	Wishkid 4/30	The Waltons 5/22	Name that Tune 2/14	Name that Tune 2/15	Name that Tune 3/23	Name that Tune 1/20
10:00 am	Masters of the Maze 5/13	Mario All Stars 10/16	Trivial Pursuit 10/31	700 Club 5/9	700 Club 5/17	Trivial Pursuit 11/10	Face the Music 2/3
10:30 am	That's My Dog 4/29	In Touch 3/12	Trivial Pursuit 3/20	Trivial Pursuit 11/1		700 Club 6/8	Trivial Pursuit 2/10
11:00 am	Big Brother Jake 1/28	Masters of the Maze 4/23	Boggle 10/17	700 Club (con't)	Split Second 3/15	Split Second 2/9	
11:30 am	Bordertown 2/4		Let's Make a Deal 10/17	Let's Make a Deal 11/8	Cable Health Club 4/26	Cable Health Club 5/4	Let's Make a Deal 2/17
12:00 pm		Punky Brewster 11/6	The Waltons 1/16	The Waltons 3/14	The Waltons 3/22	The Waltons 10/20	The Waltons 12/9
12:30 pm							
1:00 pm	High Chaparral 2/11		700 Club 10/31	700 Club 10/25	700 Club 11/2	700 Club 11/3	700 Club 11/11
1:30 pm		Bright Eyes 5/21					
2:00 pm	Young Riders 10/22	Happy Feeling 5/28					
2:30 pm		Bright Eyes 1/29	Cable Health Club 12/5	700 Club 1/17	Cable Health Club 2/15	Let's Make a Deal 5/4	Cable Health Club 3/10
3:00 pm	Rifleman 1/21		Black Stallion 3/6	Black Stallion 4/25	Black Stallion 5/3	Black Stallion 3/9	Black Stallion 2/10
3:30 pm	Rifleman 3/4		Punky Brewster 5/1	Black Stallion 2/14	Punky Brewster 2/8	Punky Brewster 2/2	Punky Brewster 3/10
4:00 pm	Big Valley 1/21	Miracle of the Heart 10/30	I'm Telling 1/30	I'm Telling 1/31	I'm Telling 5/24	I'm Telling 2/16	I'm Telling 3/17
4:30 pm			Masters of the Maze 5/15		That's My Dog 10/26	Masters of the Maze 3/9	Masters of the Maze 3/24
5:00 pm	Bonanza 10/15		Maximum Drive 10/24	Maximum Drive 11/8	Maximum Drive 5/24	Maximum Drive 3/16	Maximum Drive 1/27
5:30 pm			That's My Dog 5/8	That's My Dog 5/2	That's My Dog 1/25	That's My Dog 6/8	That's My Dog 2/17
6:00 pm	Snowy River 1/14	Snowy River 2/5	Rin Tin Tin K9 Cop 1/30	Rin Tin Tin K9 Cop 1/24	Rin Tin Tin K9 Cop 2/1	Rin Tin Tin K9 Cop 4/27	Rin Tin Tin K9 Cop 12/9
6:30 pm			New Lassie 3/6	New Lassie 5/2	New Lassie 1/18	New Lassie 3/23	New Lassie 3/17
7:00 pm	Bordertown 5/13	Madeline 11/6	The Waltons 4/24	The Waltons 3/21	The Waltons 2/8	Evening Shade 10/20	Evening Shade 10/14
7:30 pm	That's My Dog 3/18	Mrs. Lambert Remembers 3/19				Evening Shade 10/13	Evening Shade 10/21
8:00 pm	The Wonderful Country 10/29	That's My Dog 10/9	Evening Shade 2/6	The Waltons 10/18	Evening Shade 5/3	Evening Shade 3/16	Stand By Your Man 11/4
8:30 pm		Mrs. Lambert Remembers (con't)	Evening Shade 5/29		Evening Shade 2/1	Evening Shade 1/26	
9:00 pm		Country Music Spotlight 3/5	△ Rescue 911 10/10	Rescue 911 5/16	△ Rescue 911 10/19	△ Rescue 911 10/13	
9:30 pm							
10:00 pm	The Bridge at Remagen 5/27		700 Club 2/6	700 Club 10/11	700 Club 10/12	700 Club 10/19	700 Club 10/14
10:30 pm	Snowy River 1/28						

Key: △ Advisory   ¥ MPAA Rating   «» Violence Code

FOX	SATURDAY	SUNDAY	MONDAY	TUESDAY	WEDNESDAY	THURSDAY	FRIDAY
6:00 am	Swat Kats 10/29	Infomercial 5/14	News 10/24	News 11/1	News 1/25	News 6/8	News 10/14
6:30 am	Not Just News 5/6	Infomercial 10/23					
7:00 am	Power Rangers 3/11	In Touch 3/12	Good Day LA 10/31	Good Day LA 10/11	Good Day LA 5/31	Good Day LA 3/16	Good Day LA 12/9
7:30 am	Power Rangers 3/18						
8:00 am	Animaniacs 3/11	Infomercial 3/19					
8:30 am	Eek! Thunderlizard 11/5	Infomercial 1/22					
9:00 am	Spiderman 3/18	Ever Increasing Faith 4/30	I Love Lucy 5/29	I Love Lucy 5/16	I Love Lucy 6/7	OJ Trial 3/9	I Love Lucy 10/21
9:30 am			I Love Lucy 6/5	I Love Lucy 10/18		I Love Lucy 2/2	
10:00 am	X-Men 1/21		OJ Trial 3/20	Andy Griffith 6/6	Andy Griffith 5/17		OJ Trial 3/17
10:30 am	Batman & Robin 2/11			Andy Griffith 1/17	Andy Griffith 6/7		
11:00 am	Megaman 10/22	NFL Football 10/30	Beverly Hillbillies 4/24	Beverly Hillbillies 6/6	Dennis Prager 10/12	OJ Trial 3/23	Beverly Hillbillies 5/19
11:30 am	Sweet Valley High 10/15			Beverly Hillbillies 6/6	OJ Trial 3/15		OJ Trial 5/12
12:00 pm	WWF 1/14		Gordon Elliot 10/17	Gordon Elliot 4/25	Gordon Elliot 2/1	Gordon Elliot 10/27	Gordon Elliot 11/4
12:30 pm							
1:00 pm	Road to the Superbowl 1/28		Small Wonder 5/22	Small Wonder 6/6	Small Wonder 5/24	Small Wonder 6/1	Small Wonder 5/26
1:30 pm		WWF 10/9	Small Wonder 5/29	Small Wonder 6/6	Small Wonder 10/26		Small Wonder 2/10
2:00 pm	Gilligan's Island 1/21			Cubhouse 5/23		Cubhouse 6/1	Cubhouse 4/28
2:30 pm	Gilligan's Island 1/28	NFL 11/6	Bobby's World 1/16	Bobby's World 6/6	Bobby's World 5/24		Bobby's World 5/12
3:00 pm	Three's Company 2/11		Tiny Toons 1/16	VR Troopers 6/6	Tiny Toons 12/7	VR Troopers 5/25	VR Troopers 2/10
3:30 pm	Three's Company 4/22		Tazmania 10/10	OJ Trial 5/9	Tiny Toons 3/22	Tiny Toons 6/8	Tazmania 10/28
4:00 pm	Family Ties 10/15	Overtime 11/6	Tazmania 6/5	Animaniacs 1/17	Tazmania 6/7	Tazmania 6/1	Tazmania 4/28
4:30 pm	Family Ties 10/22	Family Ties 2/5	Animaniacs 5/22	Power Rangers 10/18	Animaniacs 2/15	Aladdin 10/20	Animaniacs 3/10
5:00 pm	I Love Lucy 2/4	NHL Hockey 4/23	Power Rangers 2/13	Power Rangers 3/21	VR Troopers 11/9	VR Troopers 12/8	VR Troopers 10/14
5:30 pm	I Love Lucy 10/8		Wonder Years 3/13	Wonder Years 3/7	Wonder Years 5/10	Wonder Years 3/9	Wonder Years 1/27
6:00 pm	I Love Lucy 2/4	Sightings 2/5	Married with Children 3/6	Married with Children 2/14	Married with Children 11/9	Married with Children 2/16	Married with Children 2/17
6:30 pm			Δ Cops 5/8	Δ Cops 2/14	Δ Cops 4/26	Δ Cops 10/13	Δ Cops 10/21
7:00 pm	Married with Children 1/14	Δ Encounters: The Hidden Truth 12/4	Married with Children 10/10	Married with Children 2/7	Married with Children 10/12	Married with Children 4/27	Married with Children 2/17
7:30 pm	Δ Trauma Center 10/29		Simpsons 1/30	Simpsons 1/31	Simpsons 3/22	Simpsons 5/4	Simpsons 3/24
8:00 pm	Δ Cops 5/6	Simpsons 2/12	Melrose Place 1/23		Beverly Hills 90210 10/19	Martin 1/26	M.A.N.T.I.S. 1/27
8:30 pm	Δ Cops 10/8	House of Buggin' 1/22				Living Single 2/9	
9:00 pm	America's Most Wanted 3/4	Married with Children 10/16	Party of Five 11/7	Δ Alien Nation: Dark Horizon 10/25	Party of Five 11/2	NY Undercover 1/19	X-Files 10/28
9:30 pm		Dream On 3/19					
10:00 pm	News 11/5	News 10/16	News 12/5	News 1/24	News 10/26	News 10/20	News 1/20
10:30 pm							

Key: Δ Advisory   ¥ MPAA Rating   «» Violence Code

HBO	SATURDAY	SUNDAY	MONDAY	TUESDAY	WEDNESDAY	THURSDAY	FRIDAY
6:00 am			¥ «» Dr. Mordrid 2/13		¥ «» Running Man 2/15		Δ¥ «» Fire in the Sky 5/26
6:30 am	¥ The Nutcracker Prince 10/8	¥ Dave 1/22	¥ Daffy Duck's Quackbusters 10/10	¥ Big Girls Don't Cry They Get Even 10/18	¥ Rainbow Brite & the Star Stealer 2/1	¥ The Adventures of Milo & Otis 11/3	¥ «» Airborne 10/28
7:00 am							
7:30 am						¥ Sideout 2/9	Shakespeare 10/14
8:00 am	Stop the Smoggies 10/15	Stop the Smoggies 10/9	Stop the Smoggies 2/6	Stop the Smoggies 3/14	Stop the Smoggies 3/15	Stop the Smoggies 3/9	Stop the Smoggies 1/20
8:30 am	Encyclopedia 3/11	Encyclopedia 2/12	Encyclopedia 2/13	Legend of White Fang 5/23	Encyclopedia 2/15	Legend of White Fang 5/4	Legend of White Fang 4/28
9:00 am	¥ «» So I Married... 3/18	Arthur Ashe 10/9	¥ «» Almost an Angel 3/6		¥ «» Uptown Sat. Night 10/26	¥ «» The Abyss 2/2	¥ «» Sommersby 1/27
9:30 am	¥ Stay Tuned 10/15			¥ «» Pelican Brief 1/24			
10:00 am		¥ The Sandlot 4/30					
10:30 am		¥ «» The Seventh Coin 1/15					
11:00 am	Inside the NFL 1/28		¥ Labyrinth 12/5				¥ «» Space Hunter: The Movie 10/21
11:30 am		¥ «» Protocol 11/7		¥ «» Geronimo 1/17	¥ «» Sommersby 1/18	¥ «» The Poseidon Adventure 1/26	
12:00 pm		¥ «» Delirious 12/4					
12:30 pm	¥ Daffy Duck's Quackbusters 10/22		«» Making of Bram... 10/24		¥ If Looks Could Kill 1/25		
1:00 pm		¥ Coneheads 3/5	Protocol {con't)	¥ «» Twilight Zone 3/7		¥ Casey's Shadow 2/16	¥ «» Woman with a Past 3/10
1:30 pm	¥ «» A Perfect World 1/14						
2:00 pm			¥ «» If Looks Could Kill 1/16		Life Stories 1/25		«» Blue Ice 4/28
2:30 pm	«» In the Line of Duty 3/11	¥ «» Star Trek III 10/30		¥ «» M*A*S*H 11/8	¥ «» The Butcher's Wife 2/8		
3:00 pm					¥ «» Almost an Angel 3/15	¥ «» Rocky II 10/27	¥ «» Rocky II 10/14
3:30 pm			¥ «» Star Trek III 10/24		Ice Castles 4/26	¥ «» 1492 3/16	
4:00 pm	¥ He Said, She Said 4/29			¥ «» Critters IV 11/1			
4:30 pm		¥ «» Sommersby 10/16			¥ Blue Chips 3/22	Ordinary Magic 3/9	¥ «» Toys 2/10
5:00 pm			¥ 2001: A Space Odyssey 10/31	¥ «» Solar Crisis 1/31			
5:30 pm	¥ «» Twilight Zone 3/4				¥ School Ties 10/19		
6:00 pm		¥ «» Lean On Me 5/7					¥ Robinhood, Men in Tights 2/17
6:30 pm						¥ «» Absence of Malice 10/13	
7:00 pm	¥ That Night 2/4	Black Beauty 5/14	¥ Sideout 2/6	¥ The Witches 10/25	¥ Samantha 3/8		Inside the NFL 1/20
7:30 pm		Happily Ever... 5/21					
8:00 pm						¥ «» Weekend at Bernies II 10/20	
8:30 pm	¥ The Age of Innocence 10/29	¥ «» Weekend at Bernies II 1/29	¥ «» Bram Stoker's Dracula 10/17	¥ Ace Ventura: Pet Detective 2/7	¥ «» South Central 10/12		¥ «» The Vanishing 2/3
9:00 pm							
9:30 pm		Judicial Consent 3/12				¥ «» Night of the Running Man 1/19	
10:00 pm		¥ «» Double Threat 10/23	¥ «» Rising Sun 3/13	«» Dangerous 2/14	Dream On 5/3		«» Citizen X 3/24
10:30 pm	¥ «» Falling Down 5/20		¥ «» Geronimo 1/23		Larry Sanders 5/3	«» Strapped 3/23	

Key: Δ Advisory ¥ MPAA Rating «» Violence Code

KCAL	SATURDAY	SUNDAY	MONDAY	TUESDAY	WEDNESDAY	THURSDAY	FRIDAY
6:00 am	Wonderland 5/6	Infomercial 5/7	Talespin 6/5	Talespin 1/17	Talespin 6/7	Talespin 1/26	Talespin 2/3
6:30 am	Chip N' Dale 2/11	Morris Cerullo 3/19	Captain Planet 5/8	Captain Planet 3/7	Captain Planet 6/7	Captain Planet 4/27	Bill Nye 3/24
7:00 am	Duck Tales 3/4	Coral Ridge Hour 3/12	Transformers 1/30	Transformers 11/8	Transformers 6/7	Transformers 6/1	Transformers 5/12
7:30 am	Bill Nye 1/28		Mighty Max 1/30	Mighty Max 1/24	Mighty Max 5/24	Mighty Max 1/26	Mighty Max 6/9
8:00 am	Infomercial 10/29	Bayless Conley 2/12	Toontown Kids 2/6	Toontown Kids 10/25	Toontown Kids 1/18	Toontown Kids 3/9	Toontown Kids 10/28
8:30 am	Infomercial 10/29	Feed the Children 10/30					
9:00 am	Infomercial 1/14	Kenneth Copeland 1/15	OJ Trial 6/5	OJ Trial 6/6	OJ Trial 6/7	OJ Trial 6/8	OJ Trial 6/9
9:30 am	Infomercial 3/11	It is Written 10/9					
10:00 am	Infomercial 4/22	Hour of Power 10/30	Jerry Springer 5/29	OJ Trial 6/6	OJ Trial 6/7	Richard Bey 2/9	Rolanda 12/9
10:30 am	Infomercial 3/11						
11:00 am	American Gladiators 1/28	Feed the Children 4/30	OJ Trial 5/8	OJ Trial 6/6	Susan Powter 11/9	Judge for Yourself 1/19	OJ Trial 6/9
11:30 am		Infomercial 4/30				Jones & Jury 11/10	
12:00 pm	Blade Warriors 10/8	Boogies Diner 4/23	Jane Whitney 1/23	News 10/18	News 5/3	News 2/2	OJ Trial 6/9
12:30 pm		Bill Nye 4/23					
1:00 pm	K9000 10/15	Hogan Family 11/6		Maury Povich 11/8	Maury Povich 2/1	Maury Povich 11/3	Maury Povich 3/17
1:30 pm		Toon Town Kids 5/14					
2:00 pm		Flintstones 5/7	Marilyn Kagen 2/13	OJ Trial 6/6	OJ Trial 6/7	OJ Trial 6/8	Judge for Yourself 11/4
2:30 pm		Scooby Doo 3/19					
3:00 pm		Beach Clash 1/29	Darkwing Duck 6/5	OJ Trial 6/6	OJ Trial 6/7	Darkwing Duck 10/13	Darkwing Duck 4/28
3:30 pm			Goof Troop 10/24	OJ Trial 6/6	OJ Trial 6/7	OJ Trial 6/8	Goof Troop 2/17
4:00 pm	Beach Clash 1/14	American Gladiators 11/6	Toon Town Kids 6/5	Bonkers 11/1		Bonkers 3/16	Gargoyles 3/10
4:30 pm		Perfect Strangers 2/12	Aladdin 11/7	Aladdin 3/21		OJ Trial 6/8	Aladdin 10/21
5:00 pm	American Gladiators 3/18	Who's the Boss 12/4	Who's the Boss 3/6	Susan Powter 10/11	Who's the Boss 2/15	Who's the Boss 6/1	Who's the Boss 2/3
5:30 pm		WKRP 2/5	△ Top Cops 6/5	Jones & Jury 10/11	Jones & Jury 10/12	Jones & Jury 10/13	Top Cops 6/2
6:00 pm	NBA Basketball 11/5	The Portrait 1/22	Rescue 911 1/16	Rescue 911 5/30	Rescue 911 4/26	Inside Edition 11/10	Rescue 911 5/12
6:30 pm			Rush Limbaugh 6/5	Rush Limbaugh 5/9	Rush Limbaugh 4/26	Rush Limbaugh 6/8	Rush Limbaugh 6/2
7:00 pm		Golden Girls 12/4	Inside Edition 6/5	Inside Edition 6/6	Inside Edition 6/7	△ Top Cops 10/20	Inside Edition 5/26
7:30 pm		The Portrait (con't)	Rush Limbaugh 1/16	American Journal 6/6	American Journal 6/7	American Journal 5/18	American Journal 5/5
8:00 pm	News 3/4	News 3/5	News 4/24	News 4/25	News 10/19	News 5/25	News 1/27
8:30 pm							
9:00 pm	△ Texas Chainsaw Massacre 10/29	World of Nature 10/23	News 10/31	News 11/1	News 10/26	News 10/27	News 10/14
9:30 pm							
10:00 pm		National Geographic 10/16	News 5/22	News 2/14	News 11/2	News 3/23	News 5/5
10:30 pm							

Key: △ Advisory   ¥ MPAA Rating   «» Violence Code

KCOP	SATURDAY	SUNDAY	MONDAY	TUESDAY	WEDNESDAY	THURSDAY	FRIDAY
6:00 am	Infomercial 10/29	Pick Your Brain 1/22	700 Club 1/23	700 Club 5/16	700 Club 5/31	Bots Master 10/27	700 Club 1/20
6:30 am	Infomercial 10/29	LA Kids 3/19		Conan 10/25		700 Club 2/9	
7:00 am		Blinky Bill 4/23	Biker Mice 5/15	Biker Mice 4/25	Biker Mice 5/10	Biker Mice 5/4	Biker Mice 12/9
7:30 am	Infomercial 2/4	Huey 10/30	Exosquad 10/24	Exosquad 5/9	Exosquad 2/15	Exosquad 6/8	Exosquad 6/2
8:00 am	Infomercial 2/11	Mutant League 3/12	Sonic the Hedgehog 5/15	Sonic the Hedgehog 3/7	Sonic the Hedgehog 2/15	Sonic the Hedgehog 11/10	Sonic the Hedgehog 6/2
8:30 am	Infomercial 3/4	Creepy Crawlers 4/23	Pink Panther 5/22	Pink Panther 1/17	Pink Panther 2/8	Pink Panther 6/8	Pink Panther 3/24
9:00 am	Infomercial 3/11	King Arthur 10/9	Conan 2/13	Conan 1/24	Conan 5/10	Garfield 10/13	Conan 5/26
9:30 am	Infomercial 3/4		Infomercial 5/29	Infomercial 1/17	Infomercial 10/19	Growing Pains 5/11	Infomercial 6/2
10:00 am	Infomercial 2/11	Double Dragon 1/29	Ricki Lake 10/17	Richard Bey 2/7	Richard Bey 1/25	Richard Bey 3/16	Ricki Lake 10/14
10:30 am	Infomercial 10/8	Double Dragon 4/30					
11:00 am	Infomercial 3/11	Monster Force 1/29	Jenny Jones 11/7	Jenny Jones 11/1	Jenny Jones 3/15	Jenny Jones 10/20	Jenny Jones 11/4
11:30 am	Infomercial 3/18	Battletech 10/30					
12:00 pm	Time Trax 10/15	Thunder in Paradise 3/19	Jane Whitney 5/8	Jane Whitney 1/31	Jane Whitney 2/1	Jane Whitney 5/25	Jane Whitney 5/19
12:30 pm		700 Club 1/22					
1:00 pm	Airplane 2/4	Thunder in Paradise 11/6	Montel Williams 3/6		Montel Williams 5/17	Montel Williams 2/2	Suzanne Sommers 10/28
1:30 pm							
2:00 pm	The Gauntlet 11/5	Δ The Exorcist 10/9	Jenny Jones 10/10	Jenny Jones 2/14	Jenny Jones 5/24	Jenny Jones 2/16	Jenny Jones 5/12
2:30 pm							
3:00 pm			Richard Bey 10/24	Richard Bey 3/14	Richard Bey 4/26	Richard Bey 3/9	Richard Bey 5/5
3:30 pm							
4:00 pm	Δ The Lost Boys 10/8	Class Act 10/16	Montel Williams 2/6	Montel Williams 11/8	Montel Williams 5/3	Montel Williams 10/13	Montel Williams 2/17
4:30 pm							
5:00 pm			Ricki Lake 2/13	Ricki Lake 10/18	Ricki Lake 2/8	Ricki Lake 1/19	Ricki Lake 10/21
5:30 pm							
6:00 pm	Δ The Siege of the Fire . . . 1/14	Private Benjamin 10/23	Roseanne 5/8	Roseanne 5/23	Roseanne 1/18	Roseanne 6/1	Roseanne 12/9
6:30 pm			Cosby Show 1/16	Roseanne 4/25	NBA Basketball 3/22	Roseanne 5/11	Roseanne 3/24
7:00 pm	NBA Basketball 1/21		Star Trek 3/13	Star Trek 10/11		Star Trek: The Next Generation 3/23	Star Trek: The Next Generation 1/27
7:30 pm							
8:00 pm	Δ The Borrower 10/29	Star Trek Voyager 2/5	Star Trek Voyager 4/24	The Witches of Eastwick 10/25	Babylon 5 10/12	Babylon 5 1/26	Pointman 2/10
8:30 pm							
9:00 pm		University Hospital 3/5	Star Trek Deep Space Nine 10/31		Kung Fu 11/2	Kung Fu 5/18	Baywatch 2/3
9:30 pm							
10:00 pm	Hawkeye 1/28	Babylon 5 5/28	News 1/16	News 3/7	News 10/26	News 6/1	News 10/28
10:30 pm			OJ Tonight 5/1	OJ Tonight 5/23		OJ Tonight 4/27	OJ Tonight 4/28

Key: Δ Advisory ¥ MPAA Rating «» Violence Code

KTLA	SATURDAY	SUNDAY	MONDAY	TUESDAY	WEDNESDAY	THURSDAY	FRIDAY
6:00 am	Weekend Gallery 5/20	Infomercial 10/30	News 1/16	News 10/18	News 11/9	News 5/11	News 11/11
6:30 am	Pacesetters 5/6	Infomercial 10/30					
7:00 am	Infomercial 10/15	Captain Planet 1/29		News 12/6	News 1/25	News 11/10	News 10/21
7:30 am	Infomercial 2/11	Phantom 4/30					
8:00 am	Infomercial 5/27	Ironman 2/5					
8:30 am	Infomercial 3/18	Fantastic Four 3/12					
9:00 am	Ironman 3/4	Samurai Sybersquad 10/30	OJ Trial 6/5	OJ Trial 6/6	OJ Trial 5/24		
9:30 am	Making It 5/13	Samurai Sybersquad 4/30		Happy Days 12/6	Happy Days 10/26		
10:00 am	Soul Train 5/6	18 Again 1/22	OJ Trial 5/15	Magnum, P.I. 11/1	OJ Trial 6/7	Magnum, P.I. 10/13	OJ Trial 6/2
10:30 am	Big Spin 11/5						
11:00 am	Soul Train 10/29		Little House on the Prairie 10/24	Little House on the Prairie 10/25		Little House on the Prairie 10/20	Little House on the Prairie 12/9
11:30 am							
12:00 pm	Samurai Sybersquad 3/18	Baseball 5/7	News 5/22	News 6/6	Brady Bunch 1/18	News 6/8	News 5/12
12:30 pm	Baseball 5/27	California Dreams 10/16			News 6/7		
1:00 pm		The Legend of the Lone Ranger 12/4	Brady Bunch 4/24	21 Jump Street 11/8	OJ Trial 6/7	Brady Bunch 1/26	Doogie Howser 5/5
1:30 pm			Brady Bunch 2/13		OJ Trial 5/10	Brady Bunch 6/1	Brady Bunch 2/10
2:00 pm	The Pride of the Yankees 4/22		In the Heat of the Night 5/29		OJ Trial 6/7	OJ Trial 6/8	In the Heat of the Night 10/28
2:30 pm							
3:00 pm		Beverly Hills 90210 2/12	Northern Exposure 10/17		Northern Exposure 11/2	OJ Trial 6/8	Beverly Hills 90210 1/27
3:30 pm	¥ Fatal Beauty 5/13						
4:00 pm	California Dreams 2/11	Harry & the Hendersons 10/9	Beverly Hills 90210 10/31	Charles Perez 1/17	Beverly Hills 90210 10/19	Brady Bunch 6/1	Charles Perez 3/17
4:30 pm	Saved by the Bell 10/22					Charles Perez 6/1	
5:00 pm	Baseball 5/20		Doogie Howser 10/31	Baseball 6/6	Doogie Howser 10/12		
5:30 pm			Family Matters 5/1	Family Matters 3/21	Family Matters 5/17	Family Matters 6/1	Brady Bunch 3/10
6:00 pm			Full House 2/13	Baseball (con't)	Full House 3/8	Full House 1/19	Full House 3/10
6:30 pm		Bill & Ted's Excellent Adventure 11/6	Family Matters 3/20	Family Matters 4/25	Family Matters 5/17	Family Matters 3/23	Family Matters 3/24
7:00 pm			Fresh Prince 3/20	Fresh Prince 2/14	Fresh Prince 3/8	Fresh Prince 10/27	Fresh Prince 3/24
7:30 pm			Coach 10/10	Coach 1/24		Coach 5/18	Coach 2/10
8:00 pm	Beverly Hills 90210 12/3	Hercules Minotaur 1/15	Life Stinks 10/10	Amazing Stories 10/11	Amazing Stories 10/12	Twins 11/3	Bill & Ted's Excellent Adventure 11/4
8:30 pm							
9:00 pm	Vanishing Son 3/11						
9:30 pm							
10:00 pm	News 2/4	News 1/29	News 11/7	News 1/24		News 1/19	News 1/20
10:30 pm							

Key: Δ Advisory   ¥ MPAA Rating   «» Violence Code

LIF	SATURDAY	SUNDAY	MONDAY	TUESDAY	WEDNESDAY	THURSDAY	FRIDAY
6:00 am	Infomercial 1/14	Infomercial 11/6	Infomercial 4/24	Infomercial 3/7	Infomercial 2/15	Infomercial 5/18	Infomercial 3/24
6:30 am	Infomercial 10/15	Infomercial 12/4	Infomercial 1/23	Infomercial 3/7	Infomercial 5/31	Infomercial 1/26	Infomercial 3/10
7:00 am	Infomercial 3/4		Infomercial 1/30	Infomercial 4/25	Infomercial 2/15	Infomercial 1/26	Infomercial 3/17
7:30 am	Infomercial 5/13		Everyday Workout 1/23	Everyday Workout 10/18	Everyday Workout 5/31	Everyday Workout 5/4	Everyday Workout 11/4
8:00 am	Infomercial 3/18	Infomercial 1/29	Old MacDonald's Sing Along 3/20	Old MacDonald's Sing Along 4/25	Old MacDonald's Sing Along 10/26	Old MacDonald's Sing Along 3/9	Old MacDonald's Sing Along 3/17
8:30 am	Infomercial 1/21	Infomercial 10/16	What Every Baby Knows 11/7	Your Baby & Child 5/23	What Every Baby Knows 5/3	Your Baby & Child 5/11	What Every Baby Knows 4/28
9:00 am	Infomercial 1/28	Infomercial 10/23	Sisters 10/31	Sisters 1/24	Sisters 1/18	Sisters 2/9	Sisters 1/27
9:30 am	Infomercial 3/11	Infomercial 3/5					
10:00 am	Infomercial 3/11	Infomercial 12/4	Our Home 2/6	Our Home 10/11	Our Home 3/22	Our Home 11/3	Our Home 10/21
10:30 am	Infomercial 12/3	Infomercial 5/7					
11:00 am	What Every Baby Knows 3/4	The Commish 1/22	Barbara Walters 5/8	Barbara Walters 5/9	Marriage Counselor 11/9	Barbars Walters 3/16	Barbars Walters 2/17
11:30 am	Your Baby & Child 3/18		Tracy Ulman 5/22	Tracy Ulman 5/9	Tracy Ulman 2/1	Supermarket Sweep 10/20	Supermarket Sweep 11/11
12:00 pm	Supermarket Sweep 11/5		Live from Queens 11/7	Live from Queens 11/8	Live from Queens 2/8	Live from Queens 1/19	Live from Queens 3/24
12:30 pm	Shop 'Til You Drop 10/15	Locked Up 10/9					
1:00 pm	In the Name of Love 10/8		Designing Women 1/30	Designing Women 10/18	Designing Women 10/26	Designing Women 5/11	Designing Women 3/10
1:30 pm	Ooh La La 2/11		Designing Women 10/24	Designing Women 3/21	Designing Women 6/7	Designing Women 5/18	Designing Women 1/27
2:00 pm	Δ Unsolved Mysteries 10/22	LA Law 5/7	Spenser for Hire 5/29	Our Home 10/25	Our Home 4/26	Our Home 10/20	Our Home 1/20
2:30 pm							
3:00 pm	Donor 4/22	Δ Unsolved Mysteries 10/16	Thirtysomething 1/16	Thirtysomething 2/7	Thirtysomething 5/10	Thirtysomething 2/2	
3:30 pm							
4:00 pm	Deceptions 1/21	The People Across the Lake 10/30	Agatha 10/24	I Love You Perfect 2/14		Imagine: John Lennon 12/8	
4:30 pm							
5:00 pm	Δ A Cry for Help 10/8						
5:30 pm							
6:00 pm			Supermarket Sweep 4/24	Supermarket Sweep 3/21		Supermarket Sweep 5/4	Supermarket Sweep 12/9
6:30 pm		Deadly Matrimony 5/21	Shop 'Til You Drop 3/20	Shop 'Til You Drop 1/31	Shop 'Til You Drop 3/8	Shop 'Til You Drop 3/16	Shop 'Til You Drop 10/21
7:00 pm	Compromising Positions 1/14		Designing Women 3/13	Designing Women 5/2	Designing Women 3/22	Designing Women 10/13	Designing Women 5/5
7:30 pm					Designing Women 2/1	Designing Women 3/23	Designing Women 2/3
8:00 pm	Swimsuit 2/11		Unsolved Mysteries 10/17	Δ Unsolved Mysteries 11/1		Unsolved Mysteries 3/23	Unsolved Mysteries 11/4
8:30 pm							
9:00 pm	In the Name of Love 10/22	A Cry in the Dark 2/12	Runaway Father 10/10	Spenser - A Savage Place 1/17	And Then There Was One 11/9	The Penthouse 10/27	Δ Silkwood 10/14
9:30 pm	Swimsuit (Cont.)						
10:00 pm	Designing Women 4/29	The Commish 10/23					
10:30 pm	In tne Name of Love 1/28						

Key: Δ Advisory   ¥ MPAA Rating   «» Violence Code

MTV

Time	SATURDAY	SUNDAY	MONDAY	TUESDAY	WEDNESDAY	THURSDAY	FRIDAY
6:00 am	Videos 5/6	Video Countdown 10/16	Rude Awakening 3/6	Rude Awakening 12/6	Rude Awakening 2/1	Rude Awakening 2/9	Rude Awakening 12/9
6:30 am	Brothers Grunt 1/14						
7:00 am	Speed Buster 1/14		The Grind 3/13	The Grind 10/18	The Grind 3/15	The Grind 3/16	The Grind 3/17
7:30 am	Video Countdown 10/8		Rude Awakening 10/24	Rude Awakening 11/1	Rude Awakening 1/25		Rude Awakening 10/21
8:00 am		MTV Sports 1/15					
8:30 am		Sandblast 1/29					
9:00 am		Oddities 6/4	Videos 10/31	Videos 1/17	Videos 10/19	Videos 10/13	Celebrity Interviews 2/17
9:30 am	MTV Sports 3/4	Week in Rock 6/4		Best of the 90's 5/2			
10:00 am	MTV Sports 10/22	Jams Countdown 5/21	Jams 10/10	Jams 2/7		Jams 10/20	Jams 1/20
10:30 am	Oddities 2/11						
11:00 am	Jams Countdown 4/29	Singles 5/28					Videos 11/11
11:30 am							
12:00 pm	Real World 5/6	Jams Countdown 4/30	Videos 12/5	House of Style 2/14	Videos 2/15	Videos 5/4	Videos 10/14
12:30 pm	Week in Rock 10/22			Videos 3/21		Videos 5/4	MTV's Winter Carnival 3/10
1:00 pm	Paul-O-Ween 10/29	Real World 10/23	Videos 1/16	MTV News 2/14	Videos 11/9	Videos 10/27	Videos 12/9
1:30 pm		Week in Rock 1/15	Videos 11/7	Videos 3/21	Videos 2/8	Videos 1/19	Video Countdown 1/27
2:00 pm	Top Jams of the 90's Countdown 3/11	Videos 10/9	Videos 2/6	Videos 10/11		Videos 10/27	
2:30 pm		House of Style 3/12	Videos 2/13	Nirvana Tribute 3/7	Videos (cont. 2/15)	Videos 5/11	
3:00 pm		My So Called Life 5/7	Videos 1/23	Videos 1/31	Videos 4/26	Videos 1/26	Videos 2/3
3:30 pm		Real World 3/19					
4:00 pm	Free Your Mind 3/18		The Grind 10/24	The Grind 11/8	The Grind 3/8	The Grind 3/9	The Grind 5/12
4:30 pm		Top Jams 11/6	Sandblast 3/13	Sandblast 3/7	Sandblast 3/8	Sandblast 3/23	Singled Out 3/24
5:00 pm		House of Style 10/23	Real World 10/17	Real World 2/7	Real World 5/3	Real World 12/8	Beauty & the Beach 3/24
5:30 pm	MTV Jams 11/5	Top Jams (con't.)			Most Wanted Jams 3/22	Most Wanted Jams 2/16	Most Wanted Jams 2/3
6:00 pm	Summer Vids 5/27	Videos 10/9	Most Wanted 10/17	Most Wanted 10/25	Videos 1/18	Videos 1/19	Videos 1/27
6:30 pm	Real World 10/15	My So Called Life 5/7			Videos 3/22	Sandblast 2/2	Videos 2/10
7:00 pm	The State 2/4	NBA Wrap Up 6/4	Yo! MTV Raps 11/7	Yo! MTV Raps 1/17	My So Called Life 5/31	Sandblast 2/9	My So Called Life 4/28
7:30 pm		Unplugged 2/5	Alternative Nation 1/16	Liquid Television 10/18	Mariah Carey 3/15	The State 3/23	Week in Rock 10/14
8:00 pm	Madonna 12/3	MTV Sports 4/23	Prime Time 1/30	Prime Time 11/8	My So Called Videos 5/31	Prime Time 2/2	Video Countdown 10/28
8:30 pm		Led Zepplin 10/16					
9:00 pm	The State 4/22				Prime Time 5/31		
9:30 pm	MTV Sports 4/22	REM 1/29					
10:00 pm	Δ Beavis & Butthead 3/11	Beavis & Butthead 10/30	Oddities 2/13	Straight Dope 1/24	Real World 6/7	MTV's Winter Carnival 3/9	The State 2/10
10:30 pm	Beavis & Butthead 10/15	Δ Beavis & Butthead 3/12	The State 5/1		Real World 6/7		Δ Beavis & Butthead 3/10

Key: Δ Advisory ¥ MPAA Rating «» Violence Code

NBC	SATURDAY	SUNDAY	MONDAY	TUESDAY	WEDNESDAY	THURSDAY	FRIDAY
6:00 am / 6:30 am	Today 3/4	Today 1/29	News 1/23	News 5/9	News 2/8	News 11/3	News 10/28
7:00 am / 7:30 am	News 10/15	Meet the Press 2/5	Today 6/5		Today 11/2	Today 1/19	Today 1/27
8:00 am / 8:30 am	News 2/4	News 5/21					
9:00 am	Saved By the Bell 3/11	Weekend Travel Update 10/30	The Otherside 10/17	The Otherside 5/30	Δ The Otherside 6/7	Δ The Otherside 5/4	Δ The Otherside 4/28
9:30 am	NBA Showtime 4/29	NFL Playoffs 1/15					
10:00 am / 10:30 am	NBA Playoffs 5/13			Leeza 5/2	Leeza 5/31	Leeza 10/20	Leeza 10/21
11:00 am / 11:30 am	College Football 10/29		Another World 5/29	Jane Whitney 10/11	Marilu 5/10	Marilu 3/16	Marilu 11/4
12:00 pm		News For Kids 10/30	Days of Our Lives 3/6	Days of Our Lives 1/31	Days of Our Lives 5/3	Days of Our Lives 5/25	Days of Our Lives 5/19
12:30 pm		NFL (con't.)					
1:00 pm	Women's Golf 10/29	Golf 10/16	Another World 5/15	Another World 5/23	Another World 10/19	Another World 5/11	Another World 12/9
1:30 pm							
2:00 pm / 2:30 pm	Horse Racing 10/8		Phil Donohue 6/5	Phil Donohue 3/7	Phil Donohue 5/24	Phil Donohue 6/1	Phil Donohue 2/17
3:00 pm	Skiing 3/18	American Adventurer 5/28	Sally Jesse Raphael 11/7	Sally Jesse Raphael 5/16	Sally Jesse Raphael 11/9	Sally Jesse Raphael 6/8	Sally Jesse Raphael 3/17
3:30 pm	Home Again 11/5	Emergency Call 5/28					
4:00 pm	Weekend Travel 1/28	News 10/9	News 1/16	News 11/1	News 4/26	News 2/16	News 5/5
4:30 pm	Big Spin 5/27						
5:00 pm / 5:30 pm	News 1/21		News 5/8	News 6/6	News 6/7	News 10/27	News 5/12
6:00 pm	News 3/11	Extra 3/5	News 4/24	News 2/14	NBA Finals 6/7	News 5/18	News 3/17
6:30 pm	McLaughlin Group 3/18		NBC News 6/5	NBC News 10/18	NBC News 1/25	NBC News 2/16	
7:00 pm	A Current Affair 2/11	Earth 2 11/6	Extra 3/20	Extra 6/6	Extra 1/25	Extra 2/9	Extra 5/12
7:30 pm			New Price is Right 10/24	OJ: The Trial 6/6	NBA Finals (con't)	OJ: The Trial 3/16	OJ: The Trial 2/17
8:00 pm	Empty Nest 1/28		The Fresh Prince 2/6	Wings 1/17		Mad About You 5/18	Δ Unsolved Mysteries 10/14
8:30 pm	Empty Nest 12/3		In the House 5/15	Something Wilder 6/6	Cosby Mysteries 10/26	Friends 11/10	
9:00 pm	Sweet Justice 4/22	A Family Divided 1/22	Ray Alexander: A Menu for Murder 3/20	Frasier 1/17	Dateline NBC 5/17	Seinfeld 2/2	Dateline NBC 3/24
9:30 pm				Pride & Joy 3/21			
10:00 pm / 10:30 pm	Sisters 1/14		Seduced & Betrayed 4/24	Dateline NBC 6/6	Law & Order 2/1	ER 4/27	Homicide 2/3

Key: Δ Advisory   ¥ MPAA Rating   «» Violence Code

NIK	SATURDAY	SUNDAY	MONDAY	TUESDAY	WEDNESDAY	THURSDAY	FRIDAY
6:00 am	Lil' Bits 1/14	Lil' Bits 4/23	Mr. Wizard's World 6/5		Mr. Wizard's World 5/10	Mr. Wizard's World 5/18	
6:30 am	Lassie 3/11	Lassie 5/14	Flipper 3/13	Flipper 5/30	Flipper 5/10	Flipper 6/8	Flipper 2/3
7:00 am	Arcade 1/28	Flipper 10/9	Bullwinkle 2/13	Bullwinkle 4/25	Bullwinkle 3/15	Bullwinkle 6/8	Bullwinkle 10/14
7:30 am	All Star Challenge 10/15	Gumby 12/4		Wild & Crazy Kids 5/9	Wild & Crazy Kids 5/3	Looney Tunes 11/10	Looney Tunes 10/21
8:00 am	Doug 6/3	Adventures of Tin Tin 10/23	Weinerville 5/29		Weinerville 3/22	Weinerville 5/4	Weinerville 4/28
8:30 am	Rug Rats 11/5		Gumby 2/13	Gumby 3/21	Gumby 1/18	Gumby 6/1	Gumby 11/11
9:00 am	Muppet Babies 3/4	Looney Tunes 2/12	Rug Rats 1/30	Rug Rats 10/18	Rug Rats 3/15	Rug Rats 6/1	Rug Rats 10/21
9:30 am	Muppet Babies 5/27	Looney Tunes 10/16	David the Gnome 5/15	David the Gnome 6/6	David the Gnome 5/24	David the Gnome 11/10	David the Gnome 5/12
10:00 am	Beetlejuice 6/3	Rug Rats 4/23	Muppet Babies 6/5	Muppet Babies 5/30	Muppet Babies 10/12	Muppet Babies 2/2	Muppet Babies 3/17
10:30 am	Gumby 2/4	Rocco's Modern Life 10/30	Muppet Show 11/7	Muppet Show 1/31	Muppet Show 5/31	Muppet Show 1/26	Muppet Show 2/3
11:00 am	Alvin Show 3/4	Aaah! Real Monsters 3/12	Allegra's Window 5/8	Allegra's Window 1/17	Allegra's Window 11/9	Allegra's Window 2/16	Allegra's Window 5/12
11:30 am	Adventures of Tin Tin 10/8	Ren & Stimpy 3/19	Gullah Gullah Island 5/1	Gullah Gullah Island 5/16	Gullah Gullah Island 5/31	Gullah Gullah Island 5/11	Gullah Gullah Island 10/28
12:00 pm	Hey Dude 5/13	Adventures of Pete & Pete 1/22	Papa Beaver 12/5	Eureka's Castle 10/11	Train Mice 12/7	Rumplestiltskin 2/2	Snow White 5/5
12:30 pm	My Brother & Me 1/28	Secret World of Alex Mack 3/5	Papa Beaver 5/8	Papa Beaver 5/2	Papa Beaver 6/7	Water of Life 10/13	Lil' Bits 3/10
1:00 pm	Looney Tunes 4/29	All That 3/19	Eureka's Castle 5/22	Eureka's Castle 2/7	Eureka's Castle 5/17	Eureka's Castle 5/11	Eureka's Castle 5/26
1:30 pm		Wild Side 11/6	Lassie 6/5	Lassie 5/2	Lassie 10/19	Lassie 3/9	Lassie 2/17
2:00 pm	What Would You Do 3/18	U to U 5/7	Gumby 5/22	Gumby 3/21	Gumby 1/25	Gumby 6/1	Gumby 12/9
2:30 pm	Wild & Crazy Kids 6/3	Wild & Crazy Kids 5/14	Adventures of Tin Tin 6/5	Muppet Babies 11/8	Adventures of Tin Tin 6/7	Muppet Babies 10/20	Adventures of Tin Tin 12/9
3:00 pm	Weinerville 10/22	Wild Side 10/23	Looney Tunes 3/6	Looney Tunes 3/7	Looney Tunes 5/3	Looney Tunes 10/13	Looney Tunes 10/14
3:30 pm		Hey Dude 1/29	Beetlejuice 5/29	Beetlejuice 6/6	Beetlejuice 1/18	Beetlejuice 2/9	Beetlejuice 10/28
4:00 pm	Welcome Freshmen 4/29	Welcome Freshmen 5/7	Muppet Babies 5/15	Muppet Babies 2/7	Muppet Babies 1/25	Muppet Babies 2/16	Muppet Babies 3/24
4:30 pm	Beetlejuice 10/29	Family Double Dare 1/29	Legends of the Hidden Temple 6/5	Welcome Freshmen 2/14	Legends of the Hidden Temple 2/1	Legends of the Hidden Temple 3/23	Legends of the Hidden Temple 1/20
5:00 pm	Guts 4/22	Guts 2/5	Looney Tunes 6/5	Clarissa Explains it All 11/8	Adventures of Pete & Pete 2/8	Looney Tunes 6/1	Clarissa Explains it All 11/4
5:30 pm	U to U 5/6	Are You Afraid of the Dark 4/30	Clarissa Explains it All 10/10		Clarissa Explains it All 11/2	Clarissa Explains it All 6/8	Clarissa Explains it All 1/27
6:00 pm	Doug 5/6	Rocco's Modern Life 10/16	Salute Your Shorts 1/16	Hey Dude 1/17	Salute Your Shorts 10/12	Salute Your Shorts 6/8	Salute Your Shorts 4/28
6:30 pm	Rocco's Modern Life 5/20	My Brother & Me 3/5	Rug Rats 10/17	Rug Rats 10/11	Rug Rats 2/15	Rug Rats 1/19	Rug Rats 3/24
7:00 pm	Aaah! Real Monsters 12/3	Are You Afraid of the Dark 10/30	Are You Afraid of the Dark 10/31	Doug 10/25	Doug 4/26	Doug 3/23	Doug 5/5
7:30 pm	Rugrats 6/3	Roundhouse 1/15		Looney Tunes 1/31	Looney Tunes 10/26	Looney Tunes 10/27	Bing 1/27
8:00 pm	Secret World of Alex Mack 10/8	Nick News 10/9	I Dream of Jeannie 2/6	I Dream of Jeannie 5/16	I Dream of Jeannie 11/2	I Dream of Jeannie 10/20	I Dream of Jeannie 2/10
8:30 pm	All That 2/11	Taxi 11/6	Bewitched 3/20	Bewitched 6/6	Bewitched 6/7	Bewitched 11/3	Bewitched 11/4
9:00 pm		Taxi 11/6	I Love Lucy 10/24	I Love Lucy 6/6	I Love Lucy 10/26	I Love Lucy 1/26	I Love Lucy 2/10
9:30 pm	Are You Afraid of the Dark 2/11	Mary Tyler Moore 4/30	Mary Tyler Moore 3/20	Mary Tyler Moore 5/23	Mary Tyler Moore 5/17	Mary Tyler Moore 3/16	Mary Tyler Moore 3/10
10:00 pm	I Love Lucy 3/18	Mary Tyler Moore 3/12	Taxi 1/23	Taxi 6/6	Taxi 2/8	Taxi 4/27	Taxi 2/17
10:30 pm	Lucy Show 6/3	Dick Van Dyke 12/4	Taxi 1/30	Taxi 5/23	Taxi 6/7	Taxi 1/19	

Key: Δ Advisory   ¥ MPAA Rating   «» Violence Code

MAX

Time	SATURDAY	SUNDAY	MONDAY	TUESDAY	WEDNESDAY	THURSDAY	FRIDAY
6:00 am	¥ «» Body Snatchers 5/13	¥ «» Flesh & Bone 5/28	¥ «» Transformations 10/10	Desperate Journey 11/8	¥ Hollywood Knights 5/17	¥ The Big Chill 10/27	«» Crush 5/19
6:30 am							
7:00 am	¥ «» Space Hunter 3/18	Un Cour en Hiver 10/16	Arsenic & Old Lace 10/31		Night & the City 1/25		¥ Star 1/27
7:30 am						Crazy Movies 5/18	
8:00 am	¥ Side Out 11/5			Broken Arrow 3/7		¥ Hook Line & Sinker 3/16	
8:30 am							
9:00 am		The Secret Garden 3/12	¥ «» Free Willy 3/20		¥ «» Deal of the Century 2/8		
9:30 am		¥ «» The Abyss 11/6		The Letter 10/25			¥ «» Superman II 11/4
10:00 am						¥ «» Star Trek III 2/9	
10:30 am	Zoo in Budapest 5/27	¥ Nothing But Trouble 10/30			¥ «» An Officer & a Gentleman 3/8	¥ The Adventures of Milo & Otis 3/23	¥ PCU 3/17
11:00 am			¥ The Sandlot 10/17				
11:30 am				Far Away, So Close 1/31		¥ «» The Bride 3/9	¥ «» A Perfect World 5/5
12:00 pm			¥ «» Project X 3/13				
12:30 pm	¥ «» Enemy Mine 10/8	A Guy Named Joe 2/5			Divorce American Syle 2/1		¥ Wrestling Hemmingway 2/10
1:00 pm				¥ «» Buck the Preacher 2/13		¥ Hot Shots! Part Deux 1/19	
1:30 pm					¥ «» Reckless Kelley 5/3		
2:00 pm		«» The Alamo 3/5	«» Dis. of Nora 1/16			Reflections 2/16	
2:30 pm	A League of Their Own 10/22						¥ Groundhog Day 2/17
3:00 pm			¥ «» Prophecy 1/23	¥ A League of Their Own 10/11		¥ «» Geronimo 5/11	¥ «» A Gnome Named Gnorm 4/28
3:30 pm		¥ «» Phantom of the Paradise 1/22			The Competition 4/26		¥ «» Krull 3/10
4:00 pm	¥ Hot Shots Part Deux 10/29						
4:30 pm		¥ Welcome Home Roxy . . . 12/4	The Power of One 12/5	¥ «» Rocky II 2/7		¥ A River Runs Through It 10/13	
5:00 pm					¥ «» Addams Family Values 2/15		
5:30 pm	¥ Groundhog Day 2/11						
6:00 pm							¥ «» Million Dollar Mystery 10/21
6:30 pm				¥ Leap of Faith 10/18	¥ «» National Lampoon's Last Resort 5/31		
7:00 pm	¥ «» Beverly Hillbillies 3/4	¥ Remains of the Day 1/29	¥ «» So, I Married an Ax Murderer 2/6			¥ «» Fire in the Sky 10/20	¥ Stayin' Alive 10/14
7:30 pm							
8:00 pm						¥ «» A Bronx Tale 1/26	
8:30 pm		¥ «» Innocent Blood 10/23	¥ «» Lightning Jack 5/1	¥ «» Nowhere to Run 1/24	¥ «» The Secret Rapture 5/10	¥ Tequilla Sunrise 4/27	¥ «» Watchers III 5/26
9:00 pm							
9:30 pm							
10:00 pm	¥ «» Ring of Steel 1/28	¥ Made in America 2/12	¥ «» Ghost & the Machine 1/30	¥ «» Sweet Justice 11/1	¥ «» A Liptstick Camera 1/18	¥ «» Chained Heat II 5/4	¥ «» Criminal Passion 6/2
10:30 pm						«» Sins of Desire 11/10	

Key: Δ Advisory   ¥ MPAA Rating   «» Violence Code

PBS	SATURDAY	SUNDAY	MONDAY	TUESDAY	WEDNESDAY	THURSDAY	FRIDAY
6:00 am	Plaza Sesamo 5/27	Plaza Sesamo 4/30	Sesame Street 2/6	Sesame Street 1/17	Sesame Street 2/8	Sesame Street 11/3	
6:30 am	Sesame Street 3/4	Sesame Street 3/19					
7:00 am			Barney & Friends 3/6	Barney & Friends 10/18	Barney & Friends 1/25	Barney & Friends 2/2	Barney & Friends 5/12
7:30 am	Sesame Street 10/8	Kidsongs 5/14	Storytime 5/8	Storytime 5/2	Shining Time Station 10/26	Storytime 5/4	Storytime 5/12
8:00 am	Barney & Friends 5/20	Magic School Bus 1/29	Lambchop's Play Along 10/10	Lambchop's Play Along 1/24	Lambchop's Play Along 2/8	Lambchop's Play Along 2/16	Lambchop's Play Along 10/14
8:30 am	Puzzle Place 6/3	Puzzle Place 1/29	Mister Rogers 2/13	Mister Rogers 2/7	Mister Rogers 5/24	Mister Rogers 5/11	Mister Rogers 2/3
9:00 am	Storytime 4/29	Storytime 2/12	Barney & Friends 5/1	Barney & Friends 4/25	Barney & Friends 6/7	Barney & Friends 6/1	Barney & Friends 11/11
9:30 am	Vet Medicine 5/27	Δ Tony Brown's Journal 10/30	Storytime 10/10	Puzzle Place 1/31	Puzzle Place 1/18	Puzzle Place 1/26	Puzzle Place 3/10
10:00 am	New Garden 5/20	Life & Times 2/12	Sesame Street 1/30	Sesame Street 11/1	Sesame Street 11/2	Sesame Street 10/27	Sesame Street 12/9
10:30 am	Victory Garden 2/11	Life & Times 10/23					
11:00 am	Cooking in France 2/11	Masterpiece Theatre 4/30	Sesame Street 11/7	Storytime 5/2	Storytime 3/22	Storytime 6/1	Storytime 3/17
11:30 am	Look & Cook 10/29			Shining Time Station 3/14	Shining Time Station 3/22	Shining Time Station 2/16	Reading Rainbow 4/28
12:00 pm	America's Rising Star Chefs 1/14		Storytime 12/5	Puzzle Place 3/21	Storytime 11/9	Puzzle Place 5/25	Puzzle Place 5/5
12:30 pm	Frugal Gourmet 1/28	Locked Up 2/12	American Adventure 10/24	Encore 1/24	American Adventure 10/26	Psychology: Study of Human Behavior 10/20	Earth Revealed 10/21
1:00 pm	To the Contrary 10/15						
1:30 pm	To the Contrary 11/5						
2:00 pm		National Geographic 5/14					
2:30 pm	Covert Bailey: Smart Exercise 12/3	Nature 2/5	Destinos 6/5	Sales Connection 10/25	Wild America 1/25		Universe: The Infinite Frontier 3/24
3:00 pm			MacNeil Lehrer 3/13	MacNeil Lehrer 10/11	MacNeil Lehrer 5/17	MacNeil Lehrer 3/16	MacNeil Lehrer 2/3
3:30 pm	Life & Times 10/29						
4:00 pm	Adam Smith 10/15		Ghostwriter 1/16	Ghostwriter 1/31	Ghostwriter 5/24	Ghostwriter 10/27	Ghostwriter 10/14
4:30 pm	Thinktank 4/29	American Experience 10/16	Carmen Sandiego 5/1	Carmen Sandiego 3/7	Carmen Sandiego 2/1	Carmen Sandiego 6/1	Reading Rainbow 1/27
5:00 pm	New Workshop 1/21		Bill Nye 1/23	Bill Nye 10/25	Bill Nye 5/3	Bill Nye 2/9	Reading Rainbow 3/17
5:30 pm	This Old House 4/22		Todays Gourmet 3/20	Todays Gourmet 3/21	Look & Cook 2/1	Look & Cook 2/9	Frugal Gourmet 2/17
6:00 pm	Visiting with Huell Howser 5/6	Space Age 10/30	Nightly Business Report 3/6	Nightly Business Report 11/8	Nightly Business Report 2/15	Nightly Business Report 1/26	Nightly Business Report 1/20
6:30 pm			MacNeil Lehrer 10/31	MacNeil Lehrer 5/9	MacNeil Lehrer 11/9	MacNeil Lehrer 2/2	MacNeil Lehrer 1/20
7:00 pm	American Cinema 5/13	Pandora's Box 1/22					
7:30 pm	Nova 10/22	California's Gold 4/23	Life & Times 1/23	Life & Times 11/8	Life & Times 1/18	Life & Times 5/11	Life & Times 2/17
8:00 pm	Nature 1/21	Nature 5/7	Future Quest 2/13	Δ Nova 2/14	Long Shadows 5/31		Washington Week in Review 3/10
8:30 pm			Future Quest 1/16				Wall Street Week 2/10
9:00 pm	The Glass Key 1/28	Masterpiece Theatre 1/15	Ken Burns Baseball 4/24	Δ Frontline 10/18		Mystery 1/19	Making Welfare Work 1/27
9:30 pm							
10:00 pm		Δ Frontline 10/23			American Exp. 10/12		Memories & Dreams 10/28
10:30 pm						Women's Voices 10/13	

Key: Δ Advisory   ¥ MPAA Rating   «» Violence Code

SHO	SATURDAY	SUNDAY	MONDAY	TUESDAY	WEDNESDAY	THURSDAY	FRIDAY
6:00 am	△¥ Butterflies are Free 2/11		△¥ Benny & Joon 10/17	The Devil & Daniel Webster 1/24	△«» Rookies 1/25		Henry's Cat 4/28
6:30 am						Bunch of Munsch 11/3	
7:00 am	Shelly Duval's Stories 2/11	Bunch of Munsch 3/5	Owl TV 1/16			Owl TV 4/27	Busy World of Richard Scary 5/5
7:30 am		Mrs. Piggly Wiggly 1/29		Mr. Bean 12/6	Owl TV 5/31	Mrs. Piggly Wiggly 4/27	
8:00 am	△¥ A Fine Romance 11/5	△¥ Oh What a Night 10/23	△¥ «» Hercules in New York 2/6	△¥ «» Still of the Night 10/25	△¥ «» Juggernaut 1/18	God is My Co-Pilot 3/23	△¥ «» Thunder Road 11/4
8:30 am							
9:00 am							
9:30 am			△¥ Lucky Lady 1/23			Marilynn Hotchkiss 12/8	
10:00 am	△¥ «» Every Breath 1/28	△¥ «» Wilder Naplam 1/29		△¥ «» Josh & S.A.M. 1/31	△ Gentleman Marry Brunettes 11/2	In This Our Life 6/8	Frankie & Johnny 11/11
10:30 am						△¥ Orlando 6/1	
11:00 am							
11:30 am	Degrassi Jr. High 3/11		△¥ Conrack 5/1			△¥ «» Natural Causes 1/19	△¥ Peggy Sue Got Married 3/10
12:00 pm	Still of the Night 10/8	△¥ «» Desire & Hell at the Sunset Motel 10/9			△¥ «» Mystery Date 2/15	△¥ Poseidon Adventure 5/11	△¥ «» Secret of Santa Victoria 10/14
12:30 pm			What Did You Do In the War, Daddy? 5/8				
1:00 pm							
1:30 pm	△¥ Indian Summer 1/14		△ «» Impasse 1/30				
2:00 pm		Always 11/6				△¥ Butterflies are Free 2/2	
2:30 pm					The Corn is Green 2/8		Time Bandits 3/17
3:00 pm	Huck & the King of Hearts 10/22						
3:30 pm				Objective Burma 3/7			What Did You Do In the War, Daddy? 1/20
4:00 pm		△¥ Blind Date 2/5	Huck & the King of Hearts 10/31		¥ Adventures of Milo & Otis 3/15	△¥ «» Car 54 Where are You? 2/9	
4:30 pm			△¥ «» Love Field 3/20	What Did You Do In the War, Daddy? 10/18			
5:00 pm	¥ Look Who's Talking Too 1/21	Ready or Not 2/12	△¥ Avalon 2/13		△¥ «» Solar Crisis 10/25	Here to Eternity 5/18	Busy World of Richard Scary 2/3
5:30 pm		Degrassi Jr. High 2/12					We All Have Tales 2/10
6:00 pm	△¥ «» Born Yesterday 5/6		¥ △ «» Twilight Zone 1/16			△¥ «» Coma 11/3	△¥ «» Still of the Night 2/3
6:30 pm		△¥ «» Across the Tracks 3/5			△¥ A Wedding 3/8		
7:00 pm				△¥ Nothing in Common 11/1			
7:30 pm	△¥ Indian Summer 5/13		¥ The Adventures of Milo & Otis 11/7		Degrassi Jr. High 11/2		
8:00 pm	△¥ «» American Cyborg Steel Warrior 3/4			△¥ «» The Joy Luck Club 10/11		△¥ «» Universal Soldier 10/27	The Bedroom Window 10/28
8:30 pm		△¥ Threesome 5/21	△¥ «» The Dark Half 3/6				
9:00 pm							
9:30 pm						Confessions of a Sorority Girl 10/13	
10:00 pm	△¥ «» The Joy Luck Club 3/18	△¥ Son in Law 3/19		△¥ «» Sins of the Night 2/7	△¥ Bird 2/1		△¥ «» Showdown 1/27
10:30 pm			△¥ «» Fit to Kill 10/24				

Key: △ Advisory   ¥ MPAA Rating   «» Violence Code

TNT

Time	SATURDAY	SUNDAY	MONDAY	TUESDAY	WEDNESDAY	THURSDAY	FRIDAY
6:00 am	How the West was Won 1/28	Bugs Bunny 3/19	Pink Panther 11/7	Pink Panther 11/8	Pink Panther 3/15		
6:30 am		Gilligan's Island 10/16		Jetsons 3/7	Jetsons 10/26	Pink Panther 5/11	
7:00 am	Wild Wild West 5/6	In the Heat of the Night 1/15	Bugs Bunny 10/17	Bugs Bunny 5/16	Bugs Bunny 5/3	Bugs Bunny 5/11	Bugs Bunny 1/27
7:30 am							
8:00 am	Wild Wild West 10/15	Avenging Angel 1/29	Knot's Landing 4/24	Knot's Landing 4/25	Knot's Landing 3/15	Knot's Landing 2/2	Knot's Landing 12/9
8:30 am							
9:00 am	The Good Ol' Boys 3/18		Chips 5/15	Chips 3/7	Chips 2/15		
9:30 am							
10:00 am		Lakota Woman 10/23	Kung Fu 5/8	Chips 11/1	Kung Fu 2/1	Kung Fu 2/9	Kung Fu 2/3
10:30 am							
11:00 am		A Woman of Substance 5/14	How the West was Won 3/13	How the West was Won 1/17	How the West was Won 5/24	How the West was Won 3/23	How the West was Won 1/20
11:30 am	Kung Fu 2/11						
12:00 pm	Terror of Mechagodzilla 1/14	High Noon 5/7	Wild Wild West 1/23	Wild Wild West 2/7	Wild Wild West 5/31	Wild Wild West 5/4	Wild Wild West 2/10
12:30 pm							
1:00 pm		Charlie's Angels 10/9	Man from Laramie 10/10	Day of the Evil Gun 10/25	The Badlanders 1/25	Best of Badmen 1/19	Rocky Mountain 2/17
1:30 pm							
2:00 pm	Bugs Bunny 3/4						
2:30 pm							
3:00 pm		The Devil at 4:00 3/12	Starsky & Hutch 1/16	Starsky & Hutch 3/14	Starsky & Hutch 5/10	Starsky & Hutch 5/18	Starsky & Hutch 4/28
3:30 pm							
4:00 pm	In the Heat of the Night 3/11	Daisy-Head Mayzie 2/5	Kung Fu 11/7	Kung Fu 10/11	Kung Fu 10/26	In the Heat of the Night 4/27	In the Heat of the Night 3/10
4:30 pm		Devil at 4:00 (con't)					
5:00 pm	Charlie's Angels 2/4	The Blue Lagoon 5/21	Avenging Angel 1/30	The Hanging Tree 10/18	The Unforgiven 11/2	NFL Football 10/13	Geronimo 10/21
5:30 pm							
6:00 pm							
6:30 pm							
7:00 pm	It's a Mad Mad Mad Mad World 11/5		Track of the Cat 3/6				NBA Basketball 11/11
7:30 pm		The Master Gunfighter 2/12		Cannon for Cordoba 12/6	△ Some Kind of Hero 4/26		
8:00 pm					Inside the Academy Awards 3/22		Bite the Bullet 3/17
8:30 pm							
9:00 pm			Burnt Offerings 10/31		Cat Ballou 1/18		
9:30 pm							
10:00 pm	△ Escape from NY 1/21	Avenging Angel 1/22		△ Fighting Back 1/31			
10:30 pm			Ambush Bay 5/29				Gog 5/12

Key: △ Advisory   ¥ MPAA Rating   «» Violence Code

USA

	SATURDAY	SUNDAY	MONDAY	TUESDAY	WEDNESDAY	THURSDAY	FRIDAY
6:00 am	Bob Winkleman 10/8	Cartoon Express 10/23	First Business 3/13	First Business 5/30	First Business 3/15	First Business 5/18	First Business 5/26
6:30 am	Bob Winkleman 10/8	Cartoon Express 10/23	Cartoon Express 10/31	Cartoon Express 10/18	Infomerical 5/31	Cartoon Express 10/20	Cartoon Express 10/21
7:00 am	Infomercial 11/5	Cartoon Express 1/29	Cartoon Express 2/13		Cartoon Express 5/24		
7:30 am	Infomercial 3/11	Cartoon Express 1/29	Cartoon Express 3/20	Ninja Turtles 11/1	Cartoon Express 5/24	Cartoon Express 5/11	Cartoon Express 5/12
8:00 am	Infomercial 1/28	Cartoon Express 4/23	Cartoon Express 3/13	Cartoon Express 5/16	Cartoon Express 5/24	Cartoon Express 1/19	Cartoon Express 5/5
8:30 am	Infomercial 3/4	Cartoon Express 10/23	Cartoon Express 3/13	Cartoon Express 4/25	Cartoon Express 5/24	Cartoon Express 1/19	Cartoon Express 5/5
9:00 am	C/Net Central 5/13	Cartoon Express 10/23	MacGyver 5/8	MacGyver 3/14	Cartoon Express 10/26	Cartoon Express 10/20	Cartoon Express 10/14
9:30 am	Hollywood Insider 5/6	Cartoon Express 5/7	MacGyver 5/8	MacGyver 3/14	Cartoon Express 10/26	MacGyver 2/16	Cartoon Express 10/14
10:00 am	WWF 10/15	Cartoon Express 5/14	Murder, She Wrote 5/1	Major Dad 10/25	Major Dad 10/26	Murder, She Wrote 2/9	Murder, She Wrote 2/10
10:30 am	WWF 10/15	Cartoon Express 5/14	Murder, She Wrote 5/1	Murder, She Wote 2/14	Murder, She Wrote 1/25	Murder, She Wrote 2/9	Murder, She Wrote 2/10
11:00 am	Knight Rider 11/5	Cartoon Express 2/12	Murder, She Wrote 10/24	Odd Couple 1/17	Murder, She Wrote 11/2		The Odd Couple 1/27
11:30 am	Knight Rider 11/5		Murder, She Wrote 10/24	Major Dad 5/16	Murder, She Wrote 11/2		Major Dad 2/3
12:00 pm	Δ Halloween II 10/29	WWF 10/9	French Open 5/29	Scrabble 10/25	Quantum Leap 5/10	Scrabble 10/27	Quantum Leap 12/9
12:30 pm	Δ Halloween II 10/29	WWF 10/9	French Open 5/29	Quantum Leap 3/21	Quantum Leap 5/10	Quantum Leap 3/9	Quantum Leap 12/9
1:00 pm	Δ Halloween II 10/29	WWF 10/9	Magnum, P.I. 1/30	Magnum, P.I. 1/31	Westminster Dog Show 2/15	Magnum, P.I. 5/4	Magnum, P.I. 1/20
1:30 pm	Δ Halloween II 10/29	WWF 10/9	Magnum, P.I. 1/30	Magnum, P.I. 1/31	Westminster Dog Show 2/15	$100,000 Pyramid 10/13	$100,000 Pyramid 10/14
2:00 pm	The Outlaw Josey Wales 1/21	Smokey Mountain Christmas 12/4	$25,000 Pyramid 10/17	Uptown Swing 3/7	$100,000 Pyramid 1/18	$100,000 Pyramid 4/27	$100,000 Pyramid 2/3
2:30 pm	The Outlaw Josey Wales 1/21	Smokey Mountain Christmas 12/4	Free 4 All 10/31	Free 4 All 11/1	Quicksilver 1/18		Free 4 All 10/21
3:00 pm	Tall, Dark & Deadly 2/4	Cocktail 1/15	Press Your Luck 10/17	Tatooed Fighters 3/14	Press Your Luck 2/1	Press Your Luck 11/10	Press Your Luck 11/4
3:30 pm	Tall, Dark & Deadly 2/4	Cocktail 1/15	Scrabble 6/5	Scrabble 11/8	Westminster Dog Show (con't)	Scrabble 5/11	Scrabble 12/9
4:00 pm	Tall, Dark & Deadly 2/4	Cocktail 1/15	MacGyver 2/6	MacGyver 5/2	MacGyver 2/8	Golf: Players Championship 3/23	MacGyver 2/17
4:30 pm	Tall, Dark & Deadly 2/4	Cocktail 1/15	MacGyver 2/6	MacGyver 5/2	MacGyver 2/8	Golf: Players Championship 3/23	MacGyver 2/17
5:00 pm	The Companion 10/22	Swimsuit USA 2/5	Knight Rider 1/16	Quantum Leap 10/18	Knight Rider 5/17	Knight Rider 3/16	Golf 3/24
5:30 pm	The Companion 10/22	Swimsuit USA 2/5	Knight Rider 1/16	Quantum Leap 10/18	Knight Rider 5/17	Knight Rider 3/16	Golf 3/24
6:00 pm	Naked Gun 2/11	Wings 5/7	Knight Rider 1/23	Knight Rider 5/23	Tatooed Fighters 2/1	Knight Rider 4/27	Knight Rider 4/28
6:30 pm	Naked Gun 2/11	Wings 4/30	Knight Rider 1/23	Knight Rider 5/23	Tatooed Fighters 2/1	Knight Rider 4/27	Knight Rider 4/28
7:00 pm	Wings 10/22	Lady Killer 3/5	Wings 1/23	Wings 11/8	Wings 10/19	Wings 10/27	Wings 1/27
7:30 pm	Wings 1/28	Lady Killer 3/5	Wings 3/6	Wings 1/17	Wings 5/31	Wings 2/2	Wings 3/17
8:00 pm	Kindergarten Cop 12/3	Lady Killer 3/5	Murder, She Wrote 5/22	Murder, She Wrote 1/24	Murder, She Wrote 6/7	Murder, She Wrote 12/8	Murder, She Wrote 10/28
8:30 pm	Kindergarten Cop 12/3	Lady Killer 3/5	Murder, She Wrote 5/22	Murder, She Wrote 1/24	Murder, She Wrote 6/7	Murder, She Wrote 12/8	Murder, She Wrote 10/28
9:00 pm	Kindergarten Cop 12/3	The Companion 10/16	WWF 10/10	Boxing 10/11	Sketch Artist 11/9	Caught in the Act 11/10	Trading Places 3/17
9:30 pm	Kindergarten Cop 12/3	The Companion 10/16	WWF 10/10	Boxing 10/11	Sketch Artist 11/9	Caught in the Act 11/10	Trading Places 3/17
10:00 pm	Weird Science 1/14	Silk Stalkings 3/19	Silk Stalkings 5/15	Boxing 10/11	Sketch Artist 11/9	Caught in the Act 11/10	Trading Places 3/17
10:30 pm	Super Dave 1/14	Silk Stalkings 3/19	Silk Stalkings 5/15	Boxing 10/11	Sketch Artist 11/9	Caught in the Act 11/10	Trading Places 3/17

Key: Δ Advisory   ¥ MPAA Rating   «» Violence Code

VH-1

Time	SATURDAY	SUNDAY	MONDAY	TUESDAY	WEDNESDAY	THURSDAY	FRIDAY
6:00 am	Top 10 Countdown 10/29	Hard Rock 3/19	Videos 10/17	Videos 2/7		Videos 11/10	Videos 11/11
6:30 am			Videos 1/30	Videos 6/6	Videos 5/3	Videos 11/10	Videos 2/17
7:00 am	Big 80's 5/13	Jam 10/9	Videos 5/15	Jam 10/11	Videos 5/3	Jam 10/13	Videos 5/26
7:30 am	My Generation 3/4	Videos 10/16	Videos 5/15	Videos 6/6		Videos 2/2	Videos 5/26
8:00 am	Big 80's 10/22				Videos 4/26	Vidos 2/16	Videos 6/2
8:30 am			Videos 11/7	Videos 5/2	Videos 2/1		Videos 1/20
9:00 am	Top 10 Countdown 5/27		Big 80's 2/6	Big 80's 3/14	Big 80's 5/10	Big 80's 6/1	Big 80's 12/9
9:30 am	Flicks 4/29	Videos 10/30	Number Ones 3/13	Videos 1/24	Videos 10/19	Videos 5/4	Videos 3/17
10:00 am	Fashion TV 5/6	Videos 10/16	Naked Cafe 2/6	Videos 4/25	Jam 10/12	Videos 3/16	Videos 3/17
10:30 am	Last Word 3/4		Top 10 Countdown 3/13		Videos 11/2	Videos 2/2	Videos 5/12
11:00 am	Top 21 Countdown 10/15	Big 80's Marathon 1/29	Videos 10/31	Videos 5/9	Videos 11/9	Videos 1/26	Videos 5/12
11:30 am		Women in Music 5/28	Fashion TV 5/1	Videos 12/6	Videos 3/15	Videos 1/19	Videos 5/19
12:00 pm			Videos 10/17		Videos 10/26	Big 80's 4/27	Gump Videos 4/28
12:30 pm			Videos 4/24	Videos 10/25	Videos 4/26		Videos 11/4
1:00 pm	Videos 5/20	Melissa Etheridge 2/5		Videos 10/25	Videos 12/7	Videos 12/8	Videos 12/9
1:30 pm			Videos 10/24	Videos 10/18	Videos 2/15	Jam 10/13	
2:00 pm	Bring on the Night 1/21	Videos 10/23	Videos 1/30	Videos 1/31	Videos 10/19	Videos 10/27	Videos 2/3
2:30 pm			Videos 10/31	Videos 2/14	Videos 1/25	Videos 2/16	Oscar Preview 3/24
3:00 pm			Videos 3/20	Videos 3/14	Videos 11/2	Videos 12/8	Flicks 5/5
3:30 pm			Videos 5/8	Videos 5/2	Videos 3/15	Videos 3/16	
4:00 pm	Naked Cafe 3/11	Fashion TV 2/12	Big 80's British Invasion 3/6	Big 80's 5/9	Big 80's 3/22	Big 80's 3/23	Top 21 Countdown 10/14
4:30 pm	Fashion TV 4/22	Last Word 1/15		Videos 5/30	Number Ones 12/7	Naked Cafe 1/19	
5:00 pm	Eagles Family Tree 5/6	Paul Reiser 11/6	Naked Cafe 2/13	Videos 1/31	Jam 10/12	Videos 3/23	
5:30 pm			Videos 11/7		Videos 3/8	Videos 10/20	
6:00 pm	Big 80's 1/28	Videos 2/12	△ Stand Up Spotlight 5/8	Videos 2/7		△ Stand Up Spotlight 5/4	Videos 6/9
6:30 pm			Videos 10/24	△ Stand Up Spotlight 5/16	Videos 10/26	△ Stand Up Spotlight 5/25	Videos 10/21
7:00 pm	Videos 12/3		Buster's Happy Hour 10/10	Don Kirschner's Rock Concert 6/6	△ Stand Up Spotlight 3/22	Don Kirschner's Rock Concert 5/11	Number Ones 1/20
7:30 pm				△ Stand Up Spotlight 1/24		Big 80's 5/11	△ Stand Up Spotlight 1/27
8:00 pm	△ Stand Up Spotlight 1/14	Eric Clapton 1/15	Top 10 2/13		△ Stand Up Spotlight 1/25	Big 80's 3/9	
8:30 pm		Sheryl Crow 3/5	Crossroads 3/20	Crossroads 5/23	History of Meatloaf 6/7	Bruce Springsteen 5/18	Crossroads 3/24
9:00 pm	Soul of VH-1 2/4	△ Stand Up Spotlight 3/5	Videos 1/16	Videos 11/8	Videos 11/9	Videos 1/26	Videos 3/10
9:30 pm					Videos 2/8		
10:00 pm	Videos 4/29	Top 10 Countdown 1/22	△ Stand Up Spotlight 1/23	△ Stand Up Spotlight 10/18	△ Stand Up Spotlight 5/10		△ Stand Up Spotlight 6/2
10:30 pm	Videos 3/11		Videos 1/23	Videos 1/17	△ Stand Up Spotlight 5/31		Videos 11/11

Key: △ Advisory   ¥ MPAA Rating   «» Violence Code

Appendix 2

Codebook for Television Violence

in Programming Overall

DEFINITION OF VIOLENCE

Violence is defined as any overt depiction of a credible threat of physical force or the actual use of such force intended to physically harm an animate being or a group of beings. Violence also includes certain depictions of physically harmful consequences against an animate being (or group of beings) that occur as a result of unseen violent means. Thus, there are three primary types of violent depictions: credible threats, behavioral acts and harmful consequences.

KEY TERMS OF DEFINITION SUMMARIZED

1.1 <u>Intentionality</u> refers to a character's state of mind or reason for engaging in violent behavior. To be classified as violence, a character's actions must be carried out with the desire or goal to cause physical harm to an animate being.

1.2 <u>Overt depiction</u> means that violence is shown or heard in the program content. Verbal recounting of previous threats/acts of physical force or talking about violence does not count as violence.

1.3 <u>Physical force</u> refers to a character's use of his/her/its own physical power (either human or supernatural) or the use of an object or device to cause physical harm to an animate being. Physical force must be initiated by an animate being; physical force or harm that occurs as a result of an act of nature (e.g., earthquake) is *not* counted as violence. Physical force can be perpetrated against the self or against another.

1.4 <u>Physical harm</u> occurs when a character experiences pain or bodily injury. Psychological, emotional, or social harm are not included.

1.5 <u>Credible threat</u> occurs when a perpetrator displays a serious intent to harm a target <u>AND</u> (1) the perpetrator communicates a serious intent to harm a target either directly to the target or to a person interested in protecting the target's welfare; or (2) the perpetrator possesses the means to accomplish harm to the target <u>AND</u> the target is in the immediate vicinity of the perpetrator and/or the perpetrator's weapon.

1.6 <u>Animate being</u> refers to any human, animal, supernatural creature or anthropomorphized being (e.g., possess human like characteristics). A group of animate beings can involve several characters or more abstract collections of beings such as institutions or governments. Violence must involve <u>at least one human, anthropomorphized being, or supernatural creature,</u> either as perpetrator or as target. When two or more animals threaten or harm each other it is not considered violence so long as the animals are not anthropomorphized. Human versus animal violence and animal versus human violence will be counted under some, but not all conditions.

1.7 <u>Accidents</u> involving physical harm are considered violence <u>only</u> when they occur in the context of an ongoing violent sequence (e.g., a criminal mistakenly shoots an innocent bystander in the process of fighting another criminal).

1.8 <u>Physical force against property</u> (e.g., breaking a window, setting a fire) will be considered violence <u>only</u> when it is committed in order to intimidate or threaten physical harm to an animate being. Property damage that occurs as an accident, even in the context of an ongoing violent sequence, will not be considered as violence.

1.9 <u>Harmful Consequences</u> are those visual depictions of physical harm that occur as a result of "unseen" violent means. Harmful consequences occur when a violent behavioral act is not overtly shown or heard in the plot, but the aftermath of violence is portrayed.

KEY TERMS OF DEFINITION EXPLICATED

1.1 INTENTIONALITY

Intentionality refers to a character's state of mind or reason for engaging in violent behavior. To be coded as violence, a character's actions must be carried out with the <u>desire</u> or <u>goal</u> to cause physical harm to an animate being. There are both overt and covert cues that indicate intentionality.

> 1. 11 **Overt Cues:** Various cues can be used to determine whether there is an intent or desire to harm. The most obvious is when a character expresses verbally his/her/its serious desire to hurt someone (e.g., a character discusses plans to harm someone in an earlier scene or directly threatens harm to a target).

> 1.12 **Covert Cues:** In many cases, the intent will not be overtly conveyed so one must use other cues to infer it. Cues that help in determining intent include: the initiator's <u>motive</u> or reason for violence, <u>emotional reactions</u>, or <u>extent of physical force used</u>, and the <u>target's reactions</u> to the force.

>> 1.121 <u>Motive:</u> In terms of motive, if a character engages in physical force in order to protect self or another, one can assume an intent to harm the attacker if for no other reason than to stop the attack.

>> 1.122 <u>Emotional Reactions:</u> In terms of emotional reactions, if a character expresses rage or anger toward another, this may also signal an intent to harm. So might an expression of jealousy or hate.

>> 1.123 <u>Extent of Physical Force:</u> In terms of the extent of physical force, cautious and limited force may be used more to restrain an animate being than to harm it. In contrast, excessive or extreme uses of force are likely to signal an intent to harm. For example, a parent who pulls a child away from a toy may not be using enough force to signal an intent to harm, but a parent who slaps a child or pushes a child to the ground in the same context is exhibiting more than simple restraint behaviors--the extent of force implies intent to harm.

>> 1.124 <u>Target's Reactions:</u> In terms of the <u>target's reactions</u>, pain or obvious wounds usually signal that force has been used. A target, however, might express pain even if there was no intent to harm (e.g., in an accident) so one must be careful in using the target's reaction by itself as a cue. The target's reactions should be used in conjunction with other cues, like the extent of force and the motive for the force. Lastly, remember that a target does not always show harm or pain (e.g., cartoons often fail to shown such pain cues) so don't assume that there must be obvious pain or harm in order for intent to be present.

>> 1.125 <u>Examples of Force Lacking an Intent to Harm:</u> Examples of the use of physical force that lack intent to harm include: practical jokes, accidents and natural disasters.

1.2 OVERT DEPICTIONS

Overt depictions of violence are those credible threats, violent acts or harmful consequences that can be <u>seen</u> or <u>heard</u> within the context of a program. There are three types of overt depictions: Visual, auditory and atypical.

1.21 **Visual depictions:** Visual depictions of violence are presented either in the foreground or background of the on-screen portrayal.

1.211 <u>Foreground Depictions:</u> In most cases, credible threats, violent acts and/or harmful consequences will be <u>seen</u> within the context of a program. Usually, these visual depictions will occur as the <u>primary focus</u> of the plot. Common examples include two characters getting into a fist fight, a shooting match between two outlaws or a bar room brawl.

1.212 <u>Background Depictions:</u> Other times, however, overt depictions of violence may be visually depicted in the <u>background</u> of an unfolding scene. For example, two bad guys may be in front of a saloon "staring each other down" prior to a gun fight while two other characters are brawling in the scene's background. Or, a character may walk into a room with a dead and bloody corpse lying in the corner. These background portrayals of violence should also be counted as overt depictions of violence.

1.22 **Auditory Depictions:** Depictions of violence may also be <u>heard</u> occurring within the context of an ongoing violent sequence but not actually seen. In these cases, violence that is heard will only be coded as an overt depiction when it involves an identifiable perpetrator and/or target. If a scream is heard coming from an off screen room in which a perpetrator or target is known to be present, then the scream is coded as an overt depiction of violence, presuming that all other criteria for defining violence (e.g., intent to harm is present) appear to have been met, taking into account the complete context of the program. If, however, gunshots are heard in the background of a scene and the perpetrator or target is not known, then the gunshots would not be coded as overt depictions of violence.

1.23 **Atypical Overt Depictions:** There are times when violence will be portrayed in a program in atypical forms. Examples of atypical depictions include violence enacted by characters assuming secondary roles in a program, violence within still photographs, artwork containing violence on background walls, and violence occurring on a character's TV screen.

For these depictions to qualify as "overt," they must be the <u>primary focus</u> or the <u>focal point</u> of an unfolding narrative. This is usually accomplished in one of two ways.

1.231 First, a <u>character may acknowledge, make a reference to, talk about the violent depiction or enact a secondary role involving violence.</u> For example, a police officer may use still photographs of a mutilated body in a discussion with an FBI agent. The harmful consequences portrayed in those photos would qualify as overt and could then be coded as violence, presuming that all other necessary criteria are met. Or, Bart and Homer may watch, laugh and comment as Itchy and Scratchy engage in violent behaviors on the Simpson's TV set. Because Bart and Homer react to the program depicted on their TV screen, Itchy and Scratchy's physically forceful actions would be coded as overt depictions of violence.

And finally, a character may assume a secondary role within a program. That is, a character may be acting out a "play within a play." This might occur, for example, if Alex Keaton in "Family Ties" were to take the lead role of "Clyde" in the school play "Bonnie and Clyde." All of Alex's violent actions as Clyde would be coded, provided that Clyde had an intent to physically harm his target in the play.

1.232 Second, the program's visual presentation may foreground or <u>focus in on a still photo, artwork or violence depicted on a character's TV screen</u>. For instance, two wanted criminals running from the law may be avidly watching the news to see if law authorities are on their trail. After watching for quite some time, the characters leave to go get something to eat. Immediately after they leave, <u>the camera pans and focuses in on a news story</u> as it describes the two wanted characters and shows a picture of them holding a bank teller at gun point. The picture on the news program would count as an overt depiction of violence (i.e., picture illustrates a credible threat), because it is the primary focus of the program's visual element.

In contrast, a program may background or present peripheral depictions of violence in still photographs (e.g., photo hanging on a wall of the L.A. Riots), artwork placed on background walls (e.g., painting depicting two Roman Gladiators fighting) or in portrayals on characters' TV screens (e.g., TV news story in background depicting a homicide). Because these violent depictions are not the <u>focal point</u> of the unfolding narrative, they will <u>not</u> be coded as violence.

1.3 PHYSICAL FORCE

Physical force refers to a character's use of physical power or capabilities in an effort to inflict physical harm. Physical force must include an intent to harm in order to be considered as violence. Physical force that occurs in a game or is playful in nature would not be considered violence even if it accidently resulted in physical harm (e.g., Homer Simpson hits Bart in the arm during a game of tag; Bart expressed pain but this would not count as violence because Homer did not display an intent to harm). There are two primary types of physical force: force by natural means and force by weaponry.

1.31 **Natural Means:** First, a character can use his/her/its own <u>natural means</u> or abilities to inflict harm. Common examples include kicking, hitting with the fist, slapping with a hand, biting, yanking or wrestling. In all these examples, the character enacts the physical force by using some part of the body and its inherent capabilities. Characters who are supernatural creatures may possess supernatural powers that they can also use to inflict harm. For example, a supernatural character may be able to direct laser beams from his eyes to inflict harm. This would be an example of the character using his/her/its own natural abilities (as defined in the context of the show), which happen to be supernatural.

1.32 **Weaponry:** Second, a character can use a <u>weapon</u> to inflict harm. In such cases, the character is using more than his/her/its own body and intrinsic physical force to accomplish violence, employing an object or device external to, or independent of, the body. A subsequent section will address the use of weapons.

1.33 **Four Special Types of Physical Force:** There are four types of physical force that may or may not qualify as violence. Those four include kidnapping, physical restraint, chases, and sporting events. Below you will find rules that demarcate when these types of physical acts will count as violence and how to quantify them.

1.331 <u>Kidnapping</u>: Kidnapping another character against his/her will may or may not include an overt use of physical force (e.g., a character could grab a child or entice a child into a car or two thugs could grab a character and throw him/her into a van and speed away), and may or may not include an overt intention to harm (e.g., a character may threaten an abducted child immediately or wait to threaten the child's parents over the phone in the future). Kidnapping by strangers or acquaintances for the purpose of personal gain (e.g., money, sexual gratification) contains an implicit intent to jeopardize if not harm the victim. Thus, kidnapping will be considered violence so long as it is serious and not part of a joke or game. There are times, however, when parents intentionally kidnap their children (e.g., during a child custody case, when running from the law) but do not intend to harm them. Although the kidnapping in this context is serious, it lacks an intent to harm and thus will not count as violence.

1.332 <u>Physical Restraint:</u> In most cases, physical restraint per se will not be considered violence because there is no intent to harm. For example, a parent may pull a child back from a candy bin in a grocery store. This action involves physical force but no obvious intent to harm. Similarly, a police officer may briskly put handcuffs on someone, again without an intent to harm. The only time that physical restraint will be considered violence is when a) the target displays an active physical <u>resistance</u> to the restraint <u>AND</u> b) the perpetrator employs physical force to overcome the resistance in a way that is likely to cause harm as defined herein. So, a parent who grabs a child in a way that looks like he/she is trying to cause the child pain would be engaging in violence. Likewise, a police officer who shoves a resisting suspect's face into the cement in order to temporarily inflict harm to overcome the suspect's resistance would be engaging in violence during the restraining process.

1.333 <u>Chases:</u> In many chase scenes, it is unclear why one character is pursuing another so it is impossible to determine if there is an intent to harm. Because of this ambiguity, chases will <u>not</u> be considered violence unless they are <u>preceded</u> by a credible threat or violent act and thus occur within an ongoing violent sequence. Even when chases are preceded by a credible threat, they will not be coded as violence, per se. Alternatively, a chase or pursuit will simply keep the duration of the violent sequence rolling until the imminent threat or actual use of violence ends.

1.334 <u>Sports:</u> Sports programming is not included in the sample. However, sporting activities and events will be encountered in the context of some entertainment programming. When this occurs, apply the following rule:

1.334a *Sports Rule:* For organized games/sports, such as a basketball or football game, assume that the characters are <u>not</u> intending to harm one another when they exchange physical contact so long as the exchange occurs within the normal bounds of the game and there is no specific evidence that indicates an intention to harm.

For example, in the context of a football game, one football player may tackle another player aggressively and knock him out. If this occurs in the regular course of play, then the act is <u>not</u> considered violence because one must assume no intention to harm. If, however, the prior scene depicted the tackler telling his teammates he was going to send the opponent to the hospital on the next play, that particular evidence would rebut the assumption and the act could be considered violence. For this to occur, the evidence of intent to harm must be serious. For instance, a baseball batter who yells to the pitcher that he's going to knock the next ball down the pitcher's throat would not be taken as serious; it is an aggressive euphemism that is common in sports but is not a serious threat of intention to harm.

1.334b *Key exception to the Sports Rule:* For sports that involve competition geared toward overcoming or debilitating an opponent through physically harmful means (e.g., boxing or karate), consider all physical blows to an opponent as intentional attempts to harm.

1.4 PHYSICAL HARM

Physical harm refers to injury, damage or pain inflicted against an animate being's body. The harm must be directed toward the physical body; acts designed to harm a character's emotional well-being, psychological or social well-being are _not_ considered physical harm. For example, if a character yells at someone or verbally harasses someone in order to embarrass him/her, it is not considered violence. Acts must be directed toward damaging or causing pain to an animate being's body.

1.41 **Duration of Harm:** Physical harm need not be permanent or lasting to be considered violence. For example, slapping someone in the face may cause only temporary redness or pain but still should be considered violence. Signs of physical harm include bruises, red marks, screams of pain, wounds, blood, organ or appendage damage, and death.

1.42 **Implied Harm:** In some cases, physical harm will not be shown explicitly in a sequence. For example, a psychotic killer on a shooting spree may be shown gunning down people one after the other as s/he heads down the street, but with only a brief glimpse provided of each victim being shot. As the camera follows the killer, no further information is provided about the harm that is suffered by an apparent victim of the gunfire.

In cases where a violent act is depicted but little if any information is provided about the harm that has occurred, one should draw the most reasonable inference about the likely impact of the act. For cases in which gunfire appears to have struck a victim, assume harm has occurred. For other types of physical assault, with or without the use of weapons, assume the most likely outcome that would be associated with acts of a similar type, taking into account all the relevant contextual information available from the program/plot. For example, if a trap drops someone into a small but deep pond of water, and no follow up about the outcome of the predicament is shown, one would draw different inferences about the likely outcome if the victim was known to be a non-swimmer than if the victim was a strong swimmer.

1.43 **Unrealistic Depictions of Harm:** Many programs, in particular cartoon and other children's shows, present highly unrealistic depictions of the physical consequences associated with violent acts. For example, one character may push another off of a steep cliff, sending the victim to a tremendous fall that would normally cause severe harm or death. In an unrealistic cartoon portrayal, however, the character suffers no harm and walks away. Or, a character like Elmer Fudd may shoot himself in the face, with the only consequence being that his face is blackened; he is otherwise unharmed by an act that would cause serious harm or death in the real world.

1.431 Realistic Inference Standard: In any case in which there is a patently unrealistic depiction of physical harm, the act that preceded the unrealistic depiction should be judged according to the principle noted above: one should draw the most reasonable inference about the likely impact of the act in realistic terms. Thus, all acts that would be likely to cause harm under normal circumstances in the real world (such as the two examples above) will be considered as violent, regardless of the actual depiction of an unrealistic outcome that is lacking in any harm.

1.432 <u>Special Note:</u> Improbable yet clearly possible "escapes" or safe outcomes associated with dangerous acts should still be considered as realistic. Only those depictions that are clearly unrealistic should be judged by the reasonable inference standard.

1.5 CREDIBLE THREAT

A **credible threat** occurs when a perpetrator evidences a serious intent to harm a target <u>AND</u> either one of the following two conditions are met: 1) the harmful intent is communicated or 2) there is an imminent threat. Each of these two types are explicated below.

1.51 **Harmful Intent Communicated:** The perpetrator must communicate a serious intent to harm either (a) directly to the target, or (b) to a person interested in protecting the target's welfare.

1.511 <u>Direct Communication:</u> Direct Communication may take the form of a telephone call, written message, or face to face verbal confrontation.

1.512 <u>Target or Person Protecting Target:</u> There are two possible recipients of communicated credible threats. The first and most obvious is the target. However, threats will also be considered credible when they are delivered to a person close to or interested in protecting a target. A person interested in protecting a target's welfare would typically include parents and/or family members, but could also include persons who are obliged to protect a particular target, such as a bodyguard or a law enforcement officers.

1.513 <u>Special Note:</u> To be considered credible, a threat must be serious and have a reasonable possibility of being carried out. Threats that could not possibly be fulfilled would be excluded. For example, when a criminal convicted in court screams to the prosecutor "you're a dead man" as s/he is being led away for a life sentence in prison, the threat would still be considered credible because the criminal could be paroled or could order others to accomplish the murder. When judged from this perspective, most serious threats would be included because it is difficult to know if they could possibly be fulfilled. However, any case in which it would be impossible to carry out a threat should not be counted. The timing for any possible delivery on a threat is not relevant. Threats that may be accomplished immediately or at any point in the future are both equally credible.

1.52 **Imminent Threat:** The perpetrator possesses the means to accomplish harm to the target <u>AND</u> the target is in the immediate vicinity of the perpetrator and/or the perpetrator's weapon. In this case, the focus is on overt behavioral actions that threaten, rather than any direct communication of a threat to the intended victim. Thus, it is irrelevant <u>whether or not the target is aware of the threat.</u> In addition to an intent to harm and an available means to harm, the target must be in the immediate vicinity of the perpetrator and/or the perpetrator's weapon.

1.521 <u>Immediate Vicinity:</u> Immediate vicinity refers to close physical proximity that would permit the threat to be carried out either at the time or imminently. For example, if a killer is on the rooftop of a building with a rifle waiting for an intended victim to arrive in a car, the threat is not credible until the victim appears at this location. In contrast, if the intended victim was known to be inside of a building across the street and could walk out of the building at any moment, coming into the possible line of fire, the threat would be considered credible. In this latter case, the victim is in the vicinity and the threat may be carried out at an imminent moment. In the former case, one would have no way of knowing if the intended victim would ever appear at the scene, and thus imminence is not present.

Another example would be in a scene from "Jaws," when a person is shown walking slowly toward the water's edge, possibly to take a swim. This scene is juxtaposed with shots of the shark swimming menacingly toward the shore. These scenes would <u>not</u> be counted as containing a credible threat until it is clear that the person is actually going to enter the water, which in this case would comprise the relevant "vicinity."

1.522 <u>Exception to Immediate Vicinity:</u> Violence can sometimes be accomplished even without the perpetrator being in the immediate vicinity. This can be done, for example, by remote control (e.g., planting bombs that have a timer) or by laying traps (e.g., digging a pit, covering it, and waiting for the victim to pass by; planting a snake in a empty vehicle that the victim will return to shortly). Because of this, it is not necessary for the perpetrator to be present if his/her weapon is still capable of accomplishing violence. In such cases, a threat becomes credible as soon as a victim is in the immediate vicinity of the weapon involved.

1.53 **Four Types of Special Threats:** There are four special types or instances of threats that are oftentimes difficult to assess. Those four types include: contingency threats, threats within the range of a perpetrator's weapon, a target/perpetrator's belief in an unrealistic/realistic threat and threats from a stalker. Necessary conditions must be met for each type of threat to be coded as violence. Each of the four types are explicated below.

1.531 <u>Contingency Threats:</u> There are times when perpetrators deliver credible threats that are contingent upon the target's response. In these cases, perpetrators have an intent to harm, possess the means to accomplish the harm, but choose to engage in physically forceful actions that purposefully "just miss" the target. In essence, the "just miss" communicates that the perpetrator has an intent to harm, possesses the means to harm, and will harm if the target does not comply. These strategically calculated "just misses" or contingency threats will be considered credible and should be coded as violence.

For example, a sharpshooter may purposefully shoot the gun out of an approaching target's hand. This action directly communicates that the sharpshooter purposefully chose to miss the target, has the means to shoot again and will shoot again if the target does not comply with his/her/its demands. Similarly, a perpetrator may be holding an individual hostage in a house surrounded by police officers. To escape safely with the hostage, the perpetrator may shoot a few feet in front of the police officers' barricade. By shooting purposely in front of the barricade, the perpetrator is communicating to the officers that he/she can and will physically harm them if they try to stop his/her escape.

1.532 <u>Within Range of the Weapon:</u> A target does not necessarily have to be present in order for a threat to be credible. When a serious threat is involved, and the perpetrator <u>believes</u> that the target may be within range (e.g., police with guns drawn kick in a door but there is no one home), or may appear at any moment (e.g., police climb several flights of stairs with weapons drawn as they head to a suspect's apartment on an upper floor), we will consider that threat to be credible, even if the target turns out not to be present.

1.532a *Within the Range of the Weapon Rule:* Whenever handheld guns are drawn (taken out of their holsters and held ready for use, even if not pointed), or other obvious weapons are brandished, and a target is either present or believed to be in the immediate vicinity, then a credible threat occurs.

1.532b *Exception to Within the Range Rule:* Be cautious applying the "within the range of the weapon rule" when you see characters carrying large rifles or semi-automatic weapons in their arms. Because these guns are too big and can not fit in holsters, most characters carry them freely in their arms. When you see a large gun being carried out in the open, do not code the mere presence of that weapon as a credible threat. Rather, wait until you see the character raise the rifle to his shoulder or motion in some way that suggests he believes the actual threat of violence is imminent.

1.533 <u>Belief in Threat:</u> When either the perpetrator <u>or</u> target of a threat believes the threat to be serious, the threat will be considered credible. So, if a perpetrator points a gun at a target and either person knows the bullets have been emptied, it would still be considered a credible threat so long as one of the participants believed it to be serious.

1.534 <u>Stalking:</u> Because it is often difficult to discern whether a person is following another for observational purposes, for purposes of inflicting psychological harm, or for more malicious reasons, we will <u>not</u> consider repeated stalking behaviors to be credible threats in and of themselves. Stalking behavior will only be considered as a credible threat under the following two conditions:

1.534a *When the stalker communicates an intent to harm directly to a target.* Thus, crank calls, heavy breathing and other similar behaviors that do not reflect an intent to physically harm (only an intent to frighten or to psychologically harm) will not be counted as violence.

1.534b *When the stalker displays a serious intent to harm a target and the target is within the range of an available weapon or otherwise able to be physically harmed by the stalker.* A stalker frightening a target by parking outside his/her house or by following him/her to the grocery store in an attempt to psychologically harm would not be counted. However, if the stalker was depicted as having an intent to harm the target physically and was in possession of a weapon at either of these times, and the target was within the range of this weapon at any time, then a credible threat would exist at that moment when harm becomes possible.

1.6 ANIMATE BEINGS

An **animate being** refers to any human, animal, anthropomorphized being, or supernatural creature. A group of animate beings can involve several characters or more abstract collections of beings such as institutions or governments.

1.61 **Human Being:** A human being is a homosapien with no supernatural or super biological characteristics or features. A human character may be real or fictional, presented in any   form including live action and animation. Examples of human beings include Dirty Harry, Elmer Fudd, Al Bundy and Marcia Brady.

1.62 **Animal:** An animal refers to all mammals, reptiles, birds, fish, sharks, and amphibians. Members of this group may be depicted in any form, including live action and animation. They possess only the natural characteristics and abilities native to each species. Examples include but are not limited to dogs, pigs, dolphins, and lizards.

1.63 **Supernatural Creature:** A supernatural creature is any being that (1) does not naturally exist in this world; (2) exceeds its biological limitations in regard to size or from; and/or (3) possesses supernatural powers and abilities that are not native to its species. Examples of supernatural creatures include but are not limited to giant animals, the Blob, and the dinosaurs from *Jurassic Park* (e.g., dinosaurs are supernatural creatures because their modern day presence is not natural or possible).

1.64 **Anthropomorphized Being:** An anthropomorphized being is any animal or supernatural creature that possesses human like characteristics. There are several characteristics that render a being anthropomorphic. If the character talks, then it is automatically considered anthropomorphized. If it does not talk, then it must overtly display at least two other human like characteristics. Such characteristics include but are not limited to: cooking food, wearing clothes, using sophisticated tools, possessing an interior monologue, walking in an erect manner, or using its upper extremities to grasp objects in a way that the animal it portrays would not naturally do.

There are two types of anthropomorphized beings: <u>animals</u> and <u>supernatural creatures</u>.

1.641 <u>Anthropomorphized Animals:</u> Anthropomorphized animals are those animals that possess relatively normal biological features along with human-like characteristics. Common examples of anthropomorphized animals include Bugs Bunny, Daffy Duck and Tweety Bird.

1.642 <u>Anthropomorphized Supernatural Creatures:</u> Anthropomorphized supernatural creatures are those supernatural creatures that possess human-like characteristics. Common examples include super heroes (e.g, Batman, Superman), human-like ghosts (e.g., *Casper*), and martians (e.g., Alf or Mork from *Mork and Mindy*).

1.65 **Animate Beings and Violence:** Violence must involve at least one human, anthropomorphized character, or supernatural creature, either as a perpetrator or a target. When two or more animals threaten or actually harm each other it is not considered violence so long as the animals are not anthropomorphized. Animals committing violent acts against humans and humans committing violent acts against animals will be counted under *some*, but not all, conditions. To ascertain what violent incidents involving animals will be coded as violent, refer to the following rules:

1.651 <u>Rule One - Animal Against Animal Violence:</u> When an animal threatens to harm or actually harms another animal, it will <u>not</u> be counted as violence. Common examples of animals acting violently against other animals include: dog fights, killer whales eating seals, and vultures devouring cow carcasses.

For this rule to apply, it does not matter if the animal in the program is portrayed in live action or animation. For example, the movie *The Lion King*, depicts two animated lions that do not possess any anthropomorphic characteristics attacking one another. This attack would <u>not</u> be coded as violent because the animated animals are not anthropomorphized.

If a human uses an animal as a weapon to harm another animal, the animal's aggression will <u>not</u> be coded as violence.

1.652   Rule Two - Animal Against Human Violence: For violence by animals against humans to be counted, <u>one</u> of the two following conditions must be met:

1.652a *Animal is Used as a Weapon Against a Human*: An animal would be considered a weapon when it is used by a human as an instrument to threaten or to actually harm another human. This can be accomplished in at least two different ways. The first and most common way would be a human commanding or controlling an animal that has been trained to act in an aggressive fashion. An animal is controlled when the animal's behavior is a response to a human's verbal or physical instructions or is otherwise clearly influenced by the human's will, training, or command.

An animal may also be used as a weapon when one character places another in a situation in which she/he would be *immediately vulnerable to animal attack* . Common examples include actually throwing a person into a pool of piranhas and placing a poisonous snake into an individual's car with the intent to harm the driver.

1.652b *Violent Animal is Central Theme of Program:* An animal's violent pursuit of a human or human-like character is the *central theme of the program,* with the animal's violent attempts at harm occurring in a *repeated or recurring* fashion. This distinguishes isolated animal attacks against humans, which are generally attributed to instinct (e.g., seeking food or protecting the animal's habitat or offspring from human encroachment) from attacks that occur in a *repeated and recurring* fashion, hence placing the animal in the role of an aggressive protagonist.

Examples of animals that will be coded as perpetrators of violence against humans are Jaws and Cujo. Conversely, examples of animal violence against humans that would <u>not</u> count include a single shark attack in a program or a single random lion attack in a jungle adventure show.

1.653   Rule Three - Human Against Animal Violence: In most cases, humans attacking animals will count as violence. However, there are five exceptions to this rule.

1.653a *Exception One:* Humans killing animals in an effort to obtain food (e.g., farming and/or agricultural programs) does not qualify as violence.

1.653b *Exception Two:* Portrayals of humans engaged in legal hunting will not count as violence.

1.653c *Exception Three:* Mercy killing of an animal (e.g., killing animals that are sick, injured, and/or near death in an effort to alleviate the animal's suffering) will not qualify as violence.

1.653d *Exception Four:* Accidental road kill (e.g, human driving over an animal on the freeway) should not be coded as violence.

1.653e *Exception Five:* Killing bugs and/or insects (e.g., swatting a mosquito biting a character on the arm) is not to be coded as violence. Note: Insects are not considered animals and thus are not animate beings for the purposes of this study.

1.7 ACCIDENTS

In most programming, **accidents** will <u>not</u> count as violence because they usually lack the most important element of our definition --- intent to harm. Thus, when physical harm occurs to an animate being as a result of a mishap, negligence or fluke, it will <u>not</u> be coded as violence. For example, a person who accidently hits a pedestrian because he was speeding or because he was intoxicated, would not be coded as violence. Although the driver was engaging in risky behavior, it is not violence unless there is a clear intent to harm someone. If a person purposefully drives into a pedestrian, however, it does count as violence.

Or, a child may accidently throw a ball or toy into a friend's face while playing. Such an act would not be coded as violence because it lacks an intent to harm. If you can tell from the plot (e.g., a character's facial expressions, earlier information about motives), however, that the child purposefully aimed the ball at another's face with a clear intent to cause harm, the same act would be counted as violence.

1.71 **Inclusion Rule:** There is only one special case when accidents will be considered violence: Accidental physical harm that occurs in the context of an ongoing violent sequence will be coded as violence. Such harm, though technically not intended, still qualifies as violence because it occurs within a violent sequence that itself was triggered by someone's intent to harm. There are two types of accidents that may occur within a violent sequence.

    1.711 <u>Accidents Resulting from an Act of Violence:</u> The first type of accidental harm is that which occurs as a direct result of a specific behavioral act of violence. For example, a criminal might mistakenly hit a bystander in the process of trying to beat up another criminal. Similarly, a police officer might accidently shoot a dog while trying to shoot a criminal. Finally, a perpetrator might accidently shoot himself in the foot while trying to fire a pistol at a target. All of these accidents occurred as a direct result of a particular act of violence (i.e., hitting, shooting) that was aimed at one target but accidently harmed someone else. The key is that the accidental harm that occurred can be directly connected to a specific violent act.

    1.712 <u>Accidents Resulting from a Calamity within a Violent Sequence:</u> The second type of accidental harm is *not* caused by a specific violent act but rather occurs because of some misfortune or calamity within a violent sequence. For example, a character might be chasing someone and accidently trip and hurt himself. Or, a character might flee from the police in a speeding car and accidently hit a bystander who is crossing the street. These accidents occur within a violent sequence but are not themselves caused by a specific act of violence. Chasing someone does not typically constitute a violent act unless a gun is raised during the chase. Similarly, fleeing from someone is not an act of violence. Yet, if harm occurred within the context of a violent sequence, it would need to be coded.

    Accidental harm that is caused either by a violent act or by a mishap <u>should</u> be coded as an accident so long as it occurs within a violent sequence.

1.72 **More Harm than Intended:** If a perpetrator is trying to harm a target and the resulting harm turns out to be more serious than intended, this does <u>not</u> qualify as an accident. For example, if a perpetrator is trying to wound a target but the gun is poorly aimed and the act results in death, this does not qualify as an accident. Even if the perpetrator shows remorse, it will not count as an accident so long as there was an intent to harm the target and a specific behavioral act was engaged in.

1.73 **Accidental Property Damage Within a Violent Sequence:** Accidental property damage that occurs during a violent sequence will <u>not</u> be coded as violence. The accidental harm must involve an animate being. So, if a criminal smashes a lightpost or drives into a building while chasing someone, the damage to the property will <u>not</u> be coded as violence *unless* an animate being also gets harmed in the process.

1.8 PHYSICAL FORCE AGAINST PROPERTY

Under most circumstances, **physical force against property** will be <u>not</u> be considered violence. There is only one exception to this rule.

1.81 **Physical Intimidation Rule:** If the property damage is being committed in order to physically intimidate or threaten to harm an animate being, it will be considered violence. Thus, if a person is angry and in that frustration walks along the street smashing car windows, it would <u>not</u> be considered violence. However, if a character was intentionally smashing the windows of a specific target's home in order to threaten that person, it would be considered violence. The key here is that the property damage must be committed with an intent to physically intimidate or threaten physical harm to an animate being. Overall, property damage should be assessed by the two following rules.

1.811 <u>Accidental Property Damage:</u> Property damage that occurs as an accident will <u>never</u> be counted as violence (e.g., a person accidently blows up a car or runs into a parked car).

1.812 <u>Property Damage within a Violent Sequence:</u> Property damage that occurs within an ongoing violent sequence will <u>not</u> be considered violence (e.g., during a car chase, a person runs into a stop sign) unless it is used to threaten physical harm to an animate being.

1.9 HARMFUL CONSEQUENCES

If a violent behavioral act is overtly shown, then it should be coded accordingly and any depiction of harmful consequences that follow should be coded separately. If, however, a violent behavioral act is <u>not</u> overtly shown or heard in the plot, but the aftermath of the violence is portrayed, then it should be coded as a "stand-in" for the violent behavioral act. In other words, a depiction of a violent aftermath *implies* that violence has occurred and should be treated as an "unseen" violent act. An aftermath is defined as the visual depiction of physically **harmful consequences** experienced by an animate being or beings as a result of violence that is unseen but clearly implied.

In many cases, the plot will reveal immediately that the harmful consequences are the result of unseen violence. However, in other cases it will not be immediately clear whether a dead body or a pool of blood is a result of violence or due to an accident, natural causes or a disease. When in doubt, coders should make the most reasonable inference about the cause of harmful consequences based upon the cues in the plot and/or the type of program.

In cases where there is a suspicion of foul play or violence in the unfolding narrative, coders should assume that harmful consequences are a result of violence even if this is uncertain. Similarly, when harmful consequences are depicted in programs that feature violence and foul play (e.g., crime adventure, police shows, action movies, mysteries), coders should assume that any portrayal of physical injury is due to unseen violence. For example, a dead body shown in the opening scene of a murder mystery television series can usually be assumed to be the result of violence given the nature and conventions of this genre.

1.91 **Forms of Harmful Consequences:** Harmful consequences may come in one of four forms: verbal/nonverbal expressions, physical injury, a dead corpse, and/or blood/gore. Each of these types are explicated below.

1.911 <u>Verbal/Nonverbal Expressions:</u> An animate being can express physical pain or suffering, either verbally (e.g., screaming in pain) or nonverbally (e.g., facial expression of anguish).

1.912 <u>Physical Injury to a Body can be Shown:</u> For example, a character may exhibit organ or appendage damage, open wounds or bruises. Bodily injury need not be accompanied by pain or suffering in order to be coded as harmful consequences. For instance, a person may be physically wounded but unconscious. Or, a cartoon character may walk around with a broken leg but show no pain because of the unrealistic nature of the program.

1.913 <u>Dead Bodies:</u> A dead body covered by a sheet would be coded as harmful consequences because the form of the body can be seen where as a body buried underground would not. Preserved body parts (e.g., skeleton), no matter how old they are, should be coded as harmful consequences <u>only</u> when there is a reasonable inference that death was caused by violent means. So, for example, skeletons in a medical lab or Halloween decorations would <u>not</u> be coded as harmful consequences.

1.914 <u>Blood and Gore:</u> Any depiction of blood (e.g., trails, pools, stains) or gore (e.g., internal organs, viscera) when no body is present would also be coded as harmful consequences so long as there is a reasonable inference that the blood and/or gore is a result of violence.

1.92 **Second Hand Representations of Harmful Consequences:** Second hand representations, such as talking about a victim's pain and suffering or showing photographs of the physical harm that results from violence, may or may not be coded as harmful consequences.

1.921 <u>Verbal Representations:</u> Verbal representations (e.g., talking about a person's pain or suffering, an injured body, a corpse, or artifacts of injury without showing any of these) do <u>not</u> count as harmful consequences.

1.922 <u>Pictorial Representations:</u> Pictorial representations of harmful consequences (e.g., photographs of a dead body) count only when they are shown to the viewer and are a focal point in the scene. In other words, characters must refer or react to pictures or the camera must reframe the scene to orient the viewer to the pictures in a way that gives special meaning to them. A background painting of a dead person or a background TV show depicting harmful consequences would not normally be coded as harmful consequences.

1.93 **Coding Harmful Consequences:** Harmful consequences to a given character are sometimes shown repeatedly over the course of a narrative. Such consequences should only be coded once, the first time they are depicted. For example, when a character first appears with a bloody face, it should be coded as harmful consequences/violence. However, when a character is shown in subsequent sequences getting medical treatment and recovering from scars, these portrayals should <u>not</u> be coded as additional harmful consequences.

Characters may experience multiple manifestations of harm as a result of a single act. For example, a character may first express pain from a gunshot wound and later in the scene he dies. These two manifestations of harm (pain and then death) from the same unseen act should only be coded once.

2.0 LEVELS OF ANALYSIS

2.1 PAT LEVEL

The micro-ordinate unit of analysis is the **violent incident**. A violent incident is an interaction between a perpetrator and target involving a violent act. Incident, then, is a <u>summary</u> unit of analysis comprised of the interaction of three subcomponents: a perpetrator (P), an act (A), and a target (T). A convenient acronym for this perpetrator/act/target interaction unit is the **P A T.** All variables that are coded at the PAT level of analysis will be explicated in section 3.0 of the code book.

2.2 SEQUENCE LEVEL

A **violent sequence** is a related sequence of violent behaviors, actions or depictions that occur without a significant break in the flow of actual or imminent violence. A related sequence means that one behavior, action or depiction complements another (e.g., by serving a similar goal or purpose), is clearly connected to another, or is a direct response to another. In a scene, character X may hit character Y who then turns around and hits back. This string of behaviors is related and forms a sequence, even if there are momentary pauses between the actions. The important aspect about a sequence is that it represents a narrative flow of events or depictions that are connected to one another. Because of this relational aspect, violent sequences typically occur in the same general setting among the same characters or types of characters.

2.21 **Sequence Begins:** A violent sequence **begins** with an initial depiction of violence. In other words, a violent sequence starts when 1) a credible threat occurs, 2) a violent behavioral act is initiated, or 3) the physically harmful consequences that result from unseen violent means are first depicted in the plot. You should start the "clock" on the sequence at the point that you see or hear one of these three things:

2.211 <u>Credible Threat:</u> Any verbal or nonverbal behavior that is depicted and qualifies as a credible threat of violence would begin a sequence. So, for example, when a character communicates a threat directly to a target or displays a weapon in the proximity or range of a target, a violent sequence begins.

2.212 <u>Violent Action:</u> Any behavior that meets the definition of violence would also trigger the beginning of a sequence. So, for example, if a person hits or slaps a target, the sequence begins when that hit or slap first goes into motion.

2.213 <u>Depiction of Harmful Consequences:</u> A sequence begins the first time any harmful consequences that are a result of unseen violent means (e.g., a dead body, a wounded body or blood) are depicted. Even if people are talking about a body in a room, the sequence does not begin until it is actually *shown* to the viewer.

2.22 **Sequence Continues:** Once a violent sequence begins, it **continues** in duration so long as there is contiguity or connectedness in the primary characters' violent interactions. In most cases, sequences will occur in the same setting and with the same characters. However, it is important to note that exceptions may occur.

2.221 <u>Exception One:</u> Characters who are battling may be shown in a setting that is <u>*in motion.*</u> For example, a wrestling match may start in a bar and the characters may tumble outside into a new setting. Moving from inside to outside or driving through various locations does <u>not</u> disrupt the sequence so long as the characters maintain an ongoing flow of consistent engagement.

2.222 <u>Exception Two:</u> New characters may enter the setting and join the violence. The sequence continues in this case so long as the flow of action is not halted.

2.23 **Sequence Ends:** A violent sequence **ends** when a **significant break** in the flow of action occurs. A break is considered significant when either 1) the threat of violence, the actual violent behavior and/or the harmful consequences of violence stop or cease within a scene or 2) the primary setting shifts in time or place in a way that extensively interrupts the flow of related action in the sequence. Each of these two demarcations will be explicated below.

2.231 <u>Cessation Rule:</u> A significant break occurs when the imminent threat of violent action, the violent action, and/or the harmful consequences <u>stop</u> or <u>cease</u> within a scene.

For example, the aggressor or the target might flee from the setting. Alternatively, police may enter the scene and stop a battle. Or, an aggressor may decide to put down a weapon or engage in an alternative method to resolve conflict. In addition to the imminent threat of violence and/or violent actions ceasing, there must be an end to the depiction of harmful consequences within a scene. For example, characters may remove a dead or wounded body from a scene. Thus, the sequence ends at the precise point within a scene when the threat or violent behaviors have been resolved <u>AND</u> when the harmful consequences are no longer shown.

Momentary interruptions in a string of related threats, actions, or depictions of harmful consequences within a scene <u>do not</u> end the sequence. For example, temporary breaks to reload weapons or momentary camera pans away from a dead body do not signal the end of the sequence. The sequence ends only when the violence (threat, acts, or consequences) has clearly come to some resolution within the scene.

Oftentimes in cartoons and other types of "comic book" or "formulaic" programs, production conventions will be used to demarcate the specific beginning and/or ending of a scene. In many cartoons, the standard convention used to end one scene immediately before beginning another is a complete fade to black on-screen (i.e., both audio and visual). All fade to blacks that occur within an on-going violent sequence will signal the ending of that sequence.

This "fade-to-black" technique is often used in *Tom & Jerry* cartoons. After getting his head waffled by Jerry, Tom is shown stunned with burn marks immediately before the on-screen depiction fades to black. Right after the screen fades to black, a new scene begins with Tom prowling after Jerry. Although this interruption was only momentary, the on-screen fade to black indicates that the violent actions and behaviors in one scene have completely stopped or ceased and new actions or behaviors are about to begin.

2.232 <u>Extended Interruption Rule:</u> A significant break occurs when the primary <u>setting shifts</u> in <u>time</u> and/or <u>place</u> in a way that <u>extensively interrupts</u> the flow of related action in the sequence. In this case, the violence itself does not necessarily stop but the focus of the plot moves away from the setting in an abrupt and extended way. For example, if a criminal is shown stabbing a target and the scene cuts to a new setting involving a family eating dinner, the violent sequence involving the stabbing ends at the cut away. The key is that the interruption or scene change must represent an extended shift away from the violence in order to terminate the sequence.

We have defined an extended interruption as a shift in time and/or place that lasts <u>at least 30 seconds in duration</u>. Thus, the family dining scene must last at least 30 seconds in order for it to terminate the stabbing sequence (if the camera next returns back to the stabbing). However, in some instances a violent sequence will be temporarily interrupted by flashbacks or cross-cuts back and forth between two or more time/place settings. When these cross-cuts to new places or times are less than 30 seconds in duration, they do not constitute a significant break and you should continue coding one long (although somewhat disrupted) violent sequence.

2.3 PROGRAM LEVEL

The macro-ordinate unit of analysis is an entire **program**. A program is considered violent if it features one or more violent interactions within the context of the plot. There are two types of violent programs in the sample. Each of these types will be explicated below.

2.31 **First Type of Program in the Sample:** The **first** and most common type of "program" contains *one* thematic story or unfolding narrative whose beginning, middle and end is presented across an entire block of time. These types of programs typically begin and end their time slots with standard production credits and/or conventions (e.g., teasers, previews, promos). The unfolding narrative or plot in these shows usually contains one or several reoccurring main characters who are featured throughout most of the story. While the plotline within these types of programs may be rather developed and include several rich subplots, they are presented as a part of one coherent story or narrative whose scenes are interrelated and interconnected by either character, setting and/or location.

2.311 <u>Examples of First Type of Program:</u> The examples of shows that would be categorized as this first type of program are limitless. Examples would include most sitcoms (e.g, *Seinfeld, Roseanne, I Love Lucy*) dramas (e.g, *NYPD Blue, Murder She Wrote, Northern Exposure, Picket Fences*), daytime soap operas (e.g, *General Hospital, Days of Our Lives*), and network and cable movies.

2.32 **Second Type of Program in the Sample:** In contrast, the **second** type of "program" features *two or more* self-contained stories whose unfolding narratives are each segmented and told independently of one another within a specific block of time. For a program to be considered segmented, <u>each independent story segment nested within the program must be introduced and separated from all other stories in the time block by standard production credits</u>. For all segmented content, all program level variables <u>must</u> be assessed at the end of each story in the time slot.

In segmented programs, the plotline, characters, and/or geographical locations in each segment typically vary from one story to the next. While each of the stories are independent of one another, they are usually assembled and presented around a larger program theme, focus, or title. Five types of programs within the sample may contain segmented content. Those five types of programs include, but are not be limited to, cartoons, music videos, reality based shows, news magazines and sketch comedies.

2.321 <u>Cartoons:</u> The first type of programs usually containing a series of segmented independent narrative units are cartoons. Cartoons are typically short, self-contained animated stories. Due to their short duration in length, many stations present a number of cartoons back-to-back within a certain block of time.

For example, you may be assigned to code a half an hour of *Cartoon Express*. After watching several minutes, you will realize that this program is really a half an hour of back-to-back *Looney Tunes* cartoons that are introduced by an animated narrator. Or, you may be assigned to watch the hour long *Tom & Jerry Show*. This show, in actuality, is a compilation of fifteen *different Tom & Jerry* cartoons. In both of these examples, each individual cartoon is "nested" within the larger show or time block. and is introduced by its own production and cast credits.

Not all cartoon programs contain segmentized stories within their time blocks, however. That is, you may be assigned to code an episode of *Cartoon Express* that only contains one long dramatic cartoon like *Scooby Doo*, *Ninja Turtles* or the *Smurfs*. In these types of cartoons, only one thematically developed, self-contained story is usually presented within a specified time block.

2.322   Music Videos: The second type of program usually containing a series of segmented units are music videos. Just like cartoons, music videos are typically short, self-contained stories or unfolding narratives that contain their own production credits that demarcate the band's title, song and producer. Due to their short duration in length, most stations assemble several music videos and present them back-to-back within a certain block of time.

For example, you may be assigned to code the hour long MTV program, *Rude Awakening*. Once you put in the tape, however, you realize that *Rude Awakening* is really an hour long compilation of different music videos. Because the music videos within *Rude Awakening* are preceded/introduced by production credits, then each video should be coded as a separate program or story.

2.323   Reality Based Programs: The third type of content that may or may not contain segmented material is reality based media fare. Reality based programs *typically* present two or three independent stories that feature different characters from different geographical locations. In some instances, the segments on reality shows will be introduced by production credits. When this occurs, code each narrative unit as a separate program. If production credits do not precede each story, then simple code the entire time slot or show as one program. Examples of reality based programs include *Cops, America's Most Wanted*, and *Rescue 911*.

2.324   News Magazines: The fourth type of programs that may contain segmented units are news magazines   Like reality based programming, news magazines typically cover or report on three or four stories about unrelated characters and/or issues. If the news magazine you are assigned to code separates the stories by standard production credits, then code each story segment as a separate program. If production credits do not precede each story, then code the entire program or time slot as one program. Examples of news magazines include *60 Minutes, Date Line, Hard Copy* and *Inside Edition*.

2.325   Sketch Comedies: And finally, the last type of programs in the sample that may contain segmentized content are sketch comedies. For example, programs such as *Saturday Night Live, American's Funniest Home Videos* and *Stand-Up Spotlight* are just a few examples of sketch comedies that typically contain a variety of self-contained, independent narrative stories or skits. Usually, the stories or skits that are contained within each of these programs will <u>not</u> be coded as independent units.

That is, skits on *Saturday Night Live* or humorous events presented on *American's Funniest Home Videos*, are rarely, if ever, preceded by production credits. As a result, each story would <u>not</u> be coded separately as an independent segment and program level evaluations should be made at the end of the entire show.

2.33 **Coding Program Level Variables:** The type of program you are assigned to code will directly influence when, where, and how you assess program level variables. If you are assigned to code a program containing only one thematic story or plotline across one time slot (2.31 above), then you should assess all program level variables after watching the entire show.

If you are assigned to code a program that has independent segments nested within it (2.32 above) that are separated by production credits, then you should fill out separate PAT, sequence and program level coding forms for each of the segments viewed. All introductory material and teasers should still be assessed using the decontextualized scheme. As a rule, all decontextualized coding at the *beginning* of an episode should be filled out on the PAT coding form for the first program segment. If a teaser occurs somewhere within a program, then decontextualized assessments should be written on the PAT form for the segment it occurs immediately before or after. All decontextualized coding at the end of an episode should be written on the PAT coding form of the last program segment.

3.0 PAT LEVEL VARIABLES

The micro-ordinate unit of analysis is the **violent incident.** A violent incident is an interaction between perpetrator and target involving a violent act. Incident, then, is a <u>summary</u> unit of analysis comprised of the interaction of three subcomponents: a perpetrator (P), an act (A), and a target (T). A convenient acronym for this perpetrator/act/target interaction unit is the **P A T.** Several variables are coded at the PAT level. All PAT level variables and any relevant information needed on how to code those variables is explicated below.

PAT LEVEL VARIABLES

3.1	Types of Act
3.2	Visual Depiction of Act
3.3	Sexual Assault
3.4	Means of Implementing Act
3.5	Classifying Means
3.6	Use of Multiple Means
3.7	Extent of Means
3.8	Perpetrators and Targets
3.9	Single, Multiple and Implied P/T's
3.10	Size of Multiple P/T's
3.11	PAT Line of Data
3.12	Coding Frames of Reality
3.13	Coding Accidents
3.14	Coding Bombs
3.15	Reasons for Violence
3.16	Consequences of Violence

ACT RELATED VARIABLES

3.1 TYPE OF ACTS

A **violent action** is any overt verbal or nonverbal behavior or depiction that qualifies as violence according to our basic definition. Violent actions can be classified into three primary types: credible threats, behavioral acts and harmful consequences. These three types are explained below.

3.11 **Credible Threat:** A credible threat is any overt verbal or nonverbal behavior or string of behaviors that represent a credible threat of physical force and meet the basic definition of violence.

3.12 **Behavioral Act:** A behavioral act is any overt verbal or nonverbal behavior or string of behaviors that involve the actual use of physical force and meet the basic definition of violence.

3.13 **Harmful Consequences** (of an unseen violent act): Physically harmful consequences are those depictions that portray the aftermath or results of unseen violence.

3.2 VISUAL DEPICTION OF VIOLENT ACTION

This measure assesses whether violence is depicted **on-screen** or entirely **off-screen**. Recall that an overt depiction of violence must be either shown or heard within the context of the plot. This measure distinguishes violence that can literally be seen (at least in part) from those depictions that are merely heard or otherwise implied. <u>The basis for the judgment is whether or not any portion of the means (see section 3.5 for complete description of means used) by which the violence is accomplished is depicted visually.</u>

> 3.21 **Off-Screen:** This category applies for all those depictions that are based on overt audio cues only or are otherwise implied.
>
> For a depiction to qualify as off-screen, no part of the <u>means</u> by which the violent threat/act occurs is shown on-screen. An example of this type of depiction would include a scene that portrays two characters walking into a room. The camera view remains outside the room the characters just entered. Then, a gunshot is heard coming from inside the room. From the context of the plot, it is apparent that one character has just shot another. The perpetrator emerges from the room and walks away. Because no part of the means by which the violence occurred was ever depicted visually, the act is classified as "off-screen."
>
> Another example of an off-screen depiction would include the depiction of a perpetrator threatening a target without showing the perpetrator's means on-screen. For instance, a character may be shown from the shoulders up threatening a target. In the background, however, the target is heard saying "don't shoot, don't shoot." Immediately after the target's plea, one solitary gun shot is heard. This depiction would be coded as off-screen because at no time during or immediately after the violent act was the perpetrator's gun visually depicted on-screen.
>
> Another example of an off-screen depiction of violence includes the portrayal of harmful consequences. Harmful consequences are those depictions of the physically harmful results of "unseen" violent means. In other words, a depiction of a violent aftermath implies violence has occurred and should be treated as an "unseen" violent act. By definition, then, all depictions of harmful consequences should be coded as "off-screen."

> 3.22 **On-Screen:** This category applies when any portion of the means by which violence is accomplished is depicted visually on-screen.
>
> For the means to count as on-screen, it must be observed in action or immediately adjacent to the action. In the example noted above, imagine that immediately after the shot is heard, the camera shows a close-up view of the shooter holding the gun still aimed at the victim. This would be considered an example of seeing the means immediately adjacent to the act, and thus the depiction would be classified as on-screen. If, however, the above example added a scene in which the shooter walks out of the room while tucking a gun into his/hers pants, the depiction would be considered as off-screen. The view of the means (e.g., gun) was not shown during or immediately adjacent to the act.

3.3 VIOLENT ACTS INCLUDING SEXUAL ASSAULT

After classifying a violent act as a credible threat, behavioral act, or harmful consequences, the coder must indicate whether or not the act represented on each PAT line of data involved a **sexual assault**. An act will be classified as sexual assault when violence is employed by the perpetrator for the purpose of engaging in a sexual act with a target against the target's will.

3.31 **Defining a Sexual Act:** A sexual act is defined as any behavior including at least <u>one</u> of the following elements: (1) intimate physical contact that involves sexual and/or erotic overtones, including acts such as touching, fondling, caressing, kissing; (2) sexual intercourse; and (3) other erotic touching or physical contact intended to arouse and/or sexually gratify the perpetrator.

3.32 **Acts that do <u>not</u> Count:** Physical suggestiveness (e.g., dancing, strip-teasing) and/or verbal suggestiveness (e.g., double entendre, seductive talk) alone will not be considered sexual assault. At least some form of physical contact as indicated above must occur to fulfill the definition.

3.33 **Targets Incapable of Expressing Will:** Targets that are not capable of resisting or expressing their will (e.g., unconscious, physically or mentally disabled) will be presumed to <u>not</u> have consented to the sexual act, unless it is clear from the context that this presumption is untrue.

3.4 MEANS OF IMPLEMENTING VIOLENT ACTS

The **means** by which credible threats, violent behaviors, and harmful consequences are accomplished must be accounted for. This judgment hinges on the <u>weapon used</u> in the act. A weapon is defined as any object (including the human body) or device used to accomplish or threaten harm against an animate being. The rules for ascertaining whether or not a weapon should be considered "used" are delineated below.

3.41 **Credible Threats:** For a credible threat, a weapon will be considered "used" when it is poised and ready for use at the time the credible threat occurs. For <u>natural means</u> such as the use of fists, the fists must be raised at the time of a threat and be ready to strike or punch. For <u>handheld weapons</u> such as a gun or a knife, this would mean that the weapon is held in the hands, touched by the hands or fingers continuously even if not pointed directly at the target. For <u>larger weapons</u>, like rifles and other large guns, simply carrying the weapon would not signal a credible threat. In these cases, the perpetrator must do something with the rifle (e.g., point or aim it at the target) for the threat to be coded as credible. Weapons that are readily available, although not poised and ready for use (e.g., gun laying on table in front of perpetrator, gun in holster, or gun tucked into belt, rifle carried by soldier) would not be counted as "used."

3.42 **Behavioral Acts:** For behavioral acts, "use" shall refer to the weapon actually being employed to accomplish or attempt to accomplish harm.

3.43 **Harmful Consequences:** For harmful consequences, the weapon used can only be judged by inference. Here it is important to consider the <u>context</u> of the harmful consequence. Consider verbal references to the body and its injury, the presence of blood, the type of wound, the extent of injury or any information that provides a clear indication of the means used. Many times this information will not be provided or cannot be deduced from the context. In these cases refer to the "means unknown" category listed below.

3.5 CLASSIFICATION OF MEANS USED

When a character engages in violence, you will need to code each **means used**. There are eight different categories of means. Each of these eight types are explicated below.

3.51 **Natural Means:** Natural means refers to violence or the threat of violence accomplished by a character only using his/her/its body and/or normally-endowed capabilities (e.g, hitting, punching, kicking, biting, shoving, head butting, grabbing, tripping, hurling to the ground, headlock) without the aid of a device or an object of any kind.

Natural means for other characters, such as a supernatural being, will be relative to the character as it is defined in a program. If, for example, a supernatural character could burn people with its x-ray eyes, such an act would be categorized as "natural means" so long as it was accomplished by the character's body (and its attributes/abilities) without the use of any external object or device.

For anthropomorphized creatures, the natural means framework should reflect a composite of the appropriate animal/human characteristics applicable to the specimen. For example, Bugs Bunny could punch (a human characteristic) or hop (a rabbit characteristic) in order to inflict harm; either action would be considered natural means.

Note: Violence accomplished by actual animals against humans by natural means would be classified here only if the animal was acting independently. Violence accomplished by animals that are under the command or direction of a person would be a case of "animal as weapon," which would be classified as an unconventional weapon (see below).

3.52 **Unconventional Weapon:** An unconventional weapon is an everyday object or device that is not commonly used to inflict harm, such as a baseball bat, rope, chain, waffle iron, or pillow. Virtually any object (e.g., book, ashtray, pencil) may be employed to inflict harm when held by a person and used to strike or stab another, so there is no limit to the bounds of this category. The key element is that the object is used to attempt and/or inflict harm on another. Four global types of unconventional weapons are illustrated below.

3.521 Elements and Specialized Devices: This category includes the use of elements and/or specialized devices like chemicals, fire, water (e.g, drowning), traps, snares, cages and pits. Any action that forces a target to encounter any of these agents (e.g., placing a poisonous snake in a person's car) or other similar hostile environments that inevitably result in harm would be classified in this category, even though it might be accomplished by a simple push or other natural means.

3.522 Vehicles as Weapons: This category also includes instances when a vehicle of any sort (used for air, land, or sea travel) is used to inflict harm. Examples include: running down a target with a car/truck, boat, or plane; placing targets in a vehicle and sending the vehicle off on a harmful course such as a car sent over a cliff.

3.523 Animal as Weapon: An animal is considered a weapon when it is under the influence or command of another and it is used as an instrument to accomplish harm. Examples would include a police attack dog responding to instructions from its handler or an animal that responds to ESP commands from supernatural characters. If the animal is the agent that accomplishes the harm, the animal is the weapon and the person controlling the animal is the perpetrator of the violence.

3.524 Unconventional Use of a Firearm: Finally, when a gun or other firearm is used in an unconventional way, such as to strike another, it should be counted in this category.

3.53 **Conventional Weapon / Non-Firearm:** A conventional weapon/non-firearm is an object, device, or instrument that is commonly used to inflict harm. Examples include police batons, harpoons, knifes, swords or other stabbing instruments. The device may have other applications, such as a bow and arrow which might be used for target practice. Nonetheless, a bow and arrow would be considered a conventional weapon because it is designed in a way that inflicts harm when <u>used as intended</u>.

    3.531 <u>Exception Rule:</u> An important exception to the "used as intended" concept is that <u>a knife will always be counted as a conventional weapon</u>, even if it is a kitchen knife as opposed to a switchblade. Even though all knives may have other conventional applications, it is common knowledge (and a common occurrence) that they may be used as weapons, and thus they will be counted in this category.

3.54 **Conventional Weapon / Handheld Firearm:** Handguns, firearms, pistols, rifles, ray guns, laser guns, and even bazookas fall under this category. The key element is that they are held and manipulated by an individual character, and are not fixed or mounted on the ground or on a vehicle. It is not relevant whether or not the weapon is an "automatic" firearm. Machine guns that shoot rapid or automatic fire may be handheld and thus, would be coded as a handheld firearm. Similar machine guns that are mounted on the ground or fixed on a vehicle (such as an open army jeep), however, are to be considered as heavy weaponry.

3.55 **Heavy Weaponry:** Firearms that are <u>not</u> capable of being handheld fall under this category. Examples of heavy weaponry include tanks, cannons, airplane missiles and submarine torpedoes. Hand grenades, although they can be thrown from the hand, are also to be coded as a form of "heavy weaponry."

3.56 **Bombs:** A bomb is defined as an explosive or incendiary device. There are two primary types of bombs: timer and manual control bombs. Both can be devised, set and triggered with human hands. Timer bombs and manual control bombs come in many forms and can be constructed from a wide range of materials, although there is no need to distinguish among the many possible variations.

3.57 **Means Unknown:** Only use this category when it is impossible to know what specific type of means was used. The most common application of "means unknown" would be for classifying depictions of <u>harmful consequences</u> from unseen violence.

3.58 **Credible Threat/Verbal Only (CTVO):** This is a special coding option that is used exclusively for classifying credible threats that are accomplished solely by a verbal statement or utterance without the use of any weapon. Apply the rules indicated above to determine weapon "use." For example, when a character says to another "Move an inch and I'll blow your brains out" but leaves his/her gun lying on the table in front of him throughout the scene, the act would be classified as CTVO; this is because the gun would not qualify as having been used in that case. In contrast, a scene in which a character utters the same line <u>with a gun in his/her hand</u> would be properly classified as 3.54 above (conventional weapon/handheld firearm).

In employing this category, bear in mind that any character always possesses the natural means to make good on many threats of physical harm. It is possible, however, to utter a threat to strike another person (such as "Move an inch and I'll knock your head off") in which the means would be classified as CTVO. This would occur in cases where the perpetrator <u>did not</u> display any evidence that the natural means weapon involved, for instance a fist, was poised and ready for use. When fists are raised at the time a threat to strike or punch is uttered, then the act would be properly classified as "natural means."

3.6 USE OF MULTIPLE MEANS

At times, characters may engage in acts of violence by employing **multiple means** from several of the different categories presented above. For example, a perpetrator might be kicking an opponent he has wrestled to the ground, then reach for his gun and shoot the individual. The rule for coding multiple means is described below.

3.61 **Rule for Coding Multiple Means:** When two or more categories of means are employed, code <u>all means that are used</u>. This rule applies across all three types of violent acts (e.g., credible threat, behavioral act, depiction of harmful consequences). For a credible threat, apply the special definition presented above to determine whether or not a weapon/means should be considered as "used." For harmful consequences, when injuries/death occur by multiple means (e.g., a body has been stabbed and shot, or shot and burned), code all applicable weapons/means based on all knowledge provided during the relevant sequence and any preceding contextual information.

3.7 EXTENT OF MEANS USED FOR BEHAVIORAL ACTS

This variable applies to behavioral acts only. <u>There is no assessment of extent of means used for credible threats or depictions of harmful consequences.</u> **Extent** will be assessed within each applicable means category for any given PAT incident (involving behavioral acts). Consider the following scene as an example: Character X shoots character Y twice, then shoots character Z once, and then shoots character Y three more times. The first PAT interaction unit (or line of data) has X as the perpetrator and Y as the target. The means used for the behavioral act is "handheld firearm" and the extent judgment would be based on the total of 5 shots directed by X against Y. A second, entirely separate PAT interaction unit has X as perpetrator and Z as target. Once again, the means used for the behavioral act is "handheld firearm" and the extent judgment would be one.

No matter how many times the violence by one character against another is interrupted by intervening violence involving other characters, the extent scale continues to accrue so long as the PAT remains constant (same perpetrator, same type of act and means, and same target) within a given sequence. Put differently, there should never be two PAT incidents reported within the same sequence which have the same perpetrator, same act, and same target.

3.71 **Extent Values:** Coders must take into consideration two types of action when determining extent. One type is the discrete actions such as individual punches or gunshots. These can usually be counted and an extent category is easy to select. A second type is continuous action. Oftentimes, it is impossible to count discrete acts of aggression when the nature of the violence is ongoing and contiguous. Examples of continuous violent actions would be wrestling matches and automatic gun fire from a machine gun. For continuous actions, coders should count the number of seconds the means is actually "in use."

Discrete and continuous counts of extent can be combined within the same category of means so long as the P and T are held constant. Thus, 7 seconds of "continuous" wrestling followed by 3 discrete punches (all of which are natural means) would combine to a total extent value of 10.

There are five different values for the extent variable. Those five values are delineated below.

3.711 <u>One:</u> For discrete behaviors, this category would only include a single example of the means used. That is, one single punch thrown or one single shot fired. For continuous action/s that cannot be counted, such as pouring poison into a body of water, the smallest possible amount of the activity (i.e., pouring a single drop or one second of continuous action) would be captured in this category.

3.712 <u>Some:</u> For discrete behaviors, this category would include between 2 and 9 examples of the act. For continuous actions that cannot be counted, such as automatic gunfire or wrestling, "some" would range from between 2 and 9 seconds of the activity.

3.713 <u>Many:</u> For discrete behaviors, this category includes 10 to 20 examples of the act. For continuous actions that cannot be counted, however, "many" will range from 10 to 20 seconds of the activity.

3.714 <u>Extreme:</u> For discrete behaviors, this category includes 21 or more examples of the act. For continuous actions that cannot be counted, "extreme" will include 21 or more seconds of the activity.

3.715 <u>Not Applicable:</u> For credible threats and harmful consequences, code extent as not applicable.

3.8 PERPETRATORS AND TARGETS OF VIOLENCE

When credible threats, violent behavioral acts, or harmful consequences are depicted, there is <u>by definition</u> a perpetrator and a target.

3.81 **Perpetrator of Violence:** A perpetrator (P) is the character who engages or enacts the threat or violent behavior. In the simplest example, a character who shoots someone with a gun is the perpetrator of a violent act. Perpetrators of violence may come in single, multiple or implied forms.

3.82 **Target of Violence:** A target (T) is the character to whom the violent threat/act was directed. The target may or may not incur physical harm or injury as a result of a violent act (e.g., the gunshot may miss) but nevertheless, the individual fired at is still defined as the target. Targets of violence may come in single, multiple or implied forms.

3.9 SINGLE, MULTIPLE AND IMPLIED P'S AND T'S

Characters considered perpetrators and targets of violence may come in **single**, **multiple**, or **implied** forms. In cases where a single individual acting alone or independently accomplishes a violent act against another individual, the PAT interaction unit should be applied at the level of an individual character; that is, isolating a single character as the P or the T involved in any violent incident.

In some cases, however, it will be necessary to group characters together and treat the group as a single unit (P $_{multiple}$ or T $_{multiple}$). This should be done when groups of characters act collectively in a way that makes the observation of their individual behaviors either inconsequential or impossible to differentiate.

And finally, there will be times when perpetrators or targets are not shown overtly but must be inferred from the context of the sequence. In this case, they are said to be implied in the sequence rather than depicted.

All of the rules demarcating when to code a P/T as single, multiple or implied are delineated below.

3.91 **Multiple Perpetrators (P $_{multiple}$, A, T):** The actions of a group of characters who perpetrate acts of violence should be considered as P $_{multiple}$ when **ALL** of the four following criteria are met:

    3.911 <u>Common Goals:</u> The characters share a common goal/purpose to physically harm an animate being or group of animate beings. Examples that fit include police officers in pursuit of a criminal, soldiers fighting together, members of a gang committing a violent crime, and a diverse group of townspeople who search for, find, and lynch a suspected murderer.

    3.912 <u>Characters Actions</u>: The perpetrators must either a) all act violently against the same target, OR b) all work together so that one or more characters can enact violence because of the physical assistance of others.

    To fulfill the requirements of section (b) above, two or more individuals must accomplish a violent act by working together in a cooperative or interdependent fashion in the <u>same physical location</u>. It is not required that all perpetrators in a group must commit the same act/s, or even any violent acts, nor must they all be armed in the same way. To be considered a part of the group, each character must engage in a physical act which either (1) is violent, or (2) directly facilitates the violent actions of others.

    Examples that fulfill this part of the group definition include: one person driving a car while another fires a gun in a drive-by shooting; a jet piloted by one character with the weapons operated by another; one character standing on the shoulders of another in order to reach high enough to fire a rifle over a tall fence; one police officer using a battering ram to knock down a door; allowing a second officer to enter and confront a suspect; or a group surrounding a target so s/he can't run away, which then allows a single perpetrator to commit violence against the target.

    When considering aggression associated with large vehicles (e.g., submarines or spaceships firing weapons), assume that a large vehicle such as an airplane, ship, or space ship, etc. represents a group action and classify the perpetrator as P $_{multiple}$ unless information to the contrary has been provided in the context of the program (e.g., a plane is known to be a single pilot fighter jet).

    3.913 <u>Production Conventions:</u> The productions conventions (e.g., camera focus, framing) must encourage the viewer to see characters collectively on the screen in a setting.

    The focus and framing of the camera (or other aspects of the visual presentation) emphasize more than one perpetrator at a time. We are looking here for scenes in which the viewer is likely to interpret the target as being a group. This occurs when the camera view encompasses the group or when the visual presentation moves quickly from one character to the next without emphasizing any one individual. Momentary "cuts" that place emphasis on individual perpetrators do not detract from a group focus so long as they are brief. A longer "cut" to an individual perpetrator, however, would represent a production convention that signals an emphasis on a single character and thus would require a shift to a new PAT line with a single (rather than multiple) P.

3.913a *Ten Second Rule:* To enhance the consistency of judgments regarding when to code violence as involving a $P_{multiple}$, and/or when to code the actions of individuals in a group as P_{single}, coders will consider any visual portrayal that includes a single camera view that <u>exceeds 10 seconds in length</u> (e.g., 11 seconds or more) to represent an important production convention.

Thus, when it has already been established that violence is being committed by a group ($P_{multiple}$), and the presentation of that violence includes a "cut" depicting a single member of that group engaging in violence for more than 10 seconds, the behavior in the "cut" will represent a separate PAT interaction (coded as an individual if only one perpetrator is included in that "cut").

The presence of the "cut" reflects the producer's effort to emphasize the actions of the individual over the actions of the group, and our coding must capture this aspect of the content. After that depiction, if a series of short (e.g.,10 seconds or less) "cuts" of the other members of the group are shown one after the other, the coder would return to classifying the depictions as $P_{multiple}$.

3.913b *Note:* There are a wide range of production conventions that can encourage the viewer to interpret the actions of people as a group. These must be evaluated by the coder on a case by case basis to judge whether a particular portrayal meets this requirement.

3.914 <u>Simultaneous or Sequential Actions:</u> Violent actions, if enacted by multiple characters, occur either simultaneously or in rapid sequential fashion such that it is difficult to isolate individual perpetrators.

The simplest example of this type of situation would be two or more individuals acting in truly simultaneous fashion, such as two women breaking into a room side by side while both are firing machine guns at a target, with the actions of both clearly visible at all times. In fact, however, the actions of a group are often portrayed with brief camera shots of one individual and then another and then another, each providing a view of the contributions of that character to the group effort. While such depictions would not meet the requirement of *simultaneity* indicated above, they should be judged as *rapid sequential* portrayals so long as each camera "cut" <u>does not exceed 10 seconds in length</u>.

In contrast, depictions with "cuts" of individual actors engaging in violence that last longer than 10 seconds will be considered staggered or asynchronous. This type of depiction will not qualify as rapid sequential and thus could not be considered as a $P_{multiple}$ situation, at least for that portion of the content.

3.914a *Note:* For incidents involving a $P_{multiple}$, code all weapons/means that are employed by all individuals who are a part of the group.

3.92 **Single Perpetrators:** The preceding information indicates when to classify violent actions of a $P_{multiple}$ group. The rules below present the contrasting perspective, and reiterate that when the above criteria are not met, any violent depiction must be classified as P $_{single}$. Code Perpetrators as Singles when any <u>ONE</u> of the following occurs:

3.921 <u>Goals Differ:</u> Characters do not share common goals or common characteristics. Examples include: 1) one perpetrator trying to hurt one target while another is trying to save a person, and 2) one perpetrator is trying to kill a target or capture him first before others can get him.

3.922 <u>Characters Actions:</u> Characters are not all acting violently or assisting others in violent behavior. Bystanders, mere observers or people who are "with" the perpetrator but not assisting should not be included in P count.

3.923 <u>Production Conventions:</u> The production conventions encourage the viewer to see a character as a separate individual from the group (a camera "cut" includes depiction of a single character that exceeds 10 seconds)

3.924 <u>Violent actions:</u> Violent actions, if enacted by multiple characters, are asynchronous or staggered. For example, one perpetrator acts violently and then stops, is killed or pushed away, and then another perpetrator attacks.

3.93 **Multiple Targets:** A group of characters should be considered T$_{multiple}$ when **ALL** of the following criteria are met. If any one of the four conditions is <u>not</u> met, then the target/s would be coded as single.

3.931 <u>Targeted Collectively:</u> Two or more characters are targeted collectively by a perpetrator who seeks to accomplish a particular goal or purpose.

The important aspect here is that the perpetrator intends to harm/threaten a group and not just a single individual. There may in fact be differing reasons for why a perpetrator is targeting multiple characters. For example, a criminal may want to murder a witness and thus may also have to harm a bodyguard in order to get to that individual. Even though there may technically be differing reasons why the perpetrator in this case would attack each of these individuals, they should still be coded as a multiple target so long as the perpetrator engages them collectively. The driving force behind the perpetrator's violence against both is to accomplish the goal of silencing the witness.

3.932 <u>Harm to More Than One Character:</u> More than one character is actually being harmed or threatened by a perpetrator.

This element is meant to screen out bystanders, mere observers, or people who are with the target but are not being harmed/threatened directly by the perpetrator.

3.933 <u>Production Conventions:</u> Production conventions (e.g., camera focus, framing) encourage the viewer to see the characters collectively on the screen/in a setting in a way that makes them seem like a group.

The focus and framing of the camera (or other aspects of the visual presentation) emphasize more than one target at a time. We are looking here for scenes in which the viewer is likely to interpret the target as being a group. Momentary "cuts" to individual targets that have already been established as a group should not count as a shift to a single T so long as these "cuts" do not exceed 10 seconds in length. A longer "cut" to an individual target (e.g., 11 seconds or more) however, would represent a production convention that signals an emphasis on a single character and thus would require a shift to a new PAT line with a single (rather than multiple) T.

3.934 <u>Simultaneity or Sequentiality:</u> The violent actions occur either simultaneously or in rapid sequential fashion such that it is difficult to isolate individual targets.

The simplest example would be two/more individuals who are harmed/threatened simultaneously, such as two people being shot at by a machine gun. However, perpetrators often move from one target to another sequentially, even though the characters are dealt with essentially as a group. This will still constitute a multiple T situation so long as the movement from one target to another is "rapid" and the camera does not isolate individuals for longer than 10 seconds. An example would be a tough youth assaulting a group of children gathered on the playground, attacking one after another, with several quick "cuts" that each spend less than 5 seconds with any one target.

3.94 **Implied Perpetrators and Targets (P implied, A, T) (P, A, T implied):** At times, perpetrators and targets are not shown overtly but must be inferred from the context of the sequence. In this case they are implied in the sequence rather than depicted.

3.941 <u>Most Common Occurrences:</u> The most common instance of an implied perpetrator will involve depictions of harmful consequences in which the perpetrator (as well as the act and the means) is not seen. In these instances, the perpetrator is coded as "implied."

3.942 <u>Inference of P/T from Context:</u> At times, perpetrators or targets are not overtly shown but their existence can be inferred from the context of the sequence. Two examples include a bomb blown up on a bus, with no passengers seen; or a credible threat such as a cop at the door, gun drawn, no target seen. In these instances the target is coded as "implied."

3.943 <u>Coding Implied P/T's:</u> It should be noted that an implied perpetrator or target is neither coded as single or multiple. Rather, they are simply coded as "implied."

3.10 SIZE OF MULTIPLE PERPETRATORS OR TARGETS

For each PAT line of data, the size of each P or T multiple engaged in violence must be measured. Precise counting should be pursued up to the bottom threshold of category 3 (10 to 99) or a total of 10 characters. Beyond that, estimates must be rendered based upon the coders estimate of the number of P/T's involved. In cases where group size changes during a given sequence (e.g., police reinforcements arrive), always record the highest or largest number involved in violence.

3.101 **Codes for Size of Multiple:**

3.101a <u>Two Characters</u>

3.101b <u>3 to 9 Characters</u>

3.101c <u>10 to 99 Characters</u>

3.101d <u>100 to 999 Characters</u>

3.101e <u>1000 or more Characters</u>

3.11 CODING VIOLENT INCIDENTS: USE OF PAT LINES

In general, when the coder first observes any violence, s/he must focus initially on establishing the boundaries of the sequence that surrounds the violent depiction. The next task is to re-view that sequence as many times as necessary in order to establish how many individual **PAT lines** are required to properly record all the violent interactions contained within the sequence. Once that issue is resolved, the coder then re-views the entire sequence, recording all information on one PAT line at a time. Once one line of data is complete, the tape is rewound to the beginning of the sequence in question and re-viewed again, recording observations for the next PAT line, and so on until all PAT lines within the sequence have been completed.

3.111 **Creating a Line of Data:** A "line" of data or "case" is first created when the coder observes one of the examples of violence described above (e.g., credible threat, behavioral act, or harmful consequences). Information about the perpetrator, the nature of the act (e.g., means used, extent of means used) and the target is recorded, creating a PAT line. A crucial decision for the coder is determining how much information to "load" on a single PAT line and when to switch to a new line of data indicating that a new PAT unit has been observed.

In general, all violence that occurs within a given sequence in which the P (perpetrator), A (act) and T (target) remain constant will be recorded on a single line of data. This holds true regardless of whether or not interruptions occur in the flow of violent interactions such that a delay exists between some violence initiated by P_1 against T_1 early in the sequence and some additional violence committed later in the sequence. All violence within a sequence continues to be "loaded" on a single PAT line so long as the P, A, and T are constant.

Extent will continue to accrue throughout an entire sequence for all acts of the same type employing the same means involving the same P and same T. When the means change from one classification to another, this does not require a new line of PAT data. Rather, record this new information in the "means B" column on the PAT coding form. If a third means is used, move to the "means C" column. If any additional means are employed by the same perpetrator against the same target within the same type of act, make a "means D" [and so on as needed] notation in the margin of the form and record all necessary information on the back of the PAT coding form.

3.112 **Changing PAT Lines:** An additional PAT line is needed when violence occurs that involves a new or different P, A, or T. The following will help to clarify when to add an additional PAT line within a given sequence.

3.1121 When the Perpetrator Changes: This would include the three following examples:

3.1121a *A New/Different Character Commits Violence.*

This could occur if the initial target retaliates and becomes a perpetrator, or if an entirely new character engages in violence.

3.1121b *When the P shifts from Single to Multiple.*

This would require a new line of data because the P would differ from the previous line. Note that once established, multiples are considered to remain constant so long as at least two members of the group remain involved. Thus, while a new line is required when one cop who is initially a single perpetrator is joined in violence by another officer, no additional lines are required when other back-up officers arrive subsequently and join the fray (presuming the portrayal fulfills the criteria for a P multiple for all of the officers). In this case, simply "load" all the actions of the entire group of officers on a single PAT line of data so long as their actions hold Act (e.g., behavioral act) and Target constant.

3.1121c *When the P shifts from Multiple to Single.*

This would require a new line of data because the P would differ from the previous line. Note that once established, multiples are considered to remain constant so long as at least two members of the group remain involved, even though the actual size of the group may diminish. For example, if a group of four police officers assault a suspect and the suspect kills two of them immediately, the violent actions of the remaining two officers are still loaded on the same PAT line as the actions of the group of four. The same P multiple line is employed until such time as only a single individual is involved. At that point, the P would shift from multiple to single, which represents a new Perpetrator and hence a new PAT line of data. This example presumes that all criteria for depiction of P multiple are met throughout the incident.

Reminder: In all cases in which group size varies within a given PAT line for either P multiple or T multiple, always record the largest size of the group that is portrayed at any time.

3.1122 When the Type of Act Changes: This would include the following examples.

3.1122a *A Credible Threat shifts to a Behavioral Act.*

Some violent acts are preceded by a momentary pause in which one may perceive a credible threat has occurred. In order to be sure that insignificant pauses do not inflate our count of violent acts, we will take a conservative approach to coding credible threats that are followed almost immediately by violent behavioral acts.

A 10 second rule will be used to isolate a credible threat that is followed by a violent act. This rule is applied in two ways: to account for the gap between a credible threat and an act and to time the length of the threat itself. Each of these applications are explained below.

If a credible threat occurs immediately before a related behavioral act, it is only counted as a separate act if (a) there is at least a 10 second gap between the threat and the act (i.e. a threat followed by a 10 second or longer cut-away to an unrelated scene and then returning to the scene of the threat where a violent act then occurs); or (b) if the threat itself endures for longer than 10 seconds before the violent behavior is enacted (i.e. a hitman slowly lines up his target in the scope of his rifle for 10 seconds or longer and then shoots at his target).

If a threat is followed by any act of violence by the same perpetrator to the same target in less than ten seconds from the beginning of the threat, then the act will be said to supersede the threat, and the threat will not be coded.

Note: If a perpetrator has already engaged in overt violent behavior towards a target then later threatens the same target within the same sequence using the same means (i.e. cop shoots at robber, misses, then chases robber with gun drawn), this and following threats to the target will not be coded as a credible threat. The threat can be used to extend the duration of the sequence (provided there is not a significant break or pause, or a 30 second cut away). However, <u>if the perpetrator threatens the same target with a different type of means within the same sequence, then the credible threat should be coded.</u>

> 3.1122b *A Credible Threat shifts to a Depiction of Harmful Consequences.*
>
> Whenever a threat escalates into the depiction of harmful consequences such that it is clear that the perpetrator who threatened the target is responsible for the consequences depicted later, a new line of data will be formed. An example of this would be when a perpetrator points a gun at a target, followed by a brief cut away to an unrelated scene or to a commercial, and then the camera returns and portrays the target lying dead from a gunshot wound.

3.1123 <u>When the Target Changes:</u> This would include the following examples.

> 3.1123a *A New/Different Character is the Target of Violence.*
>
> 3.1123b *When the T shifts from Single to Multiple.*
>
> 3.1123c *When the T shifts from Multiple to Single.*

3.12 CODING DIFFERENT FRAMES OF REALITY

There are multiple levels of reality that may be represented in television programming. At the first level, which occurs in most fictional programming, there are actors and actresses who portray characters. For example, Michael J. Fox portrays the character Alex Keaton in *Family Ties*. The actions portrayed by Fox (in the character of Keaton) are to be assessed by the coder literally as they are depicted <u>from the perspective of the character role that the actor has assumed</u>. If the character of Alex Keaton were to slap someone and that action was depicted as intended to harm within the context of the show, then a violent act would be coded.

3.121 **Assuming Secondary Roles:** An additional level of artificial reality may be introduced into television programs when actors such as Fox who are already portraying fictional characters assume a secondary fictional role -- a sort of "play within a play." This might occur, for example, if the character of Alex were to take the role of a leading star in the school play *Bonnie and Clyde*. Imagine a scene in which Fox, playing Alex Keaton, assumes the role of gangster Clyde -- and shoots a toy gun at a police officer who is seemingly killed by the action. Even though this action was not intended to harm from the frame of reality of Alex Keaton, it <u>was</u> intended to harm from the frame of reality of the gangster Clyde. Thus, this action -- the violence contained within the "play within a play" -- would be classified as violent.

That frame of reference is to be taken seriously in the same way that one takes seriously the actions of an actor such as Fox when he assumes the first-level role of Alex Keaton. When the criteria for violence is met from the perspective of the character being portrayed, then the violence will be included in our analysis.

3.122 **Observing Secondary Levels of Reality:** Another example of a secondary frame of reality would be when a fictional character observes another level of fiction being depicted, such as when a fictional character watches a segment of television content. An example would be the Simpsons tuning into the *Itchy and Scratchy Show*. All violence depicted involving Itchy and Scratchy would be coded, provided that it meets the criteria for an overt depiction. That determination would be made from the perspective of the

Itchy and Scratchy characters.

3.123 **Sequencing Issues:** There will be times when violence will occur adjacent or simultaneously at multiple levels of reality. For example, consider the *Simpsons* illustration noted above. If Bart bites Lisa, while at the same time they are watching violence on their television set between Itchy and Scratchy, then both levels of reality will be coded. In such a case, these two types of violent depictions would be considered a single sequence so long as there was a continuous or consistent flow of violence without a significant break. This would hold even though the violence cuts across two differing levels of reality.

Consider a more complicated example: an episode of *Beverly Hills 90210* in which Kelly and Brandon rehearse for the school play. Kelly and Brandon may be shown rehearsing a scene from *Romeo and Juliet* three or four times. Any violence in the scene is, therefore, depicted multiple times. You must determine whether or not the separate rehearsals are the same or separate sequences. To make this determination, follow the basic rules for defining sequences in terms of breaks in continuous flow of action. If, for example, characters "break out" of their secondary roles (Romeo and Juliet) between scenes before rehearsing again, then the action would be coded as three separate sequences because there would have been three breaks in the flow of continuous action. If someone dies in this scene, then according to your coding sheet, they would die three times.

3.13 CODING A SPECIAL TYPE OF ACT - ACCIDENTS

There are two types of accidents that should be coded when they occur within the context of an ongoing violent sequence. Those two types of accidents include: 1) those that are caused by a specific violent act and 2) those that are caused by a mishap or fluke. In terms of PAT, these two different types of accidents need to be accurately captured on a line of data.

3.131 **Coding Accidents Caused by a Violent Act:** For the first type of accident (e.g., accidental harm that is caused directly by a specific violent act), the perpetrator is that character who engages in the violent act that caused the accidental harm. The act type is coded as "accident." The target is that character who is accidently harmed by the perpetrator's act. The reason should reflect the perpetrator's reason for engaging in violence toward the intended target, not the accidental target (e.g., if a police officer is trying to protect society by shooting at a killer but accidently shoots a child, then the reason should be coded as "protecting others"). Thus, a criminal who shoots at an enemy in order to get money but accidently harms a bystander should be coded as : P (criminal); Act Type (accident); T (bystander); reason (personal gain).

3.132 **Coding Accidents Caused by a Mishap:** For the second type of accident (e.g., harm that occurs because of a mishap within a violent sequence and not because of a specific violent act), the perpetrator would be coded as P$_{none}$. The act type is coded as accident. The character who was accidently harmed by the mishap would be coded as the target. The reason should be coded as "accident" because there is no specific behavioral act that directly caused the harm. To illustrate, if while chasing someone, a criminal accidently falls off a cliff and hurts himself, then this incident should be coded as: P (none); act type (accident); target (criminal); and reason (accident).

3.14 CODING A SPECIAL TYPE OF MEANS - BOMBS

When a **bomb** is involved as a weapon, code a <u>credible threat</u> when the <u>bomb is first put in place</u>, provided it is clear from the context of the program that there is a serious intent to harm, or there is an effort to destroy property with the intent to intimidate an animate being. Code the actual detonation of a bomb, should an explosion occur, as a behavioral act.

More detailed observations regarding bombs must also be made, but these judgments differ according to the type of bomb employed. Determine whether the bomb is to be activated (or potentially activated) by a **timer** or a **manual control**, such as a hand operated trigger, lighting a fuse, or a remote control device. Then proceed to judge and record all subsequent coding of the use of any bomb applying the rules for the appropriate sub-group.

3.141 **Timer bombs:** After coding the initial placement of the bomb as a credible threat, classify any subsequent depictions of the bomb as additional credible threats, holding constant the perpetrator, means, and target. For a subsequent depiction to be coded as a credible threat, it must include either visual or auditory evidence of the bomb itself by portraying 1) any portion of the bomb, 2) the location (e.g., vehicle/building) where the bomb has been planted, and/or 3) the targets reactions to the planted device.

If these visual references are made within the same sequence in which the bomb was originally planted, then no additional coding is necessary because extent is not applicable for a credible threat. If these references are made at a time later than the original sequence in which the bomb was placed, then create a new line of data and code an additional credible threat that reflects the relevant information for the perpetrator/target/etc.

If a timer-bomb does not explode (for example, due to the intervention of a hero) no behavioral act will be coded. If the bomb actually explodes, code a behavioral act indicating the relevant information for the perpetrator/target/etc.

3.142 **Manual Control bombs:** Coding for manual control bombs is handled using all of the rules indicated above for timer bombs, but an additional rule is also applied. With manually controlled bombs, also code as a credible threat any depiction in which the perpetrator physically manipulates a device or mechanism (such as a remote control) that is capable of detonating the bomb.

NOTE: The very last (or several of the very last) depictions of either the bomb itself or the person at the controls may "wash-out" as a credible threat if the bomb is successfully detonated within the same sequence (provided that the depictions occur within 10 seconds of the explosion).

CHARACTER VARIABLES

3.15 REASONS FOR VIOLENCE

This measure classifies a perpetrator's primary **reason** for engaging in violence. It is judged solely from the perspective of the perpetrator. Human behavior is complex and you will certainly encounter instances in which more than one reason could be applied to account for a given violent behavior. In such instances, you must select the most important or predominant reason that influenced the perpetrator's violent action. If the character seems to be motivated by two (or more) reasons, consider each reason alone and determine which more fully accounts for the character's violence. Use all available information and cues within the program to reach this judgment. You may consider all events leading up to the violent act, the perpetrator's comments made by/to/about the target, or any information regarding the perpetrator's state of mind.

3.151 **Protection of Life:** This reason includes all those violent acts intending to protect the self or others against actual, potential, or perceived physical harm. For this reason to apply, the perpetrator must engage in violence to either protect the self and/or another character from actual, potential or perceived physical harm. For protection of self, the target must always be the actual agent or perceived agent of harm. It is only self-defense if the perpetrator commits a violent act against the target because the target has already or is presently threatening/harming that particular individual. An example of self-defense from actual harm would be if a character is attacked on the street and decides to fight back.

This category also includes violence committed by a character who believes himself or herself to be in danger, even if that character has not been the recipient of any violent behavior. Take, for example, a situation in which a man is surprised from behind by a woman and becomes extremely frightened. If he threatens or attacks the woman, it is considered self-defense, even if the woman had no intent to harm.

Also included in this category are those acts designed to protect others from physical harm. A perpetrator is protecting an other when he/she/it uses violence to intervene, overcome, counteract, or subvert the actual or threatened violent actions of a target. Threatened acts may be imminent but need not be. For example, when the police track down and arrest a murderer, it is implicit that they are seeking to protect others; the presumption is that someone who has murdered once is a high risk of murdering again.

Protection of others includes all other characters whether or not they are identified or abstract. Identified others include those in the scene or known in the program. Abstract others include broad, anonymous collections of individuals, such as the citizens of a community or country. Examples of protecting abstract others include soldiers who are fighting battles to defend their country and police who are fighting crime to protect the community.

3.152 **Anger:** This reason for violence includes all those acts that were triggered by feelings of hostility, rage or resentment on the part of the perpetrator. This category includes those acts of violence that are committed by a perpetrator out of anger. Anger may be short-term and occur within a sequence or it may be long-term and endure throughout an entire program. As a result, there are specific rules as to when and how this reason applies.

3.1521 Short-Term: Short-term anger occurs when a perpetrator acts violently against a target within the same sequence he/she/it was angered or frustrated. The anger within the sequence may be the result of anything the target did or said to the perpetrator that angered him/her/it. To illustrate, consider the following example: X insults Y or a person close to Y. Out of anger, Y immediately punches X in the face. Or, X may hit Y in the face. Because he is angered by X's actions, Y instantaneously slugs X in the face. In both of these examples, the reason for violence would be anger because the perpetrator immediately aggresses against the target within the same sequence.

Short-term anger is a *very* different reason for violence than is protection of self or personal gain. That is, the perpetrator in this case is NOT protecting him/her self from violence but is reacting to something the target did or said. Consider the following example: a character slugs the Terminator in the face. The only effect of the character's action is that the Terminator's sun glasses are jostled on his face. In anger, the Terminator turns to the character, lifts him up, and throws him against the wall. Because he is larger and stronger than the other character, it is obvious that the Terminator is not protecting himself from the target. While the Terminator may gain the satisfaction of harming the target, his violent actions were triggered by and are in immediate response to his anger or frustration towards the target. Based upon this rationale, the primary reason for the Terminator's violence in this example would be "anger."

3.1522 <u>Long-Term:</u> Long-term anger, however, occurs when a perpetrator acts violently for being previously wronged by a target prior to the violent sequence when the previous wrong was <u>NOT</u> a physically violent action. Rather, the catalyst for long-term retribution is anything done or said to the perpetrator (or another) that the perpetrator does not like. For example, a character may be convicted of a crime he/she did not commit. While in prison, the character contemplates his/her revenge against the prosecuting attorney who persuasively convinced the jury of the criminal's guilt. When the criminal is finally set free, he/she tracks down the lawyer and kills him. Because the previous wrong was not physically violent and occurred prior to the violent sequence, the character's primary reason for violence should be coded as "anger."

If the previous wrong done to the perpetrator was a physically violent action that occurred prior to the violent sequence, then the reason for violence would not be coded as anger. Rather, the reason for violence would be coded as retaliation which is defined in the next section.

3.153 **Retaliation:** This category includes all those violent acts that are triggered by feelings of retribution <u>only</u> when those feelings are the result of previous acts of physical violence against the present perpetrator.

In order for the reason for violence to be coded "retaliation," two criteria must be met. First, the perpetrator must commit a violent act in order to "settle the score" for a previous harm done to a person. The present violence is not a "first strike" against the target: instead, the target must have delivered the first strike in an earlier sequence. For example, if A hits B then B immediately hits A back, this should not be coded as retaliation. However, in the following example the reason for violence would qualify as retaliation. X hits Y and knocks him unconscious. Y is taken to the hospital to recover where he gains consciousness and begins plotting to get even with X. Later, Y sees X and hits him.

Second, the previous harm must have been caused by physical violence; it cannot be harm exclusively of a psychological or emotional nature. If the previous harm wasn't of a physically violent nature, then the reason should not be coded as retaliation. For example, if A insults B and then B thinks about this hurt for most of the program then later hits A because of the initial insult, this is not retaliation.

3.1531 <u>Implied "First Strike" Rule:</u> The "first strike" of physical violence can be implied, and it need not be shown in the program itself. For example, a program may open with A having B tied up as A tells B about how she plans to stab B because B slapped her several weeks previously. If this motive is made clear to the viewer (even though the previous slapping is not overtly shown), then retaliation would still be coded as the reason for violence.

3.1532 <u>Target of the "First Strike" Rule:</u> The target of the "first strike" can be either the present perpetrator or a person close to the perpetrator (e.g., a family member or a very good friend).

3.154 **Personal Gain:** This category includes those acts of violence accomplished for gaining material goods or objects, power or status, popularity, or affection from others.

For this reason to apply, the perpetrator must engage in violence for his/her/its own personal gain. That is, the perpetrator is acting violently because his/her/its primary goal is to take or receive external material goods/objects, power/status or affection from other individuals. Examples of trying to take or receive material gain may include a bank robber holding up a bank, a bully who punches a kid so that he may steal the kid's lunch money, or an addict trying to steal cocaine from a drug dealer.

Also included within personal gain are those violent actions that are committed to increase a perpetrator's social or political power. Violence that increases social or political power may include a gang member who kills the gang leader so that he may assume the role of leader himself, or an assassin who shoots at a political leader in order to either gain notoriety or to subvert the leader's political agenda.

Violence that increases popularity or affection from others would also be included as personal gain. Examples of violence committed to gain popularity or affection may include: a character who kills a man in order to win the attention of a woman, a boy who hits a frail child in order to be recognized and liked by a neighborhood gang, a teen who knifes a rival to win the affection of a girlfriend, and a boxer who is fighting in order to win the heavy weight title.

The motivation or extrinsic goal for committing violence in all these cases is that the perpetrator uses aggressive actions to take or receive something that will enhance him/her/it either materially, socially, and/or politically.

3.155 **Amusement/Mental Instability:** This category captures all those violent acts that are committed by perpetrators 1) to amuse the self or other, 2) who display a flagrant disregard for the basic value of human life, or 3) who lack the mental competence to value human life.

This category includes violent acts that are committed for either amusement or due to mental instability. Amusement usually includes those juvenile <u>antics</u> designed to situationally amuse the self or provoke humorous reactions from bystanders with <u>no other apparent extrinsic goal</u>. That is, the perpetrator cannot be attempting to fulfill any other goal such as alleviating anger, trying to protect himself or others, obtaining status, and/or gaining affection/affinity from others.

The target in this category will usually be characterized as extremely innocent or defenseless and will not have provoked the perpetrator in any way whatsoever. Examples include Beavis and Butthead playing a game of frog baseball (literally smashing frogs in mid air with a baseball bat) and Al Bundy kicking a neighbor's dog because it is ugly. The perpetrator and/or the bystanders typically will express situational enjoyment or amusement prior to, during and/or immediately after the violent act.

This category also includes violence committed by those who are mentally instable. It involves instances of violence perpetrated by characters who lack control over or proper judgment regarding their actions due to a mental impairment. For example, this would include a character who is suffering mental delusions and believes a victim has conspired to get him; or a character who harms a victim because a voice or God has commanded him/her to undertake the act.

This category should not be applied to cases in which someone who is being targeted by a stalker experiences an isolated instance of paranoia -- for example, a person thinks they are being followed and thus they threaten a stranger walking behind them. In such a case, the perpetrator would be said to be acting in self-defense, assuming the individual was acting on the belief that s/he was actually being threatened.

Note of Caution: There are times when the mentally incompetent or insane commit violent acts for other reasons besides mental illness or impairment. That is, an insane character, just as a normally functioning character, may engage in violent acts to protect the self or an other. Resultingly, coders should make sure each act that a mentally incompetent character commits is truly a result of a mental deficiency/psychopathy and not for any of the other reasons.

3.156 **Accident:** This category is reserved for those unintentional acts of violence that occur within the context of an ongoing violent sequence.

Accidents are coded only when they occur within the context of an ongoing violent sequence. For example, if a person loses control while driving a car and hits a pedestrian, this would not be not coded as violence. However, if the driver of the car is fleeing the scene after stabbing someone (violent act within a sequence) and loses control of his/her car and hits a pedestrian, then this hit would be coded as violence and the reason would be coded as an accident.

3.157 **Other:** This category should only be used when the reason for a character's violent actions can not be adequately described by any of the options listed above. For instance, if an animal engages in violence, then it is impossible to ascertain its reason for acting violently. As such, the reason for all non-anthropomorphized animals' violent actions would be classified as "other."

There are also times when you will not know the reason why a character engages in violence. For instance, at the beginning of a program a masked man may enter a woman's bedroom and stab her to death. Because the program just began, you have absolutely no idea why this character killed the woman. As such, you would code the reason for the character's violent actions as "other."

Or, a program may begin with the depiction of harmful consequences. Oftentimes with the depiction of harmful consequences, the identity of the perpetrator and his/her/its reason for acting violently is purposefully concealed. If no information is given to you within the context of the plot about the perpetrator's motive, then you would code his/he/its reason for violence as "other."

There will also be times when a multiple engages in violence and the group members' primary reasons for acting violently are so significantly different that it is impossible to assign only one of the reasons listed above. In this case, the "other" category should also be used.

3.16 RESULTS OF VIOLENCE

Pain and harm are measures used to describe the **results** of a violent interaction recorded as a PAT line of data. Pain and harm are coded only for behavioral acts and for harmful consequences. As such, pain and harm are not coded for credible threats.

Harm refers to physical injury or damage to a target that is caused by a violent act. Two types of harm should be assessed: a) the amount of harm that is actually <u>depicted</u> on the screen, and b) the amount of <u>likely harm</u> that would occur if the violence was enacted in real life. Sometimes these codes will be similar and sometimes they will be different. Programs that depict harm to a target realistically will be coded the same across both measures--the amount of <u>depicted harm</u> will be the same as the amount of <u>likely harm</u> in real life. Programs that depict harm unrealistically (e.g., cartoons) will either overestimate or more often underestimate the amount of harm shown and the codes will reflect that (e.g., harm depicted will be less than the likely harm in real life).

3.161 **Harm Depicted:** This measure focuses on whether harm is actually depicted. Judgments of harm are based on two factors: 1) the amount of physical injury that is depicted, and 2) the character's capacity to continue to function after experiencing violence.

3.1611 <u>Physical Injury:</u> Physical injury is defined as the overt depiction of physical damage to the target's body. Signs of injury or damage must be shown on the screen. These signs can occur during and/or after the violent act. Caution should be exercised when making judgments of injury so as not to assume that damage has occurred when it is not actually depicted.

3.1611a *Inferences about Harm:* Coders should <u>not</u> infer injury based on the nature or seriousness of the violent act but should look for overt signs of physical damage. For example, most humans would be severely injured by gunfire but in a fantastic portrayal, bullets may bounce off a character's chest and cause no injury. Similarly, a cartoon character may be thrown across the room but show no signs of physical damage. Both of these examples would be coded as no injury.

3.1611b *Seriousness of Harm:* The degrees of physical injury are grounded in the degree of seriousness of the injury *as it is depicted in a sequence.* Thus, in a realistic program involving humans, a gunshot to the chest may leave a gaping wound and may be portrayed as life threatening (e.g., a character would fall down, lose blood, and require immediate medical attention). However, in a cartoon a bullet might fly right through a character, leaving a small hole in the chest as the character blinks in amazement. In the latter case, the injury is minimal and should be considered as such (the actual degree of harm would depend on character's capacity to function).

3.1611c *Special note on Cartoon Injury:* If a violent act causes a character's body to temporarily change shape in some fantastic way, this alone does not constitute physical injury. If, however, a cartoon character gets a black eye, a bump, or loses an appendage as a result of violence, these would constitute signs of physical injury. For example, if a character's head is flattened by a hot iron, this change in body shape would not be coded as evidence of harm unless it somehow hindered the character (see below) or the flattened head was accompanied by other signs of damage such as burn marks.

3.1612 <u>Capacity to Function:</u> This aspect of harm refers to the character's ability to engage in "normal" activities after violence has occurred. "Normal" activities should be judged in terms of whatever is normal for <u>that particular character.</u> For humans or anthropomorphized characters, this would include being able to walk, fight back, or flee. For supercreatures, normal activities may include the ability to fly or disappear or use laser eyes. Capacity to function normally should be distinguished from a mere inconvenience to the character. For example, if a cartoon cat is thrown across the room, hits the wall, and lands softly on his paws, then it may be inconvenienced but not incapable of functioning. Presumably, it can still continue doing all its normal activities given the nature of the landing.

3.1613 Special Notes on Coding: When coding for harm, both physical injury and capacity to function should be considered. Often only one of the factors will be relevant in a PAT. For example, a character may be shot and completely unable to function but no actual signs of injury (bullet wound) are depicted. In this case, level of harm would be based entirely on capacity to function. If there is information on both injury and capacity to function, evaluate both factors and pick the level that corresponds to the most prominent aspects of each (see below).
When coding for harm, you should consider the scene that follows the violent sequence as well. This is especially important for cartoons. Sometimes a cartoon character may *appear* to be harmed (injured or incapable of functioning) in a sequence but the very next scene shows the same character virtually unharmed or back to normal. If it is clear that no significant amount of time has passed between the sequence and the next scene, this dramatic "return to normal" should be considered in coding the level of harm.

3.1614 Codes for Depicted Harm: There are six different values for depicted harm. Each of these six values are explicated below.

3.1614a *None:*

There is a clear depiction of a target, but *no physical injury* is portrayed and the character displays a full capacity to function. Examples include: a character is hit in the face but does not show any redness, blood or bruising, and continues moving; a supercreature is shot and his body absorbs the bullet with no sign of injury and no effect on functioning; a cartoon character's arm gets smashed and it temporarily flattens but shows no signs of redness or blood, and the character continues to stand, walk, or talk.

3.1614b *Mild:*

Injury: The depiction of *minor* physical damage to the body that does not seem to require medical attention as it is depicted in the program.

Examples may include: a bloody nose/lip, minor cuts and scrapes, black eye, minor burns, or other signs of minimal damage. Note: in cartoons, minor physical damage may also include things like dismemberment and bullet holes so long as such injuries are portrayed as though they do not require medical attention.

Capacity to Function: Target is *partially* or *briefly* hindered from performing his/her normal behaviors. Examples include: someone is knocked down by a punch, but shakes it off, gets up and pursues the attacker; a cartoon character is hit and momentarily sees stars, indicating that he/she is dizzy; a cartoon character's body is flattened in a sequence such that the character can't walk or run, but in the very next scene the body is back to normal.

3.1614c *Moderate:*

Injury: The depiction of *serious physical damage* to the body that seems to require medical attention. Examples may include: deep cuts/gashes or bullet wounds to a non-vital organ/part of the body (e.g., hands, arms, legs), serious burns, broken bones, dismemberment of a finger or toe, or other signs of substantial injury. Again, whether an injury "seems" to require medical attention depends on how seriously it is treated in a given program.

Capacity to Function: Target is *substantially hindered* from performing his/her normal behaviors after the violence occurs. The portrayal should suggest that the hindrance will persist for a substantial amount of time through the sequence once the violence has occurred even if the target is not actually shown throughout. In addition, if the target is shown in the next immediate scene, he/she should also evidence some reduction in functioning unless it is clear that a significant amount of time has passed.

Examples include: when someone is knocked down by a punch, can't get up, but keeps trying to fight back while on the ground; someone is knocked unconscious and stays that way for the remainder of a sequence or for a good portion of it, but is clearly not dead or in a life threatening state.

3.1614d *Extreme:*

Injury: The depiction of *dire or critical physical damage* to the body that either results in *certain death* or appears to be *life-threatening.* Examples may include a bullet wound to a vital organ, stab wounds to the torso/heart/neck, dismemberment of an arm or leg, or major third degree burns. Whether an injury is judged as life threatening should depend upon how it is depicted in the program. A stab wound to the heart may be life threatening in a police show but depicted as minimal injury in a cartoon.

Capacity to Function: Target is obviously *dead* or rendered *essentially incapable* of performing his/her normal behaviors within that particular sequence and also in the next scene, if featured. Incapacitation should be reserved for characters who are obviously dead or who are harmed to such a great extent that they will be unable to function for a long time.

3.1614e *Unsuccessful Attempt:*

These are intentional acts of violence that were <u>not</u> at all successful in reaching the target (e.g., shooting a gun and the bullet misses the target, swinging a fist and missing).

3.1614f *Target Not Shown:*

There is <u>no</u> clear depiction of the target during or immediately after the violence such that level or degree of harm cannot be ascertained.

3.162 **Likely Harm in Real Life:** Likely harm in real life refers to how much physical injury/damage and incapacitation would occur if the same violent means were targeted toward a human in real life. In other words, this code requires an inference to be drawn about the potential seriousness of the means/violence in the real world. For example, a cartoon character might be pushed off a steep rocky cliff and land on his feet in perfect condition. The depicted harm would be "none." However, the likely harm to a human, depending on the distance of the fall and the hardness of the ground, would be either "moderate" or "extreme." Coders need to consider the four factors that follow when assessing likely harm:

3.1621 Probable Harm: Likely harm refers to the most probable type of harm that would occur in real life. Miracles may be shown in a program involving human characters but such miracles are highly improbable and should not be used to assess likely harm. For example, a character might be shot 20 times with a rifle and miraculously have none of the bullets penetrate his/her critical organs. The depicted harm could be "moderate." But in real life, the likely (most probable) harm would be "extreme." This example illustrates that a discrepancy between depicted and likely harm could exist for other genres besides cartoons and fantastic portrayals.

3.1622 Human Target: Likely harm should be assessed in terms of a human target. Even though a depiction may involve a supernatural character who is not harmed at all (depicted harm = "none"), the likely harm should be assessed in terms of what would happen in real life to a human if the same means were applied. Assume the human is a person of average strength and stamina.

3.1623 Means Used: Likely harm should be assessed according to the precise way in which the means are used in the program. If someone is shot in the head, then likely harm should be judged in terms of a bullet to the brain. If, however, a bullet grazes the ear in a program, then likely harm should be assessed in terms of a bullet grazing a human ear. Toy weapons in a program should be judged in terms of their likely harm in real life if they are used as they are in a program. Supernatural means/weapons do not exist in real life so they pose a bit more of a challenge. Coders should use inferences to estimate the likely harm to a human if a supernatural means/weapon was employed in the same manner as used in a program. For example, if a character uses a laser gun that burns through buildings, it is reasonable to assume that it would also burn through a human body and probably inflict serious injury.

3.1624 Unsuccessful Attempts: If an unsuccessful attempt is depicted, DO NOT code likely harm. Simply indicate "unsuccessful attempt" for both categories of harm.

3.1625 Codes for Likely Harm: There are five different values for likely harm. Each of these five values are explicated below.

3.1625a *None:*

No physical injury and no hindrance in normal functioning would likely occur in real life to an average human being as a result of this violence.

3.1625b *Mild:*

Injury: The violence is likely to lead to only *minor physical damage* that would not ordinarily require medical attention for an average human being (e.g., bloody nose/lip, minor cuts and scrapes, black eye, minor burns, or other signs of minimal injury).

Capacity to Function: An average human being would likely be only *partially or briefly* hindered from performing his/her normal behaviors as a result of this violence.

3.1625c *Moderate:*

> Injury: The violence is likely to lead to *serious physical damage* that would ordinarily require medical attention for an average human being (e.g., broken bones, deep cuts or gashes to non-vital organs/parts of the body, serious burns, or other signs of substantial injury).

> Capacity to Function: An average human being would likely be *substantially hindered* from performing his/her normal behaviors as a result of this violence.

3.1625d *Extreme:*

> Injury: The violence is likely to lead to *dire or critical physical damage* to an average human being that would be *life threatening* or result in *certain death* for an average human being (e.g., bullet wound to a vital organ, stab wounds to the torso/heart/neck, major third degree burns).

> Capacity to Function: An average human target would likely be killed or rendered *essentially incapable* of performing normal behaviors as a result of this violence.

3.1625e *Unsuccessful Attempt:*

> Intentional acts of violence that were not at all successful.

3.163 **Pain Depicted:** The judgment of pain is based entirely on overt depictions in the program content, and not on any inference one might draw about the degree of pain that would likely result from a particular injury. However, the coder may take into account the nature of the injury/harm depicted in interpreting the pain cues portrayed in the program content. For example, a character who is critically injured and depicted as going into shock may not scream or groan, but an ashen appearance and occasional deep gasps would be properly interpreted as indications of extreme pain (taking into account the related knowledge of a serious injury). Pain will normally be expressed by the targets of violence either audibly, visually, or by a combination of the two.

3.1631 <u>Audible Expressions</u>: Audible expressions of pain may include screams, moans, yells, and gasps, among others.

3.1632 <u>Visual Expressions:</u> Visual expressions of pain may include victims' facial expressions, body posture, clutching at a wound or injury, and limping, among others.

3.1633 <u>Codes for Pain:</u>

3.1633a *No Pain:*

> There is a clear depiction of a target either during or after violence has occurred, but the target does <u>not</u> express (either verbally or nonverbally) any pain, anguish, or suffering due to the violence.

> This judgment would apply in cases when the target seems to behave in the same manner after the violence as s/he acted before. Examples: The Terminator gets punched in the face by a guy in a bar but does not flinch; bullets bounce off Superman's chest, but his behavior indicates that this causes him no pain. This

judgment would also apply when a target is killed immediately such that there are no pain cues.

3.1633b *Mild Pain:*

Evidencing pain that appears to be transient or of a <u>very</u> slight degree.

3.1633c *Moderate Pain:*

Evidencing pain that reflects <u>substantial suffering</u> typically associated with the need to seek medical attention

3.1633d *Extreme Pain:*

Evidencing pain that reflects <u>intense suffering</u> that is depicted in a way that suggests it will be enduring and protracted.

3.1633e *Unsuccessful Attempt:*

Attempts at intentional acts of violence that were not at all successful.

3.1633f *Target Not Shown:*

There is no depiction of the target that would allow any assessment of the pain experienced (e.g., no opportunity to observe).

This judgment would apply in cases when the camera moves immediately away from the victim at the moment that harm occurs (and does not return during the sequence; also must lack any auditory cues). An example would be the Terminator throwing a victim against a wall, with the program focus shifting quickly to the Terminator's next action against another victim, providing no opportunity to observe the target's reaction to the apparent injury that would be caused from the attack (i.e., no groans, grunts, screams, depiction of target's face, or other indication of the target's pain). Another example would be a victim being pushed over the side of a cliff (or off of a building or bridge) when the scene changes just as the character goes over the side.

3.1634 <u>Special Note for Coding:</u> Occasionally there will be a range of depictions of pain and/or harm within one particular target (or within multiple targets) on the same line of data, often due to the presence of multiple means. An example would be a single target who is punched by a perpetrator and there is a depiction of only a mild wince and a bloody nose, but then later in the same sequence there is a depiction of a blood-curdling scream and a deep gash when the target is stabbed.

Another example would be an assault on a multiple target during which all are sprayed with gunfire, but only one of those targets displays an overt expression of pain. When faced with situations in which a range of harm/pain cues are depicted within the same unit of analysis (e.g, PAT) <u>always code the highest level of pain and/or harm experienced for each means used by either the single or multiple target within any given PAT interaction.</u>

4.0 SEQUENCE LEVEL VARIABLES

Sequence level variables are grouped below by act and character. Acts within a particular sequence are coded for rewards, punishments, explicitness, graphicness and humor. Each perpetrator and/or target needs to be coded for age and physical strength within each sequence. With most of the sequence level variables, you will need to watch the entire sequence and the scene (definition in section 8.0) immediately after it prior to making any coding judgments.

ACT VARIABLES

    4.1   Reinforcements for Violence
    4.2   Explicitness
    4.3   Graphicness
    4.4   Humor

CHARACTER VARIABLES

    4. 5   Age
    4. 6   Physical Strength

ACT VARIABLES

4.1 REINFORCEMENTS FOR VIOLENCE

Rewards and punishments refer to those **reinforcements** that are obtained as a result or consequence of violence. Rewards and punishments frequently are delivered to the perpetrator by other characters, but sometimes the perpetrator might engage in self–reinforcements.

Rewards and punishments do *not* refer to whether the violence was successful in achieving some goal. For example, a perpetrator may engage in violence in order to protect someone or to promote an ideology. Whether or not such a goal is achieved is independent of whether the violence is rewarded or punished. A perpetrator may successfully meet the goal of protecting someone through the use of violence and still be punished for it (e.g., put in jail). Below, rewards and punishments will be defined along with specific coding instructions on how to assess those positive and negative reinforcements for violence.

4.11 **Rewards**: A reward is a positive reinforcement that is delivered in return for violence. Rewards can occur during or immediately after the violent action. Rewards can come in several different forms. Three types of rewards are possible and each type must be coded for every violent sequence.

    4.111 <u>Self Praise:</u> Self praise is an overt verbal or nonverbal sign of approval or satisfaction that a perpetrator expresses for acting violently. The most obvious example is when a perpetrator praises himself/herself aloud. Another example is when a perpetrator exhibits obvious pleasure or gratification nonverbally (e.g., facial expression of pleasure, raised arms in victory sign) either during or immediately after acting violently.

        A perpetrator who cracks a joke or engages in sarcasm during or immediately after violence is not engaging in self praise unless such humor is accompanied by an overt sign of self approval. Self praise can occur when a perpetrator is alone or in the context of others. If at any time within a sequence or in the immediately adjacent scene, a perpetrator praises him/herself for acting violently, either verbally or nonverbally, then the sequence is to be coded as containing "self praise."

Otherwise, the sequence should be coded as not containing "self praise."

4.112 Praise from Other: Praise from other refers to any overt verbal or nonverbal sign of approval or satisfaction that observers/bystanders express towards a violent action. The most obvious example is when other characters verbally praise or cheer a violent action. In addition, others could praise violence through nonverbal means, such as a thumbs up sign, a pat on the back or a high five.

Note: It is not necessary for the perpetrator to notice or acknowledge this praise, so long as it is obvious when viewing the sequence. If at any time during a sequence or in the scene that immediately follows a perpetrator is praised from another for acting violently, then the sequence is to be coded as containing "praise from other." Otherwise, the sequence should be coded as not containing "praise from other."

4.113 Material Reward: Material reward is a tangible, physical token of compensation that is given or taken for violence. A material reward can be taken by the perpetrator (e.g., steal money) or awarded to the perpetrator by others (e.g., someone pays a hitman). Examples of material rewards include money (e.g., robbing a bank), drugs and possessions (e.g., car or a piece of jewelry).

If at any time within the sequence or in the immediately adjacent scene a material reward is given to or taken by a perpetrator for acting violently, then the sequence should be coded as containing "material reward." Otherwise, the sequence should be coded as "material reward" absent.

4.12 **Punishments**: A punishment is a negative reinforcement that is delivered in return for violence. Punishments can occur during or immediately after the violent action. Punishments come in four specific forms: condemnation from self, condemnation from others, nonviolent actions, and violent actions. All four types should be coded at the sequence level.

4.121 Self Condemnation: Self condemnation is an overt verbal or nonverbal sign of disapproval, disappointment or dissatisfaction that a perpetrator expresses for acting violently.   The most obvious example is when a perpetrator expresses remorse or guilt either during or after engaging in violence. This can be conveyed either verbally or nonverbally (e.g., words of remorse and/or facial expression of sadness). Self condemnation can occur when a perpetrator is alone or in the context of others. If at any time self condemnation appears within a sequence or in the scene that immediately follows, then the sequence should be coded as containing "self condemnation." Otherwise, the sequence should be coded as not containing "self condemnation."

4.122 Condemnation from Other: Condemnation from "other" refers to any overt verbal or nonverbal sign of disapproval, disappointment or dissatisfaction that observers/bystanders express toward a violent action. By definition, condemnation cannot be expressed by the target of violence. The most obvious example is when others verbally reprimand a perpetrator for a violent action (e.g., scold, publicly chastise).

Disapproval also can be shown nonverbally, as when others frown or shake their heads when violence occurs. Condemnation should be distinguished from other reactions that observers might have like fear or shock; such emotional responses should not be coded as condemnation of violence. Note: It is not necessary for the perpetrator to notice or acknowledge condemnation, so long as it is obvious when viewing the sequence.

If at any time condemnation from others appear within a sequence or in the scene that immediately follows, then the sequence should be coded as containing "condemnation from other." Otherwise, the sequence should be coded as not containing "condemnation from other."

4.123 <u>Nonviolent Action:</u> Nonviolent action refers to any overt nonviolent behavior that is designed to stop violence or hinder further violence by penalizing it. Typically, nonviolent action involves somehow restricting the freedom of a perpetrator. Examples include: arresting someone, putting someone in jail or prison, making someone pay restitution, and/or making someone apologize.

If at any time nonviolent action appears as a negative reinforcement of violence within a sequence or in the scene that immediately follows, then "nonviolent action" should be coded as present. Otherwise, the sequence should be coded as "nonviolent action" absent.

4.124 <u>Violent Action from Other:</u> Violent action from "other" refers to any violent threat or behavior that an observer, bystander or third party directs toward the perpetrator in order to try to stop or punish the perpetrator's previous violence towards a target. Violent action, by definition, cannot come from the target nor any target the perpetrator had threatened to harm or actually harmed within the same violent sequence. Examples include: a cop killing a criminal on a shooting spree, a body guard tackling a deviant who has threatened his client, or an older brother hitting the neighborhood bully who has slapped his younger brother.

If at any time violent actions appear as a negative reinforcement of violence within a sequence or in the scene that immediately follows, then the sequence should be coded as containing "violent action." Otherwise, the sequence should be coded as not containing "violent action."

4.13 **Coding Positive and Negative Reinforcements:** Four specific coding instructions should be applied when coding positive and negative reinforcements of violence.

4.131 <u>Must be Overtly Displayed:</u> Rewards and punishments must be <u>overtly displayed</u> or talked about in order to be coded. You should not assume anything unless you see or hear signs of such reinforcements. For example, self rewards must be shown through visible signs of pleasure on the part of a character. You should never assume that a character is feeling proud or gratified after acting violent ... you must see overt signs of pleasure being expressed (e.g., a self congratulatory statement; a broad smile of pleasure after hitting someone).

4.132 <u>Code Positive and Negative Reinforcements Separately:</u> Rewards and punishments should be coded separately within the sequence. First, examine whether the violence was rewarded within the sequence; then focus on whether the violence was punished. It is possible that violence might be <u>both</u> rewarded and punished within a sequence. It is also possible that violence will be neither rewarded nor punished.

4.133 <u>Examine All PAT's for Reinforcements:</u> A sequence may contain several violent actions conducted by different perpetrators (PATs). Rewards and punishments should be examined across all the PATs that are portrayed. If *any* of the perpetrators are rewarded and/or punished, then rewards/punishments should be coded for the sequence.

4.134 <u>Examine Immediately Adjacent Scene</u>: As with all of the sequence level coding, you should watch the entire sequence and the scene after it. Rewards/punishments can occur any time within the sequence or in the scene immediately after. Rewards and/or punishments also might occur later in the program but these would *not* be reflected in the coding done at the sequence level.

4.2 EXPLICITNESS OF VIOLENCE

Explicitness is defined as the focus, concentration or <u>details</u> of an overt violent depiction. The focus is said to be detailed when the subject matter encompasses the screen such that other elements of the portrayal are obscured or cannot be distinguished clearly. There are two types of explicitness coded at the sequence level: explicitness of the violent behavioral act and explicitness of the means-to-target impact.

4.21 **Explicitness of Violent Behavioral Act:** This measure refers to the level of detailed focus on the perpetrator and his/her/its means used in violence. A violent portrayal can be: 1) shown from a close-up, 2) shown from a long-shot, or 3) not shown.

4.211 <u>Close-Up Depictions</u>: For a depiction to qualify as "close-up", two conditions must be met: 1) over sixty-five percent of the screen must be consumed with the means and/or a portion of the perpetrator and 2) the means must actually be depicted in use by the perpetrator (e.g., gun actually shown being shot). Because the focus of the camera zooms in on the violent action, background elements such as bystanders, furniture, or other objects should <u>not</u> be clearly featured and/or defined. If background elements in the scene are clearly ascertainable, then the depiction of violence would not be coded as "close-up."

An example of a close-up focus on a violent act would include a shot of a perpetrator's hand shown pushing the button of a switch blade. Or, a close-up depiction may zoom in on the barrel of a pistol or firearm as the perpetrator pulls the trigger. And finally, a close-up may portray a boxer's fist and arm swinging at an opponent.

4.212 <u>Long-Shot Depictions</u>: Long-shots, in contrast, are those depictions that also visually portray the violent act, but the focus or concentration of the camera is not solely on the perpetrator and his/her/its means for accomplishing violence. In long-shots, background elements such as bystanders, furniture or other objects may be irrelevant but they are clearly featured and/or portrayed in the violent portrayal.

An example of a long-shot would include a depiction of two men brawling in a saloon, two boxers punching it out in a boxing ring, or a two jet fighters attacking one another. In all these instances, a long-shot depiction would include both the characters (e.g., the two bar thugs, two boxers, two planes) and some of the surrounding background atmosphere (e.g., saloon, boxing ring and perhaps audience, and clouds, ground scenery).

4.213 <u>Depictions Not Shown</u>: This category is reserved for those sequences where none of the violent action is depicted or portrayed on-screen. For instance, the camera may be focusing on a perpetrator threatening a target and then cut away right before the perpetrator pulls the trigger so that all that is seen on-screen is the target's reaction.

4.214 <u>Not Applicable</u>: This category is to be used only when a credible threat of violence or harmful consequences of unseen violence are depicted in a sequence.

4.22 **Explicitness of Means-To-Target Impact:** This variable assesses the focus or degree of detail that is portrayed on-screen when the means or weapon used actually impacts <u>and</u> damages a target's body. For means-to-target impact to be coded, the means must actually be shown penetrating or impacting a portion of the target's body. Means-to-target impact may be: 1) shown from a close-up, 2) shown from a long-shot, or 3) not shown.

4.221 <u>Close-Up Depictions:</u> In close-up depictions, the means and the target must be portrayed on-screen. For a depiction to qualify as "close-up," two conditions must be met: 1) over sixty-five percent of the screen must be consumed with the means-to-target impact, and 2) the means must be shown actually penetrating a portion of the target's body.

For example, a knife encompassing over two thirds of the screen may be shown pressing against and then penetrating a character's flesh. This depiction should be coded as a close-up portrayal of impact. In the case of natural means, a close-up portrayal may show a near full-screen fist <u>as it</u> strikes a face, or teeth as they bite down on an arm. When guns are used, a close-up portrayal may depict only the portion of a target's body where the bullet enters and his/her/its flesh tears and explodes upon impact.

4.222 <u>Long-Shot Depictions:</u> In contrast, long-shots are those depictions that visually portray the means-to-target impact but the focus or concentration of the camera is not solely on the perpetrator's means impacting or penetrating the target's body. In long-shots, background elements such as bystanders, furniture or other objects may be irrelevant but they are clearly featured and/or portrayed in violent depictions.

An example of a long-shot would include a boxing match where two heavy weights are depicted giving punches to and receiving punches from each other. Although the camera clearly portrays each boxers' fists impacting the jaws or ribs of the opponent, the depiction also includes a clear portrayal of the boxing ring, the referee in the corner and some of the fans in the crowd.

4.223 <u>Depictions Not Shown:</u> This category is reserved for those sequences where the means-to-target impact of the violent action is <u>not</u> depicted or portrayed in use on-screen. The camera does not focus at any time on the target receiving the impact of the means used.

For instance, in *Kids Killing Kids*, a young boy in the back of a school room is shown firing a small hand-gun in class. After the gun goes off, the camera cuts to the shocked look on his face while screams are heard in the background. The camera then focuses in on the targets and the harm they incurred from the young man's irresponsibility. In this instance, the means (e.g., the bullet) was not shown <u>actually</u> penetrating and/or damaging the targets' body. As such, the explicitness of the sequence would be coded as "not shown."

4.224 <u>Not Applicable:</u> This category is to be used only when a credible threat of violence or harmful consequences of unseen violence are depicted in a sequence.

4.23 **Coding Explicitness:** Explicitness is a sequence level variable. The four following coding instructions should be applied when assessing a sequence for explicitness.

4.231 <u>Entire Sequence Assessed:</u> You should view the entire sequence in order to evaluate explicitness. An explicit depiction could occur at any point in the sequence. It does not have to occur throughout the sequence in order to be counted. Even a split-second depiction of a violent act or the means impacting a target's body in an isolated portion of the sequence should be assessed for explicitness.

4.232 <u>Duration of Camera Focus:</u> The camera need not focus exclusively on the violent action or the means-to-target impact in order for the depiction to be coded for explicitness. In some cases, the violent action may <u>not</u> even be the primary focus of the scene. Regardless of cameras focus, a violent sequence should always be coded for explicitness.

4.233 <u>Multiple Depictions Within One Sequence:</u> Several depictions of violence may occur in a given sequence. If the depictions vary in the amount of explicitness portrayed, then always code the highest level that is shown on-screen.

4.3 GRAPHICNESS OF CONSEQUENCES

Graphicness is defined as the portrayal of blood, gore, or dismemberment displayed as a consequence of violence. Gore includes any inner parts of the body (e.g., muscle, organs, tissue, viscera). Partial or complete skeletons do not count as gore unless they are attached to inner body parts. Dismemberment is defined as any limb or appendage that has been severed from the body. Examples of limbs and appendages that may be dismembered include: legs, arms, noses, ears, fingers, and toes. When coding graphicness, the <u>amount</u> of blood, gore and dismemberment needs to be assessed.

4.31 **Amount of Graphicness:** Each sequence will be assessed for the amount of graphicness displayed. Amount refers to the degree or quantity of blood, gore, and/or dismemberment shown. There are four categories of graphicness: none, mild, moderate and extreme. Each of these categories are explicated below.

4.32 **Codes for Graphicness:**

4.321 <u>None:</u>

No display of blood, gore, or dismemberment.

4.322 <u>Mild:</u>

Little or trivial amount of blood or gore. For example, from one to several drops of blood that are no larger than a quarter, a small flesh wound, a surface cut that exposes a minor amount of tissue damage.

4.323 <u>Moderate:</u>

Moderate amount of either blood or gore. For example, many drops of blood, a small pool of blood, and/or a deep flesh wound that exposes muscle and/or tissue damage.

4.324 <u>Extreme:</u>

Either heavy amounts of blood and/or gore or at least one depiction of dismemberment. Examples of extreme graphicness include: scenes that depict 1) blood spattered on walls and/or other characters, 2) an excessive wound that shows body organs or blood spewing from the body, and 3) any depiction of a limb or body part that is severed from the body.

4.325 <u>Not Applicable:</u>

This category is only to be used when credible threats that are verbal only occur within a violent sequence.

4.33 **Coding Instructions for Graphicness:** Four specific coding instructions should be applied when coding the amount of graphicness in a violent sequence.

4.331 <u>Camera Focus:</u> Graphic depictions may appear in the foreground or in the background of the on-screen depiction. The camera need not focus exclusively on the blood, gore or dismemberment in order for the sequence to be coded for graphicness.

4.332 <u>Length of Time Devoted to Graphic Depiction:</u> When coding graphicness, only <u>amount</u> of blood, gore or dismemberment portrayed should be considered and <u>not</u> the length of time the depiction is shown. For example, a very bloody scene could be shown only for a brief second but would still qualify as "extreme" in terms of graphicness.

4.333 <u>Multiple Depictions of Graphicness:</u> Several depictions of blood and gore may occur in a sequence. If the depictions vary in amount, always code the highest or most intense level that is shown in the sequence. For example, if the presence of blood at the first PAT is "extreme" yet several other PAT's contain no blood at all, code the sequence as "extreme."

If several depictions that are equal in amount occur across a sequence, do not "add" these portrayals up. Several "moderate" level depictions should always be coded as "moderate." Also, if any depiction of dismemberment occurs in a sequence, then it is automatically coded as featuring "extreme" graphicness.

4.334 <u>Special Note on Grotesque Characters and Monsters:</u> There are times when monsters and ghoulish creatures are displayed in a program with bloody faces, exposed organs and/or severed limbs. These types of depictions will <u>not</u> be considered graphic provided that their grotesque appearance was not the result of observed or implied violence within the program.

If these creatures are injured in a sequence and the results are graphically displayed, then those injuries should be coded for their graphic content. So, for example, the headless horseman (who rides around carrying his head) should <u>not</u> be coded for graphicness. However, if he is decapitated <u>within</u> the program, then each sequence he appears in should be coded for the amount of graphicness displayed.

4.4 HUMOR

Humor refers to those verbal statements or nonverbal actions a character engages in that are intended to amuse the self, another character or characters, and/or the viewer. Humorous verbal statements include jokes, sarcastic assertions, absurd remarks and/or ill-informed comments. Nonverbal actions that are funny include certain types of paralinguistic sounds, gestures, and/or motions.

Humor also includes those situations that are meant to be amusing. Humorous situations usually involve occurrences that are portrayed in an absurd, exaggerated, or unrealistic fashion. Oftentimes, there may be production conventions and cues that clearly indicate to the audience that the portrayal is a non-serious, humorous, and/or a farce-like depiction. Any time production conventions like laugh tracks and/or strange noises are used, the sequence should automatically be coded as containing humor.

Humor should be coded at the end of each violent sequence. Very simply, humor is to be coded as either absent or present within a violent sequence. Unlike all other sequence level codes, we are only interested in humor that occurs <u>within</u> the violent sequence. Resultingly, do not assess the subsequent scene prior to making your coding judgment on this sequence variable.

There are three ways humor can appear in a violent sequence: (1) the humor is directed at violence, (2) a violent situation is funny or is meant to be funny, and (3) humor occurs in the sequence but it is unrelated to the violence. Humor should be coded as "present" when <u>any</u> one of the above three categories occur. Each of these three categories will be explicated below.

4.41 **Humor Directed at the Violence:** Humor that is directed towards the violence in a sequence may be done so by the perpetrator, the target, or a bystander.

4.411 <u>Perpetrator Uses Humor:</u> In these cases, the perpetrator is shown laughing at or making jokes about violence. For example, a perpetrator may crack a sarcastic joke or comment right before killing a group of targets.

4.412 <u>Target Uses Humor:</u> In these cases, the target is clearly amused by the violence and is shown laughing at or making a joke about it.

4.413 <u>Bystander Uses Humor:</u> Oftentimes, a bystander may be shown laughing at or making a joke about the violence. For example, after arriving at a crime scene and discovering a dead and bloodied body, a desensitized detective may crack a joke about the victim looking rather bad in the color red.

4.42 **Violent Situation is Funny or is Meant to be Funny:** Violent situations are considered humorous when the characters behave in a funny way or when the consequences of violent actions are portrayed in a humorous fashion.

4.421 <u>Characters Acting Funny:</u> These characters are not making jokes about the violence but they are still behaving in a funny way. Often, they are often shown either overreacting or underacting to the situation. For example, Pee Wee Herman may express extreme and protracted pain and suffering (e.g., screaming and moaning) after being intentionally hit in the face with a water balloon by the neighborhood bully. While such an action may hurt Pee Wee, his reaction is clearly exaggerated and thus extremely humorous to those watching.

Any type of slapstick also qualifies under this category of humor because the characters are acting ridiculous in the situation. Oftentimes, slapstick and comedic programs use laugh tracks to signal that the character's actions are meant to be funny. Therefore, if a laugh track is present within a violent sequence, then humor should be coded as present within the sequence.

For example, Curly may hit Mo over the head with a bowling pin. When the bowling pin strikes Mo's head, a car horn may sound in the background and a laugh track may be instantiated off-screen.

4.422 <u>Consequences are Funny:</u> Within a violent sequence, the consequences of violence *may* be portrayed in a humorous fashion. This includes many cartoon depictions that contain nonserious or farce-like violent actions that are followed by unrealistic or absurd depictions of harm. For instance,when Tom (from cartoon, *Tom and Jerry*) gets his tail stuck in the barbecue by Jerry, he runs around screaming with the barbecue in tow.

A further example is Joe Peschi's character in *Home Alone II*. He receives an anvil in the face when trying to abduct the fleeting M. Caulkin, but the only harm Peschi experiences is a branded anvil on the forehead and momentary incompetence in pursuing his young target. Such unrealistic and absurd harm is intended to be humorous to the audience.

4.43 **Humor Occurs in the Sequence but it is Unrelated to Violence:** For humor to be present within a violent sequence, it does not necessarily have to be directed towards the violence within the sequence. Often, it is purposefully unconnected in order to trivialize the serious tone of the violence. The source of humor is the contrast or juxtaposition between the violence and mundane.

For example, after two detectives engage in several rounds of gunfire that leaves several drug dealers bleeding to death, one detective may turn to another and say, "now can we please go get some lunch?" Other examples of this sort include any off-handed comments and/or jokes that are directed towards something other than the violence within the sequence.

4.44 **Codes for Humor:**

4.441 <u>No Humor Present:</u>

None of the three types of humor listed above occur at any time during the violent sequence.

4.442 <u>Humor Present:</u>

At least one of the three types of humor listed above occur at some time within the violent sequence.

CHARACTER VARIABLES

At the end of each sequence, you will need to assess two specific character variables. Those two character variables include age and physical strength.

4.5 AGE OF CHARACTER

At the end of the sequence, you will need to code the **approximate age** of each perpetrator and target involved in violence. When ascertaining a perpetrator or target's age, you will need to take into consideration character type.

4.51 **Human Characters:** Human characters should be sorted into one of four age groups: child, teen, adult, or elderly. Children are characters between infancy and 12 years of age; teens are characters between 13 and 20 years of age; adults are characters between 21 and 64; and elderly are characters who are 65 years or older. In order to determine approximate age, you should consider all available cues in the program including physical appearance, vocal characteristics, and behavioral patterns (e.g., school attendance, employment), as well as the dialogue in the plot/context that might reveal age information.

4.52 **Non-Human Characters:** For non-human characters (e.g., supernatural creatures and animals) age may be more difficult to decipher, and thus code. As a rule, you should code all characters who possess specific traits or characteristics that would clearly categorize them into one of the four groupings delineated above. For example, Superman, the Terminator, and Mork from *Mork and Mindy* are all anthropomorphized supernatural creatures who clearly possess the physical characteristics and age cues of "adults" and would be coded as such. The Wonder Twins and Batgirl, however, act and look like teenagers and thus should be coded as such.

4.53 **Other Types of Characters:** For other types of characters, like non-anthropomorphized supernatural creatures and animals, age may be impossible and inconsequential to determine. For instance, it would be impossible and meaningless to convert the age of animals into one of the four categories mentioned above. Similarly, for supernatural creatures which possess no age cues or human like features (e.g., the Blob), age is impossible and inconsequential to ascertain. In both of these instances, the age of these types of characters should be coded as "can't tell."

4.54 **Coding Multiple Perpetrators and Targets:** Age may be difficult to ascertain when multiple perpetrators and/or targets are involved in violence. Multiple P's and T's should be treated as a unit. If the P's or the T's are homogeneous and thus possess the same or are very close in age, then you should code the entire unit into one age category. For example, if a group of gang members are engaging in violence and it is clear that they are all teenagers, then you should code the entire unit as "teen." If, however, the P's and T's age are clearly different and could be coded into more than one category, then you should code the multiple unit as "mixed." For instance, if the aforementioned group of gang members had an older "adult" male as a leader, then the unit would be coded as mixed.

4.55 **Codes for Character's Age:**

   4.551 Child: A character should be coded "child" when he/she/it is between infancy and 12 years of age.

   4.552 Teen: A character should be coded "teen" when he/she/it is between 13 and 20 years of age.

   4.553 Adult: A character should be coded "adult" when he/she/it is between 21 and 64 years of age.

   4.554 Elderly: A character should be coded as "elderly" when he/she/it is 65 years of age or older.

   4.556 Mixed: This code is reserved for those multiple perpetrators and/or targets whose ages can not be classified into one and only one of the categories listed above.

   4.557 Can't Tell: This code is reserved for those characters who possess an age but it is impossible to ascertain which age group he/she/it should fit into. This code should also be used when the age of a character is irrelevant and inconsequential to ascertain.

4.6 PHYSICAL STRENGTH

At the end of a violent sequence, you will need to ascertain the **physical strength** of the perpetrator(s) engaging in violence. Physical strength/weakness refers only to physical potency; it does not include emotional strength, moral strength, or bravery.

A perpetrator's physical strength should be coded at the end of every sequence he/she/it acts violently in. Moreover, physical strength may vary from one sequence to the next. For example, Superman may be portrayed as physically strong in one sequence by overcoming with ease and power the forces of evil. For that particular sequence, he would be coded "physically strong." In the next violent sequence, however, his opponent may possess and use cryptonite which renders him completely weak and defenseless. For this sequence, he would be coded as "physically weak."

> **4.61 Codes for Physical Strength:** There are six different codes for physical strength. Each of the codes are explicated below.
>
>> **4.611** <u>Physically Strong Characters:</u> Physically strong characters are those who engage in behaviors that demonstrate physical power and might. Examples include characters who can overcome others with force easily, who can lift heavy objects, who continue fighting despite injury, who display lots of muscles or who are physically large and brawny in appearance (e.g., Sly Stallone in *Rocky*, Linda Hamilton in *Terminator 2*, creatures with supernatural powers of strength).
>>
>> **4.612** <u>Neutral Characters:</u> Most characters will not be portrayed as either strong or weak because they are normal in physical power (e.g., neither excessively strong nor weak). As such, at the sequence level they should be coded as "neutral."
>>
>> **4.613** <u>Physically Weak Characters:</u> Characters who are physically weak are portrayed as physically fragile, frail, physically vulnerable and/or helpless. Examples include characters who are scrawny, easily defeated in physical contests, helpless or easily incapacitated in the face of danger (e.g., Barney Fife on *The Andy Griffith Show*, Shaggy on *Scooby Doo*).
>>
>> **4.614** <u>Both Physically Strong and Weak Within Same Sequence:</u> There will be times when a perpetrator is portrayed as both physically strong and weak within the same sequence. For instance, at the beginning of a sequence a character may overcome his/her/its opponent with great physical power and might. At the end of the very same sequence, however, that same character may suffer an injury and become defenseless and weak. When characters possess physical strength and weakness within the same sequence, you should use the code "both physically strong and weak."
>>
>> **4.615** <u>Mixed Characters (Multiple P's):</u> Physical strength/weakness may be difficult to ascertain when multiple perpetrators are involved in violence. Multiple P's should be treated and assessed as a unit. If the P's are extremely homogeneous and thus possess the same level of physical strength/weakness, then you should code the entire unit into the category that best represents their level of physical potency. For example, if a violent sequence contains a group of "superheroes" that are all physically brawny and display extreme power and might throughout a particular sequence, then you would code the entire multiple as "physically strong."
>>
>> If the physical strength of the members in the multiple varies, then you should code the multiple unit as "mixed." For instance, a group of bad guys may contain several

strong, brawny and physically powerful members and one physically weak, defenseless fragile member. Because the level of physical potency varies within this unit, the multiple would be coded as "mixed."

4.616 <u>Can't Tell:</u> There will be times when the physical strength of a perpetrator will be impossible to ascertain. For example, a sequence may only depict the shadow or a portion of a perpetrator's body when acting violently. Or, the perpetrator's violent actions may be so brief that his/her/its physical power and might can not be accurately determined. When these and other types of depictions occur where the strength of a perpetrator can not be clearly ascertained, you should code his/her/its physical strength for the sequence as "can't tell."

5.0 PROGRAM LEVEL VARIABLES

The coding at the program level is in some senses independent of coding done at the PAT or sequence levels. It is an independent task, because coding judgments made at the program level are not simply based on or determined by the decisions made at the more micro levels. That is, you will not be "summing-up" all your micro level decisions to "compute" program levels judgments. Instead, deciding what codes to assign at the program level requires a process of thinking that is more macro, hence different, than the decision-making at the more microscopic levels of analysis.

For each of the program level variables, you must think about the meaning of the entire narrative of the show. When making your program level decisions, it is best to think about the total <u>pattern</u> of events and character interactions. However, in some programs, a single event or character might be so important that it dominated or conveyed the meaning of the entire program.

There are two types of variables that are assessed at the program level: program variables and character variables. Programs variables include: narrative purpose, realism, harm and pain, pattern of punishments and style of presentation. Character variables include type of character, sex, ethnicity, good/bad and hero status. Each of these types of variables will be demarcated below.

PROGRAM VARIABLES

5.1	Narrative Purpose
5.2	Realism
5.3	Harm
5.4	Patterns of Punishments
5.5	Style of Presentation

CHARACTER VARIABLES

5.6	Type of Character
5.7	Sex of Character
5.8	Ethnicity of Character
5.9	Good/Bad
5.10	Hero Status

PROGRAM VARIABLES

5.1 NARRATIVE PURPOSE

The **narrative purpose** assesses how and why violence is used within a specific program. To assess this variable, coders should begin by asking: what is the reason or purpose for using violence in this program? Some programs may use violence as a thematic tool designed to illustrate some moral purpose or lesson. All programs communicating a moral purpose about violence are coded as featuring an "anti-violent" theme. For instance, *Kids Killing Kids* is one specific example of a program that uses violence to communicate to adolescents the potential dangers and negative effects of involvement with firearms and weaponry.

Other programs, however, simply use violence as a means to excite and/or entertain the audience. These types of programs usually do not communicate any type of anti-violence message or moral lesson about violence. Rather, violence is used as a plot and production devise to engage viewers. As such, these shows would be coded as containing no anti-violent theme.

In deciding the narrative purpose, you will need to assess whether the program featured or did not feature an anti-violent theme. Below, you will find some rules to guide your decision making.

5.11 **Anti-Violent Theme:** Overall, the theme of a program is that violence is bad or that violence is not a good technique for solving problems (e.g., *Schindlers List*). On the micro level, there may be sequences of violence that are rewarded (or not punished) and where no negative consequences are shown. On the macro level, however, the message of the program may be that violence is wrong and it has serious and far reaching consequences. In order for a program to coded as containing an anti-violent theme, the show must have at least one of the following as a <u>strong focus</u> of the overall narrative:

5.111 <u>Alternatives to Violence Presented or Discussed:</u> The alternatives to violence are treated more favorably as a means to deal with problems than are violent actions in the unfolding narrative. A good example of a program featuring alternatives to violence is *Kids Killing Kids*. In this made for TV movie, kids are not only shown engaging in violence but the realistic consequences from acting aggressively in society (e.g., incarceration, pain and suffering of target and targets family) are also portrayed. Immediately after each violent scene has been depicted, the programs "rewinds"and the episode and presents the positive outcomes that could have resulted if the characters had chosen a non-violent alternative.

Oftentimes, characters in programs may discuss or suggest non-violent alternatives to problems that other characters choose to ignore. In these cases, the program would still be considered as containing an anti-violent theme because the non-violent alternatives were presented and stressed in a favorable manner.

5.112 <u>Main Characters Repeatedly Discuss Negative Consequences of Violence:</u> Even though main characters commit acts of violence, they almost always do so reluctantly and display neutral feelings and/or remorse over their actions. Prior to acting violently, the perpetrator may display a general reluctant or avoidance of such actions. Even though the character does not discuss specific alternatives, there is a discussion of the moral implications or negative consequences for such actions.

For example, in the program *The Rifleman,* Lucas discusses repeatedly with his son the importance of avoiding violent actions. While it is clear that Lucas has committed violence in the past, he sees violence as only a last resort. Moreover, Lucas usually displays no pleasure in having to use violence even when it is portrayed as being justified.

5.113 <u>Pain/Suffering from Violence go beyond Victim and Perpetrator to have an Impact upon their Families, Friends, and Community:</u> The program depicts the emotional pain and suffering experienced by family members and/or friends of the victims of violence. For example, in the film *Boys in the Hood*, one character is shot and killed. In the immediately adjacent scene, the victim's friends bring the lifeless and bloodstained body to his home. An extended scene is then portrayed where the victim's friends and family members display intense emotional pain and sorrow over the victim's death. This theme is then carried throughout the entire movie or program.

5.114 <u>On Balance there is a Preponderance of Punishment for Violence when Compared to Rewards:</u> The program must present many more negative reinforcements for violence than a single punishment at the end of the show. Punishment (e.g., criticisms, sanctions, remorse, etc.) need to be consistently emphasized throughout the duration of the program.

5.12 **No Anti-Violent Theme Presented:** Overall, there is no thematic statement about the harmful effects of violence. The major purpose of including violence in the program is simply to entertain. The four following elements are typical characteristics of programs lacking an anti-violent theme:

5.121 <u>Violence is Presented as an Acceptable Means to Solve Problems:</u> When violence is used in the program, it is usually successful and the characters feel good or at least experience no remorse after acting violently. Essentially, the theme of the program suggests that the ends justify the means--even when the means used are violent.

5.122 <u>Main Characters do Not Repeatedly Discuss Violence as having Negative Consequences:</u> The characters in these types of violent programs usually do not discuss the negative or harmful effects of acting violently in society. Sometimes, however, the characters may show remorse about committing violence or may sometimes act as if it is not good to use violence to get what they want. However, these portrayals are infrequent and they are in the background, while the foreground presents messages about the usefulness of violence.

5.123 <u>Pain/Suffering from Violence are Rarely Shown.</u> Overall, the program does not portray the negative consequences of violence. When negative consequences are shown, they are mostly minor, short-term, and in the background.

5.124 <u>On balance, there are Few Punishments for Violence:</u> Violence is rarely punished throughout the program. For example, action adventure programs may portray criminals getting away with numerous acts of violence before being arrested at the very end of a program.

5.2   REALISM

Realism refers to the actuality of the characters, settings, and events that are presented in a program. The focus of this measure is to distinguish realistic portrayals from more fantastic depictions. There are four categories into which shows can be classified:

5.21 **Actual Reality:** These represent all programs that show footage of actual events **always** enacted by the actual people involved in real time and **do not** include any recreations. Although editing is used in the production process, the program attempts to convey the violent events as they actually occurred. Examples include nightly news and any live broadcast (e.g., concert).

5.22 **Recreation of Reality:** Reenactments are those programs that feature stories and events that have actually occurred in the past. Typically, actors are used in place of the real people in the story, and certain events and dialogue are fictionalized. For a program to be coded as a "recreation of reality," a written or verbal statement must appear at the start or end of a show that indicates that the story is based upon real events and characters. If no such statement or information is presented, then the program should not be coded "recreation of reality."

5.23 **Fictional:** Characters and events are creative constructions of the writer and <u>not</u> based upon an actual event. However, the events and/or characters are possible and could happen in real life. *NYPD Blue*, *Seinfeld*, and *Bay Watch*, are all examples of fictional shows even though they present realistic characters in realistic settings.

5.24 **Fantasy**: Included in this category are shows that feature either characters or settings that cannot possibly happen in the real world as we know it today. Programs containing anthropomorphized animals, machines, and superhumans are to be coded within this category. Programs with settings that cannot exist (e.g., gravity free zones) or are beyond human life experiences (e.g., heaven, hell) are also to be coded as fantastic.

5.241 Distinguishing Fiction from Fantasy: Oftentimes, futuristic settings and animated characters will be presented in a program that make realism difficult to assess. As a rule, all programs containing futuristic locales in which characters experience environmental cues that do not exist in the viewer's world today (e.g., flying cars, beaming people to different locations) should be coded as fantasy.

Programs containing settings that occurred in the past will usually be coded as fictional. However, past settings must (1) have no evidence of any fantastic or supernatural elements in the plot line, (2) present in a believable manner events and characters that reflect a specific period of time or a particular place in history. Examples of programs with characters and settings from the past that would be coded as fictional include most westerns (e.g., *The Big Valley, Unforgiven*) and time period shows (e.g., *Untouchables, The Madness of King George*).

Programs featuring animated characters may be coded as fiction or fantasy. This judgment will typically hinge on what types of animated characters are presented in the program. For example, *The Simpsons* would be considered fictional because the characters are animated humans with no fantastic or supernatural powers. In contrast, a *Looney Tunes* cartoon would be coded as a fantastic because the characters are anthropomorphized animals that can not exist in this world (e.g., Bugs Bunny and Daffy Duck).

5.3   HARM/PAIN

This program level variable allows for the documentation of more realistic depictions of the aftermath of violence in terms of long-term suffering or recovery. There are two types of portrayals that should be assessed before coding program level **harm/pain**. Those two depictions include: (1) physical harm/pain, and (2) emotional, psychological and/or financial loss.

5.31 **Physical Harm/Pain:** The depictions of physical harm/pain that occur as a result of violence should first be assessed. Examples of portrayals of physical harm/pain include the healing and recovery characters experience from gunshot wounds, broken bones, and the like. For example, after being shot, Steve Martin's character in the *Grand Canyon*, limps and walks with a cane throughout the rest of the film. These types of portrayals of the consequences of violence are realistic depictions of the harm/pain that occur from severe injuries.

5.32 **Emotional/Psychological/Financial Costs:** The second type of depictions to assess are the realistic portrayals of the emotional/psychological/financial harm and pain that occur as a result of violence. Normally, the aftermath codes are associated with the target of the actual violence. For this code, however, the emotional/psychological/financial consequences can also be seen in close friends and family members of the perpetrator and/or target. Examples of the emotional/psychological/financial consequences of violence include, but are not limited to, the initial and continued grief over violence and financial hardship that results from acting aggressively in society (e.g., welfare, hospital expenses).

5.33 **Coding Harm/Pain at the Program Level:** There are three values of harm/pain at the program level.

5.331 <u>None:</u>

Usually, no portrayal of harm/pain occurs during or after most violent sequences.

5.332 <u>Within Sequence and Immediately Adjacent Scene Only:</u>

No harm/pain from the violence are shown beyond the violent sequence and immediately adjacent scene. While harm/pain are shown within the violent sequence and/or the immediately adjacent scene, there are no reminders (e.g., pain or harm cues) of the harm in any of the scenes that follow.

5.333 <u>Extended Beyond Sequence and Immediately Adjacent Scene:</u>

For a program to be coded as "extended," the harm/pain from the violence must be portrayed in a long-term or an extended fashion throughout the program. To qualify as extended, the harm/pain has to be portrayed either a) in several scenes (two or more) that immediately follow the violent sequence or b) throughout an entire program.

For example, a gun shot victim may be portrayed as injured or in pain in several scenes after being shot, but then he/she/it completely recovers and no more suffering is depicted throughout the program. Family and friends of the victim are also shown in grief and their sadness is depicted in several scenes that follow the violence. Because the harm/pain that results from violence was portrayed as lasting several scenes beyond the actual violent act, this type of program would be coded as containing "long-term" harm/pain.

Another example of extended harm/pain would include depicting a gun shot victim's injury or painful recovery throughout the duration of a program. If the target has died, then there is no potential to show continuing pain in the recovery of the victim of violence. However, subsequent scenes could depict the emotional pain and/or financial struggle of friends and family members as a result of the target's death.

5.4 PUNISHMENTS

At the sequence level, both rewards and punishments are coded. At the program level, the primary concern is with whether violence is typically **punished** or not. Coders should reflect on all the violence that has occurred in the program and decide whether or not it was discouraged or chastised. In reflecting on punishments, consider whether the perpetrators typically:

- were condemned by others
- felt remorse
- were apprehended
- were hurt or killed because of violence

Any of these would constitute punishment. In contrast, if perpetrators typically "got away" with violence or were explicitly rewarded for violence, then punishments would be absent.

Rather than focusing on any particular sequence, coders should reflect on the overall **pattern of punishments** in the narrative. For example, if violence was punished in only one or two sequences but went unpunished in the rest of the program, then the overall pattern is "never/rarely punished."

In addition, the assessment of punishments should be made across types of characters rather than focusing on any particular individual character. Separate judgments should be made with reference to each of three types of characters: bad characters, good characters, and characters who are both good and bad.

5.41 **Punishment of Bad Characters**: Consider the characters who can be defined as bad (see section 5.9) and who are prominently featured in the program (anyone who is depicted in more than one scene). If only one character fits these criteria, then judge punishments for that character. Otherwise, consider all bad characters collectively and for those who have engaged in violence, determine whether the bad characters are:

5.411 <u>Punished Throughout:</u> Bad characters predominantly are punished throughout the program. In most of the instances in which they engage in violence, the bad characters are caught, condemned, or killed. Bad characters might "get away" with violence in one or two instances, but the overall pattern is that they are punished in the majority of cases throughout the show.

5.412 <u>Punished in the End Only:</u> Bad characters go unpunished until the ending or resolution of the program. In other words, there is a narrative progression from "getting away" with violence (or actually getting rewards for it) to somehow being punished in the end. This is typical of a crime show where the "bad guys" get away with repeated violence until somehow they are finally caught/punished in the end.

5.413 <u>Never or Rarely Punished:</u> Bad characters are never or rarely punished throughout the show for violence. They almost always "get away" with aggressive actions and in some cases may actually receive rewards for them. *Natural Born Killers* is a good example of a movie that depicts bad characters who rarely get punished for violence.

5.414 <u>None of the Above:</u> Reserve this category only for those programs that do not contain any of the above patterns. For example, punishments may occur only in the beginning but not throughout, or only some of the time but not predominantly throughout.

5.42 **Punishment of Good Characters**: Consider the characters who can be defined as good (according to section 5.9) and who are prominently featured in the program (anyone who is depicted in more than one scene). If only one character fits these criteria, then judge punishments for that character. Otherwise, consider all good characters collectively and for those who have engaged in violence, determine whether the good characters are:

5.421 <u>Punished Throughout:</u> Good characters predominantly are punished throughout the program. In most of the instances in which they engage in violence, they generally feel condemnation or some other negative reinforcement. An example of this would be a program about a group of good cops who are battling a gang of teens. Each time they have to injure one of the teens, the cops feel remorse and guilt because of the young age of the victims. In other words, the good guys experience regret throughout the program.

5.422 <u>Punished in the End Only:</u> Good characters go unpunished until the ending or resolution of the program. In other words, there is a narrative progression from "getting away" with violence (or actually being rewarded for it) to somehow being punished in the end. An example of this would be an historical program in which the good guys are fighting throughout the program to protect their land or their kingdom, receiving great admiration from others, when suddenly in the end they are captured by the enemy and imprisoned for life.

5.423 <u>Never or Rarely Punished:</u> Good characters are never or rarely punished throughout the show for violence. They almost always "get away" with aggressive actions and in some cases may actually receive rewards for them. Programs that feature heros who are praised/adored and never punished as they use violence to protect others would be an example of this.

5.424 <u>None of the Above:</u> Reserve this category only for those programs that do not contain any of the above patterns. For example, punishments may occur only in the beginning but not throughout, or only some of the time but not predominantly throughout.

5.43 **Punishment of Characters who are Both Good and Bad:** In some programs, characters who are prominently featured are best categorized as both good and bad (see section 5.9). In such cases, consider these characters collectively (if there is more than one) and for those who have engaged in violence, determine whether the good and bad characters predominantly were:

5.431 <u>Punished Throughout:</u> Good/Bad characters predominantly are punished throughout the program. In most of the instances in which they engage in violence, they are generally caught, condemned, or killed.

5.432 <u>Punished in the End Only</u>: Good/Bad characters go unpunished until the ending or resolution of the program. In other words, there is a narrative progression from "getting away" with violence (or actually getting rewards for it) to somehow being punished in the end.

5.433 <u>Never or Rarely Punished:</u> Good/Bad characters are never or rarely punished throughout the show for violence. They almost always "get away" with aggressive actions and in some cases may actually receive rewards for them.

5.434 <u>None of the Above:</u> Reserve this category only for those programs that do not contain any of the above patterns. For example, punishments may occur only in the beginning but not throughout, or only some of the time but not predominantly throughout.

Note: If a program does not contain any featured characters classified as one of these three types (e.g., good, bad, or both good and bad), then mark "not applicable" for that judgment.

5.5 STYLE OF PRESENTATION

Each program's **style of presentation** needs to be ascertained. There are three types of presentational style: 1) animated action, 2) live action or 3) both live and animated action.

5.51 **Animated Action:** Animated programs are those programs that present characters, settings and/or objects that have been either artistically drawn or computer generated. Because animated programs have been drawn or generated by computers, the characters, settings and/or objects used in those shows do not look "real." Rather, characters, settings and/or objects look like characterizations or resemblances of what you would find in the "real world." Examples of animated programming includes cartoons like *Looney Tunes, Swat Cats, Smurfs, Tron,* and *Gumby* and movies such as *The Little Mermaid, Beauty and the Beast* and *Aladdin.*

5.52 **Live Action Programs:** Live action programs, on the other hand, are those programs that present characters, settings and/or objects that have been filmed in "real" time. Regardless of the fictional or factual nature of the storyline, live action characters and settings look and appear as if they could be found in the "real" world. Examples of live action programs include *Magnum P.I.*, *Power Rangers*, and *Buffy the Vampire Slayer*. Even though many live action programs/movies contain mechanistically generated characters (i.e., *Jaws, Jurassic Park, Star Trek, King Kong*) and settings, they are still filmed in real time, and thus, should be coded as live action.

5.53 **Both Live Action and Animation:** Oftentimes, a program/movie will present characters and settings in both live action and animated action. For example, movies such as *Cool World* and *Roger Rabbit* use elements of both live action (i.e., Kim Bassinger as a human in *Cool World*; Bob Hoskins in *Roger Rabbit*) and animated action (i.e., Kim Bassinger as cartoon character in *Cool World*; Jessica Rabbit in *Roger Rabbit*). Additionally, many educational programs use elements of both live action and animation as well. Usually, *Sesame Street* and *Electric Company* combine elements of both styles. If a program has elements of both live and animated action, then it should be coded as "mixed."

CHARACTER VARIABLES

Each character who is involved in violence (either as a perpetrator or as a target) is listed on the Program Level Coding Form. At the end of each program, all characters listed must be assessed for type, sex, ethnicity, good/bad motives, and hero status. When making these judgments, the general rule is to use all of the information presented in the program you viewed. This includes information derived from a) the genre or type of program, b) the opening credits, and c) the scenes that have been shown throughout the entire program.

The profile variables may be difficult or impossible to apply in cases where the perpetrator and/or target is not overtly shown in a program. One example of this is when harmful consequences of an unseen violent act are depicted. Here, the perpetrator is not shown and even if the program hints at who the perpetrator is, the viewer is never certain. Another example is when the camera purposefully conceals the identity of the perpetrator or the target, as is often the case in mysteries and horror films. When the perpetrator/target is not depicted and is unknown, coders should still list the character on the program level coding form, mark the "can't tell" category, and then skip all the subsequent codes that refer to that character.

Other times, the perpetrators or target may be partially but not completely identifiable. Coders should fill in those characteristics that are known and use the "can't tell" category for all else. For example, if a body is covered up but it is clear that it is human and that it is a male, then those profile categories can be marked as such and all others should be marked as "can't tell" (unless the target had been clearly identified in a prior sequence so the demographics are known).

Applying the character codes may also be difficult when assessing multiple perpetrators and targets of violence. Multiple P's and T's should be treated and assessed as an entire unit. If the P's or T's are homogeneous and thus possess the same demographics, then you should code the entire unit into the category that best represents either their type, sex and/or ethnicity. For example, a program may feature a group of perpetrators who are white, male and possess supernatural powers (e.g., Batman, Robin, Superman and Spiderman). This entire unit would be coded as, "supernatural anthropomorphized creature" for type, "male" for sex, and "white" for ethnicity.

If, however, any of the demographics or traits of the members in the multiple differs, then you should code the multiple unit as "mixed" on the quality or attribute that varies in the group. For instance, a group of police officers may contain several black males and one white female. In this case, the P multiple's ethnicity and sex would both be coded as "mixed" whereas type of character would be coded as "human being."

Each of the five different character variables that need to be assessed for each perpetrator and target in violence are described below.

5.6 TYPE OF CHARACTER

For every perpetrator or target listed on the program level coding form, **type of character** needs to be assessed. In most programs, character type will remain constant throughout the duration of a program. In some cases, however, a character may be presented in a false or disguised manner for part of the program. For example, three-fourths of the way through a program you find out a very powerful human is really an anthropomorphized supernatural creature. In this type of situation, you should code the "real" or "revealed" status of the character. As such, the character in the example above would be coded as a anthropomorphized supernatural creature even though it was not portrayed as such for most of the program.

   5.61 **Codes for Type of Character:** A character may be coded into <u>one and only one</u> of the seven following types:

      5.611 <u>Human Being:</u> A homosapien with no supernatural features.

      5.612 <u>Animal:</u> A live action or animated mammal, reptile, bird, fish, amphibian, or shark.

      5.613 <u>Supernatural Creature</u>: A being that exceeds biological limits and/or possesses supernatural powers.

      5.614 <u>Anthropomorphized Animal:</u> A animal with human like characteristics.

      5.615 <u>Anthropomorphized Supernatural Creature:</u> A super creature with human like characteristics.

      5.616 <u>Mixed:</u> A multiple that contains characters of more than one type.

      5.617 <u>Can't Tell:</u> This code should only be reserved when the character type is impossible to ascertain.

5.7 SEX OF CHARACTER

At the end of each program, you should code the biological **sex** of each perpetrator and target involved in violence. In most cases, it will be easy to assess sex as either male or female. For anthropomorphized characters or supernatural characters, it may be more difficult to determine sex. Physical appearance, behavioral patterns and voice intonation or cues should all be used to make this judgment.

   5.71 **Revelations:** Usually, sex will remain constant throughout a program. In some programs, however, a character's "true" sex may be concealed or may change within the program. By the end of the program, however, the character's "real" or "true" sex is revealed. When this happens, code the character's revealed or true biological sex at the program level.

   5.72 **No Biological Sex:** Some creatures do not possess a sex. For example, the Blob has no sex and neither does a monster who doesn't talk or a Martian who has no voice and no physical characteristics that indicate sex. In these cases, sex should be coded as "can't tell."

5.73 **Codes for Sex:**

    5.731 <u>Male</u>

    5.732 <u>Female</u>

    5.733 <u>Mixed</u>

    5.734 <u>Can't Tell</u>

5.8 APPARENT ETHNICITY OF CHARACTER

The **apparent ethnicity** of each perpetrator and target involved in violence will also need to be assessed. In order to determine apparent ethnicity, you should consider all available information including the physical features of the characters (e.g., skin color, hair), their language/accent, and any knowledge about their ethnicity included in the plot (e.g., a character says he/she is Asian).

In some programs, you may be sure that a character was not white but it was difficult to determine the precise ethnicity based upon the categories listed below. In these cases, you should code the ethnicity of the character as "can't tell." In other programs, the particular ethnicity of a character you observe may not be listed among the options. When a character's ethnicity is clearly known but is not listed as an option, you should code the character's ethnicity as "can't tell."

Anthropomorphized characters may or may not have an ethnicity. If a Smurf or a Ninja Turtle speaks with a Spanish accent, you should code the character's ethnicity as Hispanic. However, if anthropomorphized characters like Bugs Bunny and Mickey Mouse do not appear to have an ethnicity they should be coded as "can't tell."

Animals cannot be classified in terms of ethnicity nor can most supernatural beings (e.g., ET, a gremlin). Only with these two types of characters, should ethnicity be coded as "not applicable." No humans or anthropomorphized beings (e.g., animals or supernatural) should ever be coded as "not applicable."

5.81 **Codes for Apparent Ethnicity:** The following categories, derived from the U.S. census, should be used to code ethnicity:

    5.811 <u>White</u>

    5.812 <u>Hispanic</u>

    5.813 <u>Black</u>

    5.814 <u>Native American</u>

    5.815 <u>Asian/Pacific Islander</u>

    5.816 <u>Middle Eastern</u>

    5.817 <u>Mixed</u>

5.818 <u>Can't Tell</u>

5.819 <u>Not Applicable</u>

5.9 GOOD/BAD CHARACTERS

This code refers to whether a character is portrayed as having **good** or **bad motives**. Motives typically are demonstrated in a character's actions and words. A character should be coded as good, bad, both good and bad, neutral, or mixed.

Coders should take into account all the information that is provided about a character across PATs, sequences, and nonviolent scenes. Coders should look for general patterns in the character's actions and words. In other words, across all the sequences and scenes that feature a character/s in the program, is he/she/it portrayed as primarily good, primarily bad, both good and bad in approximately equal amounts, or neutral? When multiple characters are considered and they are not homogeneous in their motives (e.g., some are good and some are bad), they should be coded as "mixed." Each of the categories for good/bad are explicated below.

5.91 **Good Characters:** A **good** character is one who is motivated to consider the needs of others. In doing so, a good character typically acts in ways that benefit or help others. However, a good character need *not* be totally selfless in order to be labeled good. He/she/it might benefit the self at the same time that he/she/it is trying to benefit others, and this would still qualify as a good character. Examples of actions that indicate a character has good motives include: being kind, acting sympathetic, being generous, being loyal, protecting, and/or helping.

5.92 **Bad Characters:** A **bad** character is one who is motivated to act and think with self interest. Bad characters behave in ways that accommodate their own needs without concern for the needs of others. Two types of characters qualify as bad. One type is the character who is so selfish and self focused that he/she/it ignores the needs of others in an effort to fulfill personal desires. This character does not necessarily try to harm others but in the selfish pursuit of personal gain, others indeed may be harmed. For example, a character who has stolen money may shoot anyone who gets in the way of an escape.

The second type is the character who intentionally tries to harm others in an effort to satisfy personal needs (e.g., to feel better, to amuse the self, to release anger). This character appears to be motivated by evil or ill will. Examples of actions that indicate that a character has bad motives include: being cruel, acting unsympathetically, being greedy, being disloyal, and/or hurting others.

5.93 **Good and Bad Characters:** A character who shows a balance of good and bad motives should be coded as **both good and bad**. This code should be used when the character sometimes acts in a way that is considerate of others and sometimes acts selfishly or without regard for others. Often, these characters seem to be motivated by a complex set of factors and are both likeable and unlikable in the same program. For example, Kevin Costner in *A Perfect World* is a bad guy because he kidnaps a little boy and he shoots at a lot of people when he is trying to flee, but he also befriends the boy and tries to protect him. Throughout the program, he is depicted in both good and bad ways.
However, characters who are mostly good or mostly bad but act inconsistently in one or two incidents should not be coded as "both good and bad." For example, a firefighter who helps people throughout a program but in one scene gets angry and hits someone should not necessarily be coded as "both." Again, the key is to look for a pattern of motives across the incidents that are depicted.

5.94 **Neutral Characters:** A character who is portrayed as *neither* good nor bad should be coded as **neutral**. This type of code should be used when: 1) a character is featured in a program but his/her/its orientation to others cannot be determined (e.g., character is alone until he gets shot, character is not obviously showing an orientation to others), or 2) a character is not featured enough in the program to determine whether he/she is good or bad (e.g., an innocent bystander).

5.95 **Mixed Characters:** The **mixed** category should <u>only</u> be used when a multiple unit contains characters with differing motives. For example, a multiple may contain some group members who have consistently good motives and some group members who have consistently bad motives. Because the character's motives <u>within</u> the group vary, the multiple should be coded as "mixed."

The mixed category is very different from the "good and bad" category listed above. That is, a multiple would be coded as possessing both good and bad motives if <u>each</u> of the characters in the group acted both good and bad (or vice versa) uniformly. In contrast, the mixed category is used when individuals' motives within the multiple unit vary (some act good, some bad, some neutral).

5.96 **Codes for Good/Bad:**

    5.961 <u>Good</u>

    5.962 <u>Bad</u>

    5.963 <u>Good and Bad</u>

    5.964 <u>Neutral</u>

    5.965 <u>Mixed</u> (use for multiples only)

    5.966 <u>Can't Tell</u> (not known)

5.10 HERO STATUS

At the end of each program, you will need to assess if each character involved in violence was a **hero**. Most characters on television do *not* qualify as heroes. For a character to classify as a hero, he/she/it must meet three specific criteria. First, the character must be a primary or regularly featured animate being in the program. Second, the character's role must emphasize protecting others from violence. And third, the character must engage in selfless helping of others in a way that goes above *and* beyond duty or the normal requirements of a job. Each of these three criteria is explicated below.

5.101 **Primary Character:** First, the character must be a primary or regularly featured animate being in the program. That is, the character should be featured prominently throughout the program with the plot focused on his/her actions. One other clue is to examine the opening credits and introductory material in the program. Primary characters typically appear in the opening credits in a way that labels them clearly as central to the plot.

5.102 **Protection of Others Emphasized:** Second, the character must enact a role in the program that emphasizes protecting others from becoming a victim of violence (e.g., police officer, body guard). Protection refers to any action that shields or removes another character from physical harm due to violence. Heroes typically put themselves in harm's way and often are at risk themselves in the process of protecting another.

Characters such as doctors, lawyers, and even private detectives would not typically be heroes because they are not usually present when violence is initiated and therefore cannot directly interfere with or prevent it from occurring. Instead, they usually treat the consequences of violence after it occurs. Also, such characters do not typically risk their own lives in order to save the victim. For example, a doctor who operates on someone who has been shot does not actually prevent violence but rather seeks to ameliorate its consequences, and such actions usually occur after the imminent threat of violence is over. Private detectives who solve violent crimes protect other people from becoming subsequent victims; however, they do not usually place themselves directly in harm's way and risk becoming the victim in place of someone else.

5.103 **Helps Above and Beyond the Call:** Third, the character's trait in the program must be characterized by the selfless helping of others in a way that goes <u>above</u> and <u>beyond</u> duty or the normal requirements of a job. This trait should be evidenced consistently and obviously from cues in the program. Signs of selfless helping include: engaging in extremely courageous acts of protection, engaging in acts that put the protector in extreme danger, and/or engaging in acts that can be labeled as showing self sacrifice. For example, a cop who goes out on a ledge and risks his own life to crawl to a suicidal person to save him/her would be engaging in selfless helping, whereas a cop who from a distance tries to talk a suicidal victim out of killing him/herself would not.

Characters who protect others merely to receive a favor or get a reward or pick up a pay check would not be acting in a selfless way. For example, a cop who jumps reluctantly into a fight to break it up and complains about his job is not acting selflessly. A Mafia boss who protects people in order to incur favors is not acting selflessly. A soldier who fights in battle simply because she/he is following orders is not engaging in selfless behavior that goes above and beyond the call of duty; but a soldier who risks his/her life in some courageous way to save a buddy is engaging in selfless behavior that goes above and beyond the call of duty.

Examples of heros include: Bruce Willis in *Diehard*, Kevin Costner in *The Bodyguard*, Clarise in *Silence of the Lambs,* Superman, Power Rangers, the Incredible Hulk, the Ninja Turtles, and Batman.

5.104 **Coding Hero Status:** Given the above rules, most characters will not qualify as a hero. If a character clearly meets the three criteria listed above, then he/she/it should be coded as a "hero." Characters who do not meet the three above listed criteria should be coded as "not a hero." At times, a hero may be a part of a multiple that acts violently. In these cases, the entire multiple unit that contains the hero should be coded as mixed.

5.104a <u>Hero</u>

5.104b <u>Not a Hero</u>

5.104c <u>Mixed</u>

6.0 INTRODUCTORY SEQUENCES/DECONTEXTUALIZED EXCERPTS

There are different types of sequences in programming that are essentially **decontextualized** portrayals. The most typical of these include opening sequences, such as program theme songs with visual depictions of character actions occurring "behind" title credits; short segments at the beginning of a serial drama, such as *NYPD Blue*, which recap action in previous weeks by presenting a collection of very brief excerpts of past scenes; or closing credits that appear with visual action depicted behind the text. There are also decontextualized excerpts that may be inserted in the middle of a program; for example, a brief clip of violence related to a current news story might be presented as the catalyst for a discussion of the story topic on a public affairs program such as *The McLaughlin Group*, or a film clip may be shown in a movie review discussion on *Siskel and Ebert*.

The key element that links all of these examples is that the content depictions represent isolated passages that are <u>not part of an ongoing narrative flow</u> which runs throughout the program. While the movie review clip may be surrounded by a discussion of the film, the scene portrayed in the clip is a part of a larger story, and the fact that that story is not continued beyond the brief excerpt indicates that the clip should be classified as decontextualized content.

6.1 Additional Considerations for Identifying Decontextualized Segments:

6.11 <u>Opening Credits:</u> Note that the presentation of credits does not necessarily qualify for treatment under this category. Many films run credits while still maintaining the continuous narrative flow of the story by depicting information visually. This material typically maintains a context consistent with the overall flow of the content.

In contrast, television shows that have recurring introductions which are not directly related to the narrative flow of the <u>particular episode</u> of that series would be considered decontextualized. An example would be a generic opening sequence in a cartoon series, such as that included in episodes of *Teenage Mutant Ninja Turtles*.

6.12 <u>Teasers:</u> Sometimes it may be difficult to determine whether "teasers" (e.g., a segment that starts out "Tonight on *Murder She Wrote* ...") or "program promos" are actually part of the program you are coding or not. <u>You should not code any material that is not part of the relevant program.</u> Content is considered part of the program you are coding when there is no intervening non-program messages (e.g., commercials, station identifications) that separate the material in question from a more extended portion of the program.

For example: if the program *Sixty Minutes* ends, then is followed by a promo for *Murder She Wrote*, which is then followed by a commercial and then the beginning of the *Murder She Wrote* program, the promo would not be considered part of the program. If, however, the same promo segment ran and was immediately followed by the program content, then it would be considered part of the show and the segment would be evaluated using the approach indicated below for decontextualized segments.

6.2 Coding Decontextualized Depictions:
In all cases that are considered as decontextualized depictions, the coder will record only a limited range of judgments. These will be restricted to the measures of <u>type of act</u>, <u>means</u>, and <u>extent</u>. These measures will be recorded collectively for all action in the entire excerpt involving all characters, and recorded on a single line for each type of act (e.g., credible threat, behavioral act, harmful consequences) on the PAT Coding Form. There will be no tracking of PAT interactions, so it does not matter how many different persons are engaged as perpetrators or victims -- all violent acts, means, and extent will be

summarized in a single line of data so long as they are within the same category of act (e.g., credible threat, behavioral act, harmful consequences).

Because of the lack of context in many of these depictions, it may be impossible to be certain about character motivations and intentions. This will make it difficult to identify some violent actions such as a credible threat. In evaluating decontextualized depictions, the coder should always <u>draw the most reasonable inference</u> in interpreting the likely context associated with the behaviors depicted in the excerpt.

6.21 <u>Example of PAT Coding:</u> An example applying the decontextualized approach: The following brief excerpts appear during opening credits.

(a). A woman shoots at a man three times with a pistol; all the bullets hit the target.
(b). A gang of four men kick down an apartment door and assault with their fists the one man they find inside; the attack is chaotic and blows cannot be counted but the assault lasts for two seconds. At the end, the target pulls a gun and aims it at the group. The excerpt ends before there is any resolution to the situation.
(c). One man shoots once at another but misses. The target responds by jumping the perpetrator and hitting him with three clear blows to the face, all using fists only.

The above example would be recorded as two lines of data, one for the credible threat and one for all the behavioral acts. The entries are indicated below.

act	means 1	extent 1	means 2	extent 2
CT	handheld firearm	N/A	-	-
BA	natural means	some (2+3=5)	handheld firearm	some (3+1=4)

6.22 <u>Decon:</u> To indicate on the PAT Coding Form that a given line of data reports observations from a decontextualized sequence, write the term "DECON" across all five of the columns under Perpetrator at the beginning of the line.

6.23 <u>Split Screen:</u> In cases involving split-screen depictions, consider all the depictions included in all of the visual images presented. Evaluate all such split-screen portrayals as decontextualized content.

7.0 CODING INSTRUCTIONS

7.1 GENERAL PRINCIPALS

Overall, there are five **general** principals or rules that should govern all of your coding decisions.

7.11 Information Originates in Program: All information used to make coding decisions should originate from within the program you are assigned to view. You should only code a program according to the information presented to you on the tape since you pressed play. In some cases, you may be assigned to code a program you have seen one or many times before. No matter how many times or how familiar you are with a program, television series, a character's role or an actor/actress, you need to code each program naively as if it were your first time viewing the specific characters and media content.

7.12 Code in Real Time: All coding must be done in "real time." This means that you code each violent sequence as <u>the plot unravels.</u> Violent sequences should be coded by using all available information presented in the plot up until that point in the program. To code each violent sequence, however, you will need to also watch the scene that immediately follows so that you can make accurate judgments about specific contextual features of the violent portrayals (e.g., rewards and punishments, graphicness, explicitness).

7.13 Back Coding: Once you code a particular sequence, you must <u>not</u> go back and recode or change any of the assessments that have already been made based upon new information presented later in the plot. For instance, a character may be depicted in an opening sequence engaging in violence because he/she is angry with society. As such, his/her/its primary reason for engaging in violence would be coded as "anger." By the second sequence, however, the plot may reveal that the character is actually mentally deranged and seeks innocent victims to satisfy his/her/its cannibalistic appetite. In the second sequence, the character's primary reason for violence would be coded as "mental incompetence." Even though you discovered the character is mentally incompetent later in the program, you should <u>not</u> go back and recode your initial reason for his/her/its violent actions (e.g., anger) in the first sequence.

7.14 Honest Mistakes: After coding a particular sequence, however, you may discover an honest mistake was made in one of your earlier coding judgments. For instance, you may discover at the end of a program that you accidentally coded a specific "elderly" perpetrator as a "child." You should <u>always</u> change honest mistakes that are due to carelessness. More importantly, you should always check your work after all PAT, sequence and program level judgments you make.

7.15 Fast Forwarding Through Tapes: Once you begin coding, never "fast forward" or "scan" through a program "looking" or "snooping" for violence. You may be tempted to do this with certain types of programming content that you do not "think" or "believe" will contain violence. For example, situation comedies, talk shows, and educational programs often contain little, if any, violent portrayals. However, by fast forwarding through these types of programs, you may miss violence that occurs within the plot. Also, by fast forwarding through a program, you will undoubtedly miss relevant contextual information about characters and the plot that will be needed to code later violent sequences that occur.

7.2   SPECIFIC CODING INSTRUCTIONS

7.21 Arriving at the Lab: When arriving at the lab, you will be given a video tape that contains a specific episode, program or movie that needs to be coded. Because all of the tapes in the sample have been randomized and must be coded according to that random order, you will be given a tape with a specific program or movie on it that can not be traded or exchanged for another.

After receiving the video tape, you will need to fast forward or scan to the beginning of the program you were assigned to analyze. Most of the tapes contain 10-15 minutes of non-codable programming prior to and immediately following the show that needs to be coded. Some of the programming on the movie channels (e.g., HBO, Showtime, Cinemax) may have as much as 20-25 minutes of other nonrelevant programming. When you fast forward, make sure you: 1) start the program at its beginning, and 2) do not miss any relevant information that needs to be assessed (i.e., ratings, advisories, introductions and/or credits that come prior to or immediately after the beginning of a program).

7.22 Coding a Program: For each program, four specific parts will need to be coded.

7.221 <u>Ratings and Advisories:</u> First, you will need to assess if the program contains a rating and/or advisory. Ratings and advisories are usually aired right before the start of a program. Not all programs are proceeded by a rating and/or advisory, however. These informative labels are used most often on the movie and/or premium channels, and very few network programs use them. Regardless of what channel the program was aired on, you should always examine whether the media content you are coding is preceded by a rating and/or advisory.

7.222 <u>Introductions:</u> Second, you will need to code the program's introductory material. Introductions come in several different forms. Many network programs have standard introductions that are replayed every time the show is aired. Usually, these standard intro's are accompanied with a sound track and either still photos or visual video depictions (e.g., *Cheers, LA Law*). In these cases, you should code all such introductions for violence using the "decontextualized" coding scheme. That is, you should only code the means used and extent of violent acts that are depicted in the introduction without assessing any character or contextual information (e.g, no assessment of character demographics, reason for violence, harm and/or pain, etc.).

Other production conventions that are often used immediately before, after, or in place of a standard introduction on network programming also need to be coded for violence. For instance, a program's introduction may be proceeded or followed by several fast paced highlights of scenes from previous episodes and/or highlights of scenes from upcoming episodes. These programming reviews, teasers, and/or previews should all be coded for violence using the "decontextualized" coding scheme.

7.223 <u>Program Content:</u> Third, after watching and coding the program's introduction, you should begin assessing the actual plot content for violence. When you see an act that triggers a violent sequence (e.g., an act, threat, or depiction of harmful consequences) during normal programming, watch that sequence in its entirety, noting when it ends. Once you find the end of the sequence, go to the beginning of that sequence and watch it again. Pay attention to all details because you will need to code at the act level. This includes the type of act (e.g., credible threat, violent act, harmful consequences, accident), the means used to accomplish the act, extent of means used, the characters' roles as perpetrator or target, and other contextual information (e.g., harm depicted, likely harm, pain, and reason for violence). You may watch a sequence as many times as you need to in order to code all necessary information. Do this carefully because once you have coded a sequence, you should not go back and change anything.

After assessing each PAT interaction, you will need to make several sequence level contextual judgments. That is, you will need to ascertain specific character information, rewards and punishments, humor, graphicness and explicitness of each sequence. Oftentimes, however, relevant contextual information like reinforcements given or taken for violence will not be depicted in the actual violent sequence. Consequently, you should not only watch the entire sequence but also the *scene* that immediately follows it prior to coding sequence level context variables.

7.224   Incomplete Information: Often, you will not have all of the information requested on the coding form. When it is impossible to make a judgment based on the information presented, check "Unknown" or "Not Shown" on the appropriate measure. Do not check "Not applicable" because this option means that the variable is not relevant in this PAT/Sequence/Program. For example, if your character is Bugs Bunny and you are asked about his age, the appropriate response would be "Can't Tell" *not* "Not Shown" or "Unknown."

7.225   Information that Occurs Later in Program: Some types of information will not always be available to you within each sequence or in the scene that immediately follows, but will be depicted later on in the program. For example, many of the reinforcements given or taken for violence are not depicted in the sequence that the violence actually occurs in or in the scene that immediately follows it. It is quite common for rewards and punishments to be portrayed later on or at the end of a program. For information that appears at the end (e.g., overall message of violence being either rewarded or punished in the program) or throughout a program (e.g., whether a character is a hero or not) we will ask you to make program level judgments. Program level judgments include: overall rewards and punishments, specific character demographics and attributes, narrative purpose and overall harm/pain.

7.226   Closing Credits: Finally, you will need to assess the end or closing credits of each program. Most programs will just fade to black and display credits. In these cases, your coding ends when the plot ends. You will not need to code the credits. Othertimes, however, the credits will roll while still photos or "highlights" from the movie or program are being visually depicted. In these cases, all such still photos and "highlights" should be coded using the "decontextualized" coding scheme. And lastly, some programs will roll the credits while characters are interacting or action is still taking place. All these types of depictions also need to be coded and should be done by using the contextualized or regular violence coding scheme.

7.227   Checking Your Work: After assessing the closing of a program for violence, review all of the coding judgments you have made at the PAT, sequence and program level. Make sure all of your entries are legible and clearly ascertainable. After reviewing your coding sheets, rewind the program you coded to the beginning of the tape. Then, turn all your coding sheets and the video tape containing the program coded into the lab supervisor.

8.0 SCENE

Whenever coding sequence–level variables, coders should watch the entire violent sequence *plus* the **scene** immediately after the sequence. In some cases, information about specific sequence–level variables may not occur until the imminent threat of violence is actually over. For example, a perpetrator may not be punished during the violent sequence, but he may be shown getting arrested in a nearby location immediately after the violence. Coders should base sequence–level judgments on information contained within the violent sequence as well as within the scene immediately following the violent sequence.

8.1 Subsequent Scene: A **subsequent scene** is defined as a series of related or continuous events that occur in a new setting, location, or time period from the previous violence. A subsequent scene <u>begins</u> at the moment that a shift to a new setting or a new time period occurs. The subsequent scene <u>ends</u> when the related events within the new location or time frame are interrupted or terminated. Note that the subsequent scene may involve the same characters (e.g., perpetrator, target) who were in the previous violent sequence or it may involve entirely new characters.

For example, a perpetrator may be shown shooting several bank tellers in a violent sequence. The next scene may cut to the perpetrator counting all the stolen money at his hideout. The material rewards are depicted in the subsequent scene and not within the violent sequence itself. Nevertheless, according to this framework, these material rewards would be taken into account in the sequence level coding.

In some cases, a violent sequence may end well before a shift to a new scene occurs. For example, a perpetrator may kill target and then stand around and talk to a buddy about it. Though the violent sequence technically ends (e.g., the clock stops running) when the threat is over, there is still plot relevant information occurring in this setting. Coders should consider this content as well as the subsequent scene when coding sequence level variables. If the perpetrator rejoices in his deed during his discussion with the buddy, this would be counted toward the coding of rewards (praise from self). If a cut to a new scene then shows the same perpetrator being praised by another friend, this too would count toward rewards (praise from other).

8.2 Two Special Circumstances Should be Noted:

8.21 <u>Commercials:</u> If a violent sequence is followed immediately by a cut to a commercial, there is by definition <u>no</u> subsequent scene to consider in sequence level coding. Do not code the scene after the commercial in making judgments about a previous sequence.

8.22 <u>New Violent Sequence:</u> If a violent sequence is followed immediately by another violent sequence, coders should consider this new violent sequence as the subsequent scene. Thus, coders should still watch the entire subsequent scene (even though it contains violence and will have to be coded as a new sequence) prior to assessing any sequence level variables for the previous sequence.

9.0 VARIABLE GUIDES AND CODING FORMS

9.1 PAT LEVEL GUIDE AND FORMS

Below, you will find all the values for each **PAT level variable**. All variables are listed in order of entry on the PAT level coding form (see next page for actual form). When coding the PAT level variables, you should take into account all information presented to you up until that point of the program and all information within the violent sequence itself. This principal applies to all variables except depicted and likely harm. To accurately code these variables at the PAT level, you will have to also watch the immediately adjacent scene.

Perpetrators	Size of Multiple P	Reason for Violence	Sexual Assault
1 = Single	1 = 2 Characters	1 = Protect Life	0 = No
2 = Multiple	2 = 3 to 9 Characters	2 = Anger	1 = Yes
3 = Implied	3 = 10 to 99 Characters	3 = Retaliation	
4 = None	4 = 100 to 999 Characters	4 = Personal Gain	
	5 = 1000 or more Characters	5 = Mental Incompetence/Instability	
	6 = Not Applicable	6 = Accident	
		7 = Other	

Type of Act	Means Used	Extent of Means
1 = Credible Threat	1 = Natural Means	1 = One
2 = Behavioral Act	2 = Unconventional Weapon	2 = Some
3 = Harmful Consequences	3 = Conventional Weapon/Non Firearm	3 = Many
4 = Accident	4 = Conventional Weapon/Handheld Firearm	4 = Extreme
	5 = Heavy Weaponry	5 = Not Applicable
	6 = Bombs	
	7 = Means Unknown	
	8 = Credible Threat/Verbal Only	

Harm Depicted	Harm Likely	Pain	Visual Depiction
0 = None	0 = None	0 = None	0 = Off-Screen
1 = Mild	1 = Mild	1 = Mild	1 = On-Screen
2 = Moderate	2 = Moderate	2 = Moderate	
3 = Extreme	3 = Extreme	3 = Extreme	
4 = Unsuccessful Attempt	4 = Unsuccessful Attempt	4 = Unsuccessful Attempt	
5 = Not Shown	5 = Not Shown	5 = Not Shown	
6 = N/A	6 = N/A	6 = N/A	

Target	Size of T Multiple
1 = Single	1 = 2 Characters
2 = Multiple	2 = 3 to 9 Characters
3 = Implied	3 = 10 to 99 Characters
	4 = 100 to 999 Characters
	5 = 1000 or more Characters
	6 = Not Applicable

Program: _____

Name: _____

PAT Coding Form

Sequence			Perpetrator								Act																Target			
												Means A					Means B												
line	starts	ends	name	#	code	size P mult.	reason	sexual assault	type	means	extent	depicted harm	likely harm	visual pain depic.	means	extent	depicted harm	likely harm	visual pain depic.							name	#	code	size T mult.

* **Total number of PAT lines (not including decon):**

264

9.2 SEQUENCE LEVEL GUIDE AND FORMS

Below, you will find a list of all the values for each **sequence level variable**. All variables are listed in order of entry on the sequence level coding form (see next page for actual form). For most variables at this level, all coding decisions should not only be based on the content of the violent sequence but also from the information derived in the immediately adjacent scene. This does not apply to explicitness, graphicness and/or humor, however. For these three variables, you should only use the information presented to you within the sequence itself to inform your coding decisions.

Character Variables

Age of P/T

1 = Child
2 = Teen
3 = Adult
4 = Elderly
5 = Mixed
6 = Can't Tell

Physical Strength of Perpetrator

1 = Physically Strong
2 = Neutral
3 = Physically Weak
4 = Both Strong and Weak
5 = Mixed
6 = Can't Tell

Rewards

Self Praise

0 = No
1 = Yes

Praise/Other

0 = No
1 = Yes

Material Praise

0 = No
1 = Yes

Punishments

Self Condemnation

0 = No
1 = Yes

Condemnation/Other

0 = No
1 = Yes

Nonviolent Action

0 = No
1 = Yes

Violent Actions

0 = No
1 = Yes

Explicitness

Violent Action

0 = Not Shown
1 = Up-Close
2 = Long-Shot
3 = Not Applicable

Means-to-Target Impact

0 = Not Shown
1 = Up-Close
2 = Long-Shot
3 = Not Applicable

Graphicness

Blood & Gore

0 = None
1 = Mild
2 = Moderate
3 = Extreme
4 = Not Applicable

Humor

0 = No
1 = Yes

Program: _____ **Name:** _____

Sequence Coding Form

Character Codes

General Sequence Codes

Seq #	start time	end time	name	#	age	strength	humor	rewards		punishments				explictness		graphicness
								self praise	praise from other	material praise	self condemnation	condemnation from other	nonviolent action	violent action	violent action	focus on impact	blood & gore

9.3 PROGRAM LEVEL GUIDES AND FORMS

Below, you will find a list of all the values for each **program level variable**. All variables are listed in order of entry on the program level coding form (see next page for actual form). For this macro level of analysis, you should consider all information presented to you within the entire program.

Type of Character

0 = Human
1 = Animal
2 = Super Natural Creature
3 = Anthropomorphized Animal
4 = Anthropomorphized SNC
5 = Mixed
6 = Can't Tell

Sex

0 = Male
1 = Female
2 = Mixed
3 = Can't Tell

Ethnicity

0 = White
1 = Hispanic
2 = Black
3 = Native American
4 = Asian
5 = Middle Eastern
6 = Mixed
7 = Can't Tell
8 = N/A

Good/Bad

0 = Bad
1 = Neutral
2 = Good
3 = Good and Bad
4 = Mixed
5 = Can't Tell

Hero Status

0 = Not a Hero
1 = Hero
2 = Mixed
3 = N/A (P/T implied)

Narrative Purpose

0 = No anti-violent theme
1 = Anti-Violent theme

Realism

0 = Actual Reality
1 = Recreated Reality
2 = Fictional
3 = Fantasy

Harm/Pain

0 = None
1 = Within Sequence Only
2 = Extended Beyond Sequence

Style of Presentation

1 = Live Action
2 = Animated Action
3 = Both

Punishments

Bad Characters

1 = Punished Throughout
2 = Punished at End Only
3 = Never/Rarely Punished
4 = None of the Above
5 = Not Applicable

Good Characters

1 = Punished Throughout
2 = Punished at End Only
3 = Never/Rarely Punished
4 = None of the Above
5 = Not Applicable

Good and Bad Characters

1 = Punished Throughout
2 = Punished at End Only
3 = Never/Rarely Punished
4 = None of the Above
5 = Not Applicable

Program: _____   **Program Coding Form**   Name: _____

Character Codes

Character #	Name	Type	Gender	Ethnicity	Good / Bad	Hero

Program Level Codes

Narrative Purpose	Realism	Harm / Pain	Style of Presentation	Punishment of BAD characters	Punishment of GOOD characters	Punishment of good and bad characters

PART II

TELEVISION VIOLENCE IN "REALITY" PROGRAMMING: UNIVERSITY OF TEXAS AT AUSTIN STUDY

Dr. Charles Whitney
Dr. Ellen Wartella
Dr. Dominic Lasorsa
Dr. Wayne Danielson
Adriana Olivarez
Rafael Lopez
Marlies Klijn

SUMMARY

Some 384 "reality" programs were analyzed as part of the NTVS 1994-1995 television sample. Reality programs were given special emphasis because of their increasing importance as a programming category, because previous scientific research has demonstrated that programming perceived as real or realistic may have heightened impacts on viewers, because reality programming may be particularly significant in the cultivation of fear and desensitization, and because reality programs differ in form from other programming.

While reality programs were content analyzed just as fictional programming was, additional attention was paid not just to visual violence in reality programs, but also to oral descriptions of violent acts and credible threats (Talk About Violence).

Overall, 38 percent of reality programs contained some visual violence, compared with 57 percent of the full sample. An additional 18 percent contained Talk About Violence without visual depictions. Among reality programs with some violence, 3.3 percent of program time was in visually violent sequences, and 2.4 percent was in sequences talking about violence. About 10 percent of programs containing violence featured any sort of program advisory. There were substantial variations among many contextual variables: Just 13 percent of violent sequences mentioned long-term negative consequences, perpetrators of violence were punished in any way in only a third of sequences, and about a third presented violence with no indication of its causing harm or pain.

The amount and nature of violence varied substantially by time of day (visual violence is more concentrated in the evening hours), by channel type (public television has less violence overall; independent stations have more Talk About Violence), and most especially by reality-program genre, with police-reality shows emerging as the most violent reality genre, and talk shows generally as the least violent. In general, talk about violence mirrors visual violence, except that discussed violence is more likely to have resulted from "natural means" such as hitting and choking, less likely to involve guns, and less likely to feature discussion of harm and pain.

The study recommends increasing use of advisories, shifting of violent programs to later hours and considering ways to avoid and prevent violence.

TELEVISION VIOLENCE IN 'REALITY' PROGRAMMING:
UNIVERSITY OF TEXAS AT AUSTIN STUDY

From the outset, the NTVS recognized that studying television violence demanded attention not just to the fictional programs that constitute a majority of broadcast and cable television, but to nonfictional, "reality" programming as well. Certainly violence on television is not restricted to fictional shows, and because its depiction spans the schedule, any meaningful analysis of television content must include reality programming. We have no reason to believe that the *effects* of violent portrayals exclude nonfictional programming; in fact, as we detail below, it may have more impact than fictional presentations. However, we also recognized from the outset that reality programs merited specialized treatment, for a number of reasons, which we will outline below.

Reality Programming Defined

Reality programs on television are defined as nonfictional programming in which the portrayal is presumed to present current or historical events or circumstances. The production presents itself as being a realistic account.

Included are news and public affairs programming[1], interview and talk shows, entertainment news-and-review programs, documentaries, and other programs presenting themselves as recreations of "real-world" events, such as those depicting scenes of police or emergency workers, or humorous events or circumstances. Programs may be either actual or recreated depictions of events or circumstances, but in the case of the latter, the context must make it clear that efforts have been made to recapture a past event as it happened. Although not coded for this project, instructional programs featuring live actors and quiz and game shows are also considered reality programs.

Excluded are "docu-dramas" featuring invented or composite characters or dialogue which it can be reasonably inferred did not occur, and other programming in which the dramatic or humorous intent of the program outweighs intent to re-present actual events or circumstances; docudramas were coded as dramatic or movie programming by the Santa Barbara team.

Since its inception, television programming has of course included nonfictional fare, and most of its early genres--news, documentaries, and entertainment shows such as

---

1. Regularly scheduled news programs (e.g., *ABC World News Tonight*), national and local news "drop-ins" on morning news programs, and news preemptions of regularly scheduled programming are not coded, a proviso included as part of the original contract between NCTA and the researchers. Other exclusions (e.g., game shows) are noted in the sampling sections of the Santa Barbara report.

Allen Funt's *Candid Camera* and Art Linkletter's *People are Funny* have been stock television features since its early days.[2]

However, reality as a genre of broadcast content has exploded in the recent past, and this is significant for two reasons. First, a once-clear distinction between "entertainment" and "informational" or news programming has blurred: In the middle now are tabloid news shows (e.g., *Hard Copy*), and reality-based entertainment news shows (*Entertainment Tonight*).

Not only is there more reality programming, more of what is available is violence-related. The growth sectors have been in three areas--syndicated talk shows (there are now more than 20 such series), in prime-time network newsmagazines which increasingly have featured "tabloid" staples of sex and crime, and in reality-based police shows (e.g., *Cops, Top Cops, Real Stories of the Highway Patrol*). The recent past has featured the post-program murder of a *Jenny Jones* guest, the not-infrequent coming to blows on *Geraldo* and *Jerry Springer,* the intentional confrontational situations created by talk-show programmers, and the raw footage appearing nightly on reality-based police shows. As a recent *New York Times* article noted (B. Weinraub, Aug. 16, 1994, B1, cited in Ghanem & Evatt, 1995):

> From Diane Sawyer's interview of Charles Manson to Stone Phillips' interview of Jeffrey Dahmer--between Feb. 17 and May 17 of this year [1994] alone--'reality-based' tabloid network news shows such as 'Inside Edition,' 'Hard Copy,' 'A Current Affair' and 'Prime Time Live' broadcast 45 stories that graphically focused on murders, spree killers and their victims.

Most importantly, although such programs have infrequently been studied for their effects on viewers, what research evidence there is suggests that realism as a contextual feature of television programs *heightens* involvement, arousal and aggression (Paik & Comstock, 1994; Atkin, 1982; Condry, 1989; O'Keefe, 1984). Moreover, such programs in their verisimilitude and appearance as a "window on the world" heighten viewer perceptions of the real world, and to the extent that violence is present in reality programming, viewers will perceive the real world as violent (Gerbner and Gross, 1976; Potter, 1986, 1988; Slater & Elliott, 1982). Tamborini, Zillmann and Bryant (1984), moreover, found both short-term (immediate post-test) and longer term (three days later) increases in both personal judgments of crime victimization and in societal-level risk for a televised crime documentary, while two different fictionalized dramas showed no enduring impact.

---

2. The first "reality entertainment" program was probably Allen Funt's *Candid Camera*, which, like most other early reality-genre programs had its predecessor in radio (*Candid Microphone*). But the term "reality programming" dates from the period shortly after the introduction of ABC's *Real People* in April 1979 (Horace Newcomb, interview, September 1995). We hope it is clear that we nowhere suggest that "reality" as we apply it to television programming necessarily "reflects reality" in any direct sense. The *range* of the degree of social construction of reality in television, from the syndicated *Unsolved Mysteries* to network news programming, is great, but all television presentations of "reality," we would argue, involve social constructions.

Moreover, reality programming deserves special attention because its audiences and potential effects vary systematically from much other television. Almost no reality programming is directed specifically at children, the audience for whom the most robust effects-research findings exist; when children are in the audience for most reality programming, they are considerably more likely to be viewing with adults than when they watch most child-oriented fare, and such joint viewing mediates potential effects. Further, as noted in the Santa Barbara literature review, perceived reality is an extraordinarily important factor in potential effects, and "reality" is the stock in trade of reality television.

We study "reality" violence because we believe there is much of it in the television world. We study it because we believe that there is significant potential for it to have impact on the audience it reaches. And we study it because it has been studied far too little by previous researchers describing violence on television.

Previous research

Perhaps surprisingly, relatively little prior research has focused on the content of American televised reality programming. Two content studies, however, are of particular note.

Mary Beth Oliver's (1994) analysis of 57.5 hours of five reality-based police programs (*Top Cops, America's Most Wanted, Cops, FBI: The Untold Story, American Detective*) in 1991-1992 compared their presentations to "real-world" census and FBI Uniform Crime Report data and found that the programs overreported violent crime and overreported the percentage of crimes that were solved. Oliver did not study other forms of reality programming.

While the Gerbner *et al.* studies are the largest database of TV content, they have focused on prime time non-reality programming and daytime cartoons and soap operas. One recent study, however, Lichter and Amundson's (1994) comparison of a single day of 1992 and 1994 TV content, included both reality and fictional programming. Moreover, it recognizes and accounts for two important differences between fictional and reality based programing: 1) *Their differences in narrative context units:* Fictional entertainment programming is most often presented in unitary programs, while in reality programs, stories or segments may bear no relation to one another. 2) *Their modes of depiction of violence:* Most usually, fictional programs *visually depict* violence; reality programs typically supplement depiction in a variety of ways--by *recreating* past violent scences and by *reporting on* and *orally describing* violent incidents.

Lichter & Amundson report that while nonfiction programs generally contain less violence than fictional fare (22 percent of 1994 programs contained at least one violent scene[3]) there was substantial variation by reality-program genre, with tabloid and reality shows roughly twice as likely to feature a violent scene than news stories and newsmagazine stories. And almost one quarter (22.7%) of all violent scenes in 1994

---

3. Compared with 100% of theatrical movies, 81% of TV dramas, 77% of cartoons, 67% of cartoons, 67% of made-for-TV movies and 39% of situation comedies. (Lichter & Amundsen, 1994, p. 14).

television programs, excluding commercials and promotions, appeared in reality programming. Moreover, the study finds both similarities between fictional and reality-based TV violence: Guns and other weapons account for more than a third of fictional violence and a majority of reality-based violence, but 71% of reality-based violence scenes link violence to physical harm, compared with 40% of fictional scenes. However, reality-violence was no more likely to show suffering as a result of violence (20% of scenes) than was fictional violence (23%)(Lichter & Amundson, 1994: 38-40).

While the Lichter-Amundson study is an important precursor to the present one, it has significant limitations. First, it examines but a single day of programming and has been widely faulted for its limited and possibly unrepresentative sample. Second, while it takes into account TV genre (fictional vs. reality-based) differences in narrative unit and mode of depicting violence, it fails to report these distinctions with precision: First, Lichter and Amundson do not, in reporting their data, distinguish legitimate news stories from other reality-based programs in describing reality shows. Second, when dealing with news and public affairs shows, each individual news item is coded for the presence or absence of violence, and violence in these news segments is reported and equated with the presence or absence of violence in an entire fictional program (cf. Lichter and Amundson, 1994: 14). Clearly these two units of analysis are unequal. Further, while Lichter and Amundson conceptually distinguish visual and oral portrayals of violence in reality programming, nowhere do they report differences--or similarities--of kinds or natures of violent portrayals in the two types; they sum across them.

In principle, there is every reason to expect reality-based television to have the same cognitive, affective and behavioral impacts on audiences as fictional television. Further, at least one recent analysis (Oliver & Armstrong, 1995) found that punitive attitudes about crime, higher levels of racial prejudice and higher levels of authoritarianism were associated with more frequent viewing of, and enjoyment of reality-based police programs but not with enjoyment of fictional crime programming. Further, a recent study of agenda-setting on crime in the state of Texas, has found that newspaper and television coverage of crime is a far stronger predictor of public *salience*, or judgment of civic importance, of crime as an issue, than is actual incidence of crime (Ghanem & Evatt, 1995).

Violence in Televised Reality Programming

For these reasons, in studying reality programming, we believe that several, critical considerations are warranted, in that *violence* in television reality content has its own characteristic features.

In the description of violence in reality programming, we will distinguish between *talking about* violence and visual portrayals of violence. Much like Lichter, we observed that in talk shows, in particular, violence is often the topic of conversation even when the actual visual depiction of violence is not present. We believe that such discussions in and of themselves might contribute to viewers' perceptions of the amount of violence in the real world. Moreover, in news programming, *reporting* is the characteristic mode of discourse, relating the prominent features of past events. While in television, much reporting features visual depictions of the consequences of violence where the original violent event was not captured on tape or film, reporting also involves having sources, frequently victims or witnesses--or news reporters--*describe* an event. Failing to consider such "word pictures" as descriptions of violence struck us as unwise and invalid, though we recognize that ultimate impact on audiences might differ for visual and verbal violence depictions. Therefore, in our analyses, we separately code *visual violence*, which is coded in reality-based programs as it is coded in other TV fare, and *talk about violence*, which is coded using measures appropriate to the oral description of violence. No content is "double-coded" as both visual and oral violence.

Further, in coding television violence, multiple units of meaning exist. In much fictional entertainment programming, the *program itself* is the most salient unit for understanding the meaning of violence in the show. In a variety of reality-based programs, however, the program is subdivided into multiple *segments* each of which discusses a different topic. For example, *Sixty Minutes* typically comprises four to six "stories" during the hour-long program. Similarly, *Rescue 911* usually contains two to three segments. Each of these segments consequently should be studied separately for its portrayal of violence. Therefore, in reality based programs we will describe both the topic and violent portrayals present not just in overall programs but also in program *segments*.

Just as visual violent portrayals occur within a context of character, action and audio-visual production features, a context exists for talking about violence and violence portrayals in reality based programs. We were particularly concerned that the extent to which viewers may think of reality portrayals of violence as a window on the world will depend on what world is being discussed. Therefore, in attempting to capture the context of violence in reality shows, we coded the nature of the topic under discussion and a variety of measures of identification specific to reality based programs which that engender viewer identification with the violence depictions.

Finally, perhaps the single most important context unit in understanding violence in reality program is the reality *genre*. We have noted that a variety of such genres exist on television: 1)News which in this study excludes the *bona fide* newscasts but includes newsmagazines, news-interview shows such as *Meet the Press*, and the non-hard-news segments of morning news shows); 2) Tabloid news show such as *Hard Copy*; 3) Entertainment news and review shows, such as *Entertainment Tonight;* 4) Entertainment non-news shows, such as *America's Funniest Home Videos*; 5) Police shows, such as *Top Cops;* 6) Documentary programs, such as the Arts & Entertainment network's *Biography*; and, of course, 6) Talk shows. Genre matters for several reasons. First, the likely audience for different genres varies, as is reflected by when they normally air: Talk shows are more likely to appear in daytime hours, news-interview shows on weekends, and many other genres in early fringe prime time. Second, we presume that how violence is presented varies as well, and it became important for us to analyze genres for their characteristic modes of presentation of violence. Finally, while we have little evidence across genres, there is evidence that existing attitudes and expected gratifications affect attention to at least one genre--the reality based police show--and the authors of one study speculate that attention to shows in this genre may reinforce such attitudes (Oliver & Armstrong, 1995).

MEASURING VIOLENCE IN REALITY PROGRAMS

Violence Defined

With one exception, the definition of televised violence for reality programs is the same as it is for entertainment programs: *Evidence of a credible threat of physical force or the actual use of such force intended to physically harm or intimidate an animate being or group of beings. Violence also includes certain depictions of physically harmful consequences against an animate being that occur as a result of violent means.*

The one exception is that in reality programming, *Talk About Violence* is also coded. *Talk About Violence* is defined as *the verbal recounting of threats, acts and/or harmful consequences by a person or person-like character appearing on screen or heard from off screen. Verbal abuse* per se *is not coded as Talk About Violence.*

We would note in passing that in reality programming (as in all other programming), accidental or unintentional physical harm is not considered violence. Hence in a reality program such as *America's Funniest Home Videos,* unintentional harm is not considered a violent act or consequence.

Levels of Analysis

Reality-based programs are analyzed at three levels--the *program*, the *segment* and the *violent sequence.* Unlike the Santa Barbara coders, we do not code at the Perpetrator-Action-Target level, and many of the context variables coded at the PAT level in their analysis were coded at the sequence level in ours.

Program : At the program level of analysis, coding is virtually identical with that described in the Santa Barbara report: Genre, Network, Time of Broadcast, Program Name, Day and Date, Program Length, and Presence of Ratings and Advisories.

Segment : As noted above, reality programming is frequently segmented. A segment is defined as "a coherent part of a broadcast, a partitioned narrative within a program that exhibits unity within itself and separation, by topic and/or central focal character, from other segments within a program." For instance, separate "stories" within a newsmagazine program or police-reality show are coded as separate segments.

We were interested describing the nature of the topics discussed in these segments. For example, we have coded the main theme, subject or issue under discussion in each segment, as well as secondary themes that might be present. Each segment is coded for the amount of attention paid to the following: International politics; national politics; espionage/surveillance; war/armed forces; business, industry, labor; financial stress/success; law enforcement and crime; science and technology; education; communications; health and medicine; religion; family; leisure, sports, tourism, culture; nature; manmade disasters and accidents; supernatural; minority groups and people; death and dying; sexual interaction.[4] Attention was measured as 1) No attention paid to

---

4. Adapted from Gerbner, *et al.,* 1994, p. 8-10. These data, and the topic and locale data noted below, are not reported in the present study but will be reported upon in later analyses.

the theme or subject; 2) minor attention to the theme; or 3) major theme of the segment. Secondly, segments were coded for the *locale* of the main topic--where the action described occurred--including major regions of the world and of the United States--and for *social setting*--whether the segment took place outside the United States, in a U.S. city, suburb, small town or rural area. The locale and social setting are coded as context variables, in that they may influence viewer *identification* with the violence described; presumably violence in a circumstance with which a viewer might identify would be more pertinent than that which occurs at a great remove.

All segments, whether they contain violence or not, are coded for topic, locale and social setting, in order to give us a basis of comparison for describing violent and nonviolent reality segments. Coders then identify segments as containing visual violence sequences and/or talk-about violence sequences, both, or neither.

Several contextual variables are coded at the *segment* level: The presence of reenactments; rewards and punishments; program realism; pain cues; and overall harm and pain.

Finally, *characters involved in violence* are coded at the segment level. At the segment level, characters are coded by gender, age, race, citizenship or national origin, and their authority or official status (e.g., whether they are a program's narrator or host, another journalist, an expert or professional, a police or law enforcement official, other government authority, or have no official status). As noted below, characters are further coded at the sequence level.

When Talk About Violence or Visual Violence is present in a segment or program, that violence is further described by sequence coding.

The Violent Sequence : The first determination made at the sequence level is whether that sequence is to be coded as a Talk or a Visual Violence sequence. The sequence is coded as a *Visual Depiction of Violence* sequence as described in the Santa Barbara report. A *Talk About Violence* sequence is defined as *a conversation related to violence. A sequence begins with an intial utterance concerning a violent act and continues so long as that conversation is centered on that act or closely related acts. The introduction of a new character may or may not signal the end of a sequence; it signals the end of a sequence if the new character changes the discussion, either by introducing a new topic or by changing the focus of the discussion.*

A Visual Violence sequence takes precedence over a Talk About Violence sequence; for example, during a talk show, when there is talk about violence, it is often accompanied by a visual depiction which shows the consequences of that act. The Talk About Violence sequence begins as defined above and ends when the violence is shown or there is a shift to a nonviolent topic. Any discussion related to the visual after it is shown is still part of the visual violence sequence. The visual violence sequence ends when the focus of the discussion shifts to an unrelated topic. The segment is classified as Talk about Violence only when no visual violence sequences are coded.

Thus, as noted, no sequence of events or discussion is ever coded by both the visual codes described in the Santa Barbara code and the Talk-About Violence codes we now describe below:

Violent talk is coded for the *graphicness of the discussion of violence*, as being either concrete and physical in detail or as being general and vague and for the *level of testimony*--whether the account involves *first person* description, of a violent act that involved the speaker as perpetrator or victim, an eyewitness or *second-person* account of the observation of violence or its aftermath, or a *third-person* account of violence which occurred elsewhere. As with our segment-level coding of locale and setting, we suggest that first- and second-person reports are more involving than third-person ones (cf. Davison, 1983).

At the violent sequence level, *characters* are coded for their relationship to violent acts--whether they are victims, relatives of or spokespersons for victims, perpetrators[5] of violence, relatives of or spokespersons for perpetrators, or witnesses of violent acts. These are "dummy codes," meaning that someone who was, in a sequence, both a perpetrator and a victim or target of violence, would be coded as both. Finally, in addition, perpetrators of violence are coded for sixteen reasons or motivations for violent activity.

SAMPLING

The sampling procedure is described in detail in the Santa Barbara report. Once programs were sampled and taped, a determination was made as to whether a program was to be considered an entertainment program or a reality program; entertainment programs were shipped to Santa Barbara and reality programs to Austin. In cases where there was a question or disagreement as to whether programs were entertainment or reality, a resolution was reached by conferral between the two sites.

As elsewhere noted, not all sampled reality programs were coded. Excluded were regularly scheduled news programs such as the *NBC Nightly News,* instructional programs, religious programs, sports, and "infomercials." In addition, two categories of material *within* programs were also excluded: Commercials, in all programming, and news "drop-ins" in reality programming.[6] When breaking news preempted sampled programs, the programs, but not the news preemptions, were coded if the interruption was 10 minutes or less. When preemptions were longer, the program slot was returned to the sample pool and the program was not coded.

The total number of reality programs to be coded across the 1994-1995 season on 23 network, independent, basic cable and premium cable channels was 620. Slightly more than a third of sampled reality shows were not coded because the programs fell

---

5. In all cases, characters were coded as perpetrators if they were *actual or alleged* perpetrators of violence; thus a defendant in a case of violent crime would be considered a perpetrator.

6. *Program pauses*, for commercials, news drop-ins, station promos and public service announcements were noted so that time allotted to them could be deducted from program time.

into categories (network and local newscasts; sporting events; hobby, cooking and instructional programming; travelogues; religious programming; infomercials) excluded from the analysis. Our 1994-1995 sample thus comprises 384 coded programs.

METHODS

The University of Texas at Austin research team consisted of four professors who began working on the project from the onset. We appointed four graduate students as research assistants on the project. The faculty and research assistants developed and implemented the coding procedure described herein. The research assistants also began the initial coding of programs. During the period Feb. 16-28, 1995, we hired 10 coders, the large majority of them graduate and undergraduate Communication students, to do the bulk of the coding. Coders were paid at an hourly rate and were expected to work on coding for a minimum of 10 hours per week and a maximum of 19 hours per week. The research assistants trained the coders and supervised coding sessions. During the summer of 1995, six coders left the project and two additional coders were hired. One research assistant also left the project, and we hired another graduate student to take his place. Three additional coders were hired in October 1995 to facilitate computer data entry.

Typical coding sessions lasted from about one hour to four hours. During a coding session, the coder would be assigned certain programs, segments or sequences to watch and to code. Coding was done in three "passes" through a program: a) In the first pass, a graduate research assistant coded all program-level codes and identified the beginning and ending times of each segment. b) In the second pass, a coder coded the segment and segment-level character codes and identified sequences containing Visual and Talk-About violence. c) In the third pass, a coder coded violence sequences and sequence-level character coding.

All coding was done in the project office on the University of Texas campus. The office maintained during this period four to six sets of television monitors, videocassette recorders and headphones, so that four to six coders could work simultaneously.

Coders received a copy of the reality program codebook, a 32-page document covering all coding procedures.

RELIABILITY

Content analysis as a method of science was originally developed for studying written messages. Later, the technique was extended to include simple transformations, such as the analysis of transcribed oral messages. More recently, attempts have been made to extend the use of the method to more complicated forms of messages, including those involving multidimensional stimuli such as the audio-visual content of television and film.

These more complex forms of content present special challenges to the analyst. One difficulty involves the attempt to turn continuous streams of message stimuli into discrete packets of information. In a newspaper, for example, the various message units such as headlines, bylines, leads and stories, can be clearly defined in space. That makes measurement relatively easy, compared to the various message units in a TV program, which may contain separate segments, sequences or other message units that are defined not in space but in time. Thus, while it is fairly easy to locate the boundaries of a headline, so that we can say, "Yes, this is the headline," it is often more difficult to locate the bounds of, say, a violent sequence: when does it begin, where does it end? This problem is further compounded when dealing with multi-dimensional stimuli such as a messages that contain both auditory and visual information simultaneously or independent of each other.

In other words, one of the major challenges facing a content analysis of multi-dimensional continuous data such as television programming is the very issue of locating the analytical units themselves. Only after we have reliably found and identified the units can they be reliably analyzed further.

Therefore, we really face two questions of reliability. The first question is reliably finding the units to be further coded; the second is reliably coding the content in the units found.

Generally, the reliability of the coding process was estimated by examining the agreements and disagreements among the coders in the various decisions they made in coding a subsample of the sample of television programming used in this project.

For our reliability test, the five coders who were working at the time of the test coded the same three programs. The three programs represented each of the three major genres of reality programming in the sample: talk shows, documentaries and reality drama shows. An attempt was made also to select programs with different levels and kinds of violent programming. Of the five segments within the five programs that were coded overall, two segments contained both visual violence and talk about violence, one segment contained only visual violence, one contained only talk about violence and one contained neither visual violence nor talk about violence.

In a preliminary reliability assessment, we discovered that coders were having a difficult time identifying the beginning and ending times of sequences containing visual violence or talk about violence. The problem seemed to be not with the code itself but with the training the coders had received to help them locate sequence beginnings and endings. We decided to solve this problem in the future by giving some coders special training in the identification of program, segment and sequence boundaries, and to use those coders to determine the boundaries of the units to be coded further. For coding already completed, however, the problem had something of a cascading effect. If one coder failed to identify a segment as containing talk about violence, for example, whereas another coder did, the coders disagreed not just on one coding decision (the presence of talk about violence in a segment) but on all other coding that was precipitated by the identification of the talk about violence sequence. It was to avoid this cascading effect problem in the future that we decided to make sure that coders were specially trained in the difficult task of identifying unit boundaries.

The following table shows the initial problem. As can be seen, coders disagreed on the number of talk about violence sequences, the number of visual violence sequences, the number of characters in a violent segment and the number of characters in a violent sequence.

	Coders				
	A	B	C	D	E
Talk Sequences	5	4	9	6	3
Visual Sequences	11	11	15	10	9
Characters in Segment	57	36	38	29	28
Characters in Sequence	68	45	43	38	34

Again, this reliability problem will be dealt with in future coding by having coders specially trained in identifiying these units. Other coders will then be told where the units are located and will code those units further.

The percentage of intercoder agreement was computed by adding the number of times each pair of coders agreed in their coding divided by the total number of variables codes. When one coder did not code a certain variable, the corresponding data were considered as missing values and, therefore, they were not included in the total percentages. For example, if Coder A did but Coder B did not see a perpetrator in a violent sequence, the two were considered to have disagreed on the presence of a perpetrator. The two, however, were not considered to have disagreed on the nature of the weapon used by the perpetrator, since Coder B would not have ever gotten to the point of considering that question as a coding decision.

A total of 1,314 variables were coded in the reliability test; this included 155 variables at the segment level, 168 characters at the segment level, 416 sequence variables, and 575 character variables at the sequence level.

At the segment level, a total of 155 variables were coded, not counting the special coding done on characters within segments. The percentages of intercoder agreement for coding done at the segment level ranged from 86.45 to 92.26:

	Coder				
	A	B	C	D	E
A		88.39	90.97	92.26	87.74
B			89.68	89.68	87.10
C				88.39	86.45
D					87.10

Coding of characters at the segment level involved a total of 168 coding decisions. The percentages of intercoder agreement for this coding phase ranged between 84 and 94.23:

	Coder			
	A	B	C	D	E
A		89.51	94.23	84.62	92.00
B			88.00	84.00	88.19
C				84.03	90.58
D					83.33

At the sequence level, coders dealt with 416 variables, not counting the special coding that was done on characters within sequences. The percentages of intercoder agreement at this level ranged between 83.85 and 94.53:

	Coder			
	A	B	C	D	E
A		94.53	85.34	93.23	92.19
B			83.85	93.18	92.71
C				86.46	86.88
D					89.24

Coding of characters at the sequence level involved 575 coding decisions. The percentages of intercoder agreement for this coding phase ranged between 86.34 and 97.73:

	Coder			
	A	B	C	D	E
A		94.43	91.51	96.03	97.73
B			86.34	95.09	93.01
C				91.53	91.52
D					96.27

Finally, the following table shows the percentages of agreement among all five coders across all programs coded, all variables included. Overall, for a total of 1,314 variables coded in the reliability test, the percentages of intercoder agreement ranged between 86.18 and 94.11.

	Coder			
	A	B	C	D	E
A		93.10	89.67	93.22	94.11
B			86.18	92.41	91.49
C				88.39	89.28
D					91.35

Thus at each level of analysis, our reliability checks show high levels of intercoder agreement.

RESULTS

Data below are based on the analysis of 384 reality programs across 23 networks; within those programs were 1,672 segments, of which 269 (16%) contain one or more Visual Violence sequences, and 152 (9%) contain one or more Talk about Violence sequences.

We will begin with general descriptive data of our sampled programs. These baseline data will then be followed by an analysis of how violence is portrayed across the seven reality program genres indentified in our sample. Thus, the more contextualized analysis of violence portrayals in reality programming is offered in the examination of the different reality program genres.

Description of Sampled Programs

The "average" reality program is a one-hour show (53% of the sample), the usual length of programs in some of the most popular reality genres, the talk show, and the documentary. Thirty-nine percent of the programs are 30-minute shows, and these are concentrated among entertainment-news and review shows (e.g., *Entertainment Tonight*), police shows (e.g., *Cops,* entertainment non-news shows (e.g., *America's Funniest Home Videos)* and news shows. Most of the remainder are two-hour shows (6%). mostly morning news shows such as *Good Morning America.* As Figure 1 below demonstrates, the largest category of reality program genres represented in our sample is talk shows, followed by news and public affairs and then documentary shows.

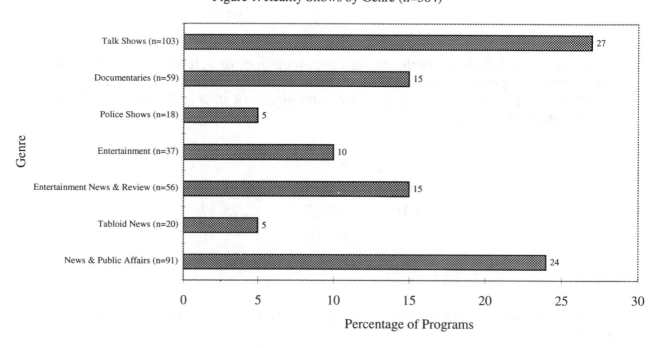

Figure 1: Reality Shows by Genre (n=384)

Reality programming is not evenly spread across channels. In general, the broadcast networks are the most frequent reality programmers. PBS airs more (n=48 in the 1994-95 sample, all but one of them documentaries or news and public affairs programs) than any of the four commercial networks. Among the commercial networks, Fox programs about two-thirds as much as the ABC and CBS affiliates, which program about equal numbers of reality shows; the Los Angeles NBC affiliate, airs about one-quarter more reality programs (n=45) than the ABC or CBS affiliates. Cable networks and independent stations show great variation. One independent, KCOP, airs the largest number of reality shows (n=43) of any non-network channel, 91% of them talkshows, while another, KTLA, airs very few (n=6). On basic cable, Lifetime and the Arts & Entertainment Network program the most reality programming, while most show little or none. In particular, family- and child-oriented channels (Nickelodeon, Cartoon Network, Disney, The Family Channel) have little or no reality programming. Premium cable (HBO, Cinemax, Showtime) likewise has almost none.

Two-thirds of all reality shows appear on network stations and basic cable channels, but there are substantial variations in the appearance of reality genres on different channel types. For instance, police shows appear primarily on network and independent stations. On the other hand, entertainment shows (e.g., MTV's *Real World*, the syndicated *Trauma Center*, Fox's *Sightings*) are found primarily on basic cable. Network television presents all genres, and public TV concentrates on news and documentaries. Basic cable looks much like network TV, and premium cable programs very few reality shows, concentrating on theatrical films.

Figure 2: Program Genre by Channel Type (n=384 programs)

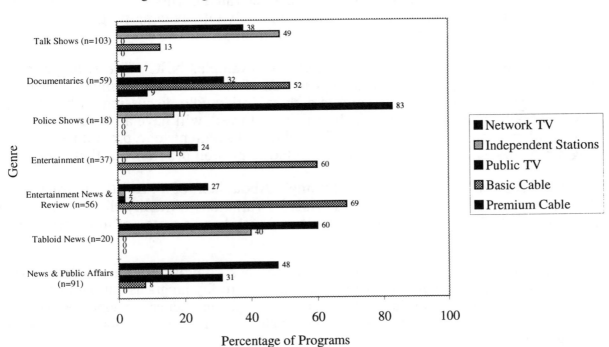

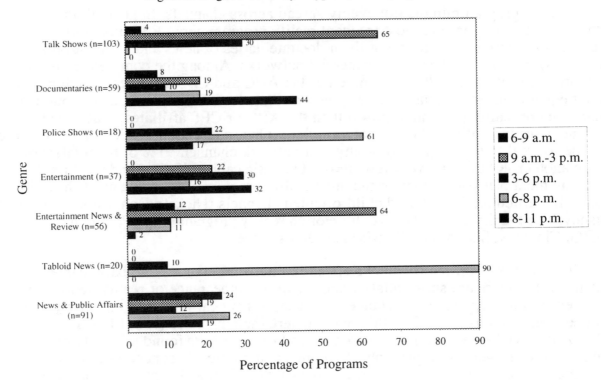

Figure 3: Program Genre by Daypart (n=384 programs)

Just as reality programming varies by channel, there are substantial variations by dayparts. News and public affairs are spread across the day, but few other genres are. Tabloid news and police shows are concentrated in the early evening. Entertainment news and review shows, and talkshows are concentrated during the day--9 a.m.-6 p.m. Entertainment and documentary programs are largely late-evening programs, but they do spread across the day except for the early morning.

Many reality programs are *segmented*. For example, NBC's *Today* program may move from a Washington, DC, studio discussion of the conflict in Bosnia to a health-spa location segment to discuss skin care, to a New York studio discussion with the author of a new book on airline travel. Each of these "stories" will have an internal unity that the overall program does not exhibit. To analyze all segments of a program as if the program were a unified whole strips segmented-television programs of their context.

How segmented *is* reality programming? About half of all reality programs contain multiple segments.[7] Clearly, there is substantial variation: Virtually all news programs are segmented (Two-hour morning news shows may have a dozen or more segments; the

---

7. In our coding scheme, introductory "teaser" sections of programs were coded as separate segments, where programs had them--and almost all reality programs (all but two of our 259 programs) do. If one considers segments just as separate "stories" or topic/treatment unities withink programs, 52% of programs are single-topic unsegmented shows, and 48% are segmented.

largest number in the 1994-95 season was a morning news show with 15), as are virtually all reality-based police programs; at the opposite pole, most talkshows and documentaries are unsegmented. To be able to discuss variables that "make sense" in some programs at the program level--that is, the program is not composed of separate segments but in other programs make sense only within specific segments, we choose here to describe these variables as segment-level variables, bearing in mind that where programs are unsegmented, they are in fact program-level variables.

Analyzed here are 1,669 segments, a mean of 4.3 segments per program.[8] At the segment level of analysis, we code the segment/program *topic,* and its *locale.* All segments of all reality programs were coded for these variables, so that meaningful comparisons could be made between violent and nonviolent programming. We now turn attention to baseline data on the presence and amount of violence in reality programs.

Presence of Violence in Reality Programs

Sixty-two percent of televised reality programs we coded in our sample depict *no* visual violence. Thirty-eight percent of televised reality programs contain at least some

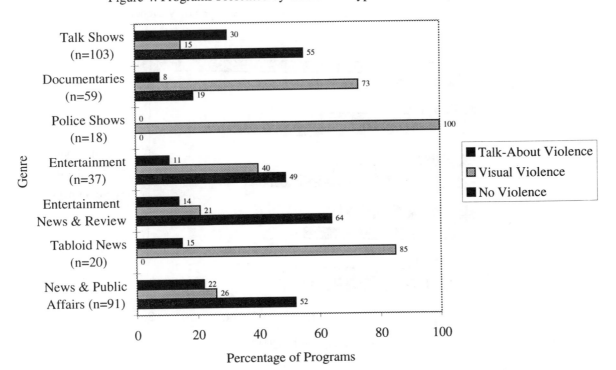

Figure 4: Programs Presented by Genre and Type of Violence (n=384)

_____

8. Here, we include the "teaser" or program introduction as a separate segment; removing these would mean that the mean number of segments per program was 3.3, not 4.3.

visual violence--that is, they have at least one sequence during the program with violence as defined in this project. Another 18% contain at least one Talk About Violence sequence but no visual violence. Recall, however, that the sample excludes from analysis some genres which are likely to contain violence such as *bona fide* network and local news shows and sports programs, as well as programs that likely do not depict violence such as instructional, nature, religious, travel and game shows.

There is a great deal of variation, among those genres which contain some violence, in the amount and types of violence they *do* contain. Figure 4 shows that police shows and tabloid news shows stand out from other genres in overall presence of violence-- *every* police show in our sample contained visual violence, and every tabloid news show contained visual (85%) or talk about (15%) violence sequences. As well, four of five of the documentaries we coded contained either visual violence or talk about violence. For the remaining genres, between half and nearly two thirds of the programs contained no violence. Talk shows are noteworthy both because they contain proportionately less violence than other genres and because most of what is there is in the form of talk about violence only. Documentaries show surprisingly high proportions of visual violence. Within the news category, morning newsmagazine shows were slightly more likely than other news shows to feature visual violence, evening magazines were substantially more likely to do so, and news talk and interview shows contained no visual violence, and news discussion shows, nearly none.

Figure 5: Programs Presented by Type of Channel and Type of Violence (n=384)

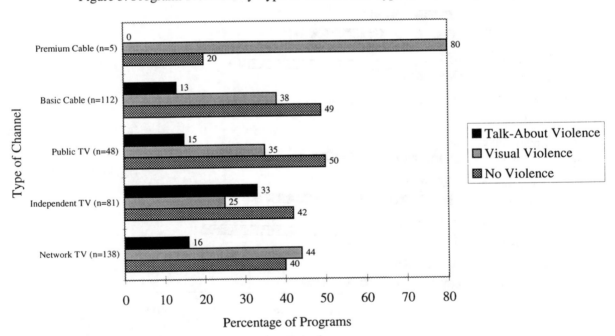

We can examine how violence in reality programs varies by channel type. We should point out again, that network television here includes all programming appearing on network affiliated stations, whether they are produced by the network or the station. Figure 5 indicates that there is some variation in the presence of violence on reality programming on different channels. Reality shows on public television (98% of which are either news and public affairs or documentary programs) are the least violent, although 35% do depict some visual violence. Independent stations are noteworthy for their relatively low levels of visual violence and high levels of Talk about Violence. This is one clear instance where station or channel type, type of violence and reality genre interact. Almost two-thirds of *all* independent-station reality programming analyzed for this report was of talk shows, a genre comparatively high on talk violence but low on visual violence. While premium cable appears to show the highest level of violence with this relatively crude measure, there are few reality programs *on* premium cable in our sample (n=5, all documentaries, most of them depicting the making of movies).

There are differences in the types and amounts of violence in reality programs across the broadcast day. See Figure B in the Appendix. These differences are so great that it is not meaningful to present the percentage of violent shows that appear in each time block without noting the genre of program and the type of channel. See Figures C and D.1-D.5 in the Appendix. For instance, police shows, which are among the most violent reality programs, predominate in the 6 p.m.-11 p.m. hours where 60% of those in our sample can be found. Overall, daytime hours have by far the lowest level of visual and talk violence. The 9 a.m.-3 p.m. daypart, when school-age children are in school, but younger children are more likely to be watching, are marked both by the lowest levels of *visual* violence (four out of five daytime programs have none) and the lowest levels of overall violence (three of five have none.). Early-morning hours (6 a,m. to 9 a.m) rank second in lowest overall levels of violence (53% of early-morning reality programs have none, but show higher levels of visual violence (32% of programs), owing to the predominance of morning newsmagazines during this time. A morning newsmagazine would be classified as containing visual violence, as would any other reality show, if *any one* segment in the program contained a violent sequence, and the probability that any one segment in a two-hour program would be higher than for shorter programs. In fact, when the index of violence is the presence of violent *segments* rather than violent *programs,* the early-morning period has the least violence. During afterschool hours (3 p.m. to 6 p.m.), 38% of reality programs shown have no violence, while 38% show some visual violence and 24% have talk about violence only. This is the time period when talk shows predominate. Evening hours have dramatically more programs than other dayparts with some visual violence. Three-fifths do, and there is no significant difference between the 6-8 p.m. and 8-11 p.m. blocks, owing to the predominance of genres--especially documentaries, newsmagazines and reality-drama programs--that are higher than average in violent depictions. Just one third of evening reality programs contain no violent talk or depictions.

It should be clear, too, that genres vary substantially by the proportion of violence that is in Talk About Violence (TAV) and Visual Violence (VV) sequences. Overall, 53% of violent sequences are Visual Violence sequences, and 47% are Talk About Violence sequences. Genres in which most violence is in Visual sequences are Police shows (79% VV, 21% TAV), Entgertainment News and Reviews (79% VV, 21% TAV) and Tabloid News (66% VV. 34% TAV). Programs roughly balanced between visual and talk violence are Documentaries (58% VV, 42% TAV), and Entertainment Non-News programs (46% VV, 54% TAV). Genres in which Talk About Violence predominates are Talk Shows (17% VV, 83% TAV) and News and Public Affairs (35% VV, 65% TAV).

How much *time* is devoted to violence in reality programs? Very little, On average, only two minutes of violence (mean visual violence per program =1.1 minutes, s.d., 2.0, n=215); mean talk about violence per program = .96 minutes, s.d., 1.8, n=215) is presented in those reality programs containing violence. Recognizing that some programs are 30 minutes in length while others are two hours or longer, the average amount of time that violence is seen or heard is small. Expressed as a *proportion,* 3.3% of the program time in reality programs, *excluding commercials and other nonprogram content,* is in visual violence sequences, and 2.4% is in talk-violence sequences.

Moreover, talk about violence and visual violence vary systematically by reality program genre. Police shows devote five times *more* of their time to visually violent sequences than the average reality show, and talk shows about ten times *less* than the average. Using the proportion of time in violent sequences measure, police shows rank highest in talk violence as well, Talk shows are about average for reality genres in the proportion of time devoted to violent sequences. Entertainment news-and-review shows feature fairly low levels of time devoted to visual and talk violence, and tabloid news shows spend about average amounts of time in visual violence sequences and below-average amounts of time in talk violence sequences. This is notable, for as we show below, these genres are noteworthy for the intensity of violence when violence is depicted. See Figure A in the Appendix.

There is only one significant variation by channel type in the proportion of sequence time within programs displaying violence: Public television reality programs devote 1.8% of their time to visual violence sequences compared with an overall mean of 3.3%. See Figure B in the Appendix. The 9 a.m.-3 p.m. daypart features the smallest proportion of time--by a factor of four--(1% vs. an overall mean of 4%) devoted to visual violence, and the 6 a.m.-9 a.m. block has about half as much Talk About Violence time as any other daypart. See Figure C and Figures D.1-D.5 in the Appendix.

Contextual Factors in Violent Portrayals

Figures 6 and 7 illustrate two aspects of the depiction and description of violence-- the acts of violence in television reality programming overall, and the weapons used to accomplish those acts. In Figure 6 we present data which indicate that hitting and use of guns are by far the most common means of committing violence in both talk and visual violence, and by and large, talk and visual violence are quite similar in means by which violence is committed, with two major exceptions: Talk violence is far more likely to involve sexual assaults. Visual violence, largely in documentaries and news-and-public-affairs programming, is more likely to take the form of mass violence or war.

By genre, police reality shows and talk shows disproportionately--in comparison with other reality genres- involve hitting; police and other reality dramas and tabloid news programs disproportionately feature generalized mass violence or acts of war involving multiple means of violence. About 30% of means are "natural," i.e., involving use of hands or fists (hitting and punching, choking and strangling), and 14% of talk sequences and 6% of visual sequences involve nonconsensual forcible acts (kidnapping, sexual assault). Sexual assault and rape is featured almost exclusively in three genres--

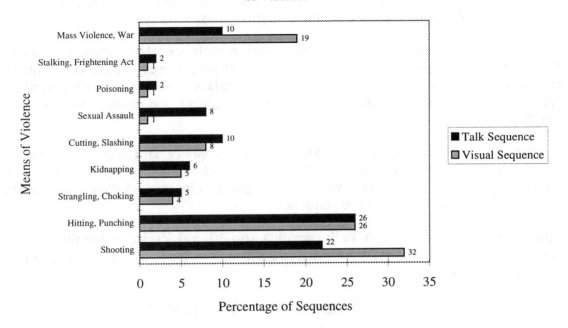

Figure 6: Percentage of Talk and Visual Sequences Depicting Different Means of Violence

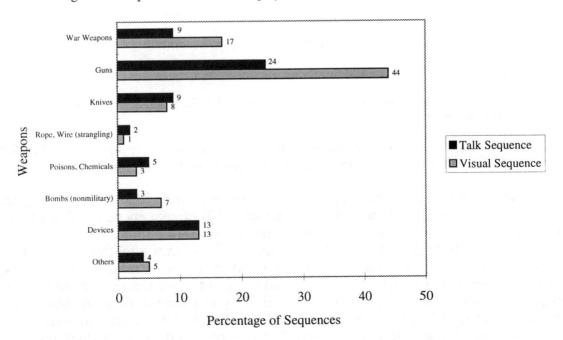

Figure 7: Weapons Discussed or Displayed in Reality Programming Sequences

talk shows (half of all depictions and mentions of rape among sampled programs), entertainment reality shows and news programs. As might be expected, most cases of rape (84%) are discussed in talk sequences, though in four cases, visual depictions of the consequences of rape are presented on talk programs.

Figure 7 presents data on weapons used in violence. Here there are some differences between talk and visual depiction. Visual sequences are substantially more likely to feature guns and war weapons than are talk sequences, and indeed visual sequences are more likely than talk sequences to feature one or more weapons in the sequence.

We use two measures of how extensive the impact of violence in sequences. First is the extent of injury, to the point of death, in a sequence. If more than one person is killed or injured, the most extensive injury is coded. The second measure is the number of persons killed or injured in the sequence.

Table 1: Extent of Injury in Talk (n=590) and Visual Violence (n=607) Sequences, in percents, read vertically. Excluded are sequences (n=282) in which extent could not be ascertained.

	Talk Sequence	**Visual Sequence**
None*	26%	33%
Minor injury	14	17
Injury, extent indeterminate	8	11
Moderate injury	8	6
Severe injury	4	5
Suicide	3	1
All other deaths	37	27
	100%	100%

_____ ____

*Includes credible threats not involving actual violence and unsuccessful attempts at violence such as firing a gun and missing the target.

Clearly, the distribution of extent is bimodal at either no injury or death. Forty percent of Talk violence sequences lead to deaths and 28% of visual sequences do.

A second index of extensiveness is the number of individuals harmed. Excluding violent sequences in which no one was harmed, 72% of sequences involve harm to a single individual, and another 15% involve harm to two (a number that likely is disproportionately high in 1994-1995 because of significant attention to the O.J. Simpson case in news and talk-show genres). At the other extreme, 22 sequences, all of them involving war, described the death and injury of more than a hundred persons. In general, sequences in entertainment-oriented programs tend to describe harm to one or two individuals, and news-oriented programs to substantially larger numbers, owing to their coverage of mass violence. When data are truncated to avoid skewing distributions (when more than 100 persons are harmed, the sequence is coded as having harmed 100), the average number harmed in the various genres ranges downward from News and Public Affairs (12.9 per violent sequence) to Documentaries (5.2), Entertainment News & Reviews (2.5), Police shows (2.4), Tabloid News (1.9), Talk shows (1.5) and Entertainment Non-News shows (1.2).

As noted in the UC-Santa Barbara report, the addition of humor to a violent sequence is a significant contextual variable, and this year's data seem to indicate that humorous violence is virtually restricted to entertainment programming: Just 3% of reality programs coupled violence with humor, and 90% of these cases were in four genres--Talk Shows (7% of sequences), Documentaries (3% of sequences), and Entertainment News and Review shows (11% of sequences, again film clips) and Tabloid News (5%). Overall, humor-in-violence is about equally prevalent in talk and visual sequences.

Context Features in Reality Program Visual Violence

We examined, at the sequence level in 765 visual violence sequences, four contextual features of violence depictions: Whether or not the depiction was a reenactment or recreation; whether violence occurred on- or off-screen; the degree of intensity of depicted violence; and depiction of the graphicness of the consequences of violence.

Reenactment-Recreation: Just over one in five reality sequences is a reenactment of a violent event. Three-quarters of these occur in two genres, the police show (41% of its 180 violent sequences are reenactments) and its cousin, the non-news reality entertainment program, which includes such "police-like" shows as *Emergency Call, Trauma Center* and *Rescue 911* and shows about occult and paranormal phenomena (e.g., *Sightings, Unsolved Mysteries*) (59% of 76 sequences).

On- or Off-Screen Depictions: Visual violence in reality programming is overwhelmingly depicted on-screen: just 28 of 765 violent sequences (4%) are off-screen violence, and half of these are in the entertainment non-news genre.

Intensity of Visual Violent Acts: Visually violent sequences were coded as depicting mildly (49%), moderately (40%) or extremely intense (11%) depiction. There are few substantial variations from these average percentages by genre, though news and public affairs sequences are more likely to depict mild violence (60%), and talk shows are bipolar, with 57% showing mild violence and 20% showing extremely intense violence.

Graphicness of Consequences of Violence: Sixty percent of reality-program sequences show *no* consequences of violence. Another 33% show somewhat graphic consequences, and 7% show very graphic consequences. Two genres stand out for their failure to show graphic consequences--the police show, in which three-quarters show no consequences, and the entertainment news-and-review program, in which almost seven-eighths show none. They do so for different reasons: The police show is the most likely genre to show credible threats of violence, with its frequent display of drawn guns. The entertainment news-and-review show's violence is markedly in decontextualized film clips, which show violent acts but rarely their consequences. As we note elsewhere, these shows are not especially high, in comparison with other reality genres, in the prevalence of their visual violence (averaging one-half violent sequence per program, compared with two violent sequences per show among all reality programs), but violent sequences in such programs tend to be distilled.

Context Features in Reality Program Talk Violence

We considered two other characteristics of talk about violence to be important contextual features. First was the *graphicness* of the discussion of violence. Just as visual violence may vary in its graphicness, so too may talk, from the abstract to the concrete. Vividness of detail might particularly be related to the possibility that violent descriptions might instill fear. Overall, 62% of violent Talk sequences (N=709) were at the abstract level, and 38% offered concrete or vivid descriptions of violent acts (N=481). Only one genre stands out in the vividness of detail of descriptions--the Talk Show (49% graphic description, n=160). Two stand out for *lack* of graphic detail in talk--Entertainment News and Review (28% graphic, n=25) and News and Public Affairs (26%, n=151).

We also analyzed the nature of description of violence from the standpoint of the speaker--whether the description was *first person*, i.e., describing his or her own involvement in it, *second person*, describing violence one has witnessed or in which intimates of the speaker are involved, and/or *third person* accounts, describing violence not witnessed and which occurred to unknown others (the usual mode of journalistic reporting). The more personal the testimony, the greater the emotional intensity and the potential arousal of fear, and the lesser the likelihood of desensitization. While a sequence can involve more than one sort of description, only about 5% actually do, and across all reality genres, 30% of Talk accounts were first person , 30% were second person, and 47% were third-person accounts. Genres higher than others on first-person accounts are Talk (46%, n=161), Entertainment Non-News (37%. n=88) and Police shows (35%, n=52). Genres higher than others on second-person witness and relative accounts are Tabloid News (39%, n=41) and Police shows (38.5%, n=52). Highest on third-person accounts were Entertainment News and Reviews (68%, n=25), Documentaries (61%, n=190) and News and Public Affairs (55%, n=146).

Characters Involved in Violence

In the 384 reality programs coded are 3,901 characters involved in violence. Of these, 89% are identifiable humans, 9% are crowds or groups of indistiguishable individuals, and 1% are nonhumans, primarily animals. Some 74% are male, and overwhelmingly, younger adults aged 21-44 (74%). While 68% of the characters involved in violence are white, 21% are African-American and 7% are Hispanic. Characters are also coded for their official status, if any. Fourteen percent are law enforcement officials and 15% are media representatives--program hosts, reporters and commentators. An additional 7% have some other official status, e.g., military authorities or government officials.

Table 2 displays characters involved in violence by their *presence* in the reality-show population, and by their status as perpetrators and/or victims. Some characters are perpetrators; some are victims; some are both, as when a character responds to a violent act by becoming violent; and some are neither: Within the "neither" category are, for example, witnesses, family members, reporters and commentators, experts, talkshow hosts, and attorneys representing the accused.

Among these characters are 1,328 perpetrators and 1,299 victims. Both perpetrators and victims are disproportionately younger adults: 81% of perpetrators and 72% of victims are aged 21-44. While children aged 12 and younger represent only 5% of all characters involved in violence, they are overwhelmingly more likely to be victims than perpetrators; they represent about 5% of all victims and just 1% of perpetrators.

As with age, gender also is a factor in the representation of victims and perpetrators. While women make up 26% of characters involved in violence, they represent 33% of victims but just 17% of perpetrators.

Table 2: Characters involved in violence, by Gender, Age, and Ethnicity. Excluded are nonhuman characters, crowds and characters for which a trait could not be ascertained.

	All Characters	**Perpetrators**	**Victims**
Male (n=2629)	74%	83%	67%
Female (n=910)	26	17	33
Age 0-5 (n=79)	3%	0.2%	6%
Age 6-12 (n=77)	3	1	5
Age 13-20 (n=253)	8	9.5	10.5
Age 21-44 (n=2271)	74	81	72
Age 45-64 (n=388)	13	8	7
Age 65+ (n=16)	0.5	0	0.5
White (n=2167)	68%	64%	65%
Black (n=652)	20.5	23	22
Hispanic (n=237)	7	9.5	8

A wealth of data exists oncharacters involved in reality-program violence, much of it yet to be analyzed in much depth or detail. However, a few significant contextual details emerge from crosstabulations of character data with other contextual variables: Males are far more likely to be involved in acts of violence involving guns; females are proportionately more likely to be involved, as perpetrators or victims, in acts involving hitting and cutting or slashing; black perpetrators disproportionately use knives; child perpetrators under 12 hit or push; teenagers disproportionately use knives and are disproportionately likely to commit sexual assaults. While a majority of sexual assaults are perpetrated by whites (n=21), blacks commit a disproportionate (n=15) number given their representation among all chararacters or among perpetrators.

Table 3: Gender of Perpetrators and Victims in Talk and Visual Violence, 1994-1995 Reality Programs. Characters who are neither perpetrators nor victims are excluded.

	Talk About Violence				Visual Violence				
	Perpetrators		Victims		Perpetrators		Victims		Total
Genre	Male	Female	Male	Female	Male	Female	Male	Female	%F.
Police Shows (561 characters)	78%	22%	50%	50%	96%	4%	84%	16%	12%
Ent. Non-news (228 characters)	63	37	42	57	94	5	71	29	27%
Ent.News&Rev. (191 characters)	67	33	56	44	88	12	86	14	18%
News & P.A. (282 characters)	80	20	56	43	96	4	68	31	25%
Tabloid News (186 characters)	78	22	67	33	78	22	72	25	26%
Documentaries (768 characters)	74	26	61	39	90	10	75	25	23%
Talk Shows (355 characters)	58	42	46	53	30	70	58	42	48%
Total	**69%**	**31%**	**54%**	**46%**	**90%**	**10%**	**76%**	**24%**	**25%**
N. Characters	**280**	**123**	**268**	**228**	**793**	**92**	**576**	**180**	**2,540**

The ethnic identity of perpetrators and victims is generally proportionate to their representation in the sampe. White characters comprise 68% of the sample and they represent 64% of perpetrators and and 65% of victims. Similarly, African-American characters represent 20.5% of all characters, 23% of perpetrators and 22% of victims, and Hispanic characters, 7% of all characters involved in violence, 9.5% of perpetrators and 8% of victims. The slight overrepresentation of whites and of adults aged 45-65 in the reality-program population is due largely ot their overrepresentation in the residual categories--as experts, journalists and other mass communicators, and public officials.

The general racial balance for perpetrators and victims, however, masks some important racial differences. Fully one-fifth of characters in reality program visual violence sequences are police officers, and police officers share two important characteristics. They are largely white (83% white, 9% African-American, 8% Hispanic) and they are far more likely to be perpetrators of violence than victims or than other characters: In visual sequences, 67% of police officers are "pure" perpetrators, 7% are victims, 6% are both perpetrators and targets/victims of violence, and 21% are neither perpetrators nor targets. For other characters, 26% are pure perpetrators, 35% are pure victims/targets, 13% are both, and 26% are neither. Thus the "balance" of races as perpetrators and victims is somewhat illusory, for the modal committer of violence is a white cop but an African-American or Hispanic character with no official standing. This matters, too, for 80% of police-officer perpetrators of violence are depicted as justified in acting violently (i.e., their motivations are self-defense or protection of others), while 70% of non-police perpetrators are depicted as having non-justifiable motives.

Finally, Table 3 depicts interesting interactions between reality program genre, Visual and Talk violence and Gender for perpetrators and victims. The table shows strong gender differences by genre, by talk vs. visual violence, and in interactions between the two. Police shows are by far the most "male" genre, with Entertainment News and Review the next most "male." By a wide margin, Talk Shows are the most "female": While females constitute only a quarter of the characters involved in violence as perpetrators or victims, they are almost half of the Talk-show population. Visual violence, too, is far more male-dominated (83%: 90% of perpetrators, 76% of victims) than Talk violence (61%: 69% of perpetrators, 54% of victims). The greatest deviation from overall norms in the table is that in Talk show visual sequences, female violence perpetrators (n=21) actually outnumber male perpetrators (n=9) by more than two to one.

VIOLENCE IN REALITY GENRES

The analyses above suggest that genre is a particularly powerful contextual variable for reality programs. Consequently, further analyses of how violence is portrayed on reality shows are offered here for the seven reality program genres identified in our sample.

Police Dramas

Police shows are the most violent reality programs. Every police show we analyzed contained at least one sequence of violence, and more time was spent in violent sequences than in any other genre (3.9 minutes of visual violence or 17.8% of noncommercial program time; .96 minutes of talk violence per show or 3.9% of total time), On a number of our measures, police-show violence emerges as among the most intense violence in reality television as well. Furthermore, more than any other genre, the depiction of violence is *visual;* almost four-fifths of the violent sequences in cop shows are visual sequences, compared with a reality-program average of 53%.

Three-fifths of police shows air in the 6-8 p.m. "family viewing" time block, with the others split about equally between late afternoon and late evening.

Some 61% of the 170 violent sequences in police shows involved credible threats, and another 51% presented violent acts themselves; only 16% present consequences of violence. Police shows are far and away the genre most likely to present violence as a credible threat, in large part because of the frequent display of weapons in police shows. Thirty percent of the visual portrayals of violence in this genre are reenactments and recreations.

More than any other genre, police shows feature guns, both in visual and talk violence. Overall, 36% of the sequences and 30% of the talk sequences in police shows involve shootings, and fully 70% of cop-show visual violence sequences show guns; in no other reality genre do more than 50% show guns.

Police programs are far different from reality programming in general in the extent to which violence is rewarded *and* punished, and this varies between visually depicted and Talk-About violence. For instance, in 62% of visual violence segments, violence is punished (versus an overall reality-genre average of 33%), and in 21%, violence is rewarded (average 9%). In visual segments, too, Police shows rank sixth among seven genres (above only Entertainment News & Review shows) in depicting pain cues. Cop show segments are somewhat more likely than average for the reality genre to show the consequences of violence, and whether these extend beyond the victim.

In talk-about violences sequences, the "word pictures" painted are more graphic than average for reality genres; 42% of talk sequences furnish concrete details and language to describe violent acts, as opposed to an overall 38% for reality talk in general. Moreover, in police-show talk, a higher proportion of the talk is first-person discussion of violence, describing one's role in violence (35% versus an overall 30%) and second-person (witness or family) description (39% vs. 30%). Combining first- and second-person depiction, Police shows virtually tie with Talk shows for personal recounting of violence.

There was only one instance in 53 segments in 18 police programs in which an alternative to violence was presented.

Overall, the portrait of police shows the data paint is of "realistic" violence, heavily visual, generally intense. As Oliver (1994) has noted, however, police-reality shows are *not* on key dimensions realistic, overemphasizing violent crime; this genre comes closer than any other to conforming to Gerbner *et al.'s* "scary world" content.

Entertainment Non-News

This category represents a range of reality shows including medical-emergency shows (*Emergency Call, Rescue 911*), cinema-verité shows (MTV's *Real World*), comedy-verité (*America's Funniest Home Videos*) and programs focusing on the paranormal (*Sightings, Unsolved Mysteries*). Forty percent of the programs contained any visual violence, and talk about violence, without visual violence occurs in 11% of the programs.

Of the 169 violence sequences in 37 programs, 54% describe the violent act itself, 40% present the consequences of violence (tying the genre with Talk shows for the most frequence portrayal of consequences), and 27% presented credible threats. Here again, guns were the dominant weapon by far, and shooting was the most common act of violence, occurring in 30% of visually violent sequences. Almost 40% of all kidnappings in visual violence reality sequences are in this genre, making it by far the most likely to present kidnappings, in goodly part because of the presence of the paranormal subgenre, and indeed, when we look at the realism of presentations, we find that 3 of 10 segments are either recreations or represent fictional depictions of events, far above the norm for other reality genres.

As is true in other genres, violence is more likely to be punished (34% of visual segments) than rewarded (one segment of 43), and overall harm and pain is depicted in 28% of the segments, about average for all reality programming.

We find two instances of programs presenting alternatives to violence in this genre.

Entertainment News and Review Programs

In some respects, violence in this genre is the most particularistic of all reality genres. While the overall *level* of violence in this genre is low (64% of programs have no violence at all), when violence appears, it does so most frequently in a particular context, as film-clips of theatrical films, many of them featuring violence. Violence in Entertainment News-and-Review shows is predominantly visual--77% of violent sequences are visual, compared with 53% of all reality sequences, a close second to Police shows.

There are multiple indicators of these conclusions: 87% of the 78 visually violent sequences show violent acts (the highest among reality genres), and 27% present a credible threat; on the other hand, only 3 of 76 visually violent scenes are of consequences of violence, as opposed to acts and threats. Guns appear in 49% of visual sequences. Other indicators that decontextualized film clips pervade violence presentations in this genre: This is one of only two genres to present fictional and fantasy-violence segments, Documentaries being the other, and it is the genre most likely to couple humor to violence (14% of sequences vs. 3% overall for reality programs). Some 41% of sequences depict no pain or injury, despite the fact that credible threats are comparatively a small part of the genre's violence. *All* visual depiction of violence, moreover, is on-screen, vs. an average of 4% off-screen for reality programming. Interestingly, the structure of talk about violence in this genre is "news-like" in that 68% of it is third-person discourse, at a remove from its subject.

Two of 47 entertainment news and review show segments presented an alternative to violence.

Documentaries

The 45 documentaries in the sample represent a hybrid genre between "real" reality and entertainment-reality programming. Some resemble news shows, while others are much more entertainment-based (e.g., the HBO presentation of "The Making of Bram Stoker's *Dracula*), with large doses of history (e.g., A&E's *Biography* and a number of war-related programs with World War II film footage). Overall, just one documentary in five showed no violence. In a quarter of all documentary visual violence, the violence is in recreations, reenactments or fictional or fantasy violence. As noted above, only Entertainment News and Review segments, within reality programming, also include fictional and fantasy segments. Violence in documentaries is more likely to be visual (58% of 265 sequences) than talk (42%).

In 265 visually violent sequences, 63% show acts themselves, 29% show credible threats and 39% show consequences. The latter is higher than for reality sequences in general (30%). This genre is like news and public affairs programming in that the means of violence are far more likely than other genres to feature general mass violence (23%) of cases) and war weapons (40%). Hand-held guns are present in 30% of visually violent sequences, below the 44% average for all reality programming). Violence is infrequently rewarded (7% of segments) or punished (21% of segments); however, harm and pain are likely to be portrayed (37% of visual segments included pain cues, second only to News and Public Affairs). Documentaries, owing to the prominence of war in the genre, are second only two news in the number of persons harmed (5.2) per sequence. Talk in documentaries is predominantly third-person description.

Six of 70 (9%) documentary segments offered alternatives to violence.

News and Public Affairs

Our 91 news and public affairs programs, we must emphasize, do not include regularly scheduled network, national or local newscasts or news "drop-ins" in morning news shows; they do include the morning programs themselves, newsmagazines such as ABC's *20/20* and interview programs such as *Meet the Press*.

This is one genre of reality programming were it is important to distinguish between the talk about violence (n=145, 65% of all news sequences) and those containing visual violence (n=78, 35%); thus the genre is second only to Talk shows in the proportion of violence which is in talk, as opposed to visual, sequences. Violent acts are portrayed in 51% of visual violence sequences and 61% of talk about violence sequences; however, credible threats are more likely to be discussed when violence is talked about (28%) than in when violence is visible shown (12% of visual violence sequences). As well, general mass violence (portrayed in 26% of visually violent sequences) and war weapons (portrayed in 21% of visual violence sequences) are a feature of news and public affairs programs, differentiating the genre from all others except documentaries. And the average number of persons killed or hurt (almost 13 per sequence, truncating the top of the scale) is more than twice as large as for documentaries, and five times greater than for any other genre.

`News and public affairs programs contextualize violence by presenting both punishment of the perpetrator (in 46% of news segments which visually present violence and 27% of those news segments where violence is only discussed, the former figure significantly higher than any genre other than Police shows). Rewarding of violent action is infrequently presented, in 10% of visual segments and 6% of talk segments, Moroever about one-third of both the talk about violence news segments and visual violence news segments presented the extended harm or pain beyond the victim and perpetrator of the violence.

Talk sequences (n=151) in news and public affairs are the *least* likely of any reality genre to present first-person accounts of violence (20% vs. an overall average of 30%) and to present graphic and concrete details in talk violence (26% vs. an overall 38%).

Lastly, news and public affairs programs presented 11 instances in these 77 news segments (12.5%) containing violence of alternatives to the violence presented in the news segment. This is more than any other genre of reality programs.

Tabloid News

All the tabloid news programs in our sample contained violence, 85% of them visual violence.

Two-thirds of tabloid news segments with violence are visual segments. Unlike other news programs, tabloid news, however, there is little focus on war-related issues, and the number of persons harmed tends to be small (1.9 per sequence). Compared with "regular" news, tabloid programs feature less violence leading to death (37% vs. 47%), but more leading to injury (43% vs. 31%).

Tabloid news shows' visual sequences predominantly depict a violent act (81% of visual violence sequences, compared to 51% of other news shows) and less frequently depict aftermaths or consequences of violence than other news (29% vs. 56%). When violence is portrayed on tabloid news shows, it tends to focus on guns (44% of visually violent sequences show guns, compared with 26% of other news) and to actually show shootings (38% compared to 26% in regular news).

Tabloid news talk sequences are also more graphic in details than regular news (38% vs. 26%), more likely to present first-person reports (29% vs. 20%) and less likely to present third-person reports (42% vs. 55%),

None of the 56 Tabloid news violent segments presented a violence alternative.

Talk shows

Fifty-five percent of the 103 talk shows in our sample contain no violence. Some 57 violent segments were identified containing 196 different violent sequences, and five-sixths of these, unsurprisingly, are talk rather than visual sequences, making Talk shows proportionately the least visually violent reality genre: Just 0.34% of time in Talk shows is in visual violence--by a factor of four the smallest proportion of any reality genre--and sequences and 3.9% of Talk program time is in violent talk sequences, below the average of 4.3% for all reality programming Furthermore, talk shows tend to focus the violence more often on the actual violent act (76%) than on credible threats of violence (23%) and consequences of violence (16% of talk about violence sequences).

Talk shows are noteworthy for the graphicness in detail when violence is talked about: 49% of sequences offered graphic details vs. an overall mean of 38% for all reality programs. Moreover, they are the *most* likely genre to offer first-person accounts of violence (46% vs. the reality-program average of 30%) and among the *least* likely to offer up third-person "journalistic" accounts (35% vs. 47%). Talk shows are one of only two genres (Entertainment News & Review is the other) to couple humor with violence; humor is present in 7% of violent sequences compared to an overall mean of 3% of violent sequences).

The violent *acts* in Talk show violence exhibit an interesting pattern: The genre is the lowest or second-lowest of all genres in presentation of forms of violence involving weapons (shootings, mass/war violence, stabbing, poisoning); highest of all genres in violence involving hitting or punching (41% of sequences; cop shows are second at 30%), sexual assault (17%; Entertainment Non-News is second at 4%); and second highest (again to Entertainment Non-News) in choking or strangling, and stalking (to Entertainment News-and-Review). Since so much Talk-show violence involves physical force, and since so much is in Talk rather than Visual sequences, it is perhaps unsurprising that Talk shows counter the general "bimodal" no-harm-or-death trend of harm in reality shows: Talk-show violence, moreso than any other genre, describe violence involving pain, but ending short of death.

Talk show visual and talk violent segments are slightly less likely to present violence as having been punished. No talk segment presents violence as rewarded.

Four of 58 talk-show violent segments present alternatives to the violence.

SUMMARY, CONCLUSIONS AND RECOMMENDATIONS

Violence is a feature of every genre of televised reality programming, but in the 1994-1995 television and cable season, 62% reality programs contained no visually depicted violence at all. An additional 18% of programs show discussions of violence without any visual depictions. The "average" reality program contains just over one minute of visually depicted violence and about the same amount of talk about violence; expressed in percentage terms, 3.3% of the program time in reality programming, excluding commercials and nonprogram content, is devoted to sequences of visual violence, and 2.4% to talk-violence sequences.

As in fictional-entertainment programming, violence is, more often than not, presented as neither rewarded nor punished, though it is far more likely to be punished (33% of both visual and talk segments) than rewarded (9% of visual segments, disproportionately in Police shows; 4% of talk segments). In 27% of visual presentations, violence leads to death, and in 40% of discussions of violence it does so. On the other hand, in 33% of visual depictions and 26% of oral ones, violence is either only threatened or leads to no injury. Where injury and death occur, frequently they are unaccompanied by accounts of pain and suffering, either to immediate victims, or to their families or friends or to the larger society. Reality violence is overwhelmingly committed by fists and guns, and guns predominate among weapons.

There is, however, no "average" program. Reality violence is more prevalent in evening hours, especially later in the evening, parts of the day when the audience is more likely to be adults. Variations in the presentation of violence in different genres of reality programming are substantial, but in the amounts of violence depicted and described, and in the nature of the violence and its modes and means of presentation. On virtually all our indices, police reality shows are the most violent programming, particularly in the visual depiction of violence. Other genres present violence in variable amounts and in differing contexts. Documentaries emerge as a more violent genre than we had anticipated, owing largely to the subject matter chosen--war and programs depicting the making of big-budget action-adventure and horror films are staples in this genre, and clips of such films in Entertainment News-and-Review programs add brief but intense bursts of violence to an otherwise fairly nonviolent genre.

This research explored a topic new to research on television violence, that of talk about violence. Where entertainment programs *depict* violence, either on-screen or by implying it by depicting its aftermath, reality programs, particularly in news-and-public-affairs programming and on talk shows, revisit violence after it has occurred. Almost half of the instances of violence we discover in reality programs occur not in visual depictions but in oral accounts. Because there is virtually no research literature on the impacts of such presentations on audiences, we are reluctant to suggest such impact here. We do feel it is important to note that the overall structure of oral discourse on violence in programming roughly parallels visual presentation, with a few notable exceptions: Because TV talk, like real-world talk, tends to focus on salient events, talk about violence is more likely to involve real violence than threats. Further, rape and sexual assault are eight times more often talked about than visually presented on television. Pain and suffering are more often discussed than depicted. Genre differences in talk are notable, too. In police dramas, talk shows and tabloid news shows, violence is discussed up close and personal, and in vivid and concrete detail, by those who have been its victims and its perpetrators and those who have been close to it and to have witnessed it. In news, it characteristically is discussed--reported--in third-person terms: Violence is something that has happened to others.

Our research in this first year leads us to three concrete recommendations to television and cable producers and programmers:

First, we note that only 23 of 215 reality programs with violence, and only a handful of violent segments within programs, begin with any sort of advisory or warning of violent content to follow. More and better ways of informing viewers of imminent violence in reality programming are warrent. This could include informative listings in program guides and reasonably detailed advisories at the beginning of programs and program segments containing violence.

Second, violent reality programs, especially Police programs and kindred non-news entertainment reality shows, should be scheduled in later-evening time blicks. Where network-affiliated stations are unable to move programs into late prime time, they should consider moving such fare to late-night time blocks.

Finally, we note, too, the relative paucity of information about how violence might be avoided, and have but a handful of examples of this, some of them bordering on the trivial. This strikes us as one area, clearly, where reality programmers, particularly in entertainment-based genres, might furnish useful information to audiences.

APPENDIX 1: REALITY SHOWS IN THE 1994-1995 SAMPLE

GENRE	*FREQUENCY*

Police Shows

America's Most Wanted	1
Cops	7
Real Stories of the Highway Patrol	7
Top Cops	3

Entertainment Non-News Shows

America's Funniest Home Videos	2
Court TV	1
Emergency Call	1
Jones & Jury	4
Judge for Yourself	1
MTV Winter Carnival	1
Hall of Fame Awards	1
Real World	9
Rescue 911	6
Sightings	1
Time Machine	1
Trauma Center	1
Unsolved Mysteries	5
Walt Disney World	3

Entertainment News and Review Shows

American Adventurer	1
Barbara Walters Special	5
Celebrity Interviews	1
Entertainment Tonight	3
Flix News	3
Healthy Kids	1
Hollywood Insider	1
L.A. Extra	1
Main Floor	1
Mike and Maty	4
MTV News Special Report	1
Nirvana Tribute	1
Ooh La La	1
Our Home	11
Regis and Kathie Lee	4
Screen Scene	7
Siskel & Ebert	1
Suzanne Somers	1
Visiting with Huell Howser	1
Week in Rock	4
Your Baby and Child	3

GENRE	*FREQUENCY*

News & Public Affairs Shows

Adam Smith	1
Behind Closed Doors	1
Bob Navarro's Journal	1
CBS This Morning	3
City View	2
Dateline	3
Day One	1
Eye to Eye with Connie Chung	1
Front Runners	1
48 Hours	3
Good Day LA	4
Good Morning America	6
Investigative Report	2
L.A. Stories	1
Lead Story	2
Life and Times	8
MacNeil Lehrer News Hour	9
Making It	1
Marriage Counselor	1
McLaughlin News Report	1
Meet the Press	1
Midday Sunday	1
Nick News	1
Nightly Business Report	4
OJ Simpson: The Trial	3
OJ Tonight	3
One on One with Charlie Neal	1
Pacesetters	1
Primetime Live	1
Rush Limbaugh	6
Sunday Morning	1
Think Tank	1
This Week with David Brinkley	1
Today Show	4
Tony Brown's Journal	1
To the Contrary	2
20/20	1
Visit L.A	2
Wall Street Journal	1
Wall Street Week	1
Washington Week	1
Weekend Gallery	1

Tabloid News Shows

American Journal	3
Current Affair	1
EXTRA	5
Hard Copy	6
Inside Edition	5

Documentaries

American Cinema	1
American Experience	2
American Justice	3
Ancient Mysteries	1
Arthur Ashe	1
Atlantic Record Story	1
Baseball	1
Behind the Veil...Nuns	1
Biography	8
California Gold	1
Civil War Journal	1
Crazy About the Movies	1
Cuban Missile Crisis	1
David L. Wolper Presents	1
Eye on Sports	2
Frontline	2
Fun and Feel of the 50's	1
Future Quest	1
Great Depression	1
Homeward Bound	1
Howard Cossell Biography	1
In Search of...	1
Inside the Academy Awards	1
Inside the NFL	1
Internet Show	1
Intimate Portrait: Grace Kelly	1
Last Years of Marvin Gaye	1
Life Stories: Families in Crisis	1
Madonna-Making of Take a Bow	1
Making of Bram Stoker's Dracula	1
Making Welfare Work	1
Memories and Dreams	1
National Geographic	1
Newsreels	1
Nova	2
The Other Epidemic	1
Pandora's Box	1
Road to the Superbowl	1
South Bank Show	1
60 minutes	2
Street Scenes-NY on Film	1
20th Century	1
Universe: The Infinite Universe	1
With the President	1
Womens Voices	1

GENRE	FREQUENCY

Talk Shows

American Baby	1
Charles Perez	3
Dennis Prager	1
Geraldo	3
Gordon Elliott	6
Jane Whitney	7
Jenny Jones	11
Jerry Springer	1
Leeza	4
Live from Queens	5
Marilu	3
Marilyn Kagen	1
Maury Povich	4
Montel Williams	8
Oprah Winfrey	5
Other Side	6
Our Voices	2
Phil Donahue	5
Richard Bey	9
Ricki Lake	7
Rolanda	1
Sally Jesse Raphael	5
Teen Summit	1
What Every Baby Knows	4

APPENDIX 2

ANTI-VIOLENT MESSAGES IN 1994-1995 REALITY PROGRAMS

TAPE 16: Frontline (PBS)
Tuesday, October 18   9:00pm-11:30pm

Description: Race Relations at Berkeley High School

Message(s):   Student talking about how he used to get in fights, but now he directs his anger towards a sport.

Teacher tells a student that instead of acting physically against him, he should have asked him what he was doing.

TAPE 24: Civil War Journal (A&E)
Saturday, October 22   7:00am-8:00am

Description: Jefferson Davis' role in the Civil War

Message(s):   Jefferson Davis would pardon deserters instead of having them shot.

TAPE 69: 20th Century (A&E)
Saturday, October 22   9:00am-10:00am

Description: Documentary about Charles Manson

Message(s):   Police tells woman that she should have called police if there was a problem and should not have hit the other woman with a baseball bat.

Police tells woman she should have called police instead of acting violent manner to the situation.

TAPE 78: Rescue 911 (FAM)
Wednesday, October 19   9:00pm-10:00pm

Description: Segment on girl abducted by stranger

Message(s):   Police go to a local elementary school to teach them how to be careful with strangers and potential abductions.

TAPE 96: Tony Brown's Journal (BET)
Sunday, October 30   9:30am-10:00am

Description: Topic: The existence of contemporary slavery

Message(s):   The discussion about current day slavery, torture and cruelty is intended to inform the public an motivate them to do something about this.

TAPE 78: Rescue 911 (FAM)
Wednesday, October 19   9:00pm-10:00pm

Description: Segment on girl abducted by stranger

Message(s):   Police go to a local elementary school to teach them how to be careful with strangers and potential abductions.

TAPE 193: Montel Williams (KCOP)
Friday, February 17   4:00pm-5:00pm

Description: Teenagers revealing lies to their mother

Message(s):   Mother says she is trying to relocate to get her daughter away from gangs and violence.

TAPE 255: Biography (A&E)
Wednesday, January 18   9:00pm-10:00pm

Description: A profile of Pope John Paul II covering his childhood as a student in a Polish seminary during WWII.

Message(s):   People describe how the Pope never fought as a child.

The Pope organized a nonviolent reaction to the war.

The Pope insisted that Brazilian workers remain nonviolent in their protesting.

The Pope says you must be very tough, but you may never kill.

TAPE 256: MacNeil Lehrer News Hour (PBS)
Tuesday, October 11   3:00pm-4:00pm

Description: Segment on Iraq Crisis

Message(s):   "The security is trying to find ways for Iraq not to fight."

TAPE 270: Cuban Missile Crisis (A&E)
Sunday, October 16   9:00pm-11:00pm

Description: A reexamination of the 1962 U.S.-U.S.S.R standoff, during which President Kennedy ordered a blockade of Cuba.

Message(s):   Fidel Castro's ex-girlfriend tells him "no, I'm not going to kill you." She says she cannot take a life. (Is "just saying no" an alternative?)

Discussion of a proposed settlement to avoid nuclear war. The Soviets said they would remove missiles from Cuba if the US removed missiles from Turkey and pledged not to invade Cuba.

President Kennedy "just say no" to invading Cuba and negotiates with Soviets, pledging not to invade Cuba and promising to discuss removal of U.S. missiles from Turkey with NATO.

Soviets promise to remove missiles from Cuba; U.S. promises not to invade Cuba

The Washington-Moscow hotline "a safeguard against hot heads in the Cold War" is installed to ensure better communication between the super powers during a nuclear crisis.

TAPE 305: MacNeil Lehrer News Hour (PBS)
Wednesday, May 17   3:00pm-4:00pm

Description: Segment on Waco in relation to Branch Davidians

Message(s):   Criticism of ATF and FBI for Waco tragedy with David Koresh. A committee was formed to ensure if violence was necessary.

Harvard professor gives his perspective and criticism of Waco incident.

Interview with Janet Reno saying they wanted to resolve Waco incident peacefully, in a non-violent manner.

TAPE 346: 48 Hours (CBS)
Thursday, June 1   10:00pm-11:00pm

Description: Segment on daughters and mothers who feel threatened by the father of family.

Message(s):   A girl is put in a psychiatric hospital for being violent.

A girl's mother is keeping her away from her father because she believes that her daughter will become violent if she sees her father.

TAPE 361: MacNeil Lehrer News Hour (PBS)
Monday, October 31   6:30pm-7:30pm

Description: White House Security

Message(s):   Closed down Pennsylvania Avenue and several streets to prevent shooting of the White House.

Discussion on the security measures for the White House.

TAPE 391: City View (ABC)
Sunday, October 16   5:30pm-6:00pm

Description: Sal Ortiz and his "Power to Change" program for troubled kids.

Message(s):   A man named Sal tells a 14 year old boy to not fight with others. He tells him that he will only be hurting himself and that he should just drop it when other kids are looking at him funny or making him angry.

TAPE 436: Nirvana Tribute (MTV)
Tuesday, March 7   2:00pm-4:00pm

Description: A history of the band includes interviews with members, including lead singer Kurt Cobain (1967-1994).

Message(s):   Alan Ross, director of Samaritans USA, discusses alternatives to suicide. Take it seriously, talk to people you trust, reach out to family, friends, religious groups or mental health organizations. Understand that you have a problem you need to address. Get help to focus on the pain and get through it. Don't keep it to yourself or wait for it to pass. Life may not be perfect, but it has possibilities.

Kurt Loder gives suicide prevention hotline numbers.

TAPE 474: Your Baby and Child (LIF)
Saturday, March 18   11:30am-12:00pm

Description: How to help your child be more socially acceptable and get along well with others.

Message(s):   Penelope Leach tells parents that they should not tell their children to fight back when a child is bullying them.

TAPE 512: Dateline (NBC)
Wednesday, March 7   9:00pm-10:00pm

Description: Segment on man who is on trial for murder

Message(s):   The entire segment 2 is about a man who shot someone who broke into his store. There is no direct mention of an alternative to violence, but in general, it seems like the man would be better off if he had not shot the intruder.

APPENDIX 3:

TABLES AND FIGURES

TABLE A:

PROFILE OF REALITY-PROGRAM VIOLENCE ACROSS GENRES
N=384 Programs

	Over-all %	Police Shows	Ent'mnt. Non-News	Ent'mnt. News & Review	Docu-mentary	News & Public Affairs	Tabloid News	Talk Shows
% of Programs with *some* Visual violence	38%	100	40	21	73	26	85	15
% of Programs with *some* Talk violence	18%	0	11	14	8	22	15	30
Among Programs Which Contain Violence:								
% of Program time in Visual Violence sequences	3.3%	17.8	3.6	1.7	3.2	1.3	3.2	0.3
% of Program time in Talk About Violence sequences	2.4%	3.9	2.6	0.9	1.9	3.1	1.8	2.6
Violence in Visual Sequences: % of Sequences...								
Depicting Acts	61%	53	55	72	51	81	81	53
Depicting Credible Threats	34%	65	27	43	13	16	24	21
Showing No Harm or Pain	33%	60	29	41	23	9	22	27
Showing Long-Term Negative Consequences	13%	13	14	3	14	18	11	15
In Which Violence Occurs Offscreen	4%	2	18	0	6	2	1	3
In Which a Gun is Used	44%	70	49	49	26	46	30	21
In Which Perpetrators are Punished	33%	62	34	7	23	46	26	25
In Which Perpetrators are Rewarded	9%	21	3	0	11	10	5	0
In Which Violence is Extremely Intense	10%	24	8	4	11	12	10	20
In Which Violence is Very Graphic	7%	3	1	1	12	12	10	6

Table A, Continued	Over-all %	Police Shows	Ent'mnt. Non-News	Ent'mnt. News & Review	Docu-mentary	News & Public Affairs	Tabloid News	Talk Shows
Violence in Talk Sequences: % if Sequences...								
Discussing Acts	65%	43	53	87	61	61	61	81
Discussing Credible Threats	28%	43	28	17	28	44	29	16
Involving No Harm or Pain	26%	30	24	19	30	29	33	30
Discussing Long-Term Negative Consequences	13%	0	8	19	38	18	11	11
In Which a Gun is Used	24%	37	26	44	33	44	14	16
In Which Perpetrators are Punished	33%	67	15	6	77	29	47	26
In Which Perpetrators are Rewarded	4%	17	0	0	8	6	6	0
In Which Talk is Graphic, Concrete	38%	42	47	28	33	26	38	49
Involves First-Person Testimony	30%	35	38	20	22	20	29	46
Involves Second-Person Testimony	30%	38	35	8	22	35	22	29
Involves Third-Person Testimony	47%	35	31	68	60	55	42	35

TABLE B:

PROFILE OF REALITY-PROGRAM VIOLENCE ACROSS DAYPARTS
N=384 Programs

	Over-all %	6 a.m.-9 a.m.	9 a.m.-3 p.m.	3 p.m.-6 p.m.	6 p.m.-8 p.m.	8 p.m.-11 p.m.
% of Programs with *some* Visual violence	38%	32	18	38	57	61
% of Programs with *some Talk* violence	18%	21	23	24	10	10
Among Programs Which Contain Violence:						
% of Program time in VV sequences	3.3%	4.1	0.9	3.8	4.9	3.9
% of Program time in TAV sequences	2.4%	1.0	2.4	3.1	4.3	4.0
Violence in Visual Sequences: % of Sequences...						
Depicting Acts	61%	72	52	53	66	61
Depicting Credible Threats	34%	35	26	38	43	25
Showing No Harm or Pain	34%	22	26	40	44	25
Showing Long-Term Negative Consequences	13%	10	6	12	13	16
In Which Violence Occurs Offscreen	4%	0	1	1	2	9
In Which a Gun is Used	44%	47	23	46	58	35
In Which Perpetrators are Punished	33%	10	14	40	40	36
In Which Perpetrators are Rewarded	9%	15	0	14	11	6
In Which Violence is Intense	10%	7	6	11	12	11
In Which Violence is Very Graphic	7%	7	2	3	10	7
Violence in Talk Sequences: % of Sequences...						
Discussing Acts	65%	42	76	60	67	60
Discussing Credible Threats	34%	35	26	38	43	25
Involving No Harm or Pain	26%	36	20-	24	21	36

TABLE B, Continued:	Over-all %	6 a.m.-9 a.m.	9 a.m.-3 p.m.	3 p.m.-6 p.m.	6 p.m.-8 p.m.	8 p.m.-11 p.m.
Discussing Long-Term Negative Consequences	13%	11	14	11	10	20
In Which a Gun is Used	24%	23	26	13	34	22
In Which Perpetrators are Punished	32%	17	32	29	45	35
In Which Perpetrators are Rewarded	4%	6	0	0	14	5
In Which Talk is Very Graphic	38%	19	45	44	39	29
Involving First-Person Testimony	30%	7	38	37	21	30
Involving Second-Person Testimony	30%	40	33	31	38	22
Involving Third-Person Testimony	48%	52	38	44	56	54

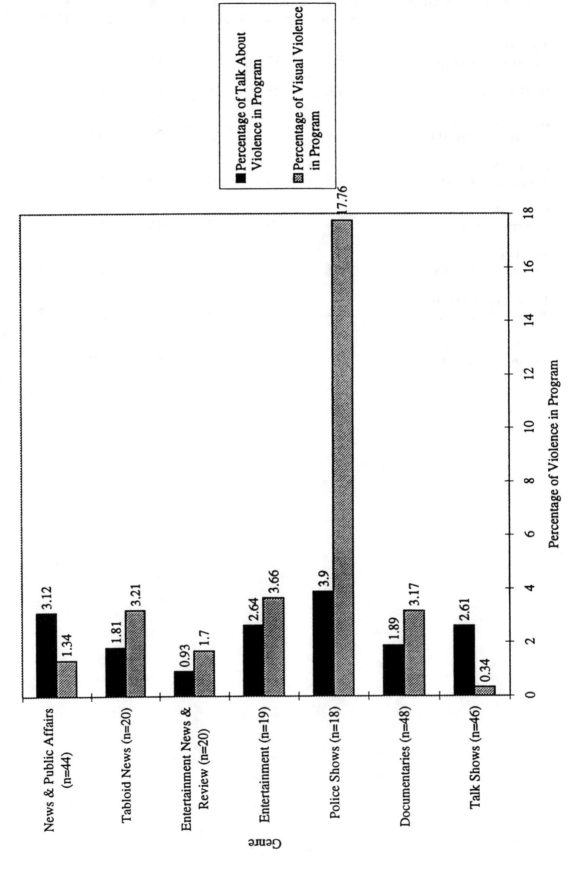

Figure A: Percentage of Violence in Program by Genre. Includes violent programs (n=215) only.

318

Figure B: Percentage of Violence in Program by Daypart. Includes violent programs (n=215) only.

319

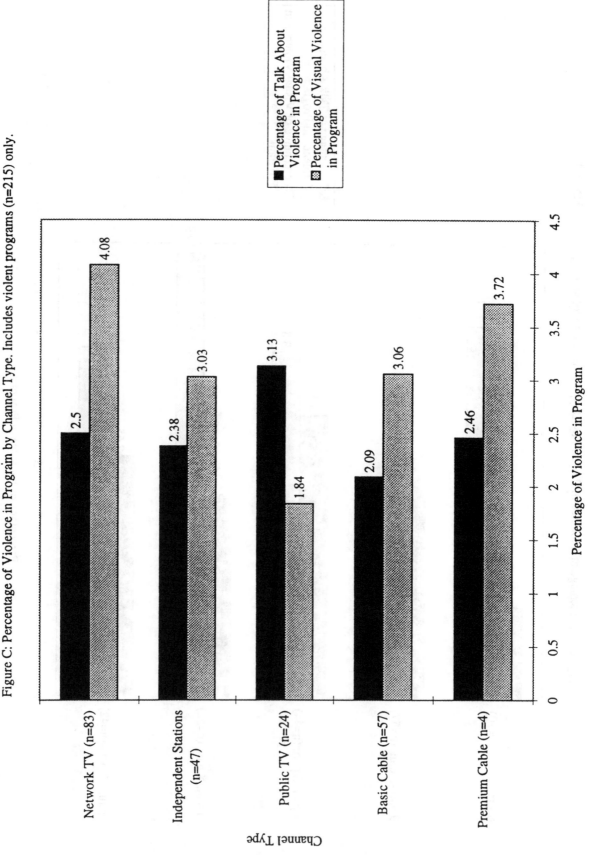

Figure C: Percentage of Violence in Program by Channel Type. Includes violent programs (n=215) only.

320

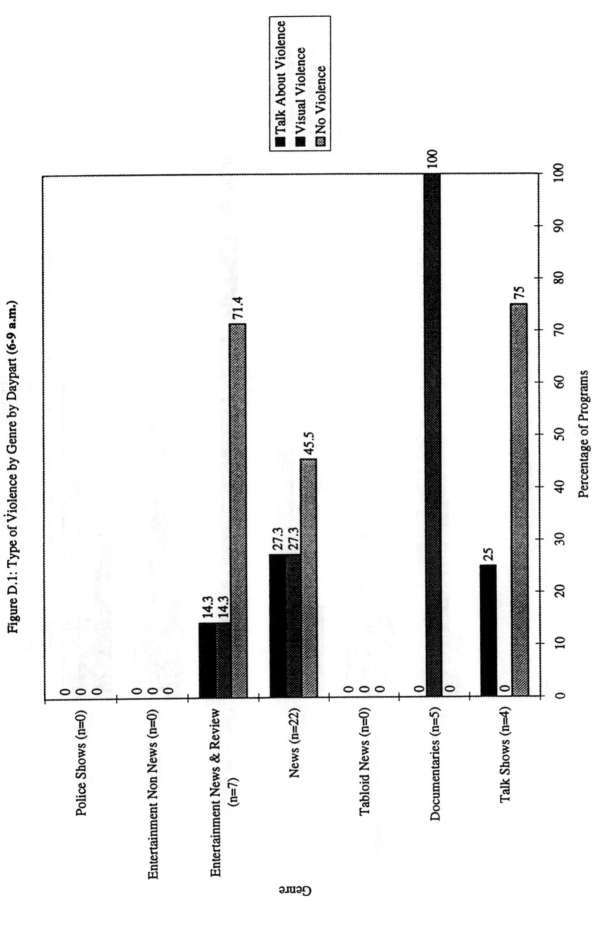

Figure D.1: Type of Violence by Genre by Daypart (6-9 a.m.)

321

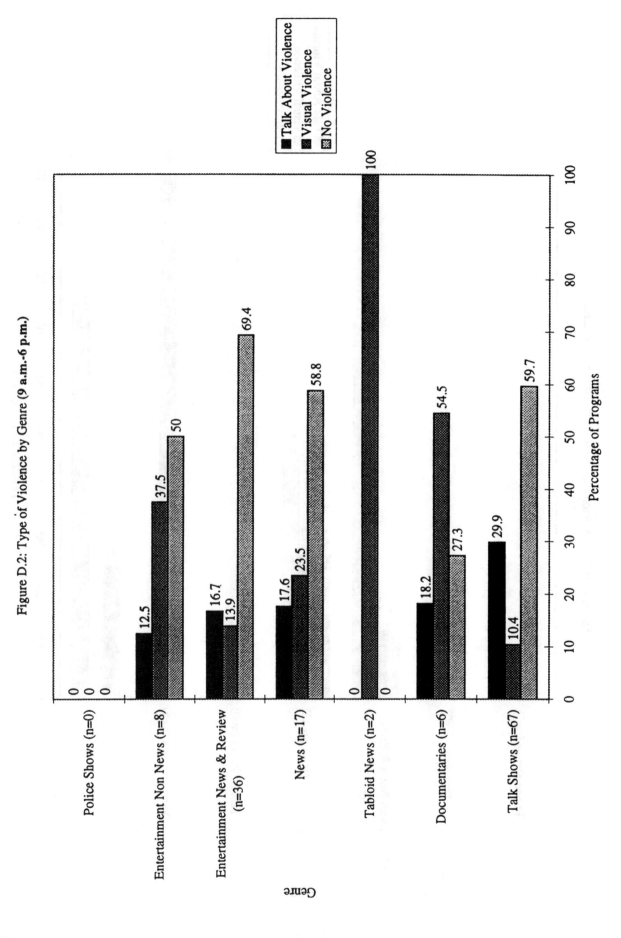

Figure D.2: Type of Violence by Genre (9 a.m.-6 p.m.)

322

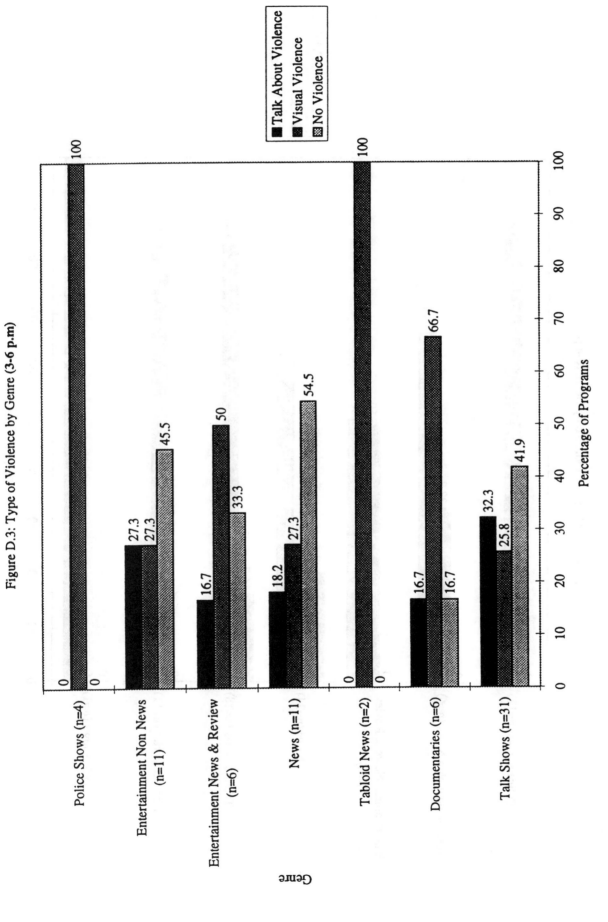

Figure D.3: Type of Violence by Genre (3-6 p.m)

323

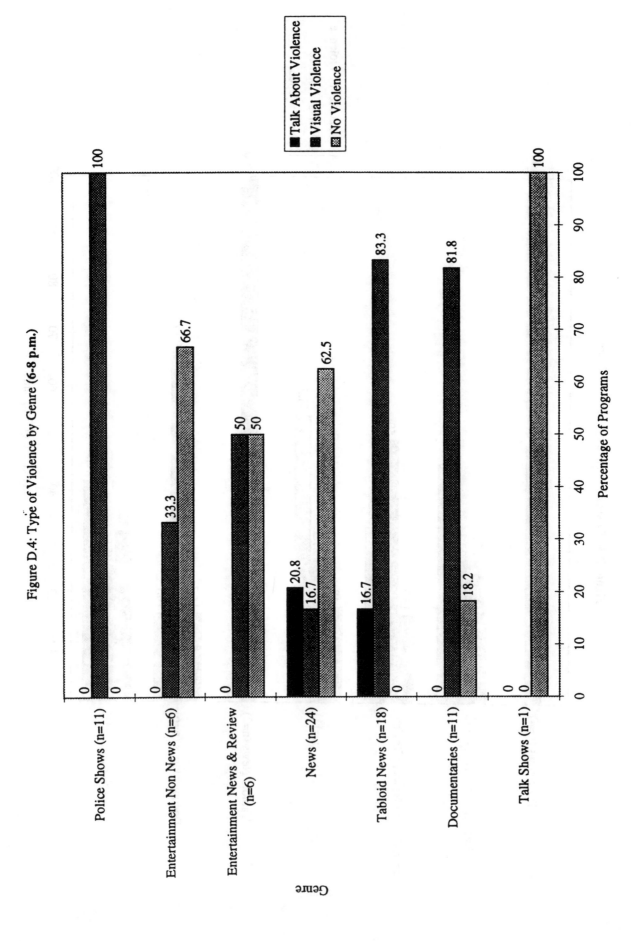

Figure D.4: Type of Violence by Genre (6-8 p.m.)

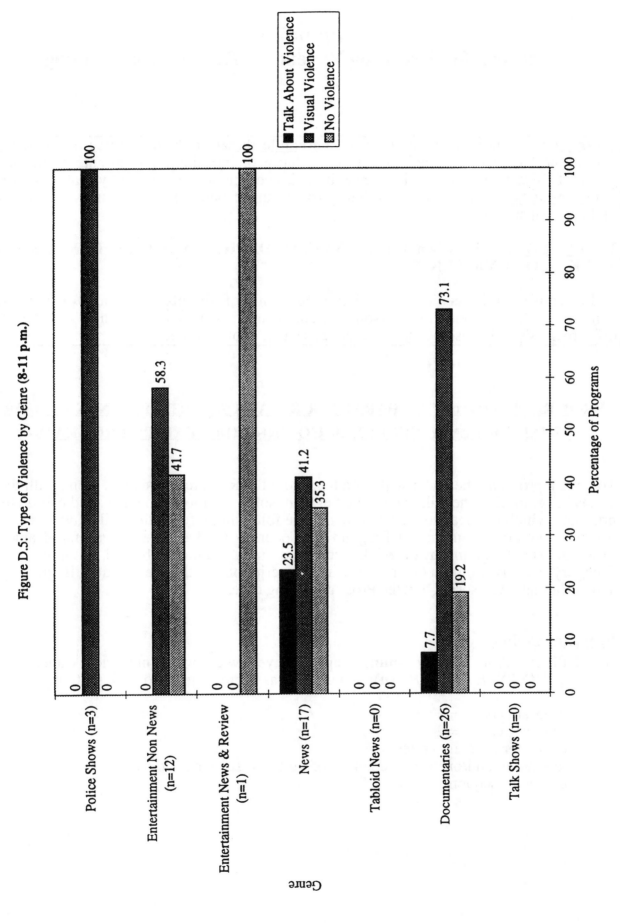

Figure D.5: Type of Violence by Genre (8-11 p.m.)

325

Appendix 4
Codebook for Television Violence in Reality Programming

__Violence__ is defined as any evidence of a <u>credible threat</u> of <u>physical force</u> or the <u>actual use</u> of such a force <u>intended</u> to physically harm or intimidate an animate being or a group of animate beings. Violence also includes certain depictions of physically harmful <u>consequences</u> against an animate being (or group of beings) that occur as a result of violent means.

__VIOLENCE__ is coded when there is a **VISUAL DEPICTION OF VIOLENCE** and/or **TALK ABOUT VIOLENCE.**

Talk about violence is the verbal recounting of threats, acts, and/or harmful consequences by a person or person-like character appearing on screen or heard from off screen. Verbal abuse <u>per se</u> is not coded as talk about violence.

<u>PROGRAM, SEGMENT, CHARACTER & TALK ABOUT VIOLENCE AND/OR VISUAL VIOLENCE SEQUENCE CODING FOR REALITY PROGRAMS</u>

To code a program, the coder will get a tape from the Research Assistant, along with the Texas Program ID; s/he will call up the Segment software, mount the tape, and call up the program, which has been logged and filed. The following information will have already been coded on the program: UT Program ID, Coder ID, MediaScope ID, Program Name, Program Date, Program Day of Week, Scheduled Time, Duration, Channel, Program Category, Reality Program Genre, TV Guide description or other description, Beginning Time, Ratings, Advisories, and the Program ending time.

<u>Program Coding:</u>

1. UT PROGRAM ID *UTID* (**nnnn**): Tape has a yellow dot with a numerical value.
2. RECORD TYPE *RECTYPE* (**n**): A number has been assigned to each section.

> program codes = 1
> segment codes = 2
> character segment codes = 3
> talk about and/or visual depiction of violence sequence codes = 4
> character sequence codes = 5

3. CODER ID *CODID* (**nn**): Each member of the research team at UT has been given a two-digit unique identification code. The team member logging in the tape should list her or his code here. The codes are:

Wayne Danielson = 01
Nick Lasorsa = 02
Ellen Wartella = 03
Chuck Whitney = 04
Shannon Campbell = 05
Marlies Klijn = 07
Adriana Olivarez = 08
Diane Quest = 20
Sylvana Fierro = 22
Neil Pollner = 26
Rafael Lopez = 28

Pamela Rivero = 29
Meredith Butler = 32
Lisa Wyatt = 34
Alison Cabral = 35
Arlene Rivero = 36
Jacqui Osman = 37
Alice Tsai = 38

4. MS PROGRAM ID *MSID* (**nnnn**): Tape label contains a five-digit unique alphanumeric code, four numbers followed by the letter "D." The program ID is the four numbers, minus the trailing "D."

5. PROGRAM NAME *NAME* (**nnnn**): Program name is contained on tape label. Use the following alphabetized list of reality programs to find the four-digit code for the program. As new programs come along, we will add them to the list by assigning them a number halfway between the two listed programs that sandwich it. For example, if the program name is "American Advertising," it gets the number 1075, halfway between "American Adventures-History" and "American Baby." Then, if we add "American Aeroplanes," it gets the number 1087, halfway between "American Advertising" and "American Baby." Thus, whenever a program is added to the list, the list of program names itself needs to be updated. (In following list, "SYN" = syndicated; "?" = unknown channel/network.)

Adam Smith = 0900
America & the Courts (?) = 1000
American Adventures-History (PBS) = 1050
American Adventurer = 1075
American Cinema = 1115
American Experience (?) = 1125
American Journal (SYN) = 1150
American Justice (A&E) = 1200
America's Funniest Home Videos (ABC) = 1250
Ancient Mysteries (A&E) = 1350
Arthur Ashe = 1375
Atlantic Record Story = 1400

Backyard America (FAM) = 1500
Barbara Walters Special (ABC) = 1550
Baseball = 1625
Behind Closed Doors (NBC) = 1675

Behind the Veil....Nuns = 1725
Biography (A&E) = 1800
Bob Navarro's Journal = 1825

California Gold (PBS) = 1950
CBS This Morning (CBS) = 2000
Celebrity Interviews = 2025
Champlin on Film (BRV) = 2050
Charles Perez (FOX) = 2075
City View (?) = 2150
Civil War Journal (A&E) = 2200
Cops (SYN?) = 2400
Court TV (SYN) = 2450
Crazy about the Movies = 2475
Cuban Missile Crisis = 2525
Current Affair (SYN) = 2550

Dateline (NBC) = 2650
David L. Wolper Presents (A&E) = 2700
Day One = 2725
Dennis Prager (?) = 2750

Entertainment Tonight (SYN) = 3000
EXTRA (SYN) = 3050
Eye on Sports = 3075
Eye to Eye with Connie Chung (CBS) = 3100

First Business = 3312
Flix News (VH-1) = 3325
Frontline (PBS) = 3375
Frontrunners = 3362
Fun and Feel of the 50's = 3388
Future Quest = 3395
48 Hours (CBS) = 3400

Geraldo (SYN) = 3500
Good Day L.A. (?) = 3550
Good Morning America (ABC) = 3600
Gordon Elliot (SYN?) = 3650
Great Depression = 3662
Great Railway Stories = 3675

Hard Copy (SYN) = 3850
Healthy Kids (FAM) = 3950
Highway Patrol (CBS) = 3985
Hollywood Insider (USA) = 4000
Homeward Bound = 4015
Howard Cossell Biography (A&E)= 4025

In Search Of ... (A&E) = 4250
Inside Academy Award = 4325
Inside Edition (SYN) = 4350
Internet Show = 4375
Intimate Portrait: Grace Kelly = 4450
Investigative Reports (A&E) = 4400

Jane Whitney (?) = 4500
Jenny Jones (SYN) = 4550
Jerry Springer (?) = 4600
Jones & Jury (KCAL) = 4700

L.A. Stories (?) = 4950
Last Years of Marvin Gaye, The (A&E) = 5025
Lead Story (BET) = 5050
Leeza (SYN?) = 5100
Life & Times (PBS) = 5150
Life Stories: Families in Crisis (HBO) = 5175

MacNeil-Lehrer (PBS) = 5350
Madonna-Making of Take a Bow (MTV) = 5375
Main Floor (?) = 5400
Making of Bram Stroker's Dracula = 5525
Making Welfare Work = 5575
Marilu (SYN) = 5550
Marilyn Kagen (KCAL) = 5552
Marriage Counselor (LIF) = 5600
Maury Povich (SYN) = 5650
Meet the Press (NBC) = 5750
Memories and Dreams = 5775
Midday Sunday = 5785
Mike and Maty (SYN) = 5800
Montel Williams (SYN) = 5850
MTV News Special Report = 6000
MTV Winter Carnival = 6050

National Geographic (PBS?) = 6100
Nature (PBS) = 6150
Newsreels (AMC)= 6175
Nightline (ABC) = 6250
Nightly Business Report (PBS) = 6300
Nirvana Tribute = 6325
Nova (PBS) = 6350

OJ Simpson: The Trial (NBC)= 6400
OJ Tonight = 6425
One on One with Charlie Neal (BET) = 6450
Ooh La La (LIF) = 6500
Oprah Winfrey (SYN) = 6550
Other Epidemic = 6560
Other Side (NBC) = 6575
Our Home (LIF) = 6600
Our Voices (BET) =6650

Pacesetters (?) = 6700
Pandora's Box = 6725
Phil Donahue (SYN) = 6850
Prime Time Live (ABC) = 7000
Psychology: The Study of Human Behavior (PBS) = 7050

Queens (LIF) = 7150

Real Stories of the Highway Patrol (SYN?) = 7250
Real World (MTV) = 7300
Regis and Kathie Lee (SYN) = 7400
Rescue 911 (CBS) = 7450
Richard Bey (?) = 7500
Ricki Lake (SYN) = 7550
Road to the Superbowl (FOX) = 7555
Rush Limbaugh (SYN) = 7700

Sally Jesse Raphael (SYN) = 7800
Screen Scene (BET) = 7900
Sightings (FOX) = 8000
Siskel & Ebert (SYN?) = 8050
Straight Dope (MTV) = 8200
Street Scenes-NY on Film (AMC) = 8225
Sunday Morning (CBS) = 8230
Susan Powter (?) = 8250

Suzanne Somers (SYN) = 8300
60 Minutes (CBS) = 8350

Teen Summit (BET) = 8400
Think Tank (PBS) =8425
This is Your Life (AMC) = 8450
This Week with David Brinkley (ABC) = 8500
Time Machine = 8525
Today (NBC) = 8550
Tony Brown's Journal (PBS) = 8600
To the Contrary (PBS) = 8650
Top Cops (?) = 8700
Trailside (PBS) = 8750
Trauma Center (?) = 8800
20/20 (ABC) = 8950
20th Century (A&E) = 9000

Universe: The Infinite Frontier
Unsolved Mysteries (LIF) = 9100

Visit L.A. (?) = 9250
Visiting with Huell Howser = 9275

Wall Street Journal Report (?) = 9300
Wall Street Week (PBS) = 9350
Walt Disney World (DIS) = 9375
Weekend Gallery = 9425
Week in Rock (MTV) = 9450
What Every Baby Knows (LIF) = 9500
With the President (DIS) = 9525
Women's Voices (PBS)= 9635
World of Nature (A&E) = 9550

6. PROGRAM DATE *DATE* (**mmddyy**): Copied from tape label.

7. PROGRAM DAY *DAY* (**n**). Day of the week on which the program was aired.

   Sunday = 1
   Monday = 2
   Tuesday = 3
   Wednesday = 4
   Thursday = 5
   Friday = 6
   Saturday =7

8. SCHEDULED TIME *TIME* (**nnnn**): Use the 24-hour clock.

      1 a.m. = 0100
      1:35 a.m. = 0135
      9 a.m. = 0900
      9:35 a.m. = 0935
      12 p.m. (noon) = 1200
      12:35 p.m. = 1235
      1 p.m. = 1300
      1:35 p.m. = 1335
      9 p.m. = 2100
      9:35 p.m. = 2135
      12 a.m. (midnight) = 2400
      12:35 a.m. = 2435

9. DURATION *LENGTH* (**nnn**) (in minutes): Copied from tape label.

10. CHANNEL *CH* (**nn**): Tape label gives network or independent channel on which program appears; translate to 2-digit code.

      ABC = 01 (American Broadcasting Company)
      AMC = 02 (American Movie Classics)
      A&E = 03 (Arts & Entertainment Network)
      BET = 04 (Black Entertainment Television)
      BRV = 05 (Bravo)
      CAR = 06 (Cartoon Network)
      CBS = 07 (Columbia Broadcasting System)
      DIS = 08 (Disney Channel)
      FAM = 09 (Family Channel)
      FOX = 10 (Fox Broadcasting Company)
      HBO = 11 (Home Box Office)
      KCAL = 12 (L.A. Independent Channel 9)
      KCOP = 13 (L.A. Independent Channel 13)
      KTLA = 14 (L.A. Independent Channel 5)
      LIF = 15 (Lifetime)
      MAX = 16 (Cinemax)
      MTV = 17 (Music Television)
      NBC = 18 (National Broadcasting Company)
      NIK = 19 (Nickelodeon)
      PBS = 20 (Public Broadcasting System)
      SHO = 21 (Showtime)
      TMC = 22 (The Movie Channel)
      TNT = 23 (Turner Network Television)
      USA = 24 (USA Network)
      VH1 = 25 (Video Hits One)

11. MS PROGRAM CATEGORY *CAT* (**nn**): A one- to three-letter code appears on the tape label. Translate it into this two-digit code.

        CA = Children's Animated Show = 01
        CL = Children's Live-Action Show = 02
        CS = Comedy Series = 03
        DAY = Daytime Serial = 04
        DOC = Documentary = 05
        DS = Drama Series = 06
        ES = Entertainment Special or Variety Series = 07
        GS = Game Show = 08
        IHS = Infomercial or Home Shopping Show =09
        IS = Instructional Show = 10
        MOW = Movie of the Week = 11
        MT = Movie: Theatrical = 12
        MV = Music Video = 13
        N   = News = 14
        NM = News Magazine = 15
        RS = Reality Show = 16
        RP = Religious Programming = 17
        S   = Sports = 18
        TS = Talk or Interview Show = 19

12. UT REALITY PROGRAM GENRE *GENRE* (**nn**): Reality programs are to be subcategorized as follows:

        CS = Court Shows = 01
        DS = Documentary Shows = 02
        ENRS = Entertainment News and Review Shows = 03
        IS = Instructional Shows = 04
        MMS = Morning Magazine Shows = 05
        NMS = News Magazine Shows = 06
        NDS = News Discussion Shows = 07
        NTIS = News Talk Interview Show = 08
        RDS = Reality Drama Shows = 09
        RES = Reality Entertainment Shows = 10
        TNS = Tabloid News Shows = 11
        TS = Talk Shows = 12

13. TV GUIDE DESCRIPTION/*TVGUIDE* (**n**): Is there a program description in the <u>TV Guide</u>?

    1. no
    2. yes

14. PROGRAM TOPIC *TOPIC* (**alpha**): Type program description as it appears in the <u>TV Guide</u>; if there isn't a description, use your own words to describe the program.

15. PROGRAMMING BEGINNING TIME *PROBEG* (**nnnn**): Record the beginning of the program as it appears on the TV monitor.

16. PRESENCE OF PROGRAM MOVIE RATING *PRESPRO* (**n**): How is the program movie rating conveyed ?

      1. oral
      2. written
      3. both oral and written
      9. none

17. PROGRAM MOVIE RATING *MRATE* (**n**): At the beginning of the program, which, if any, of the following movie-type ratings is given?

      1. G / General Audience.
      2. PG / Parental Guidance.
      3. PG-13 / Parents Strongly Cautioned.
      4. R / Restricted.
      5. NC-17 / No Children Under 17 Admitted.
      6. X
      7. NR / This movie is not rated.
      9. No movie-type rating given.

18. PRESENCE OF VIOLENCE RATING *PRESVIO* (**n**): How is the violence movie rating conveyed ?

      1. oral
      2. written
      3. both oral and written
      9. none

19. VIOLENCE RATING *VRATE* (**n**): At the beginning of the program, which, if any, of the following violence ratings is given? (Rating should include the word *violence* or *violent*. For other types of ratings, see below.)

      1. MV / Mild Violence.
      2. V / Violence.
      3. GV / Graphic Violence.
      4. Other violence rating.
      9. No violence rating given.

20. PRESENCE OF RAPE RATING *PRESRAPE* (**n**): How is the rape rating conveyed?

      1. oral
      2. written
      3. both oral and written
      9. none

21. RAPE RATING *RRATE* (**n**): At the beginning of the program, which, if any, of the following rape ratings is given?

1. R / Rape.
2. RP / Rape.
3. Other rape rating.
9. No rape rating given.

22. PRESENCE OF NUDITY RATING *PRESNUD* (**n**): How is the nudity rating conveyed?

   1. oral
   2. written
   3. both oral and written
   9. none

23. NUDITY RATING *NRATE* (**n**): At the beginning of the program, which, if any, of the following nudity ratings is given?

1. BN / Brief nudity.
2. N / Nudity.
3. Other nudity rating given.
9. No nudity rating given.

24. PRESENCE OF LANGUAGE RATING *PRESLANG* (**n**): How is the language rating conveyed?

   1. oral
   2. written
   3. both oral and written
   9. none

25. LANGUAGE RATING *LRATE* (**n**): At the beginning of the program, which, if any, of the following language ratings is given?

1. AL / Adult language.
2. GL / Graphic language.
3. Other language rating given.
9. No laguage rating given.

26. PRESENCE OF ADULT-CONSENT RATING *PRESAD* (**n**): How is the adult-consent rating conveyed?

   1. oral
   2. written
   3. both oral and written
   9. none

27. ADULT-CONTENT RATING *ARATE* (**n**): At the beginning of the program, which, if any, of the following adult-content ratings is given?

    1. AC / Adult content.
    2. SC / Strong sexual content.
    3. Other adult-content rating given.
    9. No adult-content rating given.

28. DOES IT HAVE AN ORAL PROGRAM ADVISORY *PROORAL* (**n**):

    1. no
    2. yes

29. TYPE IN ORAL ADVISORY *ORALTXT* (**alpha**): *Record <u>verbatim</u> any viewer advisories given* (e.g., "Contains some violent content; parental discretion advised." "Viewer discretion advised.") If none appears, type "none."

30. DOES IT HAVE A WRITTEN PROGRAM ADVISORY *PROWRIT* (**n**):

    1. no
    2. yes

31. TYPE IN WRITTEN ADVISORY *WRITTXT* (**alpha**) *Record <u>verbatim</u> any viewer advisories given* (e.g., "Contains some violent content; parental discretion advised." "Viewer discretion advised.") If none appears, type "none."

32. PROGRAM ENDS *PROEND* (**nnnnnn**): Record the end of the program as it appears on the TV monitor.

Segment Coding:

CODER NOW BEGINS SEGMENT CODING, BEGINNING WITH FIRST SEGMENT. The beginning and ending times of the segment will be provided for you.

You are responsible for identifying the beginning and ending times of **Talk about Violence** and/or **Visual Violence** sequences within the segment. Please write the times on the "Talk about Violence and/or Visual Violence Sequence(s)" sheet. Sequence numbers are continuous throughout the program regardless of the segment number.

A *segment* is defined as a *coherent part of a broadcast, a partitioned narrative within a program that exhibits unity within itself and separation, by topic and/or, central focal character, from other segments within a program.* All reality programs have <u>at least</u> two segments. A teaser is **always** considered segment #1. When there is no teaser, leave segment #1 blank and identify that there is "no teaser" in item 10 (segment topic). Then continue to code the next segment as #2. Examples: Separate stories within a news, news magazine or reality program, are coded as separate segments. Where stories are "roundups," as in a weather story with details or visuals of bad weather in several places, they are still considered a single segment. Most talk shows (eg, Oprah, Phil Donahue) routinely treat a single topic (e.g., guns in schools) and will be coded as a single segment. Where a talk show treats more than one topic, and the topics are readily differentiable, those topics should be coded as separate segments. Commercial breaks may or may not signal a transition from one segment to another.

Please note the *pause beginning and end times* for commercial breaks, any interruptions and the news stories in the morning news shows (i.e. Good Morning America, CBS This Morning and The Today Show). Please label "news" pauses as such.

1. UT PROGRAM ID *UTID* (**nnnn**): Tape has a yellow dot with a numerical value.
2. RECORD TYPE *RECTYPE* (**n**): A number has been assigned to each section.

    program codes = 1
    segment codes = 2
    character segment codes = 3
    talk about and/or visual depiction of violence sequence codes = 4
    character sequence codes = 5

3. CODER ID *CODID* (**nn**): Each member of the research team at UT has been given a two-digit unique identification code.

4. SEGMENT NUMBER *SEGNUM* (**nn**): Begin with 01; code each in time order in broadcast.

5. SEGMENT BEGINS *SEGBEG* (**nnnnnn**): Round to nearest second from on-screen counter.

6. DOES IT HAVE AN ORAL PROGRAM ADVISORY *PROORAL* (**n**):

    1. no
    2. yes

7. DOES IT HAVE A WRITTEN PROGRAM ADVISORY *PROWRIT* (**n**):

    1. no
    2. yes

8. TYPE IN ORAL ADVISORY *ORALTXT* (**alpha**): *Record verbatim any viewer advisories given* (e.g., "Contains some violent content; parental discretion advised." "Viewer discretion advised.") If none appears, please type "none."

9. TYPE IN WRITTEN ADVISORY *WRITTXT* (**alpha**): *Record verbatim any viewer advisories given* (e.g., "Contains some violent content; parental discretion advised." "Viewer discretion advised.") If none appears, please type "none."

10. SEGMENT TOPIC, NARRATIVE SUMMARY *SEGTOP* (**alpha**): Write a one- to two-sentence capsule description of what the segment concerns; the summary should include *what* is described, *who* is involved, and, if relevant, *when and where* it occurred.

SEGMENT TOPIC
The main themes, subjects, issues and aspects of individual stories should be coded to assess each subject's emphasis in the story. Go through the following themes (#11-30) and code each theme as the following:

    1=**no attention paid** to this theme, subject, issue in segment
    2=theme, subject, issue is present in segment, but **minor attention is given**
    3=**major theme, subject, issue** in segment

---

11. INTERNATIONAL POLITICS *INTERPOL* (**n**): Includes: international negotiations, treaty or agreement signings, international meetings of intergovernmental or nongovernmental organizations, official state visits, unofficial visits of individuals or groups, formal diplomatic procedures, alleged or confirmed treaty violations, arms negotiations <u>dealing with two or more countries</u>.

12. NATIONAL POLITICS. *NATPOL* (**n**): Includes: national and regional policy; national or regional ceremony or celebration; ceremony in one country for events in another country; appoinment, resignation or death of a public official; operations of party organizations; meetings of national and regional political organizations; national or regional elections or campaigns. Also includes operations and resolutions of national or subnational legislative bodies on legal, budgetary, or fiscal issues. <u>National politics affects only one country.</u>

13. ESPIONAGE/SURVEILLANCE *ESPION* (**n**): Police or private investigation (e.g. a detective to follow someone for personal, criminal or other reasons); domestic and international spying or intelligence agency operations and economic (including industrial) or political espionage.

14. WAR/ARMED FORCES *WARTOPIC* (**n**): Actual organized collective violence, or threat thereof. Concerns both regular and irregular armed forces. Includes irregular transfer of power, attempted coups, civil strife (violent confrontations between opposing factions or between advocates and police), civil war (factions are armed with autonomous bases of support), guerilla war (organized factions operating from largely independent bases of operations); military budget allocations, research and development, testing, and development of conventional weapons systems, aid and training for foreign military forces, war game; military personnel, organizations and style of life.

15. BUSINESS, INDUSTRY AND LABOR *BUSINESS* (**n**): Includes production, construction, transportation, finance, broad questions of economy and money.

16. FINANCIAL STRESS/SUCCESS *FINSTRES* (**n**): Includes financial hardship, unemployment, poverty, homelessness; economically "downbeat"; prizes, inheritances, raises, lottery winnings; economically "upbeat"

17. LAW ENFORCEMENT/LEGAL/CRIME/VIOLENCE *LAWENFOR* (**n**): Includes police, other agents and agencies of law, and prisons; executions and police brutality; all aspects of the judicial process, grand jury deliberations and findings, indictments or charges dropped, trials, convictions or acquittals, serving or termination of sentences, appeals processes, and deliberations of higher judicial bodies (e.g., the US Supreme Court); crimes by ordinary people and public or corporate officials; corruption; illegality, gross (criminal) injustice.

18. SCIENCE/TECHNOLOGY *SCIENCE* (**n**): Includes scientific research; announcement of death of a scientist; budgetary problems; social scientific procedures and facilities; laboratory research; "High Tech" or innovative technology, judged with respect to the story contents.

19. EDUCATION *EDUCATE* (**n**): Includes education systems and libraries; budgetary problems; schools, teachers, students, study.

20. COMMUNICATIONS *COMMS* (**n**): Includes mass media; entertainment; press, radio, tv, show business, spectator sports, books; as well as point to point interpersonal communication devices (post, telegraph, telephone, fax).

21. HEALTH AND MEDICINE *HEALTH* (**n**): Includes physical and mental health.

22. RELIGION *RELIGION* (**n**): Includes church, clergy, religious customs, rituals, paganism, satanism.

23. FAMILY *FAMILY* (**n**): Includes marriage, upbringing of children, domestic problems, inter-generational relations, children, youth, old age, pregnancy (issues such as adoption, abortion, in vitro fertilization fit into this theme).

24. LEISURE RECREATION/SPORTS AND PHYSICAL CULTURE/TOURISM/ CULTURE *LEISURE* (**n**): Includes games involving physical activity, training; fitness; professional and amateur sports. Coach travel only in the context of sightseeing or vacationing not for strictly business travel. This also includes arts and entertainment.

25. NATURE *NATURE* (**n**): Includes natural resources, astronomical phenomena, etc. Code for any appearance, mention or reference of animals in the program as well as natural disasters (includes earthquakes, hurricanes, droughts, etc.) and ecology/environmental concerns or issues.

26. MAN-MADE DISASTERS AND ACCIDENTS *MAN-MADE* (**n**): Includes transportation and industrial accidents, etc.

27. SUPERNATURAL *SUPER* (**n**): Mystical, occult; superstition, miracles, ghosts, astrology, fortune-telling, witchcraft, action of supernatural forces.

28. MINORITY GROUPS AND PEOPLE *MINORITY* (**n**): Includes racial, religious, national, ethnic, sexual and gender minorities. Homosexuals, bisexuals, gender discrimination, feminism, etc. should be coded under this theme.

29. DEATH AND DYING *DEATH* (**n**)

30. SEXUAL INTERACTION*SEX* (**n**): Includes relationships; sexual or otherwise, mistresses, dating, friendships.

31. SEGMENT LOCALE *SEGLOC* (**nn**)[1] : Code the setting of the main topic and not where the show is produced. Example: A discussion on Africa in *Lead Story*, a program produced in Washington D.C., would be coded as #4. [U.S. regions are by Census Bureau designation, which further aggregates regions into East (New England and Middle Atlantic), Midwest (E. North Central, W. North Central), South (South Atlantic, E. South Central, W. South Central) and West (Mountain, Pacific); we're separating out Washington, DC, which Census Bureau locates in South Atlantic/South.]

---

[1] Again, a summary judgement is called for. Our aim here is to establish whether the segment would suggest to an ordinary viewer *where* the segment occurred or where characters or figures described in the segment might live or call home. As with several other codes, you need to focus on the **manifest content** of the segment. That is, code only what you see and hear in the segment, using your own knowledge of the world sparingly. For example, if there are no verbal cues about the location of a segment, but you recognize in a visual shot that the city depicted is Chicago, you should code that *not* as 14: E.N. Central, but as 22: Locale in U.S. *The one exception to this general rule is if it is reasonable to assume that the average viewer, absent explicit cues, would be able to identify the locale:* For example, a story on Federal legislation showing the Capitol but not explicitly stating that it is in Washington, DC, would be coded as Washington, DC, anyway. And references to the O.J. Simpson trial would be coded as Pacific, even if no explicit reference is made to Los Angeles.

01.	No identifiable locale, NA
02.	Europe, Russia
03.	Middle East, Islamic former Soviet states (Incl. Egypt).
04.	Africa
05.	Asia, Indian subcontinent, Sri Lanka, Indonesia, Pacific Islands.
06.	Australia, New Zealand, Tasmania
07.	Canada
08.	Caribbean
09.	Mexico
10.	Central and South America.
11.	Washington, DC
12.	New England (ME, NH, VT, MA, RI, CT)
13.	Middle Atlantic (NY, NJ, PA)
14.	E. North Central (OH, IL, IN, MI, WI)
15.	W. North Central (MN, ND, SD, NE, KS)
16.	South Atlantic (DE, MD, VA, WV, NC, SC, GA, FL)
17.	E. South Central (KY, TN, AL, MS)
18.	W. South Central (AR, LA, MO, OK, TX)
19.	Mountain (MT, ID, WY, CO, NM, AZ, UT, NV)
20.	Pacific (WA, OR, CA, AK, HI)
21.	Multiple locales, all outside United States.
22.	Locale in US, focus on entire nation, multiple regions, or further subdivision impossible or irrelevant
23.	Multiple locales in U.S. and outside U.S.

32. SOCIAL SETTING *SOCSET* (**n**)[2] :

1. Outside United States, NA
2. Inside US, no cues about setting or multiple settings at different levels.
3. U.S. locale, within a city.
4. U.S., suburban or generic residential area.
5. U.S., town or village.
6. U.S., rural or uninhabited area.
7. Multiple locales in U.S. and outside U.S.

---

[2] Again, the idea is potential identity that viewers might ascribe: Does this involve someplace like where I live? As noted, all non-US locales are coded as 1. After that, look for cues about where the talk or action is located. As was true in the "Segment Locale" code, deal with manifest content only, using your personal knowledge only to the extent you are reasonably certain that the average viewer would have the same knowledge; otherwise, use the more general codes. *Studio location*--where the program was taped, as in talk shows and news-interview shows, is *not* the social setting: Rather, the setting is where the discussion is focused. A "city" is any place with large population, and any city large enough to have an airport with jet service qualifies as a city. Visual cues would include high-rise buildings, large hospitals, police stations, or city halls. Suburbs feature concentrated, but largely single family housing and the absence of high-rise buildings; largely residential areas of cities and large population areas that are primarily residential with no substantial center-city areas (e.g., Plano, Tx) should be coded as suburban. If you are unable to guess population size, but clues imply an area is residential, code it 4.
5: town or village implies a settled and organized area large enough to have a mayor, a shopping area and traffic lights. 6: Rural and uninhibited areas have open spaces, scattered housing, if any housing at all, and few streets.

33. REENACTMENT-RECREATION *REENACT* (**n**)[3] :

1. Segment contains no apparent reenactments or recreations of past events.
2. Segment contains one or more apparent reenactments.

34. TALK ABOUT VIOLENCE (TAV) *SEGTAV* (**n**): Does this segment contain talk about violence?

1. No
2. Yes (Identify beginning times on "Identifying TAV and VV" Sheet)
3. Yes, only in **teaser/promo/preview/transition** appearing in <u>second segment </u> or subsequent segments (Identify beginning times on "Identifying TAV and VV" Sheet)

35. VISUAL VIOLENCE (VV) *SEGVV* (**n**): Does this segment contain visual depiction of violence?

1. No
2. Yes (Identify beginning times on "Identifying TAV and VV" Sheet)
3. Yes, only in **teaser/promo/preview/transition** appearing in <u>second segment</u> or subsequent segments (Identify beginning times on "Identifying TAV and VV" Sheet)

If the answer to either Question 34 (SEGTAV) and/or Question 35 (SEGVV) is "2" (yes, this non-teaser-like segment contains talk about violence and/or visual depiction of violence) then the SEGMENT is analyzed further regarding the nature of the segment's talk about violence and/or visual depiction of violence, specifically, its narrative purpose, its realism, its depictions of harm and pain, and its depictions of rewards and punishments.

Please note: The first segment will probably have "teaser qualities", but it is not identified as such. In other words, response option 9 does not apply to questions 34 & 35 when coding the first segment of a program.

If the answer to Questions 34 & 35 is "no", your response to questions #36-41 is **9) Not applicable**.

---

[3]A reenactment/recreation is the use of live actors, who may or may not be the original participants in a past event, to reconstruct or relive that event; a reconstruction of the event. An oral recounting of the event is not considered a reenactment.

36. PAIN CUES *PAINCUES* (**n**)[4] : Considering the segment as a whole, does the pain and suffering of the victim go beyond the victim and perpetrator, and impact also upon families, friends or communities?

    1. no
    2. yes
    9. Not applicable

37. ANTI-VIOLENT ALTERNATIVES *ALTERNAT* (**n**)[5] : Considering the segment as a whole, are alternatives to violent action presented or considered?

    1. no
    2. yes
    9. Not applicable

38. PROGRAM REALISM *REALISM* (**n**): Code the segment into one of the following four categories:

    1. **actual reality only**--coverage of real events; program attempts to convey events as they actually occurred; no actors are used; although editing may be used in the production process, the segment uses footage of actual events; example: 60 Minutes.

    2. **recreation of reality**--reenactments of real events, although some events or dialogue may be fictionalized; example: movie JFK.

    3. **fictional**--not based on real events but the events could happen in reality; note that animated characters possessing human-like characteristics who engage in actions that could happen in reality (for example, The Simpsons) would be coded as fictional; example: Roseanne.

    4. **fantasy**--either the characters or settings are fantastic, that is, they could not exist; example: Bugs Bunny.

    9. NOT APPLICABLE

---

[4] We need to see empathy for the pain and suffering of the victim in significant others. For example, after a major character in the film *Boys in the Hood* is killed, we see an extended scene of his family members displaying significant emotional pain over his death.

[5] To pass this test, an alternative must be presented or discussed as a better way to deal with problems than is violence. A father who tells his son to fight back against a bully is NOT providing alternatives to violence. However, if he presents alternatives, even if they are not carried out, the test is met. For example, the film *Kids Killing Kids* suggests ways to resolve problems without resorting to violence.

39. OVERALL HARM/PAIN *POSTVIO* (**n**): Considering the segment as a whole, pain and/or harm that occur as a result of the violence:

    1. is not depicted.
    2. is generally depicted within the violent sequence(s) only.
    3. is generally depicted beyond the violent sequence(s) itself.
    9. NOT APPLICABLE

40. REWARDS *REWARDS* (**n**)[6]: Considering the segment as a whole, the violence is:

    1. not rewarded.
    2. rewarded only at the end of the segment
    3. rewarded
    9. NOT APPLICABLE

41. PUNISHMENT *PUNISH* (**n**)[7]: Considering the segment as a whole, the violence is:

    1. punished.
    2. punished at the end of segment.
    3. not punished.
    9. NOT APPLICABLE

42. SEGMENT ENDS *SEGENDS* (**nnnnnn**): Coder will be given the time the segment ends

Character Coding:

CHARACTER CODES: In a segment, we are coding <u>only</u> those characters involved in violence. They may or may not participate in a particular sequence, but they must play a significant role in the violence that occurs in the segment. Note, however, the time a character plays a significant role within the program determines the time the actual character appears. Groups where individuals are indistinguishable should be coded as

---

[6] A reward is a positive reinforcement that is delivered in return for violence. A reward is <u>not</u> the absence of punishment. Rewards can occur during or immediately after the violent action. Rewards can come in several different forms. There are three types of rewards: <u>self-praise</u> (an overt verbal or nonverbal sign of approval or satisfaction that a perpetrator expresses), <u>praise from other</u> (any overt or nonverbal sign of approval or satisfaction that observers/bystanders express towards a violent action), and <u>material reward</u> (a tangible, physical token of compensation that is given or taken for violence).

[7] A punishment is a negative reinforcement that is delivered in return for violence. Punishments can occur during or immediately after the violent action. Punishments come in four specific forms: <u>condemnation from self</u> (an overt verbal or nonverbal sign of disapproval, disappointment or dissatisfaction that a perpetrator expresses for acting violently), <u>condemnation from other except from the target of violence</u> (any overt verbal or nonverbal sign of disapproval, disappointment or dissatisfaction that observers/bystanders express toward a violent action), <u>nonviolent action</u> (any overt nonviolent behavior that is designed to stop vice or hinder further violence by penalizing it. Nonviolent action involves somehow restricting the freedom of a perpetrator), and <u>violent action from other</u> (refers to any violent threat or behavior that an observer, bystander or third party directs towards the perpetrator in order to try to stop or punish the perpetrator's previous violence towards a target. Violent action cannot come from the target nor any target the perpetrator has threatened to harm or actually harmed within the same violent sequence).

one character with an ID number. Only those individuals who are clearly identifiable characters, directly involved with violence, are separate characters. Character numbering will be at the program level and characters will retain their original ID number throughout the program.

*Code each character **and/or groups who play a significant role in violence,** including off-screen narrators, in the order in which they are presented in a significant role:*

Silent characters who are an <u>essential</u> part of the violence in a segment are to be coded as well. An <u>essential</u> silent character is one who is present. *If there is more than one essential silent character present,* **<u>each one</u>** *should be coded.* **Sometimes essential characters are not shown overtly but must be inferred from the context of the sequence. In this case, these characters should also be coded. For example, when a victim or perpetrator is talked about and never depicted.**

1. UT PROGRAM ID *UTID* (**nnnn**): Tape has a yellow dot with a numerical value.

2. RECORD TYPE *RECTYPE* (**n**): A number has been assigned to each section.

> program codes = 1
> segment codes = 2
> character segment codes = 3
> talk about and/or visual depiction of violence sequence codes = 4
> character sequence codes = 5

3. CODER ID *CODID* (**nn**): Each member of the research team at UT has been given a two-digit unique identification code.

4. SEGMENT NUMBER *SEGNUM* (**nn**): Type in the number of segment you are viewing.

5. CHARACTER ID: *CHARID* (**nn**): Characters are only coded once at this level; begin numbering with 01.

6. TIME APPEARS *TIMEAP* (**nnnnnn**): Record time the character first plays a significant role in the program.

7. CHARACTER DESCRIPTOR: *CHARDES* (**1 line alpha**): TYPE IN A ONE- TO FIVE-WORD DESCRIPTOR OF THE CHARACTER TO HELP RELIABILITY CODERS RELOCATE THIS CHARACTER FOR SEQUENCE CODING. For example, ID a newscaster, show host or other "known" individual by name (e.g., Diane Sawyer, Ted Koppel), "unknowns" by verbal descriptor (e.g., killer's brother, abused daughter, paramedic #1, male plainclothes detective). Be as descriptive as possible; this will allow us to go back to the character.

345

8. ANIMATE BEING *ANBEING* (**n**)[1]:

1. Animal
2. Anthropomorphized animal
3. Nonanthropomorphized super creature
4. Anthropomorphized super creature
5. Human
6. crowd/group
9. NA

9. GENDER *GENDER* (**n**)[2] :

1. Female
2. Male
9. Other, none, NA.

10. AGE *AGE* (**n**)[3] :

1. Infant or child under 6.
2. Child aged 6-12
3. Young person aged 13-20.
4. Younger adult, aged 21-44.
5. Adult, aged 45-64.
6. Older adult, aged 65+.
9. NA

---

[1] Animate beings (humanity) refers to any human, animal, anthropomorphized animal, or (non) anthropomorphized super creature. A group of animate beings can involve several creatures or more abstract collections of creatures such as institutions and governments. Definition of *anthropomorphized:* There are several characteristics which make a being anthropomorphized. If the character talks, it is automatically anthropomorphized. If it does not talk, it needs to overtly display several of the following features: 1)talking in a human voice (use of language); 2)cooking food; 3)wearing clothes; 4)using sophisticated tools; 5)presentation of interior monologue; 6)walking in an erect manner on two legs *in a way that the animal could not naturally do* ; 7)using upper extremities to grasp *in a way that the animal could not naturally do*. **Anthropomorphized Animals:** animals with relatively normal biological features that are portrayed as anthropomorphized (e.g., Bugs Bunny, Road Runner, and Mr. Ed). **Nonanthropomorphized Super Creature:** beings which do not naturally exist in this world and have no anthropomorphized characteristics. These beings are either animals which exceed their biological limitation with reagrd to size or form, beings which possess super natural powers, or objects which "come to life" (e.g., King Kong, Big Ants, ghosts who don't talk or look likepeople, Aliens (from the movie), Dinousars from *Jurassic Park*). **Anthropomorphized Super Creature:** beings which do not *naturally* exist in this world and are portrayed as anthropomorphized (e.g, Superman, super heroes, vampires, werewolves, robots (terminator), human-like ghosts, martians (little men w/ big ears), Chucky, Plant in *Little Shop of Horrors*, and Christine the Killer Car).

[2] For all speakers, use *any* cue to establish gender; use "other" only if there are no gender cues or you are coding a crowd. Cartoon characters may have genders, as may machines. Name (Tom and Jerry, Robbie the Robot) and voice (feminized or masculinized) may serve as gender cues. For transsexuals, use gender with which the character identifies himself/herself.

[3] Provide best estimate: for children, those in elementary school should be coded as 2, while those below are coded as 1. Use visual cues and, e.g., year in college to place young adults in 3 or 4. All animals or creatures should be coded as 9: Not ascertainable. If you cannot decide between two categories (e.g., you can't tell if a child is 5 or 6 years old), put the character in the *younger* category if the character number is odd, and put the character in the *older* age category if the character number is even.

11. RACE (CODE HUMANS ONLY) *RACE* (n):[4]

1. Asian/Pacific Islander/(East) Indian.
2. Black, African-American.
3. Hispanic.
4. Native American, Native Alaskan.
5. White
6. Nonhuman
9. NA

12. CITIZENSHIP/NATIONAL ORIGIN *CITIZEN* (n)[5] : CODE HUMANS ONLY:

1. U.S. citizen, regardless of ethnicity or place of residence.
2. Citizen of other nation residing in U.S. (Resident alien/immigrant).
3. Non-U.S. national not residing in U.S. (Foreign citizen).
4. Illegal immigrant
5. Nonhuman
9. NA

13. CHARACTER ROLE *CHARROLE* (n)[6] :

1. Narrator, commentator, reporter, host, observer, in employ of program or network.
2. Any other journalist or mass communicator.
3. Expert, professional (doctor, lawyer, priest).
4. Police or law enforcement officer.
5. Other official authority (military, government *officer or official*).
6. No official status.
9. NA

GO TO NEXT CHARACTER, AND CODE ALL CHARACTERS IN THE SEQUENCE BEFORE PROCEEDING.

---

[4] Code the race of off screen narrators as NA

[5] Citizenship should be where the character resides permanently, rather than where she or he is situated for the story. Longterm visitors to the United States (e.g., "foreign" students) are coded as 2; U.S. citizens are coded as 1, even if they currently reside outside the United States (e.g., soldiers stationed overseas). Immigrant status (2,4) is coded *only* if context makes it clear that one is foreign-born and has arrived in the U.S. in the past few years. If you are unclear whether the person is an immigrant (4), or a foreign citizen (3), code as citizen. The "illegal immigrant" code is reserved for persons where program context makes it unambiguous that person is in the U.S. illegally; otherwise, code the person as an immigrant.

[6] [6] Nonhuman characters *should* be coded for role if applicable. Category 1 should be reserved for individuals the employ of the program, network, or channel; other commentators and observers should be coded as 2: other journalist or 3: expert, professional. A person should be coded as 3: expert, professional *only* if offering information or opinion on a topic immediately relevant to the segment topic; someone identfied as a minister, teacher or lawyer who is not offering expert opinion should not be coded here.

5: Other official authority code should be used only in cases where a character has exercised, or is presented as able to exercise, official power and ordinarily only relatively senior officials and officers would be coded here. Lower-echelon government workers (e.g., postal employees, clerks) would not be coded in this category.

TALK ABOUT VIOLENCE AND /OR VISUAL DEPICTION OF VIOLENCE SEQUENCE CODING

Code sequences in the order they were identified at the segment level.

A **visual depiction of violence sequence** is a related sequence of violent behaviors, actions, or depictions that occur without a significant break in the flow of actual or imminent violence. A violence sequence begins with an initial depiction of violence such as 1) a credible threat that occurs, 2) a violent behavior that occurs, or 3) physically harmful consequences.

A **talk about violence sequence** is a conversation related to violence, as elsewhere defined. A sequence begins with an initial utterance concerning a violent act and continues so long as the discussion or conversation is centered on that act or closely related acts. The introduction of a new character or speaker may or may not signal the end of a sequence; it signals the end of a sequence if the new character changes the direction of the discussion, either by introducing a new topic or by changing the focus of the discussion.

PLEASE NOTE: A visual violence sequence takes precedence over a talk about violence sequence. For example, during a talk show when there is talk about violence it is often accompanied with a visual that shows a consequence of the act. The talk about violence sequence begins as defined above and <u>ends</u> when the visual is shown or there is a shift to a non-violent topic. Any discussion related to the visual, after it was shown, is still part of the visual sequence. The visual sequence will end when the focus of the discussion shifts to an unrelated topic.

1. UT PROGRAM ID *UTID* (**nnnn**): Tape has a yellow dot with a numerical value.
2. RECORD TYPE *RECTYPE* (**n**): A number has been assigned to each section.

> program codes = 1
> segment codes = 2
> character segment codes = 3
> talk about and/or visual depiction of violence sequence codes = 4
> character sequence codes = 5

3. CODER ID *CODID* (**nn**): Each member of the research team at UT has been given a two-digit unique identification code.

4. SEGMENT NUMBER *SEGNUM* (**nn**): Type the number of the segment you are viewing.

5. TALK ABOUT VIOLENCE SEQUENCE NUMBER *TSEQNUM* (**nn**): Type the number of the sequence from the sheet. If this is a <u>visual violence</u> sequence, write 99 for the number.

6. VISUAL VIOLENCE SEQUENCE NUMBER *VSEQNUM* (**nn**): Type the number of the sequence from the sheet. If this is a <u>talk about violence</u> sequence, write 99 for the number.

7. SEQUENCE BEGINS *SEQBEG* (**nnnnnn**): Round to nearest second from on-screen counter.

8. VIOLENT ACT(S) DISCUSSED OR DEPICTED *TVIOACTS* (**alpha**): In this sequence describe the **violent acts** mentioned or shown.

9. VIOLENCE DEFINITION-CREDIBLE THREAT *THREAT* (**n**): Is the violence in the form of a **credible threat**?

    1. no
    2. yes

10. VIOLENCE DEFINITION-CONSEQUENCE *CONSEQ* (**n**): Is the violence in the form of a **consequence**?

    1. no
    2. yes

11. VIOLENCE DEFINITION-ACTUAL ACT *ACTUAL* (**n**): Is the violence in the form of the **actual act itself**?

    1. no
    2. yes

NATURE OF VIOLENCE: to determine the nature of violence answer "yes" or "no" for questions #12-19.

12. SHOOTING *SHOOT* (**n**): Does this violence sequence contain <u>shooting</u>?

    1. no
    2. yes

13. KIDNAPPING *KIDNAP* (**n**): Does this violence sequence contain <u>kidnapping, other abductions and/or confinements</u>?

    1. no
    2. yes

14. STRANGLING *CHOKE* (**n**): Does this violence sequence contain <u>strangling, choking, suffocating,and/ or drowning?</u>

    1. no
    2. yes

15. HITTING/PUNCHING/PUSHING *HIT* (**n**): Does this violence sequence contain hitting, punching, pushing, kicking, biting, grabbing, etc.?

    1. no
    2. yes

16. CUTTING/SLASHING/STABBING *CUT* (**n**): Does this violence sequence contain cutting, slashing, and/or stabbing?

    1. no
    2. yes

17. SEXUAL ASSAULT *RAPE* (**n**): Does this violence sequence contain rape or sexual assault?

    1. no
    2. yes

18. POISONING *POISON* (**n**): Does this violence sequence contain poisoning?
    1. no
    2. yes

19. FRIGHTENING ACTS *STALK* (**n**): Does this violence sequence contain stalking and/or other frightening acts defined as violence?

    1. no
    2. yes

20. GENERALIZED MASS VIOLENCE *ACTWAR* (**n**): Does this violence sequence contain acts of war or generalized mass violence?

    1. no
    2. yes

21. EXTENT OF PHYSICAL INJURY AND PAIN *INJURY* (**n**)[1] : What is the most extensive physical injury in this violence sequence?

    1. No pain or injury: Credible threat only.
    2. Minor: (Examples: bloody nose, minor cuts, scrapes, burns that do not require medical attention).
    3. Moderate (Examples: bullet and stab wounds to non-vital organs, broken bones and other signs of substantial injury that require medical attention).
    4. Severe; injury to the point of physical incapacitation such as bullet and stab wounds to vital organs,

---

[1] "Physical incapacitation" means being able to ward off future harm. If a victim is able to defend against violence, the violence would be considered minor or moderate (3). #7-Pain or injury, but extent is indeterminate, should be used only if there are no cues or clues as to the extent of pain or injury, i.e. the talk is so vague that you are unable to determine the extent. It should *not* be used if you are less than absolutely certain whether injury was minor-moderate (2/3) or severe (4). In that case, use your best judgement in choosing one or the other of the three.

5. Death, other than suicide.
6. Suicide.
7. Pain or injury, but extent is indeterminate.
8. Unknown
9. Intended to cause injury, but unsuccessful attempt

22. NUMBER OF PERSONS HARMED IN THIS SEQUENCE *NUMHURT* (**nnn**)[2] :

001 - 997: Actual number
998: 998 or larger .
999: Indeterminate

WEAPONS: To determine the kind of weapons used in the sequence, answer "yes" or "no" for items # 23- 30. If the weapon used does not appear, please respond "no" to all options.

---

23. WAR WEAPONS   *WAR* (**n**): In this violence sequence are there <u>weapons of war used by military forces</u>?

   1. no
   2. yes

24. GUNS*GUNS* (**n**): In this violence sequence are there <u>guns</u>?

   1. no
   2. yes

25. KNIVES *KNIVES* (**n**): In this violence sequence are there <u>knives or other cutting instruments</u>?

   1. no
   2. yes

26. ROPE *ROPE* (**n**): In this violence sequence is there <u>rope, wire or other choking devices?</u>

   1. no
   2. yes

---

[2] In the case of credible threats, code the number that would have been harmed had the act been carried out. In all possible cases, code an *actual number, even if your number is an estimate.* If the number is expressed in an actual range (e.g. "Twenty to thirty persons injured"), use the midpoint (here, 25) as your number. If no actual range is specified, but you *infer* a range (i.e., you believe 10 - 12 persons were harmed), code the midpoint of that range (11). *Use the 999 code* (Indeterminately large number) *if and only if there are no cues as to the number of persons harmed.*

27. CHEMICALS *CHEMICAL* (**n**): In this violence sequence are there <u>chemicals or poisons</u>?

    1. no
    2. yes

28. BOMBS *BOMBS* (**n**): In this violence sequence are there <u>bombs (other than military) or incendiary devices?</u>

    1. no
    2. yes

29. DEVICES *DEVICES* (**n**): In this violence sequence are there <u>devices with other primary uses</u> (e.g., vehicles, animals used as weapons)?

    1. no
    2. yes

30. OTHER *OTHER* (**n**): In this violence sequence are there <u>other devices primarily intended to cause harm or inflict pain</u> (e.g., whips, paddles)?

    1. no
    2. yes

31. IS HUMOR USED IN THIS VIOLENT SEQUENCE *HUMOR* (**n**)[3]

    1. no
    2. yes

32. PHOTO OR VISUAL DEPICTION *DEPICT* (**n**)[4] :

    1. Sequence is not accompanied by a visual depiction of violence or consequences (TALK SEQUENCE).
    2. Single still photo, graphic depiction of violence or its consequences (VV SEQUENCE)
    3. Multiple still photos or graphics depicting violence or its consequences (VV SEQUENCE)
    4. Film or tape depicts violence or its consequences (VV SEQUENCE)

---

[3]**Humor** refers to those verbal statements or nonverbal actions a character engages in that are intended to amuse the self, another character or characters, and/or the viewer. Humorous verbal statements include jokes, sarcasm, absurd remarks and/or ill-informed comments. Nonverbal actions that are funny include certain types of paralinguistic sounds, gestures, and/or motions.

Humor also includes those situations that are meant to be amusing. These situations involve occurrences portrayed in an absurd, exaggerated, or unrealistic fashion. Oftentimes, there may be production conventions and cues that clearly indicate to the audience that the portrayal is a non-serious, humorous, and/or farce-like depiction. Any timeproduction conventions like laugh tracks and/or strange noises are used, the sequence should automatically be coded as containing humor.

[4]Depiction is of a violent act; film, photos or tape of someone talking about violence should be coded as a new talk sequence, not as a visual depiction.

If this is a <u>talk about violence sequence,</u> answer questions 33-36 and answer 9 (not applicable) to questions 37-40.

If this is a <u>visual depiction of violence sequence,</u> answer questions 37-40 and answer 9 (not applicable) to questions 33-36.

TALK ABOUT VIOLENCE

33. GRAPHICNESS OF TALK ABOUT VIOLENCE *TAVGRAF* (n)[5] :

    1. No concrete details about violence or its impact.
    2. Concrete, physical description of violent act or its aftermath.
    9. NOT APPLICABLE BECAUSE IT'S A **VISUAL VIOLENCE** SEQUENCE

LEVEL OF TESTIMONY: to determine the personal level of the talk about violence sequence, answer "no" or "yes" to questions #34-36.

34. FIRST PERSON *FIRST* (n): Does the violence sequence contain a first person speaker who is describing violence s/he committed, or was committed to her/him?

    1. no
    2. yes
    9. NOT APPLICABLE BECAUSE IT'S A **VISUAL VIOLENCE** SEQUENCE

35. SECOND PERSON *SECOND* (n): Does the violence sequence contain a second person speaker describing violence committed on others; hearsay or witness accounts?

    1. no
    2. yes
    9. NOT APPLICABLE BECAUSE IT'S A **VISUAL VIOLENCE** SEQUENCE

36. THIRD PERSON *THIRD* (n): Does the violence sequence contain a third person speaker describing unwitnessed violence and/or generalizes about violence?

    1. no
    2. yes
    9. NOT APPLICABLE BECAUSE IT'S A **VISUAL VIOLENCE** SEQUENCE

---

[5]Code for the *primary or most salient or concrete talk.* If a character talks both generally and specifically, code at the most specific and graphic level of talk.

VISUAL VIOLENCE

37. REENACTMENT/RECREATION *VVREC* (**n**): Is this visual violence sequence a reenactment/recreation of reality?

    1. no
    2. yes
    9. NOT APPLICABLE BECAUSE IT'S A **TALK ABOUT VIOLENCE** SEQUENCE

38. ON OR OFF-SCREEN DEPICTION *ONOFF* (**n**): Is this visual violence sequence:

    1.   off-screen
    2.   on-screen
    9.   NOT APPLICABLE BECAUSE IT'S A **TALK ABOUT VIOLENCE** SEQUENCE

39. DEGREE OF INTENSITY OF THE VIOLENT ACT *VVINTENT* (**n**)[6] : This measure refers to how the violent act is shown; <u>not</u> the nature of the act.

    1.   mild
    2.   moderate
    3.   extreme
    9.   NOT APPLICABLE BECAUSE IT'S A **TALK ABOUT VIOLENCE** SEQUENCE

40. GRAPHICNESS OF THE CONSEQUENCES *VVGRAF* (**n**)[6] : This measure refers to the way in which the consequence(s) is depicted.

    1.   no consequences are shown
    2.   somewhat graphic
    3.   very graphic
    9.   NOT APPLICABLE BECAUSE IT'S A **TALK ABOUT VIOLENCE** SEQUENCE

41. SEQUENCE END TIME *SEQEND* (**nnnnnn**): Coder will be given the time the sequence ends.

---

[6] To code the intensity of the violent act you have to determine the dramatic effect by taking several factors into consideration, such as camera focus, duration, music, and other editing devices. For example, when someone is killed off-screen and the act is not accompanied with music, screaming or other effects the intensity will be **mild**. While slapping somebody in the face could be coded as **extreme** because of the use of close-ups, slow motion, music and other effects.

[6] **Graphicness** is defined as the portrayal of blood, gore, or dismemberment displayed as a consequence of violence. For example, small flesh wounds, surface cuts, exposing minor amounts of tissue damage will be coded as **somewhat graphic**. **Very graphic** will include sequences depicting blood spattered on walls and/or other characters, excessive wounds, and body parts severed from the body.

CODING CHARACTERS AT THE SEQUENCE LEVEL: Use the sequence times already identified to answer the following questions about the characters. You will need to make reference to the character coding done at the segment level in order to give the character involved in the talk about violent sequence(s) the same character id. At this level, we will only <u>code characters involved</u> in a violence sequence. If a character appears in more than one sequence, he/she will be coded each time.

1. UT PROGRAM ID *UTID* (**nnnn**): Tape has a yellow dot with a numerical value.
2. RECORD TYPE *RECTYPE* (**n**): A number has been assigned to each section.

> program codes = 1
> segment codes = 2
> character segment codes = 3
> talk about and/or visual depiction of violence sequence codes = 4
> character sequence times = 5

3. CODER ID *CODID* (**nn**): Each member of the research team at UT has been given a two-digit unique identification code.

4. SEGMENT NUMBER *SEGNUM* (**n**): Type the number of the segment you are viewing.

5. TALK ABOUT VIOLENCE SEQUENCE NUMBER *TSEQNUM* (**nn**): Use the sequence numbers from the TAV and/or VV violence sequence sheet; code each in time order within segment. If this is a <u>visual violence</u> sequence, write 99 for the number.

6. VISUAL VIOLENCE SEQUENCE NUMBER *VSEQNUM* (**nn**): Use the sequence numbers from the TAV and/or VV violence sequence sheet; code each in time order within segment. If this is a <u>talk about violence</u> sequence, write 99 for the number.

7. CHARACTER ID *CHARID* (**nn**): Use the same identification number assigned during character coding at the segment level.

8. CHARACTER'S INVOLVEMENT *INVOLVE* (**alpha**): In this sequence, describe how the character was involved in the violence.

| **VIOLENCE ROLE** To identify the violence role of character answer "yes" or "no" for items #9-15. |

Code nonhumans if relevant. For purposes of this code, "perpetrator" means *actual or alleged* perpetrator: in other words, someone *accused* of a violent crime should be coded as a perpetrator. *A character may be both a perpetrator <u>and</u> a victim of violence.* A spokesperson is anyone who the context makes clear is authorized to speak in behalf of a victim or perpetrator other than a relative. An accused's attorney, for example, is a spokesperson for the perpetrator. "Relative" in this code means anyone with an affiliation to the character, whether related by blood or marriage or not; casual friends are also coded here. Witnesses may have directly observed a violent incident or its aftermath or effects. *Journalists should not be coded as witnesses, unless they are directly describing events they observed as witnesses*

9. VICTIM OF VIOLENCE *VICTIM* (**n**): Is this character a **victim of violence**?

    1. no
    2. yes

10. FRIEND OR RELATIVE OF VICTIM *FRVICT* (**n**): Is this character a **friend or relative of victim**?

    1. no
    2. yes

11. SPOKESPERSON FOR THE VICTIM *SPOVIC* (**n**): Is this character a **spokesperson for the victim**?

    1. no
    2. yes

12. PERPETRATOR OF VIOLENCE *PERVIO* (**n**): Is this character a **perpetrator of violence**?

    1. no
    2. yes

13. FRIEND OR RELATIVE OF PERPETRATOR *FRPERP* (**n**): Is this character a **friend or relative of perpetrator**?

    1. no
    2. yes

14. SPOKESPERSON FOR PERPETRATOR *SPOPERP* (**n**): Is this character a **spokesperson for perpetrator**?

    1. no
    2. yes

15. WITNESS TO VIOLENCE *WITNESS* (**n**): Is this character a **witness to violence?**

    1. no
    2. yes

> REASONS FOR VIOLENCE: The following questions need to be answered only if you are coding a character who is a **perpetrator of violence.** For other characters, answer 9-NOT APPLICABLE.

16. SELF DEFENSE *SELFDEF* (**n**): Violence intended to protect the self against actual, potential, or perceived physical harm.

    1. no
    2. yes
    9. NOT APPLICABLE

17. PROTECTION OF OTHERS *PROTECT* (**n**): Violence intended to protect other characters (either identified or abstract) from actual, potential, or perceived harm.

    1. no
    2. yes
    9. NOT APPLICABLE

18. IDEOLOGY OR BELIEF *IDEOLOGY* (**n**): Violence accomplished to promote or adhere to a religion, ideology, or a set of beliefs.

    1. no
    2. yes
    9. NOT APPLICABLE

19. EMOTION *EMOTION* (**n**): Violence triggered by feelings of hostility, rage, resentment, or other emotions on the part of perpetrator.

    1. no
    2. yes
    9. NOT APPLICABLE

20. RETALIATION *RETAL* (**n**): Violence triggered by feelings of retribution.

    1. no
    2. yes
    9. NOT APPLICABLE

21. PERSONAL GAIN (**n**): Violence accomplished for purposes of selfish enhancement or gain, including material goods/objects, power or status, popularity, or affection from others.

    1. no
    2. yes
    9. NOT APPLICABLE

22. AMUSEMENT *AMUSE* (**n**): Violence committed for the sake of one's own enjoyment or for the enjoyment of others.

    1. no
    2. yes
    9. NOT APPLICABLE

23. MENTAL INCOMPETENCE *MENTAL* (**n**): Violence committed by perpetrators who either: 1) display flagrant disregard for the basic value of human life, or 2) who lack the mental competence to value human life.

    1. no
    2. yes
    9. NOT APPLICABLE

24. COERCION *COERCE* (**n**): Violence in which the perpetrator acts, either explicitly or implicitly, because of orders from someone they perceive to be more powerful.

    1. no
    2. yes
    9. NOT APPLICABLE

REWARDS AND PUNISHMENTS OF THE VIOLENCE COMMITTED BY THE PERPETRATOR.

---

25. SELF-PRAISE *SELF* (**n**): Was the perpetrator rewarded for acting violently by verbal and/or non-verbal (such as a smile) approval or satisfaction?

    1. no
    2. yes
    9. NOT APPLICABLE

26. PRAISE FROM OTHER *PRAISE* (**n**): Was the perpetrator rewarded for acting violently by verbal and/or non-verbal (such as a smile, a pat on the back, thumbs-up sign, etc.) approval or satisfaction from observers or bystanders?

    1. no
    2. yes
    9. NOT APPLICABLE

27. MATERIAL REWARD *MATERIAL* (**n**): Was the perpetrator rewarded for acting violently by a tangible, physical token of compensation that is given (eg. someone pays a hit-man) or taken (eg. steal money or jewelry)?

    1. no
    2. yes
    9. NOT APPLICABLE

28. SELF-CONDEMNATION *SELFCON* (**n**): Was the perpetrator **punished** for acting violently by a verbal (words of remors) or non-verbal sign (facial expression of sadness) of disapproval, disappointment or dissatisfaction?

    1. no
    2. yes
    9. NOT APPLICABLE

29. CONDEMNATION FROM OTHER *CONDEM* (**n**): Was the perpetrator **punished** for acting violently by verbal and/or non-verbal sign (facial expression of sadness) of disapproval, disappointment or dissatisfaction from observers or bystanders?

    1. no
    2. yes
    9. NOT APPLICABLE

30. NON VIOLENT ACTION *NONVIO* (**n**): Was the perpetrator **punished** for acting violently by non-violent behavior that is designed to stop violence or hinder further violence by penalizing it, such as arresting someone or making somebody apologize?

    1. no
    2. yes
    9. NOT APPLICABLE

31. VIOLENT ACTION FROM OTHER *VIOLENT* (**n**): Was the perpetrator **punished** for acting violently by any violent threat or behavior from an observer, bystander, or other in order to try to stop or punish the perpetrator?

    1. no
    2. yes
    9. NOT APPLICABLE

GO TO NEXT CHARACTER, AND CODE ALL CHARACTERS IN THE SEQUENCE.

_____

PART III

RATINGS AND ADVISORIES FOR TELEVISION PROGRAMMING: UNIVERSITY OF WISCONSIN, MADISON STUDY

Dr. Joanne Cantor
Kristen Harrison

SUMMARY

Researchers at the Madison site conducted an experiment involving 297 children, ranging in age from five to 14 years, from a variety of schools in Madison, Wisconsin. Each child was given a mock channel guide. To insure that the children would tell us what they really wanted to see, we assured them of anonymity and told them that their choices would influence what we would actually show them later in the session.

Our findings indicate that advisories and ratings strongly influenced children's choices. When children were given the choice between three programs, one of which was, at random, associated with "parental discretion advised," boys, and particularly older boys (ages 10 to 14), chose the program with the advisory significantly <u>more often</u> than would be expected by chance. In contrast, when children were given the choice between three other programs, one of which was, at random, associated with "viewer discretion advised," girls, and particularly younger girls (ages five to nine), chose the program with the advisory significantly <u>less often</u> than would be expected by chance. Children were also given the choice between three movies, two of which were always rated "PG," with the third being rated "G," "PG," "PG-13," or "R" in different booklets. All groups except the older boys displayed a definite tendency to avoid the target movie when it had an "R" rating. Younger girls, in fact, chose the target movie the most when they thought it was rated "G." In contrast, not one of the older boys chose the target movie when they were told it was rated "G," but at least half of those who were told it was rated "PG-13" or "R" chose it.

In general, children who said their parents were more involved in their TV viewing and children who had been frightened by television in the past were more likely to avoid programs with restrictive advisories and ratings. In contrast, children who reported engaging in more aggression-related activities were more likely to choose programs with advisories.

In another study, we videotaped 70 parent-child pairs discussing which programs the child would watch during a similar experiment. Although almost all of the parents' comments about advisories and ratings were negative, half of the comments children made about them were favorable (e.g., "the cooler the movie, the higher the rating").

We also evaluated the use of advisories and ratings in the random sample of television programming. Very few shows (less than 4%) used advisories such as "viewer discretion advised," and the content that prompted the advisory was rarely denoted. Content information was most prevalent on the three premium channels, HBO, Showtime, and Cinemax. The majority of movies shown on these channels displayed both an MPAA rating and codes denoting specific content, such as violence or adult language.

The findings are discussed in terms of the risks and benefits of ratings and advisories, and the importance of how such messages are designed and worded.

RATINGS AND ADVISORIES
FOR TELEVISION PROGRAMMING

The Madison-based research explored how various types of ratings and advisories are used to indicate the presence of violence in programs and movies that appear on television. In addition, it investigated how children, their parents, and other adults perceive, comprehend and respond to violence ratings and advisories.

Both cable channels and network stations have promised to increase their use of messages warning the viewer of potentially problematic content in an attempt to give viewers notice of what they will be exposed to, and especially to help parents exert control over their children's violent TV intake. In 1973, a nationwide *TV Guide* survey reported that 55% of those questioned were in favor of a rating system for television programming (Wurtzel & Surlin, 1978). By 1993, a *USA Weekend* reader survey reported 73% agreement with this idea (Federman, 1993). In a telephone survey we conducted in the spring of 1994, 91% of a random sample of parents of elementary school children in Madison, Wisconsin agreed that broadcasters and cable operators should be required to issue advisories regarding violent content or give violent programs movie-type ratings.

To date, however, there is surprisingly little research regarding the impact or effectiveness of ratings and advisories. The few studies that have been conducted are described here. A major issue has been whether advisories and ratings have their intended effect, that is, to prevent people from being exposed to content that they wish to avoid, and to help parents protect their children from being exposed to problematic content. There has been concern that they might have a "boomerang" effect, that is, that they would make the content seem more interesting and exciting and attract a larger audience.

A study by Wurtzel and Surlin (1978) reported on a random survey of attitudes toward viewer advisories among adults in Athens, Georgia in 1976. Almost all respondents in this survey reported that they had seen advisory warnings on TV. However, only 24% stated that the advisories had influenced them in deciding whether to watch a show. Interestingly, of these respondents, 39% reported that the advisory resulted in their not watching the show, but 24% said that the advisory made them watch the show with increased interest.

Wurtzel and Surlin found, however, a strong difference between viewers who had children and those who did not. Thirty-four percent of respondents with children reported that their own viewing had been influenced by the warnings, compared to 17% of respondents without children. Furthermore, 54% of the respondents with children stated that the warnings had influenced their decisions about their child's viewing. The overwhelming majority (81%) of the parents who had been influenced said they had not let their children watch the program, and most of the remainder said that although they had let their children watch, they had watched the program with them.

As for the actual effects of violence ratings and advisories, that is, whether they serve their function to "protect" people from exposure to objectionable content or serve as a "magnet" for more viewers, previous research findings are decidedly mixed. A study published by Herman and Leyens (1977) reported data on Belgian television viewership between 1972 and 1975. This study looked at movies only, and compared the audience size for movies broadcast with violence advisories to those broadcast with sex advisories and without advisories. Their main finding was that films that carried violence or sex advisories had larger audiences than those that did not. Although these data might seem to support the notion that advisories attract viewers, this conclusion cannot be drawn with confidence, because the study undoubtedly confounded advisories with content. It could very well be that the programs were watched more because they contained violence and sex, not because they were broadcast with an advisory. The study thus does not permit the effect of content to be isolated from the effect of advisories.

A publication by Austin (1980) reported on a laboratory experiment in which high school students were presented with a series of four fictitious film titles and plot synopses. For different students, the same film was associated with different Motion Picture Association of America (MPAA) ratings (G, PG, R, or X). For each film description, students were asked to fill out a rating scale indicating the likelihood that they would attend the film. According to Austin's report of the findings, the ratings had no significant impact on students' desire to see the films. There are two major problems with this study, however, that render this interpretation less than conclusive. First, Austin reported only an overall data analysis that did not permit the determination of whether the ratings produced different effects for different types of plots. Second, and more importantly, it is likely that the researcher encountered a credibility problem with the participants. It seems questionable whether the same plot description could plausibly be associated with both a "G" and an "X" rating, for example. Although Austin claimed that credibility was not a problem, he did not report any of his plot synopses in his write-up.

A third study of the effect of advisories, an experiment by Christenson (1992), yielded yet a different effect. Although not a study of television, but rather of music preferences, it is relevant here because it examined the effect of parental advisory labels for popular music albums ("Parental advisory: Explicit lyrics"). In this study, adolescents gave lower evaluations of music from albums displaying advisory labels than of the same music from albums without such labels, and they reported less interest in purchasing the labeled albums.

The conflicting findings of these three studies leave us knowing very little about the impact of violence ratings and advisories on adult and child viewers' attraction to or avoidance of television programming. A recent unpublished study reported by Hamilton (1994) presents the first real contribution to general knowledge on this question. This study looked at the Nielsen ratings for prime-time movies broadcast on network television between 1987 and 1993 and used regression analysis to determine the factors that made significant contributions to the movies' ultimate audience size. In his analysis, Hamilton included a variety of characteristics that are known to have an impact on the rating a program receives, such as its scheduling, the rating of the show preceding it, and the manner in which it was described and categorized in *TV*

Guide. Hamilton's major finding was that the presence of a viewer discretion advisory was associated with a significant reduction in Nielsen ratings among viewers in the 2- to 11-year-old category. These advisories had no significant impact on the size of the teen or adult audience, however. This study represents the first successful demonstration that viewer discretion advisories can serve one of their major intended purposes, that is, to shield some of the youngest and most impressionable children from exposure to controversial content, without either increasing or reducing the size of the audience in other age groups.

A study such as Hamilton's, involving aggregate data, can tell us only about the quantitative end result of a process by which children are exposed to or protected from exposure to movies on TV. What we can't tell from such a study is how the reduction in child audience size was brought about. Did parents make decisions about their child's exposure by themselves, or were children involved in the decision to avoid these movies? It is possible that parents and children made their decisions in concert, but it is also very possible that parents made these decisions unilaterally. Some of the questions that remain unaddressed, therefore, are whether or not children knew about the advisories at all; whether, if they did, they understood what they meant; and further, whether the advisories had any effect on the children's desire to see the movies.

The research conducted at the Madison site was designed to investigate ratings and advisories in a variety of ways. The main experimental study (Part I) investigated the degree to which children understand the meaning of advisories and ratings associated with violent content, the effect of such advisories and ratings on children's desire to see programs associated with them, and whether the presence of advisories and ratings influences children's interpretations of the violence they see. Two smaller-scale studies were also included. The first (Part II) investigated how the presence of advisories and ratings for violent content influences negotiations between parents and children over what the child should watch on television, and the second (Part III) investigated the degree to which different MPAA ratings affect college students' interest in movies shown on television. Part IV of this report contains an analysis of the use of advisories and ratings in the random sample of television programming that was drawn for the content analysis of violence on television.

PART I: CHILDREN'S RESPONSES TO RATINGS AND ADVISORIES

Although it is commonly agreed that ratings and advisories are directed at adults to permit them to protect their children or themselves from objectionable content, it is difficult to ignore the question of how these messages affect children. Children's viewing decisions are often made in the absence of the parent, and anecdotal evidence suggests that children are aware of advisories and ratings. It is therefore important to determine the impact of ratings and advisories on children themselves.

For the first year of the project period, we tested those ratings and advisories that seemed most prevalent on television. Based on information supplied by the NCTA from many of the cable channels, we decided to test the following four advisories: "Parental discretion advised," "Contains some violent content; Parental discretion advised," "Viewer discretion advised," and "Contains some violent content; Viewer discretion advised." We also decided to include the four major MPAA ratings that are associated with movies shown on television: "G: General audiences," "PG: Parental guidance suggested," "PG-13: Parents strongly cautioned," and "R: Restricted." We tested the effect of these ratings and advisories on children's desire to see programs and movies. In addition, we assessed the effect of the four MPAA ratings on children's interpretation of a violent movie scene. Finally, we tested children's understanding of these eight advisories and ratings. In addition, we tested their understanding of four new content codes recently introduced on several premium channels, that are used in conjunction with the MPAA ratings for movies. They are "MV: Mild violence," "V: Violence," "G: Graphic violence," and "AC: Adult Content." The analyses compared the responses of boys and girls in two age groups, 5 to 9 years and 10 to 14 years.

Method

Participants

The sample of participants consisted of 297 children from the Madison Metropolitan School District, Madison, Wisconsin. Permission was secured from the schools and the participants' parents prior to the study. Elementary school children (grades one through five) were tested during school hours as well as during an after-school day care program located at various elementary schools. Middle school children (grades six through eight) were tested during school hours. A total of three schools and ten after-school day care sites participated in the study. An incentive was paid to the participating schools and day care programs for their cooperation.

A variety of schools were included in the sample in order to cover an adequate range of socioeconomic status (lower to upper-middle class). Participants ranged in age from 5 to 14 years. Many of the analyses compared subjects in two age groups. The "younger" group was composed of children between the ages of five and nine years (N=159; 55% male). The "older" group was composed of children between 10 and 14 (N=138; 42% male). The overwhelming majority of the children participating in the study were Caucasian.

Procedure

Each research session began with the administration of a 15-minute questionnaire, followed by a 15-minute film clip, followed by another 15-minute questionnaire. Children in first and second grades were interviewed individually by groups of trained interviewers. The older children were tested in groups of four to eight by two research assistants, with the exception of one middle school, whose students were tested simultaneously by two research assistants as one large group in a lecture hall. In all cases, children were told not to put their name on any of the booklets, and were assured that their answers would be completely anonymous.

The first questionnaire booklet consisted of two parts: a background questionnaire, including a personality inventory followed by several media use questions, and a selective exposure questionnaire in the form of a five-page mock television programming schedule. Children were instructed to choose the program they would like to view from three different program descriptions presented on each page of the programming schedule. The last page of the schedule featured three movie descriptions. Children were told that they would be shown a video clip after completing the questionnaire, and that their viewing choices would count as "votes" to help the researchers decide which video clip to show. When the children had all finished filling out the first questionnaire, the researchers tallied their "votes." All groups were shown the same video clip, regardless of their programming choices.

Children were told to gather around one or two (depending on the size of the group) large (27") video monitors to watch a video clip from the program that "won the most votes." Care was taken prior to the video presentation to make sure each child could see at least one of the screens clearly. In the single case where a large group of middle-school children viewed the tape simultaneously, the video image was projected onto a 10-foot-square screen to facilitate viewing.

Immediately after viewing the video clip, the children filled out a second booklet containing two parts: a questionnaire about their reactions to the movie clip, and a test of their understanding of various ratings and advisories commonly used in network and cable television programming. After completing this questionnaire, the children were thanked, given a small gift (a sticker or a pencil), and dismissed.

Materials

Background questions. The personality inventory consisted of self-report measures adapted from a variety of sources, including the Junior Eysenck Personality Inventory (JEPI, 1965) and Mehrabian and Epstein's measure of emotional empathy (Mehrabian & Epstein, 1972). The personality dimensions of greatest interest were aggressiveness and anxiety. Examples of the items in these dimensions are "I get into fights with other children" (aggression), and "I find it hard to sleep at night because I worry about things" (anxiety). Possible responses were "never," "some of the time," "most of the time," and "all of the time."

The media exposure questions following the personality inventory asked for the children's assessment of whether their parents ever watched TV with them or discussed it with them, and whether their parents set limits on their TV viewing.

Selective exposure questionnaire. The second segment of the first booklet consisted of a TV program listing grid similar to those featured in such publications as *TV Guide* and daily newspapers. The first page of listings described three reality-based crime shows with fictional names: *Countdown*, *On Camera*, and *L.A.P.D.*, each associated with a short description of the plot of an episode (e.g., "A gun dealer who is selling illegal firearms is taken into custody after a shoot-out.") Fictitious names that sounded like real programs were used because in initial testing, young children automatically chose programs whose names they recognized, such as Rescue 911, and would not even listen to the program descriptions before making their choices. Children were told that all the programs were real, but that some were not currently being broadcast locally. (A measure of the program titles' credibility can be seen in the fact that an average of 17% of the children in the sample stated that they had seen these programs before). On the first page, one of the programs and its description was followed by an advisory that read "Parental discretion advised" (parental advisory) or "Contains some violent content; parental discretion advised" (parental violence advisory). The program that contained an advisory was randomly varied, as were the advisory version (with or without the mention of violent content) and the order of the show descriptions.

After reading the descriptions (or, in the case of first and second graders, listening to an interviewer read the descriptions), the children marked their viewing choice and indicated whether they had ever seen any of the shows described. The procedure for completing pages 2 through 5 was identical to that of the first page. The second page of listings described three situation comedies with real names and plausible episode descriptions: *Full House, The Nanny*, and *Home Improvement*. This page was presented as filler material, and contained no advisories.

The third page of listings described three crime dramas with fictional names: *RIVALS, Keep the Peace*, and *Chicago Underground*. (An average of 12% of the participants said that they had seen these programs before.) These program titles were also followed by episode descriptions (e.g., "An assassin pursues the daughter of an African ambassador.") One of these descriptions was always followed by an advisory that read "Viewer discretion advised" (viewer advisory) or "Contains some violent content; viewer discretion advised" (viewer violence advisory). Again, the show description containing the advisory was randomly varied, as was the advisory version and the order of presentation of the show descriptions. The fourth page of listings described three more situation comedies with real names and plausible episode descriptions: *Mad About You, Saved by the Bell*, and *Martin*. This page was also presented as filler material, and contained no advisories.

The fifth page of listings described three feature-length movies whose names and plot descriptions contained both real and fictional elements. The titles were *Hidden Island, Cold River*, and *The Moon-Spinners*. The descriptions for *Hidden Island* and *Cold River* were always followed by the MPAA rating "PG: Parental guidance suggested." The MPAA rating for *The Moon-Spinners* was randomly varied to read one of four ways: "G: General audiences," "PG: Parental guidance suggested," "PG-13: Parents strongly cautioned," or "R: Restricted." As on the first and third pages, the order of presentation of the movie descriptions was randomly varied.

Video clip. All groups of children saw the same video clip: a 15-minute edited version of the 1964 Disney movie *The Moon-Spinners*. It should be noted that, depending on the questionnaire version they received, children were led to believe that the movie they were about to see was rated "G," "PG," "PG-13," or "R." The movie's rating was actually "G."

The video clip depicted the story of an adolescent girl (played by Hayley Mills), who helps a young man who had earlier been framed for a jewel theft. Together, they catch the criminal who really stole the jewels and safely return them to their owner. The 15-minute clip was edited to contain enough of the entire plot to make sense as a story. It contained two fight scenes between the young man (the "hero") and the older male criminal (the "villain"). The fight scenes depicted fist-fighting between the hero and villain, with the villain also using a fishing harpoon and a motor boat as weapons. The second fight scene ended with the story's resolution, in which the villain is arrested and the hero is vindicated.

Questionnaire on reactions to violent video. The first segment of the movie-rating questionnaire began with items measuring participants' liking for the video clip, how exciting they thought the scenes were, how much they would like to see the whole movie, and how violent they thought the scenes were. Responses ranged from 0 ("not at all") to 4 ("very, very much"). Participants were also asked to think back to the two fight scenes and to estimate, for each scene separately, how hard the hero and villain were hitting each other, how hurt they each were, and how right or wrong it was for them to be hitting each other. The hero and villain were referred to by name and appearance (e.g., "Mark, the young man in the white shirt") and not designated in the questionnaire as "hero" or "villain." In addition, participants' feelings during the viewing session were assessed with a battery of items measuring how happy, sad, angry, excited, scared, and surprised they were while viewing the fight scenes. Finally, a question measuring memory for the rating of the video clip (as described in the selective exposure questionnaire) was included as a manipulation check.

Questionnaire assessing interpretation of ratings and advisories. The final segment of the experiment was designed to measure children's understanding of three types of advisories and ratings commonly associated with commercial media fare. Each child was shown one of each of the three types of advisories. The particular form of each type of advisory a child received was determined at random. The first advisory was one of four written warnings: "Parental discretion advised," "Viewer discretion advised," "Contains some violent content; parental discretion advised," or "Contains some violent content; viewer discretion advised." The second message to be interpreted was one of four MPAA movie ratings: "G: General audiences," "PG: Parental guidance suggested," "PG-13: Parents strongly cautioned," or "R: Restricted." The third message was one of four content codes recently introduced on some premium channels: "MV: Mild violence," "V: Violence," "GV: Graphic violence," or "AC: Adult content."

The advisories were presented as illustrations of how they are commonly displayed--in white letters on a black television screen. After reading each advisory, the children were asked open-ended questions about the meaning of the advisory and what they would expect a program or movie associated with it to contain. Children then answered a question regarding whether the advisory would make them want to watch a program more or less, and how much so. After giving their responses on the three advisories, one to a page, they were presented with the same three advisories a second time, this time followed by questions with multiple-choice responses. First, they were asked to choose the phrase that came closest to the meaning of the message. Second, they were given a list of 13 types of content, and were asked to circle all those things that they would expect to see in a program that was preceded by that advisory or rating. The types of content were: punching, fighting, kissing, explosions, drinking alcohol, sex, swearing, shooting, kicking, smoking, monsters, drugs, and people dying.

In both questionnaire booklets, all of the pages that involved random assignment of advisories, ratings, and orders were independently randomized so that there would be no systematic effects of questionnaire structure. For example, there were 18 different versions of page 1 of the selective exposure booklet (2 advisory types X which of 3 programs was associated with an advisory X 3 orders of presentation). A series of random orders of 18 numbers was generated by computer and the versions of that page were stacked in these orders. A separate randomization was carried out for each page that included random assignment to conditions, and booklets were collated from these randomly ordered stacks of page versions. As a result, random assignment to conditions was independent for each manipulated variable. In other words, a participant's assignment to a parental advisory condition was entirely independent of his or her assignment to a viewer advisory condition and to an MPAA rating condition in the selective exposure portion. Moreover, it was also independent of his or her assignment to a condition in the latter portion of the experiment, testing comprehension of advisories and ratings.

Results

Selective Exposure

The first set of analyses we conducted dealt with whether children's choices of programs and movies to view during the experiment were affected by the presence of advisories or MPAA ratings.

Parental discretion advisories. The first page of the TV program listings included three fictitious programs that sounded like "reality-action" programs. To determine whether the presence of the advisories "Parental discretion advised" or "Contains some violent content; Parental discretion advised" influenced children's choices of these programs, binomial tests were employed, assessing whether the observed pattern of choices differed significantly from chance, that is, from what would be expected if there were no effect of advisories. Since there were three possible program choices, and the advisories were associated with each title at random, a chance outcome would occur if one-third of the children chose a program with an advisory. Thus, the percentage of children choosing the program with an advisory was compared to the chance expectation of 33.3%. A number higher than 33.3% would indicate that more kids chose the program with an advisory; a lower percent would indicate that fewer children chose it. The standard probability level of .05 was set to determine whether the percent choosing the program differed significantly from chance.

The first analyses included both versions of the parental advisory (combining the version with and without the mention of violence). Overall, 104 children chose programs with the advisory, while 189 did not. This represents an observed value of 36%. Although slightly higher than the 1/3 comparison figure, this value did not even approach significance ($\underline{p}$=.47, two-tailed).

Further analyses were performed to determine how the patterns of interest in programs with parental advisories compared in the four age-by-sex groupings, that is, younger girls, younger boys, older girls, and older boys. These patterns are displayed in <u>Figure 1</u>. The data revealed that younger and older girls were highly similar, with 27% and 28%, respectively, choosing a program with a parental advisory. In contrast, boys showed more interest in programs with parental advisories. Although more than one-third of both younger and older boys chose such shows, the preference of older boys was much stronger. Thirty-nine percent of the younger boys, but 51% of the older boys, chose a program with a parental advisory. The binomial tests revealed the percent for the older boys to be significantly different from chance (p<.01). The percent in the other three groups did not differ from chance expectations (all p's>.29).

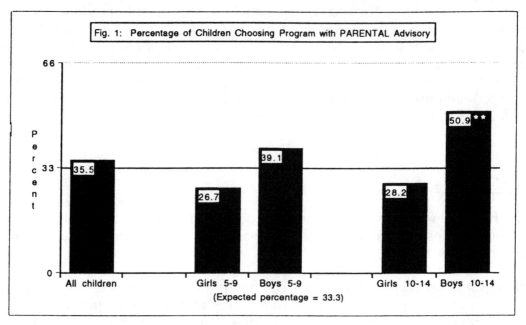

NOTE: ** p < .01

When the data were analyzed by gender of participant, collapsing age, it was found that the percentages of boys choosing a program with a parental advisory significantly exceeded that of girls (44% vs. 28%, ($\underline{X}^2$(2, N=293)=7.73, p<.01, phi=.17). Furthermore, the percentage for boys was significantly higher than chance levels (p=.01). When the percentages were analyzed by age, collapsing gender, there was no significant difference between the age groups (p=.53).

The two versions of the parental advisory (mentioning violence vs. not mentioning violence) were also analyzed separately. These analyses showed that the two types of parental advisories exerted highly similar effects, with 35% of subjects choosing a program with the parental advisory and 36% choosing a program when it had the parental violence advisory (p=.86). The only real difference between the effects of the two forms of the parental advisory was that the difference between boys and girls was larger for the parental violence advisory (47% vs. 25%) than for the parental advisory that did not mention violence (40% vs. 30%). The former comparison was significant ($\underline{X}^2$(2, N=143)=6.47, p<.01).

In summary, boys, and especially older boys, showed significantly more interest in reality-action programs with parental discretion advisories than would be expected by chance, and boys showed significantly more interest than girls in these programs.

Viewer discretion advisories. Next, the "viewer discretion advised" warnings from the third page of the TV booklet were analyzed in the same fashion. The programs on this page were made to sound like crime dramas. As can be seen from Figure 2, overall, 27% of the children chose a drama associated with one of the two forms of viewer discretion advisories, and this percent was lower than chance levels, approaching significance (p=.07).

The data within the four age-by-sex groupings are also shown in Figure 2. As the figure shows, younger girls chose programs with a viewer discretion advisory at the lowest rate (21%) and this rate was significantly different from chance (p<.05). The percentages in the other three conditions did not differ from chance expectations (p>.3).

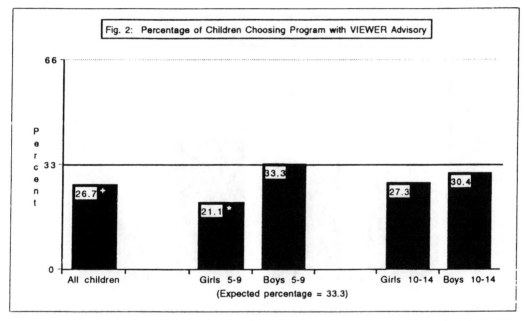

NOTE: * p < .05   + p < .07

When the patterns for both genders were looked at, collapsing age, the proportion of girls choosing a program with a viewer advisory (24%) was significantly lower than chance expectations (p<.05). However, the pattern for girls did not differ significantly from that for boys. The choices of the younger and older groups (combining sexes) did not differ from chance, nor did the two age groups differ significantly from each other.

When the two forms of the viewer advisory were compared, there was a tendency to choose the one mentioning violence more often (30% vs. 27%), but this difference did not even approach significance (p=.67).

Overall, then, there was a tendency to avoid crime dramas with viewer discretion advisories, approaching significance, and this effect was predominantly due to a significant tendency for girls, and especially younger girls, to avoid dramas with viewer discretion advisories.

MPAA ratings. Children's movie choices as a function of MPAA ratings were analyzed by chi square. It will be recalled that only one movie, *The Moon-Spinners*, was associated with a manipulated rating, and the rating was varied in four ways (G, PG, PG-13, R). The other two movies were always rated "PG."

The first analysis compared the percentage of all children who chose the target movie *(The Moon-Spinners)* when it was given the different ratings. As can be seen from Figure 3, *The Moon-Spinners* was chosen by 22%, 28%, 33%, and 14% of children when it was rated "G," "PG," "PG-13," and "R," respectively. The chi square computed to determine whether this pattern was different from chance expectations (i.e., that the movie was equally attractive with the different ratings) was of borderline significance (X^2(3, N=291)=7.45, p=.059, Cramer's V=.16).

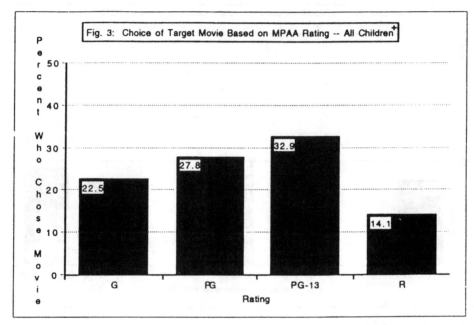

NOTE: + p < .06

Figures 4a and 4b report the movie choice data broken down by gender and by age, respectively. Figure 4a shows that for girls, choice of the target movie was approximately equal when the movie was rated "G," "PG," or "PG-13," but it was much lower when the movie was rated "R." This pattern differed from what would be expected by chance, approaching significance (X^2(3, N=148)=6.70, p=.08, Cramer's V=.21). In contrast, for boys, the "G" rating made the target movie the least popular, and interest in the movie peaked at the "PG-13" rating. This pattern was not significantly different from chance. However, when the patterns for boys and girls were compared to each other in a chi square based on proportions, the choice patterns for the two sexes were significantly different (X^2(3)=15.22, p<.01).

Figure 4b reports the data on the impact of MPAA ratings on selective exposure, broken down by age. As the figure shows, the pattern for the younger group is remarkably similar to the pattern for girls; and the pattern for the older group is very similar to the pattern for boys. For the younger group, exactly 25% chose the target movie when it was rated "G," "PG," and "PG-13," but fewer than 5% selected it when it was rated "R." The chi square on these frequencies was significant ($\underline{X}^2$(3, N=157)=7.74, $\underline{p}$=.05, Cramer's V=.22). For the older group, as with the boys, interest in the target movie again was lowest when it was rated "G" and peaked at "PG-13." This pattern did not differ significantly from chance ($\underline{X}^2$(3)=4.39, N=134, $\underline{p}$=.22). However, when the proportions for the two age groups were compared in a chi square, the pattern for younger and older groups did differ significantly ($\underline{X}^2$ (3)= 13.39, $\underline{p}$<.01).

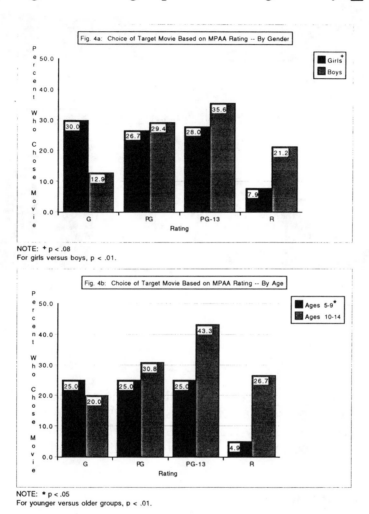

Fig. 4a: Choice of Target Movie Based on MPAA Rating -- By Gender

NOTE: + p < .08
For girls versus boys, p < .01.

Fig. 4b: Choice of Target Movie Based on MPAA Rating -- By Age

NOTE: * p < .05
For younger versus older groups, p < .01.

The similarity of the patterns for younger children and girls is not due to a confounding of gender with age. In fact, the younger group had a higher percentage of males than the older group (55% vs. 42%). Figures 5a through 5d show the patterns of choice within the four age-by-gender groupings. Perhaps because of the smaller sample sizes, the patterns in three of the four groups did not reach statistical significance, but these patterns show similarities to the analyses by age group and by gender. The only pattern that is significantly different from chance is that of the older boys ($\underline{X}^2$ (3,N=56)=9.02, $\underline{p}$<.05, Cramer's V=.40). It seems particularly remarkable that in this group, none of the boys who were told the movie was rated "G" chose it, but 53% of those who were told it was rated "PG-13," and 50% of those who were told it was rated "R" wanted to see it.

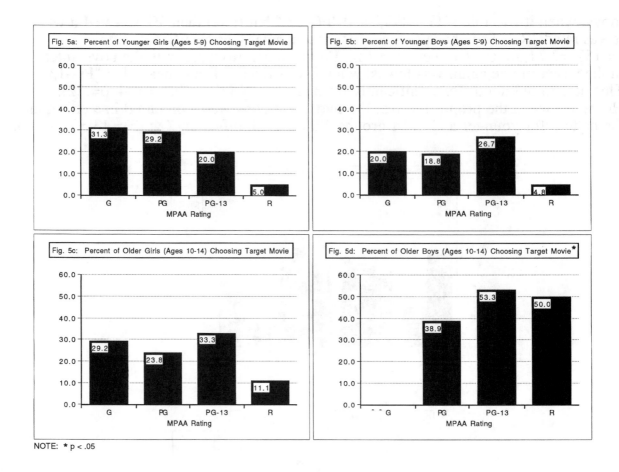

Fig. 5a: Percent of Younger Girls (Ages 5-9) Choosing Target Movie

Fig. 5b: Percent of Younger Boys (Ages 5-9) Choosing Target Movie

Fig. 5c: Percent of Older Girls (Ages 10-14) Choosing Target Movie

Fig. 5d: Percent of Older Boys (Ages 10-14) Choosing Target Movie*

NOTE: * p < .05

Overall, these data show that the rating the movie received influenced the degree to which children expressed a desire to see it. Although younger children and girls showed a tendency to shy away from the movie when it had the restrictive rating "R," older boys were attracted to the more restrictive ratings and avoided the "G" rating.

Interpretation of Violent Content

Responses to the questions assessing reactions to the video clip from *The Moon-Spinners*, and specifically to its violent content, were analyzed in factorial analyses of variance with age (younger, older), sex, and the MPAA rating associated with the video (G, PG, PG-13, R) as independent factors. Over all the analyses, there were many differences attributable to age and sex. For the most part, the movie and its violence were appreciated by younger more than by older participants and by boys more than by girls. However, since gender and age differences *per se* were not a focus of this research, significant main effects of these factors are not reported here.

The results revealed that the movie's MPAA rating had very little effect on children's interpretations of the movie scenes. With only one exception, there were no significant effects or interactions involving the MPAA rating factor on any of the questions about children's evaluations of the movie, their interpretations of the violence, or the emotions they felt while viewing.

The one significant effect of the movie ratings was in response to the question about how hurt the hero was by the end of the first violent scene. This analysis revealed a significant main effect of the movie's rating ($F(3,267)=4.38$, $p<.01$). Figure 6 shows the pattern of means over the four conditions. As can be seen from the figure, children who had been told that the movie they were seeing had been rated "R" thought that the hero was significantly more hurt during his violent encounter with the villain than children in the other three conditions. This finding is of interest because it suggests that ratings may have the potential to focus attention on the negative consequences of violence. However, in light of the fact that only one significant effect was observed over the four-page questionnaire, such an effect needs to be replicated in future studies before we place much confidence in it. The manipulated rating did not affect children's enjoyment of the movie, the degree to which they thought it was, overall, violent, their moral evaluations of the violence, or the emotions they reported while viewing it.

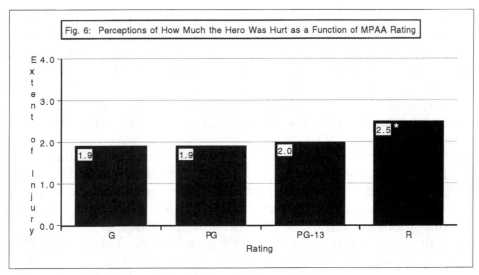

Fig. 6: Perceptions of How Much the Hero Was Hurt as a Function of MPAA Rating

NOTE: * Significantly different from all other groups at p < .05.

One possible reason for the minimal effect of the ratings on responses to the movie may be that although we have reported strong evidence that the ratings influenced movie choice, children may not have been sufficiently conscious of the movie's rating to remember it during the viewing portion. Since children in the groups worked at different rates of speed, there was some delay for many children between choosing which movie they wanted to see and watching the video clip. And because the groups of viewers were composed of children who were told the movie was rated differently, it was not feasible to remind children of the rating as we showed the clip to them.

By the time children had seen the movie and filled out the questionnaire on their responses to it, they indeed revealed poor memory for the rating the movie had been assigned in the selective exposure questionnaire, which they had filled out approximately 20 minutes earlier. Overall, only 30% of the children accurately reported the movie's rating at the end of the movie-evaluation questionnaire. Twenty-six percent responded that they did not know what the rating was. One aspect of the procedure that must have contributed to the low accuracy is the fact that the two non-target movies were always given a "PG" rating. It is no wonder then, that 40% of the subjects remembered the target movie as being rated "PG" (vs. 10%, 15% and 10% respectively for "G," "PG-13," and "R"). To determine whether the lack of significant rating effects on evaluations of the movie might be due to poor memory of the rating, one-way analyses of variance on children's responses to the movie were run using only those 82 participants who accurately remembered the rating. These findings did not differ in any substantial way from the findings reported on the entire sample.

Interpretations of Advisories and Ratings

Comprehension. Children's forced-choice answers regarding the meanings of the various advisories and ratings are shown in Figures 7 through 9.

In responding to the question about the parental and viewer advisories, subjects could choose from the following responses: A) "people shouldn't watch it" B) "kids need a grownup's permission to watch it," C) "parents should be careful in deciding whether to let their kids watch it," D) "people should be careful in deciding whether to watch it," and E) "don't know." Since the two versions of each advisory (with and without the mention of violence) had essentially the same literal meaning as far as the advisory was concerned, the data for the two versions were combined.

Figure 7a compares the distribution of chosen meanings for the parental discretion advisory for younger vs. older children. The literal meaning of this advisory is closest to choice C, indicating that parents should exercise care in deciding whether their children should watch the program. Although this alternative was chosen most frequently by the older children (52%), a sizable number of this group (41%) said the advisory meant that children needed a parent's permission. Almost half of the younger group chose the latter option, while 27% chose the option that was literally correct. The distributions of the two age groups differed significantly from each other ($\underline{X}^2$ (4, N=129)=12.04, $\underline{p}$<.05).

Figure 7b compares the two age groups in their understanding of the viewer discretion advisories. Although the literal meaning of this advisory is closest to alternative D, that people should consider whether they want to watch the program, almost half of the older children interpreted this as a parental advisory, and less than one-fourth chose the literal meaning. Again, the most frequent choice for the younger group was that children need a parent's permission. The distribution of responses in the two age groups was significantly different ($\underline{X}^2$ (4, N=145)=12.12, $\underline{p}$<.05).

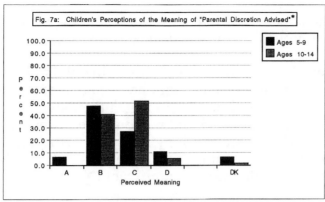

Fig. 7a: Children's Perceptions of the Meaning of "Parental Discretion Advised"*

NOTE: *Patterns for age groups significantly different at the p < .05 level.

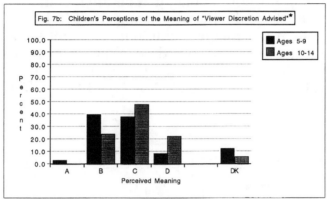

Fig. 7b: Children's Perceptions of the Meaning of "Viewer Discretion Advised"*

NOTE: *Patterns for age groups significantly different at the p < .05 level.

PERCEIVED MEANING KEY: A -- People shouldn't watch
B -- Kids need a grownup's permission to watch
C -- Parents should be careful in deciding whether to let their kids watch
D -- People should be careful in deciding whether to watch
DK -- Don't know

In responding to the question regarding the meaning of the four MPAA ratings, subjects could choose from the following: A) "anyone can watch it," B) "parents should decide whether their kids can watch it," C) "parents should be very careful about letting their kids watch it," D) "kids shouldn't watch it without a parent," E) "no kids are allowed to watch it," and F) "don't know."

Figures 8a through 8d show the distribution of responses for younger and older children among these response categories. As can be seen from Figure 8a, all of the older children who were asked about the meaning of "G: General audiences" knew that it meant that anyone can watch the movie. Only half of the younger children gave the correct answer to this question, with another quarter of the sample saying it meant that parents should make the decision. The difference between the age groups was significant ($\underline{X}^2$ (5, N=61)=17.73, $\underline{p}$<.01).

Figure 8b shows the distribution of chosen meanings for "PG: Parental guidance suggested." Among the older children, the highest proportion (40%) chose the literal meaning, that parents should decide if their children should watch. However another 35% chose the option "anyone can watch." Although this is not the literal meaning of the message, it does reflect the fact that a "PG" rating does not actively restrict any child's access. Younger children's responses to this question were more spread out over the options, and 14 percent of this group said they did not know what the rating meant. Although there are apparent differences in the patterns for the two age groups, the difference between the groups was not significant ($p<.20$).

From <u>Figure 8c</u> it can be seen that almost half of the older children chose the literal meaning of "PG-13: Parents strongly cautioned" that parents should be very careful in deciding whether their children should watch the movie, and most others chose the option indicating that parents should make the decision. In contrast, the responses of the younger children were much more evenly distributed across the options, indicating a very low rate of comprehension of this rating. The difference between the younger and older children was significant (X^2 (5, N=90)=14.55, $p<.05$).

<u>Figure 8d</u> shows that for older children, the most typical (42%) understanding of "R: Restricted" was the literally correct one, that children could not watch without a parent. More than one-fourth chose the literal meaning of "PG-13" as the meaning of "R," however, and 15% thought it meant that children could not see an R-rated movie at all. Younger children's responses were spread out almost equally over most of the options, which suggests that they may have been guessing. The difference between the two age groups approached significance (X^2 (5, N=61)=10.19, $p=.07$).

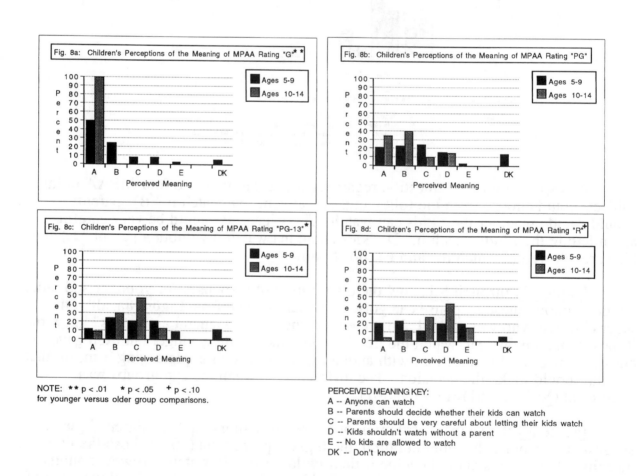

NOTE: ** p < .01   * p < .05   + p < .10
for younger versus older group comparisons.

PERCEIVED MEANING KEY:
A -- Anyone can watch
B -- Parents should decide whether their kids can watch
C -- Parents should be very careful about letting their kids watch
D -- Kids shouldn't watch without a parent
E -- No kids are allowed to watch
DK -- Don't know

The response choices for the meaning of the premium channel content codes were as follows: A) "No fighting, shooting, or hurting," B) "A little fighting, shooting, or hurting," C) "Some fighting, shooting, or hurting," D) "Lots of fighting, shooting, or hurting," and E) "Don't know." Figure 9a shows that the largest number of children in the older group thought "MV: Mild violence" meant a small amount of violence, and most of the others thought it meant "some" violence. In contrast, the responses of the younger children were spread between "a little," "some," and "lots," and one-fifth of them either did not know what it meant or said it meant there was no fighting. The difference between younger and older children was not significant, however (p=.13).

Figure 9b shows that the overwhelming majority of children in both age groups thought that "V: Violence," meant "lots of fighting, shooting, and hurting." Even more younger than older children chose this option, but the difference between the age groups was not significant (p=.22). Figure 9c shows that "GV: Graphic violence," was less well understood by the younger children. Although 82% of this group thought that "V: Violence" meant "lots of fighting...," only 48% thought "GV: Graphic violence," had this meaning. They apparently perceived "graphic" as a minimizing modifier rather than an intensifier. One possible explanation for this misunderstanding is that they confused the "G" in "GV" with the MPAA rating of "G." One younger child, in fact, commented confidently that "graphic violence" was violence that anyone could see. Showing greater comprehension, slightly more of the older children chose "lots of fighting..." as a meaning for GV than had chosen it for V. The difference between the younger and older groups was significant ($\underline{X}^2$ (4, N=87)=10.60, p<.05).

Finally, Figure 9d shows that younger and older children perceived "AC: Adult Content" differently. Although there is no "correct" response to this item since "adult" content may or may not involve violence, it is interesting to see how the age groups interpreted its meaning. The most typical response for both age groups was "lots of fighting ..." The overwhelming majority of older children chose this option, while half of the younger children did. The difference between the two groups was significant ($\underline{X}^2$ (4, N=64)=10.24, p<.05).

Effects on attractiveness of TV offerings. Children's responses to the question regarding whether the advisories and ratings would make them more or less likely to want to see the program or movie were subjected to factorial analyses of variance with advisory type, sex, and age group as independent factors. The responses to this question could range from 1, "very very much less," to 9, "very very much more," with 5 indicating the neutral point.

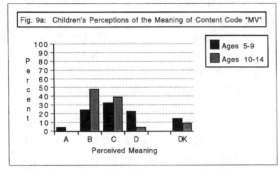

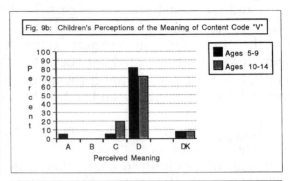

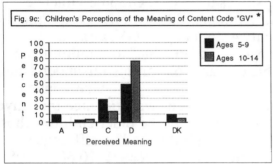

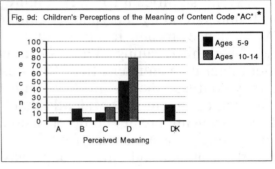

NOTE: * p < .05 for younger versus older group comparisons.

CONTENT CODE KEY:
"MV" -- Mild violence
"V" -- Violence
"GV" -- Graphic violence
"AC" -- Adult content

PERCEIVED MEANING KEY:
A -- No fighting, shooting, or hurting
B -- A little fighting, shooting or hurting
C -- Some fighting, shooting, or hurting
D -- Lots of fighting, shooting, or hurting
DK -- Don't know

The analysis of the four parental and viewer discretion advisories revealed that there were no differences between the four advisories in their effects on children's rated interest in programs ($p > .5$). There were, however, strong effects of both sex and age. As might be expected, older children reported that these advisories would make them want to see a program "a little bit more," and younger children said they would make them want to see it "a little bit less," (5.6 vs. 4.6, $F(1,257) = 16.99$, $p < .001$). Boys also said they would make them more interested (5.8) and girls said they would make them less interested (4.4, $F(1,257) = 28.04$, $p < .001$). There were no significant interactions in this analysis. The analysis came out essentially the same when the two parental advisories were combined and contrasted to the two viewer advisories, that is, there were no differences in the expected effects of the two types of advisories. This analysis indicates that children's expectations of the effect of these messages differed from the effects these messages actually had when the children chose programs to view.

The analysis of children's reported interest in movies with the various MPAA ratings yielded a significant main effect of ratings ($F(3,249) = 5.33$, $p = .001$), and significant interactions between ratings and age ($F(3,249) = 4.39$, $p = .01$) and between ratings and sex ($F(3,249) = 5.39$, $p = .001$). Figure 10a shows the interaction between ratings and gender. Post-hoc Scheffé comparisons within gender revealed that girls expressed less interest in "R"-rated movies than in "G"- or "PG-13"-rated movies. The differences were not significant for boys. However, Figure 10a shows that the pattern of reported interest as a function of sex and MPAA rating is highly similar to the pattern of actual choices by these groups. Figure 10b shows the interaction between MPAA Rating and age group. The Scheffé comparisons revealed that older children expressed a preference for "PG-13" over "G" and "R." Differences within the younger group were not significant. Again these patterns were very similar to the data on movie choice.

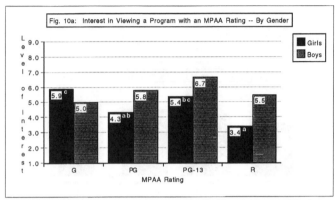

NOTE: Means without common superscripts are significantly different at the p < .05 level. No means for boys are significantly different.

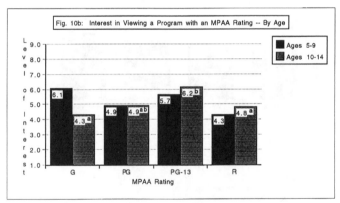

NOTE: Means without common superscripts are significantly different at the p < .05 level. No means for children ages 5-9 are significantly different.

The analysis of the content codes revealed only main effects of sex and age. As we have seen for the other advisories, younger children expressed less interest than older children in viewing programs associated with these advisories (4.3 vs. 5.1, $F(1,252)=8.49$, $p<.01$), and girls showed less interest than boys in such programs (4.1 vs. 5.3, $F(1,252)=22.01$, $p<.001$).

Expected content of televised offerings with advisories and ratings. For each set of advisories and ratings, the percentage of children expecting each of the content types was computed, and the four forms of each type of advisory or rating were compared in chi square analyses.

For the parental and viewer discretion advisories, only two violent content variables were associated with significant differences as a function of which version the child was responding to. As can be seen from <u>Figures 11a</u> and <u>11b</u>, the percentage of children expecting punching or kicking in a program increased over the four forms of advisory, from "Parental discretion advised" to "Contains some violent content; viewer discretion advised." The chi squares computed on these data were as follows: punching, $\underline{X}^2$ (3, N=280)=20.26, $\underline{p}$<.01; kicking, $\underline{X}^2$ (3, N=280)=10.77, $\underline{p}$<.01. There was only one significant difference between the two age groups on these variables: significantly fewer younger than older children expected punching in a program preceded by the parental violence advisory.

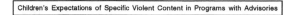

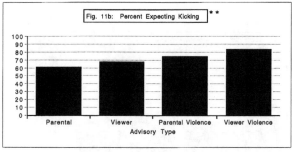

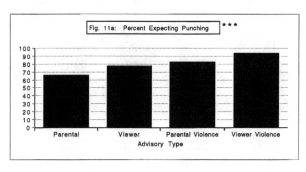

NOTE: *** p < .001   ** p < .01

ADVISORY TYPE KEY:
Parental -- "Parental discretion advised"
Viewer -- "Viewer discretion advised"
Parental Violence -- "Contains some violent content; parental discretion advised"
Viewer Violence -- "Contains some violent content; viewer discretion advised"

Although it is not surprising that the phrase "contains some violent content" would increase the number of children expecting punching and kicking, it is interesting that a greater proportion of children rating the viewer advisories than the parental advisories expected these behaviors. Part of the reason for the different effects of these two types of advisories may be, then, that "viewer discretion advised" suggests more violent content than "parental discretion advised."

The analyses of the MPAA ratings revealed that these ratings exerted significant effects on expectations of content for all of the violent content variables (and for all other content variables as well). <u>Figures 12a</u> through <u>12f</u> show the percentage of children expecting each type of violent content (punching, fighting, explosions, shooting, kicking, and people dying) as a function of the four MPAA ratings. All the chi squares computed on these distributions were highly significant ($\underline{df}$=3, N=280, $\underline{p}$<.001), ranging from a high of 83.16 for shooting to a "low" of 49.05 for punching. For all these variables, the percentage expecting the violent content is lowest for the "G" rating and increases dramatically to the "PG-13" rating. The percentage levels off or declines somewhat in the group that evaluated the "R" rating. The only significant difference between younger and older groups occurred with regard to the "G" rating. More younger than older children expected to see punching, explosions, shooting, and kicking in "G"-rated movies.

Children's Expectations of Specific Violent Content in Movies with MPAA Ratings

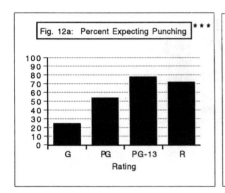

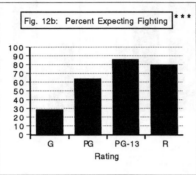

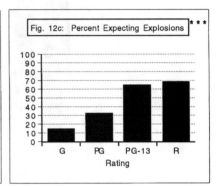

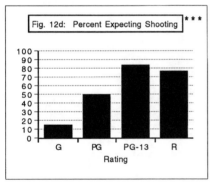

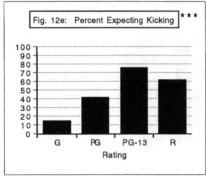

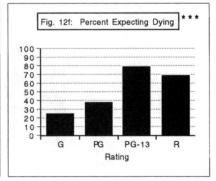

NOTE: *** p < .001

With regard to the content of movies with the different MPAA ratings, the findings with regard to expectations of sexual content are of interest. The percentage of children expecting to see sex in a movie increased from "G" through "R": (G: 10%, PG: 20%, PG-13: 52%, R: 66%). Moreover, older children were significantly more likely than younger children to expect sex in "R"-rated movies (92% vs. 46%, $\underline{X}^2$ (1, N=61)=12.36, $\underline{p}$<.001). This age difference in expectations of sex did not occur in relation to "PG-13."

Figures 13a through 13c display the violent content variables that were perceived by children to be differentially likely in programs as a function of the different content codes: fighting, explosions, and people dying. The chi squares associated with these effects ranged from 11.11 ($\underline{p}$<.01) for fighting to 15.17 ($\underline{p}$<.001) for explosions (df=3, N=278). The patterns for these variables are similar, with the highest proportion of children expecting these violent contents with the "V" and "GV" advisories. The only significant difference between younger and older groups occurred with regard to "AC: Adult content." Fewer younger than older children expected to see fighting and people dying in movies so designated.

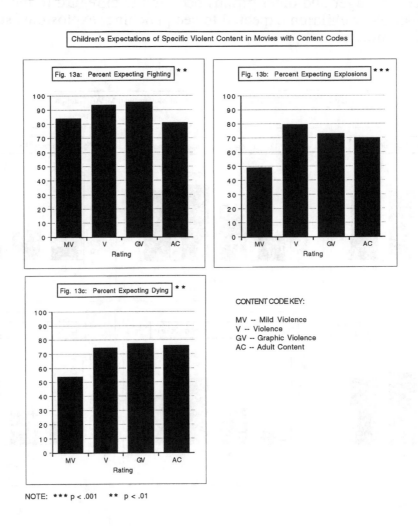

Children's Expectations of Specific Violent Content in Movies with Content Codes

Fig. 13a: Percent Expecting Fighting **

Fig. 13b: Percent Expecting Explosions ***

Fig. 13c: Percent Expecting Dying **

CONTENT CODE KEY:

MV -- Mild Violence
V -- Violence
GV -- Graphic Violence
AC -- Adult Content

NOTE: *** p < .001   ** p < .01

Impact of Background Variables

Parental involvement in child's TV exposure. Four questions on the background questionnaire dealt with the degree to which children said their parents were involved in their television viewing, from which a scale of parental involvement was developed. There was one multiple-choice question: "my mom or dad watches TV with me" (response choices: never, some of the time, most of the time, all of the time). The latter two responses were assigned a value of 1, and the former two were given the value of zero. There were three yes-no questions: For "my parents talk to me about the TV shows I watch," a "yes" response was given a value of 1. For "my parents let me watch whatever TV shows I want," and "my parents let me watch TV for as long as I want," a "no" response was given a value of 1. Analyses of these responses demonstrated that the level of parental involvement differed over the range of behaviors. Only 36% of children indicated that their parents watched television with them most or all of the time. Forty-six percent said their parents talk with them about the shows they watch, 58% said their parents do not let them watch anything they want, and 74% indicated that their parents do not let them watch as long as they want.

The scale combining these responses thus ranged from 0 to 4, with 0 indicating that the parents set no limits on viewing and are uninvolved, and 4 indicating the highest level of involvement. The scores over these five values tended toward a normal distribution, with 10%, 19%, 29%, 29% and 12% reporting scores of 0, 1, 2, 3, and 4, respectively.

To determine whether the degree to which parents were involved in their children's television viewing was related to the child's tendency to choose a program with an advisory, a multiple regression analysis was conducted, in which the dependent variable was whether or not the child chose a program with a "parental discretion" advisory. Age group and gender were entered into the equation on the first step, and as expected, gender was associated with choosing a program with a parental advisory, with males more likely to make such a selection (Beta=.17, $p<.01$, $\underline{R}^2= .03$). More importantly, when parental involvement was entered on the second step, it contributed significantly and negatively to the variance in choice of programs with a parental advisory (Beta=-.15, $p=.01$, $\underline{R}^2_{change}=.02$). What this means is that children who rated their parents as more involved in their TV viewing were less likely than other children to choose a program with a parental discretion advisory.

When the same type of regression analysis was conducted on the choice of programs with viewer discretion advisories, none of the variables were significantly related to choice of a program with a viewer advisory.

To perform a similar analysis on children's choices of movies with ratings indicating more "mature" content, we ran the same type of regression analysis on the data for children in the conditions in which *The Moon-Spinners* was rated "PG-13" or "R." In this analysis, age group, gender, and the measure of parental involvement were all significantly related to children's choice of *The Moon-Spinners* when it had a more restrictive rating. As expected, males (Beta =.20, $\underline{p}<.05$) and older children (Beta = .27, $\underline{p}<.001$, $\underline{R}^2=.10$) chose the movie more often. In addition, after age and gender were accounted for, children whose parents were more involved in their television viewing were less likely to choose the movie when it had these more restrictive rating (Beta =-.17, $\underline{p}<.05$, $\underline{R}^2_{change} =.03$).

Child personality variables. Two aspects of the child's responses on the personality questionnaire were explored. The first personality characteristic, which we referred to as "aggressiveness," was based on respondents' scores on the following items: "I get into fights with other kids," "I like rough and tumble games," and (reverse coded): "I am very careful not to hurt other kids when we play." Although they were intended to form a scale, the reliability of the three items together was quite low (alpha=.39). Because of the low reliability, each of the items was entered separately on the second step of regression analyses predicting the selection of a program with a parental advisory and a viewer advisory and the selection of *The Moon-Spinners* when it was rated "PG-13" or "R."

In the first analysis, when liking "rough and tumble games" was entered after the effects of age group and gender (R^2=.03), it was a positive predictor of the tendency to choose a program with a parental discretion advisory (Beta=.15, p<.05, R^2_{change} =.02). Neither of the other aggression-related items made a significant contribution. In the analysis of the tendency to choose a program with a viewer discretion advisory, neither age group nor gender were significant predictors. Children's responses to the item "I get into fights with other kids," was positively related to choosing such programs, approaching significance (Beta=.12, p=.059, R^2_{change} =.03). Thus, children who reported more often behaving aggressively tended to show more interest in programs with a viewer advisory. Neither of the other aggression-related items made a significant contribution to these choices.

In the third analysis, both gender (Beta = .19, p<.05) and age (Beta = .27, p<.001, R^2=.10) were significant predictors of choosing *The Moon-Spinners* when it was rated "PG-13" or "R," with boys and older children choosing it more often. None of the three aggression-related personality items were significant further contributors to this choice.

The second personality characteristic that we explored was labeled "anxiety." It involved responses to the following four items: "I have nightmares (bad dreams)," "I find it hard to get to sleep at night because I worry about things," "I get nervous when I'm in a strange place," and "seeing scary things on TV upsets me." Since the reliability of a scale based on these items was low (alpha=.58), these four items were entered separately on the second step of regression analyses predicting program and movie choice.

For the analysis predicting choice of programs with parental discretion advisories, gender was a significant predictor on the first step (Beta=.18, p<.01, R^2=.03), with boys choosing such programs more. When entered on the second step, the tendency to report being upset by scary television contributed significantly to the choice of such programs in a negative fashion (Beta=-.18, p<.01, R^2_{change} =.03). In other words, kids who reported getting upset more often by scary television were less likely to choose a program with a parental discretion advisory.

Neither age group nor gender predicted the tendency to choose programs with viewer discretion advisories. However, having been upset by television was again a significant negative predictor (Beta=-.18, p<.01, R^2_{change} =.04), that is, children reporting that scary television upsets them were less likely to choose a program with a viewer advisory.

In the third analysis, the only significant predictor of the choice of *The Moon-Spinners* when it was rated "PG-13" or "R," was gender (Beta=.21, p=.01, R^2=.10), with boys choosing it significantly more. None of the anxiety-related items contributed to these choices.

PART II: EFFECTS OF ADVISORIES AND RATINGS ON PARENT-CHILD DISCUSSIONS OF TELEVISION VIEWING CHOICES

Joanne Cantor & Marina B. Krcmar

In the context of a larger investigation of family communication patterns and patterns of parent-child discourse, a dissertation by Marina Krcmar, we gathered some data on the effect of the presence of advisories and ratings on the television-viewing choices that parents and children make together. In this study, parent-child dyads were brought into the experimental laboratory, ostensibly to study the child's reactions to television. Parents and children were given the choice of which programs the child would watch, and as they discussed the choices available to them in a channel guide similar to the one used in the main experiment, their interactions were videotaped. Although the overall dissertation explored the relationship between family communication patterns and the participants' communication strategies in discussing what the child would view, this report will provide data on the effects of advisories and ratings on the viewing choices of different subgroups of the sample, the way parents and children referred to ratings and advisories in discussing these choices, and the degree to which such joint decisions were complied with in the absence of the parent.

It must be acknowledged here that there are major differences between this experiment and the one conducted on children alone. Most important is the fact that in the children's study, children made their choices in complete anonymity. In the parent-child study, the participants not only could not be treated anonymously; they knew that their conversations were being videotaped. Therefore, a very high rate of avoidance of the programs with restrictive advisories was expected in the parent-child study. This rate should not be considered readily generalizable to normal home-viewing, and should not be directly compared to the rate observed in the main experiment. Moreover, the samples for the two studies were drawn from different types of schools. Rather than comparing the findings of this study to the larger one, we are making comparisons between different groups within this study.

Four questions were of particular interest regarding the issues involved in the overall research on ratings and advisories. The first was whether the rate of avoidance of programs with restrictive advisories would be higher in dyads involving younger children than in dyads involving older children. Parents were expected to be more protective of younger than older children. The second was whether the rate of avoidance would be greater for dyads involving female than male children. Based on the results of the main experiment, it might be expected that boys would be more interested in restricted programs, which might result in a higher choice rate for restricted programs in dyads involving boys than in those involving girls.

The third question was whether the discussions of programs with advisories and restrictive ratings would reveal differences in the attitudes of children and parents toward the programs associated with them. For example, would the advisories provoke more positive evaluations from the children than from their parents? Would boys be more likely than girls to make positive comments about a restrictive rating?

The fourth question was whether children would be more or less likely to comply with decisions made regarding programs with advisories than programs without advisories. In other words, would a program that was rejected that had an advisory become more tempting than a program that was rejected that did not have an advisory?

Method

Participants

The sample included 70 parent-child dyads who were recruited from five parochial schools in the Madison, Wisconsin area. Thirty-six of the dyads included children in the younger group, who were attending kindergarten or first grade. They ranged in age from 5 to 7, with a mean age of 6.2 years. Thirty-four of the dyads, the older group, involved children in fourth or fifth grade. These children ranged in age from 9 to 11, with a mean age of 9.3 years. Within each age group, there was an equal number of girls and boys. The sample of parents contained 4 fathers and 66 mothers. Participants were recruited by letter, and parents' informed consent was obtained prior to their participation.

Procedure

Parents and children were brought into an empty classroom at the child's school. They were seated on chairs in front of a television, a VCR, and a camera. The session was described as a study of children's responses to television, and it was explained that we wanted to be more realistic by giving the participants a choice of several programs to view. The participants were also asked for their permission to be videotaped during the session.

After agreeing to the procedures, the pair was given a television program guide booklet, somewhat similar to the one used in the main experiment. The participants were told to select one program on each page of the booklet. In addition, they were invited to indicate whether, for each non-chosen program, they felt "neutral" about it or actively rejected that choice. Finally, they were asked to rank-order their choices among all programs that were not rejected.

The experimenter left the room while the parent and child made their decisions. After the choices had been made, the experimenter returned and escorted the parent out of the room to fill out some questionnaires, taking the choice booklet with her. At this time, a second experimenter entered the room to show the child a program. She brought with her a booklet similar to the one the child had seen, but this one had not been filled out. She stated that she did not know which programs had been chosen, and asked which of the programs on Page 3 of the booklet the child wanted to watch. The experimenter then appeared to look for that tape and professed not being able to find it. She then gave the child a choice among the three situation comedies listed on Page 1 of the booklet. The child was then shown a scene from the chosen sitcom.

After viewing the program, the child filled out a brief questionnaire tapping measures not directly relevant to the violence project. After completing the questionnaire, the child was given a small gift and reunited with the parent. Both were then thanked for their participation.

Materials

The viewing-choice booklet described three available programs on each of four pages. Pages 1 and 2 contained descriptions of three real situation comedies and three current violent cartoons, respectively. Page 3 contained titles of three fictitious reality-action programs. These programs were given the titles *Criminals at Large, Cop Scenes from the Street*, and *Detectives Live!* Each title was followed by a brief description of the episode. In each booklet, one of these programs, at random, was given the advisory "Contains some violence. Parental discretion advised."

Page 4 contained the fictitious titles of three animated violent movies. These movies were titled *Mission Pilot X, Robot Renegades*, and *Kombat III*, and each title was followed by a brief plot description. One of these movies, at random, was given the rating of "PG-13: Parents strongly cautioned." The other two were assigned a "PG" rating.

Measures

Parent-child viewing choices were recorded as the dyad's first choice on Pages 3 and 4 of booklet. Any programs or movies that were rejected were noted as well. When the child made a choice of what to view when the parent was out of the room, the child's behavior was considered noncompliant if he or she chose a program that had been rejected earlier by the dyad.

The videotaped discussions were coded for comments made by the parent and child about the advisory or the "PG-13" rating. These comments were categorized as "favorable," (e.g., "Cool!"), "unfavorable," (e.g., "not 'PG-13'") or "neutral" toward the advisory. A second coder categorized a randomly selected subset of 23% of the videotapes. Scott's pi, computed on these categorizations, was .88.

Results

Parent-Child Viewing Choices

Programs with parental discretion advisories. As expected, there was a strong tendency to avoid choosing the program with the advisory when parents and children made their decisions in concert. Out of the 70 dyads, only five (7%) chose a program with an advisory, and this percentage was dramatically and significantly below chance expectations of 33.3% ($p<.001$). Because of the small number of dyads choosing a program with an advisory, comparisons between subgroups were destined to fall short of statistical significance. Dyads involving both younger and older children chose programs with advisories significantly below chance levels. Only one dyad out of the 34 involving a younger child chose a program with the advisory (3%, $p<.001$), and only four out of the 36 dyads involving older children did so (11%, $p<.01$). Similarly, dyads involving both boys and girls chose such programs significantly below chance levels. Only one of the 34 dyads involving boys selected a program with the advisory (3%, p<.001), and 4 of the 36 dyads involving girls did so (11%, p<.01).

In these data on parental discretion advisories, then, there is only a slight suggestion that parents were more "protective" of their younger than their older children. The expectation that dyads with boys would choose programs with advisories more often than dyads with girls received even less support, since the significance of the tendency to avoid such programs was stronger among dyads with boys than among dyads with girls.

Movies with "PG-13" ratings. The tendency to avoid movies with "PG-13" ratings when pitted against others rated "PG" was not as strong as the tendency to avoid programs with advisories. Out of the 70 dyads, ten (14%) chose the movie that had the "PG-13" rating, and this number was significantly below the 33.3% that would be expected by chance (p=.001). In these data, choice of "PG-13" was significantly below chance for dyads involving younger, but not for those involving older children. Three of 34 dyads with younger children (9%) chose the "PG-13" movie (p<.01), while 7 of 36 dyads with older children (19%) did so (p=.11). As for the impact of the child's gender, the tendency to avoid the "PG-13" movie only approached significance in dyads with boys, but it was significant in dyads with girls. Six out of 34, or 18% of the dyads with boys chose the movie with the "PG-13" rating (p=.08), while 4 out of 36, or 11% of the dyads with girls chose such a movie (p<.01).

The Role of Advisories and Ratings in Parent-Child Discussions

Parents' comments about advisories and ratings. Parents made many comments about the advisory and the "PG-13" rating, and these comments were almost entirely negative. Eighteen parents in dyads with younger children (50%) made comments about the advisories. All of these comments were unfavorable, indicating that the content was inappropriate or that the child could not see the program. Three of these parents mentioned the child's age as a reason to avoid the program (e.g., "that means it's for big kids"); six referred to the violence in the advisory (e.g., "it says there's violence. I don't think we'd like that"); one mentioned that it would be frightening ("it means it's scary"). The remaining parents gave nonspecific negative references [e.g., "not with that" (pointing to the advisory)]. Fifteen parents in dyads with older children (44%) made comments about the advisory, and all of these comments, too, were negative. Two of these parents referred to the violence (e.g., "Says it contains violence and so no"). The remainder of the negative comments did not specify why (e.g., "parental discretion. I'd probably say not.")

Twenty parents in dyads with younger children (56%) made comments about the "PG-13" rating, and all of these were negative. Seven of these referred to the child's age as an issue (e.g., "you're not old enough"); and three others said that it would be frightening (e.g., "it means it's scary"). The remainder made nonspecific negative comments (e.g., "Not PG-13"). Fifteen parents in dyads with older children (44%) made comments about the "PG-13" rating. One of these comments had a positive tone, but it may have been tongue-in-cheek ("I'm strongly cautioned, so that's the one!"

[laughing]). All of the remaining comments made nonspecific negative references to the "PG-13" rating (e.g., "You've seen PG. PG-13 has a lesser chance.")

Children's comments about advisories and ratings. The children did not comment on the advisory or the "PG-13" rating nearly as often as their parents, but when they did, their comments were more evenly split between favorable and unfavorable judgments. In dyads with younger children, 4 children (11%) made unfavorable references to the advisory (one suggesting it would be "scary") and 1 (3%) made a favorable reference (saying "oh yes, please???" after reading the advisory). In contrast, in dyads with older children, 3 (9%) made unfavorable references to the advisory (e.g., "sounds violent"), but 7 (20%) made favorable references (e.g., after reading the advisory, "that's awesome!" and "they all say that. It's fine. They just all say that.") The difference between younger and older children in their tendency to make favorable references to the advisory was significant ($X^2(1, N=70)=4.70, p<.05$).

A similar pattern was observed in children's references to the "PG-13" rating, although the difference between older and younger children was not significant. Among dyads with younger children, 4 children (11%) made unfavorable references to the "PG-13" rating (e.g, "does it mean bad?") and 2 (6%) made positive references (e.g., after reading the advisory, "I'll take it"). Among dyads with older children, one child (3%) said something negative about the "PG-13" rating ("PG-13. Adios"), and 6 (18%) said something positive about it (e.g., "PG-13. Choose that one"). One older girl said, "those two [PG-rated movies] are little loser ones. They rated *Home Alone* 'PG.' The cooler the movie, the higher the rating."

It is not surprising that positive comments about the advisory and the "PG-13" rating were more frequent among older than younger children. However, the expected gender difference in these comments did not materialize. The favorable comments about the advisory and the "PG-13" rating were equally split between girls and boys.

Compliance with Joint Decisions

When the children were given the choice, outside their parent's presence, between the three reality-action programs, 16 of them (23%) chose a program that had been rejected during the joint decision-making process. However, choosing a program that had been rejected was no more likely when the rejected program had an advisory than when it did not: Seven of the noncompliant children chose a rejected program that had an advisory, while nine children chose a rejected program that did not have an advisory. Five of the seven children who chose a rejected program that had an advisory were boys (4 older and one younger); the two girls were both younger. Of the nine children who chose a rejected program that did not have an advisory, six were boys (four older and two younger); of the three girls, two were older and one was younger.

There is thus no evidence from these data that a program with an advisory that is rejected becomes more tempting than one without an advisory that is rejected.

PART III: COLLEGE STUDENTS' INTEREST IN MOVIES ON TELEVISION AS A FUNCTION OF MPAA RATINGS

A third study was conducted (with the help of Nick Van Straten) to determine the degree to which information about a movie's MPAA rating would influence college undergraduates' desire to see the movie. A large sample of college students participated in an experiment in which they gave ratings of how interested they would be in seeing a series of five movies if they were to appear on television. Different types of movies were selected, some containing violence, some sex, and some, both sex and violence. In different booklets, the same movie was associated with a different MPAA rating. Some movie descriptions were ambiguous enough that they could credibly be assigned to a wide range of ratings. Others were confined to a narrower range. In addition to variations in MPAA ratings, one of the movies also contained variations in the new content codes being used on some premium channels. The effect of MPAA ratings on students' evaluations of a movie scene was also examined.

Method

Participants

Five hundred seventy-four University of Wisconsin-Madison students were recruited from classes in the Business School and in the Departments of Communication Arts and Journalism. Participants received extra class credit in exchange for their participation. Approximately 44% of the sample was male. The mean age of the sample was 20.3 years.

Procedure

Participants reported to testing sessions in groups ranging from 10 to 25. They were told about the procedures to be followed and signed consent forms regarding their participation.

Participants each filled out a movie-interest booklet. They were told that they would read descriptions of five movies as they might be presented in the television listings. They were asked to indicate how interested they would be in seeing each movie if it were shown on television. There were five films, each described on a separate page. After indicating their level of interest in the five movies, they were told that they would see some film clips from the last movie described. Because this movie had been associated with different ratings in different booklets, different subjects were led to believe the movie they were seeing had been differentially rated. After seeing the movie segment, subjects filled out a questionnaire assessing their judgments and evaluations of the movie. They were also asked about their recall of the rating of the movie.

Materials

The first movie in the booklet, titled *Shadowman*, was about a jewel theft and a falsely accused man attempting to find the real criminals. In different booklets it was rated "G," "PG," "PG-13," or "R," or no rating was indicated. The second movie, titled *Lost in London*, was about an "alienated art student" being introduced to "sensual pleasures." It was rated "PG-13" or "R," or was not associated with a rating.

The third movie, titled *Witnesses*, was described as a "gritty melodrama" pitting small-town policemen against drug-dealing killers. The film was rated either "PG-13" or "R," and each of these ratings appeared by itself or was paired with "MV: Mild Violence," "V: Violence," or "GV: Graphic Violence." In addition to these eight conditions, there was a condition in which the movie received no rating.

The fourth movie, titled *Love Hurts*, was described as a story about a woman who introduces a "womanizing disc-jockey" to a sensual world of pain mixed with pleasure. This movie, which suggested a mixture of sex and violence, was rated "PG-13," "R," or "NC-17," or had no rating.

The final movie was called *Rage*. It was described as portraying a blind Vietnam veteran who takes on a gang of Mafia killers. Like the fourth movie, it was rated "PG-13," "R," or "NC-17," or had no rating.

The movie scene that was shown was introduced as an excerpt from *Rage*, but it was actually from *Blind Fury* (1989). The scene involved the blind Vietnam veteran, played by Rutger Hauer, coming to the aid of the widow of one of his army buddies as she and her son are attacked by vicious killers. Although blind, he has a keen "sixth sense" and is able to overcome his attackers when they think he is the most vulnerable. The movie was originally rated "R."

Measures

Participants indicated their interest in seeing the movie on a 7-point scale ranging from 1, labeled "not at all," to 7, labeled "very very much." After viewing the movie segment, they were asked to indicate the following on the same seven-point scale: 1) how much they liked the segment, 2) how violent they thought the segment was, 3) how much they wanted to see the whole movie, 4) how violent they thought the movie would be, and 5) how sexually explicit they thought the movie would be. They were also asked to indicate what they remembered the movie's rating to have been.

Results

Interest in Movies

Overall, students' reported interest in the movies described in the booklets was only minimally affected by the ratings the movies were assigned. Analyses of variance were conducted on ratings of interest in the movies, with the participant's gender and the movie's rating as the independent variables. For the first movie, *Shadowman*, about the jewel theft, which was associated with "G," "PG," "PG-13," "R," or no rating, there were no significant effects of ratings, gender, or the interaction.

For *Lost in London*, the movie whose description suggested sex but not violence, there was a significant effect of gender ($\underline{F}(1,550)=9.19$, $\underline{p}<.01$). Males expressed more interest in the movie than females (4.3 vs. 3.9 on a 7-point scale). Although the main effect of ratings ("PG-13," "R," or no rating) was not significant, there was a significant ratings by gender interaction ($\underline{F}(2,550)=4.10$, $\underline{p}<.05$). Males showed greater interest in the movie when it was rated "R" or had no rating than when it was rated "PG-13." Females, in contrast, showed greater interest in the movie when it was rated "PG-13," than when it was rated "R" or had no rating. However, Scheffé tests revealed that these differences between means were not significant.

In a three-factor analysis of variance of interest in *Witnesses*, involving rating (PG-13, R), violence code (none, MV, V, or GV), and gender of subject, there were no significant effects of rating, violence code, or their interaction. The only significant effect was that of gender ($\underline{F}(1,476)=36.73$, $\underline{p}<.001$), with males showing significantly greater interest in this violent movie than females (4.3 vs. 3.4). Gender did not interact with either rating or violence code in this analysis. When the no-rating condition was included in an analysis involving three levels of rating (no rating, PG-13, R) and gender, the results were essentially the same. There was again a strong main effect of gender, but no effect of ratings, and no interaction between ratings and gender.

There were no significant effects in the analysis of *Love Hurts*, a movie whose description suggested a mixture of sex and violence, and was associated with "PG-13," "R," "NC-17," or no rating.

Interest in the final movie, *Rage*, was marginally affected by its purported rating (PG-13, R, NC-17, or no rating), with the F-ratio only approaching significance $\underline{F}(3,557)=2.12$, $\underline{p}=.10$) in spite of the very large sample size. Subsequent tests revealed that none of the means of the ratings conditions differed significantly. There was a highly significant effect of gender ($\underline{F}(1,557)=61.08$, $\underline{p}<.001$), with males more interested in the movie than females (4.0 vs. 3.0).

Evaluation of Movie Clip

Participants' evaluations of the movie clip were only minimally affected by the rating they were told the movie had. Analyses of variance were conducted on the participants' responses to the five questions asked after the movie was seen. These analyses involved the participant's gender and the movie's purported rating (no rating, PG-13, R, or NC-17) as independent variables. For four out of the five questions, the only significant effect was a main effect of gender. Males liked the movie clips significantly more than females ($\underline{F}(1,557)=70.57$, $\underline{p}<.001$), with men giving the movie a mean "liking" rating of 4.2 vs. 2.9 for women. Males expressed significantly more interest than females in seeing the whole movie ($\underline{F}(1,558)=38.44$, $\underline{p}<.001$; males, 3.9; females, 2.9). Females saw the movie as significantly more violent than males did ($\underline{F}(1,558)=17.42$, $\underline{p}<.001$; males, 5.5; females, 5.9), and they expected the whole movie to be more violent ($\underline{F}(1,557)=27.18$, $\underline{p}<.001$; males, 5.5; females, 5.9).

The only response to the movie that was affected by the movie's rating was participants' expectations of how sexually explicit the whole movie would be. These responses were affected by both the movie's rating and the participant's gender. Males expected the movie to be less sexually explicit than females ($F(1,557)=10.67$, p<.001; males, 3.1; females, 3.5), and expectations of sexual explicitness increased as the ratings became more restrictive. The means were as follows: no rating, 3.0; "PG-13," 3.1; "R," 3.3, and "NC-17," 3.6. Scheffé comparisons revealed that the movie was expected to be significantly more sexually explicit in the "NC-17" condition than in the no-rating and "PG-13" conditions.

Memory for Movie's Rating

Like the children in the main experiment, the college students in this experiment did not have good recall of the rating they were told the movie had. Overall, by the end of the session, only about 40% answered correctly when asked what the rating of *Rage* was, and slightly over one-fourth said they did not recall the rating. Correct recall was higher in the conditions in which the movie was rated "R" (51.4%) and "NC-17" (52.4%), than when it was rated "PG-13" (23.4%) or had no rating (32.1%).

When the ratings of interest in the movie *Rage* were reanalyzed, including only the 229 participants who remembered the movie's rating correctly, the results were essentially the same as those reported above, with the exception that in the smaller analysis, the effect of ratings did not even approach significance. In addition, analyses of evaluations of the movie including only those 229 participants were essentially the same as analyses computed on the entire sample, with one exception. In the smaller analysis, there was a significant effect of the movie's rating on expectations of the level of violence in the whole movie ($F(3,218)=2.79$, p<.05). The means of the four conditions were as follows: no rating, 5.7; "PG-13," 5.3; "R," 5.7; "NC-17," 5.9. Scheffé comparisons indicated that the whole movie was expected to contain significantly more violence when it was rated "NC-17" than when it was rated "PG-13."

Overall, the most compelling aspect of the results of this study of college students is the paucity of significant effects of ratings. Put simply, these ratings had very little impact on these students' expressed interest in these movies. The lack of significance is especially striking given the very large sample size involved in this study. These findings are in some sense consistent with the earlier findings of Austin (1980), who also reported no significant impact of MPAA ratings on college students' interest in movies. Although that study was criticized earlier for a potential problem in the credibility of the manipulation, our experiment also reported essentially null findings.

One procedural similarity between these two studies is that both posed viewing choices hypothetically rather than giving students choices that would result in their viewing of the selected movies. Therefore, research should be conducted in which actual choices are measured before we can finally conclude that MPAA ratings have minimal effects on college students' viewing choices.

PART IV: THE USE OF ADVISORIES AND RATINGS IN THE COMPOSITE WEEK OF TELEVISON

The final part of this report describes the use of advisories, ratings, and content codes in the random sample of television that was taped in Los Angeles and content analyzed in Santa Barbara and Austin. It should be kept in mind that the Year 1 analysis constitutes mainly a base-level against which Years 2 and 3 can be compared. At present, the use of these ratings, codes and advisories cannot be evaluated in relation to the violent content of these programs, so statements about the appropriateness of these messages would be premature.

A description of the sampling procedures and the overall characteristics of the random sample is contained in the report from the Santa Barbara site. When programs were screened by the content coders in Santa Barbara and Austin, they were given codes for the presence of advisories, MPAA ratings, and the more specific content codes recently adopted by some premium channels. The coders also indicated whether these messages were communicated orally, in written form, or both orally and in writing. The text of all advisories was written down verbatim. This text was then further categorized by coders at the Madison site. Because occasionally there were problems with the taping of programs, which resulted in the initial minute or so of the program not being included on the tape, a small proportion of programs could not be evaluated regarding the use of ratings and advisories. The data to be reported here reflect an analysis of only those tapes for which the entire introductory portion of the program was available.

Coding of Advisories

Advisories refer to short verbal messages that precede programs and can take a variety of forms, but typically involve advocating caution or discretion regarding the upcoming program, e.g., "viewer discretion advised." A few advisories characterize the program in other ways, such as involving actual footage or dramatizations of real events. Advisories were analyzed separately from the MPAA Ratings (G, PG, PG-13, and R), and the content codes (e.g., MV: Mild Violence). The data sets that were assembled at Santa Barbara and Austin indicated whether or not an oral advisory was aired with a program and whether or not a written advisory was present. One coder at the Madison site categorized the text of the advisories on a series of variables. A randomly selected subset consisting of 20% of the advisories was categorized by a second coder. The coding variables are described below. Agreement was 100% for all variables.

Whose Discretion Is Advocated?

The advisories were first coded according to whether or not discretion was advised, and further, according to whose discretion was being advocated. Advisories were coded as advocating "parental" discretion (e.g., "parental discretion advised"), "viewer" discretion, (e.g., "viewer discretion advised"), "discretion" without a specific target (e.g., "discretion advised"), as presenting a "warning" or other admonition, but no mention of discretion (e.g., "warning: this program contains ..."), or as including no reference to discretion or warnings.

Unsuitable for Which Viewers?

Independent of the presence of "discretion" or "warnings," the advisories were coded for whether they indicated that the program might be inappropriate for specific viewer categories. Advisories were coded as indicating that the content might be inappropriate for children, (e.g., "portions of the following may not be suitable for younger audiences") or for unspecified viewers, not including children (e.g., "the following movie [contains graphic scenes and] may be too intense for some viewers"), or as not indicating any inappropriate viewer categories.

Content Mentioned

Five variables indicated whether or not the advisory mentioned the following content: violence, language, sex or nudity, adult themes, or unspecified inappropriate content. An example of the latter category is "the following program contains certain scenes [which may be too intense for young children]".

Humor

A final variable indicated whether or not the advisory seemed to be presented in a "tongue in cheek" fashion, rather than in a serious mode. For example, the following advisory aired on MTV: "Beavis & Butthead are not role models. They're not even human. They're cartoons. Some of the things they do would cause a person to get hurt, expelled, arrested, possibly deported. To put it another way: Don't try this at home.").

Use of Advisories in the Sample

Presence of Oral and Written Advisories

A frequency analysis of the presence of advisories presented orally indicated that 98, or 4.0% of the 2445 programs that could be evaluated were aired with oral advisories. Slightly more, or 105 programs (4.2%) were aired with written advisories. The overwhelming majority of advisories were presented in both oral and written form, and contained essentially the same information in both modes. Figure 14 shows the distribution of written advisories over the channels in the sample. There were differences between the number of oral and written advisories on only three channels. FOX had nine written but only two oral advisories; Lifetime had five written but three oral advisories; and NBC communicated one advisory in writing, but aired four orally.

A review of Figure 14 also reveals that 8 of the 23 channels did not use advisories in their sampled programs at all. Moreover, 50 or 48% of the advisories in the sample came from one channel, Showtime.

Text of Advisories

Figure 15 displays the frequency with which various types of discretion were advocated in the advisories. Although the figure reports data from both oral and written advisories, percentages mentioned in this description will refer to written advisories for the sake of simplicity. In terms of the content of these advisories, "viewer discretion" was advocated most frequently, with 63% of the written advisories advocating viewer discretion. It should be acknowledged here, however, that 50, or 77% of these advisories were on one channel, Showtime. "Parental discretion" was advocated for 8% of the programs with written advisories. Two advisories advocated discretion without a specified target. Fourteen percent of the advisories involved a warning without further mentioning discretion.

Figure 16 displays the distribution of other content features of the verbal advisories in the sample. As can be seen from the figure, 10% mentioned the unsuitability of the content for children, and only one advisory mentioned viewer groups not involving children. The mention of the specific content that was responsible for the advisory was relatively rare, with only 5% mentioning violence, 4% mentioning language, and even fewer mentioning sex and adult themes.

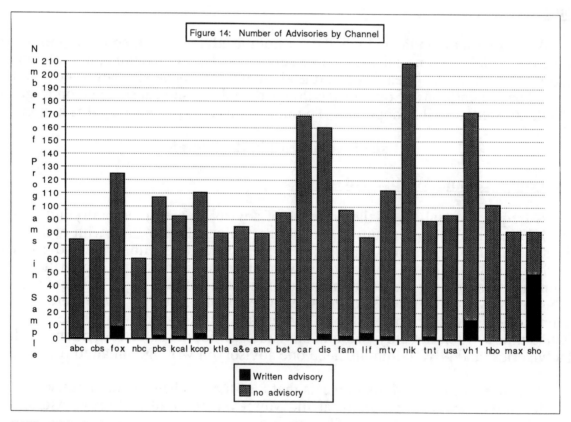

NOTE: Advisories involve phrases such as "viewer discretion advised."

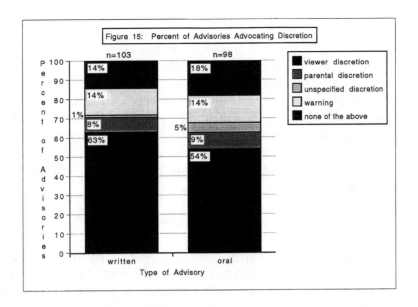

Figure 15: Percent of Advisories Advocating Discretion

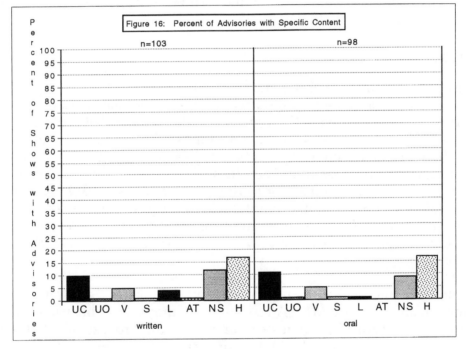

Figure 16: Percent of Advisories with Specific Content

KEY: UC - unsuitability for children
      UO - unsuitability for others
      V - mention of violence
      S - mention of sex
      L - mention of language
      AT - mention of adult themes
      NS - nonspecific subject matter
      H - humor

Finally, 17% of the advisories involved humor. Three of these were on MTV and involved the Beavis and Butthead disclaimer quoted above, and 14 were on "Stand-Up Spotlight" on VH1, and involved the following language: "Warning. The following material may not be suitable for small children, some adults, a few senior citizens, many farm animals, and most household appliances."

In summary, a small proportion (4%) of the programs in the Year 1 sample involved advisories, and almost half of these came from one premium channel. About three-fourths of all advisories advocated someone's "discretion." Approximately 10% of advisories advocated parental discretion and the same proportion suggested that the content might not be suitable for young viewers. Combining these two types of advisories, approximately 13% indicated that children were a concern, that is, they either advocated parental discretion or indicated a concern for young viewers, or both. For the most part, the advisories were not specific about the nature of the content that prompted the advisory. Five percent of the verbal advisories mentioned violence, and this was the content type mentioned most.

Coding of Ratings

All complete programs in the sample were screened by the content coders in Santa Barbara and Austin for the presence of MPAA ratings and specific content codes. Ratings and content codes were coded according to their mode of presentation, that is, written only, oral only, or both oral and written. They were also coded according to which rating or code was used.

MPAA Ratings

Because these ratings are associated with movies only, the analyses to be reported here are based on the 442 programs in our sample that were designated by the content coders as movies. Of the 442 programs in the sample that were designated as movies, 180, or 41% were shown with MPAA ratings. All but one of these ratings were shown on the three premium movie channels in the sample. Figure 17 shows the distribution of movies with these ratings on these channels. As can be seen from the figure, all three channels gave ratings for most of their movies. HBO presented MPAA ratings on 90% of their movies in the sample; Cinemax gave ratings for 78%, and Showtime gave ratings for 75%. Almost all of these ratings were presented both orally and visually. In addition, one movie, on KTLA, was broadcast with an "R" rating, in written form only.

It should be acknowledged here that there may be a good reason for the failure of nonpremium channels to use MPAA ratings when they show theatrical movies. If these channels typically edit the movies for television, the process of altering the movies' contents makes the initial MPAA designations no longer applicable.

Combining the three premium channels, 30% percent of the movies were rated "PG," and 31% were rated "PG-13." Only 4% were rated "G," and 16% were rated "R." In 19% of the cases, no rating information was provided. There were no "X"-rated or "NC-17"-rated movies in the sample.

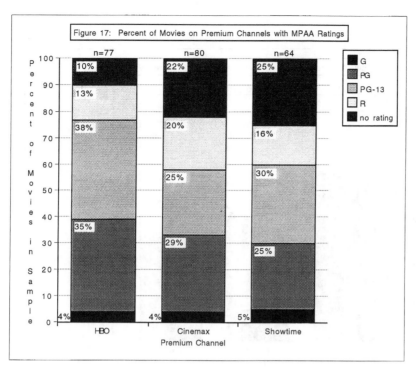

Figure 17: Percent of Movies on Premium Channels with MPAA Ratings

Content Codes

Content codes are independent of any MPAA designation, and are assigned to a movie by the channel carrying it. The content code data was contributed by the coders at Santa Barbara, and analyzed at the Madison site. The codes involved notations for violence, language, nudity, adult content, and rape.

Figure 18 shows the percentage of movies broadcast on the three premium channels that used content codes for violence. This figure shows that the violence codes were used quite heavily by these channels. Combining the three premium channels, more than half of all movies shown on these channels bore one of these codes. The "V: Violence" code was used most by all three channels. A total of 39% of the movies on these channels were so designated. Sixteen percent of the movies used the "MV: Mild Violence" code, and 2% used the "GV: Graphic Violence" code.

Figure 19 shows the percentage of movies broadcast on the premium channels that used the other content codes. Again, it can be seen that these labels were frequently applied to movies. The language codes were the most heavily used, with 65% of the movies aired on these channels featuring the code "AL: Adult Language." The "AC: Adult Content" code was also heavily used, with 52% of movies being so designated. Nudity notations were applied to almost one-fourth of the movies on these channels, with 13% of movies carrying the "BN: Brief Nudity" code and another 10% carrying the "N: Nudity" code. The codes for Graphic Language (GL), Strong Sexual Content (SC), and Rape (R) were used very rarely.

Showtime presented all the content codes both visually and orally. In contrast, most of the content codes that were presented on HBO and Cinemax were presented visually only.

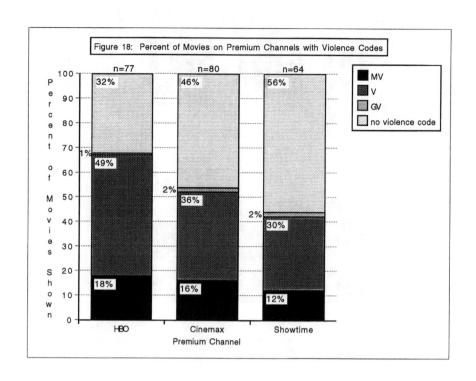

Figure 18: Percent of Movies on Premium Channels with Violence Codes

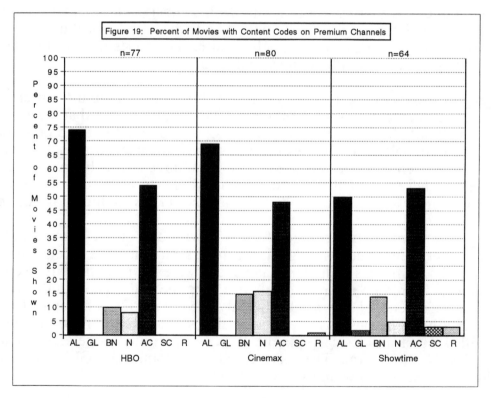

Figure 19: Percent of Movies with Content Codes on Premium Channels

KEY: AL - adult language
GL - graphic language
BN - brief nudity
N - nudity
AC - adult content
SC - strong sexual content
R - rape

Scheduling of Advisories, Ratings, and Codes

To determine how programs with advisories were distributed throughout the day, days were divided into dayparts consistent with the analyses being conducted at the other sites. Programs were placed into dayparts as a function of the time a program began. The dayparts are as follows:

1: 7-9, early morning
2: 9-3, daytime
3: 3-6, late afternoon
4: 6-8, early evening
5: 8-11, prime time.

Because the 9-3 daypart is during school hours during weekdays but not during weekends, analyses were initially done separately for weekdays and weekends. However, the two analyses yielded results that were extremely similar. Therefore, only the results for the entire week are reported here.

An analysis of the timing of advisories revealed that the use of advisories tended to increase over the course of the day. Figure 20 shows the percent of programs in each daypart that were shown with advisories. These percentages range from 1.3% in the early morning to 10.5% in prime time. However, given the small number of advisories overall and the fact that almost half came from one channel (Showtime) and 14% came from one comedy show ("Stand-up Spotlight"), these trends over time probably do not reflect any general trends in the industry as a whole.

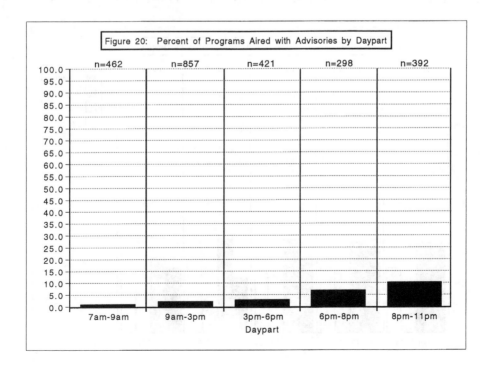

Figure 20: Percent of Programs Aired with Advisories by Daypart

Figure 21 shows the distribution of each of the four observed MPAA Ratings over the dayparts. As the figure shows, the highest proportion of "G"-rated films were presented in the early morning, and the overwhelming majority of "R-Rated" movies were shown in prime time.

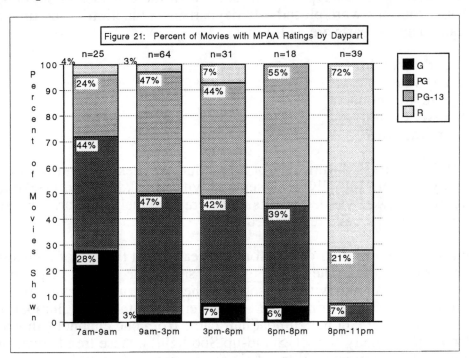

Figure 22 shows the distribution of the various content codes over the same dayparts. This figure shows no marked variations across the time periods.

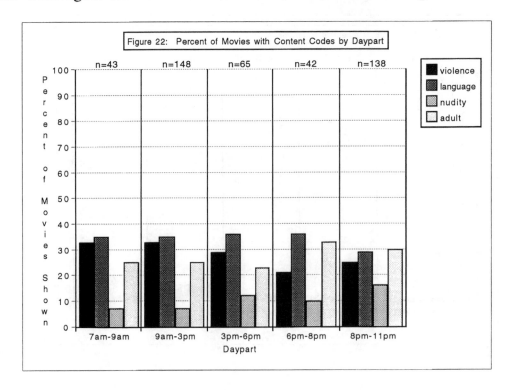

In summary, then, advisories advocating discretion are rarely used, and when they are used, they are seldom specific about the nature of the content that prompted the advisory. MPAA ratings and specific content codes for movies are used much more frequently, but these appear almost exclusively on the three premium channels in the sample. Whether or not the advisories, restrictive ratings, and content codes are used to signal the most problematic content on television must await further analyses on the content of the sample.

GENERAL DISCUSSION OF FINDINGS AND IMPLICATIONS

Effects of Advisories and Ratings on the Attractiveness of Programs

The results of the main experimental research project indicate unequivocally that ratings and advisories can have a significant impact on children's choices of programs and movies on television. Precisely what that impact is depends on a number of things, including aspects of the advisory or rating and characteristics of the child making the choices.

The well known admonition, "parental discretion advised" had a strong and positive effect on boys' interest in viewing reality-action programs, and the effect was strongest for boys in the older group. This same advisory had no impact on girls' tendency to choose such programs. In contrast, another frequently used advisory, "viewer discretion advised," did not increase boys' interest in viewing police-detective shows, but it decreased girls' (and especially younger girls') choices of such programs.

The MPAA ratings "G," "PG," "PG-13," and "R" also strongly affected children's desire to see a movie. Older boys were especially interested in the target movie when it was rated "PG-13" or "R" and completely avoided it when it was rated "G." In contrast, younger girls were most interested in the movie when it was rated "G." For older girls and younger boys, interest in the movie peaked when it was rated "PG-13."

All of the selective exposure data suggest, then, that ratings and advisories are important contributors to children's desire to view or avoid viewing television programming. Although this study does not provide direct answers to the question of why this occurs, some of the findings appear suggestive of various explanations. One question concerns the issue of why "parental" and "viewer" advisories produced such different effects. One possible explanation comes from the data on expectations of the content of programs with advisories. The percentage of children expecting certain forms of violent content was higher for the viewer discretion advisories than for the parental discretion advisories (see Figures 11a and 11b). Perhaps what was considered mild and more manageable violence was attractive to boys, but higher levels were expected to be too intense.

A related question concerns the reason for children's differential interest in the target movie as a function of its MPAA rating. The data on expectations of violent content in movies with different ratings were very consistent, and indicated that expectations of a variety of forms of violent content were lowest for the "G" rating and peaked at the "PG-13" rating (see Figures 12a through 12f). It is interesting to note that this pattern of expectations of violent content exactly mirrors the pattern of interest in the movie among boys as a group, and among older children as a group (see Figures 4a and 4b).

A second possible explanation for the effects of the two forms of the advisory on children's selective exposure deals with the literal meanings of the two messages. "Parental discretion advised" is a message to parents to shield their children, whereas "viewer discretion advised" exhorts the viewer to take care of him- or herself. Perhaps the boys in this experiment, and particularly the older boys, resented being "treated like children," and took the advisory as a challenge to overcome rather than good advice. Perhaps the viewer advisory was not perceived as so demeaning, and perhaps the boys, being told to decide for themselves, were more willing to accept the message at face value. The data on children's perceptions of the meanings of these two advisories show that although the majority of children in both age groups thought the message implied a parental decision, 22% of children in the older group interpreted the viewer advisory as directed at the viewer ("people"), while only 5% interpreted the parental advisory this way (see Figures 7a and 7b).

Responses to the MPAA ratings are relevant here as well. One explanation for the boys' and older children's interest in the movie when it had the more restrictive ratings of "PG-13" and "R" may be that these ratings signify that the content is explicitly not for children. Children's perceptions of the meaning of the MPAA ratings revealed that all of the older children selected "anyone can watch" as the meaning of a "G" rating. As the level of the rating increased, so too did older children's perception that the message indicated that younger children's viewing was to be avoided. With the exception of the "G" rating, younger children seem not to have had a clear view of the meaning or intention of the MPAA ratings (see Figures 8a through 8d).

It seems likely that both of these explanations, the expectation of more violence and the desire not to be treated as a child, are in part responsible for the pattern of viewing decisions among boys and especially older boys. An additional possible explanation comes from the study of parent-child discussions of viewing choices. The fact that children made positive comments about advisories and the more restrictive of the two ratings involved, characterizing them as "cool" and "awesome," may reflect that such messages endow programs with a nonspecific aura of attractiveness.

These explanations are speculative at this juncture. Future research needs to be done to determine more definitively the mechanisms underlying these effects.

The Role of Background Variables

This research also revealed some interesting relationships between parental involvement, characteristics of children, and the children's responses to ratings and advisories, even after the contributions of gender and age were accounted for. Children whose parents set limits and were more involved in their television viewing were less likely than other children to choose programs with parental advisories and movies with more restrictive ratings. This finding suggests that parental involvement may become internalized and have beneficial effects even when the child selects programming without adult supervision.

It is also interesting and encouraging that children in some instances behaved sensibly and in their own best interest. Specifically, children who reported experiencing fright reactions from television were more likely to avoid programs with both parental and viewer advisories. These children have apparently learned from their previous experiences and used these messages as they were intended -- to shield themselves from future emotional upsets.

A more disturbing result related to the personality variables was the relationship between program choices and two items tapping aggressive tendencies. The more benign item, "I like rough and tumble games," was positively associated with choosing a program with a parental advisory. The more directly aggression-related item, "I get into fights with other kids," was positively related to choosing a program with a viewer advisory, although this relationship only approached significance. If this relationship holds up under replication, it suggests that advisories may be attracting just those viewers who are of prime concern in our desire to reduce the contribution of violence on television to violence in our society. Research has repeatedly shown that children who are already aggressive are the most likely to become even more violent as a function of exposure to television violence.

Limitations to Generalizability

We must, of course, acknowledge the limitations to the generalizability of the findings of the experiments. The study demonstrated that ratings and advisories can have an impact on children's viewing choices, but the specific effects we observed would not necessarily occur in all groups of children. The children we tested came from a moderately-sized midwestern community, and the children who participated, although representing a range of socioeconomic neighborhoods, were predominantly Caucasian. Research to be conducted next year will involve samples of children from a larger city and of a more diverse ethnic mix, and will include both inner-city and suburban children.

The different findings for "parental" vs. "viewer" discretion must be explored further and these messages must be tested in the context of different types of programs. In this experiment, the parental advisories were tested with reality-action shows, while the viewer advisories were tested with police-detective dramas. Although there is no theoretical reason to expect that it is the show type rather than the advisory type that is responsible for the differential effects, this alternative should be tested in future years. It would also be worthwhile to test these advisories and other types of advisories, ratings, and codes in the context of other types of program descriptions.

Implications for Industry Decisions and Public Policy

Even though there are important questions that remain to be answered, the findings regarding the effect of advisories and ratings on children's choices of programs should lead us, at the very least, to use caution in assigning ratings and advisories to television offerings where children are concerned. Since in our experiment, the presence of "parental discretion advised" and the "PG-13" and "R" ratings increased boys' interest in programs and movies, the possibility that such messages might attract viewers should be kept in mind when considering the various options for informing the public about problematic content on television.

On the other hand, since "viewer discretion advised" was used in a sensible fashion by girls and children who frequently experienced fright reactions to television, the potential value of such messages when used by children should not be overlooked. It may be somewhat reassuring to note that in our sample, the advisory that produced the "boomerang" effect ("parental discretion advised") was used rarely, and less frequently than other messages advocating discretion.

In terms of public policy, we should consider alternatives involving better communication with both parents and children about television content, and future research should explore the most effective strategies. In addition, we should be willing to consider the feasiblity of technological alternatives that would allow the parent to unilaterally restrict access without calling the child's attention to the restricted content.

Finally, the content analysis of the use of ratings and advisories constitutes an initial step toward an awareness of how such messages are currently being used by the providers of television fare. This report provides us with an analysis of the frequencies with which advisories, ratings, and codes are being used and by whom. Future reports will provide information on how appropriately these messages are placed in terms of signalling the content that presents the highest risk to viewers and will let us compare the industry's use of these messages over the course of three years.

PART IV

ASSESSMENT OF TELEVISION'S ANTI-VIOLENCE MESSAGES: UNIVERSITY OF NORTH CAROLINA AT CHAPEL HILL STUDY

Dr. Frank Biocca
Dr. Jane Brown
Fuyan Shen
Jay M. Bernhardt
Leandro Batista
Karen Kemp
Greg Makris
Dr. Mark West
Dr. James Lee
Howard Straker
Dr. Henry Hsiao
Elena Carbone

Summary

Can television help "deglamorize" violence? Seven studies tested a systematic sample of 15 antiviolence public service announcements (PSAs), and an award-winning program promoting conflict resolution. More than 200 adolescents drawn from a training school, a middle school, and a university viewed and responded to the antiviolence messages. The interim analysis of more than one million data points, 22 hours of videotaped interviews, and more than 350 pages of focus group and interview transcripts yielded the following preliminary findings:

Attitudes toward violence. No evidence was found that either the antiviolence programs or PSAs significantly altered the adolescents' attitudes toward the appropriateness of using violence to resolve conflicts.

Interest and mood. On average, nine of the 15 antiviolence PSAs were rated as "slightly" to "very interesting" by adolescent viewers. The PSAs affected the mood of audiences, arousing most, and making some feel less pleasure and less personal dominance. However, exposure to some of the PSAs embedded in an action and adventure film did not alter college students' interest in viewing violent scenes shown after the film. The longer educational program also was not significantly more interesting than a fire safety video shown to a control group.

Comprehension of PSAs. Although some celebrity endorsers stimulated interest, the lack of credibility of some other celebrities, especially those who were perceived as violent in real life or in their jobs (e.g., sports, acting), sometimes confused or undermined the antiviolence messages.

These findings suggest that TV may be only modestly effective in decreasing violent attitudes and behavior among youth. The finding that exposure to nine antiviolence PSAs in a ninety-minute film could not diminish interest in subsequent violent scenes suggests that antiviolence PSAs may never be aired frequently enough to achieve their objectives. Messages that deglamorize violence may be overwhelmed by messages that glamorize violence. Given these findings, and previous research on effective health communication campaigns, it is recommended that antiviolence media campaigns: 1) pretest messages with target audiences while in production; 2) reduce reliance on celebrities, especially those previously associated in their life or work with violence; 3) increase portrayals of powerful nonviolent figures, peer-driven shame, and non-lethal effects of violence such as paralysis and family suffering; 4) target younger audiences of 8 to 13 years old who may be more open to alternatives to violence; 5) better coordinate campaigns with schools and youth organizations that are also working to reduce violence.

1. RESEARCH QUESTIONS AND TASKS

1.1 The Central Questions

The cable industry will devote significant financial resources to an antiviolence education campaign -- targeted to young viewers -- that deglamorizes violence. In addition, the industry will seek alliances with third-party educational organizations to extend the reach and impact of its efforts (National Cable Television Association, 1994, p. 7).

In the 1990s there is evidence that the American public is extremely concerned about violence, especially among the young. The United States has the highest level of homicide of any industrial country and is just two positions away from having the highest per-capita homicide rate in the world (Reiss & Roth, 1993). This unfortunate distinction has led many to ask what forces are creating a culture of violence in the United States. Some believe that the gun is often portrayed as a means of self-expression, an effective solution to interpersonal conflict, and as a symbol of power and respect. On the streets, some of America's youth don't just *view* the culture of violence, they live it. The Surgeon General's office has called violence an epidemic in America.

If violence is an epidemic, what is the treatment? Television? Can television be a part of the cure? When television is at its best, can powerful antiviolence messages provide an antidote to the effects of repeated viewing of TV violence? If violent television programming has contributed to a *culture of violence*, can antiviolence programming contribute to a culture of peace and self-restraint?

1.1.1 Television's Social Experiment With Antiviolence Programming: Can It Work?

In the 1990s the television industry has attempted to respond to the problem of violence in America in the way it knows best--*communication.* As we record below, almost every broadcast and cable television network has aired antiviolence programs and/or public service announcements (PSAs). This multimillion dollar investment has created a large *social experiment*, a social intervention that attempts to use television to prevent violence in America.

Some may argue that these messages are only dim, flickering candles in the dark, violent world of television. One campaign called their messages *Voices Against Violence*. *Are these voices heard?* If they are heard, are they convincing?

The studies described here attempted to look at the effectiveness of this wave of antiviolence messages. We asked: Is there any evidence that these messages have an effect on the violent attitudes of young Americans? If so, which approaches work best and which approaches are less effective?

1.1.2 What Does It Mean to Say That an Antiviolence Message Is Effective?

Antiviolence messages can be said to be effective if their intended audiences:

- ⊙ are *interested* in the messages,
- ⊙ *understand* the messages,
- ⊙ *remember* the messages,
- ⊙ *change their attitudes and norms* about violence as a result of viewing the messages,
- ⊙ feel they could *control* their violence-related behaviors after viewing the messages.

If violence is "glamorized," adolescents may hold false norms, role models and expectations about the value of violent behavior. We were particularly interested in whether antiviolence messages could affect the social norms and attitudes of adolescents, whether the messages gave these viewers concrete behavioral models, and whether the messages left viewers feeling that they could control their behavioral choices (behavioral self-efficacy).

However, messages can be *ineffective* for a variety of reasons and may have unintended negative consequences. We also examined whether messages inadvertently:

- ⊙ increased *anxiety, depression*, and *hostility*,
- ⊙ increased *fears of being a victim* of violence,
- ⊙ increased the *perception of the world as a dangerous and violent place.*

Increases in any of these areas indicate reduced likelihood that antiviolence messages had the intended effect. Of course, it is hoped that the messages will also reduce violent behavior. This desirable outcome is, however, difficult and costly to assess because it would require longitudinal studies that are not possible with the allocated resources. Therefore, the possibility of behavioral change is assessed only indirectly with measures of attitudes and behavioral intentions.

2. ARCHIVE OF THE TELEVISION INDUSTRY'S ANTIVIOLENCE EDUCATIONAL PROGRAMMING AND PUBLIC SERVICE ANNOUNCEMENTS

Our research team was charged with assessing television's antiviolence educational programming and helping guide antiviolence message producers (NCTA, 1994). Although funded by the cable industry, we were advised by Mediascope to assess the antiviolence educational efforts produced by *all* segments of the television industry. The study was national in scope. We confined our analysis to programs and PSAs that received *national* distribution. With a few exceptions, we focused our year one analysis on antiviolence programming that aired during the fall of 1994 and the spring of 1995.

We have begun gauging the range and volume of the television industry's antiviolence educational programming. Below we describe how PSAs and programs were selected for inclusion in the studies conducted in year one.

2.1 The Messages: Scope of Antiviolence Programming Considered in This Project

The antiviolence programming we assessed was produced to achieve a variety of goals. Some of the programming was directed at adolescent viewers and clearly designed to *alter their attitudes and norms about violence*. Some of the programming, such as news and documentaries, aimed to inform the public, contribute to public debate and social action, and possibly influence *public policy*. Both of these approaches have potential for influencing violent behaviors. Some of the antiviolence programming may have had *public relations* goals and was intended to influence the public's perception of the programming participant, producers, and networks rather than to influence violent behaviors. These different goals are not necessarily mutually exclusive and may support each other.

What is an antiviolence educational program? It can include programs from a number of genres:

- ⊙ public service announcements,
- ⊙ news and information programs,
- ⊙ talk shows,
- ⊙ reality programming,
- ⊙ entertainment programming with an antiviolence message.

For example, one network listed the movie *Going My Way*, a moralistic tale in which a priest assists wayward youths, as an antiviolence program. This has some general validity, but such a definition of antiviolence educational programming was too broad and unmanageable for use in this study. It equates *nonviolent* programming with *antiviolence* educational programming. A program that simply lacks violent actions or images does not necessarily affect viewers' attitudes or beliefs about violence.

We chose a more focused and precise definition of antiviolence educational programming. We wanted to focus on messages that were *designed to have a direct effect on violent behavior by influencing the norms and attitudes* of adolescent viewers. We refer to this subset of all antiviolence programming as Proactive Antiviolence Programming.

To be considered for study, antiviolence programs or PSAs had to:

⊙ be targeted for *adolescent* viewers,
⊙ be explicitly *educational*,
⊙ be explicitly designed to change adolescent *attitudes or norms* about violent behavior.

We excluded most entertainment programming with an antiviolence message from possible analysis and testing because such programs were difficult to distinguish. For example, the show *Kung Fu: The Legend Continues* has numerous violent scenes, but the main character can be said to advocate nonviolence. Therefore, it is not clear whether the program, as opposed to its main character, truly communicates an antiviolence message. Also, using the criteria above, most entertainment programming is not explicitly designed to change adolescents' norms or attitudes about their own or their peers' violent behavior. Entertainment programs that appeared explicitly designed to influence the violent norms and attitudes of adolescent viewers were set aside for possible further study.

Many news, documentary and talk-show programs on violence are designed to inform viewers about the social reality of violence, stimulate debate, and/or indirectly influence public policy. We recognize that such programs have potential social value. However, programs that simply provided basic information on crime were noted, but not submitted for study in the first year. News programs are viewed primarily by adult audiences (Papazian, 1995) and are not designed primarily to have *direct* effects on adolescent viewers' violent attitudes or norms, propensity to commit violence, or actual violent behavior. Programs that appeared designed to have direct effects on adolescents' violent attitudes were set aside for consideration in later studies.

We excluded most reality programming (e.g., *Rescue 911, America's Most Wanted*) from our sampling frame and further study. This kind of programming is designed primarily for entertainment and to assist law enforcement in the identification and apprehension of criminals. Reality programming may have some indirect effect on violence by demonstrating the penalties of violent crime, but this kind of programming is not *designed* primarily to directly impact adolescents' attitudes toward violence.

2.2 The Range and Scope of the Industry's Efforts

Evaluating the range and scope of the industry's antiviolence efforts has proven challenging. Although we had been hired to test antiviolence educational programming, the programming had not been identified and no arrangements had been made to provide the research team with any systematic sample of the industry's work. With the help of Mediascope and the National Cable Television Association, we spent part of the first year assembling the sample. Numerous independent organizations have provided the research team with a variety of materials. We have begun building an archive of the television industry's antiviolence educational programming and developing techniques to systematically sample the industry's antiviolence efforts.

2.2.1 Method Used to Construct the Sampling Frame

In the first year we began to construct mechanisms for identifying as many of the antiviolence PSAs and antiviolence programs as possible. Our goals were:

- to construct a sampling frame from which we could pick a representative sample of all the antiviolence PSAs and programs aired in 1994-1995,
- to assess the extent of the television industry's antiviolence educational efforts.

Antiviolence PSAs were harder to identify than educational programs. Network representatives reported that there are few and incomplete records of their production, date and time of airing, and frequency of airing.

We used the following two approaches to identify and obtain samples of PSAs and educational programs:

Direct contact with broadcast and cable networks. Mediascope, in conjunction with the NCTA, identified key decision makers in broadcast and cable networks. Identification of antiviolence programming in the cable industry was aided by the development of combined industry efforts such as *Voices Against Violence Week.*

In the Spring of 1995, Mediascope contacted key decision makers in each of the major cable and broadcast networks via mail and telephone. We also requested that the National Cable Television Association contact each of its members and ask them to send us all programming associated with *Voices Against Violence Week*. This approach led to the accumulation of numerous tapes of antiviolence PSAs and programs in the UNC Center for Research in Journalism and Mass Communication.

Identification from program listings. Using weekly program listings, we attempted to systematically identify programming whose *primary focus* was antiviolence education. This provided us with another pool of possible test programming.

2.3 Public Service Announcements

As of September 1995 we had gathered 89 antiviolence PSAs from 14 organizations, most of which were cable networks. Almost all of these PSAs aired during the 1994-1995 season. This is a preliminary list. Tapes continue to come in.

Table 2.1 lists these PSAs, along with a categorization by genre, the network on which it aired, its length in seconds, and the campaign during which it aired, if any and if known.

Table 2.1: Public Service Announcements in the Archive of the UNC Center for Research in Journalism and Mass Communication

	TITLE	GENRE	SEC.	SPONSOR	CAMPAIGN
1	Brownstone	Celebrity	30	The Box	VAV Week
2	Gloria Estefan	Celebrity	30	The Box	VAV Week
3	Redman	Celebrity	30	The Box	VAV Week
4	Salt & Pepa	Celebrity	20	The Box	VAV Week
5	Hammer	Celebrity	30	The Box	VAV Week
6	Rob Halford	Celebrity	20	The Box	VAV Week
7	Duran Duran	Celebrity	25	The Box	VAV Week
8	Changing Faces	Celebrity	30	The Box	VAV Week
9	Jamie Walters	Celebrity	30	The Box	VAV Week
10	Mike Bivens	Celebrity	30	The Box	VAV Week
11	Sammy Hagar	Celebrity	30	The Box	VAV Week
12	Ice Cube & K-Dee	Celebrity	30	The Box	VAV Week
13	Subway	Celebrity	30	The Box	VAV Week
14	Lay Down Your Guns	Expository/image	35	The Box	VAV Week
15	Boys II Men	Celebrity	20	The Box	VAV Week
16	Genocide	Expository/image	30	The Box	VAV Week
17	Luke	Celebrity	30	The Box	VAV Week
18	Heartbeat/Locker Slam	Narrative/fiction	30	Cartoon/Turner	
19	Protest	Narrative/ documentary	30	Child. Def. Fund	
20	Walter Cronkite	Celebrity	30/15	Disc./Learning	VAV Week
21	Et Tu Brutus	Narrative/fiction	60	HBO/Warner	Peace: Live It
22	Good Kids	Narrative/fiction	60	HBO/Warner	Peace: Live It

23	Hero	Narrative/doc.	30	HBO/Warner	Peace: Live It
24	Chuck D	Celebrity	30	HBO/Warner	Peace: Live It
25	Nikki & Khalif	Fiction/Celebrity	60	HBO/Warner	Peace: Live It
26	Stray Bullet	Narrative/fiction	60	HBO/Warner	Peace: Live It
27	These Walls Have No Prejudice	Expository/image	30	HBO/Warner	Peace: Live It
28	What Are You, Stupid?	Celebrity	60	HBO/Warner	Peace: Live It
29	MLK/Mandela	Narrative/doc.	30	History Channel	VAV Week
30	History/Peace	Narrative/doc.	30	History Channel	VAV Week
31	Crime Boy	Narrative/doc.	60/30	TNT	
32	Barbara Boxer 1	Celebrity	60	Lifetime	VAV Week
33	Barbara Boxer 2	Celebrity	30	Lifetime	VAV Week
34	Henry Rollins	Celebrity	30	MTV	Enough is Enough
35	Low Rider Bicycle	Narrative/doc.	30	MTV	Enough is Enough
36	Moments of Glory (chalk outlines)	Narrative/fiction	30	MTV	Enough is Enough
37	Salt & Pepa 2	Celebrity	15	MTV	Enough is Enough
38	Ballots not Bullets/ Peter Gabriel	Celebrity	30	MTV	Enough/Rock the Vote
39	Ballots not Bullets/Various Artists	Celebrity	30	MTV	Enough/Rock the Vote
40	Before/After Hospital	Narrative/doc.	20	MTV	Enough is Enough
41	Derrick Coleman	Celebrity	15	MTV	Enough is Enough
42	Guns/Heart	Expository/image	12	MTV	Enough is Enough
43	Dennis Grant	Narrative/doc.	135	MTV	
44	Martin Luther King	Expository/image	20	MTV	Enough is Enough
45	Positive Rap - Lalo	Celebrity	30	MTV	Enough is Enough
46	Somewhere in America-Rapper	Real person	30	MTV	Enough is Enough
47	Zlata- America is Great	Celebrity	30	MTV	Enough is Enough
48	Adam-Spider and Fly	Exp image/real pers.	15	Nickelodeon	VAV Week
49	Andrew-Be Different	Exp image/real pers.	15	Nickelodeon	VAV Week
50	Antonia-Hugs	Exp image/real pers.	15	Nickelodeon	VAV Week
51	Beth- Flyers	Exp image/real pers.	15	Nickelodeon	VAV Week
52	Bryan-Guns into Dimes	Exp image/real pers.	20	Nickelodeon	VAV Week
53	Christina-Laws	Exp image/real pers.	20	Nickelodeon	VAV Week
54	Elizabeth-Schools	Exp image/real pers.	15	Nickelodeon	VAV Week
55	Gary-Clubs	Exp image/real pers.	20	Nickelodeon	VAV Week
56	Genevieve-I love you	Exp image/real pers.	15	Nickelodeon	VAV Week
57	Hoops	Exp image/real pers.	20	Nickelodeon	VAV Week
58	James-Crime/Freedom	Exp image/real pers.	20	Nickelodeon	VAV Week
59	Johnny-Stop Selling Guns	Exp image/real pers.	20	Nickelodeon	VAV Week

60	Katoya- Dr. King	Exp image/real pers.	15	Nickelodeon	VAV Week
61	Mike-Sports	Exp image/real pers.	15	Nickelodeon	VAV Week
62	Paul-Rabbit	Exp image/real pers.	20	Nickelodeon	VAV Week
63	Sarah-Jail	Exp image/real pers.	15	Nickelodeon	VAV Week
64	Shavon-In our Hands	Exp image/real pers.	15	Nickelodeon	VAV Week
65	Starlen-Super Bird	Exp image/real pers.	15	Nickelodeon	VAV Week
66	Whitney-All Against Violence	Exp image/real pers.	15	Nickelodeon	VAV Week
67	Pro-peace VAV -- Bully	Music video	60	Nick at Nite	VAV Week
68	Pro-peace VAV-- Brother	Music video	60	Nick at Nite	VAV Week
69	Pro-peace VAV-- Bus	Music video	60	Nick at Nite	VAV Week
70	Jobeth Williams	Celebrity	30	Showtime	VAV Week
71	Julie Brown	Celebrity	30	Showtime	VAV Week
72	Lynn Whitfield	Celebrity	30	Showtime	VAV Week
73	Martin Landau	Celebrity	30	Showtime	VAV Week
74	Nick Charles	Celebrity	30	Showtime	VAV Week
75	President Clinton 1	Celebrity	33	Showtime	VAV Week
76	President Clinton 2	Celebrity	34	Showtime	VAV Week
77	Samuel Jackson	Celebrity	30	Showtime	VAV Week
78	Susan Rook	Celebrity	30	Showtime	VAV Week
79	Alyssa Milano	Celebrity	30	Showtime	VAV Week
80	Boyd Matson	Celebrity	30	Showtime	VAV Week
81	Alan Jackson	Celebrity	30	Showtime	VAV Week
82	Erase the Hate/Had Enough	Narrative/doc.	30	USA	
83	Basketball	*	30	Advert. Council	
84	Children-Montage	*	60	Advert. Council	
85	Neighbors	*	60/30	Advert. Council	
86	Prisoner	*	30	Advert. Council	
87	Scruff Beats the Scary Streets	*	60/30	Advert. Council	
88	Weapon	*	15/10	Advert. Council	
89	Wedding	*	15/10	Advert. Council	

These ads are not categorized because we do not have the equipment to view them in the format in which they arrived. After they are transferred to standard videotape, they will be added to the archive.

2.3.1 Categorization of the PSAs

We categorized the PSAs into several broad genres. Most ads relied primarily on one approach, but some combined methods. The genres were:

⊙ *Narrative.* These ads told a story. Ads based on true stories were categorized as *narrative/documentary.* Those that were not based on real persons or events were categorized as *narrative/fiction*.

⊙ *Celebrity*. A well-known public figure presented the message. Although celebrities could have been used in narrative ads, in almost all cases, celebrity PSAs were of the "talking head" variety in which the celebrity directly addressed the viewer. Thirty-nine of the 89 PSAs in the archive are of this type.

⊙ *Real person*. These PSAs relied on non-celebrities to present an antiviolence message.

⊙ *Music video*. These ads used music or rap to convey an antiviolence message.

⊙ *Expository-image*. This broad category included PSAs that were information-oriented--facts and figures on crime for example--as well as ads composed primarily of collages of meaningful or symbolic images.

2.4 Educational Programs

As of September 1995 we had collected 64 antiviolence educational programs produced by 19 organizations. Most of these programs aired during the 1994-1995 season. These programs can be categorized broadly into various genres, including news/documentaries, fiction, talk shows, variety shows, docudramas and music videos. Table 2.2 lists these antiviolence programs, along with a categorization of each program by genre, the network on which it aired, its length in minutes, and the campaign during which it aired, if known. Many of these belong to genres we did not study in year one, but they are included to present a picture of the range of materials being produced.

**Table 2.2: Educational Programs in the Archive of the
UNC Center for Research in Journalism and Mass Communication**

	TITLE	GENRE	MIN	SPONSOR	CAMPAIGN
1	Prime Time Violence	News/Doc.	120	A&E	VAV Week/ Cable in Class
2	American Justice--Juvenile Justice	News/Doc.	60	A&E	VAV Week
3	Invest. Reports: Shot By a Kid	News/Doc.	60	A&E	VAV Week
4	Rap City/Teen Summit	Talk	120	BET	VAV Week
5	Rap City: Stop the Violence	Rap videos	97	BET	VAV Week
6	Kids Killing Kids	Fiction	60	CBS/Fox	Stop Kids Killing Kids
7	VAV Week Anchor Show 1	News/Doc.	30	CNBC	VAV Week
8	VAV Week Anchor Show 2	News/Doc.	30	CNBC	VAV Week
9	VAV Week Anchor Show 3	News/Doc.	30	CNBC	VAV Week
10	VAV Week Anchor Show 4	News/Doc.	30	CNBC	VAV Week
11	Tim Russert	Talk	30	CNBC	VAV Week
12	Cal Thomas	Talk	30	CNBC	VAV Week

13	Equal Time/Mary Matalin	Talk	30	CNBC	VAV Week
14	Real Personal/Bob Berkowitz	Talk	30	CNBC	VAV Week
15	Dick Cavett	Talk	30	CNBC	VAV Week
16	Rivera Live	Talk	57	CNBC	VAV Week
17	Charles Grodin	Talk	15	CNBC	VAV Week
18	Talkback 1	Talk	60	CNN	
19	Talkback 2	Talk	60	CNN	VAV Week
20	News Segment 1	News/Doc.	5	CNN	VAV Week
21	News Segment 2	News/Doc.	5	CNN	VAV Week
22	News Segment 3	News/Doc.	5	CNN	VAV Week
23	News Segment 4	News/Doc.	5	CNN	VAV Week
24	News Segment 5	News/Doc.	5	CNN	VAV Week
25	Class Action--Getting Physical	News/Doc.	57	Court TV	VAV Week/ Cable in Class
26	Kids and Guns: Who's Responsible?	News/Doc.	60	Court TV	VAV Week
27	Instant Justice--Domestic Violence	News/Doc.	56	Court TV	VAV Week
28	Eight Tray Gangster	News/Doc.	60	Discovery	VAV Week
29	Choices	News/Doc.	60	Discovery	VAV Week
30	Mickey Mouse Club	Fiction	24	Disney	VAV Week
31	Adventures in Wonderland/ Pie Noon	Fiction	28	Disney	VAV Week
32	Our Violent Games	News/Doc.	55	ESPN	
33	Home is Where the Hurt Is	News/Doc.	26	Faith&Values VISN	VAV Week*
34	Choices: Impact of Violence on Youth	News/Doc.	29	Faith&Values VISN	VAV Week*
35	Violence in the Media	Talk	27	Faith&Values VISN	VAV Week
36	The Church in a Violent Society	Talk	57	Faith&Values VISN	VAV Week
37	Broken Vows	News/Doc.	56	Faith&Values VISN	VAV Week*
38	Lifestyle Mag.: Media Violence	Talk	25	Faith&Values VISN	VAV Week
39	Take 2: You Want In?	Fiction/ talk	26	Faith&Values VISN	VAV Week
40	Heroes of Street: Survivors	News/Doc.	45	Family	VAV Week
41	Heroes of Street: Lost Generation	News/Doc.	45	Family	VAV Week
42	Heroes of Street: Reclaim. Neighbor	News/Doc.	45	Family	VAV Week
43	Break Silence: Kids Against Abuse	News/Doc.	28	Family	VAV Week
44	5 American Handguns, 5 American Kids	News/Doc.	60	HBO	VAV Week
45	Strapped	Fiction	98	HBO	VAV Week

46	No Visible Bruises	Docu-drama	30	HBO	VAV Week
47	P.O.W.E.R.: The Eddie Matos Story	Docu-drama	29	HBO	VAV Week
48	Gunplay: Last Day in the Life of Brian...	News/Doc.	29	HBO	VAV Week
49	Guns: Day in Death of America	News/Doc.	48	HBO	VAV Week
50	V. in Schools: Solutions that Work	News/Doc.	30	Learning Channel	VAV Week
51	Life From Queens	Talk	16	Lifetime	VAV Week
52	Straight from the Hood	News/Doc.	46	MTV	
53	Racism: Point of View	News/Doc.	25	MTV	
54	A Generation Under the Gun	News/Doc.	24	MTV	Enough*/Cable in Class.
55	Enough is Enough	News/Doc.	24	MTV	Enough*/Cable in Class.
56	Forum with the President	Talk	24	MTV	Enough*/Cable in Class.
57	Straight Dope	News/Doc.	24	MTV	Enough*/Cable in Class.
58	Hate Rock	News/Doc.	23	MTV	
59	Gangsta Rap	News/Doc.	23	MTV	Enough is Enough
60	Nick News: Are You What You Watch?	News/Doc.	29	Nickelodeon	VAV Week
61	Roundhouse	Variety	27	Nickelodeon	VAV Week
62	State of Sport: Sports -An Alt. to Violence	News/Doc.	23	Prime	VAV Week
63	Zooman	Fiction	120	Showtime	VAV Week
64	Erase the Hate	News/Doc.	44	USA	

* These programs were known to have aired previously.

2.5 Selection of the Test Samples

2.5.1 Sample of PSAs

Five of the eight studies described below tested the effectiveness of the antiviolence PSAs. The "antidote" study was conducted first, in the Fall of 1994. In it, we used PSAs from the HBO campaign exclusively, because they were the first PSAs supplied by the cable industry, and because they were believed to represent some of the industry's best work.

The other PSA studies used a random sample stratified by campaign. A total time value was calculated based on the sum of all the ads in the campaign. Ads were selected within each campaign with the total number of ads weighted by the total time for the campaign. This strategy guaranteed that the sample would represent diverse message styles and would prevent an over-representation of 15-second spots. The sample was drawn in the Spring of 1995 from the sampling frame available at that time.

A total of 15 PSAs were systematically sampled, representing 22 percent of the sampling frame. They were *Before and After Hospital, Brownstone, Chuck D, Derrick Coleman, Et Tu Brutus, Gloria Estefan, Heartbeat/Locker Slam, President Clinton, Redman, Salt & Pepa, Samuel Jackson, Somewhere in America-Rapper, Stray Bullet, These Walls Have No Prejudice and Zlata--America is Great* (See Table 2.1 for descriptions). We estimate that this sample was 10 percent of the total number of antiviolence PSAs that aired in 1994-95.[1] The sample size and systematic sampling procedure should allow us to make some stable generalizations about the population of antiviolence educational PSAs.

2.5.2 Sample of Educational Programs

Our budget allowed us to test only a small set of educational programs. In year one we wanted to test superior antiviolence educational programs, because if superior antiviolence educational programs produced minimal effects, it was unlikely that the inferior programs would perform better.

For these studies we used a judgment sample based on what members of the industry would recognize as some of their best efforts. We selected educational programs that: (a) were the product of **significant organizational effort and cost**, (b) had received industry **awards** and significant **recognition** and **publicity**, and (c) were aired more than once or **received significant distribution**. Based on these criteria, we selected *Kids Killing Kids* and *Forum with the President* to test in our studies.

---

[1] It appears that we have received most of the PSAs used by the cable industry in 1994 and 1995, when the cable industry launched a number of antiviolence programming initiatives. We are in the process of acquiring antiviolence PSAs produced by the broadcast networks. It is unlikely that this number will exceed the number produced by the cable networks. Based on that preliminary assumption, we estimate that the total number of antiviolence PSAs aired by the television industry in the 1994-1995 season does not exceed 150. Therefore, our sample would constitute at least 10% of the total number of antiviolence PSAs produced in the year.

3. AN INTEGRATED MODEL FOR CONSIDERING THE POTENTIAL EFFECTS OF ANTIVIOLENCE MESSAGES

The causes of violence are multiple and complex (Gilbert, 1994; Reiss & Roth, 1993). Contributing factors include poverty, unemployment, racism, access to firearms, low self-esteem, fatalism (Houk & Warren, 1991; Novello, 1991), biological (Daly & Wilson, 1994) and/or hormonal drives (Turner, 1994), parenting, geography, social capital (Reiss & Roth, 1993), and exposure to media violence (Jo & Berkowitz, 1994; Strasburger, 1993). Individual and social factors thought to contribute to violence are depicted in Figure 3.1.

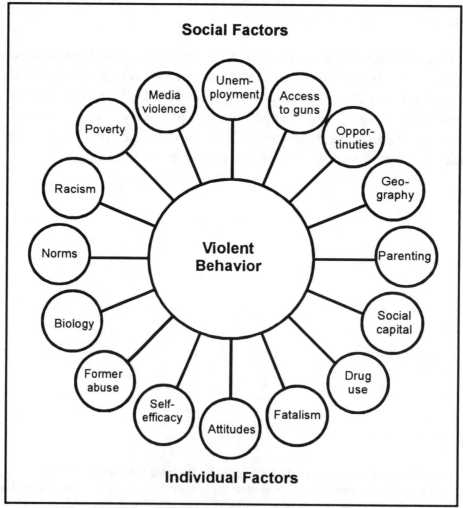

Figure 3.1: Factors that contribute to violence

Educational programs and PSAs capitalize on the persuasiveness of the television medium to present violence prevention messages. Television can be a powerfully persuasive medium, but previous research on antiviolence interventions suggests that we can expect programs and PSAs to only *moderately* affect viewers (Reiss & Roth, 1993).

In year one, we have begun to construct an integrated model with which to approach the testing of antiviolence messages. To understand how antiviolence messages work, we must understand the full communication context within which audiences receive them. Most producers of antiviolence messages hope that the messages will help curb violent attitudes and behaviors. Therefore, we have taken an approach that concentrates on how communication messages influence attitudes about violence and how these potentially contribute to increasing or decreasing violence in society.

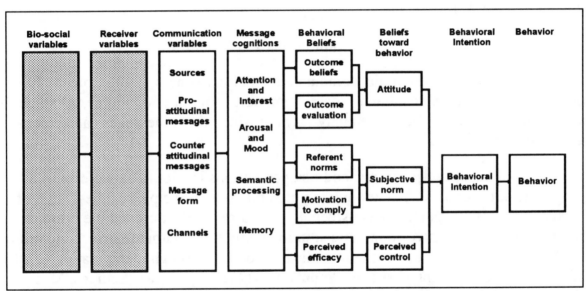

Figure 3.2: Theoretical model for the evaluation of antiviolence messages.

The working model for year one attempts to consider the full context in which antiviolence public health messages work (Figure 3.2). This model is a synthesis of work on persuasion and mass communication (Azjen, 1985; Ajzen & Fishbein, 1980; Biocca, 1991; Fishbein & Ajzen, 1975; McGuire, 1989), and other work on communication campaigns described below.

3.1 Bio-Social & Receiver Variables

Any discussion of the success of an antiviolence television campaign must acknowledge the constraints imposed by bio-social factors. Bio-social factors influence the individual's proclivity to violence, and biological factors play an important role in determining who commits violence. Violence worldwide is largely a male province

(Archer, 1994) and males constitute more than 89% of arrests for violent crimes. Most violent acts are committed by young males between the ages of 15 and 30 (Federal Bureau of Investigation, 1991, p. 37; Reiss & Roth, 1993, p. 72, 73). This pattern is found worldwide and historically. Such consistency suggests that biological factors do play an important role.

Social factors also influence the likelihood of violence in young males. The United States is a violent nation. It has the third highest homicide rate in the world (Reiss & Roth, 1993, p. 52), the highest among developed countries, and more than four times the homicide rate of most European and Commonwealth countries. Factors associated with the community in which an individual lives influence the likelihood that the individual will be either a perpetrator or victim of violence. Unemployed young males in economically distressed areas are more likely to be both perpetrators and victims of violence (Reiss & Roth, 1993).

3.2 Communication Variables

This study focuses on the communication effectiveness of antiviolence PSAs and programs. Each commercial and program embodies a number of source, message form and content variables. There are many ways in which these messages can be constructed and delivered.

Changing attitudes, norms, and risk perceptions is a lot to expect from PSAs and programs, but success will be more likely if some basic principles of the design of persuasive communication are considered. McGuire (1989) outlined the basic components of persuasive communication in an input and output matrix. According to the McGuire model, persuasive communication occurs through manipulation of attributes of the communication process (i.e., "inputs"). These "inputs" are Sources, Messages, Channels and Receivers. The communication variables will affect the "output," or dependent variables--what McGuire called the "response steps mediating persuasion." In our model (Figure 3.3), we labeled the dependent variables or receiver outputs *message cognitions* and *behavioral beliefs*. McGuire identified 12 steps in the process that begins with exposure to the communication, continues with attention, interest, comprehension and skill acquisition, and finally leads to attitude change and behavior. The number and complexity of the steps alone suggest the difficulty of affecting behavior exclusively through communication. We have measured a number of the output variables identified by McGuire in our studies as diagrammed in Figure 3.3.

Not all messages compel viewers to complete each of the steps in the persuasion process. Some messages may focus only on increasing awareness about an issue, others may suggest alternative behaviors. In our studies, adolescents were exposed to the messages, so to some extent, the first step in the process--attention--was ensured. But simply viewing the messages isn't sufficient. Interest in the message and emotional arousal are important steps in persuasion. We also measured comprehension and retention of the messages, changes in beliefs, norms, attitudes, probability assessments, and behavioral intentions.

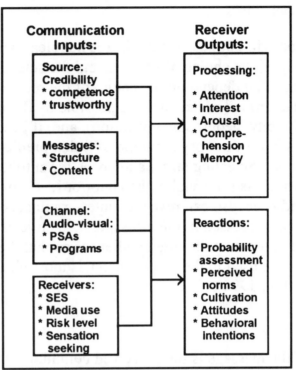

Figure 3.3: Measures included from McGuire's Model of Communication Inputs and Outputs.

Appropriate manipulation of the input variables McGuire identifies will increase the probability that messages will have the desired effect. Years of research on each of these components of the communication process (source, message, channel, and receiver) have resulted in some basic guidelines about what works and what doesn't work. Persuasive communication requires attention to so many factors that successful application is often considered more art than science. Nevertheless, there are basic principles that if adhered to will guide assessment and increase the probability that messages and campaigns are successful. The target audience is the most important piece of the puzzle, and choices about source, message and channel must be made in the context of these receivers.

3.2.1 Receivers/Audiences

In health communication campaigns, target audiences typically are chosen by considering which segments of the population are affected most by the health issue or problem, or which groups appear to have the least information. Sometimes a campaign is targeted at those who might influence others (e.g., parents, teachers). Social factors have been considered in the targeting of antiviolence messages, but the very same factors influence how much and in what ways antiviolence messages can be effective in changing violent attitudes and behaviors.

Communication will not be effective if it is not clear who the audience is. The construction of messages, the choice of sources, and the selection of appropriate communication channels all depend on the nature of the receiver. Target audiences should be selected and defined as narrowly as possible by demographic characteristics (age, gender, race/ethnicity, geography, education), and, if possible, by other kinds of indicators (sometimes known as "psychographics") that predict potential reactions and message comprehension. Selecting target audiences for antiviolence messages might be based on risk factors such as prior violent behavior or levels of sensation seeking. Understanding the audience also can reveal counter-arguments and other forms of resistance that could be addressed in the message. Effective campaigns engage in extensive formative evaluation with target audiences so that the most appropriate messages and sources are used in the media channels most likely to reach the intended audience (Flay & Burton, 1990).

3.2.2 Sources

The source of the message is the perceived communicator, i.e., to whom the audience attributes the message. In these studies, two different communicators might be perceived--the producing source (e.g., MTV, HBO), and the speaking source (e.g., the celebrity in endorsement PSAs or the primary actors in the educational programs and dramatic PSAs). Most research has focused on speaking sources and perceived credibility: "Should I believe this speaker?"

Extensive research suggests two basic dimensions of source credibility: competence and trustworthiness (O'Keefe, 1990). Competence is the extent to which the source is seen as having expertise and the qualifications for speaking about the subject. The receiver asks, "Is the communicator in a position to know the truth? To know what is right or correct?" A competent source typically would be ranked high on attributes such as experience, training, and intelligence.

Sources will be rated high on trustworthiness if they are perceived as having personal integrity and character, and are considered honest, just, fair and unselfish. The receiver asks, "Can I trust this person to tell me the truth?" Some research suggests that liking the source contributes to a perception of trustworthiness, but that liking is not as powerful a predictor of persuasion as trustworthiness (O'Keefe, 1990). The physical attractiveness of a source may contribute to liking of the source, and thus indirectly contribute to the source's effectiveness. Credibility is not intrinsic to the source because one source may be perceived as credible by some audiences but not by others.

Some handbooks on message design suggest that sources will be more effective when they are similar to the receiver (Making PSAs Work, 1984), but research suggests that dissimilar sources may be judged as more competent. For example, suburban youth may find urban youth to be more competent on the danger of guns, even though they do not perceive the urban youth to be similar to themselves.

In general, the most successful sources will be those who are perceived as both competent and trustworthy. The receiver asks, "Does this person know the truth and can I trust him or her to tell me the truth?" Sources may be perceived as trustworthy but not competent, or competent but not trustworthy. Celebrities are sometimes problematic because few retain such status for long, especially among the young, and may be considered hypocritical or untrustworthy if they themselves have engaged in the prohibited behaviors. The viewer may ask, "Why should I listen to someone who says I shouldn't be doing what he's getting paid to do?" Celebrities may help attract attention, however, especially when the target audience is initially not very involved with the topic (Atkin, 1979).

3.2.3 Pro- and Counter-attitudinal Messages

Television is filled with messages about violence. This project concentrated on messages that promoted antiviolence attitudes and behaviors. But it is important to consider that these antiviolence messages are often surrounded by messages that implicitly support violent attitudes and behaviors. Both compete to shape attitudes.

According to Petty and Cacioppo's (1986) model of persuasive communication, messages should be constructed differently depending on the audience's level of involvement in the topic. Involved audiences who perceive that an issue is personally relevant and bears directly on their own lives should receive rational appeals that include logical arguments and information. Uninvolved audiences who do not perceive the issue as affecting their own lives should receive emotional appeals (fear, humor, sadness, excitement) that may then lead to involvement and a willingness to engage with messages more cognitively. For example, anti-drug ads that used stimulating production techniques such as loud music and quick cuts have been found to be more effective with drug users (Donohew, Lorch & Palmgreen, 1991).

Fear is the most typically used emotional appeal in health-related messages. In general, the more fear generated in the audience by the message, the more effective the message (Boster & Mongeau, 1984). Theorists today make a distinction between the fear appeal of the message and the degree of fear aroused in the audience. Too much gruesome material in a message may contribute to audience distraction or disbelief and thus, be less persuasive. But, if anxiety and fear are generated in the audience, the message will be more effective than if fear is not generated. It is not clear at this point whether fear appeals are effective because of the emotional reaction they generate, or because the fear causes greater cognitive processing of the message (O'Keefe, 1990). Research does suggest that messages including a fear appeal are more effective behaviorally if the audience is provided with some reasonable way to offset the fear (e.g., "talking it out") rather than being simply left with the fear (Job, 1988).

How a message is structured may effect how persuasive it is. In general, it makes little difference whether the message's most important arguments are put at the beginning or at the end of the message, but messages will be more persuasive if explicit conclusions are drawn and recommendations for action are clear (O'Keefe, 1990). Research also shows that messages that present both sides of an issue or relevant opposing arguments are more effective than messages that include only supporting arguments. Messages that first present the supportive information and then refute relevant opposing arguments generally are more persuasive than those that refute and then support (O'Keefe, 1990). Information in messages will be more effective when presented in case history form, or as an example that describes some event or object in detail, rather than as a statistical summary of a large number of events or objects. The individual case is more compelling than averages (Taylor & Thompson, 1982).

In general, the key outcome variables of attention, acceptance and change can be maximized if messages: 1) discuss the potential risks and benefits of the desired behavior, particularly those that are most immediate and most probable; 2) present an opportunity to act and guidelines for action; and 3) demonstrate that the action is feasible (Flay & Burton, 1990).

3.2.4 Channels

In this context, the selection of channels is somewhat irrelevant because the messages are designed for television. Yet, even within television as a channel, selection of more specific channels is important. The most appropriate channels are those the target audience watches. Unfortunately, public communication campaigns frequently rely on donated media time and messages are shown at times when few members of the target audience are watching (Flay & Burton, 1990).

3.3 Message Cognitions

The effectiveness of a message begins on contact with the receiver. Ads influence the receivers' moods as the viewer immediately begins to construct the meaning of the message (*semantic processing*). The antiviolence campaigns tested in this study are part of a multimillion dollar battle over meaning. Antiviolence ads struggle to realign the meanings of violence, male identity, handgun use, gangs and numerous other interrelated concepts in the mind of the violence-prone adolescent. The ability of antiviolence messages to influence beliefs about violence and violent behavior largely will be decided by how receivers construct the meaning of the ad, and how that relates to the meanings the receivers assign to themselves, people around them (such as peers and family), certain behaviors (such as gang membership), and certain artifacts (such as guns). To fully grasp the function and effectiveness of the antiviolence commercial, it is necessary to better understand the interaction between the program or PSA and the adolescent. Viewed in cognitive terms, the struggle over the meaning of violence is the struggle over the semantic processing of antiviolence messages.

The meaning of a message is not "received," it is extracted, inferred, worked on and constructed. A commercial can be thought of not as a piece of video but as *mental models* (Johnson-Laird, 1983) constructed in the minds of different target audiences. In this interaction there is no fixed commercial, no set meaning (Eco, 1976; Fiske, 1987; Harteley, 1982), but a family of meanings. The meanings are not random. For any specific cultural community the patterns of meaning cluster statistically around a typical or shared pattern of meaning. The variations in viewers' psychological models ("readings") of the message may be due to:

- ⊙ *socio-cultural variations* in the use of codes, including those used to process television. This is described in literature on "cultural schema and scripts" (Kintsch & Greene, 1978), "interpretive communities" (Lindlof, 1988; Morley, 1980a) and the presence of "sociolects" (Labov, 1972);

- ⊙ *individual differences* in knowledge of the rules of reference--that is viewers vary in their competence in using and translating television's codes [For example, see the discussion of "competence" and "cognitive skills" (Salomon, 1979), or the accessibility of schema (Fiske & Kinder, 1981; Fiske, Kinder, & Larter, 1983)];

- ⊙ *knowledge-based differences* in the extent and nature of viewer's inference making [For example, schema instantiation in news and political communication (Conover & Feldman, 1986; Gunther, 1987)];

- ⊙ factors in the *viewing situation* that influence the allocation of attention or vary the context of semantic processing for the viewer (see discussion of "context effects," e.g., Higgins & King, 1981).

The viewer's internal representation of the imagery of antiviolence commercials, with their depictions of gangs, guns, and risk-taking youths, can be mapped. The meaning can be represented by networks of semantic nodes and markers. The audience member always "reads into" the message. Using the literature on schema use, Biocca (1991) postulates a set of schematic frames where various components of the meaning of a television message are calculated. These include the possible world frame, agent frame, narrative frame, discursive frame, point-of-view frame, ideological frame and self-schematic frame.

Quantitative and qualitative methods can be used to examine the pattern of meanings common in any community of viewers. In year one, we attempted to explore the mental models that viewers derived from the messages using qualitative methods, such as one-on-one interviews, focus groups and open-ended questions. Based on this preliminary exploration of the semantic space in which adolescents interpret these antiviolence ads, we plan to explore the structure of the mental models of the PSAs, as well as the receivers' memory, using reaction time measures in year two.

3.4 Behavioral Beliefs and Attitudes Toward Behavior

The Theory of Planned Behavior (Azjen, 1985) predicts a person's behavioral intention, and is represented in the right portion of Figure 3.2. Three factors predict the strength of a person's behavioral intention: norms, attitudes, and self-efficacy. *Subjective norms* toward the behavior are determined by a person's perception of the beliefs of important others and his or her own motivation to comply with those perceived beliefs. *Attitudes* toward the behavior are determined by a person's beliefs about the behavior and his or her evaluation of the perceived outcome of enacting the behavior. *Self-efficacy* toward the behavior is determined by a person's belief that he or she can achieve the behavior, and how much control he or she perceives having.

Unlike other models of the persuasion process, this theory takes into account the social context in which an individual is acting. It assumes that acting out a behavior is a rational process and that behavioral intention accurately predicts behavior (Carter, 1990). Although "conscious deliberation" may not always play a part in the violence some adolescents engage in, it may influence the construction of behavioral intentions. These behavioral intentions may be activated in contexts that elicit violent or antiviolence behavior. Not all violent behavior results directly or indirectly from planned action. But this approach may be more applicable to antiviolence attitude change. The contributing factors to planned and unplanned acts of violence, such as impulsiveness and sensation seeking, must be inhibited by a self interested, if not perfectly rational actor.

Thus, we assume a model of a purposive, quasi-rational actor who examines his world to see the extent to which violent behavior is practiced and condoned. The adolescent considers whether key people in his environment (real or in the media) believe that he should or should not behave violently (normative beliefs). If those key people are clear about condemning violence and the adolescent wants their approval (motivation to comply), he may perceive what the theory calls a *subjective norm* of nonviolence. We would expect that these norms will carry primary weight for most adolescents, perhaps even overriding the adolescent's own attitudes. Many of the PSAs included in the studies used celebrity role models to present positive norms about non-violence.

436

The adolescent also has an *attitude* toward violence that is based on his assessment of whether violence results in desirable consequences (e.g., power, control, status vs. death, disfigurement, loss of status) and his evaluation of the perceived outcome (his personal judgment that engaging in violent behavior is good or bad, or that he is in favor of or against behaving violently). These attitudes come from scripts or schema that model the social meaning and potential outcomes of various behavioral models that the adolescent considers. Gilbert (1994) suggests consideration of how the hierarchy of the following such scripts and schema influences the meanings of violent behavior: cultural patterns and scripts, life scripts, relationship models, episodes (models of interpersonal communication routines), speech acts, and (message) content. Many of the PSAs included in the studies showed examples of violent behavior and recommended that the viewer "think about it" (i.e., the consequences of violent behavior).

The adolescent's *perceived behavioral efficacy (self-efficacy)* is based on his previous experiences with violence and his interpretation of his relative successes and failures during those experiences. If he was in previous situations where he did not want to use violence but felt powerless to stop himself, he now may feel little efficacy regarding his power to control his behavior. Alcohol or other drugs may reduce perceived power and self-control, as well as the strength of positive norms and/or attitudes.

According to the theory of planned behavior, the relative weight of an adolescent's subjective norms, attitudes, and self-efficacy will result in *behavioral intentions* to act violently or not. Tests of the theory have found that measures of behavioral intentions are strong indicators of actual behavior. It is advantageous both socially and methodologically to be able to measure one step short of actual violent behavior.

In the context of the theory of planned behavior, television messages may moderately influence the individual's attitudes about the value of violent behavior. The messages also may serve as a window on cultural norms, especially when the messages include role models that adolescents admire. We measured the effects the programs and PSAs had on individual attitudes and norms in these studies, and saw some indication of self-efficacy in the qualitative studies.

Clearly, both violence and antiviolent behavior will be influenced by *beliefs regarding the outcomes of violence* and the individual's *evaluations of the outcomes*. Many antiviolence messages directly attempt to influence the target audience's perception of the risk of violent behaviors. The risk and benefits of violent and non-violent behavior may have played a major role in the evolutionary psychology of violent behavior (Daly & Wilson, 1994) and the behavioral considerations of the high-risk adolescent. The beliefs that people hold about their susceptibility to harm are prominent constructs in several theories that explain self-protective behavior, including the Health Belief Model (Janz & Becker, 1984), Theory of Reasoned Action (Ajzen & Fishbein, 1980; Fishbein & Ajzen,

1975), Theory of Planned Behavior (Azjen, 1985), and Subjective Expected Utility (Sutton, 1982). Nonetheless, there are several other factors that moderate these beliefs (e.g., experience with the hazard). Among these factors, one that is very relevant is the differentiation between the personal and social dimensions of risk perception.

One important aspect of risk perception is that it has both societal level and personal level judgments (Tyler, 1980). The societal judgment of risk considers the risk to the whole society, whereas the personal level judgment is how an individual positions himself in relation to that risk. For example, some believe that violence is a widening problem in society (societal level judgment), although they do not feel that their own risk of victimization is increasing (personal level judgment). The increase in risk perception at one level does not necessarily produce an increase at the other. Moreover, personal judgment is affected primarily by interpersonal communication, whereas societal judgment is affected primarily by mass mediated messages (Tyler & Cook, 1984).

Decisions at each level can affect *behavioral intentions* and subsequent *behavior*. Research on home radon testing found that both perceived susceptibility (personal) and perceived severity (social) were significant predictors of risk-reducing behavior. However, failure to perceive personal susceptibility is a stronger barrier to adopting precautionary behavior. In this study we attempted to see if the antiviolence PSAs significantly affected perceptions of social or personal risk as potential precursors to behavioral change.

4. DESCRIPTION OF THE TEST AUDIENCES

A great deal of violence is committed by America's youth, and the amount of violence perpetrated by young adolescents is increasing. Males between the ages of 12 and 25 commit most of the violent crimes worldwide (Archer, 1994; Reiss & Roth, 1993). According to Gilbert (1994), "male violence may even outrank disease and famine as the major source of human suffering." He reports that more than 89% of violent crime is committed by males. It makes sense that many of the antiviolence messages created by the industry attempted to reach those who commit violence. The vast majority of broadcast and cable network campaigns were "targeted to young viewers" (National Cable Television Association, 1994) and most addressed males.

Can antiviolence messages reach high school students, troubled teens tottering on the edge of violence, young college students contemplating date rape, adolescent gang members, or adolescents who already have committed murders or armed robberies? Since such different audiences may respond to antiviolence messages in different ways, diverse audiences were used as test audiences in year one.

4.1 Criteria and Overview

The exploratory interviews and experiments in year one were designed to yield qualitative and quantitative data on adolescents' responses to every second of several antiviolence messages. The studies required controlled exposure to the stimuli, and, in some cases, interviews or procedures lasting 2 hours. Our budget for year one did not allow us to draw a prohibitively expensive national or regional sample of adolescents that would require flying in hundreds of adolescents for these experiments. We chose instead to select a series of non-probability judgment samples. To help validate the results we replicated some of studies across more than one audience. We selected diverse audiences that fulfilled one or more of the following criteria:

1) matched the apparent target audiences for the PSAs and programs,[1]
2) had committed violence, or were more likely than average to commit violence,
3) reflected the age distribution of the young television audience.

Our study participants were drawn from a population ranging in age from 8 to 30. Judging from the actors, tone, and format of the antiviolence PSAs and programs, most of

---

[1] In some cases, the intended target audience was derived from discussions with the producers. In other cases, the target audience was inferred by (1) the age and social characteristics of the behavioral models, when present, (2) the maturity and tone of the presentation, and (3) the complexity of the message or apparent assumptions about the experience or knowledge of the audience.

the messages were targeted to mid-to-late adolescents 14 to 18 years old, while a few were targeted to early adolescents 12 to 14 years old. For five of the eight studies discussed below, participants were adolescents aged 12-18 years. The majority of study participants were male.

4.2   Test Audience 1: Training School Students
(North Carolina Division of Youth Services)

After long and protracted negotiation with university, state, and correctional authorities, our research team obtained access to adolescents in a high security training school in North Carolina. Run by the North Carolina Division of Youth Services, this institution houses youth who were part of the serious offender program. In this program 70% have been committed to the training school for violent crimes (murder, non-negligent manslaughter, forcible rape, armed robbery, aggravated assault), 49% have been adjudicated for other person offenses (negligent manslaughter, simple assault, sexual assault), and 30% for property crimes (burglary, arson, larceny, forgery, counterfeiting, etc.).[2] See Tables 4.1 and 4.2 for a summary of the test samples' self-reported exposure to violence and their violent behavior, and Table 4.3 for the age distribution of the training school students.

The antiviolence messages would have their *greatest social value* if they could interest and influence youth who have a history of violence or who, as a group, have an above average probability of committing violence. A study conducted by Lewis et al. (1994) with a population of incarcerated adolescent males found that a decade after they were released, 94% went on to have adult criminal records and 73% were later involved in *violent* crimes. Other studies have found similar rates of reincarceration ranging from 60-95% with many finding rates of 70% or above (see Lewis et al., 1994). Using Dean et al.'s (1995) predictive classification scheme developed with the North Carolina training school population, the majority of the subjects in this sample would be classified as having a high risk of recidivism (76% and above) (Dean, et al., 1995) with some subjects exhibiting characteristics that would give them a 90% probability of recidivism (Dean & Brame, 1992).

Many of these adolescents have been exposed to harsh family and social environments. Another study of training school students in North Carolina found that 20% report child abuse, 37% have family members with a criminal history, 75% use illegal drugs, and 82% come from single parent households (Dean & Brame, 1995). Studies of incarcerated youth suggest that as many as 6% will die before they are 25, as

---

[2] The sum adds to more than 100% because some participants have been adjudicated for more than one crime.

440

compared to only 1.5% of U.S. 15-year-old males (National Center for Health Statistics, 1992). Thus, there would be great social value if antiviolence messages could *influence even a small percentage of these adolescents* before they are either victims or repeat perpetrators of violence.

Table 4.1: Exposure to Violence (Self-report)

Question/Response	Sample 1: Training School Students: NC Div. of Youth Services (N =41)	Sample 2: High School Students: Githens Middle School (N =77)
Witnessed someone shooting at another person		
One or more times	87%	16%
Five or more times	56%	4%
Threatened by a gun		
One or more times	45%	11%
Five or more times	20%	3%

Table 4.2: Past Violent Behavior (Self-report)

Question/Response	Sample 1: Training School Students (N =41)	Sample 2: Middle School Students (N =77)
Carried gun		
One or more times	87%	4%
Five or more times	83%	3%
Joined others to beat someone		
One or more times	93%	32%
Five or more times	73%	11%
Threatened someone with gun		
One or more times	80%	7%
Five or more times	53%	3%
Shot gun at someone		
One or more times	77%	3%
Five or more times	50%	0%

Table 4.3: Age Distribution of Training School Students

Age	Frequency	Percentage
13	1	2%
14	5	12%
15	15	37%
16	11	27%
17	9	22%

4.3 Test Audience 2: Middle School Students (Githens Middle School, Durham, NC)

Middle school students are also part of the target populations for the antiviolence messages. This judgment sample of 77 students came from Githens Middle School in Durham, NC. The age distribution of students is presented in Table 4.4. This sample varies in their exposure to violence and levels of violent behavior. As a group they reported far less violent experience than the training school students (See Tables 4.1 and 4.2).

But the specter of violence loomed over these students as well. Just prior to our study, the brother of a favorite seventh grade math teacher was shot and killed. This school, situated in the city of Durham, has had to deal with students who bring guns to school. Durham is the "regional distribution center" for heroin, according to press reports and Capt. Paul Martin of the Durham Police Department (Eli Shiffer, 1995, p. 12A). Our sample was not drawn from a school in one of the highest-risk communities, but from a suburban middle school perceived in the community as being relatively safe. However, police incident report statistics showed that more assault reports came from the suburban school's patrol zone in 1994 and the first half of 1995 than from two other middle schools in the school system (Durham Police Department, 1995).

Table 4.4: Age Distribution of Middle School Students

Age	Frequency	Percentage
12	25	33%
13	44	57%
14	8	10%

4.4 Test Sample 3: College Males
(University of North Carolina at Chapel Hill)

A sample of 144 college males was drawn from the student body of the University of North Carolina at Chapel Hill. Subjects responded to ads offering a financial incentive to participate in the study. The age breakdown of this sample is described in Table 4.5.

Table 4.5: Age Distribution of College Students

Age	Frequency	Percentage
17	1	1%
18	40	28%
19	34	24%
20	28	20%
21	21	15%
22	12	8%
23-30	7	5%
Missing	1	1%

4.5 Test Sample 4: Children and Young Adolescents
(Non-sectarian rural school, Henderson, NC)

An allied study reported here used a sample of 20 children aged 8-14 from a private, non-sectarian school in rural Hendersonville, NC. The school and the rural area where the subjects live have below average crime rates.

5. RESEARCH METHODS AND MEASURES USED IN YEAR ONE

5.1 Methods

The year one studies used a variety of quantitative and qualitative research methods to gather data, including experiments, focus group, and in-depth interviews. The exact use of the methods is described in greater depth in the sections describing each of the studies.

5.2 Measures

5.2.1 Measures of Bio-social & Receiver Variables

Measures of violent behavior and victimization. A set of items was constructed to measure past violent behavior. Items were grouped into two sets of scales, those that measured violent behavior involving weapon use and those that measured how often the respondent was a victim of violence.

Sensation seeking scale. Sensation seeking is an individual trait defined by the need for varied, novel, complex sensations and experiences, and the willingness to take physical and social risks for the sake of such experiences. The sensation seeking scale was developed by Marvin Zuckerman from 1964 to 1978 (Zuckerman, 1979). During this period five scales were progressively developed in his search for a tool to show "that people differ in their optimal levels of stimulation and arousal and that these differences influence their choice of life activities" (Zuckerman, 1979, p. 95). The latest form of the scale (Form V) is a set of 40 items combined into four factors: Thrill and Adventure Seeking (TAS), Experience Seeking (ES), Disinhibition (D), and Boredom Susceptibility (BS). Each factor has 10 items. The scale has good overall internal reliability that ranges from .83 to .86, measured by Cronbach's Alpha in two samples (one of American individuals and one of British). Individual factors have lower internal reliability.

Hirschfield impulsivity scale. The Hirschfield Impulsivity Scale measures impulsivity (low self-censoring) through 19 statements, to which respondents answer either "true" or "false." The items are: "I like to keep moving around," "I don't make friends quickly," "I don't like to wrestle and play rough," "I like to shoot with bows and arrows," "I think I'm a pretty good talker," "Whenever there's a fire engine going someplace, I'd like to follow it," "My home life is always happy," "When things get quiet, I like to stir things up," "I am restless," "I think I'm as happy as other people," "I don't get into trouble at Halloween," "I like being 'it' when we play games like that," "It's fun to push people off the edge into the pool," "I never lay out of school," "I like to hang out with lots of other kids, not just one," "I like throwing rocks at things," "It's hard to stick to the rules if you're losing the game," "I don't like to dare kids to do things,"

"Teachers think I'm a hard worker." Impulsivity Scale scores have been observed to correlate significantly with teacher ratings of student impulsivity and scores have test-retest correlations of .85 (Hirschfield, 1965).

Children's perceived self-control scale. The Children's Perceived Self-Control Scale, or CPSC, is an 11-item instrument that uses a cognitive-behavioral perspective to examine self-control. Perceived self-control has been shown to be related to behaviors that promote adolescent adjustment (Humphrey, 1982).

Media use measures. Measures used in previous surveys of early adolescents (Brown, Walsh-Childers, et al., 1990; Klein, et al., 1993) of respondents' typical patterns of television viewing were updated to include current shows. Measures assessed both number of hours spent viewing television in general and content-specific preferences, to determine whether respondents who typically were exposed to more violence in media responded differently to educational programming.

Demographic questionnaires. Each respondent was asked a set of simple demographic questions that included where they had lived for most of the time they were growing up (rural to urban area), their gender and age. College students were asked how well they were doing in school (grades) and students at the training school were asked how long they had been living at the school.

5.2.2 Measures of Behavioral Beliefs and Attitudes Toward Violence

Normative Beliefs About Aggression Scale. This is a 20-item scale designed by Huesman and his colleagues to measure a child's, adolescent's and young adult's perception of how acceptable it is to behave aggressively both under varying conditions of provocation and when no conditions are specified (Huesman, Guerra, Miller & Zelli, 1992). The scale is designed for a broad range of individuals, from preschool to college-age. The scale is readily adaptable to this broad age range through minor changes in the wording of the questions (e.g., changing the nouns from boys to young men). It has proven to be a reliable and valid measure of beliefs about the appropriateness of aggression.

The items on the scale were derived through a process of pilot-testing and revision and have been used on subjects from age 6 to 30 in a variety of countries and ethnic groups. The scale consists of 12 items assessing approval of aggression in response to specific provocations, plus eight items assessing approval "in general" when no provocations are mentioned.

All items are worded in the "It is OK" direction and in the "It is Wrong" direction. They were scored: 1 = Really Wrong, 2 = Sort of Wrong, 3 = Sort of OK, 4 = Perfectly OK. The scale score is obtained by calculating the subjects' average response to the items on the scale (Huesman, Guerra, Miller & Zelli, 1994).

There are three ways to aggregate the items to evaluate beliefs about aggression:

⊙ *Retaliation beliefs.* This set of questions describes a brief scenario such as: "Suppose a boy says something bad to another boy, John," and asks questions such as, "Do you think it's OK for John to scream at him?" Answers range from "It's perfectly OK" to "It's sort of OK."

⊙ *General beliefs.* This set of questions are straightforward questions such as, "In general, is it wrong to hit other people?" Answers range from "It's sort of wrong" to "It's really wrong."

⊙ *Total approval of aggression.* All questions are combined to develop a measure of total approval of aggression.

Probability Assessment of Risk. A scale was developed based on theories of the perception of risk developed in Chapter 3. Respondents were asked about their perception of being victimized by crime on a scale of 1 to 100. Separate items measured personal and social perceptions of risk. For example, one of the questions was: "What do you think is the probability that you will be mugged in the next 10 years?" The social counterpart of this question was "What do you think is the probability that an average person living in a big city will be mugged in the next 10 years?" Two other sets of questions asked the probability of being shot and the probability of being burglarized.

Mean World Index (MWI) & Cultivation Scale. The Mean World Index (MWI) is a three-item measure drawn from the media cultivation literature. The index is designed to measure perceptions of mistrust and alienation and comes originally from the National Opinion Research Center's General Social Surveys and a five-item Faith-in-People scale developed by Rosenberg (1957). Reliability estimates of the three-item scale have been reported between .66 and .68 (alphas) when used with American adults (Gerbner, Gross, Morgan & Signorielli, 1980; Morgan, 1986) and an average inter-item correlation of .22 when used with Australian children (Pingree, 1983). Criterion-related validity tests have found small relationships: Gerbner et al. (1980) found that an original correlation of .12 between overall TV viewing and the MWI dropped to .04 after controlling for eight demographic and individual characteristics. Pingree (1983) found a .04 correlation using a six-item version of the scale (Rubin, Palmgreen & Sypher, 1994). We also used the related Cultivation scale, a four-item measure of the perceived probability of real world violent acts or violence-related phenomena (Gerbner, Gross, Morgan & Signorielli, 1980).

5.2.3 Measures of Message Cognitions

Continuous Audience Response Measurement. Several of the studies used a continuous response measurement system (Biocca, David, West, 1994). The system measures participants' moment-to-moment evaluations of their cognitive states, usually a mood, interest level, or simple opinion. The hardware for the measure includes a computer and a set of handsets. Each participant continuously evaluated their *level of interest* in the programming by moving a seven-point dial on the handset. The seven points allowed viewers to signal the following levels of interest: 1) very uninterested; 2) moderately uninterested, 3) slightly interested; 4) neutral, neither interested nor uninterested; 5) slightly interested; 6) moderately interested, and 7) very interested. The computer sampled the viewers' interest in the programming every second.

Multiple Affective Adjective Checklist. The Multiple Affective Adjective Check List (MAACL) consists of 132 adjectives designed to provide brief state and trait measures of study participants' moods before and after exposure to the stimulus material (Zuckerman & Lubin, 1965). The list items can be coded to measure such constructs as anxiety (e.g. afraid, shaky), depression (e.g., alone, wilted) and hostility (e.g., angry).

The MAACL is simple and brief, requiring about five minutes to administer. All words are at or below an eighth grade reading level. MAACL has been used in a variety of clinical, experimental, field and epidemiological studies to measure anxiety, depression and hostility. A bibliography compiled by Lubin, Zuckerman & Woodward (1985) listed 716 published references to studies using the MAACL.

Self-Assessment Manikin. To assess levels of affective response, subjects completed the Self-Assessment Manikin or SAM (Lang, 1980). Lang describes the SAM as three five-point visual-based semantic differential scales for different affective factors. The scale for arousal depicts five conditions from excited (eyes open with raised eyebrows and exploding insides) to calm (eyes closed and stable). The scale for pleasure depicts five conditions from happy (smile and raised eyebrows) to sad (frown and knitted eyebrows). The scale for dominance or control depicts five conditions from powerless (very small) to powerful (very large).

The SAM scale for arousal was found to have a correlation of .937 with the Mehrabian standardized affective dimensions (Lang, 1980). Lang also reported that children easily identify with a SAM figure. Greenwald, Cook III & Lang (1989) similarly found that SAM split-half reliability for arousal correlated at .928. They found mean arousal ratings were similar across two administrations ($r=0.64$, $p<.001$). They also found larger mean skin conductance changes were related significantly to increased SAM arousal ratings by regression analysis ($F(1,46)=21.26$, $p<.00005$).

Memory. Some of the middle school students were given memory tests after they viewed the PSAs. They were asked to write down brief descriptions of as many of the PSAs as they could remember at the end of the viewing session. The memory score was calculated by counting the number of PSAs participants could remember.

6. STUDIES 1 AND 2: QUALITATIVE IN-DEPTH INTERVIEWS WITH TRAINING SCHOOL AND MIDDLE SCHOOL STUDENTS FOLLOWING EXPOSURE TO ANTIVIOLENCE PSAS

These studies combined qualitative and quantitative approaches to explore the meanings, moods and reactions that the antiviolence PSAs triggered in various adolescent audiences. Two studies were conducted to assess responses to and understanding of a sample of PSAs. In Study 1, students from a training school (Sample 1) were shown a randomly selected set of 12 PSAs and were interviewed one-on-one to learn how each PSA was interpreted and how sources were perceived. In Study 2, students from a middle school (Sample 2) were shown the same PSAs and also were interviewed one-on-one.

In addition to the one-on-one interviews, group responses also were elicited from students who had viewed the 15 PSAs in groups Study 3 and 4 (see Chapter 8). Their comments about each PSA are included in this chapter.

6.1 Research Questions

6.1.1 Semantic Processing of Each Antiviolence PSA

- ⊙ How are the PSAs received and understood by target audiences?
- ⊙ Are the sources used in the antiviolence PSAs perceived as competent and trustworthy?
- ⊙ Does the form of the PSA affect interest and comprehension?
- ⊙ Do audiences' interpretations and comprehension serve or undermine the attitudinal goals of the campaigns?

6.2 Methods

Because Study 2 is a replication of Study 1, both studies used the same methods. They are described together here, although analyses were conducted separately.

6.2.1 Participants

Eight students in the training school (see the description of Sample 1 in Chapter 4) participated in Study 1 and 14 middle school students participated in Study 2 (see the description of Sample 2 in Chapter 4). The students interviewed in Study 1 were all male, with an average age of 15.3 years old, who had spent an average of 11.5 months in the training school. In Study 2, nine male and 5 female middle school students were interviewed. They were generally younger (average age 12.9 years old) than the training school students. Results from group interviews with students from the two schools are also included.

6.2.2 Apparatus

Stimulus materials: Antiviolence PSAs. Students were shown a tape of antiviolence PSAs. The PSAs were randomly selected from the stratified pool of PSAs described in Chapter 2. The middle school students viewed six PSAs selected from 12 random orders. The training school students viewed 12 PSAs at a time out of six random orders. We increased the number of PSAs viewed at the training school because the middle-school students (who completed the study before the training school students) had shown no sign of fatigue in responding to six PSAs. The groups of students in Studies 3 and 4 viewed a total of 15 PSAs in two random orders. Tables 6.1 through Table 6.15 describe each of the PSAs used in Studies 1 through 4.

Tables 6.1- 6.15

PSAs Tested: 5 Narratives

Table 6.1: Before and After Hospital

Description
Teen gang leader is shown dancing at a party (before) and lying paralyzed in a hospital bed (after). Captions tell that he was felled by a single gunshot wound. He whispers, "It's hard. It's hard."

Main Character	Time	Type	Approach	Network
Male; 16-25 years old; victim and perpetrator	20 sec.	Attitudinal	Friendly advice	MTV

Table 6.2: Et Tu Brutus

Description
Teens play basketball on a city street. Car drives up, assailant with handgun jumps out, chases and corners one. Assailant's hood slides off and teen is staring at himself. James Earl Jones voice-over: "Stop. You're only killing yourself."

Main Character	Time	Type	Approach	Network
Male; 16-25 years old; victim and perpetrator	60 sec.	Attitudinal	Fear/ personal danger	HBO/Warner

Table 6. 3: Locker Slam

Description				
Boy in school hall is deliberately bumped by another. Color turns neon as imagined fight begins and victim pulls knife. Scene returns to normal as victim decides to "Pick up my books and walk away."				
Main Character	*Time*	*Type*	*Approach*	*Network*
Male; about 15 years old; victim	30 sec.	Behavioral	Self-help/ reform	Cartoon

Table 6.4: Stray Bullet

Description				
Boy playing with gun fires shot. Camera tracks bullet speeding down street, smashing car windows and a TV set in a living room and zeroing in on a baby in a high chair.				
Main Character	*Time*	*Type*	*Approach*	*Network*
Multiple	60 sec.	Attitudinal	Fear/ personal danger	HBO/Warner

Table 6.5: These Walls Have no Prejudice

Description				
Camera pans over bodies in morgue as Leonard Nimoy (voice-over) recites statistics on gun violence. Notes that guns are "everybody's problem." Ends with a shadowy figure firing at viewer.				
Main Character	*Time*	*Type*	*Approach*	*Network*
Multiple; all ages; all races; narrator is male, 40-60 years old	30 sec.	Attitudinal	Fear/ personal danger	HBO/Warner

10 Celebrity Endorsements/Testimonials

Table 6.6: Brownstone

Description				
Members of musical group tell viewers to "Take control, stop the violence and give peace a chance." Scene of them sitting alternates with rapid graphics, statistics on gun violence.				
Main Character	*Time*	*Type*	*Approach*	*Network*
Females; 16-25 years old; celebrity	30 sec.	Attitudinal	Friendly advice	The Box

Table 6.7: Chuck D

Description				
Leader of Public Enemy (rap group) on street corner: "A gun don't make you hard, bucking the odds make you hard. ... Do this for our community."				
Main Character	*Time*	*Type*	*Approach*	*Network*
Male; 26-40 years old; celebrity	30 sec.	Attitudinal	Friendly advice; racial pride	HBO/Warner

Table 6.8: Bill Clinton

Description				
Clinton, in office, says federal government is doing its job to try to stop crime. "You have to do your part too ... our country, our problem. Let's solve it together." Ends with VAV Week logo.				
Main Character	*Time*	*Type*	*Approach*	*Network*
Male; 40-60 years old; authority figure	30 sec.	Attitudinal	Self-help/ reform; affiliation/ community	Showtime

Table 6.9: Derrick Coleman

Description				
Basketball player tells viewers, "To increase the peace, start with yourself. Stay strong."				
Main Character	*Time*	*Type*	*Approach*	*Network*
Male; 26-40; sports celebrity	15 sec.	Attitudinal	Friendly advice	MTV

Table 6.10: Gloria Estefan

Description				
Musician tells viewers to stop the violence. Scene of her sitting in chair is intercut with rapid graphics, statistics on gun violence.				
Main Character	*Time*	*Type*	*Approach*	*Network*
Female; 26-40 years old; celebrity	30 sec.	Attitudinal	Friendly advice	The Box

Table 6.11: Samuel Jackson

Description				
Jackson (sitting on chair in studio) talks about difference between movie violence, real violence. "Violence doesn't solve anything. Think about it."				
Main Character	Time	Type	Approach	Network
Male; 30-50 years old; celebrity	30 sec.	Attitudinal	Friendly advice	Showtime

Table 6.12: Redman

Description				
Rap artist talks about violence. Shots of him alternate with fast-moving graphics, statistics on gun violence. "Numbers don't lie." Some segments appear shot in a jail.				
Main Character	Time	Type	Approach	Network
Male; 16-25 years old; celebrity	30 sec.	Attitudinal	Friendly advice	The Box

Table 6.13: Salt & Pepa

Description				
Musicians tell viewers, "Think about the mothers. Brothers, please stop the violence." Shots of them are intercut with fast-moving graphics, statistics on gun violence.				
Main Character	Time	Type	Approach	Network
Females; 26-40 years old; celebrities	20 sec.	Attitudinal	Friendly advice	The Box

Table 6.14: Somewhere in America (rapper)

Description				
Rapper walks down hallway. Excerpt: "Men used to fight like men. Now everybody owns a Mac 10. Be for peace, take it to the street, gotta look at life in a whole new light."				
Main Character	Time	Type	Approach	Network
Male; 16-25 years old; non-celebrity	30 sec.	Attitudinal	Friendly advice	MTV

Table 6.15: Zlata - America is great

Description				
Girl from war-ravaged Sarajevo whose diary was published sits on a beach and tells viewers to "think before they do things" and "give peace a chance."				
Main Character	Time	Type	Approach	Network
Female; 16-25 years old; victim	30 sec.	Attitudinal	Friendly advice	MTV

Video monitor. Students viewed the antiviolence PSAs on a 19-inch video monitor.

Video camera. During the one-on-one interviews, a camcorder was used to record each viewer's reactions to and explanations of the PSAs. Back-lighting and silhouettes were used to preserve the anonymity of the respondents.

Audio tape recorder. Students' reactions also were recorded on audio-cassette tapes.

6.2.1 Procedure

More than three days before the studies, students completed a questionnaire that measured demographic variables, media use, probability assessment of risk, beliefs about aggression and past violent behavior. Each student and his/her parent and/or guardian had previously completed an informed consent procedure.

Students entered the interview room on the day of the study and were greeted by the interviewer, who provided verbal instructions about the study. After the student viewed each antiviolence PSA, the interviewer paused the tape. Participants were then asked open-ended questions about the PSA's characters and sources, the sequence of actions, and their interpretation of the PSA. Where appropriate, the interviewer added additional questions to clarify or probe the viewer's responses. All responses were audio and videotaped. In both school settings, an assistant was also in the room during the interview to help the interviewer with equipment and taping.

6.2.2 Qualitative Analysis

A total of 350 pages of transcripts of the one-on-one and group interviews were reviewed. Comments on the PSAs were organized by PSA and respondent ID number. In the analyses reported here, direct quotes from the interview participants are identified by randomly selected names assigned to each student. The names were adopted strictly as an aid in distinguishing between respondents, and have no relationship to the respondents' real names.

Because this was an exploratory study and the number of subjects at the two schools was small, we have also included comments from focus group interviews with the training school and middle school students from Studies 3 and 4. (The group comments were found to be highly consistent with the one-on-one interviews, and are used here to reinforce the comments of the individual students.) These quotes are all labeled "group" to show they come from the focus groups in Studies 3 and 4.

6.3 Results

6.3.1 Study 1: Training School Students

The training school students, although initially somewhat reticent given their currently restricted and closely monitored lives, were remarkably candid in their assessments of the PSAs. An evaluation of their responses was conducted by examining reactions to the celebrities and/or central figures in the testimonial PSAs, and then analyzing how the form of the messages and other factors affected response and comprehension.

Sources. Some sources were perceived as more credible than others by the training school viewers. Several of the celebrity sources, such as Gloria Estefan and Derrick Coleman, weren't even recognized by most of the viewers. Other sources, like Samuel Jackson, were considered untrustworthy because they have either portrayed violent characters or have participated in violence themselves.

The most credible sources, in general, were perceived as similar in age and interests/activities to the training school audience. Sources were also considered trustworthy if they had either always been for peace, or could be trusted to speak against violence out of personal conviction rather than financial gain. Trustworthy sources included Chuck D and Redman:

> (group response) "Well he (Chuck D) is (credible) 'cause he has always been about 'stop the violence' from day one."

> (group) "He (Redman) is legit, man."

Demographic similarity. The age and gender of the sources did make a difference in both recognition and attention to the messages' sources. The training school viewers were most likely to recognize and relate to testimonials by younger (e.g., Chuck D, Redman) rather than older (e.g., President Clinton, Samuel Jackson) celebrities. The gender of the sources also made a difference. Probably because they live in an all-male environment, the training school viewers especially liked hearing from and looking at the female celebrities (e.g., Salt & Pepa, Brownstone). As two of the respondents said:

> (Tom) "Yea (I would watch)...for one it had some females on there and they were kind of cute."

> (Jim) "Anyone would pay attention to that right there...that is Salt n' Pepa right there."

But the physical appeal of women may also have had a negative effect on attention to the message itself:

(Tom) "They were females--I would look at (it) just to look at them--I didn't really pay any attention to what they were saying."

Music as a professional role. Celebrities who engaged in respected musical genres attracted more attention than those who did not. For example, rap artists scored high on both interest and arousal among training school students, who frequently indicated a preference for rap music. When asked how to make an effective PSA, the students responded with:

(group) "I'll...make a rap out of it man."

(group) "I'd put a little video together, and a couple of rappers together...like a rap song."

But not just any rap will draw attention or be judged as credible. Although well-known rap artists (Chuck D, Redman) earned high scores among respondents who liked rap music, lesser-known (and perhaps less talented) rap artists (as in "Somewhere in America") were not as well received:

(group) "No, he can't rap."

(Adam) "He ain't nobody I'd look up to or nothin' like that."

(Tom) "The way he was doing it was just whack [boring or poorly done]."

(group) "He thinking that just because everyone listen to rap, they'll listen to what he's saying."

The athlete and politician celebrities were not well-received. Few of the respondents recognized basketball star Derrick Coleman, and those who did suggested that he might not be an appropriate antiviolence spokesperson because of his desire for financial gain and his overall attitude and behavior:

(Bill) "He got the money, he got the shoes, he got so much money it's pitiful."

(Mike) "He seemed like the type of person that's out there doing violence by himself."

President Clinton was sometimes laughed at by the training school students, who saw him as hypocritical and doing too little to solve problems:

(group) "He fake man. He fake...He just doing this 'cause he the president. He lied to get in the president spot."

(group) "I believe he probably doing some of the same stuff we used to do in the crib [at home]..."

(group [sarcastically]) "I smoked pot, but I didn't inhale it."

(group) "Besides killing, all the stuff we used to do at the crib, I believe he do the same thing, man."

(group) "He don't know what's going on. I believe he can do more than what he's supposed to be doing, anyway."

Celebrity actors who portray violent characters also were suspect. Many of the respondents appreciated Samuel Jackson's message, but suggested that actors who play violent roles in television and film are being hypocritical when they offer antiviolence messages:

(Mike) "In the movies I see...he out there...with guns and everything. Regardless if it's fake or not, they're still broadcasting violence...to me he out there demonstrating violence and at the same time...he telling people to stop the violence...he's confusing people that's watching these movies and these commercials or whatever."

Actors also were considered hypocrites because they are frequently involved in behaviors in their personal lives that run contrary to the messages they are trying to convey:

(group) "...trying to stress a point to us saying no to drugs, then the next thing you know, you hear about them in the news...they caught selling drugs."

In sum, the celebrity sources got mixed reviews. The celebrities who were similar demographically and shared musical tastes with the respondents were more readily recognized and listened to. Even favorite celebrities were not credible, however, if they had portrayed or participated in violence or related activities, or were suspected of being paid for saying the right thing.

Message form and comprehension. Both the testimonial and narrative PSAs had positive and negative characteristics, depending on specific content elements and audience variables. In general, narratives were more likely to be well-received, but also were more vulnerable to misinterpretation. Testimonials, on the other hand, were not as interesting, but their messages appeared to be more clearly understood and recalled.

Narrative PSAs. Narrative PSAs attracted and engaged the training school viewers. The viewers were aroused by the action taking place, and often recounted the individual stories and recalled specific details. The respondents frequently related the narrative stories to experiences in their own lives and referred to real-life violence that paralleled the narrative images. Students from the training school reacted to the narrative PSAs *Stray Bullet* and *Et Tu Brutus* PSAs with the following comments:

> (Joe) "I can relate to that, I can picture one of my family members that...young getting shot."

> (group) "I know an incident that happened and the baby got killed--I can relate to that."

> (group) "We were all out playing having fun. And it went off, and went through the van, and shot a little girl in the back."

> (Mike) "I know a few people...I have a few friends and family members shot...in my family, I have two that were shot and killed ... I have about four or five that were shot at..."

Although the narratives maintained the attention of viewers and the stories were often recalled, the relative "openness" of the narrative form allowed frequent misinterpretation by the target audiences. The individual interviews revealed several cases where training school respondents had extracted different or "unintended" meanings from the PSAs, and had decoded pro- rather than antiviolence messages. For example, a number of viewers of *Brutus* didn't see that the killer was the same person as the victim until it was pointed out during a second viewing.

Viewers of *Stray Bullet* didn't agree on whose gun the boy was playing with or whether anyone was killed in the end, and some viewers thought the message was that parents should keep their guns out of reach of their children, while fewer thought the message was they shouldn't have guns in the first place:

> (group) "Don't leave gun around kids. If you gonna have it, don't leave your gun around kids."

Some respondents thought the message was simply that "a bullet has no name" and that even innocent children can get killed.

The training school viewers also drew on their personal experience to critique the PSAs' depictions of guns and/or violent confrontations. A number of the training school students who viewed *Stray Bullet* were skeptical that a bullet could do what that particular bullet did:

> (Mike) "I doubt if it would ricochet and go that far."

> (group) "I don't think a bullet can travel that far."

They also thought the depiction of a boy walking away from a fight in the school hall in the *Locker Slam* PSA was unrealistic:

(Chris) "If somebody come bumps against me when I'm in school...I'm gonna do something about it."

(Tom) "It ain't in my nature to walk away--I've been used to fighting. That's all I know to do is fight. If I want to fight, I'm going to fight."

Training school respondents frequently focused on peripheral rather than central themes. For example, comments from the students after seeing *Stray Bullet* and *These Walls* included:

(Ted) "They want us to put the gun down--but they were showing how to load it up."

(Mike) "That's a fine .38...I ain't never had a .38...Yeah, I might use...I want to check out...something like that when I get out."

The two PSAs with the clearest story lines (*Stray Bullet* and *Et Tu Brutus*) may also have been misinterpreted because they incorporated the same production techniques and styles as full-length programs and films. The sophisticated narrative structure and production techniques appeared to have reminded viewers of action adventure movies designed purely for entertainment; thus, they did not process what they viewed as information. One training school student, commenting on *Et Tu Brutus*, said:

(Chris) "...maybe if you was just seeing it, you'd think they got a new movie out ...they could have taken it as kinda like a new gangsta movie."

Testimonial PSAs. Despite the varying interest in specific sources discussed above, the messages of the celebrities were frequently and clearly recalled by the training school respondents. This was true even in cases where the respondents were disinterested in or even critical of individual celebrities. In contrast to the narrative PSAs, the straight-forward, informative approach of the testimonials left a more precise impression on the respondents--much less subject to misinterpretation. However, the viewers were typically less involved or moved by the messages.

The training school students did appear to be especially sensitive to depictions and discussion about families. They appreciated celebrities like Salt & Pepa commenting that families are hurt by violence:

(Tom) "We need to think about our mother...and all that will come down on her... or the next man's mother."

(Chris) "I liked the idea that families getting close."

In contrast, however, the same viewers were matter-of-fact about the violent crime statistics presented in the celebrity spots, and often were skeptical that such messages could be expected to reduce violence:

> (Tom) "I don't really get no message--it's just like the rest of them...Stop the violence."

> (Chris) "No man, that ain't effective. I ain't gonna try and hear it, you know what I'm saying."

Effectiveness of production methods. Production techniques appeared to help emphasize mood and character of some of the antiviolence messages. The use of quick edits, for example, appealed to the younger "music video" generation. But over-editing sometimes resulted in poor understanding of message themes, as can be seen by these reactions to the *Derrick Coleman* PSA:

> (group) "Too quick times two...can't get any of it."

> (Bill) "He said it so quick, I didn't understand it."

> (Chris) "I don't know man...the thing went by so fast."

Others took little notice of the production techniques, and simply dismissed television's role as neither part of the problem:

> (Tom) "Hey-- teenagers ain't at home. They out in somebody's neighborhood at a party or something-- trying to have fun. They ain't at home looking at no TV."

> (group) "Yeah, most of them don't even look at the TV...not that much, anyway."

> (group) "Violence--some people get it off television. Some people are just violent."

...nor the solution:

> (group) "They can make commercials, regardless, people still going to do what they want to do."

> (group) "Cause people going to do what they want to do regardless of what somebody say. People see the commercials all day and go out and shoot somebody, it don't make no difference."

459

6.3.2 Study 2: Middle School Students

Middle school students in general were both interested in and often frightened by what they viewed in the PSAs. Frequently they noted little similarity between themselves and the sources or the situations depicted, and suggested that most of the portrayals were inconsistent with their own personal experiences.

Sources. The middle school students responded most favorably to celebrity spokespersons who were similar to them in age or interests/activities. They also appeared to be rather receptive to messages from celebrities who were involved in professional endeavors (such as performing rap music) that the viewers were not necessarily interested in or familiar with. Some spokespersons were viewed by the students as being sincere but inappropriate for the messages they were delivering, while others were perceived as hypocritical or untrustworthy.

Demographic similarity. The middle school viewers tended to favor the testimonials by younger rather than older celebrities:

> (Susan, commenting on *Zlata*) "...I think she touched us, because she's like...I think she's a teenager. Since she's a very young person giving us the message, we would probably understand it better."

Music and roles. Musical acts generally were well-received by the middle school viewers, even though few of the respondents indicated being familiar with or interested in rap or R&B music during the interviews:

> (Diane) "I don't particularly like rap. But it still did catch my attention."

Unfamiliarity with the genre did, however, occasionally contribute to difficulty in understanding the message:

> (John) "I don't listen to rap music. I'd have to listen to it twice before I caught all of what he's saying."

Among the other celebrity endorsers, few of the middle school respondents recognized basketball star Derrick Coleman, and those who did were not sure that he was a particularly good antiviolence spokesperson:

> (group) "Lots of times they do it for money."

> (Michelle) "He looks sort of big and violent to me..."

President Clinton was fairly well-respected by the middle school viewers, but even viewers who felt the President was a credible spokesperson ("He's very dedicated to improving our country. He really wants to make things change") thought a "real person" would be more effective:

> (John) "I mean, sometimes when you think of the president, you don't think that a real person-- you think that he's just there...you just think that if it was a common person you could really relate to it like an average American."

Samuel Jackson, the lone actor in the sample PSAs, was generally viewed by the middle school viewers as sincere in his message, but some perceived him as being hypocritical or disinterested:

> (Cathy) "A person that's against violence. Good talker, that's all."

> (group) "They may be saying don't do drugs, but then they may be actually involved in it."

Message Form and Comprehension. The middle school students appeared to be generally receptive to both narrative and testimonial approaches. They often noted that the narrative depictions were both arousing and frightening, though frequently unfamiliar in terms of setting or situations. The testimonials were viewed as being perhaps less exciting, but offering useful and memorable information.

Narrative PSAs. The middle school viewers generally were aroused by the action taking place, and were often able to discuss specific details of the narrative PSAs. The respondents also appeared quite interested in the narrative story lines, but were not likely to draw comparisons between the PSA characters and their own life experiences. Sometimes they relied on stereotypes to fill in for lack of experience:

> (Mark [commenting on *Et Tu Brutus*]) "These people who were playing basketball they looked like gang members. I'm not trying to stereotype, but by the way they looked, they were curious."

Although not living in a totally crime-free environment, the students were unable to identify with the violent scenes or locations depicted or discussed in the PSAs. Often they relied on their perceptions of what a crime-ridden area might look like. Comments on the *Et Tu Brutus* and *These Walls* PSAs included:

> (Tracy) "I guess there's a pretty big chance (of seeing violence) in one of the broken down places, or junkier places, like there where gangs like to hang out."

> (Jennifer) "If I maybe go to the wrong neighborhood..."

> (John) "The reason I can't relate to any of these is because it looked like a place like New York."

For some of the middle school students, the fear appeals in narrative PSAs such as *Et Tu Brutus* proved to be powerful--and may have been a bit overwhelming:

(Michelle) "It's really, actually really scary....it was really, really scary."

The narrative form also resulted in different or misinterpretations by the middle school audience. For example, some of the viewers of *Stray Bullet* thought the message was that parents shouldn't have guns around the house in the first place, while others thought that it just meant parents should keep their guns out of reach of their children:

(Kim) "That you should take better care of your gun or guns if you have them, and keep them in a safe place where children can't get a hold of them."

Other misinterpretations of the messages also occurred. One student inadvertently referred to a narrative PSA as a "movie":

(Mark) "Kids watch these *movies* and try to do the same thing."

Some of the middle school students were also critical of the themes depicted in the narratives, as several respondents thought the depiction of the boy walking away from a fight in the school hall in *Locker Slam* was unrealistic:

(John) "It's just not realistic...he wouldn't be happy if he was confronted by a bully that was going to turn his face into mush."

However, several students did agree with the PSA's message:

(Susan) "I wouldn't get in a fight...I would definitely walk away."

Testimonials. Although the middle school students did not relate personally to many of the celebrity spokespersons, they sometimes recalled the messages of the celebrities verbatim. Several of the respondents were able to remember the specific statistical data presented by celebrities, and appeared genuinely impressed by the violent crime figures cited in some testimonial PSAs:

(Michelle) "The facts are really scary. I mean the fact that there is a new...gun (manufactured) every 20 seconds is really scary."

(Patricia) "They said that over 900,000 handgun crimes were committed last year..."

(Diane) "I think it's really startling that every 20 seconds someone is injured by a handgun..."

Effectiveness of production methods. Several viewers reacted to the use of certain production techniques in the PSAs. They sometimes appeared to be affected by the incorporation of such elements as special lighting and sound effects, such as those used in the *These Walls* PSA:

> (Susan) "...the background light, very dim, and the sound effects, make it very effective."

> (Diane) "It was a good voice--fairly deep, and deep voices gain more attention."

The use of quick "music video" edits was also appealing to most middle school students; however, the over-editing of some PSAs--such as the *Derrick Coleman* testimonial--resulted in poor reception of message themes:

> (Denise) "He's saying the right thing (but) I think it might have been too short."

6.4 Discussion

The **training school** responses show that the students are selective in terms of the sources they respect and the types of PSAs they are more likely to respond to. Younger male and female musical artists (particularly rap artists) received the most interest and attention. Several of the sources were considered hypocritical for having financial incentives or having previous involvement in violent or antisocial activities.

Narratives appeared to be more appealing to the training school students than testimonials, although message interpretation was clearest for the testimonials. Many of the students were able to relate to the narrative PSAs from personal experiences, but most were also pessimistic about the potential effectiveness of these PSAs--as several respondents indicated that the solutions being offered were unrealistic, and that the problem of violence comes from sources other than television portrayals.

The **middle school** responses indicated that although sources are important in attracting interest and attention, similarity is not the only necessary attribute. The students were interested in many of the messages, even those that featured celebrities involved in activities they were not familiar with. They were also, however, suspicious of the motives of some spokespersons who they thought might be speaking for the wrong reasons.

The middle school students were impressed with the severity of the problem as presented by the statistics in some of the testimonials. Apparently, however, these PSAs spoke less directly to this audience about themselves and more about others who they perceive as more likely to be involved in violence. Only the PSA featuring kids in school, *Locker Slam*, invoked any projection of self into the situation--but this PSA was frequently seen as presenting an unrealistic solution to a real-world dilemma.

7. STUDIES 3 & 4: EXPERIMENTAL TESTS OF THE EFFECT OF INDIVIDUAL ANTIVIOLENCE PSAS ON THE INTEREST LEVEL, AROUSAL AND MOOD OF TRAINING SCHOOL AND MIDDLE SCHOOL STUDENTS

7.1 Research questions

7.1.1 Moment-to-Moment Patterns of Interest

⊙ Which PSAs are of greatest interest to and maintain the attention of the viewers?

7.1.2 Arousal & Mood

⊙ Which of the PSAs are most arousing?
⊙ Which PSAs are the most pleasing?
⊙ Which PSAs leave the viewer feeling dominant and/or in control of his/her own behavior?

7.1.3 Memory

Which PSAs are best remembered?

7.2 Methods

Two separate experiments were conducted in the training school and the middle school. The within-subjects variable for each experiment was type of message (15 PSAs). The dependent variables were level of interest, pleasure, arousal, dominance, comprehension and memory (memory was tested only at the middle school). Because both studies used the same methodology, the section below applies to both.

7.2.1 Participants

Sixteen training school students and 25 middle school students participated in the study. The training school students watched two randomly ordered tapes of 15 PSAs in 4 small groups; the middle school students watched the same PSAs in two groups. Groups were assigned according to either students' cottage in the training school or class in the middle school. The training school students included 15 males with an average age of 15.5 years old who had spent an average of 6.9 months in the school. The middle school participants included 20 females and 5 males with an average age of 12.8 years old.

7.2.2 Apparatus

Participants completed pre- and posttest measures of beliefs about aggression. Pretests also included measures of violent behavior, media use and demographics. (For descriptions of these measures, see Chapter 5.) Participants were then shown 15 antiviolence PSAs. The PSAs were randomly selected from a sampling frame of all antiviolence PSAs (see Chapter 2). The 15 PSAs were edited into two tapes, each with a random order of the PSAs. Each ad appeared once separated by 10 seconds of video black.

A continuous response measure was used to gather moment-to-moment self-reports of the level of interest for each PSA. (See Chapter 5 for a description of the measure.) The Self-Assessment Manikin (SAM) was used after each PSA to measure arousal, pleasure and dominance. (See Chapter 5 for a description of the measure.)

7.2.3 Procedure

More than three days before the experiment, study participants completed a questionnaire that measured demographics, media use, beliefs about aggression, and past violent behavior. Each participant and his/her parent and/or guardian had previously completed an informed consent procedure.

On the day of the experiment, participants viewed the PSAs in groups. They were first instructed on how to use the continuous response handsets. Each viewer held a handset (Biocca, David & West, 1994) and was instructed to evaluate each second of the video on a seven-point, uninteresting-to-interesting scale. Participants communicated their evaluations by continuously turning a seven-position dial on the handset. The participants then viewed the 15 antiviolence PSAs. After each PSA, the experimenter paused the tape and participants completed a SAM sheet. After viewing the PSAs, participants in both schools were also asked about their perceptions of each PSA.

At the middle school, students completed the SAM sheet and also individually wrote short responses to two questions about each PSA on a questionnaire attached to the SAM sheet. The middle school subjects also were given a surprise memory test. After viewing the entire tape, they were asked to list as many of the PSAs as they could remember.

At the training school, a significant percentage of the subjects had poor reading and writing skills. Therefore, after viewing each PSA, they were asked to comment on it orally. These comments were audiotaped. No written memory test was used with this group.

7.3 Results

The SAM measure is divided into three dimensions: arousal, pleasure and dominance. The results reported here follow these three dimensions. All three analyses of covariance were conducted using the same model, i.e., a single factor experiment with repeated measures on the same element: 15 (PSAs), using a baseline measurement as the covariant to control for initial differences.

7.3.1 Study 3: Training School Students

Interest, arousal & mood scores. Exposure to the 15 PSAs had an effect on the mood of the training school participants. After exposure, participants were more aroused than before (see Table 7.1), but there appeared to be no overall effect on feelings of pleasure or dominance.

Table 7.1: Pre- and posttest of SAM Measurement

SAM	Pretest	Posttest	diff	T	p<
Arousal	1.88	2.49	0.61	7.33	0.001
Pleasure	3.38	3.39	0.01	0.05	0.96
Dominance	3.81	3.82	0.01	0.11	0.91

Table 7.2 provides a summary of the scores of the training school students for the measures of interest, arousal, pleasure and dominance for each of the PSAs. (The order of the PSAs in the table is based on the ranking of each PSA on the interest measure.)

Table 7.2: Training school scores on interest, arousal, pleasure and dominance*

PSA	Interest	Arousal	Pleasure	Dominance
Brownstone	6.1	2.9	3.8	4.2
Et Tu Brutus	5.8	3.1	3.9	4.4
Chuck D	5.7	3.1	3.5	4.2
Redman	5.6	2.7	3.7	4.1
Salt & Pepa	5.5	2.8	3.8	4.4
Stray Bullet	5.4	2.9	2.8	3.3
These walls have no prejudice	5.4	2.6	3.3	4.1
Before and after hospital	5.3	2.0	2.8	3.3
Samuel Jackson	5.2	2.4	3.4	3.9
Somewhere in America	4.9	2.6	3.9	4.1
Locker Slam	4.9	2.1	3.4	3.8
Gloria Estefan	4.6	2.1	3.3	3.2
Derrick Coleman	4.4	2.0	2.9	3.4
Zlata	4.1	2.3	3.3	3.7
President Clinton	2.5	1.6	2.9	2.9

* The continuous response measurement scale for interest runs from 1 (very uninterested) to 7 (very interested). For all other measures, the SAM scale runs from 1(low) to 5 (high).

Interest. As can be seen in Table 7.2, the training school students showed strongest interest in PSAs that featured younger celebrities and male or female rap artists. Four of the top 5 PSA scores were earned by celebrities who are involved in either rap or R & B music.

Arousal. The narrative format was more arousing than the celebrity PSAs (see Table 7.2). All of the narrative PSAs scored in the top 50 percent of the sample, while the *Et Tu Brutus* PSA tied with the *Chuck D* (rap artist) testimonial for "most arousing." The *President Clinton* PSA was by far the least arousing, scoring a full half-point lower than any of the other testimonials.

Analysis of Covariance (ANCOVA) on the arousal dimension showed that there was a statistically significant difference among the PSAs ($F_{(14,206)}$=3.18; p<0.0002). A follow-up Tukey's test showed that the *President Clinton* PSA was statistically different from four other PSAs: *Et Tu Brutus, Locker Slam, Stray Bullet,* and *Chuck D* (see Table 7.3).

Pleasure. Viewers experienced more pleasure after viewing the narrative PSAs, the rap artist testimonials, and especially the female rapper testimonials (see Table 7.2). Several of the narratives, however, and in particular *Stray Bullet* and *These Walls*, received low pleasure scores. This was the only dimension on which the *President Clinton* PSA did not receive the lowest score. However, the analysis of difference among means revealed that only the PSA *Stray Bullet* was statistically different from two other PSAs: *Et tu Brutus* and *Somewhere in America*.

ANCOVA results revealed a statistically significant difference among the PSAs overall ($F_{(14,207)}$=2.95; p<0.0004), with *Stray Bullet* registering significantly less pleasure than *Et Tu Brutus* and *Somewhere in America* (see Table 7.3).

Dominance. Analysis of the dominance dimension revealed that the female rap and R&B spokespersons resulted in the strongest feelings of having power and being in control (Table 7.2). Several of the narratives also drew relatively high scores. The testimonials featuring Gloria Estefan, Derrick Coleman, and President Clinton accounted for three of the five lowest scores.

The scores on dominance also were statistically significantly different among the PSAs ($F_{(14,236)}$=4.39; p<0.0001). The analysis of difference among means revealed that *President Clinton* was the most distinctive by being present in 7 out of 11 pairs of statistically different scores (in all cases lower). *Salt & Pepa* was the next most distinctive (in all cases higher)(see Table 7.3).

Table 7.3 Differences between PSAs on SAM Measures*

PSA	1	2	3	4	5	6	7	8	9	10	11	12	13	14	15
1. Et Tu Brutus															
2. Gloria Estefan															
3. Somewhere in America															
4. President Clinton	ad		d												
5. Brownstone				a											
6. Locker Slam				ad											
7. These Walls				d											
8. Samuel Jackson															
9. Derrick Coleman															
10. Redman				d											
11. Stray Bullet	dp		p	a											
12. Before & After Hospital	d														
13. Zlata															
14. Salt & Pepa				d							d	d			
15. Chuck D				d											

*Letters in the cells indicate significant pairwise difference on each of the three SAM scales. *a* stands for Arousal, *d* for Dominance, and *p* for Pleasure.

7.3.2 Study 4: Middle School students

Interest, arousal and mood scores. Exposure to the 15 PSAs affected middle school students on all three dimensions of mood. Students were more aroused, felt less pleasure and felt less in control after seeing the set of PSAs (see Table 7.4).

Table 7.4: Pre- and posttest of SAM Measurement

SAM	Pretest	Posttest	diff	T	p<
Arousal	2.05	2.56	0.51	4.97	0.0001
Pleasure	3.87	3.20	-0.67	-7.49	0.0001
Dominance	3.61	3.11	-0.50	-6.82	0.0001

Table 7.5 provides a summary of the scores of the PSAs for the measures of interest, arousal, pleasure and dominance. (The order of the PSAs is based on their ranking on interest.)

Table 7.5: Middle school scores on interest, arousal, pleasure and dominance*

PSA	Interest	Arousal	Pleasure	Dominance
Locker Slam	5.9	2.2	4.0	3.8
Et Tu Brutus	5.7	4.0	2.1	2.5
Stray Bullet	5.7	4.4	1.7	1.9
Salt & Pepa	5.2	1.8	3.9	4.2
These walls have no prejudice	5.0	3.4	2.6	2.6
Before and after Hospital	4.9	3.2	2.6	3.0
Redman	4.9	2.3	4.1	4.1
Brownstone	4.6	3.5	2.0	4.0
Derrick Coleman	4.4	2.2	3.4	3.0
Chuck D	4.3	2.3	3.7	3.6
Somewhere in America	3.9	1.5	3.6	3.2
Samuel Jackson	3.8	2.1	3.3	3.4
Gloria Estefan	3.5	2.1	3.3	3.2
Zlata	3.3	2.1	3.6	3.4
President Clinton	1.8	2.0	3.3	2.6

* The continuous response measurement scale for interest runs from 1 (very uninterested) to 7
(very interested). For all other measures, the SAM scales run from 1 (low) to 5 (high).

Interest. The results for the middle school respondents indicate high interest for narrative PSAs (see Table 7.5). Four of the top 5 scores were earned by narratives. Results were moderate for younger rap or R & B musicians. The three lowest scoring PSAs featured Gloria Estefan, Zlata and President Clinton.

Arousal. The narrative PSAs were most arousing for the middle school students. Two of the narratives (*Et Tu Brutus* and *Stray Bullet*) were substantially more arousing than any of the other PSAs (see Table 7.5). All of the narrative PSAs were in the top 30 percent of the sample. Unlike the results for the interest measure, the rap celebrities scored particularly low on the arousal measure. The *Salt & Pepa* and *Somewhere in America* (Rapper) PSAs were the least arousing.

Some ads were more distinctive than others ($F_{(14,294)}$=15.34; p<0.0001). The analysis of differences among the means revealed that *Et Tu Brutus, Stray Bullets* and *These Walls* were the most distinctive on the arousal dimension. Pairwise differences are displayed in Table 7.6.

Table 7.6: Differences between PSAs on SAM Measures*

PSA	1	2	3	4	5	6	7	8	9	10	11	12	13	14	15
1. Et Tu Brutus															
2. Gloria Estefan	ap														
3. Somewhere in America	ap														
4. President Clinton	ap														
5. Brownstone	adp			d											
6. Locker Slam	adp														
7. These Walls Have No Prejudice		a	ap	a	adp	ap									
8. Samuel Jackson	ap						a								
9. Derrick Coleman	ap						a								
10. Redman	adp			d			dp								
11. Stray Bullet		adp		ap	adp	adp		adp	adp	adp					
12. Before & After Hospital			p		p	p				p	ad				
13. Zlata	ap						ap				adp	p			
14. Salt & Pepa	ap			d			adp				adp	dp			
15. Chuck D	adp						p				adp	p			

*Letters in the cells indicate significant pairwise difference on each of the three SAM scales. *a* stands for Arousal, *d* for Dominance, and *p* for Pleasure.

Pleasure. In contrast to the other variables, pleasure scores were higher for celebrity testimonials than for narrative PSAs (see Table 7.5). Many of the rap artists and other entertainers were pleasing to the middle school audience members, and even *President Clinton* scored among the top half of the PSAs. In contrast, several of the narratives, such as *Stray Bullet, Et Tu Brutus* and *These Walls*, received very low pleasure scores. The violent action narratives appeared to leave the viewers feeling very little pleasure, as they accounted for 3 of the lowest 4 scores. Some of the PSAs were more distinctive on this dimension than others $(F_{(14,207)}= 10.91; p<0.0001)$. However, the difference among means was particularly prominent between *Et Tu Brutus* and most of the other PSAs (see Table 7.6).

Dominance. The results for dominance indicated that female musicians left the middle school students with the strongest feelings of power and control (see Table 7.5). Several of the male rap artists also drew relatively high scores. Many of the narratives scored low on this dimension, however. The narrative PSAs left the viewers feeling little power or control, as these depictions accounted for 3 of the 4 lowest scores. There is a statistically significant difference among the PSAs $(F_{(14,207)}= 10.91; p<0.0001)$ on this dimension. *Stray Bullet* was the most distinctive PSA, leaving viewers feeling the least dominant. A comparison between the PSAs are presented in Table 7.6.

Memory. As can be seen in Table 7.7, three of the four PSAs most frequently remembered used a narrative format. The one celebrity PSA in the top four was *Brownstone*, the female rap group. As expected, memory scores were positively correlated with arousal (r=.69, p<.01). Unexpectedly, however, memory scores were not significantly correlated with average interest (as measured by the CRM). Memory was negatively correlated with both dominance (r=-.51, p<.05) and pleasure (r=-.63, p<.01), and positively correlated with the PSA length (r=.81, p<.001). T-tests indicated that there was no significant order effect, meaning that PSAs shown at the beginning or end of the tapes were not remembered more frequently than those appearing in the middle.

Table 7.7: Ranking of PSAs by Memory Score

PSA	Memory score
Stray Bullet	24
Et Tu Brutus	22
Brownstone	14
Locker Slam	14
Somewhere in America	12
Chuck D	10
Salt & Pepa	9
These Walls Have No Prejudice	9
President Clinton	9
Gloria Estefan	8
Zlata - America is Great	6
Before & After Hospital	6
Derrick Coleman	6
Redman	3
Samuel Jackson	2

7.3.3 PSA-by-PSA Descriptive Analysis of Interest, Arousal, Pleasure and Dominance For Students in Studies 3 and 4

In this exploratory descriptive data analysis we looked at differences in the moment-to-moment reactions of the two audiences (training school students and middle school students) to each second of each PSA. Because these are not samples drawn from the same population, we must be careful to not draw firm conclusions about differences until the pattern is confirmed with other samples. The comparison does provide some indication, however, of how differently audiences may respond to the same messages. Each PSA is described with a percentile ranking on each dimension of arousal, pleasure and dominance, and a graph showing moment-to-moment patterns of interest for each group. Percentile ranking results were obtained by comparing each PSA to all other PSAs on the dimension. Quotations are from the one-on-one interviews and group discussions.

Before and After Hospital

Percentile Ranking of Viewers' Responses

Group	Interest	Arousal	Pleasure	Dominance
Training School	50%	7.1%	7.1%	21.4%
Middle School	64.2%	71.4%	21.4%	28.5%

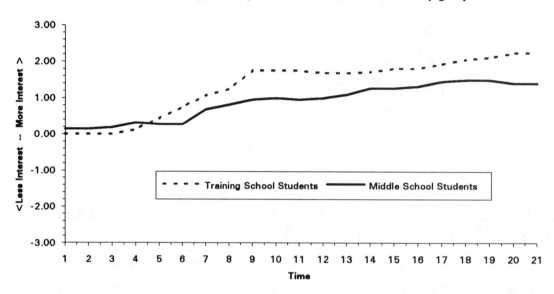

Before and After Hospital: Interest in PSA over time by group

The middle school students were both aroused by and interested in this PSA, while the training school group showed only moderate interest and little arousal. As with the other PSAs that contained tragic consequences or young victims, both groups found little pleasure in or felt in control after viewing the PSA. The training school students appeared to be particularly disturbed by the images, as their pleasure and dominance scores were especially low. Typical responses included:

Training School:
> (group) "...If you're paralyzed...you gotta suffer...he paralyzed...can't do nothing."
> (group) "Can't get out and do what you want to do...you just got to be around the house looking stupid."

Et Tu Brutus

Percentile Ranking of Viewers' Responses

Group	Interest	Arousal	Pleasure	Dominance
Training School	92.8%	92.8%	100%	100%
Middle School	92.8%	92.8%	14.2%	7.1%

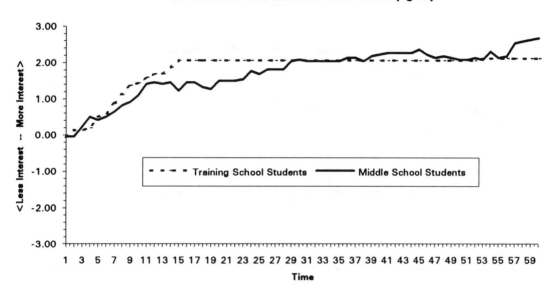

Et Tu Brutus: Interest in PSA over time by group

Both of the groups were interested in and aroused by this PSA, but there was a dramatic difference between the groups on the measures of pleasure and dominance. The training school students experienced a great deal of pleasure and feeling of control/efficacy after viewing *Et Tu*, while the middle school students appeared to be frightened and intimidated by the images and storyline. Individual responses included:

Training school:
  (Chris) "Oh yeah, I've seen a lot of that man."
  (Bill) "It affected my attention (because) it reminded me of how me and some of the guys used to stand on the street."

Middle School:
  (Michelle) "They made it look really bad...this one I didn't like."

Locker Slam

Percentile Ranking of Viewers' Responses

Group	Interest	Arousal	Pleasure	Dominance
Training School	28.5%	28.5%	50%	42.8%
Middle School	100%	50%	92.8%	78.5%

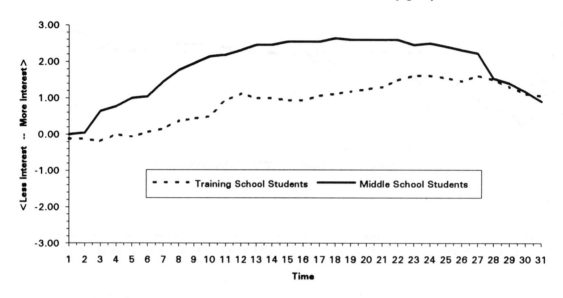

Locker Slam: Interest in PSA over time by group

The middle school students particularly were drawn to the *Locker Slam* PSA, as it received their highest score for interest, and was among the highest on both pleasure and dominance. In contrast, the training school students showed little interest or arousal, frequently indicating that the theme was simply unrealistic. Responses ranged from:

Training school:
  (group) "Ain't realistic, somebody bump into you like that, it won't be that much talking."
  (group) "If you let people just walk over you like that, they are going to try it every day."

Middle school:
  (Susan) "I wouldn't get in a fight...I would definitely walk away."

Stray Bullet

Percentile Ranking of Viewers' Responses

Group	Interest	Arousal	Pleasure	Dominance
Training School	64.2%	85.7%	0%	14.2%
Middle School	85.7%	100%	0%	0%

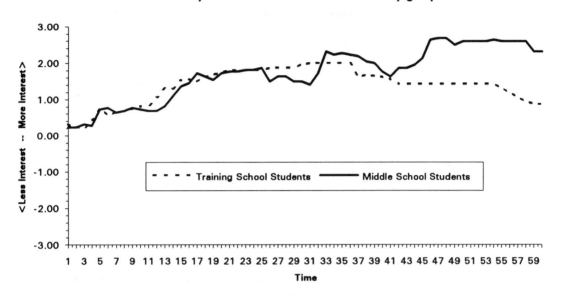

Stray Bullet: Interest in PSA over time by group

Both groups showed high levels of both interest and arousal, with the middle school group indicating that the PSA was the most arousing of the entire sample. Probably because of the seemingly tragic consequence of the narrative, and the involvement of an infant as the potential victim, neither of the two groups were left with feelings of pleasure or control. The students responded with:

Training school:
   (Joe) "What if that had been me...and my little son or nephew ...got hit by a stray bullet...don't know what I'd have did."
   (Jim) "That one right there make you think right now, the way they shot that little baby."

Middle school:
   (Kim) "It was really effective...it got my attention."
   (Tracy) "Yeah, it sounds (like) a good message...that it hurts innocent people."

These Walls Have no Prejudice

Percentile Ranking of Viewers' Responses

Group	Interest	Arousal	Pleasure	Dominance
Training School	57.1%	50%	28.5%	57.1%
Middle School	71.4%	78.5%	28.5%	21.4%

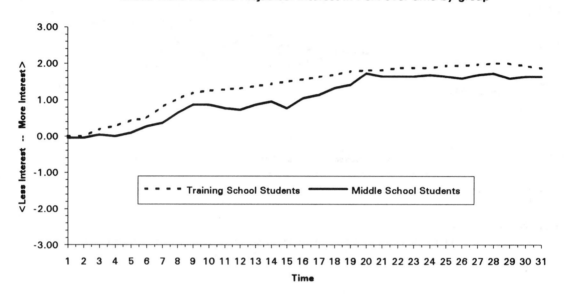

These Walls Have No Prejudice: Interest in PSA over time by group

The training school students showed only moderate interest and arousal for the *These Walls* PSA, while the middle school students gave the narrative fairly high scores in both categories. Neither group was left feeling a sense of pleasure after viewing the PSA, and only the training school students indicated a moderate level of control after viewing. The middle school students appeared to indicate that while the imagery was interesting, it was also rather intimidating. Comments included:

Training school:
   (Joe) "It affected me a little bit."
   (Chris) "That's a fat commercial...I like that."

Middle School:
   (Jen) "It's scary...I think it's a good piece, very effective."
   (Susan) "It looked scary, and that really warned me more than all the videos I've been seeing."

Brownstone

Percentile Ranking of Viewers' Responses

Group	Interest	Arousal	Pleasure	Dominance
Training School	100%	78.5%	78.5%	78.5%
Middle School	50%	85.7%	7.1%	85.7%

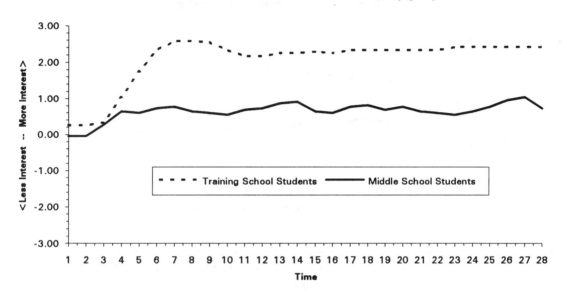

Brownstone: Interest in PSA over time by group

This PSA generated the highest level of interest among the training school students, who in the qualitative analysis said they found the female musical artists' physical appearance highly appealing. Both groups found the PSA arousing, and both indicated that the testimonial left them feeling a strong sense of control. But while the training school students found the PSA pleasurable, the middle school viewers did not. Typical comments included:

Training school:
    (Chris) "Yeah, they well...to me they tough."
    (Adam) "You see how many numbers that was...that's a lot of people got killed."

Middle School:
    (Michelle) "I think they are a rap group, but I'm not sure."
    (Tracy) "I'm familiar with them, but I don't listen to them."

Chuck D

Percentile Ranking of Viewers' Responses

Group	Interest	Arousal	Pleasure	Dominance
Training School	85.7%	100%	64.2%	85.7%
Middle School	35.7%	57.1%	78.5%	71.4%

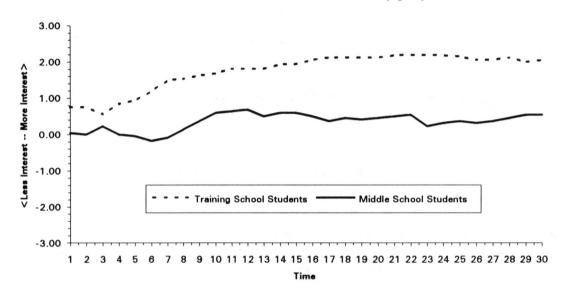

Chuck D: Interest in PSA over time by group

The *Chuck D* PSA was well-received by the training school students, who retained high levels of interest and the highest scores for arousal. In contrast, the middle school students were less interested and only moderately aroused. Both groups felt relatively high levels of pleasure and control after watching the testimonial. Training school responses included:

Training school:
   (group) "Yeah, I believe him...he convincing anyway."
   (group) "Yeah, he (is) telling the truth."

Bill Clinton

Percentile Ranking of Viewers' Responses

Group	Interest	Arousal	Pleasure	Dominance
Training school	0%	0%	14.2%	0%
Middle school	0%	14.2%	35.7%	14.2%

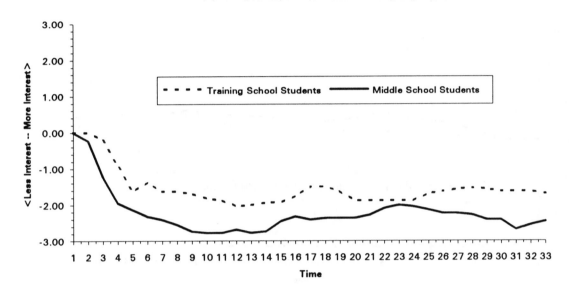

Bill Clinton: Interest in PSA over time by group

The consensus among both groups was that the President *Bill Clinton* testimonial was the least interesting and least arousing of all of the PSAs. Many of the students in the two groups suggested that the President was an inappropriate source for antiviolence messages, and few viewers appeared to relate to his perspective. The scores were particularly low for the training school students, who frequently commented that they view the President as a hypocrite. Typical comments included:

Training school:
> (group) "He don't know what's going on."
> (Chris) "He (is) just putting on a act. He ain't trying to help nobody."
> (Joe) "He (is) in a higher position. I'm in a lower position than you ever want to be in."

Middle School:
> (John) "Well, the President is just like some person who is just a figure."

Derrick Coleman

Percentile Ranking of Viewers' Responses

Group	Interest	Arousal	Pleasure	Dominance
Training school	14.2%	7.1%	14.2%	28.5%
Middle school	42.8%	42.8%	57.1%	35.7%

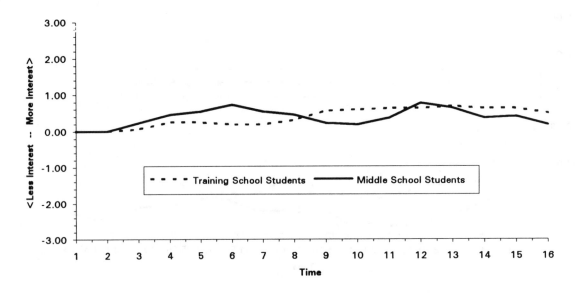

Derrick Coleman: Interest in PSA over time by group

The *Derrick Coleman* PSA was moderately well-received by the middle school students, but scored very poorly with the training school group. Scores in all four categories were in the medium range for the middle school group, but among the lowest of all of the PSAs for the training school viewers. This group frequently commented on the abbreviated nature of the testimonial, as well as on the possibility that the basketball star was a hypocrite. Neither group showed much recognition of Coleman, as most didn't even know he was an athlete. Responses included:

Training school:
    (group) "Naw, he said that he was talking 'cause they paid him to do it."
    (group) "Too short man...he didn't really say anything."

Middle School:
    (Cathy) "They (the facts) go by too fast. You can't even see them because they go by too fast."
    (Denise) "...Don't think it's as effective as the others."

Gloria Estefan

Percentile Ranking of Viewers' Responses

Group	Interest	Arousal	Pleasure	Dominance
Training school	21.4%	21.4%	35.7%	7.1%
Middle school	14.2%	21.4%	42.8%	42.8%

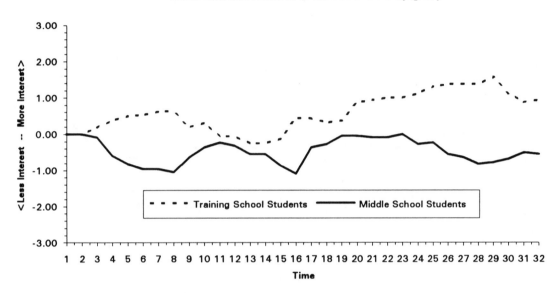

Gloria Estefan: Interest in PSA over time by group

The two groups showed little interest in or arousal for this testimonial, and only the middle school students indicated a moderate level of pleasure or control. Few of the students in either group recognized the successful musical artist. An unusual result was the very low score for dominance among the training school students, who individually appeared to show little regard for the testimonial. Comments included:

Training school:
(group) "(It's) more for (a) Latin audience...down in Miami."
(group) "Ain't never heard of it (her music)."

Middle School:
(Michelle) "I really don't know anything about her."
(Denise) "I don't know her...I think the message she's spreading is good."

481

Samuel Jackson

Percentile Ranking of Viewers' Responses

Group	Interest	Arousal	Pleasure	Dominance
Training school	42.8%	42.8%	57.1%	50%
Middle school	21.4%	28.5%	50%	64.2%

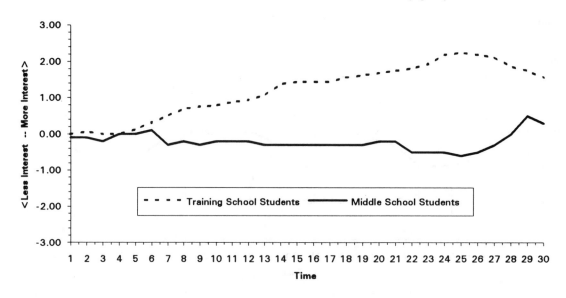

Samuel Jackson: Interest in PSA over time by group

The *Samuel Jackson* PSA scored only moderately well with either group in the majority of categories, and it was particularly weak for the measure of arousal with the middle school students. Both of the groups appeared only somewhat familiar with the actor, and several students from both groups suggested that Jackson was rather hypocritical to appear in an antiviolence PSA after playing lead roles in numerous violent films. A few others thought that this fact might add to his credibility. Responses included:

Training school:
>   (group) "They might be just doing it for the money."
>   (Chris) "Yeah, he probably do the same thing (drugs), just a front."
>   (Ted) "It's good because some people see movies...and try the same thing."

Middle School:
>   (group) "Lots of times they do it for money."
>   (Denise) "I think he is a good person to say it because he is in a lot of violent movies."

Redman

Percentile Ranking of Viewers' Responses

Group	Interest	Arousal	Pleasure	Dominance
Training School	78.5%	64.2%	71.4%	71.4%
Middle School	57.1%	57.1%	100%	92.8%

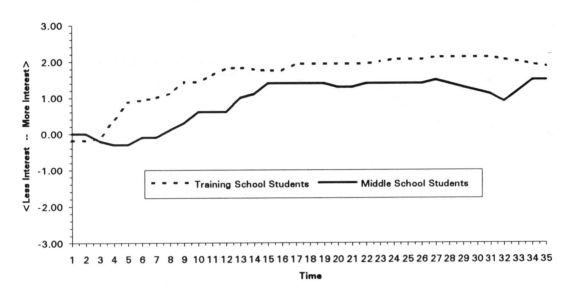

Redman: Interest in PSA over time by group

The *Redman* PSA was appealing to both of the student groups in virtually every measure, however, it scored particularly well with the training school students. Both groups also gave the PSA high scores on both the pleasure and dominance measures, with the middle school students indicating that the PSA was the most pleasing of the entire sample.

Training school:
(group) "Hey, I'd listen to Redman. I'd rather hear him talk than anyone else."
(group) "Yeah...he's alright."

Salt & Pepa

Percentile Ranking of Viewers' Responses

Group	Interest	Arousal	Pleasure	Dominance
Training School	71.4%	71.4%	78.5%	92.8%
Middle School	78.5%	7.1%	85.7%	100%

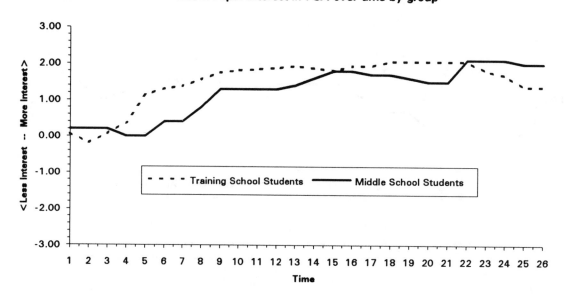

Salt & Pepa: Interest in PSA over time by group

Both groups appeared to be rather interested in the *Salt & Pepa* PSA, however, there was a large difference between the groups for the level of arousal that the PSA invoked. As with the *Brownstone* testimonial, the training school students were aroused by the female musical artists, and the middle school students were relatively unaroused perhaps because they were less familiar with the group. Both groups did indicate strong feelings of dominance after viewing the PSA, and both agreed that the video left them with strong feelings of pleasure. Typical responses included:

Training school:
   (group) "The music was alright and the message was alright, too."
   (group) "I like them...they look good."

Middle School:
   (Tracy) "I think they were rap stars. I don't really listen to rap, but I think I've heard them."
   (Denise) "I like them. I don't really like the kind of music they sing...I think it (the message) was pretty good."

Somewhere in America (Rap Music)

Percentile Ranking of Viewers' Responses

Group	Interest	Arousal	Pleasure	Dominance
Training school	35.7%	50%	92.8%	57.1%
Middle school	28.5%	0%	64.2%	42.8%

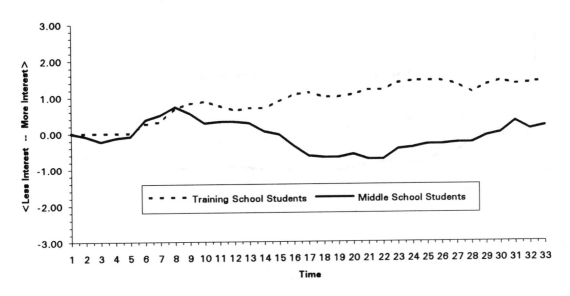

Somewhere in America: Interest in PSA over time by group

Neither group was very interested in the PSA featuring the unknown rapper, although the training school students were more aroused by the testimonial than the middle school students. Both groups gave the PSA medium scores for feelings of control, and high scores for pleasure. The training school students, who questioned the credibility of the artist, still felt pleasure after viewing the PSA. Comments included:

Training school:
   (Tom) "The rapping just caught my attention more than the rest of them."
   (Chris) "He shouldn't try to rap to us..."

Middle School:
   (group) "I don't know (him), he's just a person that knows how to rap."
   (Diane) "I think it would (get) the attention of a lot of people who like rap. I don't particularly like rap, but it still did catch my attention."

Zlata

Percentile Ranking of Viewers' Responses

Group	Interest	Arousal	Pleasure	Dominance
Training school	7.1%	35.7%	42.8%	35.7%
Middle school	7.1%	35.7%	64.2%	57.1%

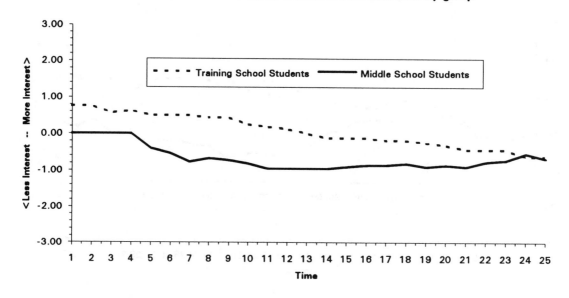

Zlata - America is Great: Interest in PSA over time by group

Overall, the *Zlata* PSA scored consistently low with both groups for the measure of arousal, and even lower for the measure of interest. Few viewers appeared to relate to the young European female spokesperson, although the middle school group did indicate fairly high scores for the dimensions of pleasure and dominance. The training school students appreciated the message, but most did not relate Zlata's perspective with their own life experiences. Responses included:

Training school:
    (group) "Hey, it don't excite me, man."
    (group) "Kind of boring to me."
    (Jim) "I probably won't listen to it."
    (Tom) "She was telling the truth. She was talking about America...we need to stop the violence."

Middle School:
    (Tracy) "I think it sort of gives the message pretty clearly."

7.4 Discussion

The *training school* students were most aroused by narrative PSAs that depicted scenes consistent with their personal life experiences, and by testimonial PSAs from young rap artists and attractive female musicians. Pleasure scores were also higher for younger female celebrities. Some of the narrative PSAs evoked pleasure, but others, such as *Stray Bullet* made viewers uncomfortable as they related what they saw to similar experiences in their own lives. The testimonials from young celebrities left the training school students feeling more powerful and in control than the narratives.

The *middle school* students showed the highest levels of interest for the narrative PSAs. For example, they were most interested in *Locker Slam,* a narrative PSA in which a teenager chooses to walk away from a confrontation in a school hallway. They were less interested in celebrity musical artists, whom most were either not familiar with or not interested in musically. The narratives also were most arousing to this group, even though the students indicated little personal connection with the depicted behaviors or consequences. They did not, however, find them pleasurable and felt little dominance or personal control after viewing them. The memory test revealed that the PSAs that were most readily remembered were longer, aroused viewers, and also disturbed them, e.g., left them feeling less dominant and less pleasure.

In particular, these analyses suggest that:

1. *Simple, straightforward messages will be remembered.* Most viewers remembered Gloria Estefan's simple message and statistics, even though few related to her personally. The MTV format of some of the messages impeded comprehension. Although comprehension might improve on subsequent showings, viewers who found the message confusing or incomprehensible may not make the effort to understand on subsequent exposures. Stories inherently are more open to interpretation than straight declarations, but narratives should be tested with target audiences to ensure that the intended message is the most likely interpretation.

2. *Celebrities should be chosen carefully.* Young viewers are critical and skeptical of adults who are telling them what to do, especially when the adult may be perceived as having engaged in similar behavior. Sources perceived as similar may be considered more competent, but also must be considered trustworthy by the target group.

3. *Music should be chosen carefully.* Even among audiences that prefer rap music, all rappers are not the same. Musical taste is diverse among the young, and an important marker of identification and social stance. Many of the middle school youth did not recognize the rap music celebrities, and unfamiliar with the genre, could not understand the rap of the anonymous rapper.

4. *Fear appeals should include clear and realistic suggestions for reducing fear and for resolving conflict.* Youth are aroused by fear appeals, but may be left with fear, rather than a changed attitude toward violence or a desire to behave in nonviolent ways. None of the messages tested presented clear recommendations about what an individual should do to "stop the violence," except *Locker Slam*, which advocated "just walking away." The training school youth thought that was an unrealistic alternative.

5. *Other kinds of appeals may be effective.* Both middle school and training school viewers found the discussion of mothers and brothers (*Salt & Pepa*) and portrayal of families and children (*Stray Bullet*) compelling. These adolescents do have families and may be affected by messages that speak to the effect of violence on their siblings and parents.

In sum, the successful PSA should include recognizable and credible sources, presented in familiar and appropriate contexts, who convey relevant and clear messages. Narratives should be clear and realistic, and should provide models or ideas for action for the viewer.

8. STUDIES 5 AND 6: AN EXPERIMENTAL TEST OF REACTIONS AMONG TRAINING SCHOOL AND MIDDLE SCHOOL STUDENTS TO AN EDUCATIONAL PROGRAM ON CONFLICT RESOLUTION

Compared to PSAs, educational programs can deliver a more powerful and complete message to adolescents, because there is greater time to elaborate and repeat key points and themes. The programs can use narratives to illustrate consequences of behavior, provide specific models of appropriate behavior in resolving interpersonal conflict, and use celebrities and testimonials to show that certain antiviolence attitudes and behaviors are the norm within the viewers' reference groups.

These studies tested the effectiveness of an antiviolence video that attempts to directly alter adolescent attitudes toward the use of guns to resolve interpersonal conflict. The program, *Kids Killing Kid/Kids Saving Kids,* was chosen to represent the industry's efforts in this area because:

- ⊙ The television industry had designated this as one of their *best programs for children* by giving it an Emmy in 1994 (Los Angeles Times, Sept. 12, 1994).
- ⊙ The antiviolence video had *reached about 13.5 million homes* because it aired several times in national and local prime time.
- ⊙ The program was specifically *designed to directly affect adolescents' attitudes toward the use of guns*.

Kids Killing Kids/Kids Saving Kids consists of a 45-minute fictional program followed by a 15-minute documentary. In the first segment, Malcolm Jamal Warner narrates a series of four vignettes showing how four teenagers' lives were irrevocably changed because of the use of a handgun. The movie features a technique whereby the teenagers are shown going back in time and getting "a second chance." During this second chance, the adolescents choose a nonviolent strategy to deal with his/her interpersonal conflict. This nonviolent strategy is depicted as leading to successful outcomes and provides viewers with concrete models of how to solve their own interpersonal conflicts.

Executive Producer Arnold Shapiro said he got the idea for the replay-your-day format from a comedy movie, *Groundhog Day*. "It's a vivid portrayal of the same situation with and without a gun, where injury and/or death is the consequence of the story with the gun, and life and a peaceful resolution are the outcome in the version without the gun" (Shapiro, quoted in Mendoza, 1994). The 15-minute *Kids Saving Kids* documentary follow-up segment showcases real teenagers involved in antiviolence efforts.

The program's commercial-free simulcast by CBS and Fox at 8 p.m. on April 26, 1994 was praised by President Bill Clinton (Bash, 1994). It also aired at 5 p.m. that same day on the Faith & Values Channel and was part of a week-long TV antiviolence campaign. The show would have ranked tenth for the week if rated by Nielsen (Nielsen does not rate commercial-free programs) (Margulies, 1994). Students in at least one California city watched the show as an assignment and later gathered for a public discussion about crime (Berg, 1994).

Writer, director and producer David J. Eagle, who has produced after-school specials for children, said he tried to interest networks in a program about kids and guns several years ago but was turned down. One executive declined "because of the NRA (National Rifle Association)," Eagle said (Rosenberg, 1994). Later, CBS united Eagle with Shapiro, who was working on an afternoon kids program about guns. According to Eagle, the comparatively low-budget show, intended as a *CBS Schoolbreak Special* in an afternoon airtime, landed in Shapiro's prime time *Rescue 911* slot because a CBS executive thought the network could earn more "brownie points" (Rosenberg, 1994). CBS also offered the show to other networks. Fox was the only one to accept.

The show was not pre-tested with its intended audience.

8.1 Research Questions

The research questions asked how well one of the best antiviolence television programs produced by the industry could influence adolescents. If this video failed to produce any significant effects, then we could infer that some other videos would possess either equal or lesser effectiveness. We asked the following basic questions:

8.1.1 Program Effectiveness: Attitude Change

- ⊙ Can an award-winning, antiviolence educational program change teenagers' attitudes about the use of violence for conflict resolution? This is the *central goal* of the video, *Kids Killing Kids*, and many other videos of the same genre.

8.1.2 Program Interest Level

- ⊙ Do teenagers like the antiviolence program more than the control program?

- ⊙ Which parts of the antiviolence program do teenagers like best? (This video was composed of separate vignettes dealing with different kinds of interpersonal conflict--from gang violence to teen suicide.)

8.1.3 Unintended Effects

- ⊙ Will viewing antiviolence programs make the world appear more violent and dangerous to teenagers? This would be an unintended consequence of the video. It might increase anxiety and decrease feelings of self-efficacy.

8.2 Methods

The studies used an experimental design. Subjects were randomly assigned to watch one of two types of program: 1) antiviolence programming, and 2) neutral (control) programming.

8.2.1 Participants

Twenty-five training school students and thirty-two middle school students participated in the studies (see chapter 4 for a description of the test samples).

8.2.2 Apparatus:

Stimulus materials. The educational, antiviolence video was *Kids Killing Kids*. The control video was a combination of two fire safety videos: *Plan to Get Out Alive*, a 45-minute video that uses footage of real fires to teach methods for surviving structure fires, and *Survive! Fire in Your Home*, a 15-minute video that shows a home fire tragedy and the steps that could have been taken to prevent it. The control video matched the experimental video in length, target audience and in its general intent to modify risky behavior.

8.2.3 Measures

Continuous Response Measure of Interest. A continuous audience response measure was used to gather moment-to-moment self-reports of the level of interest throughout the viewing of each program (see Chapter 5).

See Chapter 5 for descriptions of other measures used as well: **Self-Assessment Manikin, Probability Assessment of Risk, Measure of Violent Behavior, Media Use Measures,** and **Demographic Measures.**

8.2.4 Procedure

For both groups, each participant and his/her parent or legal guardian provided informed consent prior to the collection of data. Three days before the experiment, participants completed two questionnaires. One measured demographics and history of violent behavior, and the other measured attitudes toward violence. On the day of the experiments, participants completed the Self-Assessment Manikin measure of mood prior to viewing the program.

Participants at each school were randomly assigned to test and control conditions, and they assembled in groups where they viewed either the antiviolence or the control videotape. Each participant held a continuous response handset (Biocca, David & West, 1994) and was instructed to evaluate each second of the video on a seven-point scale measuring level of interest from uninteresting to interesting. Each participant communicated his or her evaluation by continuously turning a 7-position dial on a handset. After the programs, participants again completed the mood measure and a posttest questionnaire measuring attitudes toward violence.

8.3 Results

8.3.1 Training School Students

Program effectiveness: Attitude change. The dependent variables were the three measurements obtained using the normative beliefs about aggression scale. Because a pretest was collected on this measure, the data were analyzed controlling for the pretest measures as a baseline.

After controlling for pretest attitude level, there was no significant difference in the adolescents' attitudes toward violence as a result of watching the antiviolence television program when compared to the neutral program. These results can be seen in Table 8.1.

Table 8.1: Normative Beliefs About Aggression After Viewing

Aggression Beliefs	Antiviolence Mean	Control Mean	F (1, 22)	P<
Overall	2.43	2.47	0.23	0.64
Gen. Beliefs	2.38	2.43	0.40	0.70
Retaliation	2.48	2.51	0.28	0.78

Program interest level. We examined the difference in interest for each of the television program types by comparing the grand means of the moment-to-moment levels of interest. Although the antiviolence program did score higher, we found no significant difference in interest between the two programs. The results appear in Table 8.2.

Table 8.2: Grand Means of Interest in Each Program

Program	Grand Mean	T Value	DF	P<
Antiviolence	4.83	-1.08	23	0.29
Control	4.17			

Kids Killing Kids was composed of a number of separate segments, and we calculated the means of the moment-to-moment levels of interest for each segment (Table 8.3). The results indicate that the participants found the video to be mildly interesting, and their mean interest level did not fluctuate considerably across segments.

Table 8.3: Mean Interest Level Across Film Segments

Segment	Mean Interest Level	SD
1	5.46	1.15
2	5.47	0.88
3	4.71	1.19
4	4.73	1.19
5	4.97	1.06
6	5.51	0.97

Unintended effects. To answer the question of whether the program increased fear, an analysis of the differences between antiviolence and control programs using pre- and posttest measures was performed. Subjects' responses to two indexes, the cultivation index and the mean world index, were used to measure perceptions of the level of danger in the world.

Cultivation Index. The ANCOVA results indicated that the program type (antiviolence and control program) was not a statistically significant factor in perceptions of the probability of real world violence. These results appear in Table 8.4.

Table 8.4: Comparison of Cultivation Index by Program Type

Program	Cultivation	$F_{(1, 22)}$	p<
Anti violence	1.75	0.13	0.72
Control	1.89		

Mean World Index. The analysis of the mean world index followed the same procedure as the cultivation index above. The results indicated that type of program was not a statistically significant factor in levels of mistrust and alienation.

Table 8.5: Comparison of Mean World Index by Program Type

Program	Mean World	F (1, 22)	p<
Anti violence	5.00	0.49	0.50
Control	5.11		

8.3.2 Middle School Students

Program effectiveness: Attitude change. The study conducted with the training school students was replicated with the middle school students. The same set of analyses was conducted. The dependent variables were the three measurements obtained using the normative beliefs about aggression scale. Because a pretest was collected on this measure, the data were analyzed while controlling for the pretest measures.

After controlling for pretest attitude levels, no significant differences in attitudes toward violence between those who watched the antiviolence television program and those who watched the control program were found. The results are presented in Table 8.6.

Table 8.6: Normative Beliefs About Aggression

Aggression Beliefs	Antiviolence Mean	Control Mean	F (1, 29)	P
Overall	2.53	2.56	0.29	0.59
Gen. Beliefs	2.47	2.47	0.15	0.70
Retaliation	2.57	2.64	0.71	0.41

Program interest level. We examined the difference in liking of each of the television program types by comparing the grand means of the moment-to-moment levels of interest. We found that there was no significant difference in liking between the two types of programs. The results appear in Table 8.7.

Table 8.7: Grand Means of Interest in Each Program

Program	Grand Mean	T Value	DF	P
Antiviolence	4.83	-0.78	28	0.45
Control	4.58			

Kids Killing Kids was composed of a number of separate segments, and the moment-to-moment levels of interest were calculated for each segment. (Table 8.8). The results indicate that the participants found the video to be mildly interesting. Their mean interest level did not fluctuate considerably across segments.

Table 8.8: Mean Interest Level Across Film Segments

Segment	Mean Interest Level	SD
1	4.68	1.30
2	5.50	0.92
3	5.33	1.33
4	4.74	1.21
5	4.36	1.34
6	4.34	1.34

Unintended effects. To answer this question an analysis of the differences between antiviolence and control programs using pre- and posttest measurements was performed. Subjects' responses to two indexes, the cultivation index and the mean world index, were the dependent variables.

Cultivation Index. The results indicated that the program type (antiviolence and control program) was nearly a statistically significant factor in perception of the probability of real world violence. The results appear in Table 8.9.

Table 8.9: Comparison of Cultivation Index by Program

Program	Cultivation Mean	$F_{(1, 29)}$	p>
Antiviolence	1.94	3.51	0.07
Control	1.79		

Mean World Index. The analysis of the mean world index followed the same procedure as the cultivation index above. The results appear in Table 8.10 and indicate that the type of program was not a statistically significant factor in levels of mistrust and violence.

Table 8.10: Mean World Index by Program

Program	Mean World Mean	$F_{(1, 29)}$	p<
Antiviolence	4.47	2.29	0.15
Control	4.86		

8.3.3 Exploratory Comparison of Moment-by-moment Interest.

To understand the pattern of response by segments, moment-to-moment mean levels of interest were calculated for the middle school and training school subjects. A graph was created for each segment plotting the second-by-second level of interest of each audience (Figures 8.1 to 8.6). These must be considered only exploratory comparisons because these two samples were not drawn from the same population.

Exploratory Comparison of Moment-by-Moment Interest in Each of the Six Segments of the *Kids Killing Kids* by *Training School and Middle School Students*

Figure 8.1: Introduction

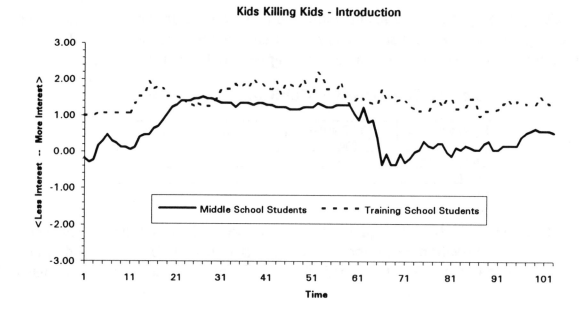

Figure 8.2: Episode I (Kid joining gang)

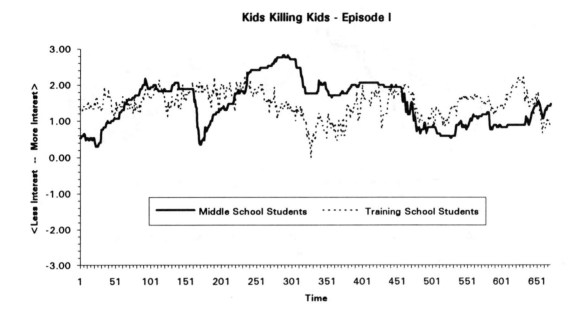

Kids Killing Kids - Episode I

Figure 8.3: Episode II (Kid taking gun to classroom)

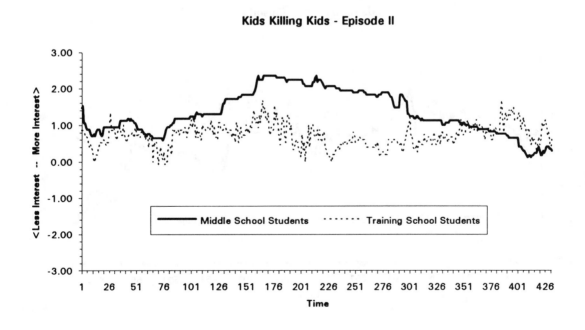

Kids Killing Kids - Episode II

Figure 8.4: Episode III (Suicide)

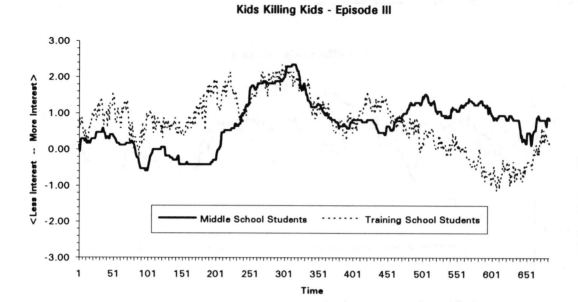

Figure 8.5: Episode IV (Baseball player)

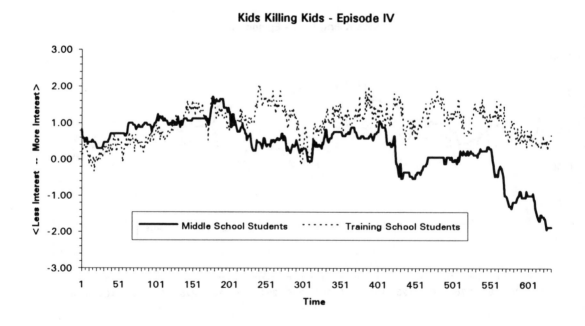

Figure 8.6: Concluding section

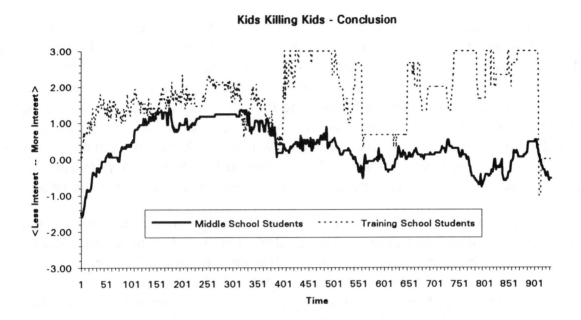

Kids Killing Kids - Conclusion

8.4 Discussion

We attempted to determine if an Emmy-award winning antiviolence television program, *Kids Killing Kids*, can influence adolescents' attitudes toward violence. The overall findings suggest that the program had little or no effect on attitudes. Neither the training school students nor middle school students who were exposed to the antiviolence program showed any significant differences in their attitudes toward violence from those who were exposed to the control program. The adolescents from the training school reported slightly more interest for the material in the antiviolence program. However, their interest for the program was not significantly greater than that for the fire safety control program. The middle school students did not show any more interest for the antiviolence program than for the control program.

The effects of the program *Kids Killing Kids* on viewers' perceptions of the real world were evaluated by the cultivation index and mean world index. The results for both groups on the two measures showed that neither the antiviolence program nor the control program had any effect on changing subjects' beliefs about the dangers of the real world.

Was the antiviolence program that we tested representative of other such programs? The antiviolence program that we tested, *Kids Killing Kids*, is an Emmy-award winning program. We infer from our findings, therefore, that other antiviolence programs would be unlikely to have a strong effect in changing attitudes toward violence.

Was the exposure to the antiviolence program sufficient to cause a change in attitudes? We tested the program through a single exposure in a controlled setting. It is possible that, when seen in a natural setting with more frequent message repetition, the program might influence adolescents' attitudes. However, the program is approximately one hour long and, according to our findings, found to be only moderately interesting. It is unlikely that any adolescents will view this program unless it is shown to them in a controlled setting. It is even less likely that they would watch it more than once. It was not possible to measure any cumulative effect of the entire antiviolence television campaign in this study. We recommend that such a study be conducted in the future.

From the graphs depicting students' interest the program, we can see that there is some difference between the training school students and middle school students in their levels of interest in different segments of the antiviolence program. The most notable difference was during the final segment. This high level of interest among the training school students may have been due to the program's characters and setting. The final segment of the program took place at Satellite High School in the South Bronx section of New York City. It featured interviews with current students on preventing violence, and on their school program called Creative Conflict Resolution. This antiviolence program may be similar to some of the therapy programs conducted at the training school. The high interest scores may have been due to the audiences' familiarity with the segments' characters, settings, and/or messages. These mediating factors were not measured in this study, but should be considered for future research.

9. STUDY 7: "ANTIDOTE" -- AN EXPERIMENTAL TEST OF THE EFFECTIVENESS OF ANTIVIOLENCE PSAS EMBEDDED IN VIOLENT PROGRAMMING

9.1 Research Questions

Antiviolence messages compete with violent television messages. Violent television messages directly or indirectly suggest violence is an effective strategy to deal with conflict, that guns lead to respect and power, and that violence is a natural expression of male identity. In our theoretical model, we expressed this as the competition between pro and anti-attitudinal messages. All public health messages must compete with messages that indirectly promote unhealthy behavior. Examples include smoking ads, movies that depict unsafe sex practices, etc. Antiviolence messages face similar challenges.

This study explored answers to the following questions about the relationship of antiviolence messages, proviolence messages and message cognitions:

⊙ Can antiviolence message compete head-on with proviolence messages?
⊙ Can antiviolence messages alter viewers' message cognitions when viewing violent programming: 1) can the messages lessen audience interest and arousal, and 2) can they change the way the violent programming is interpreted (semantic processing)?
⊙ When considering the effects on beliefs about violence, can antiviolence PSAs provide an *antidote* to the deleterious effects of violent programming?

We explored one possible answer to these questions by asking: What if antiviolence PSAs were embedded right into violent programming? Could this approach maximize the effectiveness of antiviolence PSAs? This has practical value because it may provide an answer to the following question:

⊙ What are the best ways to deliver antiviolence PSAs?

9.2 Theoretical Rationale for Embedding Antiviolence PSAs in Violent Programming

There are a number of reasons why embedding antiviolence PSAs in violent programming might be an effective strategy to maximize the impact of antiviolence PSAs and assist the goal of "deglamorizing violence."

9.2.1 Heckling Violent Behavior: The PSA as a Counter-attitudinal Message

A violent program can be seen as not just a piece of fiction. It also can be characterized as a persuasive message. Any program frames a specific view of the world. The program purposely or inadvertently promotes or condemns certain lifestyles and attitudes. If we look at the value content of the typical "action" film, we find that violent films may be interpreted by audience members as advocating some of the following positions:

- violence is an effective tool to solve interpersonal conflicts,
- a person who shows or uses a gun often gets power or respect,
- gang life is glamorous, exciting, intense, or heroic.

If a violent film is interpreted as advocating violence, then antiviolence PSAs are counter-attitudinal messages. They advocate the exact opposite message. We theorized that an antiviolence message embedded in the middle of a violent film would be the video equivalent of a heckler in the middle of a speech. At every commercial break the antiviolence PSAs would *heckle and challenge* the assumptions and messages of the film. Research on heckling has a shown that unchallenged hecklers can reduce the persuasive power of a speaker. If the antiviolence messages are equally or more powerful than the proviolence message of the film they may act as an antidote to the negative effects of the violent film. We therefore formulated our first hypothesis:

Hypothesis 1: If the PSAs are effective, then people who view antiviolence messages embedded in programming will express different attitudes about violence than individuals who see violent programming with typical commercials.

In our experiment, differences in attitudes toward violence were operationalized and measured using:

- attitude scales about the appropriateness of violent behavior,
- attitudes about a violent principal character of a film,
- inferences about the future success of a violent film character.

9.2.2 PSAs and Desensitization to Violence

One of the effects of television violence is an increased desensitization to the consequences of violence. One possible effect of antiviolence messages may be to make the audience members more sensitive to the effects of violence. Many of the antiviolence PSAs are unsettling. They make the viewer aware of the human cost and tragedy of violence. Some directly challenge the representation of violence on television. If the PSAs can make audience members aware of and sensitive to acts of violence, then embedded ads might make audience members less comfortable and more sensitive to television violence. Therefore:

Hypothesis 2: Viewers exposed to antiviolence PSAs embedded in violent programming will like the violent scenes less than viewers exposed to regular ads.

9.2.3 Media Planning Considerations: Ideal Timing for Target Audiences

Embedding antiviolence messages in the middle of violent programming is logical from a media planning viewpoint. Some advantages of this means of delivery include:

- ⊙ the PSAs directly reach viewers who seek out violent programming,
- ⊙ the PSAs directly combat the negative effects of exposure to television violence,
- ⊙ public interest organizations and networks can freely buy time on the open market to counteract the effects of television violence or reach audiences who seek and respond to violent programming.

9.2.4 Possible Boomerang Effects of PSA Embedding

Embedding antiviolence PSAs in the middle of violent programming might have some unintended consequences called "boomerang effects." The antiviolence messages might interact with the violent programming in unexpected ways. Many of the antiviolence PSAs use fear appeals to reach their audiences. We were concerned that the antiviolence ads might increase the viewer's sense that violence is a problem, that the world is dangerous, and that violence is ready to claim them or others as victims. This led to the third hypothesis:

Hypothesis 3: Viewers exposed to antiviolence PSAs embedded in violent programming may come to see the world as a more dangerous and scary place. This perception might manifest itself into a greater belief that they (the viewers) or others will be victims of violence.

Exposure to antiviolence PSAs might interact with violent programming in other ways. The emphasis on violence and its consequences in both PSAs and violent programming might influence viewers' moods by making them either more hostile, anxious, or depressed. Therefore, we decided to also explore the following hypothesis:

Hypothesis 4: Viewers exposed to antiviolence PSAs embedded in violent programming may become more anxious, hostile or depressed compared to viewers exposed to the programming with only regular ads.

9.3 Method

A Solomon four group experimental design was used. Subjects were exposed to violent programming either with (experimental group) or without (control group) embedded antiviolence PSAs. The experimental and control groups were each split in two. Only one each of the experimental and control groups received the pre-tests (see Table 9.1).

Table 9.1: Sequence of Procedures for Solomon Four Group Design

Condition	Antiviolence Commercials		Regular Commercials	
Pre-Test	Yes	No	Yes	No
Subjects(N)	36	22	37	15
Film Quest.	Yes	Yes	Yes	Yes
Health Quest.	Yes	No	Yes	No
MAACL-Pre	Yes	No	Yes	No
Audience Response	Yes	Yes	Yes	Yes
MAACL-Post	Yes	Yes	Yes	Yes
Film Ending	Yes	Yes	Yes	Yes
V-Clips-Post	Yes	Yes	Yes	Yes
Viol-Att-Post	Yes	Yes	Yes	Yes
Probability of Risk	Yes	Yes	Yes	Yes

9.3.1 Participants

All 110 study participants were male university students between the ages of 17 and 30. More than 70% were between the ages of 18 and 20. Subjects were paid to participate in the study.

9.3.2 Apparatus

Stimulus Materials.
Stimulus Violent Film. A stimulus tape was created using a violent action film titled *The King of New York*. The film portrays the violent life of a drug lord after his release from prison. Most of the characters in the film die from gun violence. Six commercial breaks were edited in the film at sections immediately preceding a violent scene. Each commercial break had four messages. In the experimental condition each commercial break included one or two antiviolence PSAs among the regular commercials. The antiviolence PSAs are described below. The film was edited to prevent subject fatigue. The ending was removed to allow the audience to write a suggested ending to the film.

Antiviolence PSAs. Seven antiviolence PSAs were used, and two of them were shown twice. All of the PSAs were from an anti-gun and antiviolence campaign produced by Home Box Office and Warner. The campaign theme was *Peace...Live it or rest in it.* The slogan was appropriate for the content of the film, which portrayed the outcome of violent criminal gang wars.

Posttest Tape of Violent Clips. A videotape composed exclusively of video clips of violent action was edited together. The tape consisted of a total of six clips varying in length from one minute to four minutes. Each clip was separated by four seconds of video black on which was superimposed the instruction, "Return your dials to 4 or Neutral."

Questionnaires. Two questionnaires were constructed. One, the "Film Questionnaire," was administered to all participants. The second, a "Health Study Questionnaire," was administered only to those conditions receiving a pretest. The film questionnaire was composed of our demographic and media-use measures (see Chapter 5). The "Health Study Questionnaire" was composed of a number of measures that were used as pretest and posttest in our Solomon four group design. The measures in this questionnaire included:

- Measures of Violent Behavior
- Sensation Seeking Scale
- Probability Assessment of Risk
- Normative Beliefs About Aggression Scale (See Chapter 5 for descriptions of the measures).

Continuous Response Measure of Interest. (See Chapter 5).

Multiple Affective Adjective Checklist. (See Chapter 5).

9.3.3 Procedure

The experiment used a cover story to recruit participants. They were told that a cable company had hired a mass communication research team to test how young males like action films, and that a number of films were to be tested. After they signed up, participants were given the film questionnaire. A randomly selected subgroup was told that they were eligible for additional money if they participated in a *separate study*, a survey being conducted by the public health school. The subgroup was told to go to a separate table to talk to the "public health researchers." This technique was used to disguise the researchers' interest in the topic of violence. All who were offered the "opportunity" to participate in the "other" study accepted and completed the health questionnaire.

All participants were scheduled for a "screening" of the test film. After they arrived, participants in the pretest group completed the mood measure (MAACL). They were instructed on how to use the continuous response system and asked to rate each second of the video on a seven-point scale: 1) very uninterested; 2) moderately uninterested; 3) slightly interested; 4) neutral, neither interested nor uninterested; 5) slightly interested; 6) moderately interested; and 7) very interested. They viewed the video, which included the film and commercials, according to condition.

Participants were told that the "film company" was considering alternative endings to the film and were asked to write how they thought the film should end. Once this was collected, all viewers were exposed to "action scenes from other films." They were then told to rate each one.

Following their exposure to the violent clips, participants completed a subsequent posttest including the mood measure (MAACL), the Normative Beliefs About Aggression Scale and the Probability Assessment of Risk.

9.4 Results

The results are presented by hypothesis.

Hypothesis 1: If the PSAs are effective, then people who view antiviolence messages embedded in programming will express different attitudes about violence than individuals who see violent programming with typical commercials.

To evaluate this hypothesis, three measurements from the Normative Beliefs About Aggression scale were used. (The higher the mean on the scale, the higher the acceptance of the aggressive behavior.)

1. A 2X2 Analysis of Variance (ANOVA) was applied to the data. The null hypothesis was not rejected. The results of the analysis are presented below in a condensed format (Table 9.2).

Table 9.2: ANOVA Results on Attitudes Toward Violence

Normative Beliefs About Aggression Scale	Mean antiviolence ads	Mean regular ads	F value	P
Overall	2.29	2.26	0.05	ns
Gen. Beliefs	1.57	1.66	0.85	ns
Retaliation	2.83	2.75	0.64	ns

2. A second analysis was conducted. An Analysis of Covariance (ANCOVA) was used. The covariant was the pre-test measurement of Normative Beliefs about

Aggression. The null hypothesis was not rejected (see Table 9.3). The results of the analysis are presented in a condensed format.

Table 9.3: ANCOVA Results on Attitudes Toward Violence

Normative Beliefs About Aggression Scale	Mean antiviolence ads	Mean regular ads	F value	P
Overall	2.24	2.34	0.30	ns
Gen. Beliefs	1.65	1.59	1.24	ns
Retaliation	2.83	2.74	0.25	ns

Hypothesis 2: Viewers exposed to antiviolence PSAs embedded in violent programming will like the violent scenes less than viewers exposed to regular ads.

To test this hypothesis, a 2 (pre-test / no pre-test) x 2 (antiviolence ads / regular ads) x 9 (violence scenes) factorial experiment was set up. The first two factors were between subjects, whereas the third factor was within subjects.

The ANOVA indicates that the violent scenes were different from each other ($F_{(8,728)}$=2.74, p<0.006), and the interaction between pre-test and the evaluation of the scenes approached significance ($F_{(8,728)}$= 1.72, p < 0.09). Overall, subjects who were pre-tested showed more interest in the violent scenes (higher scores). A t-test was performed for each scene comparing pre- and posttest subjects. Only one of the scenes was statistically different for subjects who were pre-tested and subjects who were not; two other scenes approached statistically significant difference. Table 9.4 is a summary of the mean comparison by scene:

Table 9.4: Mean Interest by Violent Scene

Scene #	Pre- and posttest Score	Posttest Score	T value	P<
1	5.63	5.46	0.64	0.52
2	5.37	5.60	-0.99	0.32
3	5.47	5.18	1.04	0.30
4	5.27	4.52	2.67	0.01
5	5.62	5.07	1.85	0.07
6	5.29	5.04	0.78	0.44
7	5.34	5.10	0.90	0.37
8	5.40	4.85	1.55	0.13
9	5.48	4.93	1.73	0.09

Hypothesis 3: Viewers exposed to antiviolence PSAs embedded in violent programming may come to see the world as a more dangerous and scary place. This

perception might manifest itself into a greater belief that they (the viewers) or others will be victims of violence.

The evaluation of this hypothesis is divided into two manifestations of risk perception: personal (how risky is it to me), and societal (how risky is it for society in general). There were two sets of three questions that were combined to form an index (average of the probabilities given on each question) for each of these perceptions of risk. Subjects answered these questions in both pre- and posttest conditions.

With the exception of the personal perception of risk pre-test, all alpha values indicate a good internal reliability of the items. Table 9.5 includes the Cronbach's Alpha values for them.

Table 9.5: Cronbach's Alpha Values

Type of risk	Pre-test alpha	Posttest alpha
personal	0.55	0.80
social	0.78	0.86

An ANOVA was performed on the data including all subjects and an ANCOVA was performed for the subjects who had both pre- and posttest measurements, using pre-test as a covariate. This hypothesis was evaluated separately by personal and societal perception of risk, following trends in the literature (e.g., Tyler & Cook, 1984).

Personal perception of risk. The analysis of variance indicated that there was a statistically significant difference among the groups ($F_{(3,104)}$=5.06; p<0.003). A Tukey evaluation for the difference among means indicated that subjects who were pre-tested scored lower in the personal perception of risk for both conditions (viewing regular ads and viewing PSAs). Moreover, these differences were statistically significant within each condition. See Table 9.6 for the mean scores.

Table 9.6: Means of Risk Perception N=170

Group	Pre-test	Mean[*]
PSAs	no	34.74[a]
PSAs	yes	24.20[b]
Regular ads	no	32.49[a]
Regular ads	yes	21.30[b]

[*] Means with the same superscripts are not statistically significantly different.

The analysis of covariance found no difference between the two groups ($F_{(1,68)}$=1.03; p<0.31, see Table 9.7).

Table 9.7: Means of Risk Perception N=70

Group	Pre-test	Mean
PSAs	yes	23.96
Regular ads	yes	21.52

Societal perception of risk. The analysis of variance for the social perception of risk showed no statistically significant difference for the two groups that were pre-tested ($F_{(3,104)}=1.21$; $p<0.31$). The same is true for the ANCOVA ($F_{(1,68)}=0.34$; $p<0.56$). Table 9.8 and Table 9.9 are the means for each condition.

Table 9.8: Means of Societal Perception of Risk, N=170

Group	Pre-test	Mean
PSAs	no	48.89
PSAs	yes	40.30
Regular ads	no	44.76
Regular ads	yes	40.28

Table 9.9: Means of Societal Perception of Risk, N=70

Group	Pre-test	Mean
PSAs	yes	39.36
Regular ads	yes	41.15

Across the two manifestations of risk perception our data showed the same trend that has been observed in the literature, and has been called optimistic bias (Weinstein, 1989), i.e., that the personal perception of risk is smaller than the societal perception of risk (see Table 9.10).

Table 9.10: Societal and Personal Perception of Risk

Condition	Societal mean	Personal mean	T value	P<
pre-test	41.80	23.60	10.57	0.001
posttest	42.66	26.50	10.85	0.001

Hypothesis 4: Viewers exposed to antiviolence PSAs embedded in violent programming may become anxious, hostile or depressed compared to viewers exposed to the programming with only regular ads.

The dependent measure of mood was the Multiple Adjective Checklist. Three scales measured feelings of anxiety, depression, and hostility. A separate analysis of variance was used for each mood. For the purposes of analysis there were four groups (see Table 9.11).

Table 9.11: Descriptions of Experimental Groups

Condition	Pre-test	N	Group
Antiviolence ads	no	21	1
Antiviolence ads	yes	35	2
Regular ads	no	17	3
Regular ads	yes	36	4

Two types of analyses were applied to the data. First, an overall analysis of variance was conducted to evaluate the difference among the groups. Second, because two out of the four groups were pre-tested, the analysis for these groups used the pre-test measurement as a covariate.

Both analyses found no statistical differences among the groups for all three traits. Anxiety was the only trait that had a marginal statistical difference among the groups for the overall analysis. The analysis of covariance did not find any significant differences in the effect of the presence of PSAs on mood.

Table 9.12: Group Differences in Anxiety, Depression and Hostility

Trait	ANOVA F	P <	ANCOVA F	P<
Anxiety	2.38 (3.106)	0.07	1.77 (1.68)	0.19
Depression	1.37 (3.106)	0.26	0.64 (1.68)	0.43
Hostility	1.03 (3.106)	0.38	2.27 (1.68)	0.14

Tukey post-hoc analyses of the differences among groups identified two pairs of groups that were statistically significantly different for the anxiety trait: groups 1 and 3 (antiviolence ads and regular ads both without pre-test), and groups 3 and 4 (regular ads without pre-test and regular ads with pre-test). However, caution should be taken when considering these results because the ANOVA results indicate only a marginal statistical difference.

9.5 Discussion

This study examined whether the presence of high quality antiviolence PSAs, with high production values, could alter how audiences think about and experience violent programming, or influence their attitudes about violent behavior. Could the presence of the ads significantly alter message cognitions not only during the antiviolent programming but, more importantly, during violent programming? The pattern of results suggests that the presence of seven antiviolence PSAs had little or no effect on viewers' responses to violent programming or their attitudes about the appropriateness of violent behavior.

Effects of antiviolence ads on message cognitions. The presence of antiviolence PSAs did not significantly influence the audience's level of interest in an extremely violent video. Despite the fact that the message of the PSAs directly challenged the implicit values of the violent film, there appeared to be no effect. It is possible that the effect diminished over time. But the analysis tested audience interest in segments of the video that directly followed the antiviolence messages. So, if the ads made audiences uncomfortable with their enjoyment or interest in violence, then we should have detected a significant drop in interest in the violent and gory scenes that followed--at least when compared to viewers who viewed only regular ads. On the other hand, it appears that the presence of the pre-test--asking people about their attitudes about violence--had more of an effect on the audience's reactions than did the presence of antiviolence ads. It appears to have primed their response to violence, made the topic of violence more salient and increased their interest.

The antiviolence messages did not have a significant effect on the mood of subjects. Subjects who viewed the antiviolence messages embedded in the violent film were not more anxious, depressed, or hostile than subjects who viewed the film with regular ads.

Effects of antiviolence ads on the attitudes about violent behavior. Some of the antiviolence ads appeared designed to influence *outcome beliefs about violence*. The ads used fear appeals to suggest that the viewer may be killed or maimed if they continue to engage in high risk behaviors such as carrying guns or belonging to a gang. If this message was effective, it might be indicated by a viewer's altered sense of the probability that they or "someone living in a large city" might be victims of violence. There is no evidence that the ads had such an effect even though a preliminary analysis of the data indicates that the film (a proviolence message) did have an effect on their beliefs about the outcomes of violent behavior.

On the other hand, it appears that the measure of risk perception was able to detect differences within the test audience. The absence of an effect for the antiviolence ads must be seen against a background of significant effects for the pre-test and a difference in the perception of individual versus social risk. Both of these effects are consistent with the literature and support the construct validity of the measure.

The ads were designed to alter young people's attitudes about the use of violence on the streets and in interpersonal relationships. In the terminology of our theoretical model, the ads attempted to alter *subjective norms about violence*. Our analysis indicated that the presence of antiviolence PSAs did not alter short term attitudes about the use of violence in interpersonal relationships. Subjects who viewed the antiviolence PSAs were neither more or less likely to report that violence is "OK" or "not OK" under different circumstances. This finding is consistent with our findings in the other studies using this measure. (See previous chapters.)

What do the findings tell us about the ability of the antiviolence campaign to significantly influence attitudes and response to violence? Although it is impossible to "prove" the null hypothesis, we are inclined to conclude that the antiviolence PSAs were not powerful or effective enough to significantly alter message cognitions about violence or to influence attitudes about violence.

Considering alternative explanations. Because the PSAs appeared to have no significant effect on viewers, it might be appropriate to consider a few possible alternative reasons for why the PSAs were not effective in these circumstances.

How representative was the campaign? The HBO campaign used in this study was one of the most expensive and professionally produced campaigns in 1994-1995. It is fair to say that it is representative of some of the best antiviolence commercials produced until now, and, in fact may be superior to the average antiviolence PSA. So the lack of effect is not due to the fact that this group of PSAs was somehow inferior to the norm. That is not to say that the PSAs were as effective as they might be. We will return to this issue below.

Did the viewers see enough antiviolence PSAs or did they pay enough attention? The experiment was conducted in a setting that should have favored the detection of an effect. Subjects viewed nine antiviolence ads in a 1 1/2 hour setting. This level of exposure is much higher than would occur in typical TV viewing, because antiviolence PSAs do not get such high levels of air time. The "dose" or ratio of pro-attitudinal messages to anti-attitudinal messages was much higher than would be seen in the normal environment. Subjects also viewed the ads in a forced viewing setting and the audience response task required that they pay attention to the video content. Their attention to the ads should have been higher than it would be in normal TV viewing. Again, this is a situation that would have increased the likelihood of detecting an effect.

Did the presence of the violent movie somehow cancel out the positive effect of the antiviolence PSAs? It is possible that the movie neutralized the effects of the ads. The counter-attitudinal, violent message of the film might have negated the pro-attitudinal messages of the PSAs. If this is the case, then the null effect would be even more discouraging for producers of antiviolence PSAs. This would mean that a mere 1 1/2 hour exposure to violent programming completely wiped out any positive effect of seven antiviolence PSAs. Consider the fact that a great percentage of TV content is dedicated to violent themes, and only a minuscule amount of air time carries antiviolence messages of all kinds, including PSAs. If the effect of antiviolence PSAs can be neutralized by one film, then this would suggest that the faint spark lit by antiviolence PSAs would be drowned in the sea of competing violent messages.

Maybe the PSAs don't work with these subjects, but would work on other people? The audience was composed exclusively of young males. Young males are the primary aggressive force in almost all societies (Archer, 1994; Reiss & Roth, 1993). These subjects were university students. But the other studies in this report included young prisoners and middle school teens. With these different audiences we also found minimal or null effects for the antiviolence PSAs.

Concluding note. These results are consistent with our findings in the other studies. Although it is impossible to be absolutely certain, the pattern of null results in this study suggests that the PSAs were not effective in influencing violent attitudes, moods, or interest in violent programming.

10. PROPOSED AND ALLIED STUDIES OF ANTIVIOLENCE TELEVISION MESSAGES

This chapter includes proposed and allied studies. Proposed studies were formally submitted for funding to MediaScope and/or the National Cable Television Association. These are included here, because the research team feels they are essential to obtaining an adequate view of the effectiveness of television's antiviolence campaigns. Without them, a significant part of the picture cannot be filled in.

Allied studies are antiviolence studies that were partially supported, assisted, or guided by the University of North Carolina research group of the National Television Violence Study. In year one, one such study was aided by the research team. In future years the research team hopes to encourage more allied research studies among colleagues and graduate students.

10.1 Proposed National Survey of Awareness, Memory and Attitude Change Following *Voices Against Violence Week*

The goal of Voices Against Violence Week is to raise awareness as well as increase debate about ways to address the problem of violence, stimulating an engaging comprehensive, national forum for serious discussions of violence (NCTA, 1995, p. 2).

Our research team proposed to measure whether *Voices Against Violence Week* did indeed "raise awareness," "increase debate," or generate a "national forum for serious discussion of violence." Another function of the week-long campaign, according to an NCTA press release, was to "heighten awareness of the initiative." In December 1994, we proposed a two-wave national survey to measure cable viewers' awareness and the influence of *Voices Against Violence Week* on attitudes. Unfortunately, we were not able to obtain additional funding from NCTA for this survey. Therefore, we were unable to determine the overall impact of this concentrated communication effort on the general public.

10.2 Allied Study on the Effect of Antiviolence Programming on Response to Violent Programming

Dr. Mark West, University of North Carolina at Asheville[1]

This study sought to examine the effects of one informational antiviolence program, produced by MTV networks, featuring an interview with U.S. President Bill Clinton. The program, produced in a talk show format, used rapid-tempo cutting, attractive modern sets and youthful moderators in an attempt to appeal to and influence a younger audience. Adolescents' impressions of the program and the effect of viewing the

---

[1] Please contact Dr. Mark West at the University of North Carolina at Asheville for more information about this study.

program upon their affective responses to violent programming are the subject of this study.

10.2.1 Research Questions

- ⊙ Can viewing an informational antiviolence program reduce young viewers' *interest* in violent programming?

- ⊙ Do degrees of *self-control* or *impulsivity* influence young viewers' reactions to an informational antiviolence program?

- ⊙ Does viewing an informational antiviolence program alter *attitudes* toward violent behavior?

- ⊙ Does amount of *media use* influence young viewers' reactions to an informational antiviolence program?

10.2.2 Methods

The research used several tools of analysis: questionnaires asking a range of demographic, psychological and behavioral questions; and continuous response measurement (CRM). The measures are described in more detail in Chapter 5. Students completed pre-tests and posttests and, during viewing, used the continuous response system to register moment-by-moment reactions to the programming.

Participants. Twenty students were selected randomly from students at a K-12, private, nonsectarian school in Hendersonville, NC. On April 28, 1995, the day arranged for the research, 18 of the 20 were present.

10.2.3 Stimulus Materials and Apparatus

Stimulus Tapes. A reference tape was prepared for student viewing, consisting of two hours of programming divided into three segments. Segment One consisted of 7.5 minutes of neutral programming (a Warner Brothers animated cartoon with neutral characters and situations), followed by the last 30 minutes of "Karate Kid I," a PG-13-rated movie aimed at adolescents with martial arts conflict as its primary theme. Segment Two was the 27-minute MTV antiviolence program discussed earlier. Segment Three was identical to Segment One, except that the initial, neutral programming was a different Warner Brothers animated cartoon, and the final 30 minutes of the segment consisted of the last 30 minutes of "Karate Kid II," a sequel to the film used in segment one and containing comparable levels of violence.

Questionnaire.

Demographic measures. The pre-test asked a series of standard demographic questions, which included age, grade, gender, household composition and family composition items. These variables will serve as controls in further analysis.

Media use measures. The pre-test also asked several questions about media use. These included preferred type of television show and approximate amounts of television viewing. In addition, a battery of questions derived from previous studies were asked concerning motivations for watching television.

Violence measures. To examine short-term cultivation effects, both the pre-test and posttest instruments included several questions designed to assess participants' perceived likelihood of being victims of violence. Another battery, also using questions developed for other studies in this series, asked about the viewers' attitudes toward violence (see Chapter 5 for description). A final set of measures in the violence subsection sought to examine participant exposure to violence within the last year.

Psychological measures. Several batteries of questions were included in the pre-test to assess prior psychological states of the respondents. The first of these was the Children's Perceived Self-Control Scale, or CPSC (Humphrey, 1982). The CPSC is an 11-item instrument that uses a cognitive-behavioral perspective to examine self-control. Perceived self-control has been shown to be related to behaviors that promote adolescent adjustment. This research project examined whether perceived self-control is a mediating variable upon affective evaluations of violent programming.

A second battery of questions comprises the Hirschfield Impulsivity Scale, an instrument that measures impulsivity (low self-censoring) through 19 statements, to which respondents answer either "true" or "false" (Hirschfield, 1965) (see Chapter 5 for description).

10.2.4 Procedure

The students were first instructed in the use of the continuous response measurement handsets (Biocca, David & West, 1994), and were then presented with the pre-test. After completing the pre-test, participants watched the referent tape, operating the handsets to indicate their moment-by-moment affective responses to the material. After evaluation of the taped programming, students completed a posttest which repeated the psychometric elements of the pre-test.

10.2.5 Results

At this point, only overall analyses of the effectiveness of the antiviolence educational program on the affective evaluation of violent programming have been conducted, and those analyses are in an initial stage. Nevertheless, an initial conclusion would be that the antiviolence programming had little effect upon adolescent viewers' affective reaction to violent programming. Before and after mean scores of liking of such programming appeared to vary little. Additionally, affective responses to the antiviolence programming were quite negative, with the lowest overall and lowest momentary evaluations of any of the programming presented. This particular antiviolence appeal, at least at this initial stage of analysis, appears to have had little effect upon viewers. In addition, these adolescent viewers disliked it enough that they probably wouldn't have watched it voluntarily.

10.2.6 Discussion

The paper-and-pencil tests generated a large quantity of data, and a good deal of analysis remains to be completed. Of particular interest are analyses of the interaction of psychological variables such as locus of self-control, overall liking of violent programming and the effects of viewing the antiviolence talk show featuring Bill Clinton. Although viewers overall were unaffected by the antiviolence program, perhaps certain types of viewers *were* affected. If such programming can reach some students, perhaps even those most at risk for violent behavior, it can have significant value despite being ineffective for most adolescents.

11. INTERIM FINDINGS AND CONCLUSIONS FOR YEAR ONE

A number of factors contribute to the effectiveness of any antiviolence campaign. Much needs to be examined before findings can be conclusive. Because the task is large--to assess the effectiveness of all of TV's antiviolence messages--and the budget modest for the task, the strategy in the first year was to explore reactions to samples of antiviolence programming through a variety of studies and with a variety of audiences. This approach was chosen over conducting one large (but necessarily more narrow) study. This is only the first year of a four-year study of antiviolence messages. The studies in year one were designed to provide insight into how audiences receive these kinds of messages, and, possibly, guide the selection of key variables for testing in a small set of larger studies in years two and three. These *interim findings are preliminary*, analysis is in progress and some of the findings will need to be confirmed.

The findings are organized according to the criteria of effectiveness defined earlier in this report.

11.1 Quantitative and Experimental Results

11.1.1 Interest.

◆ When viewed by training school students, 75% of the antiviolence PSAs were rated as slightly-to-very interesting. Middle school students found only 46% of the PSAs to be slightly-to-very interesting.

These results are based on subjects' second-by-second self-report of interest level. One PSA, *Et Tu Brutus*, stands out among the others and might be considered representative of the more successful PSAs in this genre. Researchers observed that training school students who had a history of violence were absolutely quiet and riveted when the PSA aired. The realistic narrative and slick production captured their attention. This quantitative finding can be illuminated by some of the other quantitative and qualitative data. In focus groups and experimental studies, the narrative PSAs tended to score higher as a group on measures of interest, liking, and arousal. They also tended to evoke greater commentary and self-reference in the one-on-one interviews.

◆ An award-winning program promoting conflict resolution, *Kids Killing Kids*, was not found to be significantly more interesting than a fire safety video by either training school students or middle school students.

◆ Exposure to antiviolence PSAs did not alter college students' level of interest in violent scenes that immediately followed the PSAs.

11.1.2 Arousal and Mood.

◆ Viewing the antiviolence PSAs significantly altered the self-reported mood of the viewers. Middle school students were significantly more aroused following exposure to the PSAs, but felt less pleased and less dominant. The training school students felt significantly more aroused after watching the antiviolence PSAs, but did not report any change in feelings of pleasure or dominance. Antiviolence PSAs depicting the threat or results of violence were rated as most arousing for both groups.

11.1.3 Attitudes About Violence.

◆ Measures of attitudes toward violence come closest to measuring the industry's goal of "deglamorizing violence," but no evidence was found that an award-winning program on conflict resolution had an effect on changing attitudes about aggression with either training school students or middle school students.

Two educational programs were tested in year one with a single exposure in a controlled setting. Both programs included messages clearly designed to influence attitudes toward violence. The program *Kids Killing Kids* was chosen because it was considered among the industry's best. This fine production won an Emmy award in 1994 and received broad industry praise. However, although this program explicitly tries to alter violent attitudes, we could find no evidence that it significantly influenced any of the measures of attitude toward violent behavior with two different audiences. It is possible that, when seen in a natural setting with more frequent message repetition, the program might influence adolescents' attitudes. However, the program is approximately one hour long and was found to be only moderately interesting. It is unlikely that the typical adolescent would view this program unless they are shown in a controlled setting. It is even less likely that they would watch each program more than once.

It was not possible to measure the cumulative effect of an entire antiviolence television campaign in this study. We recommend that such a study be conducted in the future, but we are not confident that such testing will find different results.

◆ Embedding nine antiviolence PSAs in the middle of a violent movie had no effect on changing attitudes about aggression among college students.

Antiviolence messages are marketing a particular world view. They directly compete with messages that present an opposing world view: violence is glamorous, guns are valuable and bring power, and violence is a way to solve interpersonal conflict. There is no doubt that the antiviolence messages produced in year one constitute a major effort on the part of the broadcast and cable industry. But if one considers proviolence messages on regular television, these antiviolence messages receive only a small sliver of air time. We requested an estimate of the percentage of air time dedicated to antiviolence messages from the content analysis study that is also part of this project. Such a number should be obtainable from the data in years two and three. By most estimates, the percentage of air time for antiviolence messages probably is less than one percent.

In Study 7 antiviolence messages were directly pitted against violent programming. The number of antiviolence messages presented in that study was much higher than in regular television. The effect of the PSAs was measured moment-by-moment immediately after the audience saw them. No effect could be found. The PSAs did not diminish interest in violence, nor did their presence affect attitudes toward violence. These results bring into question the effectiveness of the PSAs under conditions where they are diluted by surrounding violent programming.

11.1.4 Unintended Effects.

◆ No evidence was found that antiviolence programming had negative, unintended effects such as increased anxiety, depression or hostility (college students only), or fears of being a victim of violence or increased tendencies to see the world as a dangerous or violent place (all test groups).

11.2 Qualitative Results

11.2.1 Attention and Interest.

◆ Network promotions and sponsor tags attached to antiviolence messages appeared to compete for valuable message time and audience attention.

Most antiviolence PSAs are only 15 or 30 seconds in duration. Some PSAs, such as those produced by the Music Box, consumed quite a few seconds of the air time with an animated logo and station identification segment. Precious time was lost. On the other hand, HBO was notable for releasing their antiviolence messages without any organizational identification.

Sponsor identification also may be distracting to viewers. Theories on the processing of advertising suggest that the presence of network identification influences the perceived source of the message (Biocca, 1991). For example, in our focus group discussions of Music Box PSAs, some subjects commented more on the Music Box service than on the antiviolence message.

11.2.2 Attitudes About Violence.

◆ Most of the antiviolence campaign slogans, such as "Stop the violence," appeared to promote positions already held by target audiences, e.g., they already believed that violence was wrong and should be stopped.

Most of the PSA campaigns appeared designed to influence what in our theoretical model is called "outcome beliefs" and "outcome evaluations." PSAs advanced norms such as: "Stop the violence" or stressed the potential cost of violent behavior such as "Handguns kill." Target audiences--including violent viewers--appeared to already subscribe to these outcome beliefs, i.e., they already believe that in general, "violence is bad." Most were acutely aware that handguns kill, and that they themselves were potential victims. Therefore, they already shared the outcome beliefs of the PSAs: "If you use a handgun, you may die." The PSAs' exhortations may have had minimal effects because they merely echoed existing general beliefs. Only two of the more than 200 adolescents in these studies appeared to hold positions that advocated violence and the "pleasure" of committing violence. Most others easily agreed with the message but suggested that it was not something they thought about much. Some adolescent viewers treated them as truisms.

Often subjects suggested that such beliefs did not rule their behavior because the environment ("the streets," "my crib," etc.) ruled their behavior. Such comments suggest that messages targeting audience members' sense of *perceived self-efficacy* (see Figure 3.2) might have focused on attitudinal areas more in need of change. The campaigns expressed a general concern about violence but did not challenge the viewers' beliefs about personal power, self-esteem, and efficacy that motivate the use of violence. Viewers found it easy to accept the proposition that "violence is a bad thing," and that "sometime people die." As one subject reported, "Yeah, I know that."

◆ Messages promoting pacifist themes, such as "just walk away," did not seem credible to the training school students, many of whom had experience with violence, but scored higher with middle school students, many of whom had no experience with violence.

Pacifist behaviors advocated by some PSAs (i.e., "just walk away") or in some segments of the program, *Kids Killing Kids*, were seen as unrealistic or not viable by most of the adolescents with a history of violence, and with some of the other participants. The messages advocated social norms that were seen as outside what was acceptable for their group. Pacifism was seen as particularly threatening to self-esteem. Furthermore, some participants from violent environments suggested that giving in might increase the chances of personal violence by making the individual "a mark." The pattern of results suggested that the more the subjects were at risk of violence, the more such approaches were seen as not credible, believable, or viable in their subculture.

On the other hand, some of the adolescents from the middle school did see such pacifist behavior as viable and credible. The pacifist PSA, *Locker Slam*, took place in a school much like the one these students attend. The scores on interest and pleasure and one-on-one interview responses suggest an acceptance of this PSA and its message.

The results suggest that such messages will be ineffectual among violence-prone youths. Critics might question the value of PSAs that advocate nonviolence to audiences that are already nonviolent and prone to accepting the message. But these messages might reinforce such self-protective attitudes among students who might be potential victims of violence, by giving them social support for refusing to fight, even though they probably will be rejected by perpetrators of violence, or by youths who are in violent environments and feel they must be violent for self-protection.

◆ PSAs and program segments that portrayed paralysis or the death of innocent victims as an outcome of violent behavior may have been more disturbing to adolescents than the possibility of the death of people like themselves.

A few messages seemed to make viewers think in a different way about behavioral outcomes--a segment in *Kids Killing Kids* and a before-and-after commercial featured youths paralyzed by bullets. The image of paralysis may have been more disturbing to some of the viewers than the image of death. In focus group discussions and in one-on-one interviews, some of the training school students were solemn and sometimes visibly uncomfortable when viewing these segments. Imagining death is abstract; imagining a crippled body is concrete. To adolescents who are self-conscious of their body image, the possibility of living with a deformed body may have been easier to imagine and more disturbing than trying to imagine the nothingness of death.

11.2.3 Message Comprehension.

◆ Although some celebrity endorsers aroused interest, the lack of credibility of some of the celebrities, especially those who were perceived as violent in real life or in their jobs (e.g., sports, acting), sometimes confused or undermined the message.

Advertising can be effective at gaining attention, but sometimes attention comes at the expense of clear communication. A variety of celebrity sources were used in the campaigns in year one: pop music artists, actors, politicians, sports heroes, etc. Studies 1 to 4 showed that many of the ads aroused interest. But the use of celebrities had mixed and unpredictable effects on response to the messages.

The image of individual celebrities varied greatly across the test audiences. That is to be expected. But in a number of cases the lack of credibility of the celebrity undermined the message. For example, some of the PSAs featured rap artists whose music included lyrics that could be interpreted as glorifying a street culture of violence. Adolescent viewers, especially some of the training school students with a history of violence, saw a contradiction between an artist's songs and the PSA's antiviolence message. Questions about trustworthiness also appeared in PSAs featuring actors such as Samuel Jackson. Some participants were familiar with the actor's role as a paid killer in the violent film, *Pulp Fiction*. Although his scripted message insisted that his movie roles were fictional, some adolescent viewers thought he was a hypocrite. Adolescent viewers sometimes perceived hypocrisy in other messages. For example, President Clinton was perceived as hypocritical by training school subjects because: 1) they felt he was "powerful" enough to stop to violence if he "really wanted to," and 2) because he had admitted a flirtation with drugs as a youth.

◆ Narrative formats stimulated more discussion among the middle and training school students, and more association with life experiences among training school students. Although narrative formats were, on the whole, more arousing than talking heads, the messages in narratives were more frequently "misinterpreted" than those in which celebrities simply spoke to the viewers.

The narratives were often subtle and led to open-ended interpretations. In some cases, the interpretations were consistent with the antiviolent thrust of the message, in other cases they undermined the message. For example, the narrative in *Et Tu Brutus* shows an individual being chased and about to be killed by a man with a gun. The "message" required that the audience detect that the person chasing and the person running away were the same individual. But the PSA was sometimes interpreted as a story about vengeance where the victim "probably deserved it." In these cases, the anti-violence message of "You're only killing yourself" was lost. Many adolescent viewers didn't "get it." In another, the PSA titled *Stray Bullet* appeared designed to discourage playing with guns. The PSA was interpreted by a number of adolescent viewers as a message to parents about the presence of unattended guns in the house. Although this does not appear to be the producer's intended message, it is consistent with the antiviolence theme. But the PSA's strength was weakened when adolescents thought the target audience was their parents and not them. In this case there is a problem with the perceived model reader. This can significantly disrupt the cognitive processing of the message (see Biocca, 1991).

11.3 Interim Conclusions

Antiviolence PSAs are capable of attracting the interest and attention of adolescent audiences. The PSAs tested in this study varied greatly on the various criteria of effectiveness, suggesting that many could be improved. Previous communication research and the finding that an award-winning, antiviolence program had no effect on attitudes toward violence suggest that at its best and by itself, TV may be only modestly effective in decreasing violent attitudes or behavior. The finding that exposure to nine antiviolence PSAs, in one hour-and-a-half, could not diminish interest in subsequent violent scenes suggests that antiviolence PSA campaigns may not air frequently enough to achieve their objectives. Messages that deglamorize violence may be overwhelmed by messages that compellingly glamorize violence.

12. INTERIM RECOMMENDATIONS FOR YEAR ONE

These are interim recommendations. Complete recommendations will be provided at the end of the study. The following recommendations grow out of the pattern of results in the first year and accumulated research on the effectiveness of other health communication campaigns.

12.1 Recommendations Derived from the Year One Studies

◆ The effectiveness of the antiviolence PSAs could be improved if they are submitted to formative evaluation and testing before they are aired. Both quantitative and qualitative testing clearly detected several uninteresting, ambiguous and confusing PSAs. These less effective PSAs might have used valuable airtime that could have been used by more effective ads.

Many of the problems found with some of the PSAs could easily have been detected during pretests, and especially at the formative evaluation stage. We recommend that all antiviolence PSA storyboards be subject to focus group testing prior to production and airing. We also recommend that finished and produced PSAs be submitted to test audiences to determine which ones are the most effective prior to scheduling the amount of airtime per PSA. The lack of credibility of some celebrity sources could have been detected with such procedures. Audience misunderstanding of some of the narrative PSAs tested also would have been detected, and they could have been re-edited to minimize confusion.

It is sometimes argued that this would be expensive. But such expense is small relative to the cost of production and airtime. If a PSA is ineffective, then production and airtime costs are wasted. Maximizing the effectiveness of the antiviolence PSAs is particularly critical given that the PSAs receive modest airtime and must compete with expensive, professionally produced and highly seductive television messages that glamorize the use of violence to settle interpersonal conflict.

12.1.1 Sources.

◆ Campaigns should decrease heavy reliance on celebrity endorsements. Although some celebrity endorsers caught the attention of the audience, they were rarely more effective than narrative ads and sometimes their sexual attractiveness or lack of credibility or recognition distracted from or undermined the message.

Celebrity endorsers can get attention. They are particularly useful when trying to raise the visibility of low awareness issues: diabetes, cataracts, etc. But there is high awareness of the problem of violence in America. For high awareness issues, celebrity endorsers may not always be the most effective vehicle for delivering a message.

Attention to the celebrity can in some cases distract from the message. For example, incarcerated young males were captivated by female celebrities such as Brownstone and Salt & Pepa, but sometimes ignored their message.

The talking head format of the typical celebrity endorsement tends to be flat. Such PSAs were only modestly arousing or interesting to test audiences. Under such circumstances it is likely that such PSAs are subject to rapid wearout and effectiveness is sapped quickly with repeated exposure.

In some of the antiviolence campaigns, celebrities were used poorly. For example, one campaign had different celebrities saying the same "impassioned" script. Test audiences exposed to a number of these PSAs read this as a lack of sincerity. Many of the celebrities may be well intentioned, but increasingly cynical audience members may see their performance as self-promotion.

The attention-getting power of celebrities might be used more effectively in other PSA formats. For example, the few PSAs where celebrities were used in narrative formats seemed to work well. *Et Tu Brutus* used a celebrity rap artist in its narrative. The artist got the attention of our incarcerated test audiences while the narrative delivered the message. We might consider mixed format messages where a celebrity is used to draw attention while a narrative (which may not necessarily incorporate the celebrity) carries the bulk of the message.

◆ Antiviolence PSAs should avoid using celebrities who have been associated with violence in their work or personal lives. Their image may undermine the antiviolence message and the goal of deglamorizing violence.

Celebrities carry preexisting meaning (an "image"), and this meaning will be different across audiences. For some audiences, *the celebrity's lack of credibility will undermine the message.* For example, the PSA featuring what should be a credible source, the President, was among the lowest scoring PSAs with test audiences. This may have been due to adolescent reaction to an authority figure. But many in the test audiences questioned, fairly or unfairly, President Clinton's credibility. The problem also surfaced with the use of some rappers whose lyrics glorified violent street culture and with actors who had starred in violent films.

Some of the PSAs seem to want to co-opt public figures associated with a violent subculture: for example, some rap singers who had a history of violent songs (e.g., Ice T). It is probably assumed that these individuals can gain the attention and the respect of young adolescents who idolize elements of the violent subculture. But the spokesperson's past may undermine his or her credibility. The mere use of spokespersons identified with fictional or real violence *may potentially reinforce the legitimacy of a violent lifestyle.* The "formerly" proviolent source is idolized as the converted "non-violent" individual. In this social script, *the individual who has always been non-violent is not seen as a hero worthy of respect.* The use of sources with violent images may unwittingly contribute to the glamorization of the violent lifestyle.

The use of "previously violent" sources plays into the stereotype of what we call the "redeemed gunfighter": the violent individual who "really wants to do good," but sometimes "is forced" to use violence to achieve some good end. Strategies involving these sources may result in confused messages open to interpretations that may undermine the goals of the campaign.

12.1.2 Messages.

◆ Communicators should consider producing more messages that portray outcomes of violent behavior such as paralysis, the death of innocent victims, or negative consequences for members of the perpetrator's family. These consequences may be more disturbing and effective with adolescent audiences than the possibility of death of people like themselves.

Above we mentioned that the portrayal of paralysis appeared to disturb audiences more than the portrayal of death. In other instances, the death of family or noncombatants also appeared to be disturbing. The PSA *Stray Bullet* shows a scene in which a child in a baby chair apparently is killed by a stray bullet. The final scene evoked open shouts of "No!" among some of the incarcerated youths who had significant exposure to real violence. This kind of death was considered more "stupid" than the death of combatants. It also seemed to generate more discussion and consideration of the consequences of violent behavior.

Both middle and training school viewers found the themes of mothers and violence (*Salt & Pepa*) and the portrayal of the impact of violence on families and children (*Stray Bullets*) compelling. The family ideal is still a powerful force with most adolescents and sometimes the gang provides a peer-based substitute for "family." Hip maternal themes, such as the one suggested by the *Salt & Pepa* PSA, might strike a chord, as well as narratives that speak to the impact of violent behavior on the perpetrator's siblings and parents.

12.1.3 Channels.

◆ Because of the heavy competition from messages that glamorize violence, the volume of antiviolence messages will probably have to be significantly higher to cause changes in interest and attitudes about violence.

In Study 7, nine antiviolence PSAs embedded in a 1 1/2 hour violent program did not appear to alter interest in the violent, gory scenes that immediately followed the commercial break. Exposure to six antiviolence PSAs per hour is very high; it is exposure at a rate several orders of magnitude higher than has ever appeared on regular television. If exposure to antiviolence messages at these levels was unable to move the audience's interest in violence, then it is likely that the present frequency of these messages may be inadequate to achieve the desired effects.

12.2 Recommendations consistent with health communication campaign research

The following recommendations are drawn from other research on effective health communication campaigns and are consistent with our findings:

12.2.1 Sources.

◆ Messages that show an antiviolence mediator as a role model who has high social esteem, power, and who demonstrates nonviolent approaches to resolving interpersonal conflict may be effective.

Most PSAs featured either the perpetrator, the victim of violence, or "members of the community" who spoke out against violence. Few featured a powerful nonviolent mediator as a role model. Two of the most successful test segments featured such roles: a PSA featuring the antiviolence rapper Chuck D and a segment of *Kids Killing Kids* featuring an older brother who attempts to redeem and protect a drug dealing younger brother. The role of the nonviolent mediator can potentially be appealing to high risk audiences:

1) the role of antiviolence mediator can be used to *portray non-violent approaches to solving interpersonal conflict* while maintaining social esteem,

2) the role of antiviolence mediator can be used to embody an alternative role model to violent teens, *a respected--even powerful--community figure* who may not be a traditional authority figure,

3) the role of antiviolence mediator may be used to *embody a mature behavioral model* that can show young teens how to achieve goals and social esteem without the use of violence.

12.2.2 Messages.

◆ Messages should provide examples of specific, feasible and concrete behaviors that adolescents can use to decrease their likelihood of engaging in violence.

Social learning and the perception of self-efficacy is built in part on concrete models of behavior. Most PSA campaigns seemed designed to build awareness. But as we found out, target audiences were aware of the problem of violence. Most antiviolence PSAs did not provide concrete suggestions or models to guide behavior. The campaigns concentrated on influencing social norms and increasing the perceived cost of violent acts. Although this can be valuable, few messages demonstrated concrete actions for viewers who wanted to change behavior.

The program-length *Kids Killing Kids* did concentrate exclusively on providing behavioral models. This kind of approach might be valuable if incorporated into PSA campaigns so that at least some of the PSAs also provide concrete models for nonviolent conflict resolution. On other hand, the data suggest that simply advocating pacifist approaches, especially those that are seen as damaging social esteem, may not be successful. This suggest that models of nonviolent conflict resolution should be presented so that the person choosing the less violent path is elevated in social status.

◆ Messages using fear appeals should include clear and realistic suggestions for reducing fear and resolving conflict.

Adolescents are aroused by fear appeals, but may be left with fear, rather than a changed attitude toward violence or a desire to behave in nonviolent ways. None of the messages tested presented clear recommendations about what an individual should do to "stop the violence," except *Locker Slam*, which advocated "just walking away." The training school students thought that was an unrealistic alternative. Fear appeal campaigns need to build in realistic behavioral models for reducing fear or resolving conflict.

◆ Messages that increase the potential power of peer-driven shame and social stigma may be effective.

Violence is often used to achieve self-esteem among young peer members. A critique of this behavior may be more effective if the message can undermine the social value of violence among violence-prone peer groups. Violence in certain communities is associated with manliness, power, and street sophistication.

Hesitance to engage in violent or gang behavior can sometimes lead young males to suffer social shame. Campaigns can assist in changing this attitude by undermining the perceived social value of violence. This strategy may require that the PSA undermine the social value of violence using other accepted values of violence-prone peer groups and other adolescent groups.

12.2.3 Channels.

◆ The effectiveness of large-scale antiviolence TV campaigns may be greatly enhanced by coordination with other media channels including interpersonal channels such as schools and other youth organizations.

Antiviolence messages are likely to be more effective if consistent messages are reaching youth through various channels. Schools are one such communication channel. They offer not only a means of communicating more information, but also ways to practice nonviolent approaches to interpersonal conflict. The example of some networks, such as MTV's attempt to coordinate campaigns with schools, is excellent. Coordination with schools or adolescent correction centers may help maximize the effectiveness of the media campaigns.

◆ To obtain maximum distribution, messages should avoid identifying the network producing the message.

Network tags and identification appeared to be a barrier to maximizing the success of antiviolence campaigns. The sponsor tags, such as those used by the Music Box, consumed a significant portion of the PSAs' limited time. HBO's example might be followed by other networks. Their PSAs were produced without any network identification. This strategy does not squander message time on self-promotion. Also, because the messages are not linked to any network, the best PSAs can be used and reused across networks. This increases the potential utility of the strongest PSAs. If regulatory restrictions require group identification, an industry-wide umbrella organization could increase use of antiviolence messages across networks.

◆ Because a significant proportion of violent acts are committed under the influence of drugs and alcohol, linking antiviolence and antidrug campaigns should be considered.

A great many homicides are perpetrated by males under the influence of drugs. These drugs, including alcohol, lessen the perception of risk. Antiviolence campaigns may benefit by linking up with antidrug campaigns to create PSAs that stress this combined risk.

◆ All television industry antiviolence efforts could be more effective if coordinated and concentrated into short, industry-wide campaigns with a specific message targeted to specific audiences.

Antiviolence PSAs and programs constitute only a small part of television. Their effect can easily be diluted or overwhelmed by counter-attitudinal messages that glamorize violence. The limited resources might be concentrated into a short period of time. Cable's *Voices Against Violence week* is a good example of this approach. Campaigns might be timed to match the beginning of the school year and/or the beginning of summer. Short, intense, industry-wide campaigns can:

1) *maximize impact* of limited resources and share of voice during the campaign

period,
2) *increase opportunities* to mobilize industry resources,
3) allow *coordination across multiple media channels,*
4) allow for *coordination with schools* and other youth service institutions,
5) *minimize* issue and compassion *fatigue.*

12.2.4 Audiences.

◆ Younger audiences 8-13 years old may be more responsive to antiviolence messages than older audiences.

The research literature indicates that behavioral patterns related to violence may be formed early and may be hard to change in mid-to-late adolescence. Many of the PSAs target mid-to-late adolescents. PSA-based approaches may not be as effective at this point. Our training school subjects were mid-to-late adolescents. Some of the PSAs were targeted to adolescents who like them were living lives disrupted and toughened by violence. Numerous antiviolence interventions involving months of direct, face-to-face counseling and training often fail with such adolescents. It is unlikely that older adolescents with violent experience can be significantly influenced by a few television messages.

This may not be true for pre-adolescents and early adolescents. Some are still forming conflict resolution strategies. PSAs targeted at these younger, perhaps more susceptible, audiences may have more of an impact.

◆ Antiviolence campaigns may have other positive effects on other audiences.

Although the PSAs may have limited or no effect on the violent behavior of mid-to-late adolescents, there may be other positive social effects. Antiviolence PSAs may help keep the topic of violence on the political agenda. These social mobilization effects may help generate changes in the social ills that contribute to a culture of violence. Our proposed national survey would have attempted to measure such effects, but it was not funded. It is recommended that such indirect social effects be investigated.

References

Ajzen, I. (1985). From intentions to actions: A theory of planned behavior. In L. Kuhl & J. Beckman (Eds.), Action control: From cognition to behavior (pp. 11-39). New York: Springer-Verlag.

Ajzen, I., & Fishbein, M. (1980). Understanding attitudes and predicting social behavior. Englewood Cliffs, NJ: Prentice Hall.

American Psychological Association (1993). Violence and youth: Psychology's response. Washington, DC: American Psychological Association.

Archer, J. (1994). Introduction to male violence. In J. Archer (Ed.), Male violence (pp. 1-22). London: Routledge.

Atkin, C. (1979). Research evidence on mass mediated health communication campaigns. In D. Nimmo (Ed.), Communication Yearbook 3 (pp. 655-668). New Brunswick, NJ: Transation-International Communication Association.

Atkin, C. (1983). Effects of realistic TV violence vs. fictional violence on aggression. Journalism Quarterly, 60, 615-621.

Austin, B. A. (1980). The influence of the MPAA's film-rating system on motion picture attendance: A pilot study. The Journal of Psychology, 106, 91-99.

Bandura, A. (1965). Influence of models' reinforcement contingencies on the acquisition of imitative responses. Journal of Personality and Social Psychology, 1, 589-595.

Bandura, A. (1971). Social learning theory. New York, NY: General Learning Press.

Bandura, A. (1986). Social foundations of thought and action: A social cognitive theory. Englewood Cliffs, NJ: Prentice-Hall.

Bandura, A. (1994). Social cognitive theory of mass communication. In J. Bryant & D. Zillmann (Eds.), Media effects (pp. 61-90). Hillsdale, NJ: Erlbaum.

Bandura, A., Ross, D., & Ross, S. A. (1961). Transmission of aggression through imitation of aggressive models. Journal of Abnormal and Social Psychology, 63, 575-582.

Bandura, A., Ross, D., & Ross, S. A. (1963a). Imitation of film-mediated aggressive models. Journal of Abnormal and Social Psychology, 66 (1), 3-11.

Bandura, A., Ross, D., & Ross, S. A. (1963b). Vicarious reinforcement and imitative learning. Journal of Abnormal and Social Psychology, 67 (6), 601-607.

Baron, R. A. (1971a). Aggression as a function of magnitude of victim's pain cues, level of prior anger arousal, and aggressor-victim similarity. Journal of Personality and Social Psychology, 18, 48-54.

Baron, R. A. (1971b). Magnitude of victim's pain cues and level of prior anger arousal as determinants of adult aggressive behavior. Journal of Personality and Social Psychology, 17, 236-243.

Baron, R. A. (1978). The influence of hostile and nonhostile humor upon physical aggression. Personality and Social Psychology Bulletin, 4 (1), 77-80.

Baron, R. A. (1979). Effects of victim's pain cues, victim's race, and level of prior instigation upon physical aggression. Journal of Applied Social Psychology, 9 (2), 103-114.

Baron, R. A., & Ball, R. L. (1974). The aggression-inhibiting influence of non hostile humor. Journal of Experimental Social Psychology, 10, 23-33.

Baron, R. A., & Richardson, D. R. (1994). Human Aggression (2nd. ed). New York, NY: Plenum.

Baxter, R. L., Reimer, C. D. Landini, A., Leslie, L., & Singletary M. W. (1985). A content analysis of music videos. Journal of Broadcasting & Electronic Media, 29, 333-340.

Berger, A. A. (1988). Humor and behavior: Therapeutic aspects of comedic techniques and other considerations. In B. D. Ruben (Ed.), Information and Behavior (Vol. 2, pp. 226-247). New Brunswick, NJ: Transaction Books.

Berkowitz, L. (1970). Aggressive humor as a stimulus to aggressive responses. Journal of Personality and Social Psychology, 16, 710-717.

Berkowitz, L. (1973). Words and symbols as stimuli to aggressive responses. In J. Knutson (Ed.), Control of aggression: Implications from basic research. Chicago, IL: Aldine-Atherton.

Berkowitz, L. (1984). Some effects of thoughts on anti- and prosocial influences of media events: A cognitive-neoassociation analysis. Psychological Bulletin, 95 (3), 410-427.

Berkowitz, L. (1990). On the formation and regulation of anger and aggression: A cognitive neoassociationistic analysis. American Psychologist, 45, 494-503.

Berkowitz, L., & Alioto, J. T. (1973). The meaning of an observed event as a determinant of its aggressive consequences. Journal of Personality and Social Psychology, 28, 206-217.

Berkowitz, L., & Geen, R. G. (1966). Film violence and the cue properties of available targets. Journal of Personality and Social Psychology, 3, 525-530.

Berkowitz, L., & Geen, R. G. (1967). Stimulus qualities of the target of aggression: A further study. Journal of Personality and Social Psychology, 5, 364-368.

Berkowitz, L., & LePage, A. (1967). Weapons as aggression-eliciting stimuli. Journal of Personality and Social Psychology, 7, 202-207.

Berkowitz, L., & Powers, P. C. (1979). Effects of timing and justification of witnessed aggression on the observers' punitiveness. Journal of Research in Personality, 13, 71-80.

Berkowitz, L., & Rawlings, E. (1963). Effects of film violence on inhibitions against subsequent aggression. Journal of Abnormal and Social Psychology, 66 (5), 405-412.

Berkowitz, L., & Rogers, K.H. (1986). A priming effect analysis of media influences. In J. Bryant and D. Zillmann (Eds). Perspectives on media effects (pp. 57-82). Hillsdale, NJ: Erlbaum.

Berndt, T. J., & Berndt, E. G. (1975). Children's use of motives and intentionality in person perception and moral judgment. Child Development, 46, 904-920.

Biocca, F. (1991). Viewer's mental models of political commercials: Toward a theory of the semantic processing of television. In F. Biocca (Ed.), Television and political advertising: Psychological processes (Vol. 1, pp. 27-90). Hillsdale, NJ: Lawrence Erlbaum Associates.

Biocca, F., David, P., & West, M. (1994). Continuous response measurement (CRM): A computerized tool for research on the cognitive processing of communication messages. In A. Lang (Ed.), Measuring psychological responses to media messages (pp. 15-64). Hillsdale, NJ: Lawrence Erlbaum Associates.

Boster, F. J., & Mongeau, P. (1984). Fear-arousing persuasive messages. In R. N. Bostrom (Ed.), Communication Yearbook 8 (pp. 330-375). Beverly Hills, CA: Sage.

Boyatzis, C. J., Matillo, G. M., & Nesbitt, K. M. (1995). Effects of "The Mighty Morphin Power Rangers" on children's aggression with peers. Child Study Journal, 25 (1), 45-55.

Broder, J. M. (1995, June 1). Dole indicts Hollywood for debasing culture. The Los Angeles Times, pp. A1, A15.

Brown, J. D., & Campbell, K. (1986). Race and gender in music videos: The same beat but a different drummer. Journal of Communication, 36 (1), 94-106.

Brown, J. D., Walsh-Childers, K., Bauman, D. E., & Koch, G. G. (1990). The influence of new media and family structure on young adolescents' television and radio use. Communication Research, 17, 65-82.

Bryant, J., Carveth, R. A., & Brown D. (1981). Television viewing and anxiety: An experimental examination. Journal of Communication, 31 (1), 106-119.

Cantor, J. (1991). Fright responses to mass media. In J. Bryant & D. Zillmann (Eds.), Responding to the screen (pp. 169-198). Hillsdale, NJ: Lawrence Erlbaum.

Cantor, J. (1994). Fright reactions to mass media. In J. Bryant & D. Zillmann (Eds.), Media effects (pp. 213-245). Hillsdale, NJ: Lawrence Erlbaum Associates.

Cantor, J., & Hoffner, C. (1990). Forewarning of a threat and prior knowledge of outcome. Human Communication Research, 16, 323-354.

Cantor, J., & Sparks, G. G. (1984). Children's fear responses to mass media: Testing some Piagetian predictions. Journal of Communication, 34 (2), 90-103.

Cantor, J., & Wilson, B. J. (1988). Helping children cope with frightening media presentations. Current Psychology: Research & Reviews, 7, 58-75.

Carlson, M., Marcus-Newhall, A., & Miller, N. (1990). Effects of situational aggression cues: A quantitative review. Journal of Personality and Social Psychology, 58, 622-633.

Carver, C. S., Ganellen, R. J., Froming, W. J., & Chambers, W. (1983). Modeling: An analysis in terms of category accessibility. Journal of Experimental Social Psychology, 19, 403-421.

Centers for Disease Control. (1991). Position papers from the Third National Injury Conference: Setting the National Agenda for Injury Control in the 1990s. Washington, DC: Department of Health and Human Services.

Christenson P. (1992). The effects of parental advisory labels on adolescent music preferences. Journal of Communication, 42 (1), 106-113.

Clark, D. G., & Blankenberg, W. B. (1972). Trends in violent content in selected mass media. In G. A. Comstock & E. A. Rubinstein (Eds.), Television and social behavior: Media and content control (Vol. 1, pp. 188-243). Washington, DC: US Government Publication Office.

Cline, V. B., Croft, R. G., & Courrier, S. (1973). Desensitization of children to television violence. Journal of Personality and Social Psychology, 27, 360-365.

Collins, W. A. (1973). Effect of temporal separation between motivation, aggression, and consequences. Developmental Psychology, 8 (2), 215-221.

Collins, W. A. (1979). Children's comprehension of television content. In E. Wartella (Ed.), <u>Children communicating: Media and development of thought, speech, understanding</u> (pp. 21-52). Beverly Hills, CA: Sage.

Collins, W. A. (1983). Interpretation and inference in children's television viewing. In J. Bryant & D. R. Anderson (Eds.), <u>Children's understanding of television</u> (pp. 125-150). New York, NY: Academic Press.

Columbia Broadcasting System (1980). <u>Network prime time violence tabulations for 1978-1979 season.</u> New York: Author.

Comisky, P., & Bryant, J. (1982). Factors involved in generating suspense. <u>Human Communication Research, 9</u>, 49-58.

Comstock, G., & Paik, H. (1991). <u>Television and the American child.</u> New York, NY: Academic Press.

Condry, J. (1989). <u>The psychology of television.</u> Hillsdale, NJ: Lawrence Erlbaum.

Conover, P. J., & Feldman, S. (1986). The role of inference in the perception of political candidates. In R. Lau & D. Sears (Eds.), <u>Political cognition</u> (pp. 127-158). Hillsdale, NJ: Lawrence Erlbaum Associates.

Cumberbatch, G., Lee, M., Hardy, G., & Jones, I. (1987). <u>The portrayal of violence on British television.</u> London: British Broadcasting Corporation. Hillsdale, NJ: Lawrence Erlbaum Associates.

Daly, M., & Wilson, M. (1994). Evolutionary psychology of male violence. In J. Archer (Ed.), <u>Male violence</u> (pp. 253-288). London: Routledge.

Davison, W. P. (1983). The third-person effect in communication. <u>Public Opinion Quarterly, 47</u>, (1), 1-15.

Dean, C., & Brame, R. (1992). <u>Assessing post-release failure risk for institutionalized juvenile delinquents (1988-1989)</u>. Unpublished study, University of North Carolina at Charlotte, NC.

Dean, C., & Brame, R. (1995). <u>Criminal propensities, discrete groups of offenders, and persistence in crime</u>. Unpublished study, University of North Carolina at Charlotte, NC.

Dean, C., Bryson, D., Smith, A., Fortos, M., Brame, R., & Clary, R. (1995). <u>Developing an information system for the North Carolina Division of Youth Services: A Working Paper</u>. University of North Carolina at Charlotte, NC.

Deckers, L., & Carr, D. E. (1986). Cartoons varying in low-level pain ratings, not aggression ratings, correlate positively with funniness ratings. <u>Motivation and Emotion, 10</u> (3), 207-216.

Dominick, J. (1973). Crime and law enforcement on prime-time television. Public Opinion Quarterly, 37 (2), 241-250.

Donohew, L., Lorch, E., & Palmgreen, P. (1991). Sensation seeking and targeting of televised anti-drug PSAs. In L. Donohew, H.E. Sypher, & W.J. Bukoski (Eds.), Persuasive communication and drug abuse prevention (pp. 209-228). Hillsdale, NJ: Lawrence Erlbaum Associates.

Donnerstein, E., Slaby, R., & Eron, L. (1994). The mass media and youth violence. In J. Murray, E. Rubinstein, & G. Comstock (Eds.), Violence and youth: Psychology's response (Vol. 2, pp. 219-250). Washington, DC: American Psychological Association.

Dorr, A. (1983). No shortcuts to judging reality. In J. Bryant & D. R. Anderson (Eds.), Children's understanding of television (pp. 199-220). New York, NY: Academic Press.

Drabman, R. S. & Thomas, M. H. (1974). Does media violence increase childrens' toleration of real-life aggression? Developmental Psychology, 10, 418-421.

Durham Police Department Division of Crime Analysis, August 1995, personal communication.

Dubanoski, R. A., & Kong, C. (1977). The effects of pain cues on the behavior of high and low aggressive boys. Social Behavior and Personality, 5 (2), 273-279.

Eco, U. (1976). A theory of semiotics. Bloomington, IN: Indiana University Press.

Eysenck, S.B.G. (1965). Junior Eysenck Personality Inventory. Educational and Industrial Testing Services: San Diego, CA.

Federman, J. (1993). Film and television ratings: An international assessment. Unpublished Report. Studio City, CA: Mediascope.

Feshbach, S. (1972). Reality and fantasy in filmed violence. In J. P. Murray, E. A. Rubinstein, & G. Comstock (Eds.), Television and social behavior: Television and social learning (Vol. 2, pp. 318-345). Washington, DC: US Government Publication Office.

Feshbach, N. D., & Roe, K. (1968). Empathy in six- and seven-year-olds. Child Development, 39, 133-145.

Fishbein M., & Ajzen, I. (1975). Belief, attitude, intention, and behavior. Reading, MA: Addison-Wesley.

Fiske, J. (1987). Television culture. London: Methuen.

Fiske, S., & Kinder, D. (1981). Involvement, expertise, and schema use: Evidence from political cognition. In N. Cantor & J. F. Kihlstrom (Eds.), Personality, cognition, and social interaction (pp. 171-192). Hillsdale, NJ: Lawrence Erbaum Associates.

Fiske, S., Kinder, D., & Larter, W. (1983). The novice and expert knowledge based strategies in political cognition. Journal of Experimental Social Psychology, 19, 381-400.

Flavell, J. H. (1985). Cognitive development (2nd ed.). Englewood Cliffs, NJ: Prentice-Hall.

Flavell, J. H. (1986). The development of children's knowledge about the appearance-reality distinction. American Psychologist, 41, 418-425.

Flay, B. R., & Burton, D. (1990). Effective mass communication strategies for health campaigns. In C. Atkin & L. Wallack (Eds.), Mass communication and public health (pp. 129-146). Newbury Park: Sage Publications.

Foa, E. B., & Kozak, M. J. (1986). Emotional processing of fear: Exposure to corrective information. Psychological Bulletin, 99, 20-35.

Freidrich, L., & Stein, A. H. (1972). Aggressive and prosocial television programs and the natural behavior of preschool children. Monographs of the Society for Research in Child Development, 38 (4, Serial No. 151).

Frodi, A. (1975). The effect of exposure to weapons on aggressive behavior from a cross-cultural perspective. International Journal of Psychology, 10 (4), 283-292.

Geen, R. G. (1975). The meaning of observed violence: Real vs. fictional violence and consequent effects on aggression and emotional arousal. Journal of Research In Personality, 9, 270-281.

Geen, R. G. (1981). Behavioral and physiological reactions to observed violence: Effects of prior exposure to aggressive stimuli. Journal of Personality and Social Psychology, 40, 868-875.

Geen, R. & Berkowitz, L. (1966). Name-mediated aggressive cue properties. Journal of Personality and Social Psychology, 34, 456-465.

Geen, R. G., & Rakosky, J. J. (1975). Interpretations of observed violence and their effects on GSR. Journal of Experimental Research in Personality, 6, 289-292.

Geen, R. G., & Stonner, D. (1973). Context effects in observed violence. Journal of Personality and Social Psychology, 25, 145-150.

Geen, R. G., & Stonner, D. (1974). The meaning of observed violence: Effects on arousal and aggressive behavior. Journal of Research In Personality, 8, 55-63.

Gerbner, G. (1969). Dimensions of violence in television drama. In R. K. Baker & S. J. Ball (Eds.), <u>Violence in the media</u> (Staff Report to the National Commission on the Causes and Prevention of Violence, pp. 311-340). Washington, DC: U.S. Government Printing Office.

Gerbner, G., Gross, L., Morgan, M., & Signorielli, N. (1980). Violence profile no. 11: Trends in network television drama and viewer conceptions of social reality. Philadelphia: Annenberg School of Communications, University of Pennsylvania.

Gerbner, G., et al. (1994, June 7). Cultural Indicators project: TV message analysis recording instrument. Philadelphia: Annenberg School of Communications, University of Pennsylvania.

Gerbner, G. (1992, December). Testimony at Hearings on Violence on Television before the House Judiciary Committee, Subcommittee on Crime and Criminal Justice, New York (field hearing).

Gerbner, G., & Gross, L. (1976). Living with television: The violence profile. <u>Journal of Communication, 26</u> (2), 172-199.

Gerbner, G., Gross, L., Eleey, M.F., Jackson-Beeck, M., Jeffries-Fox, S., & Signorielli, N. (1977). TV violence profile no. 8: The highlights. <u>Journal of Communication, 27</u> (2), 171-180.

Gerbner, G., Gross, L., Morgan, M., & Signorielli, N. (1980). The 'mainstreaming' of America: Violence profile no. 11. <u>Journal of Communication, 30</u> (3), 10-29.

Gerbner, G., Gross, L., Morgan, M., & Signorielli, N. (1986). Living with television: The dynamics of the cultivation process. In J. Bryant & D. Zillmann (Eds.), <u>Perspectives on media effects</u> (pp. 17-40). Hillsdale, NJ: Lawrence Erlbaum.

Gerbner, G., Gross, L., Morgan, M., & Signorielli, N. (1994). Growing up with television: The cultivation perspective. In J. Bryant & D. Zillmann (Eds.), <u>Media effects</u> (pp. 17-41). Hillsdale, NJ: Lawrence Erlbaum.

Gerbner, G., Gross, L., Signorielli, N., & Morgan, M. (1986). <u>Television's mean world: Violence profile no. 14-15</u>. Unpublished manuscript, University of Pennsylvania at Annenberg School of Communication.

Gerbner, G., Gross, L., Signorielli, N., Morgan, M., & Jackson-Beeck, M. (1979).The demonstration of power: Violence profile no. 10. <u>Journal of Communication, 29</u> (3), 177-196.

Ghanem, S. & Evatt, D. (1995, August). The paradox of public concern about crime: An interim report. Paper presented to the Association for Education in Journalism and Mass Communication, Washington, DC.

Gibert, P. (1994). Male violence: Toward an integration. In J. Archer (Ed.), Male violence (pp. 352-389). London: Routledge.

Goransen, R. E. (1969). Observed violence and aggressive behavior: The effects of negative outcomes to observed violence. Dissertation Abstracts International, 31 (01), DAI-B. (University Microfilms No. AAC77 08286).

Gray, T. G., & Barry, M. (1994, November). The kindest cut? A preliminary examination of the British Film Board's policy of censoring graphic violence. Paper session presented at the annual conference of the Speech Communication Association, New Orleans, LA.

Greenberg, B. S. (Ed.) (1980). Life on television: Content analysis of U.S. TV drama. Norwood, NJ: Ablex.

Greenberg, B. S., Edison, N., Korzenny, F., Fernandez-Collado, C., & Atkin, C. K. (1980). Antisocial and prosocial behaviors on television. In B.S. Greenberg (Ed.), Life on television: Content analyses of U.S. TV drama (pp. 99-128). Norwood, NJ: Ablex Publishing.

Greenwald, M. K., Cook III, E. W. & Lang, P. J. (1989). Affective judgment and psychophysiological response: Dimensional covariation in the evaluation of pictorial stimuli. Journal of Psychophysiology, 3, 51-64.

Gunter, B. (1983). Do aggressive people prefer violent television? Bulletin of the British Psychological Society, 36, 166-168.

Gunter, B. (1985). Dimensions of television violence. Aldershots, England: Gower.

Gunter, B. (1994). The question of media violence. In J. Bryant & D. Zillmann (Eds.), Media effects (pp. 163-211). Hillsdale, NJ: Lawrence Erlbaum Associates.

Hamilton, J.T. (1994, October). Marketing violence: The impact of labeling violent television content. Paper presented at the International Conference on Violence in the Media. New York: St. John's University.

Hapkiewicz, W. G., & Stone, R. D. (1974). The effect of realistic versus imaginary aggressive models on children's interpersonal play. Child Study Journal, 4 (2), 47-58.

Harris, R. J. (1994). The impact of sexually explicit media. In J. Bryant & D. Zillmann (Eds.), Media effects (pp. 247-272). Hillsdale, NJ: Lawrence Erlbaum.

Hartley, J. (1982). Understanding news. London: Methuen.

Hawkins, R. P., & Pingree, S. (1981). Uniform messages and habitual viewing: Unnecessary assumptions in social reality effects. Human Communication Research, 7, 291-301.

Hawkins, R. P. (1977). The dimensional structure of children's perceptions of television reality. <u>Communication Research</u>, <u>7</u>, 193-226.

Head, S. (1954). Content analysis of television drama programs. <u>Quarterly Journal of Film, Radio and TV</u>, <u>9</u>, 175-194.

Herman, G., & Leyens, J. P. (1977). Rating films on TV. <u>Journal of Communication</u>, <u>27</u> (4), 48-53.

Hicks, D. J. (1965). Imitation and retention of film-mediated aggressive peer and adult models. <u>Journal of Personality and Social Psychology</u>, <u>2</u>, 97-100.

Higgins, E., & King, G. (1981). Accessibility of social constructs: Information processing consequences of individual and contextual variability. In N. Cantor & J. F. Kihlstrom (Eds.), <u>Personality, cognition, and social interaction</u> (pp. 66-122). Hillsdale, NJ: Lawrence Erlbaum Associates.

Hirsch, P. M. (1980). The 'scary world' of the nonviewer and other anomalies: A reanalysis of Gerbner et al.'s findings of cultivation analysis, part I. <u>Communication Research</u>, <u>7</u>, 403-456.

Hirsch, P. M. (1981a). Distinguishing good speculation from bad theory: Rejoinder to Gerbner et al. <u>Communication Research</u>, <u>8</u>, 73-95.

Hirsch, P. M. (1981b). On not learning from one's own mistakes: A reanalysis of Gerbner et al.'s findings on cultivation analysis, part II. <u>Communication Research</u>, <u>8</u>, 3-37.

Hirschfield, P. P. (1965). Response set in impulsive children. <u>Journal of Genetic Psychology</u>, <u>107</u>, 117-126.

Hoffner, C., & Cantor, J. (1985). Developmental differences in responses to a television character's appearance and behavior. <u>Developmental Psychology</u>, <u>21</u> (6), 1065-1074.

Hoffner, C., & Cantor, J. (1991). Perceiving and responding to mass media characters. In J. Bryant & D. Zillmann (Eds.), <u>Responding to the screen</u> (pp. 63-101). Hillsdale, NJ: Lawrence Erlbaum.

Holsti, O. R. (1969). <u>Content analysis for the social sciences and humanities.</u> Reading, MA: Addison-Wesley.

Houk, V. N. & Warren, R. C. (1991). Special section: Forum on youth violence in minority communities: Setting the agenda for prevention. A summary: Forward to the proceedings. <u>Public Health Reports</u>, 106-225.

Hoyt, J. L. (1970). Effect of media violence "justification" on aggression. <u>Journal of Broadcasting</u>, <u>14</u>, 455-464.

Huesmann, L. R., Guerra, N. G., Miller, L. & Zelli, A. (1992). The role of social norms in the development of aggression. In H. Zumkley & A. Fraszek (Eds.), Socialization and aggression (pp. 139-152). New York: Springer.

Huesmann, L. R., Guerra, N. G., Miller, L. & Zelli, A. (1994). The normative beliefs about aggression scale (NOBAGS). Chicago: University of Illinois at Chicago.

Huesmann, L. R. (1986). Psychological processes promoting the relation between exposure to media violence and aggressive behavior by the viewer. Journal of Social Issues, 42 (3), 125-140.

Huesmann, L. R., & Eron, L. D. (Eds.). (1986). Television and the aggressive child: A cross-national comparison. Hillsdale, NJ: Lawrence Erlbaum Associates.

Huesmann, L. R., Eron, L. D., Lefkowitz, M. M., & Walder, L. O. (1984). The stability of aggression over time and generations. Developmental Psychology, 20 (6), 1120-1134.

Huesmann, L. R., Lagerspetz, K., & Eron, L. D. (1984). Intervening variables in the TV violence-aggression relation: Evidence from two countries. Developmental Psychology, 20, 1120-1134.

Humphrey, L. L. (1982). Children's and teachers' perspectives on children's self-control: The development of two rating scales. Journal of Consulting and Clinical Psychology, 50, 624-633.

Hundt, R. (1995, June 5). An open letter from FCC chairman Reed Hundt. Broadcasting & Cable, 7.

Huston, A. C., Donnerstein, E., Fairchild, H., Feshbach, N. D., Katz, P. A., Murray, J. P., Rubinstein, E. A., Wilcox, B. L., & Zuckerman, D. (1992). Big world, small screen: The role of television in American society. Lincoln, NE: University of Nebraska Press.

Janz, N. K., & Becker, M. H. (1984). The health belief model: A decade later. Health Education Quarterly, 11, 1-47.

Jo, E., & Berkowitz, L. (1994). A priming effect analysis of media influences: An update. In J. Bryant & D. Zillmann (Eds.), Media effects (pp. 43-60). Hillsdale, NJ: Lawrence Erlbaum Associates.

Job, R. F. S. (1988). Effective and ineffective use of fear in health promotion campaigns. American Journal of Public Health, 78, 163-7.

Johnson-Laird, P. (1983). Mental models: Toward a cognitive science of language, inference, and consciousness. Cambridge, MA: Harvard University Press.

Jose, P. E., & Brewer, W. F. (1984). Development of story liking: Character identification, suspense, and outcome resolution. <u>Developmental Psychology</u>, <u>20</u> (5), 911-924.

Josephson, W. L. (1987). Television violence and children's aggression: Testing and priming, social script, and disinhibition predictions. <u>Journal of Personality and Social Psychology</u>, <u>53</u> (5), 882-890.

Kail, R. (1990). <u>The development of memory in children</u>. New York, NY: Freeman.

Kintch, W., & Greene, E. (1978). The role of culture-specific schemata in the comprehension and recall of stories. <u>Discourse Process</u>, <u>1</u>, 1-13.

Klein, J. D., Brown, J. D., Childers, K. W., Oliveri, J., Porter, C., & Dykers, C. (1993). Adolescents' risky behavior and mass media use. <u>Pediatrics</u>, 92 (1), 24-31.

Labov, W. (1972). <u>Sociolinguistic patterns</u>. Philadelphia: University of Philadelphia.

Lacayo, R. (1995, June 12). Are music and movies killing America's soul? <u>Time</u>, 24-30.

Lando, H. A., & Donnerstein, E. I. (1978). The effects of a model's success or failure on subsequent aggressive behavior <u>Journal of Research In Personality</u>, <u>12</u>, 225-234.

Lang, P. L. (1980). Behavioral treatment and bio-behavioral assessment: Computer applications. In J.B. Sidowski, J.H. Johnson, & T.A. Williams (Eds.), <u>Technology in mental health care delivery systems</u> (pp. 119-137). Norwood, NJ: Ablex.

Lazarus, R. S., & Alfert, E. (1964). Short-circuiting of threat by experimentally altering cognitive appraisal. <u>Journal of Abnormal and Social Psychology</u>, <u>69</u> (2), 195-205.

Lazarus, R. S., Opton, E. M., Nomikos, M. S., & Rankin, N. O. (1965). The principal of short-circuiting of threat: Further evidence. <u>Journal of Personality</u>, <u>33</u>, 622-635.

Lazarus, R. S., Speisman, M., Mordkoff, A. M., & Davidson, L. A. (1962). A laboratory study of psychological stress produced by a motion picture film. <u>Psychological Monographs: General and Applied</u>, <u>76</u>, (34) Whole No. 553.

Lefkowitz, M. M., Eron, L. D., Walder, L. Q., & Huesmann, L. R. (1977). <u>Growing up to be violent: A longitudinal study of the development of aggression</u>. New York, NY: Pergamon Press.

Lewis, M., Yeager, C., Lovely, F., Stein, A. S., & Chobham-Portorreal, C. (1994). A clinical follow-up of delinquent males: Ignored vulnerabilities, unmet needs, and the perpetuation of violence. Journal of the American Academy of Adolescent Psychiatry, 33 (4), 518-535.

Leyens, J. P., & Parke, (1974). Aggressive slides can induce a weapons effect. European Journal of Social Psychology, 5 (2), 229-236.

Leyens, J. P., & Picus, S. (1973). Identification with the winner of a fight and name mediation: Their differential effects upon subsequent aggressive behavior. British Journal of Social and Clinical Psychology, 12, 374-377.

Lichter, S. R., & Amundson, D. (1992, June). A day of television violence. Washington, DC: Center for Media and Public Affairs.

Lichter, S. R., & Amundson, D. (1994, August 15). A day of TV violence 1992 vs. 1994. Washington, DC: Center for Media and Public Affairs.

Liebert, R. M., & Baron, R. A. (1972). Short-term effects of televised aggression on children's aggressive behavior. In J. P. Murray, E. A. Rubinstein, & G. A. Comstock (Eds.), Television and social behavior: Television and social learning (Vol. 2, pp. 181-201). Washington, DC: U.S. Government Printing Office.

Lindlof, T. (1988). Media audiences as interpretive communities. In J. A. Anderson (Ed.), Communication yearbook 11 (pp. 81-107). Beverly Hills, CA: Sage Publications.

Linz, D., Donnerstein, E., & Penrod, S. (1984). The effects of multiple exposures to filmed violence against women. Journal of Communication, 34 (3), 130-147.

Linz, D., Donnerstein, E., & Penrod, S. (1987). Sexual violence in the mass media: Social psychological implications. In P. Shaver & C. Hendrick (Eds.), Review of personality and social psychology (Vol. 7, pp. 95-123). Beverly Hills, CA: Sage Publications.

Linz, D. G., Donnerstein, E., & Penrod, S. (1988). Effects of long-term exposure to violent and sexually degrading depictions of women. Journal of Personality and Social Psychology, 55, 758-768.

Liss, M. B., Reinhardt, L. C., & Fredriksen, S. (1983). TV heroes: The impact of rhetoric and deeds. Journal of Applied Developmental Psychology, 4, 175-187.

Lubin, B., Zuckerman, M., & Woodward, L. (1985). A bibliography for the Multiple Affect Adjective Check List. San Diego, CA: Educational and Industrial Testing Service.

Making PSAs that work: A handbook for health communication professionals (1984). Bethesda, MD: National Cancer Institute. NIH Publication No. 84-2485.

Malamuth, N., & Check, J. V. P. (1981). The effects of mass media exposure on acceptance of violence against women: A field experiment. Journal of Research in Personality, 15, 436-446.

Mathai, J. (1983). An acute anxiety state in an adolescent precipitated by viewing a horror movie. Journal of Adolescence, 6, 197-200.

McGuire, W. J. (1989). Theoretical foundations of campaigns. In R. E. Rice & C. K. Atkin (Eds.), Public communication campaigns (pp. 43-65). Newbury Park: Sage Publications.

Mehrabian, A., & Epstein, N. (1972). A measure of emotional empathy. Journal of Personality, 40 (4), 525-543.

Meyer, T. P. (1972). Effects of viewing justified and unjustified real film violence on aggressive behavior. Journal of Personality and Social Psychology, 23, 21-29.

Morgan, M. (1986). Television and the erosion of regional diversity. Journal of Broadcasting and Electronic Media, 30, 123-139.

Morison, P., & Gardner, H. (1978). Dragons and dinosaurs: The child's capacity to differentiate fantasy from reality. Child Development, 49, 642-648.

Morley, D. (1980). The nationwide audience: Structure and decoding. London: British Film Institute.

Mueller, C., & Donnerstein, E. (1977). The effects of humor-induced arousal upon aggressive behavior. Journal of Research In Personality, 11, 73-82.

Mueller, C. W., & Donnerstein, E. (1983). Film-induced arousal and aggressive behavior. The Journal of Social Psychology, 119, 61-67.

Mullin, C. R., & Linz, D. (1995). Desensitization and resensitization to violence against women: Effects of exposure to sexually violent films on judgments of domestic violence victims. Journal of Personality and Social Psychology, 69, 449-459.

Mustonen A., & Pulkkinen, L. (1993). Aggression in television programs in Finland. Aggressive Behavior, 19, 175-183.

National Academy of Science. (1993). Understanding and preventing violence. Washington, DC: National Academy Press.

National Cable Television Association. (Feb. 22, 1995). The voices of cable networks grow louder as they announce more than 130 programs and PSAs scheduled for Voices Against Violence Week March 19 to March 25. Washington: National Cable Television Initiative (Press release).

National Cable Television Initiative (1994). <u>Voices against violence: A cable television initiative</u>. Washington: NCTA.

<u>Health risk behaviors among our nations youth: United States, 1992</u> (1992). Washington, DC: National Center for Health Statistics.

National Cable Television Association. (1993, January). <u>Industry policy statement regarding violence</u>. Washington, DC: Author.

NCTV says violence on TV up 16%. (1983, March 22). <u>Broadcasting Magazine</u>, p. 63.

National Institute of Mental Health (1982). <u>Television and behavior: Ten years of scientific progress and implications for the eighties (Vol. I). Summary Report</u>. Washington, DC: U.S. Government Printing Office.

Network Television Association. (1992, December). <u>Standards for depiction of violence in television programs</u>. New York: Author.

Neisser, U. (1967). <u>Cognitive psychology</u>. New York, NY: Appleton-Century-Crofts.

Newcomb, H. (1978). Assessing the violence profile of Gerbner and Gross: A humanistic critique and suggestion. <u>Communication Research, 5</u>, 264-282.

Novello, A.C. (1991). Violence is a greater killer of children than disease. <u>Public Health Reports, 106</u>, 237-9.

Ogles, R. M., & Hoffner, C. (1987). Film violence and perceptions of crime: The cultivation effect. In M. L. McLaughlin (Ed.), <u>Communication yearbook</u> (Vol. 10, pp. 384-394). Newbury Park, CA: Sage.

O'Keefe, D. J. (1990). <u>Persuasion: Theory and research</u>. Newbury Park, CA: Sage Publications.

O'Keefe, G. J. (1984). Public views on crime: Television exposure and media credibility. In R. Bostrom, (Ed.), <u>Communication Yearbook</u> (Vol. 8, pp. 514-535). Beverly Hills, CA: Sage.

Oliver, M. B. (1994). Portrayals of crime, race, and aggression in "reality-based" police shows: A content analysis. <u>Journal of Broadcasting & Electronic Media, 38</u>, 179-192.

Oliver, M. B. & Armstrong, G. B. (1995). Predictors of viewing and enjoyment of reality-based and fictional crime shows. <u>Journalism Quarterly, 72</u>, 559-570.

Page, D., & O' Neal, E. (1977). "Weapons effect" without demand characteristics. <u>Psychological Reports, 41</u>, 29-30.

Paik, H., & Comstock, G. (1994). The effects of television violence on antisocial behavior: A meta-analysis. Communication Research, 21, 516-546.

Parke, R. D., Berkowitz, L., Leyens, J. P., West, S. G., & Sebastian R. J. (1977). Some effects of violent and nonviolent movies on the behavior of juvenile delinquents. In L. Berkowitz (Ed.), Advances in experimental social psychology (Vol. 10, pp. 135-172). New York, NY: Academic Press.

Perry, D. G., & Perry, L. C. (1976). Identification with film characters, covert aggressive verbalization, and reactions to film violence. Journal of Research In Personality, 10, 399-409.

Perse, E. M. (1990). Cultivation and involvement with public affairs. In N. Signorielli & M. Morgan (Eds.), Cultivation analysis: New directions in media effects research. (pp. 51-70). Newbury Park, CA: Sage.

Petty, R., & Cacioppo, J. (1986). Communication and persuasion: Central and peripheral routes to attitude change. New York: Springer-Verlag.

Piaget, J. (1952). The origins of intelligence in children. New York, NY: International Universities Press.

Piaget, J. (1960). The child's conception of the world. London, England: Routledge.

Pingree, S. (1983). Children's cognitive processes in constructing social reality. Journalism Quarterly, 60 (4), 415-422.

Plagens, P., Miller, M., Foote, D., & Yoffe, E. (1991, April 1). Violence in our culture. Newsweek, 46-52.

Potter, W. J. (1986). Perceived reality and the cultivation hypothesis. Journal of Broadcasting & Electronic Media, 30, 159-174.

Potter, W. J. (1988). Perceived reality in television effects research. Journal of Broadcasting & Electronic Media, 32, 23-41.

Potter, W. J. (1993). Cultivation theory and research: A conceptual critique. Human Communication Research, 19, 564-601.

Potter, W. J., Vaughan, M., Warren, R., Howley, K., Land, A., & Hagemeyer, J. (in press). How Real is the Portrayal of Aggression in Television Entertainment Programming? Journal of Broadcasting & Electronic Media, 41.

Potter, W. J., & Ware, W. (1987). An analysis of the contexts of antisocial acts on prime-time television. Communication Research, 14, 664-686.

Poulos, R. W., Harvey, S. E., & Liebert, R. M. (1976). Saturday morning television: A profile of the 1974-75 children's season. <u>Psychological Reports</u>, <u>39</u>, 1047-1057.

Reiss, A. J., & Roth, J. A. (Eds.). (1993). <u>Understanding and preventing violence</u>. Washington, DC: National Academy Press.

Reiss, A. J., & Roth, J. A. (1993). Patterns of violence in American society. In A. J. Reiss & J. A. Roth (Eds.), <u>Understanding and preventing violence</u> (pp. 42-97). Washington, D.C.: National Academy Press.

Rosekrans, M. A., & Hartup, W. W. (1967). Imitative influences of consistent and inconsistent response consequences to a model on aggressive behavior in children. <u>Journal of Personality and Social Psychology</u>, <u>7</u>, 429-434.

Rosengren, K. S., Kalish, C. W., Hickling, A. K., & Gelman, S. A. (1994). Exploring the relation between preschool children's magical beliefs and causal thinking. <u>British Journal of Developmental Psychology</u>, <u>12</u>, 69-82.

Rosenberg, M. (1957). <u>Occupations and values</u>. Glencoe, IL: Free Press.

Rubin, A. M., Perse, E. M., & Taylor, D. S. (1988). A methodological examination of cultivation. <u>Communication Research</u>, <u>15</u>, 107-134.

Rubin, R. B., Palmgreen, P., & Sypher, H. E. (1994). <u>Communication research measures: A sourcebook</u>. New York: The Guilford Press.

Sander, I. (1995). <u>How violent is TV-violence? An empirical investigation of factors influencing viewers' perceptions of TV-violence</u>. Paper presented at the International Communication Association conference in Albuquerque, NM.

Sanders, G. S., & Baron, R. S. (1975). Pain cues and uncertainty as determinants of aggression in a situation involving repeated instigation. <u>Journal of Personality and Social Psychology</u>, <u>32</u>, 495-502.

Schmidt, C. R., Schmidt, S. R., & Tomalis, S. M. (1984). Children's constructive processing and monitoring of stories containing anomalous information. <u>Child Development</u>, <u>55</u>, 2056-2071.

Schmutte, G. T., & Taylor, S. P. (1980). Physical aggression as a function of alcohol and pain feedback. <u>The Journal of Social Psychology</u>, <u>110</u>, 235-244.

Scott. W. A. (1955). Reliability of content analysis: The case of nominal scale coding. <u>Public Opinion Quarterly</u>, <u>19</u>, 321-325.

Shapiro, M. A. (1991). Memory and decision processes in the construction of social reality. <u>Communication Research</u>, <u>18</u>, 3-24.

Schramm, W., Lyle, J., & Parker, E. B. (1961). <u>Television in the lives of our children</u>. Stanford, CA: Stanford University Press.

Sherman, B. L., & Dominick, J. R. (1986). Violence and sex in music videos: TV and rock 'n' roll. <u>Journal of Communication</u>, <u>36</u> (1), 79-93.

Shiffer, J. E. (Sept. 24, 1995). Powerful, potent heroin has a hold on the Triangle once again (pp. 1A, 12A). <u>News and Observer</u>. Raleigh, NC.

Siegler, R. S. (1991). <u>Children's thinking</u> (2nd ed.). Englewood Cliffs, NJ: Prentice-Hall.

Signorielli, N. (1990). Television's mean and dangerous world: A continuation of the cultural indicators perspective. In N. Signorielli & M. Morgan (Eds.), <u>Cultivation analysis: New directions in media effects research</u> (pp. 85-106). Newbury Park: Sage Publications.

Slater, D., & Elliott, W. R. (1982). Television's influences on social reality. <u>Quarterly Journal of Speech</u>, <u>68</u> (1), 69-79.

Smythe, D. (1954). Reality as presented on television. <u>Public Opinion Quarterly</u>, <u>18</u>, 143-156.

Sommers-Flanagan, R., Sommers-Flanagan, J., & Davis, B. (1993). What's happening on music television? A gender role content analysis. <u>Sex Roles</u>, <u>28</u>, 745-753.

Sparks, G. G. (1986). Developmental differences in children's reports of fear induced by the mass media. <u>Child Study Journal</u>, <u>16</u>, 55-66.

Speisman, J. C., Lazarus, R. S., Mordkoff, A., & Davison, L. (1964). Experimental reduction of stress based on ego-defense theory. <u>Journal of Abnormal and Social Psychology</u>, <u>68</u> (4), 367-380.

Strasburger, V. C. (1993). Children, adolescents, and the media: Five crucial issues. <u>Adolescent Medicine</u>, <u>4</u>, 479-92.

Steuer, F. B., Applefield, J. M., & Smith R. (1971). Televised aggression and the interpersonal aggression of preschool children. <u>Journal of Experimental Child Psychology</u>, <u>11</u>, 442-447.

Surgeon General's Scientific Advisory Committee on Television and Social Behavior. (1972). <u>Television and growing up: The impact of televised violence</u>. Washington, DC: U.S. Government Printing Office.

Sutton, S. R. (1982). Fear-arousing communications: A critical examination of theory and research. In J. R. Eiser (Ed.), <u>Social psychology and behavioral medicine</u> (pp. 303-337). New York, NY: Wiley.

Swart, C., & Berkowitz, L. (1976). Effects of a stimulus associated with a victim's pain on later aggression. <u>Journal of Personality and Social Psychology</u>, <u>33</u>, 623-631.

Tamborini, R., Zillmann, D., & Bryant, J. (1984). Fear and victimization: Exposure to television and perceptions of crime and fear. In R. E. Bostrom (Ed.), <u>Communication yearbook</u>, (Vol. 8, pp. 492-513). Beverly Hills, CA: Sage.

Tan, A. S. (1986). Social learning of aggression from television. In J. Bryant & D. Zillmann (Eds.), <u>Perspectives on media effects</u> (pp. 41-55). Hillsdale, NJ: Lawrence Erlbaum.

Tannenbaum, P. H., & Gaer, E. P. (1965). Mood change as a function of stress of protagonist and degree of identification in a film-viewing situation. <u>Journal of Personality and Social Psychology</u>, <u>2</u>, 612-616.

Taylor, B. J., & Howell, R. J. (1973). The ability of three-, four-, and five-year-old children to distinguish fantasy from reality. <u>The Journal of Genetic Psychology</u>, <u>122</u>, 315-318.

Taylor, S. E., & Thompson, S. C. (1982). Stalking the elusive "vividness" effect. <u>Psychological Review</u>, <u>89</u>, 155-181.

Thomas, M. H. (1982). Physiological arousal, exposure to a relatively lengthy aggressive film, and aggressive behavior. <u>Journal of Research in Personality</u>, <u>16</u>, 72-81.

Thomas, M. H., & Tell, P. M. (1974). Effects of viewing real versus fantasy violence upon interpersonal aggression. <u>Journal of Research In Personality</u>, <u>8</u>, 153-160.

Thomas, M. H., Horton, R. W., Lippencott, E. C., & Drabman, R. S. (1977). Desensitization to portrayals of real-life aggression as a function of exposure to television violence. <u>Journal of Personality and Social Psychology</u>, <u>35</u>, 450-458.

Thompson, J. G., & Myers, N. A. (1985). Inferences and recall at ages four and seven. <u>Child Development</u>, <u>56</u>, 1134-1144.

Turner, A. K. (1994). Genetic and hormonal influences on male violence. In J. Archer (Ed.), <u>Male violence</u> (pp. 233-252). London: Routledge.

Turner, C. W., & Berkowitz, L. (1972). Identification with film aggressor (covert role taking) and reactions to film violence. <u>Journal of Personality and Social Psychology</u>, <u>21</u>, 256-264.

Turner, C. W., Layton, J. F., & Simons, L. S. (1975). Naturalistic studies of aggressive behavior: Aggressive stimuli, victim visibility, and horn honking. <u>Journal of Personality and Social Psychology</u>, <u>31</u>, 1098-1107.

Tyler, T. R. (1980). The impact of directly and indirectly experienced events: The origin of crime-related judgments and behaviors. Journal of Personality and Social Psychology, 39, 13-28.

Tyler, T. R., & Cook, F. L. (1984). The mass media and judgments of risk: Distinguishing impact on personal and societal level judgments. Journal of Personality and Social Psychology, 47, 693-708.

Valenti, J. (1987). The voluntary movie rating system. New York, NY: Motion Picture Association of America.

Walters, R. H., & Parke, R. D. (1964). Influence of response consequences to a social model on resistance to deviation. Journal of Experimental Child Psychology, 1, 269-280.

Walters, R. H., Parke, R. D., & Cane, V. A. (1965). Timing of punishment and the observation of consequences to others as determinants of response inhibition. Journal of Experimental Child Psychology, 2, 10-30.

Williams, T. M., Zabrack, M. L., & Joy, L. A. (1982). The portrayal of aggression on North American television. Journal of Applied Social Psychology, 12 (5), 360-380.

Wilson, B. J. (1995). Les recherches sur médias et violence: Aggressivité, désensibilisation, peur [Effects of media violence: Aggression, desensitization, and fear]. Les Cahiers de la sécurité Intérieure, 20 (2), 21-37.

Wilson, B. J., & Cantor, J. (1985). Developmental differences in empathy with a television protagonist's fear. Journal of Experimental Child Psychology, 39, 284-299.

Wilson, B. J., Linz D., & Randall, B. (1990). Applying social science research to film ratings: A shift from offensiveness to harmful effects. Journal of Broadcasting & Electronic Media, 34, 443-468.

Worchel, S. (1972). The effect of films on the importance of behavioral freedom. Journal of Personality, 40, 417-435.

Wotring, C. E., & Greenberg, B. S. (1973). Experiments in televised violence and verbal aggression: Two exploratory studies. Journal of Communication, 23, 446-460.

Wright, J. C., Huston, A. C., Reitz, A. L., & Piemyat, S. (1994). Young children's perceptions of television reality: Determinants and developmental differences. Developmental Psychology, 30 (2), 229-239.

Wurtzel, A., & Surlin, S. (1978). Viewer attitudes toward television advisory warnings. Journal of Broadcasting, 22, 19-31.

Zillmann, D. (1979). <u>Hostility and aggression</u>. Hillsdale, NJ: Lawrence Erlbaum.

Zillmann, D. (1980). Anatomy of suspense. In P. H. Tannenbaum (Ed.), <u>The entertainment functions of television</u> (pp. 133-163). Hillsdale, NJ: Lawrence Erlbaum.

Zillmann, D. (1982). Television viewing and arousal. In D. Pearl, L. Bouthilet, & J. Lazar (Eds.), <u>Television and behavior: Ten years of scientific progress and implications for the eighties</u> (Vol. 2, pp. 53-67). Washington, DC: U.S. Government Printing Office.

Zillmann, D. (1991). Empathy: Affect from bearing witness to the emotions of others. In J. Bryant & D. Zillmann (Eds.), <u>Responding to the screen</u> (pp. 135-167). Hillsdale, NJ: Lawrence Erlbaum.

Zillmann, D., & Bryant, J. (1991). Responding to comedy: The sense and nonsense in humor. In J. Bryant & D. Zillmann (Eds.), <u>Responding to the screen</u> (pp. 261-279). Hillsdale, NJ: Lawrence Erlbaum.

Zillmann, D., & Cantor, J. R. (1977). Affective responses to the emotions of a protagonist. <u>Journal of Experimental Social Psychology, 13</u>, 155-165.

Zuckerman, M. (1979). <u>Sensation seeking: Beyond the optimal level of arousal</u>. Hillsdale, NJ: Lawrence Erlbaum Associates.

Zuckerman, M., & Lubin, B. (1965). Manual for the Multiple Affect Adjective Check List. San Diego, CA: Educational and Industrial Testing Service.

INDEX

Potter, W. J., 17, 29, 33, 36, 37, 38, 39, 40, 273
Poulos, R. W., 36
Powers, P. C., 24
Prime Ticket:
    as antiviolence educational program sponsor, 426
Priming effects theory, 13, 19, 27
    as one-directional, 13
    appeal of, 12
    cognitive psychology and, 12
    definition of, 12
    identification with television characters and, 13
    thought activation and, 12-13
Probability Assessment of Risk, 446, 491, 505, 506
Program-level analysis, 139
Public service announcements (PSAs), antiviolence, 415, 418, 419, 421-424
    advantages of embedding in violent programming, 503
    as counter-attitudinal messages, 502
    attitudes toward violence and, 415, 521-522
    audience comprehension of, 415, 522-523
    audience interest and, 415
    audience mood and, 415
    biosocial factors and success of, 429-430
    careful selection of celebrities for, 487, 525-526
    careful selection of music for, 487
    celebrity, 421, 422, 423, 424, 436, 524-525
    desensitization to violence and, 502-503
    effect of on TV viewers, 429
    effects of on attitudes about violent behavior, 511-512
    effects of on message cognitions, 511
    elements of effective, 488
    expository-image, 421, 422, 423, 424
    family as subject of, 488, 526
    fear appeals in, 488, 528
    genres of, 423-424
    identifying, 420
    importance of simple messages in, 487
    influence of on violent attitudes, 513, 519
    influence of on violent moods, 513, 519
    influence of on violent programming, 513, 519
    music video, 423, 424
    narrative, 421, 422, 423-424
    possible boomerang effects of embedding, 503
    rationale for embedding in violent programming, 501-503
    real person, 422, 423, 424
    recommendations for improving effectiveness of, 524
    role of antiviolence mediator in, 527
    samples of, 420, 449-452
    social factors and success of, 430
    source credibility in, 432-433, 522-523, 524
    target audiences for, 440
    See also Githens Middle School students; North Carolina Division of Youth Services Training School Students; University of North Carolina at Chapel Hill study
Public television, 82
    absence of violence on, 288
    advisories, 90, 91, 147
    age of targets of violence on, 100
    age of violent perpetrators on, 95
    animated violence on, 115
    antiviolence programming on, 131, 146, 147
    attractive perpetrators on, 147
    attractive targets on, 147
    depiction of pain on, 147
    distribution of violence on, 87
    ethnicity of targets of violence on, 101
    gender of targets of violence on, 100
    gender of violent perpetrators on, 94
    graphicness of violence on, 110, 147
    humorous violence on, 127, 146, 147
    justified violence on, 147
    likelihood of violence on, 136, 151
    live-action violence on, 114, 115
    long-term consequences of violence depicted on, 126, 147
    means of violence on, 147
    motivation for violence on, 104
    no consequences of violence depicted on, 126
    percentage of violent programs on, 90, 146, 147
    realistic violence on, 113, 147
    reality-based programs on, 285, 289
    repeated behavioral violence on, 147
    short-term consequences of violence depicted on, 126
    talk about violence on, 288
    types of characters as targets of violence on, 99, 100, 103
    types of violent perpetrators on, 93, 94, 98
    unpunished violence on, 147
    unrealistic harm depicted on, 122, 123, 146, 147
    visual violence on, 288, 289, 290
    See also PBS
Pulkkinen, L., 40

Rakosky, J. J., 28
Randall, B., 20
Rankin, N. O., 28
Rawlings, E., 24
Realism, television:
    aggression and, 273
    arousal and, 273
    violent involvement and, 273

DATE DUE

MAY 0 1 2010	
GAYLORD	PRINTED IN U.S.A.